Lecture Notes in Artificial Intelligence 10351

Subseries of Lecture Notes in Computer Science

More information about this series at http://www.springer.com/series/1244

Salem Benferhat · Karim Tabia
Moonis Ali (Eds.)

Advances in Artificial Intelligence

From Theory to Practice

30th International Conference
on Industrial Engineering and Other Applications
of Applied Intelligent Systems, IEA/AIE 2017
Arras, France, June 27–30, 2017
Proceedings, Part II

 Springer

Editors
Salem Benferhat
Artois University
Lens
France

Moonis Ali
Texas State University
San Marcos, TX
USA

Karim Tabia
Artois University
Lens
France

ISSN 0302-9743   ISSN 1611-3349   (electronic)
Lecture Notes in Artificial Intelligence
ISBN 978-3-319-60044-4   ISBN 978-3-319-60045-1   (eBook)
DOI 10.1007/978-3-319-60045-1

Library of Congress Control Number: 2017943043

LNCS Sublibrary: SL7 – Artificial Intelligence

Printed on acid-free paper

This Springer imprint is published by Springer Nature
The registered company is Springer International Publishing AG
The registered company address is: Gewerbestrasse 11, 6330 Cham, Switzerland

Preface

In many industrial applications, there is a real need to develop intelligent systems that deal with complex, open, and dynamic information systems. These information systems often involve a huge amount of data that may be incomplete, heterogeneous, pervaded with uncertainty, and inconsistent with available ontologies or expert knowledge.

This volume, entitled *Advances in Artificial Intelligence: From Theory to Practice*, contains the papers presented at the 30th International Conference on Industrial, Engineering, and Other Applications of Applied Intelligent Systems (IEA/AIE 2017) which was held in Arras (France), during June 27–30, 2017. This edition continues the tradition of emphasizing applications of applied intelligent systems to solve real-life problems in all areas including engineering, science, industry, automation and robotics, business and finance, health care, agronomy, anomaly detection, human–machine interactions, etc.

In this 30th year of the IEA/AIE conference, we received 180 papers for the main and the special tracks. We accepted 70 papers as full papers and 45 papers as short papers. All accepted papers were carefully reviewed by Program Committee members. The accepted papers cover a wide array of applied artificial intelligence topics including knowledge representation and reasoning, machine learning, argumentation systems, ontological reasoning, computer animation, non-monotonic and uncertainty-based reasoning, graphical models, decision support systems, recommendation systems, meta-heuristics, planning and scheduling, practical problem solving, etc.

In addition to the list of accepted papers, the conference greatly benefited from invited lectures by three world-leading researchers in applied artificial intelligence: (a) Jian J. Zhang (Professor of Computer Graphics at the National Centre for Computer Animation, Bournemouth University, UK), who gave a talk on "Creativity for Research – An Analogy Model"; (b) Umberto Straccia (Senior Researcher at the Istituto di Scienza e Tecnologie dell' Informazione (ISTI) of the Italian National Council of Research CNR), who gave a talk on "Fuzzy Semantic Web Languages and Beyond"; and (c) Leendert van der Torre (Professor of Computer Science at University of Luxembourg, Luxembourg), who gave a talk on "Rational Enterprise Architecture."

In addition to the main track, the following special tracks were organized:

- Agronomy and Artificial Intelligence
- Anomaly Detection
- Applications of Argumentation
- Conditionals and Non-monotonic Reasoning
- De Finetti's Heritage in Uncertainty and Decision-Making
- Computational Intelligence in Databases
- Graphical Models: From Theory to Applications
- Innovative Applications of Textual Analysis Based on AI
- Intelligent Systems in Health Care and mHealth for Health Outcomes

Additionally, two affiliated workshops were also organized:

- Workshop on ASP Technologies for Querying Large-Scale Multiple-Source Heterogeneous Web Information, WASPIQ 2017 (co-chairs Odile Papini, Salem Benferhat, Laurent Garcia, and Marie-Laure Mugnier)
- Computer Animation and Artificial Intelligence, CAnimAI (co-chairs The Duy Bui, Sylvain Lagrue, Hongchuan Yu, Huu-Hoa Nguyen, Pradorn Sureephong, Mohd Shafry Mohd Rahim, and Karim Tabia)

We would like to thank the following organizations/projects for their support of the conference:

- International Society of Applied Intelligence (ISAI)
- University of Artois, France
- Centre Nationale de la Recherche Scientifique (CNRS), France
- The ANR (French National Research Agency) project ASPIQ (ASP Technologies for Querying Large-Scale Multisource Heterogeneous Web Information)
- The European RISE (Research and Innovation Staff Exchange) project AniAge (High-Dimensional Heterogeneous Data-Based Animation Techniques for Southeast Asian Intangible Cultural Heritage Digital Content).

We would like to thank all the members of the Program Committees (from the main and the special tracks), as well as the additional reviewers, who devoted their time for the reviewing process. We thank all the authors of submitted papers, the invited speakers, and the participants for their scientific contributions to the conference. Finally, we would like to thank all the Organizing Committee members (with a special thanks to Sylvain Lagrue, from CRIL, CNRS-University of Artois) for their excellent local organization, which made the IEA/AIE-2017 conference a success.

May 2017   Salem Benferhat
                                                                          Karim Tabia
                                                                          Moonis Ali

Organization

Executive Committee

General Chair

Moonis Ali, USA

International Advisory Committee

Hamido Fujita, Japan (Chair)
Enrique Herrera-Viedma, Spain
Francisco Chiclana, UK
Yinglin Wang, China
Love Ekenberg, Sweden
Imre Rudas, Hungary
Shiliang Sun, China
Vincenzo Loia, Italy
Ali Selamat, Malaysia
Bipin Indurkhya, Poland
Chris Bowman, Australia
Jun Sasaki, Japan
Ligang Zhou, Macao
Rajendra Acharya, Singapore
Levente Kovacs, Hungary

Program Co-chairs

Salem Benferhat, France
Karim Tabia, France

Local Co-chairs

Salem Benferhat, France
Sylvain Lagrue, France

Special Sessions Co-chairs

Zied Bouraoui, UK
Steven Schockaert, UK

Workshop Co-chairs

Jianbing Ma, UK
Hongchuan Yu, UK

Social Events and Local Arrangements Co-chairs

Fahima Cheikh-Alili, France
Nathalie Chetcuti-Sperandio, France
Karim Tabia, France

Web Co-chairs

Jérôme Delobelle, France
Fabien Delorme, France
Amélie Levray, France

Publicity Chair

Farid Nouioua, France

Registration and Financial Chair

Virginie Delahaye, France

Local Organizing Committee

François Chevallier, France
Jérôme Delobelle, France
Yacine Izza, France
Amélie Levray, France
Emmanuel Lonca, France
Valentin Montmirail, France
Imen Ouled Dlala, France
Éric Piette, France
Nicolas Szczepanski, France

Program Committee (Main Track)

Carole Adam, France
Mario Alviano, Italy
Youngchul Bae, South Korea
Edurne Barrenechea, Spain
Fevzi Belli, Germany
Nahla Ben Amor, Tunisia
Sadok Ben Yahia, Tunisia
Jamal Bentahar, USA
Mehul Bhatt, Germany
Isabelle Bloch, France
Leszek Borzemski, Poland
Thouraya Bouabana Tebibel, Algeria
Imen Boukhris, Tunisia

Mustapha Bourahla, Algeria
Zied Bouraoui, UK
Narhimene Boustia, Algeria
Patrick Brezillon, France
The Duy Bui, Vietnam
Stephane Cardon, France
Tristan Cazenave, France
Martine Cebiero, USA
Michael C.W. Chan, Hong Kong,
    SAR China
Darryl Charles, UK
Shyi-Ming Chen, Taiwan
Laurence Cholvy, France

Paul Chung, UK
Mike Cook, UK
Fabio Cozman, Brazil
José Valente de Oliveira, Portugal
Georgios Dounias, Greece
Florence Dupin De Saint Cyr, France
Zied Elouedi, Tunisia
Roberta Ferrario, Italy
Philippe Fournier-Viger, China
Hamido Fujita, Japan
Eric Jacopin, France
Laurent Garcia, France
Lluis Godo, Spain
Maciej Grzenda, Poland
Allel Hadjali, France
Jun Hakura, Japan
Shyamanta M. Hazarika, India
Bipin Indurkhya, Poland
He Jiang, China
Bian Jiang, USA
Vicente Julian, Spain
Gabriele Kern-Isberner, Germany
Faiza Khellaf, Algeria
Frank Klawonn, Germany
Vladik Kreinovich, USA
Amruth Kumar, USA
Bora Kumova, Turkey
Sylvain Lagrue, France
Jean-Charles Lamirel, France
Jooyoung Lee, USA
Chang-Hwan Lee, South Korea
Mehdi Kaytoue, France
Arnaud Lallouet, France
Eric Lefevre, France
Philippe Leray, France
Mark Sh. Levin, Russia
Amélie Levray, France
Vincenzo Loia, Italy
Bouzar Lydia, Algeria
Jianbing Ma, UK
Thi Chau Ma, Vietnam
Francesco Marcelloni, Italy
Joao Marques-Silva, Portugal
Arnaud Martin, France
Philippe Mathieu, France
Kishan Mehrotra, USA

Carlos Mencia, Spain
Engelbert Mephu Nguifo, France
Enrique Miranda, Spain
François Modave, USA
Yasser Mohammad, Egypt
Mohd Shafry Mohd Rahim, Malaysia
Aïcha Mokhtari, Algeria
Malek Mouhoub, USA
Thanhthuy Nguyen, Vietnam
Ngoc-Thanh Nguyen, Poland
Farid Nouioua, France
Jae Oh, USA
Santiago Ontanon, USA
Meltem Ozturk, France
Gregorio Sainz Palmero, Spain
Odile Papini, France
Rafael Peñaloza, Italy
Eric Piette, France
Don Potter, USA
Nico Potyka, Germany
Henri Prade, France
Guilin Qi, China
Chedy Raissi, France
Srini Ramaswamy, USA
Florian Richoux, France
Abdallah Saffidine, Australia
Giuseppe Sanfilippo, Italy
Paulo E. Santos, Brazil
Steven Schockaert, UK
Karima Sedki, France
Michael Spranger, France
Pradorn Sureephong, Thailand
Armando Tacchella, Italy
Choh Man Teng, USA
Le Thanh Ha, Vietnam
Ruck Thawonmas, Japan
Marco Valtorta, USA
Barbara Vantaggi, Italy
Ivan Varzinczak, France
Zsolt Janos Viharos, Hungary
Marco Viviani, Italy
Martijn Warnier, The Netherlands
Mary-Anne Williams, Australia
Safa Yahi, France
Don-Lin Yang, Taiwan
Lei Zhang, USA

Program Committees (Special Tracks)

Agronomy and Artificial Intelligence

Madalina Croitoru, France (Co-chair)
Pierre Bisquert, France (Co-chair)
Abdallah Arioua, France
Estelle Chaix, France
Liliana Ibanescu, France
Wim Laurier, Belgium
Alexandru Mihnea Moisescu, Romania
Claire Nedelec, France
Nir Oren, UK
Alun Preece, UK
Danai Symeonidou, France
Rallou Thomopolous, France
Jan Top, The Netherlands

Anomaly Detection

Ryan McConville, UK (Co-chair)
Weiru Liu, UK (Co-chair)
Frans Coenen, UK
Masud Moshtaghi, Australia
Nico Görnitz, Germany
Jun Hong, UK
Michael Davis, Switzerland
Paul Miller, UK
Zhanyu Ma, China
Jen Houle, UK
Hanghang Tong, USA
Florian Skopik, Austria

Applications of Argumentation

Federico Cerutti, UK (Co-chair)
Richard Booth, UK (Co-chair)
Leila Amgoud, France
Pietro Baroni, Italy
Ringo Baumann, Germany
Stefano Bistarelli, Italy
Claudette Cayrol, France
Wolfgang Faber, UK
John Fox, UK
Sarah Gaggl, Germany
Massimiliano Giacomin, Italy
Tom Gordon, Germany

Matti Jarvisalo, Finland
Antonis Kakas, Cyprus
Jean-Guy Mailly, France
Nir Oren, UK
Sylwia Polberg, UK
Alun Preece, UK
Guillermo Simari, Argentina
Nikos Spanoudakis, Greece
Christian Stab, Germany
Manfred Stede, Germany
Hannes Strass, Germany
Matthias Thimm, Germany
Mauro Vallati, UK
Srdjan Vesic, France
Serena Villata, France
Johannes Wallner, Finland
Stefan Woltran, Austria

Conditionals and Non-monotonic Reasoning

Gabriele Kern Isberner, Germany (Co-chair)
Christian Eichhorn, Germany (Co-chair)
Ofer Arieli, Israel
Christoph Beierle, Germany
Giovanni Casini, Luxembourg
Lupita Estefania Gazzo Castañeda, Germany
Laura Giordano, Italy
Tommie Meyer, South Africa
Odile Papini, France
Marco Ragni, Germany
Gavin Rens, South Africa
Gerhard Schurz, Germany
Niels Skovgaard Olsen, Germany
Matthias Thimm, Germany
Stefan Woltran, Austria
Renata Wassermann, Brazil
Anna Zamansky, Israel

De Finetti's Heritage in Uncertainty and Decision-Making

Giualianella Coletti, Italy (Co-chair)
Davide Petturiti, Italy (Co-chair)
Barbara Vantaggi, Italy (Co-chair)
Giuseppe Sanfilippo, Italy
Giualianella Coletti, Italy
Davide Petturiti, Italy
Barbara Vantaggi, Italy

Gernot Kleiter, Austria
Romano Scozzafava, Italy
Vladik Kreinovich, USA

Computational Intelligence in Databases

Guy De Trév, Belgium (Co-chair)
Allel Hadjali, France (Co-chair)
Mohamed Anis Bach, Tunisia
Belkasmi Djamal, Algeria
Stephane Jean, France
Karima Akli Astouati, Algeria
Zied Elouedi, Tunisia
Slawomir Zadrozny, Poland
Mourad Ouziri, France
Djamal Benslimane, France
Ludovic Lietard, France
Gloria Bordogna, Italy
Ahmed Mostefaoui, France
Arnaud Martin, France
Daniel Rocacher, France
Anne Laurent, France
Peter Dolog, Denmark
Maria Rifqi, France

Graphical Models: From Theory to Applications

Christophe Gonzales, France (Co-chair)
Philippe Leray, France (Co-chair)
Alexandre Aussem, France
Concha Bielza, Spain
Andrés Cano, Spain
Luis M. De Campos, Spain
Julia Flores, Spain
Jan Lemeire, Belgium
Anders L. Madsen, Denmark
Jose Luis Molina Gonzales, Spain
Thomas D. Nielsen, Denmark
Agnieszka Onisko, Poland
Silja Renooi, The Netherlands
Pierre-Henri Wuillemin, France

Innovative Applications of Textual Analysis-Based on AI

Yinglin Wang, China (Chair)
Xin Lin, China
Lei Duan, China

Deqing Yang, China
Hongtao Lu, China
Min Liu, China
Jian Cao, China

Intelligent Systems in Health Care and mHealth for Health Outcomes

François Modave, USA (Co-chair)
Jiang Bian, USA (Co-chair)
William Hogan, USA
Zhe He, USA
Yi Guo, USA
Xia Hu, USA
Remzi Seker, USA
Juan Antonio Lossio-Ventura, USA
Jiawei Yuan, USA
Mengjun Xie, USA
Tanja Magoc, USA
Kenji Yoshigoe, USA
Olac Fuentes, USA
Enrico Pontelli, USA
Doug Talbert, USA
Yanming Gong, USA
Yonghui Wu, USA
Lixia Yao, USA
Ramzi Salloum, USA

Sponsoring Institutions

IEA/AIE 2017 was organized by the Centre de Recherche en Informatique de Lens (UMR CNRS 8188) of Artois University, Arras, France.

Sponsored by

International Society of Applied Intelligence (ISAI)
University of Artois, France
Centre Nationale de la Recherche Scientifique (CNRS), France
The ANR (French National Research Agency) project ASPIQ (ASP Technologies for Querying Large-Scale Multisource Heterogeneous Web Information)
The European RISE (Research and Innovation Staff Exchange) project AniAge (High Dimensional Heterogeneous Data-Based Animation Techniques for Southeast Asian Intangible Cultural Heritage Digital Content)

Organized in cooperation with

Association for the Advancement of Artificial Intelligence (AAAI)
Association for Computing Machinery (ACM/SIGART)

Catalan Association for Artificial Intelligence (ACIA)
International Neural Network Society (INNS)
Italian Artificial Intelligence Association (AI*IA)
Japanese Society for Artificial Intelligence (JSAI)
Lithuanian Computer Society - Artificial Intelligence Section (LIKS-AIS)
Spanish Society for Artificial Intelligence (AEPIA)
Society for the Study of Artificial Intelligence and the Simulation of Behaviour (AISB)
Taiwanese Association for Artificial Intelligence (TAAI)
Taiwanese Association for Consumer Electronics (TACE)
Centre Nationale de la Recherche Scientifique (CNRS)
Texas State University, USA
Artois University, France

Contents – Part II

Games, Computer Vision and Animation

Annotating Movement Phrases in Vietnamese Folk Dance Videos 3
   Chau Ma-Thi, Karim Tabia, Sylvain Lagrue, Ha Le-Thanh,
   Duy Bui-The, and Thuy Nguyen-Thanh

Mining the Lattice of Binary Classifiers for Identifying Duplicate Labels
in Behavioral Data 12
   Quentin Labernia, Victor Codocedo, Céline Robardet,
   and Mehdi Kaytoue

Implementing a Tool for Translating Dance Notation to Display
in 3D Animation: A Case Study of Traditional Thai Dance 22
   Yootthapong Tongpaeng, Mongkhol Rattanakhum,
   Pradorn Sureephong, and Satichai Wicha

Dance Training Tool Using Kinect-Based Skeleton Tracking
and Evaluating Dancer's Performance 27
   Ob-orm Muangmoon, Pradorn Sureephong, and Karim Tabia

Using Program by Demonstration and Visual Scripting to Supporting
Game Design 33
   Ismael Sagredo-Olivenza, Pedro Pablo Gómez-Martín,
   Marco Antonio Gómez-Martín, and Pedro A. González-Calero

Presenting Mathematical Expression Images on Web to Support
Mathematics Understanding 40
   Kuniko Yamada, Hiroshi Ueda, Harumi Murakami, and Ikuo Oka

Chiang Mai Digital Craft: A Case Study of Craftsmanship's Knowledge
Representation Using Digital Content Technology 47
   Suepphong Charnbumroong, Pradorn Sureephong,
   and Yootthapong Tongpaeng

Uncertainty Management

A Robust, Distributed Task Allocation Algorithm for Time-Critical,
Multi Agent Systems Operating in Uncertain Environments 55
   Amanda Whitbrook, Qinggang Meng, and Paul W.H. Chung

An Efficient Probabilistic Merging Procedure Applied to Statistical
Matching 65
   Marco Baioletti and Andrea Capotorti

Interval-Based Possibilistic Logic in a Coherent Setting 75
   Giulianella Coletti, Davide Petturiti, and Barbara Vantaggi

Conjunction and Disjunction Among Conditional Events 85
   Angelo Gilio and Giuseppe Sanfilippo

A Gold Standards-Based Crowd Label Aggregation Within
the Belief Function Theory 97
   Lina Abassi and Imen Boukhris

Experimental Evaluation of the Understanding of Qualitative Probability
and Probabilistic Reasoning in Young Children 107
   Jean Baratgin, Giulianella Coletti, Frank Jamet, and Davide Petturiti

A Set-Valued Approach to Multiple Source Evidence 113
   Didier Dubois and Henri Prade

Graphical Models: From Theory to Applications

On the Use of WalkSAT Based Algorithms for MLN Inference
in Some Realistic Applications 121
   Romain Rincé, Romain Kervarc, and Philippe Leray

Applying Object-Oriented Bayesian Networks for Smart Diagnosis
and Health Monitoring at both Component and Factory Level 132
   *Anders L. Madsen, Nicolaj Søndberg-Jeppesen, Mohamed S. Sayed,
   Michael Peschl, and Niels Lohse*

Graphical Representations of Multiple Agent Preferences 142
   Nahla Ben Amor, Didier Dubois, Héla Gouider, and Henri Prade

A Probabilistic Relational Model Approach for Fault Tree Modeling 154
   Thierno Kante and Philippe Leray

Incremental Method for Learning Parameters in Evidential Networks 163
   Narjes Ben Hariz and Boutheina Ben Yaghlane

aGrUM: A Graphical Universal Model Framework 171
   Christophe Gonzales, Lionel Torti, and Pierre-Henri Wuillemin

Anomaly Detection

Improving Card Fraud Detection Through Suspicious Pattern Discovery   181
Fabian Braun, Olivier Caelen, Evgueni N. Smirnov, Steven Kelk,
and Bertrand Lebichot

Contextual Air Leakage Detection in Train Braking Pipes   191
Wan-Jui Lee

K-means Application for Anomaly Detection and Log Classification
in HPC   201
Mohamed Cherif Dani, Henri Doreau, and Samantha Alt

Information Quality in Social Networks: A Collaborative Method
for Detecting Spam Tweets in Trending Topics.   211
Mahdi Washha, Aziz Qaroush, Manel Mezghani, and Florence Sedes

Agronomy and Artificial Intelligence

Bayesian Model Averaging for Streamflow Prediction
of Intermittent Rivers.   227
Paul J. Darwen

A Mixed Integer Programming Reformulation of the Mixed Fruit-Vegetable
Crop Allocation Problem   237
Sara Maqrot, Simon de Givry, Gauthier Quesnel,
and Marc Tchamitchian

Data Collection and Analysis of Usages from Connected Objects:
Some Lessons.   251
Sara Meftah, Antoine Cornuéjols, Juliette Dibie, and Mariette Sicard

Assessing Nitrogen Nutrition in Corn Crops with Airborne Multispectral
Sensors   259
Jaen Alberto Arroyo, Cecilia Gomez-Castaneda, Elias Ruiz,
Enrique Munoz de Cote, Francisco Gavi, and Luis Enrique Sucar

Multidimensional Analysis Through Argumentation? Contributions
from a Short Food Supply Chain Experience   268
Rallou Thomopoulos and Dominique Paturel

Combined Argumentation and Simulation to Support Decision:
Example to Assess the Attractiveness of a Change in Agriculture   275
Rallou Thomopoulos, Bernard Moulin, and Laurent Bedoussac

Applications of Argumentation

Analysis of Medical Arguments from Patient Experiences Expressed
on the Social Web.   285
    Kawsar Noor, Anthony Hunter, and Astrid Mayer

A Dynamic Logic Framework for Abstract Argumentation:
Adding and Removing Arguments.   295
    Sylvie Doutre, Faustine Maffre, and Peter McBurney

Combining Answer Set Programming with Description Logics
for Analogical Reasoning Under an Agent's Preferences   306
    Teeradaj Racharak, Satoshi Tojo, Nguyen Duy Hung,
    and Prachya Boonkwan

Modeling Data Access Legislation with Gorgias   317
    Nikolaos I. Spanoudakis, Elena Constantinou, Adamos Koumi,
    and Antonis C. Kakas

dARe – Using Argumentation to Explain Conclusions from a Controlled
Natural Language Knowledge Base.   328
    Adam Wyner and Hannes Strass

Intelligent Systems in Healthcare and mHealth for Health Outcomes

Exploring Parameter Tuning for Analysis and Optimization
of a Computational Model   341
    Julia S. Mollee, Eric F.M. Araújo, and Michel C.A. Klein

Empirical Validation of a Computational Model of Influences
on Physical Activity Behavior.   353
    Julia S. Mollee and Michel C.A. Klein

Detecting Drinking-Related Contents on Social Media by Classifying
Heterogeneous Data Types.   364
    Omar ElTayeby, Todd Eaglin, Malak Abdullah, David Burlinson,
    Wenwen Dou, and Lixia Yao

Estimating Disease Burden Using Google Trends and Wikipedia Data.   374
    Riyi Qiu, Mirsad Hadzikadic, and Lixia Yao

Knowledge-Based Approach for Named Entity Recognition in Biomedical
Literature: A Use Case in Biomedical Software Identification.   386
    Muhammad Amith, Yaoyun Zhang, Hua Xu, and Cui Tao

Interweaving Domain Knowledge and Unsupervised Learning
for Psychiatric Stressor Extraction from Clinical Notes 396
    Olivia R. Zhang, Yaoyun Zhang, Jun Xu, Kirk Roberts,
    Xiang Y. Zhang, and Hua Xu

Innovative Applications of Textual Analysis Based on AI

Active Learning for Text Mining from Crowds. 409
    Hao Shao

Chinese Lyrics Generation Using Long Short-Term Memory Neural
Network. 419
    Xing Wu, Zhikang Du, Mingyu Zhong, Shuji Dai, and Yazhou Liu

CN-DBpedia: A Never-Ending Chinese Knowledge Extraction System 428
    Bo Xu, Yong Xu, Jiaqing Liang, Chenhao Xie, Bin Liang,
    Wanyun Cui, and Yanghua Xiao

Aspect-Based Rating Prediction on Reviews Using Sentiment Strength
Analysis. 439
    Yinglin Wang, Yi Huang, and Ming Wang

Using Topic Labels for Text Summarization. 448
    Wanqiu Kou, Fang Li, and Zhe Ye

Pair-Aware Neural Sentence Modeling for Implicit Discourse Relation
Classification 458
    Deng Cai and Hai Zhao

Author Index 467

Contents – Part I

Invited Talks

Fuzzy Semantic Web Languages and Beyond 3
  Umberto Straccia

Rational Enterprise Architecture 9
  Leendert van der Torre and Marc van Zee

Constraints, Planning and Optimization

Cluster-Specific Heuristics for Constraint Solving 21
  Seda Polat Erdeniz, Alexander Felfernig, Muesluem Atas,
  Thi Ngoc Trang Tran, Michael Jeran, and Martin Stettinger

Car Pooling Based on a Meta-heuristic Approach 31
  Fu-Shiung Hsieh, Fu-Min Zhan, and Yi-Hong Guo

Reactive Motion Planning with Qualitative Constraints 41
  Domen Šoberl and Ivan Bratko

A New System for the Dynamic Shortest Route Problem 51
  Eisa Alanazi, Malek Mouhoub, and Mahmoud Halfawy

M-NSGA-II: A Memetic Algorithm for Vehicle Routing Problem
with Route Balancing 61
  Yuyan Sun, Yuxuan Liang, Zizhen Zhang, and Jiahai Wang

A Matrix-Based Implementation of DE Algorithm: The Compensation
and Deficiency 72
  Jeng-Shyang Pan, Zhenyu Meng, Huarong Xu, and Xiaoqing Li

A Bayesian Model of Game Decomposition 82
  Hanqing Zhao, Zengchang Qin, Weijia Liu, and Tao Wan

Two-Timescale Learning Automata for Solving Stochastic Nonlinear
Resource Allocation Problems 92
  Anis Yazidi, Hugo Lewi Hammer, and Tore Møller Jonassen

A Hybrid of Tabu Search and Simulated Annealing Algorithms
for Preemptive Project Scheduling Problem 102
  Behrouz Afshar-Nadjafi, Mehdi Yazdani, and Mahyar Majlesi

Elitist Ant System for the Distributed Job Shop Scheduling Problem   112
  Imen Chaouch, Olfa Belkahla Driss, and Khaled Ghedira

Fuzzy Reinforcement Learning for Routing in Multi-Hop Cognitive
Radio Networks   118
  Jerzy Martyna

FJS Problem Under Machine Breakdowns   124
  Rim Zarrouk, Imed Bennour, Abderrazak Jemai, and Abdelghani Bekrar

A Dijkstra-Based Algorithm for Selecting the Shortest-Safe Evacuation
Routes in Dynamic Environments (SSER)   131
  Angely Oyola, Dennis G. Romero, and Boris X. Vintimilla

Replication in Fault-Tolerant Distributed CSP   136
  *Fadoua Chakchouk, Julien Vion, Sylvain Piechowiak, René Mandiau,
  Makram Soui, and Khaled Ghedira*

Optimal Route Prediction as a Smart Mobile Application of Gift Ideas   141
  Veronika Nemeckova, Jan Dvorak, Ali Selamat, and Ondrej Krejcar

Data Mining and Machine Learning

Machine Learning Approach to Detect Falls on Elderly
People Using Sound   149
  *Armando Collado-Villaverde, María D. R-Moreno, David F. Barrero,
  and Daniel Rodriguez*

A Novel *k*-NN Approach for Data with Uncertain Attribute Values   160
  Asma Trabelsi, Zied Elouedi, and Eric Lefevre

On Combining Imputation Methods for Handling Missing Data   171
  Nassima Ben Hariz, Hela Khoufi, and Ezzeddine Zagrouba

Supervised Feature Space Reduction for Multi-Label Nearest Neighbors   182
  Wissam Siblini, Reda Alami, Frank Meyer, and Pascale Kuntz

Stock Volatility Prediction Using Recurrent Neural Networks
with Sentiment Analysis.   192
  Yifan Liu, Zengchang Qin, Pengyu Li, and Tao Wan

Incremental Quantiles Estimators for Tracking Multiple Quantiles   202
  Hugo Lewi Hammer and Anis Yazidi

Forecasting Passenger Flows Using Data Analytics   211
  Nang Laik Ma

Co-location Rules Discovery Process Focused on Reference Spatial
Features Using Decision Tree Learning   221
  Giovanni Daián Rottoli, Hernán Merlino, and Ramón García-Martinez

Virtual Career Advisor System with an Artificial Neural Network   227
  Tracey John and Dwaine Clarke

Implicit Knowledge Extraction and Structuration
from Electrical Diagrams   235
  Ikram Chraibi Kaadoud, Nicolas Rougier, and Frederic Alexandre

An Energy-Aware Learning Agent for Power Management
in Mobile Devices.   242
  Ismat Chaib Draa, Emmanuelle Grislin-Le Strugeon, and Smail Niar

Sensors, Signal Processing and Data Fusion

An Empirical Study on Verifier Order Selection in Serial Fusion
Based Multi-biometric Verification System.   249
  Md Shafaeat Hossain and Khandaker Abir Rahman

Characterization of Cardiovascular Diseases Using Wavelet Packet
Decomposition and Nonlinear Measures of Electrocardiogram Signal.   259
  Hamido Fujita, Vidya K. Sudarshan, Muhammad Adam, Shu Lih Oh,
  Jen Hong Tan, Yuki Hagiwara, Kuang Chua Chua, Kok Poo Chua,
  and U. Rajendra Acharya

Biometric Keystroke Signal Preprocessing Part I: Signalization, Digitization
and Alteration.   267
  Orcan Alpar and Ondrej Krejcar

Robust Sensor Data Fusion Through Adaptive Threshold Learning   277
  Bing Zhou, Hyuk Cho, and Adam Mansfield

An Application of Fuzzy Signal-to-Noise Ratio to the Assessment
of Manufacturing Processes   283
  Shiang-Tai Liu

Biometric Keystroke Signal Preprocessing Part II: Manipulation   289
  Orcan Alpar and Ondrej Krejcar

Computational Intelligence Techniques for Modelling the Critical Flashover
Voltage of Insulators: From Accuracy to Comprehensibility   295
  Evangelos Karampotsis, Konstantinos Boulas, Alexandros Tzanetos,
  Vasilios P. Androvitsaneas, Ioannis F. Gonos, Georgios Dounias,
  and Ioannis A. Stathopulos

Recommender Systems

Replication and Reproduction in Recommender Systems Research -
Evidence from a Case-Study with the rrecsys Library   305
  Ludovik Çoba and Markus Zanker

A New User-Based Collaborative Filtering Under the Belief
Function Theory   315
  Raoua Abdelkhalek, Imen Boukhris, and Zied Elouedi

Aggregating Top-K Lists in Group Recommendation Using Borda Rule   325
  *Sabrine Ben Abdrabbah, Manel Ayadi, Raouia Ayachi,
  and Nahla Ben Amor*

An Analysis of Group Recommendation Heuristics
for High- and Low-Involvement Items   335
  *Alexander Felfernig, Muesluem Atas, Thi Ngoc Trang Tran,
  Martin Stettinger, Seda Polat Erdeniz, and Gerhard Leitner*

SemCoTrip: A Variety-Seeking Model for Recommending Travel
Activities in a Composite Trip   345
  *Montassar Ben Messaoud, Ilyes Jenhani, Eya Garci,
  and Toon De Pessemier*

Decision Support Systems

A New Dynamic Model for Anticipatory Adaptive Control of Airline Seat
Reservation via Order Statistics of Cumulative Customer Demand.   359
  Nicholas Nechval, Gundars Berzins, and Vadims Danovics

A Multi-Criteria Decision Support Framework for Interactive Adaptive
Systems Evaluation   371
  *Amira Dhouib, Abdelwaheb Trabelsi, Christophe Kolski,
  and Mahmoud Neji*

Application of Multi-Criteria Decision Making Method for Developing
a Control Plan   383
  Fadwa Oukhay, Hajer Ben Mahmoud, and Taieb Ben Romdhane

Efficient Matching in Heterogeneous Rule Engines   394
  Kennedy Kambona, Thierry Renaux, and Wolfgang De Meuter

Towards Extending Business Process Modeling Formalisms
with Information and Knowledge Dimensions.   407
  Mariam Ben Hassen, Mohamed Turki, and Faïez Gargouri

Adaptive Planning in-Service Inspections of Fatigued Structures in Damage
Tolerance Situations via Observations of Crack Growth Process   426
  Nicholas Nechval, Gundars Berzins, and Vadims Danovics

Introducing Causality in Business Rule-Based Decisions   433
  Karim El Mernissi, Pierre Feillet, Nicolas Maudet,
  and Wassila Ouerdane

Model-Based Diagnosis in Practice: Interaction Design of an Integrated
Diagnosis Application for Industrial Wind Turbines.   440
  Roxane Koitz, Johannes Lüftenegger, and Franz Wotawa

A New Model to Implement a SWOT Fuzzy ANP   446
  Mounira Souli, Ahmed Badreddine, and Taieb Ben Romdhane

Knowledge Representation and Reasoning

Argumentative Approaches to Reasoning with Consistent
Subsets of Premises.   455
  Ofer Arieli, AnneMarie Borg, and Christian Straßer

Volunteered Geographic Information Management Supported
by Fuzzy Ontologies and Level-Based Approximate Reasoning   466
  Gloria Bordogna and Simone Sterlacchini

Regular and Sufficient Bounds of Finite Domain Constraints
for Skeptical C-Inference   477
  Christoph Beierle and Steven Kutsch

On Transformations and Normal Forms of Conditional Knowledge Bases . . .   488
  Christoph Beierle, Christian Eichhorn, and Gabriele Kern-Isberner

ADNOTO: A Self-adaptive System for Automatic Ontology-Based
Annotation of Unstructured Documents   495
  Laura Pandolfo and Luca Pulina

Ontologies in System Engineering: A Field Report   502
  Marco Menapace and Armando Tacchella

An Argumentative Agent-Based Model of Scientific Inquiry.   507
  AnneMarie Borg, Daniel Frey, Dunja Šešelja, and Christian Straßer

Navigation, Control and Autonomous Agents

Development of a Novel Driver Model Offering Human like
Longitudinal Vehicle Control in Order to Simulate Emission
in Real Driving Conditions.   513
   Aymeric Rateau, Wim van der Borght, Marcello Mastroleo,
   Alessandro Pietro Bardelli, Alessandro Bacchini, and Federico Sassi

Consistency Check in a Multiple Viewpoint System for Reasoning
About Occlusion.   523
   Ana Paula Martin, Paulo E. Santos, and Marjan Safi-Samghabadi

An Advanced Teleassistance System to Improve Life Quality
in the Elderly   533
   Fernando Ropero, Daniel Vaquerizo, Pablo Muñoz,
   and María D. R-Moreno

Learning the Elasticity of a Series-Elastic Actuator for Accurate
Torque Control.   543
   Bingbin Yu, José de Gea Fernández, Yohannes Kassahun,
   and Vinzenz Bargsten

The Effect of Rotation in the Navigation of Multi-level Buildings:
A Pilot Study   553
   Giulia Mastrodonato, Domenico Camarda, Caterina De Lucia,
   and Dino Borri

NAO Robot, Transmitter of Social Cues: What Impacts? The Example
with "Endowment effect".   559
   Olivier Masson, Jean Baratgin, and Frank Jamet

Arduino as a Control Unit for the System of Laser Diodes.   569
   Jiri Bradle, Jakub Mesicek, Ondrej Krejcar, Ali Selamat,
   and Kamil Kuca

Sentiment Analysis and Social Media

Timeline Summarization for Event-Related Discussions on a Chinese
Social Media Platform.   579
   Han Wang and Jia-Ling Koh

Evidential Link Prediction in Uncertain Social Networks Based
on Node Attributes   595
   Sabrine Mallek, Imen Boukhris, Zied Elouedi, and Eric Lefevre

Arabic Tweets Sentimental Analysis Using Machine Learning   602
   Khaled Mohammad Alomari, Hatem M. ElSherif, and Khaled Shaalan

Getting Frustrated: Modelling Emotional Contagion
in Stranded Passengers.   611
    C. Natalie van der Wal, Maik Couwenberg, and Tibor Bosse

An Agent-Based Evacuation Model with Social Contagion Mechanisms
and Cultural Factors   620
    C. Natalie van der Wal, Daniel Formolo, and Tibor Bosse

A Consensus Approach to Sentiment Analysis   628
    Orestes Appel, Francisco Chiclana, Jenny Carter, and Hamido Fujita

Way of Coordination of Visual Modeling and Mental Imagery
in Conceptual Solution of Project Task   635
    P. Sosnin and M. Galochkin

Author Index   639

Games, Computer Vision and Animation

Annotating Movement Phrases in Vietnamese Folk Dance Videos

Chau Ma-Thi[1(✉)], Karim Tabia[2], Sylvain Lagrue[2], Ha Le-Thanh[1], Duy Bui-The[1], and Thuy Nguyen-Thanh[1]

[1] HMI Lab, VNU University of Engineering and Technology, Hanoi, Vietnam
ma.thi.chau@gmail.com
[2] Artois University, CRIL - CNRS UMR 8188, Arras, France

Abstract. This paper aims at the annotation of movement phrases in Vietnamese folk dance videos that were mainly gathered, stored and used in teaching at art schools and in preserving cultural intangible heritages (performed by different famous folk dance masters). We propose a framework of automatic movement phrase annotation, in which the motion vectors are used as movement phrase features. Movement phrase classification can be carried out, based on dancer's trajectories. A deep investigation of Vietnamese folk dance gives an idea of using optical flow as movement phrase features in movement phrase detection and classification. For the richness and usefulness in annotation of Vietnamese folk dance, a lookup table of movement phrase descriptions is defined. In initial experiments, a sample movement phrase dataset is built up to train k-NN classification model. Experiments have shown the effectiveness of the proposed framework of automatic movement phrase annotation with classification accuracy at least 88%.

Keywords: Video annotation · Movement phrase · Vietnamese folk dance

1 Introduction

Dance notation which has been used by dance trainers and choreographers can be considered as an effective intermediate tool to fill the gaps between human's readability and machine's one in dance analysis. Choosing and using a suitable dance notation, we could make sense of data in processing dance videos by transforming unstructured videos into semantic video.

Vietnamese folk dances are various and plentiful because Vietnam is a country having a rich diversity of ethnics, regions and cultures. Folk dance performance and training are indispensable in preserving and promoting this type of folk art. Vietnamese folk dances are decomposed into poses and basic movements. Similar postures and movements can be done repeatedly with some modifications, depending on the context, performers' emotional status and age. Nowadays in Vietnam, dance videos in general, and folk dance ones in particular, have

© Springer International Publishing AG 2017
S. Benferhat et al. (Eds.): IEA/AIE 2017, Part II, LNAI 10351, pp. 3–11, 2017.
DOI: 10.1007/978-3-319-60045-1_1

become a main resource to be exploited. The big issue in teaching and training folk dances is how to extract movement phrases and basic dance primitives from videos provided by famous folk dance masters themselves in art school's archives [13]. Another practical problem in folk dance video processing is the heterogeneity of different resources to be integrated in the dance analysis training and per-formed with different video recording tools of different quality levels.

Our objective is to build up an initial vocabulary of Vietnam folk dance primitives. For that purpose, we will carry out a segmentation of dances in videos into movement phrases, then into dance primitives. Then, each movement phrase, dance primitive will be interpreted in a notation framework such as Benesh notation [7,8] or Labanotation [1,4]. It will also give initial descriptions in Vietnamese folk dance ontology building. Notations of movement phrases, movement primitives and the Vietnamese folk dance ontology can be used for searching, retrieving and matching dances in practical folk dance training and preserving.

In this paper, we propose an automatic framework of movement phrase annotation in Vietnamese folk dance videos. We present a process of constructing sample Vietnamese folk dance phrase dataset, which is used to train a movement phrase classification model. We also suggest a feature detection suitable to movement phrase detection and classification based on characteristics of Vietnamese folk dances. Then, we annotate movement phrases using predefined descriptive lookup table. This paper is organized as follows. Section 2 briefly presents about Vietnamese folk dance structure. Section 3 shows related works on video annotation and video shot detection. In Sect. 4, we present the proposed framework for Vietnamese folk dance phrase annotation. Experimental results are presented in Sect. 5.

2   Vietnamese Traditional Folk Dance

The analysis of Vietnam folk dances is based on four main terms [13]: movement phrases, movement primitives, basic dance poses, and dance orientations. There are eight dance orientations including $ort1$, $ort2$, $ort3$, $ort4$, $ort5$, $ort6$, $ort7$, $ort8$ (Fig. 1a). First orientation, $ort1$ is the direction from the stage where dancer performs dance to audience. Two consecutive orientations make an angle value 45^0C. Basic dance poses are postures of hands, arms, legs at a time in sequence of movements. Figure 1b shows 6 arm poses. Movement primitives are shot movements which change between basic dance poses. Movement primitives include basic hand movements, upper/lower arm ones, feet ones, upper/lower leg ones, head ones, and arm-leg ones. A movement phrase is a simple movement which changes position, orientation of the whole body of dancer in space. Vietnam traditional folk dance is different from modern one by the fact that there is no movements which lift dancer on the air. So, movement phrases in Vietnamese folk dance are not too complicated: the dancers move only on the stage and change their positions only on a plane. Therefore, a movement phrase has trajectory in the form of a line, an arc or a dot on a plane. Movement phrases include moving spot, translation, and rotation. Moving spot can be in eight orientations. Translation can be in one of eight orientations. There are two types of rotation: clockwise and counter clockwise [13].

Fig. 1. a, Dance orientation. b, Arm poses.

3   Related Works

3.1   Movement Phrase Detection

Movement phrase detection in dance video is one kind of video shot detection. A shot is defined as consecutive series of frames that present continuous actions. "Shots can be effectively considered as the smallest indexing unit where no changes in scene content can be perceived" [2]. To detect shots, features are extracted from each frame in video. Then, the resemblance measurement is done to compare consecutive frames, using extracted features. Shot boundaries are detected as frames where their features are not similar to those of previous frames. There are three main steps in shot detection: feature extraction, resemblance measurement and extracting boundary [9]. In shot detection, features are in the form of motion vectors, color histograms [10], block color histogram, and edge change ratio [11], scale invariant feature transform [19], salient map [17], corner points [16]. In order to determine a resemblance degree between frames, represented in the form of extracted feature vectors, Euclidean distance, chi-squared similarity, 1-norm cosine dissimilarity and the histogram intersection are most commonly used similarity metrics [6]. In addition, the earth movers distance [10], shared information [5] are also used as similarity measures. Besides, [6] suggested a pairwise similarity which measures the resemblance among consecutive frames and similarities among frames within a window. Shot boundary can be identified by the comparison of calculated resemblance among frames.

In shot detection, camera motion affects significantly on the results because in addition to foreground, we must also consider the background. In videos with illumination changes and motion, features of color histograms are more variable as compared to edges. Motion vector can be influenced by object motion and camera one. In general, edge features, and motion features are outperformed by color histogram. Especially, shot detection depends on shot definition related to application domain. Different from usual video shot detection, video dance shot detection gives out a new challenge how to segment dance videos into meaningful shots (phrase movements, here in this paper).

3.2   Movement Phrase Annotation

Movement phrase annotation is the main task in Vietnamese folk dance video annotation problem, which is fundamental to information sharing, exchanging and reusing. Annotation gives descriptions both at syntactic level and at semantic one, involving structural and low-level video features and the analysis of visual contents.

For different purposes, there are lots of video annotation tools with different techniques. [15] proposed effectively semi-automatic video content annotation technique. A video was represented using a hierarchy. An algorithm combining visual contents and semantics was proposed to visualize and refine the annotation results. Various video indexing strategies describing video contents are: (1) High level indexing; (2) Low level indexing; and (3) Domain specific indexing. Video contents were described using four content descriptors: video description, group description, shot description and frame one. In [12], a dynamically changing topic technique which represented the relationship between video frames and associated text labels was acquired by using hierarchical topic trajectory model. This technique incorporated cooccurrences among video information and temporal dynamics of videos. In [18], texts and captions were detected by a corner based approach from videos. Corner points were discriminating features. In detecting moving captions, motion features were extracted by optical flow, combined with text features to detect the moving caption patterns. No text regions formed by the corner points appeared in the background, text regions can be filtered out efficiently. In [14], a semi-supervised learning approach was proposed for interesting event video annotation by means of information from the Internet. Three features were used: Event recognition, Event Localization and Semantic search and navigation. A fast graph-based semi-supervised multiple instance learning algorithm was proposed to tackle difficulties in a generic framework for various video domains. It explored small scale expert labeled videos and large scale unlabeled videos to train the models. Resemblance measure was multiple instance learning induced similarity. Videos were represented in the form of multiple instances. [20] used the concept of semantic diffusion to efficiently refine large scale images and video annotation. Graph diffusion formulation was used to improve concept annotation scores. Input to the system was the labels tagged by web users. Semantic graph was built. The graph was then applied in semantic diffusion to refine concept annotation results. In [3], an automatic video annotation technique was proposed to introduce the video retrieval and sharing process in smart TV environments. Two types of ontologies were described: ontologies for content description and ontologies for domain knowledge acquisition. Video annotation concentrated on analysis of video contents including colors, shapes, illumination, and texts. Most of video annotation systems are semi-automatic because it needs human's decision for semantic meaning. In Vietnamese folk dance video annotation, we focus mainly on dancer's movement, expressed in basic dance primitives, dancer's trajectories which will be gathered in dance vocabularies.

4   A Framework for Vietnamese Folk Movement Phrase Annotation

Assume we have a set of Vietnamese folk dance videos. Each video has one dancer and the background is static (see Sect. 5 for details).

A framework for determining movement phrases and corresponding annotation, with input video performed by trainees or non-professional amateurs, has 3 main parts: Movement phrase detection, Movement phrase classification and Movement phrase annotation/interpretation.

Movement Phrase Detection: Vietnamese folk dance movements are gentle and slow, dancers change pose very quickly, stopping a movement phrase and starting a new one in some instants. Features used to detect shots from videos express mainly dancer movements (moving object), especially sudden changes in movements. Motion vector is chosen as a suitable feature. At the frame t, the corresponding motion vector element $P(t)$ on moving object is a couple of Mag and Ort, that stand for Magnitude and Orientation, respectively. Magnitude of the vector is calculated mainly from moving pixels (belong to dancer), given in the form of a curve by the time. We find out all extreme of the curve. Frames in video, which are corresponding to extreme, give boundaries of shot partitions.

Movement Phrase Classification: Phrase Feature Extraction: Based on folk dance documents and ex-pert discussions [13], there are 11 main phrase: $Spot\_mov$, Tr_O1, Tr_O2, Tr_O3, Tr_O4, Tr_O5, Tr_O6, Tr_O7, Tr_O8, R_CW and R_CCW, corresponding to spot moving, translation in eight orientations, moving in a counter clockwise/clockwise arc. Figure 2 shows some frames of Tr_O1. Orientation corresponding to the largest magnitudes (only on moving object) of

Fig. 2. Movement phrase Tr_O1.

movement phrases in motion vector are considered features in classifying movement phrases. So, each sample movement phrase dataset element includes orientation of phrase movement vector and corresponding labels. Denote the sample movement phrase dataset as $\Phi = \{\Phi_1, \Phi_2..., \Phi_N\}$, where $\Phi_i = (P(t_i).Ort, l_i)$, N is the number of sample movement phrases and l_i is class label.

Training on labeled phrase dataset: Given a collection of labeled Vietnamese folk movement phrases, training algorithms aims at building up parameters in a chosen supervised model, such as SVM, k-NN,... for making a class label as a function of orientation attribute (see Fig. 3a).

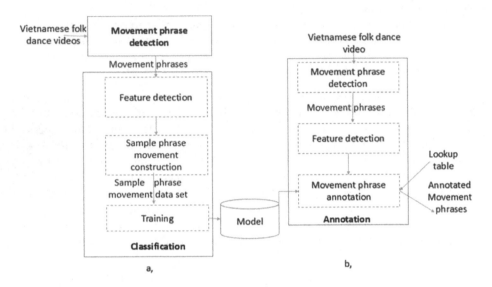

Fig. 3. Movement phrase classification model and annotation.

Classification: Given as input an orientation of a movement phrase, extracted from movement phrase video, chosen supervised models give the result label, corresponding to its features.

Annotation and Interpretation: Lookup table (see Table 1) shows descriptions of Vietnamese folk dance movement phrases, correspondent to 11 movement phrases for Vietnamese folk dances. In annotation stage, movement phrases are extracted from a dance video input, then classified using trained model to obtain a corresponding label and description in the lookup table (see Fig. 3b).

5   Experiments

For experiments, we used MatLab R2016a with Image Processing Toolbox and Computer Vision Toolbox. We divide videos into shots which are corresponding to movement phrases. Optical flow is a projection of the real world 3D motion

Table 1. Lookup table of movement phrase description.

No	MP names	Corresponding descriptions
1	*Spot_mov*	Dancer performs arm/leg movements while his body position doesn't change
2	*Tr_O1*	Dancer moves in trajectory of a line in *ort1* while dancing
3	*Tr_O2*	Dancer moves in trajectory of a line in *ort2* while dancing
4	*Tr_O3*	Dancer moves in trajectory of a line in *ort3* while dancing
5	*Tr_O4*	Dancer moves in trajectory of a line in *ort4* while dancing
6	*Tr_O5*	Dancer moves in trajectory of a line in *ort5* while dancing
7	*Tr_O6*	Dancer moves in trajectory of a line in *ort6* while dancing
8	*Tr_O7*	Dancer moves in trajectory of a line in *ort7* while dancing
9	*Tr_O8*	Dancer moves in trajectory of a line in *ort8* while dancing
10	*R_CW*	Dancer moves in trajectory of an arc in clockwise while dancing
11	*R_CCW*	Dancer moves in trajectory of an arc counterclockwise while dancing

onto 2D images. In this paper, we use optical flow as an approximation of the motion vector. In optical flow, magnitudes are large at the indexes corresponding to pixels of dancer in videos. We apply optical flow to movement phrase detection in Vietnamese folk dance videos. We only use M biggest magnitude values on moving objects. M is calculated as flows. In first five frames in the input video, we track dancer. M is defined as the average number of pixels belonging to the dancer. The orientation component in the optical flow with the largest magnitudes expresses also the trajectory of moving objects, hence, it is used as feature in movement phrase classification.

For each among 11 labels of movement phrases, we get 10 sample videos. The experimental classification model, used for labeling movement phrases in our experimentation, is k-NN. Given a Vietnamese folk dance video, movement phrases are extracted from input video. They are matched with others in the dataset, finding k nearest neighbors. To evaluate movement phrase annotation, for testing each label, we use 3 movement phrase videos. These movement phrase videos are shown to experts, dance masters and proposed to be labeled using 11 labels as said above. We determine the confusion matrix C of the classification result, given by k-NN, of which each element c_{ij} means the ratio of samples of ith label recognized as j^{th} one. In this experimentation, c_{ij} are 0.93, 0.98, 0.88, 0.96, 0.88, 0.97, 0.89, 0.95, 0.89, 0.92, 0.88 for $i = 1$ to 11 respectively. There are only 21 values $c_{ij} > 0$ for $i <> j$, of which the biggest one is $c_{11} = 0.1$ and the smallest one is $c_{21} = c_{27} = c_{45} = 0.01$.

6   Conclusion

Vietnamese folk dances are various and rich in ethnic, region and culture characteristics. Folk dance performance and training, preserving and promoting folk dances request applying advanced technologies to making sense of folk dance videos gathered, stored and used at art schools. This work aims at the classification and annotation of movement phrases in Vietnamese folk dance videos using motion vector as features. An expert based investigation of Vietnamese folk dance allows using optical flow as good movement phrase features. Furthermore, dance orientation is shown effective for movement phrase classification. Initial experiments with a built-up sample movement phrase dataset, k-NN classification model have shown the effectiveness of the proposed framework of automatic movement phrase annotation with acceptable classification accuracy. In the near future, we will expand the experiments with different features, and different models. We also broaden dataset and test on folk dances from different regions of Vietnam.

Acknowledgments. This work has received support from the European project H2020 Marie Sklodowska-Curie Actions (MSCA) research and Innovation Staff Exchange (RISE): AniAge (High Dimensional Heterogeneous Data based Animation Techniques for Southeast Asian Intangible Cultural Heritage Digital Con-tent), project number 691215.

References

1. LaViers, A., Bai, L., Bashiri, M., Heddy, G., Sheng, Y.: Abstractions for design-by-humans of Heterogeneous Behaviors. In: Laumond, J.-P., Abe, N. (eds.) Dance Notations and Robot Motion. Springer Tracts in Advanced Robotics, vol. 111, pp. 237–262. Springer, Switzerland (2015)
2. Patel, D.H.: Content based video retrieval: a survey. Int. J. Comput. Appl. **109**(13), January 2015
3. Jeong, J.-W., Hong, H.-K., Lee, D.-H.: Ontology-based automatic video annotation technique in smart TV environment. IEEE Trans. Consum. Electron. **57**(4), 1830–1836 (2011)
4. El Raheb, K., Ioannidis, Y.: A labanotation based ontology for representing dance movement. In: Proceedings of the 9th International Gesture Workshop (2011)
5. Bai, L., Lao, S.-Y., Liu, H.-T., Bu, J.: Video shot boundary detection using Petrinet. In: 2008 International Conference on Machine Learning and Cybernetics, vol. 5, pp. 3047–3051. IEEE (2008)
6. Cooper, M., Liu, T., Rieffel, E.: Video segmentation via temporal pattern classification. IEEE Trans. Multimedia **9**(3), 610–618 (2007)
7. Neagle, R.J.: Emotion by motion: expression simulation in Virtual Ballet. Thesis of Doctor of Philosophy. The University Of Leeds School of computing. United Kingdom (2005)
8. Saad, S., De Beul, D., Mahmoudi, S., Manneback, P.: An ontology for video human movement representation based on benesh notation. In: International Conference on Multimedia Computing and Systems (2012)
9. Chantamunee, S., Gotoh, Y.: University of Sheffield at trecvid 2007: Shot boundary detection and rushes summarization. In: TRECVID. Citeseer (2007)
10. Hoi, S.C., Wong, L.L., Lyu, A.: Chinese university of hongkong at trecvid 2006: shot boundary detection and video search. In: TRECVid 2006 Workshop, pp. 76–86 (2006)

11. Porter, S.V.: Video segmentation and indexing using motion estimation. Ph.D. dissertation, University of Bristol (2004)
12. Nakano, T., Kimura, A.: Automatic video annotation via hierarchical topic trajectory model considering cross-modal correlations. In: IEEE 2011 (2011)
13. Ngoc, T.T.: CHEO dance curriculum. Hanoi Academy of Theatre and Cinema (1998)
14. Zhang, T., Xu, C., Zhu, G.: A generic framework for video annotation via semi-supervised learning. IEEE Trans. Multimedia 14(4), 1206–1219 (2012)
15. Zhu, X., Fan, J., Xue, X., Wu, L., Elmagarmid, A.K.: Semi-automatic video content annotation. In: Proceeding of Third IEEE Pacific Rim Conference on Multimedia, pp. 37–52 (2008)
16. Gao, X., Li, J., Shi, Y.: A video shot boundary detection algorithm based on feature tracking. In: Wang, G.-Y., Peters, J.F., Skowron, A., Yao, Y. (eds.) RSKT 2006. LNCS, vol. 4062, pp. 651–658. Springer, Heidelberg (2006). doi:10.1007/11795131_95
17. Wu, X., Yuen, P.C., Liu, C., Huang, J., Detection, S.B.: An information saliency approach. In: 2008 Congress on Image and Signal Processing, pp. 808–812 (2008)
18. Zhao, X., Lin, K.-H., Yun, F., Corners, T.F.: A novel approach to detect text and caption in videos. IEEE Trans. Image Process. 20(3), 2296–2305 (2011)
19. Chang, Y., Lee, D.J., Hong, Y., Archibald, J.: Unsupervised video shot detection using clustering ensemble with a color global scale invariant feature transform descriptor. EURASIP J. Image Video Process. 2008, 1–10 (2008)
20. Jiang, Y.G., Dai, Q., Wang, J., Ngo, C.W.: Fast semantic Diffusion for large scale context based image and video annotation. IEEE Trans. Image Process. 21(6), 3080–3091 (2012)

Mining the Lattice of Binary Classifiers for Identifying Duplicate Labels in Behavioral Data

Quentin Labernia, Victor Codocedo, Céline Robardet, and Mehdi Kaytoue[✉]

Université de Lyon, CNRS, INSA-Lyon, LIRIS UMR5205, 69621 Lyon, France
mehdi.kaytoue@insa-lyon.fr

Abstract. Analysis of behavioral data represents today a big issue, as so many domains generate huge quantity of activity and mobility traces. When traces are labeled by the user that generates it, models can be learned to accurately predict the user of an unknown trace. In online systems however, users may have several virtual identities, or duplicate labels. By ignoring them, the prediction accuracy drastically drops, as the set of all virtual identities of a single person is not known beforehand. In this article, we tackle this *duplicate labels identification problem*, and present an original approach that explores the lattice of binary classifiers. Each subset of labels is learned as the positive class against the others (the negative class), and constraints make possible to identify duplicate labels while pruning the search space. We experiment this original approach with data of the video game STARCRAFT 2 in the new context of Electronic Sports (eSport) with encouraging results.

Keywords: Binary classification · Label duplicate · Data quality

1 Introduction

Sensors are nowadays part of our daily life, hidden in our cars, phones or watches and recording our position, speed, bio-signals, etc. Professional athletes may have position sensors in their shoes when playing soccer, or in their racket when playing tennis. Alone or combined together, these (mobile) devices generate rich behavioral data which, properly analyzed by means of data mining, machine learning and visualization techniques, can help answering several industrial challenges and inventing new services and applications for the common good.

In this article, we are interested in user identification techniques from behavioral data. Such methods are useful for security applications (fraud detection, targeted marketing, identity usurpation) and privacy preserving issues (e.g., for evaluating data anonymization techniques). There are indeed several domains for which it was established that the user who has generated a trace can be found through data analysis techniques: only a few points of interest in space

S. Benferhat et al. (Eds.): IEA/AIE 2017, Part II, LNAI 10351, pp. 12–21, 2017.
DOI: 10.1007/978-3-319-60045-1_2

and time uniquely identify a person [2]; typing patterns allow to recognize a person typing his password [7] or even playing a video game [9], etc.

However, especially on the Web, it often happens that a user has several identities (called *avatar aliases* in the remainder of this paper) and that the mapping between users and aliases is not known beforehand. For example, one issue for targeted marketing applications is to identify that several Web cookies from different devices (tablet, smart phone, laptop, computer...) belong to the same individual [5]. In this work, we consider behavioral data from video games, as such data are extremely rich, freely available on the Web and without privacy preserving issues. Moreover, the video game industry is in crucial need of automatic methods to be able to detect cheaters, that is, users usurping an avatar [8]; as well as electronic sport structures seek to identify professional athletes hiding their tactics behind avatars when training on the Internet (more details are given in [1]).

It was shown in the context of online gaming by [9] that prediction models learned from particular typing patterns (keyboard usage while playing) can very accurately identify a player. Accuracy however strongly degrades in presence of avatar aliases: when individuals use several virtual identities the model hardly detects that two labels (or more) in the data describe the same user, that is, these two labels are avatar aliases. We refer in what follows to this problem as the *duplicate labels identification problem*: given a set of behavioral traces labeled by avatars, output groups of avatars that each denotes the same user.

Problem. Consider a set of users U and a set online identities L called avatars, the duplicate labels identification problem consists in discovering the mapping $f : U \rightarrow \wp(L)$ that corresponds to the set of identities assigned to each user. Note that $\wp(L)$ is the power set of L. The objective is to partition L into a set of label sets, each label block corresponding to an unknown yet unique user.

Recently, Cavadenti et al. presented an original approach to solve this problem [1]: it relies on mining the confusion matrix yielded by a supervised classifier, and exploiting the confusion the classifier has in presence of avatar aliases. Whereas this method has interesting results for identifying avatar aliases, it has a drawback we propose to address in this paper: it operates as a post-processing of a unique classification model and under exploits the power of classification algorithms by considering a static target value. Consequently, some classes, especially unbalanced ones, cannot be properly learned. Our intuition is that, when merged with their aliases, these classes should be properly learned.

Consequently, the approach we introduce takes advantage of the power of classification algorithms by recomputing the model for all target generalizations. We thus explore the lattice of binary classifiers, where each set of labels (duplicate candidate) is evaluated against all the other labels. For each new generated subset, the confusion matrix is compared to those of its subsets to tell us either (a) that the label subsets (i.e. positive examples) belongs to a same user, or (b) to prune the search space by stopping the enumeration of it supersets. To do so, we study the evolution of (i) the F1-measure and (ii) the distribution of the data objects in the positive/negative classes while generalizing label subsets.

2 Method

We propose an original method that considers the lattice of binary classifiers, where each element is a model learned from positive and negative examples that are respectively the instances of a subset of labels B and their complementary instances. This constitutes the search space of our problem and each binary classifier forms a potential group of avatar duplicate. We propose an efficient way to traverse the lattice of binary classifier to output the set of *duplicate label sets*.

2.1 The Lattice of Binary Classifiers

Consider a set of traces T. Each trace is labeled by an avatar $label(t) = l$, with $t \in T, l \in L$. Consider now an arbitrary subset of labels $B \subseteq L$. Its corresponding binary classifier ρ_B is learned from positive and negative examples. The positive class is given by $B \subseteq L$ and the negative class by $\bar{B} = L \backslash B$. The data instances of the positive class are thus the set traces labeled by any $b \in B$, i.e.

Table 1. Confusion matrix of a binary classifier ρ_B.

		Prediction	
	C^{ρ_B}	$+$	$-$
Reality	$+$	α_{++}	α_{+-}
	$-$	α_{-+}	α_{--}

$\mathcal{I}_+(B) = \{t \in T \mid label(t) \in B\}$, while the instances of the negative class are the remaining ones, i.e. $\mathcal{I}_-(B) = T \setminus \mathcal{I}_+(B) = \{t \in T \mid label(t) \in \bar{B}\}$.

Definition 1 BINARY CLASSIFIER AND CONFUSION MATRIX. *For any $B \subseteq L$, we define a classifier $\rho_B \colon T \longrightarrow \{+, -\}$. The confusion matrix C^{ρ_B} of this binary classifier is given in Table 1 where each score α_{ij}, with $i, j \in \{+, -\}$, counts the number of traces with class i classified as class j. Incidentally, it is easy to observe that α_{++} corresponds to true positives, α_{+-} to false negatives, α_{-+} to false positives and α_{--} to true negatives.*

Definition 2 SCORES OF A BINARY CLASSIFIER. *Given a non-empty subset of labels $B \subseteq L$ and its binary classifier ρ_B. From the confusion matrix of the classification of traces, we compute two scores $\varphi_B \in [0, 1]$ and $p_B \in \mathbb{N}$ such that*

$$\varphi_B = \frac{2 \cdot \alpha_{++}}{(2 \cdot \alpha_{++}) + (\alpha_{+-}) + (\alpha_{-+})} \qquad p_B = (\alpha_{++}) + (\alpha_{+-}) + (\alpha_{-+})$$

Intuitively, φ_B corresponds to the F1-score or the harmonic mean of the precision and recall measures associated to the classification of traces. The score p_B counts the number of "similar traces" according to the model, i.e. traces that are well classified in the positive class as well as the confusion.

Definition 3 LATTICE OF BINARY CLASSIFIERS. $\mathcal{L} = (\wp(L), \subseteq)$ *constitutes a Boolean lattice where each element B is associated to a classifier ρ_B.*

Our method relies on the study of the changes of the measures φ_B and p_B while enumerating the search space in a bottom up fashion (from singletons $B = \{l\}, l \in L$ towards $B = L$). The main idea is to find out maximal elements B (the most general) for which a set of constraints holds, such that one can assume that B is the set of avatar aliases of a single user $f(u) = B, u \in U$.

2.2   Constraining the Set of Binary Classifiers

The general idea is to enumerate the lattice of binary classifiers and evaluate each element to assess if it represents a set of duplicate labels or not. As the number of elements is exponential w.r.t the number of labels, it is not acceptable to enumerate all of them. We introduce two constraints a classifier should respect so that it represents an actual set of duplicate labels. These constraints rely on the evolution of the $F1$-measure and the distribution of the data objects in the positive and negative classes within its downset. It implies an algorithm with a bottom-up enumeration (from $\emptyset$ to L) of the lattice, which is affordable as duplicate labels sets are rather small in most of the applications (we could not find an application where an individual has hundreds of different aliases).

The first constraint relies on the following intuition. If $E \subseteq L$ is set of duplicates, its binary classifier ρ_E should be more robust than any of its subsets. Rewriting $E = C \cup D$, if it exists a subset $C \subset E$ such that $\varphi_C \geq \varphi_E$, it means that merging together C and D must be avoided. More formally, a set $E \subseteq L$ is valid if it respects Constraint 1.

Constraint 1. *Consider a label set $E \subseteq L$ and its associated classifier ρ_E. E is a valid set of labels iff it respects the following constraint, $\forall C, D \subseteq E, E = C \cup D$, $\varphi_E \geqslant max(\varphi_C, \varphi_D)$.*

Note that φ_E is not monotone, but Constraint 1 is. However, this constraint alone is not sufficient. Indeed, we may have robust classifiers merged together which does not consider similar set of positive and negative examples, that is, better classifier but which does not merge duplicates labels. Still considering the sets $C, D \subseteq E$, we need another constraint to control that indeed the instances assigned to E are those assigned to C and D. To be more robust, rather than observing directly the set of instances, we show how the score p_E should be expressed in terms of p_C and p_D so that the classifier ρ_E is valid.

For all $B \subset L$, P_B is the set of traces well identified to be duplicates (true positives) along with the traces confused by the classifier ρ_B (false positives and false negatives). Two traces confused by the classifier can belong to the same duplicated labels, but sometimes they can belong to different labels (the classifier can make a mistake confusing two traces they are not as similar as it seems w.r.t. other traces). Thus, if the set $E = C \cup D$ is a set of duplicates, then we consider that we can reasonably write $P_E = (P_C \cup P_D) \cap \mathcal{E}$, where $\mathcal{E}$ is the set of traces that are confused by ρ_C or ρ_D but not by ρ_E. Intuitively, this property we defined considers that if the set E is a set of duplicates, the merging between two of its subsets C and D results in that P_E does not contain traces that are not in P_C or P_D, i.e., P_E is a subset of $(P_C \cup P_D)$. So, it gives that $|P_E| \leq |P_C \cup P_D|$, with $|P_E| = p_E$. The formula $|P_E| = |P_C| + |P_D| - |P_C \cap P_D|$ always holds and enables us to estimate the upper bound of the validity interval of p_E. Also, it is clear that the set P_E contains at least the elements within P_C or P_D: the lower bound of the validity interval is $|P_E| \geq max(|P_C|, |P_D|)$.

Constraint 2. *We introduce* $\mu\colon \wp(P)^2 \longrightarrow \mathbb{N}$ *and* $\theta \in [0,1]$ *such that*

$$|P_C \cap P_D| = \mu(P_C, P_D) \cdot \theta \tag{1}$$

where θ *represents the overlapping factor between* P_C *and* P_D *given a arbitrary measure* μ*. We have then naturally the following constraint,* $\forall C, D \subset E$*,* $E = C \cup D$*,*

$$max(|P_C|, |P_D|) \leqslant |P_E| \leqslant |P_C| + |P_D| - \mu(P_C, P_D) \cdot \theta \tag{2}$$

$$\mu(P_C, P_D) \leqslant min(|P_C|, |P_D|) \tag{3}$$

We can choose for example $\mu(P_C, P_D) = min(|P_C|, |P_D|)$ *and* $\theta = min(\varphi_C, \varphi_D)$ *as a way to estimate its value.*

In Eq. 1, rewriting the upper bounds allows us to control a minimal overlapping factor between the instances of C and D: when this overlapping factor is zero, it means that p_C and p_D do not have to overlap. On the flip side, the more the overlapping factor, the stronger the similarity constraint. In practice, it is required to set an increasing similarity constraint because experience has shown that the confusion of singleton classifier $\rho_{\{l\};l\in L}$ is less accurate than that of a classifier ρ_B with B a set of a higher cardinality. This is why we choose to express θ in function of φ.

In the end, we introduce the two mappings $C_1 : L \to \{true, false\}$ and $C_2 : L \to \{true, false\}$ telling if a subset of labels verifies respectively Constraint 1 and Constraint 2. A subset $B \subseteq L$ is valid iff $C_1(B) = true$ and $C_2(B) = true$.

2.3   Characterizing the Result

Remembering that our goal is to discover the avatar set $f : U \to \wp(L)$ for any user $u \in U$. As we have no information about the users, our output shall be a set of label sets, each one belonging to a unique and unknown user. It means that we are looking at a partition of L. We construct our result as follows. Firstly, the set of all valid label sets is given by $\mathcal{V} = \{ B \subseteq L \mid C_1(B) = true \wedge C_2(B) = true\}$.

The final result we are looking for is the set of maximal elements of $\mathcal{V}$ w.r.t. set inclusion: $\mathcal{R} = \{v \in \mathcal{V} \mid \nexists v' \in \mathcal{V} \text{ s.t. } v \subseteq v'\}$. $\mathcal{R}$ is an anti-chain of the lattice $(\wp(L), \subseteq)$, hence it is not necessarily a partition of the label set. $\mathcal{R}$ is here a tolerance relation, that is a set of sets that covers L but that can overlap (as opposed to a partition or equivalence relation where parts cannot overlap). We could as such enforce the fact that our result is a partition, e.g. by choosing some elements to remove, or adding constraints in the definition of the set $\mathcal{V}$. However, given our initial hypothesis and the choice of our constraints we should observe in practice that $\mathcal{R}$ is a partition as (i) only duplicates labels should be merged together (no intersecting parts), (ii) the singletons cannot be pruned by the constraints by definition (parts covering L). The only possible explanation for not having a partition is the case an avatar would be shared between several users: it shall be pruned early and not joined with another set respecting C_1 and C_2, we check this assumption in the experiments. Finally, note that it could be shown that $\mathcal{L} = ((\mathcal{V} \cup \emptyset \cup L), \subseteq)$ is a lattice, and that $\mathcal{R}$ is the anti-chain composed of all co-atoms.

2.4   Algorithm

The theoretical search space is the power set of labels $(\wp(L), \subseteq)$. We explore this lattice in a level-wise manner. Firstly, "*singleton*" classifiers $\rho_{\{l\}, l \in L}$ are generated. These singletons are pairwise combined to generate the next level, and so on. The new model is learned and tested to be valid or not. If the new classifier is valid, it will be used to generate the next level. If the classifier is not valid, the set is marked as irrelevant and none of its super sets shall be considered. The algorithm continues until there is no more possible merging. The worst-case complexity is $O(h \cdot 2^{|L|})$ where h depends on the classification method ρ used.

3   Experiments

This section reports an evaluation of our approach through both quantitative and qualitative experiments. As we study the video game STARCRAFT 2 and seek to identify groups of avatars belonging to the same player, we consider the same data of [1]. All experiments were performed on a 2,5 GHz Intel Core i7 with 8 GB main memory running OSX. The basic enumeration algorithm was coded in python. We used the Weka's implementations of several supervised classification methods to build the models $\rho_{B \subseteq L}$ [4].

3.1   Data and Experimental Settings

Replay collections. There are two collections of replays: C_1 and C_2. A replay is a game record which contains all actions made by the players, hence several behavioral traces each labeled by an avatar. The first collection is composed of the 955 games made by 171 expert players during the *2014 World Championship Series*. The rules of this tournament ensure us that there is no avatar aliases in this collection. We use this collection to build a ground truth, that is, inserting avatars aliases. The second collection is composed of 10,108 one-versus-one games taken on a specialized website entailing 3,805 players. We use this collection as real-world settings.

Features and classification models. We use the same features than two previous works to train the classifiers $\rho_{B \subseteq L}$. We briefly recall them and refer the interested reader to the work of [1,9]. The game allows the player to customize its usage of the keyboard in a limited way (change the function associated to keys 0 to 9). There are three ways to use a key given the current state of the game which implies 30 features counting the frequency of the different key usage by the player. A few other features were also added, such as the number of actions per minutes made by a player (up to 300 for expert players). When there is no avatar duplicates in the replay collection under study, it was indeed shown that these features allows to predict the avatar with an accuracy over 95%. Although our method is independent of the choice of a classification method, we report with several techniques (knn, J48, Multilayer Perceptron, Naive Bayes, RandomForest and SMO) and their basic *Weka* implementations ([4]). In the end, we learn the model $\rho_{B,B\subseteq L}$ from a set of traces with positive (a set of avatars) and negative (the other avatars) examples and use a using 10-cross validation for building the confusion matrices. Then, the scores φ_B and p_B are computed. Note that a unique classification method is used for each full run of our algorithm (we do not "mix" classification models while enumerating the lattice).

Parameters. Concerning the avatar aliases identification problem, we consider three additional parameters also used the previous work of [1]. We consider only the τ first seconds of a game when computing the features as it was show to have an impact in the learning phase (the best being between 10 and 20 s). Second, there are labels with a very few instances which leads to bad average accuracy: we consider a trace in the dataset if its associated avatar has at least $\Theta \in \mathbb{N}$ examples, i.e. $\forall \ell \in L, |T_{\{\ell\}}| \geqslant \Theta$. It was previously shown that good predictions require $\Theta \geq 10$. Finally, a threshold $\Lambda \in [0;1]$ permits the selection of $R \in \mathcal{R}$ iff. $\varphi_R \geqslant \Lambda$. This cut on $\mathcal{R}$ is able to increase precision introduced now.

Ground-truth and evaluation. Given a set of labels, our method aims at finding the set of label sets $\mathcal{R}$ for which each part $R \in \mathcal{R}$ represents duplicate labels (avatar aliases of an unknown, yet unique user). As there exists no ground-truth (for privacy preserving issues the mapping between users and their avatars is not available), we build one. For that matter, we consider datasets built from the collection $\mathcal{C}_1$, where there is no duplicate labels. First, we choose the γ first labels that have the more instances. For each of such labels, we split their set of instances into several parts, each part being an avatar alias. In other words, we replace each of these γ labels by p new labels $(\ell_i)_{i\in[1;p]}$ and a family or *proportions* $(r_i)_{i\in[1;p]}$ such that $\forall i \in [1;p], |T_{\{\ell_i\}}| = \frac{r_i \cdot |T_{\{\ell\}}|}{\sum_{j\in[1;p]} r_j}$. We will use the following notation to explain a split: 1_1_2 means that each label l (with at least γ instances) is replaced by three labels: having respectively 25%, 25% and 50% of the instances of l (randomly distributed). This allow us to study balance issues.

To evaluate a result $\mathcal{R}$ w.r.t. the ground truth $\mathcal{G}$, we proceed as follows. The powerset of labels $\wp(L)$ is cut into positive and negative examples : $\mathcal{G}^+ = \{X \subseteq G, \forall G \in \mathcal{G}\}$ while $\mathcal{G}^- = \wp(G) \backslash \mathcal{G}^+$ and this is our ground truth. We operate similarly to partition the observed result : $\mathcal{R}^+ = \{X \subseteq R, \forall R \in \mathcal{R}\}$ while $\mathcal{R}^- = \wp(R) \backslash \mathcal{R}^+$. We can thus compare the ground truth w.r.t. the observed results : TP, FP and FN (resp. standing for true positives, false positives and false negative) can be defined as usual, as well as the classical evaluation metrics of precision, recall and F1-measure.

This evaluation roughly consists in comparing two partitions. However, $\mathcal{R}$ is not necessarily a partition but may be a tolerance. As explained before, this should not happen. Moreover, a null precision and recall penalize these cases in the experiments.

3.2   Experimental Results

Parameter selection. Before giving our first results, we explain how the main parameters were chosen. We use the collection $\mathcal{C}_1$. The parameter γ is fixed to

10, $\Theta = 15$ and all classifiers were used (except SMO that has bad results). This experiment sets the value of parameter Λ as threshold over the elements of $\mathcal{R}$. This choice is based on the third quantile of false positive series, i.e., elements of $\mathcal{R}$ which are false positives. It ensures to drop 75% of these false positives. The true positive dropped elements rate can be shown on Fig. 1 as a function of τ. The best result is for $\tau = 200$ matching with $\Lambda = 0.78$. Figure 2 illustrates the FP and TP distribution for this final setting. These two figures gives distributions that have been aggregated for all classifiers (without SMO).

Finally, four ways are explored to calculate θ as a function of φ_C, φ_D, $C, D \subseteq L$. These are: $\theta = 0$ (null), min, mean and max. The table on the right side shows aggregated results with parameters $\Gamma = 10$, $\Theta = 20$, $\tau = 200$ and all classifiers used. Although the results have a low mean/high variance (as aggregated results between good and bad clas-

θ	Precision	Recall
null	0.76 ± 0.28	0.69 ± 0.28
min	0.50 ± 0.50	0.22 ± 0.28
mean	0.39 ± 0.49	0.17 ± 0.26
max	0.35 ± 0.48	0.16 ± 0.26

sifiers), it clearly appears that $\theta = 0$ draws the best result. Some classification methods perform particularly well (we have indeed a 97%-precision and 61%-recall for the Naive Bayes classification algorithm with $\theta = 0$, while SMO is an outlier).

Run-time and memory analysis. Given the chosen parameters, we build several ground truth $\mathcal{G}$ with different proportions, some fully balanced other unbalanced. Recall that, e.g., (1_1_1_1) means that an original class was cut into 4 subclasses, each with the same amount of instances, while (1_4) means that a class was cut into two, with an unbalanced distribution of 20% vs. 80%. For all classification method we used, the number of generated nodes in the lattices of binary classifiers was less than a thousand which is insignificant w.r.t. the size of the theoretical search space 2^{171}. This means that our constraints allows very early pruning which makes the method possible in practice: Except for the method SMO, all run times were below 50 s.

Efficiency analysis. Still with the same parameters, we show some aspects on how efficient the method is. Figure 3 plots the precision and recall of our method when comparing the obtained results $\mathcal{R}$ with the ground truth $\mathcal{G}$. The main result is that the *Naive Bayes* implementation gives the best results, favors precision over recall, and is robust with unbalanced classes. Actually, as our method requires that the two constraints C_1 and C_2 are valid for any subset, our method favors precision in general. In an unreported experiment, we observed that the method favors recall if we set the restriction to the existence of only at least two different direct subsets that respect the two constraints. However, the goal in user identification is generally to favor precision.

Qualitative experiment. Until now, the goal of the experiments was to study how our method can retrieve a ground truth: traces of Collection C_1 had no duplicate, we inserted some in a controlled way and observed how they can be retrieved. In this last experiment, we run our method on the collection C_2 which

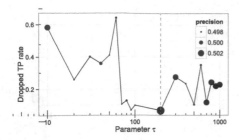

Fig. 1. % of dropped TP as a function of parameter τ when setting Λ as the third quantile of each FP series. The dashed line shows the best solution $\tau = 200$.

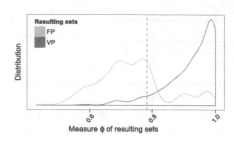

Fig. 2. TP and FP distribution for $\tau = 200$. The dashed line shows the third quantile of FP serie. This solution implies around only 6% of dropped TP.

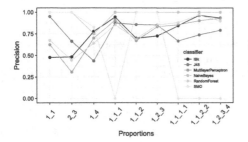

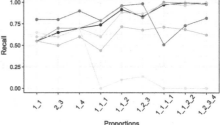

Fig. 3. Precision and recall with different ground truths (label distributions)

corresponds to real-world settings. We ran our algorithm with several parameters and report here only our first results. The settings were the following: we choose the Naive Bayes classification algorithm as it experimentally favors precision over recall, and behaves the better for imbalanced classes that we suspect to occur in $\mathcal{C}_2$. We set $\tau = 200$ and $\theta = mean(\varphi_C, \varphi_D)$ and $\Lambda = 0$ after several trials. We order the label sets of the result w.r.t. the robustness of their classifier, i.e. $\mathcal{R} = \langle R_1, ..., R_n \rangle$, where $\varphi_{R_i} \geq \varphi_{R_{i+1}}$, for $1 \leq i \leq n - 1$. After a run of $1,017$ s, out of the $|L| = 58$ initial avatars labeling $|T| = 5,883$ traces, we find 7 aliases of size 2, i.e. $|\mathcal{R}| = 51$. For four of the found pairs, we have that the avatars share a same ID, so we are sure that it is the same user account: we omitted that information when building the dataset, and we kept only the avatar names. For example, we found the avatar names *EGStephanoRC*, a famous ex-professional player associated with the avatar name *lIlIlIlIlIII* (a name not recognizable on purpose). One pair of avatars share a same name (pro-player *LiquidHero*), but not the same ID: we can assume with high confidence that this is a true positive. Finally, two false positives, for which we cannot advance anything, but just assume that the same player is behind each of these pairs; these are actually the most interesting avatar aliases we are looking for.

4 Conclusion

In several online applications, a single user may have different virtual identities. When this mapping is not known, we face the duplicate label identification problem, whose resolution has applications in targeted marketing, online systems security, etc. Whereas this problem has similar goals as entity resolution techniques [3,6], we treat it in a new way, taking into account the user behavior hidden in the data traces by building a model for each possible subset of label (in theory). Indeed, behavioral traces generated by the users can help building accurate prediction models that only confuse avatars of a same user. We proposed a method that takes advantage of this idea, by generating a binary classifier for each possible subset of labels. Using a bottom-up generation of the label sets, appropriate constraints ensure that we generate few accurate classifiers that each depict the same user. We experimented the implementation of our approach with behavioral data of a video game where players use several identities to play online. The results are encouraging although more experiments and comparisons remain to be done.

Acknowledgments. This work has been partially financed by the projects FUI AAP 14 Tracaverre 2012–2016, VEL'INNOV (ANR INOV 2012) and GRAISearch (FP7-PEOPLE-2013-IAPP).

References

1. Cavadenti, O., Codocedo, V., Boulicaut, J.F., Kaytoue, M.: When cyberathletes conceal their game: clustering confusion matrices to identify avatar aliases. In: International Conference on Data Science and Advanced Analytics (DSAA) (2015)
2. De Montjoye, Y.A., Hidalgo, C.A., Verleysen, M., Blondel, V.D.: Unique in the crowd: the privacy bounds of human mobility. Nature Sci. Rep. **3**(1376), 779–782 (2013)
3. Getoor, L., Machanavajjhala, A.: Entity resolution: theory, practice & open challenges. PVLDB **5**(12), 2018–2019 (2012)
4. Hall, M.A., Frank, E., Holmes, G., Pfahringer, B., Reutemann, P., Witten, I.H.: The WEKA data mining software: an update. SIGKDD Explor. **11**(1), 10–18 (2009). http://doi.acm.org/10.1145/1656274.1656278
5. ICDM Contest: Identify individual users across their digital devices. In: IEEE International Conference on data mining (2015)
6. Mugan, J., Chari, R., Hitt, L., McDermid, E., Sowell, M., Qu, Y., Coffman, T.: Entity resolution using inferred relationships and behavior. In: IEEE International Conference on Big Data, pp. 555–560 (2014)
7. Peacock, A., Ke, X., Wilkerson, M.: Typing patterns: a key to user identification. IEEE Secur. Priv. **2**(5), 40–47 (2004)
8. Von Eschen, A.: Machine learning and data mining in call of duty (invited talk). In: European Conference on Machine Learning and Knowledge Discovery in Databases (ECML/PKDD) (2014)
9. Yan, E.Q., Huang, J., Cheung, G.K.: Masters of control: behavioral patterns of simultaneous unit group manipulation in starcraft 2. In: 33rd Annual ACM Conference on Human Factors in Computing Systems (CHI 2015), pp. 3711–3720. ACM (2015)

Implementing a Tool for Translating Dance Notation to Display in 3D Animation: A Case Study of Traditional Thai Dance

Yootthapong Tongpaeng[1(✉)], Mongkhol Rattanakhum[1(✉)], Pradorn Sureephong[1(✉)], and Satichai Wicha[2(✉)]

[1] College of Arts, Media and Technology, Chiang Mai University, Chiang Mai, Thailand
yootthapong@kic.camt.info, mongkhol@kirly.org, dorn@camt.info
[2] School of Information Technology, Mae Fah Luang University, Chiang Rai, Thailand
santichai@mfu.ac.th

Abstract. In Southeast Asia, Thai dance is a living traditional art form that belongs to the Intangible Cultural Heritage listed by UNESCO. This unique and stylized traditional dance portrays its history, culture, emotional expression, body movement etc. To archive the knowledge of the Traditional Thai dance, a dance notation known as "Labanotation" has been widely used to record and archive the unique essence of dance knowledge. In addition, many researchers have worked on reproducing and showcasing the dance movements. Currently, there is no such system that is available for us to demonstrate our Thai Dance Notation Score in 3D animation. Specifically, displaying the hand and finger movement is an issue. The aim of this paper is to present the process of implementing a tool to translate the dance notation into a 3D animation focusing on hand and finger movements of the traditional Thai dance.

Keywords: Archive knowledge · Traditional thai dance · Intangible cultural heritage · Dance notation · Labanotation · Translate · 3D animation · Hand and fingers movement

1 Introduction

The idea of recoding the dance began in the 1960s by Michael Noll using digital computer and an electronic pencil. The computer translated the information on screen as a form of stick figure and recoded the pattern of ballet dance [1]. Zella Wolofsky was the first person who took the challenge to applying Labanotation to computer. It was an interpretation of selected Labanotation commands to convert the selected movement of the dance notation symbol into numerical representations of the body's position in 1974 [2]. In 1984, Ohio State University developed an entirely new form of notation called the "LabanWriter" program [3, 4]. Recently, LabanDancer has been developed to translate the LabanWriter scores and convert them to 3-dimension animation [5]. LabanEditor is also another software, as an interactive graphical editor where the user can use five main functions: input, edit, print, display and export data [6, 7]. In Asia, the Labanotation system is also available to recode the Asian dances. For instance, Indian dance,

© Springer International Publishing AG 2017
S. Benferhat et al. (Eds.): IEA/AIE 2017, Part II, LNAI 10351, pp. 22–26, 2017.
DOI: 10.1007/978-3-319-60045-1_3

Vietnamese dance, Taiwanese dance and Thai dance due to the similarity of the dance gestures using hand and finger movements [6, 8]. The Asian dances were recoded and the Labanotation scores were created to preserve the cultural heritage of the countries and transfer the knowledge from generation to generation. Learning from the dance notation score is quite difficult, the dance students must understand the Labanotation symbols to read, write and perform the dance movements. In 2013, Worawat Choensawat and his co-researchers published the new symbols for Thai dance generating a collection of new symbols for hand and finger movements which allow Thai notators and students to read easily and write the scores faster with more accurately. Thai dance notation scores are difficult to translate into 3D animation and it must have a specific software and method to decode the score to animation. Besides, there is no available software for the notation scores to precisely represent the finger and hand gestures. Therefore, this paper focuses on the implementation of a tool to translate the Thai dance notation and represent it in 3D animation.

2 Literature Review

2.1 Thai Dance Notation Score

Chommanad Kijkhum had been awarded a scholarship to study three training courses of Labanotation. She developed a set of new symbols that described all the movements and fundamentals of the Thai dance. This was important due to the complexity of Laban symbol combinations for hand and finger movements. Chommanad created a new design in terms of efficiency and comprehensibility called *"Thai dance notation system"*. Figure 1 shows an example of a hand gesture together with the developed new Thai Labanotation symbol design for assigned to the gesture. The Thai dance notation symbols represent all the basic hand gestures and describe the precise postures of the classical Thai dance such as Wong, Jiib and foot lifting [6].

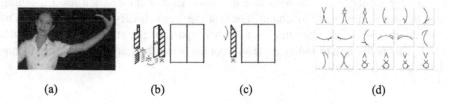

| (a) | (b) | (c) | (d) |

Fig. 1. Thai dance notation score for hand gesture (wong): (a) Thai dancer showing a hand gesture, (b) Original Labanotation, (c) Thai notation score. A set of new design of the Thai Labanotation symbols for describing Thai dance (d).

2.2 Translation into 3D Animation

The LabanWriter program was developed by the Ohio State University in 1984 and it was implemented for Macintosh computers to create dance notation scores, edited and stored on the computer's hard drive [3, 4]. Using the LabanWriter program was a big improvement for the notators and an important step forward from analog representation, which means drawing the notation score on paper, to digital representation, that is typing on the keyboard and using the mouse to drag the Laban symbol to the staff and save it as a digital file. This breakthrough offered an opportunity to all scholars to implement the 3D animation representation based on Labanotation. One of the first 3D translator program was LabanEditor introduced by Hachimura and his research team to convert Laban notation scores into 3D animation corresponding to the notation score [6]. Similarly, LabanDancer was developed to translate the LabanWriter scores to 3D animation [5]. Nevertheless, the uniqueness of the stylized traditional dance reflects the historical cultural knowledge, emotion expression etc. To recode and represent such stylized traditional dance, Labanotation is an available system. However, representing the dance movement according to the notation score is difficult. Hand and finger movements are hard to decode and translate into 3D animation using the LabanEditor or the Laban-Dancer programs. These stylized traditional dances, like the Thai dance represent emotions with hand and finger movements. A special system of translation is needed to decode the complex Thai notation scores.

3   Methodology

As regards the Thai dance notation score with new symbols, implementing a specific tool to translate the notation score is more appropriate for the Thai stylized traditional dance. Using six steps of the translation model of Michael C. and his colleagues [9] serves as our guideline to implement our Thai translation program. Besides, our six steps of implementing the Thai notation score translation includes the following explanation:

3.1   Parsing the LabanWriter File

To understand the LabanWriter file, we have to look at the numeric element of the file where all the symbols are decoded into numbers. Each number signifies a meaning related to each symbol and movement. The first step is to classify each symbol such as the direction symbols, the column for each body part, or the start-end time for each symbol. This is the key to indicate the symbol allowing the translation of the Laban-Writer file to CG animation.

3.2   Creating Laban Symbols

The next step is to create Laban symbol pictures to be imported in the Unity 3D program (Fig. 2) and to generate a code name for each symbol. All the directional symbol pictures must be created to indicate the direction of each limp movement. Every image created by using Adobe Illustrator is saved as a vector image in Portable Network Graphics (PNG) file format. Similarly, each column specifies a body part, such as the left arm, left leg, right arm, right leg, head and body. This is an important step to generate the symbols and it is represented on the screen while displaying the notation scores and 3D model in motion.

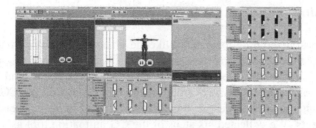

Fig. 2. Each directional symbol is imported in the Unity 3D program with several separate folders.

3.3   Creating a 3D Model and Setting up the Skeleton

In the Unity 3D program, the project continues with working on both the human figure's 3D model and the skeleton. The human figure's 3D model is imported in the Unity 3D program to set up the model in T-Post gesture. Then, the skeleton's axis is modified using the programming language to control each skeleton conferred to each column. Every skeleton axis must be set to zero so that it is ready for the next step, which is setting up the rule for a particular condition.

3.4   Using a Basic Rule to Interpret Laban Symbol

After creating Laban symbols and setting up the 3D model, assigning a rule to each symbol is the next step to give a particular task to each Laban symbol. Besides, each symbol is interconnected to symbols and a column. For each symbol, the rule controls the 3D model representing the limited movement or dance gesture.

3.5   Generating Animation

Subsequently, setting an animation to the 3D model gives the model the control of direction for each joint or skeleton. This is a corresponding between symbols with the rule and animation control of 3D model.

3.6   Generating a User Interface (UI)

Last, a simple User Interface is built to display the output of the translated notation scores. The available function of the program is the manual input of the LabanWriter file, displaying both the Labanotation score on the left side of the screen and the 3D model on the right side. In the 3D space, the user can rotate the angle of the 3D model to see the movement of the 3D animation. To play the animation, the user has to press the play button to activate the program which reads the notation score and the movement will be shown according to the notation score. Play and pause functions are also available.

4   Conclusion

In conclusion, a stylized traditional dance like the Thai dance is difficult to archive and represent in CG animation. Using the Labanotation system to recode the gesture movement is more helpful and can be precisely recoded into systematic symbols, however for the translation of notation scores from LabanWriter files into the CG animation a specific tool must be used to decode the complex Thai gestures, especially hand and finger movements. We collected six steps of the CG animation tool as a step-by-step assistance to be followed by programmers. Our approach uses the Unity 3D program as a tool to translate the notation scores of Thai dance movements into 3D Animation. It can read basic notation scores like leg and hand movements of various directions by manually importing the notation score file and displaying a user interface for the user to control, play and pause the GC animation referring to the notation score. As regards future work, we continue working on representing 3D Animation of figure movement, basic Thai dance gestures and on improving our back-end program to import more complex Thai notation scores.

Acknowledgement. This study would never be successful without the support from Knowledge and Innovation Laboratory (KIRLY), College of Arts, Media and Technology, Chiang Mai University, Thailand. Moreover, this work is partially funded by EU H2020 project-AniAge (691215).

References

1. Noll, M.: Choreography and Computers. Dance Magazine, pp. 43–45, January 1967
2. Wolofsky, Z.: Computer Interpretation of Selected Labanotation Commands. M.Sc. thesis, Simon Fraser University (1974)
3. Kasey, J.L.: Capturing dance- the art of documentation (An exploration of distilling the body in motion). http://ro.ecu.edu.au/cgi/viewcontent.cgi?article=1076&context=theses_hons. Accessed 25 May 2016
4. Department of Dance, The Ohio State University. "LabanWrier". https://dance.osu.edu/research/dnb/laban-writer. Accessed 25 May 2016
5. Wilke, L., Calvert, T., Ryman, R.: From Dance Notation to Human Animation: The LabanDancer Project. http://www.sfu.ca/~tom/Papers/LabanDancer1.pdf. Accessed 25 May 2016
6. Choensawat, W., Sookhanaphibarn, K., Kijkhun, C., Hachimura, K.: Desirability of a teaching and learning tool for Thai dance body motion. In: Marcus, A. (ed.) DUXU 2013. LNCS, vol. 8013, pp. 171–179. Springer, Heidelberg (2013). doi:10.1007/978-3-642-39241-2_20
7. Kojima, K., Hachimura, K., Nakamura, M.: LabanEditor - Graphical Editor for Dance Notation. http://ieeexplore.ieee.org/stamp/stamp.jsp?arnumber=1045598. Accessed 28 Jan 2016
8. Annemtte, P.K.: Labanotation for Indian Dance, in particular Bharata Natyam, In: 11th European Conference on Modern South Asian Studies, Amsterdam (1990)
9. Michael, C., Diego, S.M., Tom, C.: A Tool for Translating Dance Notation to Animation. http://www.oplopanax.ca/Downloads/Skigraph2002_DanceNotationTranslation.pdf. Accessed 28 Jan 2016

Dance Training Tool Using Kinect-Based Skeleton Tracking and Evaluating Dancer's Performance

Ob-orm Muangmoon[1,2(✉)], Pradorn Sureephong[1,2(✉)], and Karim Tabia[1,2(✉)]

[1] College of Arts, Media and Technology, Chiang Mai University, Chiang Mai, Thailand
ob-orm@kic.camt.info, dorn@camt.info, tabia@cril.univ-artois.fr
[2] CRIL UMR CNRS 8188, Université d'Artois, Arras, France

Abstract. In this preliminary work, we propose a system prototype for Thai Dance training. This paper considers the problem of teaching traditional dances from Thailand. This is particularly useful given the lack of teachers and tools for teaching dances. In order to build a software tool helping people learn Thai dances, the main problems are (i) how to represent the dance gestures and movements of the dance to teach, (ii) how to display it for the learner and how to rate the performance of the learner and provide him useful feedback. Fortunately, Natural User Interfaces (NUI) enables users to interact with a system in a natural and intuitive way. For instance, a user can interact with the system by his body through postures and movements. In this study, we developed a working prototype of a system teaching users traditional Thai dances. The system requires Kinect-based device to enable real-time skeleton tracking. For the reference postures/movements dataset, we collected dance movement from experts by Motion Capture System and used the collected data to represent the dance in the system. Moreover, the system is designed such that it rates the user's performance and provides helpful and real-time feedback to the user.

Keywords: Microsoft kinect · Skeleton tracking · Thai dance

1 Introduction

The work reported in this short paper is carried out in the framework of a European research project called AniAge dealing with High Dimensional Heterogeneous Data based Animation Techniques for Southeast Asian Intangible Cultural Heritage Digital Content. The AniAge Project aims to tackle challenging problems such as archiving and reproducing style-preserved intangible cultural heritage (ICH) contents. The overall aim of AniAge is to develop novel techniques and tools to reduce the production costs and improve the level of automation without sacrificing the control of the artists; in order to preserve performance arts related ICHs of Southeast Asia.

Southeast Asia is one of the most rapidly growing regions in the world. The coastal states have a population of around six hundred millions and are very rich with natural and cultural resources. The United Nations Educational, Scientific and Cultural Organization (UNESCO) now lists many of the living traditional art forms in these countries

© Springer International Publishing AG 2017
S. Benferhat et al. (Eds.): IEA/AIE 2017, Part II, LNAI 10351, pp. 27–32, 2017.
DOI: 10.1007/978-3-319-60045-1_4

as intangible cultural heritages (ICH) needing preservation. Examples include traditional dance and local operas.

Thailand is located in Southeast Asia and it is one member of the AniAge project. This country is very rich with cultural and performance arts. Especially, the dramatic arts have played important role in Thailand. Dramatic arts in Thailand are generally transmitted from the ancestors for next generations orally. The curriculum of education in Thailand enforces students to study Thai Dance, which is one of dramatic arts. Unfortunately, shortage of teachers of traditional Thai dances and lack of alternative tools for helping student to learn Thai dances don't allow reaching such an objective.

In this work, we deal with three main issues. The first one aims to represent the postures and movements of some Thai Dances in the training system. We study some of data collection process and represent the postures and movements with 3D characters. In the second, we study the problem of evaluating and rating the user's performance in real-time through skeleton tracking with Microsoft Kinect device. Microsoft Kinect device is low-cost and learner can accessible. We developed this software prototype using Unity, which a popular tool in game development industry. The third issue is how to provide useful feedback for users such that they can efficiently improve their performance.

This paper is organized as follows: In Sect. 2, we briefly describe a Thai Dance Data set. In Sect. 3, we describe the dance data collected from Microsoft Kinect and some information about mapping the captured data with 3D models. In Sect. 4, we provide Thai Dance Training Tool System Architecture. In Sect. 5, we describe the system prototype with some of user interface and how to evaluate dance performance. Finally, in Sect. 6, we proposed some future work of this the system.

2   Thai Dance Dataset

The movements in Thai Dance are motion gestures imitating nature for meaningful use. The gestures need the whole body to perform. The motion gestures play the same role as words such that the audience can understand. Thai Dance have multiple types of motion gestures. For example, gestures may express pronouns; "I", "You", "We", "Go", "Come", gestures may express actions; "Standing", "Walk", "Sit", "Pray", gestures may express emotions; "Glad", "Sad", "Angry", "Love", "Cry", and some gestures are used for imitating animals like "Bird", "Fish", "Horse" and "Elephant".

In this work, we used a dataset from Thai Dance experts performing a popular Thai dance including Northern Thai Dance and Central Thai Dance. This involves recording Thai Dance captured with various systems, including Microsoft Kinect sensors. The dataset includes records of 2 experts Dance (a male and a female) performing Thai. In our prototype, the dataset is composed of 11 gestures: Go In (Come), Go Out (Go), Happy, Love, Sad, Shy, Smile, Walk, Angry, Laugh, Cry and 2 songs which we captured using Motion Capture System making use of 42 markers set on the performers' bodies.

3 Microsoft Kinect

The Kinect motion controller technology, developed by Microsoft Corporation, tracks the skeleton of a person standing in front of the device. It has a set of IR and RGB cameras. The IR cameras are used for sensing the skeleton and hence the body postures irrespective of the color of the performer's dress or distance from the camera [1]. Skeleton data contain 3D position data for human skeletons. Each joint position in the skeleton space is represented as three coordinates (x, y, and z). The skeleton space coordinates are expressed in meters [2]. The real-time skeleton tracking using OpenNI SDK provides among others, a high-level skeleton tracking module, which can be used for detecting the captured user and tracking his/her body joint. More specifically, the OpenNI tracking module produces the positions of 17 joints (Head, Neck Torso, Left and Right Collar, L/R Shoulder, L/R Elbow, L/R Wrist, L/R Hip, L/R Knee and L/R Foot), along with the corresponding tracking confidence [3].

3.1 Kinect in Education

Hui-Mei J. explores the potential of Kinect as interactive technology and discusses how it can facilitate and enhance teaching and learning. Kinect is examined in terms of its affordances of technical interactivity, which is an important aspect of pedagogical interactivity. As it utilizes gesture-based technology, Kinect can support kinesthetic pedagogical practices to benefit learners with strong bodily-kinesthetic intelligence. As far as a teaching tool is concerned, due to the multiple interaction types it supports, Kinect has the potential to enhance classroom interactions, to increase classroom participation, to improve teachers' ability to present and manipulate multimedia and multimodal materials, and to create opportunities for interaction and discussion. In addition, students can utilize the bodily information gathered by Kinect with software programs to create highly interactive multimedia works [4].

3.2 Kinect for Teaching Dance

Emiko C. et al. presented a study comparing a dance instruction video to a rhythm game interface. This research explores the player's perceptions of their own capabilities, their capacity to deal with a high influx of information, and their preferences regarding body-controlled video games. The results indicate that the game-inspired interface elements alone were not a substitute for footage of a real human dancer, but participants overall preferred to have access to both forms of media [5].

Zoe M. et al. proposed the Super Mirror, a Kinect-based system that combines the functionality of studio mirrors and prescriptive images to provide the user with instructional feedback in real-time. In this study, they developed a working prototype of their system, which records ballet movements (also called "positions" and "poses") and contains step-by-step illustrations of individual movements, captures live motion. The fundamental purpose of the Super Mirror is to render the useful features of mirrored reflection and modeled instruction in a clear and informative way [6].

4   Thai Dance Training Tool System Architecture

The system diagram of Thai Dance Training Tool, in our proposed system is shown in Fig. 1. The end-user (player or learner) can interact with the system to be installed on the user's computer or available on-line. The user's computer is equipped with Microsoft Kinect. Figure 1 shows the architecture of the proposed system. The optical Motion Capture system is used to capture the movements of the Thai Dance expert performer. The motion data is then stored into a database. For each posture and gesture of a dance to teach, we captured some samples from the expert performer. The database represents the reference motion data of the dances. Such reference samples are used to rate the learner's performance using posture and motion recognition techniques. When the end-user performs in front of his Kinect device, his postures and movements are displayed on the screen while the system analyzes the performance to provide useful feedback.

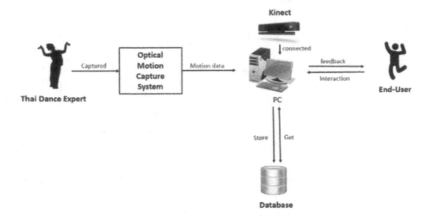

Fig. 1. Thai dance training tool architecture

Note that the reference dataset of postures and gestures is captured only once and offline. As said earlier, in our system, we rely on 2 Thai dance experts to perform the motion of Thai traditional dance. We captured 11 gestures since the experts teaching Thai dance in the college.

Figure 2 shows the motion capture system and Thai dance expert while they were performing and the system was capturing.

Fig. 2. Capturing Thai dance expert motion

5   System Prototype

We proposed a system prototype for training people Thai dance and we have implemented the interactive training tools system. In our application, the dataset contains two types of Thai dance (Central Thai dance and Northern Thai dance) as shown in Fig. 3. The graphical user interface of the system includes:

- Main menu (dance type choice): When a user chooses the type of the Thai dance he wants to learn, the gestures selection page shows 22 motion gestures and 1 song as shown in Fig. 4.
- Gestures menu: When a user selects the gesture, the system shows the reference 3D model captured using the motion capture system and the learner's model on the right side. The user should try to match the pose on the left, then the system provide performance feedback for user. Moreover, user can play gesture animation before perform as shown in Fig. 5.

Fig. 3. Main menu   **Fig. 4.** Gestures selection page

Fig. 5. Reference model and learner's model

In addition to the user interface, the prototype involves reference Thai dance posture and gesture samples captured from the experts. When learning, the system tracks the skeleton of the learner in real time and compares it with the chosen gestures or postures to learn. In order to do such comparison, we have reference model on the left side for the 3D model which have each joint and for each joint can be connected and make the bone for the comparison we use the angle of each bone. We compare the reference bone with the Learner's model bone in real-time and calculate the difference each bone. We supposed to max angle different is 90°. For difference degree of each bone, we summarize overall difference angle and give grade for Learner. Moreover, the prototype can show list of each joint which low performance for Learner to improve their dance performance.

Note that the result of the comparison is a global score... which we graphically represent in colors and text message (such as: Good, bad...). In addition, in order to point out the exact p arts of the body where the performance went wrong, the concerned joints of the skeleton are highlighted and displayed directly on the screen.

The proposed prototype has been successfully implemented and tried in realistic conditions on the two captured Thai dances by some volunteers. The first results are very encouraging but there is need to assess empirically our system on a sample of learners and a wide range of dances in different conditions.

6   Conclusion and Future Work

The work reported in this short paper results from preliminary works in the AniAge project dealing with Asian intangible cultural heritage digital contents. This paper presented an interactive training prototype for representing basic postures and gestures of Thai dances. We provide the system description including data collection, learner's performance evaluation and providing feedback. In future works, we will address all the remaining issues, in particular how represent complex gestures, how to evaluate user performance for a whole performance and how to improve performance the rating and feedback. We will add the comparison of the system feedback with expert. We also plan to use abstract descriptions of dances instead of motion data captured from dance experts. For instance, it would be very interesting and challenging to use dance notations (ex. Labanotation) as reference models and compare the learner's performance with such notations.

References

1. Saha, S., Ghosh, S., Konar, A., Nagar, A.K.: Gesture recognition from indian classical dance using kinect sensor. In: 2013 Fifth International Conference on Computational Intelligence, Communication Systems and Networks (CICSyN), pp. 3–8. IEEE (2013)
2. Wei, T., Qiao, Y., Lee, B.: Kinect skeleton coordinate calibration for remote physical training. In: Proceedings of the International Conference on Advances in Multimedia (MMEDIA), pp. 23–27 (2014)
3. Alexiadis, D.S., Kelly, P., Daras, P., O'Connor, N.E., Boubekeur, T., Moussa, M.B.: Evaluating a dancer's performance using kinect-based skeleton tracking. In: Proceedings of the 19th ACM International Conference on Multimedia, pp. 659–662. ACM (2011)
4. Hsu, H.M.J.: The potential of Kinect in education. Int. J. Inf. Educ. Technol. 1(5), 365 (2011)
5. Charbonneau, E., Miller, A., LaViola Jr., J.J.: Teach me to dance: exploring player experience and performance in full body dance games. In: Proceedings of the 8th International Conference on Advances in Computer Entertainment Technology, p. 43. ACM (2011)
6. Marquardt, Z., Beira, J., Em, N., Paiva, I., Kox, S.: Super mirror: a kinect interface for ballet dancers. In: CHI 2012 Extended Abstracts on Human Factors in Computing Systems, pp. 1619–1624. ACM (2012)

Using Program by Demonstration and Visual Scripting to Supporting Game Design

Ismael Sagredo-Olivenza$^{(\boxtimes)}$, Pedro Pablo Gómez-Martín,
Marco Antonio Gómez-Martín, and Pedro A. González-Calero

Dep. Ingeniería del Software e Inteligencia Artificial,
Universidad Complutense de Madrid, Madrid, Spain
isagredo@ucm.es, {pedrop,marcoa,pedro}@fdi.ucm.es

Abstract. Creating the behavior for non-player characters (NPCs) in video games is a complex task that requires the collaboration among programmers and game designers. Usually these game designers are responsible of configuring and fine tuning certain parameters of the behavior, while programmers write the actual code of those behaviors. That requires several iterations between them. In this paper, we present a new approach for creating the behavior of NPCs that gives more power to the game designer to create behavior without technical knowledge using program by demonstration but preserving the designer confident of the final behavior.

Keywords: Case-based reasoning · Machine learning · Entertainment · Game AI · Program by demonstration

1 Introduction

Game AI development is a hard problem that involves two roles: programmers and designers. On the one hand, game programmers deal with low-level algorithms, perception systems or behavior representation. On the other hand, designers envision the way their characters should behave and have in mind the player experience and whether the behaviors are enjoyable or not.

To successfully accommodate both sides of the same task, programmers and designers must work together. Designers do not usually have programming skills, and this implies that building the final AIs is an iterative process where designers specify the desired behaviors, programmers develop them and designers test them. The process repeats itself over and over again until designers are satisfied.

To minimize the number of cycles, programmers have developed different mechanisms to allow designers to specify the Non-Playable Characters (NPCs) behavior in richer and richer ways, without requiring programming abilities.

A lot of formalisms have been used in game development for designing game AI. Over the last decade, however, behavior trees (BTs) [2,6] have gained

---

Supported by the Spanish Ministry of Science and Education (TIN2014-55006-R).

S. Benferhat et al. (Eds.): IEA/AIE 2017, Part II, LNAI 10351, pp. 33–39, 2017.
DOI: 10.1007/978-3-319-60045-1_5

momentum. This technique is widely used in a several games like Halo [7,8], and also in control systems and robotics [3].

Although BTs were born as a tool for designers because behaviors can be created through visual interfaces without writing code, they involve concepts that can be difficult for a game designer to fully grasp, such as parameter passing, behavior abstraction or parallel execution. Some previous studies [12] confirm that programmers are more skillful creating BT than designers and today they are primarily a programmer tool.

A different promising way for creating NPC behaviors is *Program by Demonstration* (PbD) [4], which has been gaining momentum in the academic field during the last few years [9]. Although very intuitive for designers, this approach has a main problem: either the result is too simple to be fun to play with, or it is too complex to be fully predictable.

In this paper, we describe *Trained-Behavior Bricks*, a tool which combines program by demonstration and visual scripting through behavior trees. They allow designer to first sketch a behavior by demonstration and then fine-tune a BT induced from that demonstration. To make it possible, we have extended BTs with a new type of nodes, *Trained-Query Nodes*, using *Case-based Reasoning* [1] to select the best task to run at each moment.

The rest of the paper runs as follows. Next section describes some related work on tools for visual scripting by game designers. Then, we describe the use of Trained-Behavior Bricks from the designer point of view. Afterwards a section on the underlying technology for Trained-Behavior Bricks is provided. Next we describe the experiment with game designers and finally present some conclusions and future work.

2   Related Work

The creation of tools and techniques that simplify behavior definition has been tackled in both Academia and industry for years.

On one hand, the game industry has used different approaches, always trying to reduce the development time. Today, the leading commercial game engines have available some kind of visual tool for authoring behaviors. For example, PlayMaker[1] is a plug-in for Unity3D that provides a Finite State Machine editor; CryEngine® incorporates *Behavior Selection Tree Editor*[2] and *Blueprints*[3] have replaced *Kismet* and UnrealScript in Unreal Engine®.

All of them try to simplify the game logic and the behavior authoring, using visual scripting languages.

On the other hand, in Academia significant work done under the label of *programming by demonstration* has emerged recently in the *Case-Based Reasoning* community. For example, Floyd et al. [5] present an approach to learn how to

---

[1] http://hutonggames.com/index.html.
[2] http://docs.cryengine.com/display/SDKDOC4/Modular+Behavior+Tree.
[3] https://docs.unrealengine.com/latest/INT/Engine/Blueprints/index.html.

play RoboSoccer by observing the play of other teams or Ontañón et al. [9,10] use program by demonstration for real-time strategy games.

These other approaches are focused into imitating the human play, but they are not always suitable for real-world settings due to the loss of control. Learning by demonstration is usually an *all-or-nothing* option and designers are forced to be confident of the generated emergent behavior.

Our approach tries to go beyond of visual scripting (that it also uses). Designers without programming knowledge can define behaviors using *program by demonstration* and visually adjust the learned behaviour, so a compromise between ease of use and reliability is reached.

3   Description of Trained-Behavior Bricks

As explained in the Introduction, designers envision and decide the behaviors that NPCs must follow, and programmers make those ideas reality. This requires an iterative process of refinement shared by roles.

To shorten this task, Trained-Behavior Bricks helps non-technical designers create behaviors in a more intuitive way, just by playing the game as the NPC would do. The process starts with the creation of a minimal BT using the provided BT editor. This initial BT contains a special node called *Trained Query Node*. This node can be trained by a designer in a pure game session where he simulates the intended behavior of the NPC. The knowledge acquired during this training session is later used at run-time when the player executes the game. When the execution of the BT reaches the Trained Query Node, it selects the task that better fits the actual state of the game, using the traces recorded in the training session.

For this approach to work, some basic tasks should be available, so that complex behaviors can be built using them. These basic tasks are implemented by programmers. We propose the following methodology: the designer starts with the definition of the behavior of the game NPCs using a very high level specification, for example, natural language. Using this description, designers and programmers identify the basic tasks of the NPC. These tasks are implemented by the programmers and later used by designers as *bricks* when building the behaviors. The designers then place a Trained Query Node on the BT, to create the high level behavior by demonstration, training the character in a game session and finally, validate the behavior in a running session.

4   Technology Used in Trained-Behavior Bricks

Trained-Behavior Bricks works on top of our BT infrastructure, named Behavior Bricks (BB), implemented as a plug-in for Unity game engine. The leaf nodes in behavior bricks are named *task* and can be conditions for checking the environment state, actions for changing it, and other behaviors that act as *macros*.

Trained Query Nodes are also a special type of leaf nodes, that enrich BTs with program by demonstration. They have two independent running modes:

training mode and *game mode*. During *training mode*, the node takes samples of the game environment and the actions the designer playing the role of an NPC takes. During this training process, designers must be able to pause the game and instruct the NPC to execute one of the available actions.

The training mode produces a *case base* relating the environment parameters and the corresponding actions. When run in *game mode*, the Trained Query Node chooses which action should execute next, depending on the current game state, using the collected cases. It uses the k-NN algorithm for choosing the most similar cases to the current state, comparing the environment parameters that were considered more relevant during sampling with the current ones. The similarity measure used is a *weighted Euclidean distance* among the parameters recorded while training, that was chosen because this distance is applicable to nearly any domain.

Once trained, Trained-Behavior Bricks converts the Trained Query Node into an equivalent regular BT. This feature is invaluable for designers because offers an insight of the Trained Query Node internals, bringing to light the way it takes its decisions. To achieve this, the system first generates a decision tree with the training data using the C4.5 algorithm [11]. Then, a greedy algorithm is used in order to simplify the tree, looking for, as an instance, identical sibling subtrees that can be joined together.

5   Experimental Results

Although program by demonstration has proved to be a promising technique for authoring AI behavior, our hypothesis is that it is not enough to ensure behavior fidelity and to make designers confident with the predictability of the result. Using our Training Query Nodes, program by demonstration could be used in specific and independent parts of the entire behavior, for those moments where the technique is better suited.

We have carried out an experiment for testing that a pure program-by-demonstration behavior creation fails in complex environments. In the experiment we use an in-house developed game called TowoT as a testbed. This game is a tower defense like *Orcs Must Die*[4] but the player is accompanied by an NPC (a TowoT). The goal of the experiment is the creation of the TowoT behavior.

The experiment was carried out for thirty students in a master program in game design, and was divided into three episodes.

During the first episode, the TowoT had to defend the *core*, a game element that, when destroyed, makes the game ends. This behavior was called *defensive behavior*. In the second episode, the TowoT must attack enemies far away from the core and only when the core is directly attacked, the TowoT must defend it. This behavior was called *offensive behavior*. In both behaviors, the TowoT must keep its batteries charged, otherwise it will not be able to fire. The third episode consisted of trying to get both behaviors at the same time, joining both traces in just a case base.

---

[4] http://es.omd.gameforge.com/.

At the end of each episode, users measure the quality of the behavior, putting a score between 1 and 5. In addition, we calculate the similarity between both executions (training and test), making a vector with actions executed in both of them by the TowoT and comparing them using the *Levenshtein distance*. The Pearson product-moment correlation coefficient between both measures was **0.68**, which indicates that the use of the *Levenshtein distance* was good enough.

Regarding the parameters used in the experiment, the k-NN selected the most popular task among the k more similar, where $k = 10$. We select the k value empirically. Some previous training episodes revealed that this value usually produces good results. The system stores seven parameters taken from the environment, related to the TowoT energy and the risk levels of some critical parts of the level to be attacked, including the main player character. All the values were normalized taking into account their value ranges, and had a weight depending on their relative importance in the game evolution.

The experimental results shown in Table 1 demonstrate that in the two first strategies the designers satisfaction is good and the similarity is high (86 and 71 per cent). But in the third setting results are worse. That indicates that mixing training data is not enough to determinate which strategy is better. To achieve this goal, the system needs more contextual information. In these situations, when the *Program by Demonstration* fails, the designer can generate the BT that explains the model learned by the system and use it to refine the behavior or the programmer to implement it.

Table 1. Average results using similarity and users score

	Strategy 1	Strategy 2	Union strat. 1 & 2
Similarity	0.86	0.71	0.54
Score (1–5)	3.77	3.19	2.77

6   Conclusions and Future Work

In this paper, we have presented a novel approach to facilitate the collaboration between programmers and game designers in game development. Game designers can be seen as end-user programmers that need to build a very complex software system in close collaboration with their programmer partners.

Trained-Behavior Bricks combines program by demonstration and behavior trees to put in the hands of game designers the tools for creating complex behavior for non-player characters. The proposed combination of techniques has a number of benefits:

– It is easy to use without programming knowledge. Designers can create the behavior for NPCs just by playing the game while controlling them.

- Behavior trees for designers. BTs are state-of-the-art technology for programming behavior in games, but they are usually too complex for the average game designer. Trained-Behavior Bricks proposes a BT to the designer based on his game traces, and therefore greatly facilitates the creation of the tree.
- Power to the designer. This combination of techniques put the designer at the driver's seat, providing enough control on the user experience.

Our experiments demonstrate how the use of program by demonstration can provide useful behavior in certain situations but not in every situation. Our approach to PbD uses Case-based Reasoning (CBR) to record and reuse actions to be taken in particular situations. These examples can be used as input for CBR, or be processed to generate a decision tree, that is automatically transformed into a BT, closing the gap between both techniques.

Regarding future work, we plan to test Trained-Behavior Bricks to train more complex behaviors for other types of games. In addition, we want to test our tool in a real working environment to create the attributes of a video game and to verify if the tool is useful to designers for creating behaviors without any help for programmers.

References

1. Aamodt, A., Plaza, E.: Case-based reasoning: foundational issues, methodological variations, and system approaches. AI Commun. **7**, 39–59 (1994)
2. Champandard, A.J.: Getting started with decision making and control systems. In: AI Game Programming Wisdom, vol. 4, Chap. 3.4, pp. 257–264. Course Technology (2008)
3. Colledanchise, M., Ögren, P.: How behavior trees modularize hybrid control systems and generalize sequential behavior compositions, the subsumption architecture, and decision trees. IEEE Trans. Rob. **33**(2), 372–389 (2016)
4. Cypher, A., Halbert, D.C.: Watch What I Do: Programming by Demonstration. MIT press, Cambridge (1993)
5. Floyd, M.W., Esfandiari, B., Lam, K.: A case-based reasoning approach to imitating robocup players. In: Wilson, D., Lane, H.C. (eds.) Proceedings of the Twenty-First International Florida Artificial Intelligence Research Society Conference, 15–17 May 2008, Coconut Grove, Florida, USA, pp. 251–256. AAAI Press (2008)
6. Gonzalez-Perez, C., Henderson-Sellers, B., Dromey, G.: A metamodel for the behavior trees modelling technique. In: Information Technology and Applications, ICITA 2005, vol. 1, pp. 35–39. IEEE (2005)
7. Isla, D.: Handling complexity in the Halo 2 AI. In: Game Developers Conference (2005)
8. Isla, D.: Halo 3 - building a better battle. In: Game Developers Conference (2008)
9. Ontañón, S., Mishra, K., Sugandh, N., Ram, A.: On-line case-based planning. Comput. Intell. **26**(1), 84–119 (2010)
10. Ontanón, S., Ram, A.: Case-based reasoning and user-generated artificial intelligence for real-time strategy games. In: González-Calero, P.A., Gómez-Martín, M.A. (eds.) Artificial Intelligence for Computer Games, pp. 103–124. Springer, New York (2011)

11. Quinlan, J.R.: C4.5: Programs for Machine Learning. Elsevier, San Francisco (2014)
12. Sagredo-Olivenza, I., Gómez-Martín, M.A., González-Calero, P.A.: Supporting the collaboration between programmers and designers building game AI. In: Chorianopoulos, K., Divitini, M., Hauge, J.B., Jaccheri, L., Malaka, R. (eds.) ICEC 2015. LNCS, vol. 9353, pp. 496–501. Springer, Cham (2015). doi:10.1007/978-3-319-24589-8_46

Presenting Mathematical Expression Images on Web to Support Mathematics Understanding

Kuniko Yamada[1]([✉]), Hiroshi Ueda[2], Harumi Murakami[1], and Ikuo Oka[1]

[1] Osaka City University,
3-3-138, Sugimoto, Sumiyoshi, Osaka 558-8585, Japan
k16uz90z10@st.osaka-cu.ac.jp
[2] Stroly Inc.,
7-5-1, Seikadai, Seika, Soraku, Kyoto 619-0294, Japan

Abstract. People cannot use a text search to find mathematical expressions because expressions cannot be replaced with words. Our research uses an ordinary text search and presents appropriate mathematical expression images (hereinafter called math-images) for input keywords. First we classify a set of the top ranking images from all the images in HTML files by scoring them. We focus on three viewpoints that are unique to mathematical expression images and mark the images by using these viewpoints. Then by adding bonus points to these marked images, the best three images are chosen from the set and presented with an explanation of the keyword and the surrounding information in the HTML files. We conducted two experiments to optimize the parameters of the expression giving the mark and to evaluate the effect of the bonus points. The rate of the average correct images of the best three was 79.5%.

Keywords: Mathematical expression image · Mathematics understanding · Mathematical information retrieval · Web search · SVM · Wikipedia

1 Introduction

For such fields as science, technology, or economics, searching for mathematical expressions is necessary because these concepts are explained using expressions. However, mathematical information retrieval is difficult. Since expressions are not annotated by names, we cannot search for them by names; we cannot use a text search.

Our research uses an ordinary text search given a mathematical term as a keyword and presents appropriate math-images for an input keyword. We focus on the viewpoints where important math-images are on a separate line in a document, and many of these images have unique feature quantities. Adding another viewpoint where these important images often have a keyword around them to the viewpoints, we obtain a set of the top ranking math-images. Focusing on one more viewpoint where important information often appears in the first

© Springer International Publishing AG 2017
S. Benferhat et al. (Eds.): IEA/AIE 2017, Part II, LNAI 10351, pp. 40–46, 2017.
DOI: 10.1007/978-3-319-60045-1_6

part of a document, we obtain the best three math-images from a set of the top rankings. Our experiment result showed that at least two of the best three math-images were correct images. To support mathematics understanding, the best three images are shown on a screen display with keyword explanations and the surrounding information in HTML files.

2 Approach

2.1 Mathematical Expression

General ways of writing mathematical expressions on the web use pdfs, images embedded in a HTML file, or MathML based on XML. The following is the writing style for mathematical expressions in a document. (a) A variable, a sign, or an additional expression is on a line and is expressed with math notation instead of characters because the mathematical font is special. (b) An important theorem or a formula is on a separate line, even though it is in a sentence. (c) Connected by equal signs, a mathematical expression is too long from which a theorem is derived or a calculation example is shown.

2.2 Method

In the following steps, we explain Fig. 1.

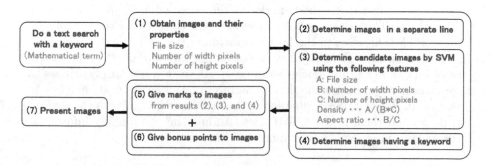

Fig. 1. Overview

(1) **Obtain images:** When the HTML files of a mathematical term are given, we obtain the images and extract the following image information: the file size, the number of width pixels, and the number of height pixels. When there is no text between the images, they are concatenated and considered as one.

(2) **Determine images on a separate line:** When an image satisfies the following two conditions, it is defined as being on a separate line: (a) An image tag to which the image belongs has no text before or after it. (b) The image tag has tags that denote a new line before and after, such as `<br>`, `<p>`, `<tr>`, `</br>`, `</p>`, `</tr>`.

(3) **Determine candidate images by SVM:** We determine whether an image is a candidate by Support Vector Machines (SVM). The features given to the SVM are file size, the number of width pixels, the number of height pixels, the density, and the aspect ratio.

(4) **Determine images having a keyword:** We search for the closest image to a keyword as the window size that is set from -80 to $+80$ Japanese characters surrounding the keyword. If it exists, the image is defined as having a keyword. However, if an image and a keyword appear in the same sentence, it is preferentially defined as having a keyword.

(5) **Give marks to images:** Each image is given a mark using (2) to (4) and ranked in descending order of points. Figure 2 shows an example of the top ranking images when the keyword is "spherical harmonics". The first two images are incorrect and the others are correct.

(6) **Give bonus points to images:** In Fig. 2, the first two happen to be incorrect, because their order is affected by the ranking of the original web pages. This order is not useful when we choose the best three or five from the top ranked images. To solve this problem, we propose a bonus point system where the important information on a keyword often appears in the first part of a document. This system gives an additional point to an image when it obtains the highest marks in the order of the appearance in the HTML file. Then the possibility increases that the actually correct image in each HTML file rises to the higher position in the set of the top rankings.

(7) **Present image:** Figure 3 shows a screen display example that has all correct images (The third image is omitted). At the top, the display shows the outline extracted from the first paragraph of Wikipedia that matches the keyword. Below it, the display shows the best three images with the information around them in the HTML files. Adding the surrounding information provides clearer explanation about the images.

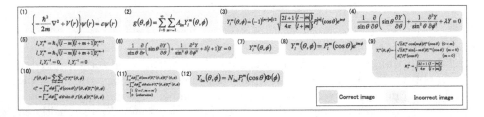

Fig. 2. Example of top ranking images for keyword: spherical harmonics

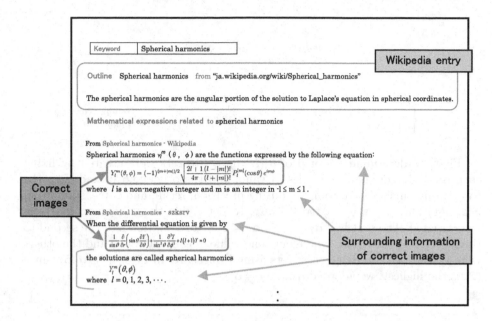

Fig. 3. Screen display example of keyword: spherical harmonics

3 Experiment

3.1 Dataset

We extracted 16 keywords from the science and engineering web syllabi of Osaka City University and obtained the top five HTML files for each keyword using a text search in Experiment 1. We added five keywords in Experiment 2, for a total of 105 web pages and 3,262 images. These images were judged manually and SVM used eight keyword search results as training data. In Experiment 1, the remaining eight keyword search results were evaluation data. In Experiment 2, 13 keyword search results including additional five keyword search results were evaluation data.

3.2 Experiment 1

To give marks to the images, we developed Expression (1), where *points* is the acquisition mark, *image* is the math-image, and α_k is the weights. When $k = 1$, an image in a separate line is correct; when $k = 2$, an image determined to be correct by SVM is correct; when $k = 3$, an image with a keyword is correct. The aim of this experiment is to optimize the values of α_k and $\delta_3(image)$ when an image is incorrect.

$$points = \sum_{i=1}^{3} \alpha_k \delta_k(image) \tag{1}$$

When $k = 1, 2$
$$\delta_k(image) = \begin{cases} 1 & (image : correct) \\ -1 & (image : incorrect) \end{cases}$$

When $k = 3$
$$\delta_k(image) = \begin{cases} 1 & (image : correct) \\ -1 \ or \ 0 & (image : incorrect) \end{cases}$$

First, to determine -1 or 0 of $\delta_3(image)$, two sets were created by fixing each $\alpha_k = 1$. One had -1 as its δ_3 value and the other had 0, and then the top ranking images were compared using precision, recall, and F-measure. From Figs. 4(1) and (2), we adopted 0. Next, to determine the α_k values, four sets were created. The first had $\alpha_1 = \alpha_2 = \alpha_3 = 1$ as its condition and the second to the fourth had conditions where only one value of each α_k was 2 and the others were 1. Then we compared these sets using F-measure. In Figs. 4(2) to (5), since (2) is the highest, we adopted $\alpha_1 = \alpha_2 = \alpha_3 = 1$.

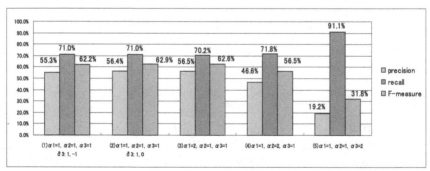

(1) and (2): Comparison of applying 0 and -1 to images without a keyword
(2) to (5): Comparison when changing weights

Fig. 4. Results of Experiment 1

3.3   Experiment 2

Expression (1) was fixed to $points = \sum_{i=1}^{3} \delta_k(image)$ and $\delta_3(image) = 0$ when the image is incorrect. Using this expression, we examined the validity of our bonus point system. In Fig. 5, adding bonus points was basically better than not adding them. Especially in Fig. 5(a), the number of correct images of the third keyword, "Gauss' law", rose to 2 from 0. The rates of the average correct images showed that the bonus point system was effective, and since the rate of the average correct images of the best three exceeded the rate of the best five, we adopted the best three to which bonus points were added.

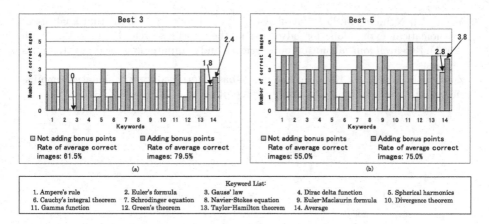

Fig. 5. Comparison of adding and not adding bonus points

4 Related Work

Even though various methods have addressed mathematical information retrieval [1], they are searching for math notations with similar structure or semantics for a given expression. Among those methods, content-based image retrieval (CBIR) inputs a digital image to search for similar images [2], and instead of using images, others use MathML [3] or LaTeX [4].

This paper's approach is quite different. Focusing on the unique features of mathematical expressions and math-images led us to use text information. Even people who are unfamiliar with handling MathML or LaTeX can use our method.

5 Conclusions

We proposed a method to present math-images with the information around them in the HTML files. Our method uses an ordinary text search that inputs a mathematical term as a keyword. To obtain the best three math-images, we developed Expression (1) and optimized its parameters. Our results showed that at least two of the best three were correct, and the rate of the average correct images of the best three was 79.5%. Then using these three images, we showed a screen display with an explanation of the keyword and information about the images to support mathematics understanding.

References

1. Zanibbi, R., Blostein, D.: Recognition and Retrieval of Mathematical Expressions. Int. J. Doc. Anal. Recogn. **15**(4), 331–357 (2012)
2. Shirmenbaatar, M., Koga, H., Watanabe, T.: Content-based mathematical formula image retrieval system. In: The 4th forum on Data engineering and Information Management (DEIM 2012) (2012)

3. Yokoi, K., Nghiem, M.-Q., Matsubayashi, Y., Aizawa, A.: Contextual analysis of mathematical expressions for advanced mathematical search. Polibits **43**, 81–86 (2011). Research journal on Computer science and computer engineering with applications
4. Zanibbi, R., Yuan, B.: Keyword and image-based retrieval for mathematical expressions. In: Proceedings of Document Recognition and Retrieval XVIII, SPIE, pp. 011–019 (2011)

Chiang Mai Digital Craft: A Case Study of Craftsmanship's Knowledge Representation Using Digital Content Technology

Suepphong Charnbumroong[✉], Pradorn Sureephong[✉], and Yootthapong Tongpaeng[✉]

Knowledge and Innovation Center, College of Arts, Media and Technology, Chiang Mai University, Chiang Mai, Thailand
{suepphong,yootthapong}@kic.camt.info, dorn@camt.info

Abstract. Chiang Mai is known as the capital city of handicraft and tourism industry of Thailand. It generates source of income and employment to the local people for a long time. Nowadays, the craftsmen have tried to exploited their wisdom, creativity, skills and technology to enhance the product's value in order to create the sustainable and higher economic growth. However, most of the time, the created value was not delivered along with the product or transferred via seller. Therefore, buyer could not perceive the wisdom, creativity, or craftsmanship skill of the purchased product. Our work aimed at applying the notion of digital content e.g. storytelling, 360-degree images, 3D-model, or augmented reality to preserve the added value and deliver to the customer. Then, the digital content was conveyed to customer through various IT tools i.e. website, web application, video streaming, and mobile application.

Keyword: Handicrafts · Digital content technology · Knowledge representation

1 Introduction

Chiang Mai is the home to prosperous crafts industries where Ceramics, textiles, wood-carvings, silverwork and lacquerware are of primary importance and look back to a long history. Over millions of visitors visited Chiang Mai in every year [1]. The attractions include historic sites, cultural ceremonies, and handcraft shopping [2]. The handicrafts product in Chiang Mai has engaged with long tradition, fine skills and great expertise regarding crafts. The craftsmanship's skill and knowledge is considered to be the most valuable added since it has been involved in many process of creativity process. This era, the creative economy has played a crucial role in economy aspect [3]. Creative economy mainly mention in creativity as the main factors which can improve value of economic good and service [4]. Therefore, these unique skills of craftsmanship have enhanced the product's value and create the higher economic growth. However, most of the time, the created value were not delivered along with the product or transferred via seller. Therefore, buyer could not perceive the wisdom, creativity, or craftsmanship

© Springer International Publishing AG 2017
S. Benferhat et al. (Eds.): IEA/AIE 2017, Part II, LNAI 10351, pp. 47–51, 2017.
DOI: 10.1007/978-3-319-60045-1_7

skill of the purchased product. Moreover, local company cannot effort the advance digital technology which is normally requested high budget of investment.

The aim of project "Chiang Mai Digital craft" applied the notion of digital content to preserve the added value of product and deliver to the customer. Moreover, the result of project would contribute positive impact, particularly in economy and cultural aspect and it would be provided a good international collaboration between United Kingdom and Thailand. In this paper, we represent the scopes of project in 3 main areas. Firstly, background area will provide the general information which is related to project. Then, the second area is the project framework which illustrates development process of each part of project. The result of project implementation within 3 years will be present in the end part of this paper.

2 Background

2.1 Chiang Mai Digital Crafts

The project Chiang Mai Digital craft was formed by the cooperation between the British Council and Thai partners, namely the Chiang Mai Creative City Initiative (CMCC), the Technology Development Center for Industry (TDCI), the Northern Handicrafts Manufacturers and Exporters (NOHMEX) and the College of Arts, Media and Technology (CAMT), Chiang Mai University. The aim was to give support to Chiang Mai's c creative crafts by establishing channels and materials to propagate them, and by raising their competitiveness through knowledge and technology exchange. Additionally, the project laid stress upon such references as tourism, arts, heritage, culture and digital content. To reach these goals, this project focused on the implementation of new digital technologies as a key to enhance the competitiveness of SMEs in Chiang Mai's creative industry. The project encourages the collaboration between the participating countries (Thailand and United Kingdom) by the exchange of knowledge, best practices, expertise and technology in the field of the creative economy. The wider public has been involved in the project by disseminating the results on seminars, meetings, workshops, publications etc.

3 Methodology

3.1 Project Framework

The project Chiang Mai Digital Crafts consisted of three main phases. In the first step, a preliminary assessment has been executed to gain a better understanding of the current situation. The preliminary assessment was based on a SWOT analysis. In the second step, the website "handmade chiangmai.com" has been created. This website was dedicated to promote the crafts online supporting Chiang Mai's traditional craftsmen with state of the art digital technologies. The third project phase focused on digital production design and the exploration of the various possibilities that the application of different 3D technologies have to offer for the crafts industry. 3D technologies with the potential to boost the competitiveness of craft products have been investigated, applied and tested in this phase.

3.2   Development Process

Phase 1: Preliminary Assessment

As an introductory step, a SWOT analysis has been executed to get a clear picture about crafts in Chiang Mai. This analysis later functioned as a guideline to define the further project phases and their operative activities. The results of the SWOT analysis are shown in Table 1.

Table 1.   SWOT analysis results

Strengths	Weaknesses
• Chiang Mai is a city with long tradition, fine skills and great expertise regarding crafts. • The products show original design and unique style and there are also attractive showrooms throughout the city.	• Production capacity was found to be insufficient. In many cases, there is a lack of in-house design expertise, and a lack of digital media and e-commerce know-how such as branding expertise. • There is a concern about copyrights and the security of internet transactions. The local use of e-commerce is turned out to be very low. • High postal cost for small batch international orders is an obstacle of competitiveness. • There is a lack of contemporary product development inspired by local traditions and cultural heritage.
Opportunities	**Threats**
• The relatively low price of local products has the capacity of profit margin growth if supported by good branding. • Topics such as the contemporary application of traditional techniques provide compelling stories to tell as regards the city, the companies and the products. • Potential of the growing foreign retail / B2C market and growing domestic market • Growth on the market of cultural products • Growing demand of products with authenticity and high design quality	• Concerns over copyrights • Internet transaction safety and security issues regarding e-commerce • Strong competition from China and Vietnam, particularly as regards quality and price • The local workforce typically associated with crafts is subject to urbanization trends and migration, following the global tendencies.

Phase 2: Digital Story-Telling Through an Interactive and Content Rich Website

As the SWOT analysis made it clear in which direction to go, the next project phase was dedicated to the creation of the website "handmade-chiangmai.com". The concept behind the website was based on the recognition of some of the difficulties related to the crafts industry in Chiang Mai. Although the city looks back to a long tradition of crafts production with high expertise, producers had disadvantages in meeting the demands of the 21st century markets and its customers in terms of branding, product design, distribution channels, online media presence and the use of digital technologies. The website aimed to function as a role model for crafts producers, emphasizing the importance of online media presence with high quality visual contents. When trying to solve the above-mentioned problems related to the crafts industry of Chiang Mai, great stress was laid upon website and storytelling, allowing the site to give its visitors an insight to local traditions and history, craftsmanship, production techniques, skills and knowledge, as well as local communities and lifestyles.

The Website Creation Process

As an early step of the Chiang Mai Digital Crafts project some of the subsectors of the crafts industry have been selected to be represented on the website with rich multimedia content. The following aspects were taken into consideration in the selection process: significance, uniqueness of the subsector, storytelling potential, availability of entrepreneurs, businesses, and artisans to participate in the online content production, just as the suitability for the next project phases. As a result of the selection process, wood, ceramics and textiles were selected to be presented online. The list has later been expanded by 3 new subsectors as follows: metals, paper, soaps and oils. The idea was to display a few companies related to each selected subsector on the website. As the final step of the website creation process, having all the sectors and companies selected, the production team created the visual content. The key elements of the visual content are the story-telling videos and the product photographs. Find more about such content under the Project Output chapter.

Phase 3: Digital Design and Production

3D technologies allow realistic experiences in virtual environments. With the fast growing popularity of e-commerce platforms this characteristic of 3D technologies potentially delivers competitive advantage [5]. Realizing their growing importance, this project aimed to seek for 3D technologies that can be implemented for an enhanced crafts design. The SWOT analysis as a preliminary assessment method of the project clearly indicated that producers in the crafts industry of Chiang Mai tend to lack knowledge on digital media and product design. Such deficiencies result in an incapacity of revealing the full market potential of the products. It was a substantial goal of the project to let the craftsmen realize the importance of product design and to make them recognize the possibilities of digital technology applications. During the project Chiang Mai Digital Crafts, the following 3D technology solutions have been investigated together with their possible ways of implementation in the crafts industry. For example, 3D printing is a process whereby solid 3D objects are produced from a digital file. This process can create almost any shape of various geometric features. The end product is almost identical with the virtual illustration [6]. 3D scanning is a device that analyzes a real-world object or environment to collect data on its shape and possibly its appearance [7]. 360° capturing allows viewers to observe the captured objects in 3D, from any angles [8]. This technology makes it possible to reveal the important characteristics of objects without their real presence.

4   Results

When trying to evaluate the results of the project Chiang Mai Digital Craft first of all we have to understand the special nature of the crafts industry and the distinguishing characteristics of the sector. The classic terms of economics like profit maximization, market extension, increase of profit margins etc. doesn't seem to have the potential to sufficiently describe the crafts markets as they by-pass some of the most crucial elements. Talking about the crafts sector of Chiang Mai as a whole, first of all we need to bear in mind that this is not just a competitive market sector. Being a source of income is only one of the many functions that can be linked to crafts. It is not just a profession in the classic way of sense but it is a lifestyle. It should not be ignored that craftsmen represent a traditional lifestyle where cultural heritage is preserved as values, knowledge and skills are passed over from generation to generation. Therefore, the key aspect of the crafts sector is sustainability in contrast with short term economic goals like the growth of sales. Sustainability means finding the balance between the rich traditions of the past or the aim of value and culture preservation and the free emergence of modern influences, the capability to meet contemporary needs. And of course, sustainability has its strong environmental and social references. Using natural resources in a sustainable manner is of primary importance in the crafts industry representing a traditional lifestyle based on harmony with nature. Nature is the supporting background from which human creativity can emerge thus it is something to be respected and protected and not to be exploited by short-term profit interests. As already mentioned, craftsmanship is passed from generation to generation which gives the social dimension a great significance. Sustainability in terms of social conditions means that the crafts sector should remain attractive for the young generations and it should cope with the challenges of rapid changes in modern societies.

Acknowledgement. Authors would like to express special appreciation and thanks to Knowledge and Innovation Laboratory (KIRLY), College of Arts, Media and Technology, Chiang Mai University, for kindly support. Moreover, this work is partially funded by EU H2020 project-AniAge (691215).

References

1. Euromonitor International: Euro monitors International's Top City Destination Ranking, January 2010
2. A Survey of Cultural Tourism by Social Research Institute, Chiang Mai University (2006)
3. Wikipedia: Creative economy. https://en.wikipedia.org/wiki/Creative_industries. Accessed 15 June 2015
4. Howkins, J.: The Creative Economy: How People Make Money from Ideas. Penguin, London (2001)
5. Cignoni, P., Gobbetti, E., Pintus, R., Scopigno, R.: Color enhancement for rapid prototyping. In: The 9th International Symposium on Virtual Reality, Archaeology and Cultural Heritage VAST (2008)
6. Kulik, A., Shergil, I.P., Novikov, P.: Stone Spray: Soil Solidifying Robot. Institute for Advanced Architecture of Catalonia, Spain (2012). http://www.stonespray.com/the-book/
7. Vosselman, G., Maas, H.-G.: Airborne and Terrestrial Laser Scanning. Whittles, Dunbeath (2010). Print
8. Chen, S.E.: QuickTime VR – an image-based approach to virtual environment navigation. In: Proceedings of SIGGRAPH 1995, pp. 29–38 (1995)

Uncertainty Management

A Robust, Distributed Task Allocation Algorithm for Time-Critical, Multi Agent Systems Operating in Uncertain Environments

Amanda Whitbrook[1]([✉]), Qinggang Meng[2], and Paul W.H. Chung[2]

[1] University of Derby, Derby, UK
a.whitbrook@derby.ac.uk
[2] Loughborough University, Loughborough, UK
{q.meng,p.w.h.chung}@lboro.ac.uk

Abstract. The aim of this work is to produce and test a robust, distributed, multi-agent task allocation algorithm, as these are scarce and not well-documented in the literature. The vehicle used to create the robust system is the Performance Impact algorithm (PI), as it has previously shown good performance. Three different variants of PI are designed to improve its robustness, each using Monte Carlo sampling to approximate Gaussian distributions. Variant A uses the expected value of the task completion times, variant B uses the worst-case scenario metric and variant C is a hybrid that implements a combination of these. The paper shows that, in simulated trials, baseline PI does not handle uncertainty well; the task-allocation success rate tends to decrease linearly as degree of uncertainty increases. Variant B demonstrates a worse performance and variant A improves the failure rate only slightly. However, in comparison, the hybrid variant C exhibits a very low failure rate, even under high uncertainty. Furthermore, it demonstrates a significantly better mean objective function value than the baseline.

1 Introduction

The ability to assign tasks well in the light of intrinsic uncertainty is very valuable for multi-agent task allocation systems. However, despite the advantages of distributed systems [1] very few robust algorithms have been developed with this architecture. To date, centralized systems have dominated research focus. This is not surprising since distributed task allocation for multi-agent systems operating in uncertain environments is a challenging problem [2]. One of the main difficulties is that the scheduling system must run independently on each agent but must generate the same schedule in each case. This can be problematic when connectivity between agents is limited or subject to change, when measurements are unreliable, or when information is imprecise or vague. These situations typically arise in Search-and-Rescue (SAR) missions where each agent may record a different location for each survivor because of inaccuracies in sensor readings, and none of the locations may be exact. Furthermore, measurements of the agents' positions and velocities may also be uncertain and different for each agent. SAR missions

S. Benferhat et al. (Eds.): IEA/AIE 2017, Part II, LNAI 10351, pp. 55–64, 2017.
DOI: 10.1007/978-3-319-60045-1_8

are time-critical and demand a low probability of failure; it is vital that the assignment is reached quickly and that it represents a robust, conflict-free solution, where every survivor is rescued within the given time-frame. The main aim of this work is to attempt to address some of these challenges by creating a robust, distributed, multi-agent task allocation system with a very low failure rate.

To achieve the aim, the Performance Impact algorithm (PI) is used as the baseline for building a more robust architecture [3]. The PI algorithm has demonstrated better performance than CBBA [4] when solving deterministic model SAR problems, but lacks any mechanism for handling uncertainty. Ponda [5] has developed a robust version of CBBA using stochastic metrics such as the expected value metric [6] and worst-case scenario metric. The approach used here to extend PI is similar, but it takes the technique a step further by using a hybrid combination of expected value and worst-case scenario metric to improve robustness. The hybrid algorithm consistently demonstrates a very low failure rate and a low number of unallocated tasks in model SAR problems. Furthermore, it has a significantly better mean objective function value when compared to the baseline PI algorithm, and uses far fewer samples than Ponda's model [5].

2   Related Work

There is an extensive body of work related to multi-agent task planning, task allocation, and scheduling with many solutions proposed. These include the Contract Net method [7], Markov Random Fields (MRFs) [8], auction-based methods [9], and Distributed Constraint Optimization methods (DCOPs) [10]. In addition, solution methods can be sub-divided into optimization and heuristic types, online and offline types, and centralized and distributed communication architectures. A good review of the different approaches is presented in [11].

Time-critical, multi-agent, task allocation problems are NP-hard [12] and are thus difficult to solve using optimization approaches such as linear programming (LP), mixed integer linear programming (MILP), MRFs, and DCOPS. A MILP solution has been attempted, but the problem is not time-constrained and only eight agents and six targets are tested [13]. Pujol-Gonzalez applies an MRF-based solution to UAV online routing using the max-sum algorithm [8], but the problem is also not time-constrained and empirical tests restrict the number of UAVs to ten surveying a limited area of 100 km^2. In general, when the number of tasks and agents increases sufficiently, the optimization approach becomes intractable because of the exponential number of constraints in the model [14].

Heuristic-based methods provide an alternative as scalability is not such a problem. Popular heuristic methods include Tabu-search [15], genetic algorithms [16], and auction-based techniques [17]. In general, heuristic systems are less complex and demonstrate relatively fast execution times, although the trade-off is that they often provide sub-optimal solutions.

Auction-based heuristic algorithms, a subset of market-based approaches [18] have been widely used for solving these problems [19]. The method is easily adapted to a decentralized architecture, although this can increase complexity and communication overheads [20]. However, auction-based approaches have many benefits including high efficiency, good scalability [21], and robustness when implemented within a decentralized paradigm.

Two particular combinatorial auction-based algorithms lend themselves to the solution of the problems of interest in this paper - CBBA [4] and the PI algorithm [3]. Both algorithms use combinatorial auctions, where bundles of tasks are formed. These combinatorial methods have exhibited superior performance to single-item auctions and have generated good results when compared to optimal centralized approaches [22]. It has been shown empirically that the baseline PI algorithm performs better than the baseline CBBA algorithm [3, 23], with PI demonstrating a much better success rate with different numbers of tasks and agents, and different network topologies. However, the papers mentioned do not examine PI's handling of uncertainty.

2.1 Incorporating Uncertainty into Task Allocation Algorithms

To account for uncertainty, many researchers use Monte Carlo sampling techniques to allow the approximation of complex distributions. Undurti and How formulate the problem as a Constrained Markov Decision Process (C-MDP) [24]. Their method allows risk, defined as the probability of violating constraints, to be kept below a threshold value whilst optimizing the reward. Simulation results showed that the algorithm performed well, but the experiments were limited to only two agents. An online MDP method is used in [25], but results are inferior to basic reactive approaches and testing is based on a much simpler problem.

Maheswaran et al. enable users to encode their intuition as guidance for the system [26]. This approach simplifies a scheduling problem by decomposing it into simpler problems that can be solved in a centralized fashion. The work of Ramchurn et al. follows a similar approach, where human decisions are encoded as additional constraints for the optimization [27]. However, in work presented here attention is restricted to solutions that do not involve human intervention.

Lui and Shell postulate an alternative method that assesses the robustness of any given solution to uncertainty given a measure of it [28]. They propose the Interval Hungarian Algorithm that provides a tolerance-to-uncertainty metric for a given allocation. In particular, they compute a set of inputs that yield the same output schedule, providing a reliable method for assessing the tolerance of the allocation to uncertainties.

Creation of a solution that can hedge against uncertainty is an alternative technique to those already listed. Ponda implements this by adding probabilistic models of uncertain variables, Monte Carlo sampling, and stochastic metrics (such as the expected-value and worst-case scenario) to baseline CBBA to improve its robustness [5]. Simulation results showed improved performance over the baseline, achieving results similar to centralized approaches. However, the experiments involved only six agents and 10,000 samples were required. In addition, beyond about twelve tasks the robust algorithms began to fail. This suggests that further research in this area is needed to address the problems.

3   Methodology

3.1   Problem Definition

The problem of interest is documented fully in [3, 23, 29, 30]. It is the optimal, conflict-free assignment of a set of n heterogeneous agents $\mathbf{V} = [v_1, \ldots, v_n]^T$ to an ordered sequence of heterogeneous tasks from an m-sized set $\mathbf{T} = [t_1, \ldots, t_m]^T$. Each task has a fixed location and a maximum (latest) start time g, i.e., the problem is time-critical. Each task requires only one agent to service it, and each agent can complete only one task at a time, although it can complete other tasks afterwards, if there is time. The objective function is the minimization of mean individual task cost over all tasks rather than mean completion time for each agent, as the former takes into account the number of tasks that benefit from the time saving. The constraints are that the number of tasks assigned to a particular agent must be less than or equal to the total number of tasks, all tasks must be assigned to an agent, each ordered sequence of allocations is a subset of the whole set of tasks, tasks cannot be assigned to multiple agents, and an agent must complete a task before its latest start time.

3.2   The PI Algorithm

The PI algorithm is a distributed, multi-agent task allocation system that runs simultaneously on each agent. As in CBBA, the tasks are grouped into bundles that are continuously updated as the auction proceeds. In CBBA, the agents bid on the bundles rather than individual tasks and the bundles are formed by logically grouping similar tasks. In contrast, the PI algorithm uses a novel concept called performance impact to score and organize the task bundles. These are incrementally built and updated by systematically swapping tasks between agents, and then measuring the benefit over all tasks using special metrics. The removal performance impact (RPI) measures the benefits of removing a task from a bundle and the inclusion performance impact (IPI) measures the benefits of adding a task. Full details of the metrics and the PI algorithm are presented in [3, 23, 29, 30]. The details are not reproduced here because of space limitations. In addition, for the purposes of this paper, the reader only needs to know that the RPI and the IPI are calculated using the time costs $c_{i,k}$ associated with each agent i and task k. In addition, creation of a robust scheduler in this way means that the methodology can be applied to other task allocation algorithms; it is not limited to the PI algorithm.

3.3   The Robust PI Variants

Each robust PI variant creates robust time cost values $r_{i,k}$ by sampling uncertain variables from a Gaussian distribution N times. A Gaussian distribution is selected because physical quantities that are the sum of many independent processes (for example measurement errors) often have distributions that are nearly normal.

In variant A, the expected values of the actual time costs are taken as the robust time costs, where the expected value of an uncertain variable ζ is calculated as follows:

$$E(\zeta) = \sum_{s=1}^{N} \zeta_s \|p_s\|. \tag{1}$$

In (1), p_s is the probability of the sample value ζ_s, and $\|p_s\|$ is the normalized value of this given by:

$$\|p_s\| = \frac{p_s}{\sum_{l=1}^{N} p_l}. \tag{2}$$

Thus, in variant A, the robust time costs are given by:

$$r_{i,k} = E(c_{i,k}) = \sum_{s=1}^{N} c_{i,k} \|p_s\|. \tag{3}$$

In (3), the probability p_s of sample s is taken as the combined probability of the component uncertain variables. Variant B makes use of the worst-case scenario metric to calculate the robust time costs so that:

$$r_{i,k} = \max_{s=1}^{N}(c_{i,k}). \tag{4}$$

Variant C uses a hybrid technique that places a buffer value ψ on the difference between the expected time cost and the maximum (latest) start time of the task g_k. If

$$g_k - E(c_{i,k}) < \psi \tag{5}$$

is true then the maximum time cost (4) is used for $r_{i,k}$; the deadline for the task is tight so it pays to be pessimistic. In other words, the algorithm is simply more cautious about accounting for uncertainty in its allocation. However, if (5) is false then the deadline is more flexible and the expected time cost can be used for $r_{i,k}$ as in (3).

It is important to note that each variant uses the same objective function as the baseline, but substitutes the robust time costs $r_{i,k}$ for the measured ones $c_{i,k}$. Apart from sampling and calculating the robust time costs, the procedural details for the robust PI algorithms follow the same pattern as the baseline.

4   Experimental Design

4.1   Scenario

The algorithms are tested on a scenario based on the rescue aspect of a SAR mission. The agents are UAVs carrying food and helicopters carrying medicine, and their mission is to rescue disaster survivors by delivering the supplies to them. Each survivor requires either food or medicine and their delivery constitutes the completion of a task. The start locations of the UAVs and helicopters are known in advance, as are the 3-dimensional locations and requirements of the survivors. The world x and

y coordinates range from -2500 m to 2500 m and the z coordinates range from 0 m to 1000 m. The helicopters travel at 30 m/s and the UAVs at 50 m/s. The mission time limit is set at 5000 s, the earliest start time for each task is 0 s, and the latest start time is a random fraction of 5000 s that cannot be less than 1500 s. The task durations are fixed at 300 s and 350 s for medicine and food delivery respectively. Forty tasks and five vehicles are tested in each case.

4.2   Uncertainty Models

Three levels of uncertainty (low, medium and high) are considered, which vary according to prescribed errors in the key uncertain variables - task location, vehicle velocity and task duration. These variables are modelled as Gaussian distributions centered on a known mean with standard deviation equal to the estimated error. Monte Carlo sampling is used to allocate a value from the distribution to each uncertain variable and this is carried out separately for each vehicle. Relatively large errors are modelled for the task location as information relies upon intelligence from mixed external sources. UAVs generally use airspeed indicators to measure their velocity [31], but these can demonstrate instrument errors of up to about 7 m/s [32]. Task durations are the most uncertain parameters since many sources contribute to them. For this reason, relatively large errors are modelled, but the uncertain values are not allowed to fall below their real values by more than 50 s as it is assumed that there is a minimum time for each. For the low uncertainty case, the errors are 50 m for task location, 5% for vehicle velocity and 10% for task duration. For the medium case they are 100 m, 10% and 25% respectively, and for the high case they are 200 m, 20% and 50% respectively.

4.3   Parameter Setting and Metrics

Preliminary trials with values between 5 s and 40 s confirmed that the best value to use for ψ in variant C is about 20 s, although the algorithm does not appear to be very sensitive to the parameter. The size N of the samples is maintained at 100 throughout all the experiments, which are conducted using a randomly generated network topology where half of all possible connection pairs are set as communicable. This represents a realistic structure as it is not fully connected and is not as simplistic as a row or circular structure.

Each algorithm is run 100 times to obtain a percentage failure rate. Success is measured by selecting random real values for the uncertain parameters from the known probability distributions and calculating the actual number of tasks allocated to vehicles using the robust solution. If any tasks are unassigned then the run is counted as a failure; a run is only successful when all tasks are allocated. The total number of unassigned tasks is also recorded for each algorithm and uncertainty case, as are the mean objective function values.

5   Results

Figure 1 shows the total number of unassigned tasks across all 100 runs and Fig. 2 shows the percentage failures for each algorithm and each uncertainty case.

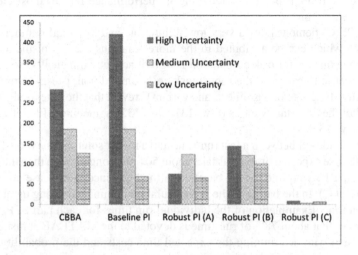

Fig. 1. Unallocated tasks for each algorithm and each uncertainty case

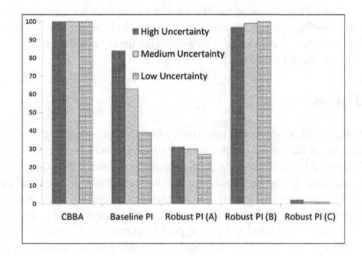

Fig. 2. Percentage failures for each algorithm and each uncertainty case

Failure to allocate tasks is a serious drawback for CBBA and baseline PI when uncertainty is modelled. For PI, the problem scales linearly with the level of uncertainty in terms of both the failure rate and the number of unassigned tasks. CBBA shows 100% failure rate for all uncertainty cases, and similar results to PI for the unassigned tasks, although it performs slightly better for high uncertainty in this respect.

Robust PI (A) improves on the baseline performance with less difference between the uncertainty cases, but the algorithm does not produce an acceptable failure rate or a low enough number of unassigned tasks. Robust PI (B)'s performance is comparable to that of CBBA in terms of the failure rate, and to Robust PI (A) in terms of the unassigned tasks. It proves 100% capable of predicting its performance but, in most cases, just predicts its own failure.

Robust PI (C) demonstrates a very low failure rate and low total number of unassigned tasks, which can be attributed to the more 'cautious' design of the algorithm. When the time margin for task completion is tight it acts pessimistically, selecting the worst-case metric to calculate the robust task costs. In addition, t-tests comparing the mean objective function for baseline PI and variant C reveal that the latter is significantly faster in all of the uncertainty cases (low: 1316 s vs 1321 s, medium: 1322 s vs 1340 s, high: 1340 s vs 1378 s).

There is a trade-off between a fast run-time and a robust solution; the robust variants (A and C) that use expected time-costs take about 50 times longer to run than the baseline (for example, a 1 s run-time for the baseline in the high uncertainty case compares to 47 s for variant C). In the baseline, the IPI-calculation dominates, taking up about 85% of execution time. Examination of the individual run times for each part of PI variants A and C shows that about 78% of run-time is devoted to the MATLAB statistical functions associated with determining the expected time costs and the probabilities of the uncertain variables. This is the key factor underlying the longer run-times. However, the IPI calculation still dominates the remaining routines, taking around 20% of total run-time, with actual time spent in the IPI routine longer than for equivalent problems solved with the baseline. Around 8 s are added to run-time, which may be attributed to the increase in complexity associated with computing the expected time costs and probabilities of the uncertain variables.

6   Conclusions

CBBA and baseline PI do not handle uncertainty well; a high percentage of the solutions fail to allocate all of the tasks, and the number of unallocated tasks is relatively high. Taking the expected value of the time costs reduces the failure rate and the numbers of unallocated tasks, but the method is still not reliable enough for time-critical problems. Using the worst-case scenario metric demonstrates poor performance, especially for high uncertainty. However, when a combination of the expected value and the worst-case scenario metric is used, the results are greatly improved, in terms of both a more robust solution (a 1% to 2% failure rate and low number of unallocated tasks) and a significantly smaller objective function value for all the uncertainty cases tested. In addition, only 100 samples are required to achieve this low failure rate, which compares very favourably to the 10,000 samples used by Ponda, [5]. However, despite the small sample size, scalability in the numbers of agents and tasks is still a problem, with variant C displaying a higher run time compared to the baseline. For the model problems tested, one run still completes in a relatively short time compared to the mission length, but there is a limit to usability in terms of the numbers of tasks and agents because of the increased computation time. Future work will aim to improve the efficiency of variant C and then provide estimates of how this scales as the number of samples, tasks and agents increases.

The study of distributed robust optimization remains wide open. Most methods designed for solution of the types of problem discussed in this paper do not consider uncertainty in their solutions. Thus, the main contribution here is the successful design and implementation of a robust distributed system for solving such problems.

Acknowledgments. This work was supported by EPSRC (grant number EP/J011525/1) with BAE Systems as the leading industrial partner.

References

1. Zhang, K., Collins Jr., E.G., Shi, D.: Centralized and distributed task allocation in multi-robot team via a stochastic clustering auction. ACM Trans. Autonom. Adapt. Syst. **7**(2), 21 (2012)
2. Horling, B., Lesser, V.: A survey of multi-agent organizational paradigms. Knowl. Eng. Rev. **19**, 281–316 (2004)
3. Zhao, W., Meng, Q., Chung, P.W.H.: A heuristic distributed task allocation method for multivehicle multitask problems and its application to search and rescue scenario. IEEE Trans. Cybern. **46**(4), 902–915 (2015)
4. Choi, H.-L., Brunet, J., How, J.P.: Consensus-based decentralization auctions for robust task allocation. IEEE Trans. Robot. **25**(4), 912–926 (2009)
5. Ponda, S.S.: Robust distributed planning strategies for autonomous multi-agent teams. PhD dissertation, Mass. Inst. Technol. (2012)
6. Grinstead, C.M., Snell, D.A.: Expected value and variance. In: Introduction to Probability, 2nd edn., pp. 936–953. American Mathematical Society, Rhode Island (1998)
7. Smith, R.G.: The contract net protocol: high level communication and control in a distributed problem solver. IEEE Trans. Comput. **C-19**(12), 1104–1113 (1998)
8. Pujol-Gonzalez, M., Cerquides, J., Meseguer, P., Rodríguez-Aguilar, J.A., Tambe, M.: Engineering the decentralized coordination of UAVs with limited communication range. In: Bielza, C., Salmerón, A., Alonso-Betanzos, A., Hidalgo, J.I., Martínez, L., Troncoso, A., Corchado, E., Corchado, J.M. (eds.) CAEPIA 2013. LNCS (LNAI), vol. 8109, pp. 199–208. Springer, Heidelberg (2013). doi:10.1007/978-3-642-40643-0_21
9. Lagoudakis, M., Markakis, E., Kempe, D., Keskinocak, P., KJleywegt, A., Koenig, S., Tovey, C., Meyerson, A., Jain, S.: Auction-Based Multi-Robot Routing. Robotics: Science and Systems, vol. 5, MIT Press (2005)
10. Fave, F.M.D., Farinelli, A., Rogers, A., Jennings, N.: A methodology for deploying the max-sum algorithm and a case study on unmanned aerial vehicles. In: Proceedings of IAAI-2012, pp. 2275–2280 (2012)
11. Khamis, A., Hussein, A., Elmogy A.: Multi-robot task allocation: a review of the state-of-the-art. In: Koubaa, A., Martinez-de Dios, J.R. (eds.) Cooperative Robots and Sensor Networks 2015: Studies in Computational Intelligence, vol. 604, pp. 31–51 (2015)
12. Bruno, J.L., Coffman, E.G., Sethi, R.: Scheduling independent tasks to reduce mean finishing time. Commun. ACM **17**(7), 382–387 (1974)
13. Atay, N., Bayazit, B.: Mixed-integer linear programming solution to multi-robot task allocation problem. Technical Report 2006-54, Washington University, St. Louis (2006)

14. Gerkey, B.P., Matarić, M.J.M.: A formal analysis and taxonomy of task allocation in multi-robot systems. Intl. J. Robot. Res. **23**(9), 939–954 (2004)

15. Glover, F., Marti, R.: Tabu search. In: Alba, E., Marti, R. (eds.) Metaheuristic Procedures for Training Neural Networks, pp. 53–69 (2006)

16. Shima, T., Rasmussen, S.J., Sparks, A.G., Passino, K.M.: Multiple task assignments for cooperating uninhabited aerial vehicles using genetic algorithms. Comput. Oper. Res. **33**(11), 3252–3269 (2006)

17. Oliver, G., Guerrero, J.: Auction and swarm multi-robot task allocation algorithms in real time scenarios. In: Yasuda, T. (ed.) Multi-Robot Systems, Trends and Development, pp. 437–456 (2011)

18. Dias, M.B., Stentz, A.: Opportunistic optimization for market-based multi-robot control. In: Proceedings of IROS-2002, pp. 2714–2720 (2002)

19. Bertsekas, D.P.: The auction algorithm for assignment and other network flow problems. Technical Report, Mass. Inst. Technol., Cambridge, MA (1989)

20. Dias, M., Zlot, R., Kalra, N., Stentz, A.: Market-based multirobot coordination: a survey and analysis. Proc. IEEE **94**(7), 1257–1270 (2006)

21. Coltin, B., Veloso, M.: Mobile robot task allocation in hybrid wireless sensor networks. In: Proceedings of IROS-2010, pp. 2932–2937 (2010)

22. Cramton, P., Shoham, Y., Steinberg, R.: An overview of combinatorial auction. ACM SIGecom Exchanges **7**(1), 3–14 (2007)

23. Whitbrook, A., Meng, Q., Chung, P.W.H.: A novel distributed scheduling algorithm for time-critical, multi-agent systems. In: Proceedings of IROS-2015, pp. 6451–6458 (2015)

24. Undurti, A., How, J.P.: A decentralized approach to multi-agent planning in the presence of constraints and uncertainty. In: Proceedings of ICRA-2011, pp. 2534–2539 (2011)

25. Musliner, D.J., Durfee, E.H., Wu, J., Dolgov, D.A., Goldman, R.P., Boddy, M.S.: Coordinated plan management using multiagent MDPs. In: Proceedings of SSDPSM (2006)

26. Maheswaran, R.T., Rogers, C.M., Sanchez, R., Szekely, P.: Realtime multi-agent planning and scheduling in dynamic uncertain domains. In: Proceedings of ICAPS (2010)

27. Ramchurn, S.D., Fischer, J.E., Ikuno, Y., Wu, F., Flann, J., Waldock, A.: A study of human-agent collaboration for Multi-UAV task allocation in dynamic environments. In: Proceedings of IJCAI (2015)

28. Liu, L., Shell, D.A.: Assessing optimal assignment under uncertainty: an interval-based algorithm. Int. J. Rob. Res. **30**(7), 936–953 (2011)

29. Turner, J., Meng, Q., Schaeffer, G.: Increasing allocated tasks with a time minimization algorithm for a search and rescue scenario. In: Proceedings of ICRA 2015, pp. 3401–3407 (2015)

30. Whitbrook, A., Meng, Q., Chung, P.W.H.: Reliable, distributed scheduling and rescheduling for time-critical, multi-agent systems. IEEE Trans. Autom. Sci. Eng. (2017, to appear)

31. Collinson, R.G.P.: Introduction to Avionic Systems, 3rd edn. Springer, London (2011)

32. Huston, W.B.: Accuracy of airspeed measurements and flight calibration procedures. Technical Report No. 919, NACA, Langley Memorial Aeronautical Laboratory (1948)

An Efficient Probabilistic Merging Procedure Applied to Statistical Matching

Marco Baioletti and Andrea Capotorti[✉]

Dipartimento di Matematica e Informatica,
Università degli Studi di Perugia, Perugia, Italy
andrea.capotorti@unipg.it

Abstract. We propose to use a recently introduced merging procedure for jointly inconsistent probabilistic assessments to the statistical matching problem. The merging procedure is based on an efficient $L1$ distance minimization through mixed-integer linear programming that results not only feasible but also meaningful for imprecise (lower-upper) probability evaluations elicitation. Significance of the method can be appreciated whenever among quantities (events) there are logical (structural) constraints and there are different sources of information. Statistical matching problem has these features and is characterized by a set of random (discrete) variables that cannot be jointly observed. Separate observations share some common variable and this, together with structural constraints, make sometimes inconsistent the estimates of probability occurrences. Even though estimates on statistical matching are mainly conditional probabilities, inconsistencies appear only on events with the same conditioning, hence the correction procedure can be easily reduced to unconditional cases and the aforementioned procedure applied.

Keywords: Probabilistic merging · Statistical matching · $L1$ constrained minimization · Mixed integer programming

1 Introduction

This contribution is a straight application of the merging procedure proposed in [1] to the statistical matching problem as presented in [6,17].

The merging procedure has been shown to be particularly meaningful whenever the probabilistic assessments come from different sources of information that share some common elements and there are some impossible configurations (the so called "structural zeroes"). These are exactly the peculiarities of the statistical matching problem. Even though the merging procedure is based on an efficient $L1$ distance minimization and such a measure was already investigated for the statistical matching problem in [3,5,6], we can reappraise its methodic use since it can legitimate and operationally obtain imprecise (lower-upper) probability

Research partially supported by the INdAM–GNAMPA Project 2016 U2016/000391.

S. Benferhat et al. (Eds.): IEA/AIE 2017, Part II, LNAI 10351, pp. 65–74, 2017.
DOI: 10.1007/978-3-319-60045-1_9

assessments, not only for the initial marginal probabilities of the common events, as already depicted in [3], but also for the corrected parts.

For the sake of completeness, we briefly review both the statistical matching problem and the efficient $L1$ merging procedure in the next Sects. 2 and 3, respectively. In the following Sect. 4 we show how the merging procedure can be systematically applied to the statistical matching problem.

2   The Statistical Matching Problem

Denote by $(X_1, Y_1), ..., (X_{n_A}, Y_{n_A})$ and by $(X_{n_A+1}, Z_{n_A+1}), ..., (X_{n_A+n_B},$ $Z_{n_A+n_B})$ two random samples, related to two sources A and B, of dimensions n_A and n_B. Samples observe three categorical variables X, Y, Z with modalities x_i, $i \in I$, y_j, $j \in J$ and z_k, $z \in K$, respectively. We suppose that the two samples are related to the same population of interest. The two samples can be supposed to be drawn according to the same sampling scheme, as done in [17], or according to different schemes and with different relevance (weight) of the two sources, as also contemplated in [3].

Let S_s (with $s = 1, 2$) be the two, possibly different, sampling schemes. From them, relevant parameters, represented by (conditional) probabilities, can be estimated: from A the probability to observe $Y = y_j$ conditional on $(X = x_i)$ (for any $i \in I$)

$$\mathbf{y}_{j|i} = P_{Y|(X=x_i)}(y_j), \tag{1}$$

and analogously from B the probability to observe $Z = z_k$ conditional on $(X = x_i)$ (for any $i \in I$)

$$\mathbf{z}_{k|i} = P_{Z|(X=x_i)}(z_k). \tag{2}$$

Moreover, from A we can estimate the probability to observe $X = x_j$ by following the first sampling scheme

$$\mathbf{x}_i^{S_1} = P_X(x_i|S_1), \tag{3}$$

while from file B by following the second one

$$\mathbf{x}_i^{S_2} = P_X(x_i|S_2), \tag{4}$$

and, by supposing that an observation can be obtained through one single sampling scheme S_s, with $s \in \{1, 2\}$ and probability $P(S_s)$, we get

$$\mathbf{x}_i = P_X(x_i) = \mathbf{x}_i^{S_1} P(S_1) + \mathbf{x}_i^{S_2} P(S_2). \tag{5}$$

Under the assumption of a common sampling scheme, estimations are obtained through partial maximum likelihood method, and the result brings to the frequencies

$$\mathbf{y}_{j|i} = \frac{n_A^{ij}}{n_A^{i\cdot}} \qquad \mathbf{z}_{k|i} = \frac{n_B^{ik}}{n_B^{i\cdot}} \qquad \mathbf{x}_i = \frac{n_A^{i\cdot} + n_B^{i\cdot}}{n_A + n_B} \tag{6}$$

with n_A^i and n_B^i cardinalities of elements with $(X = x_i)$ in samples A and B, respectively, while n_A^{ij} is the cardinality of elements in A with $(X = x_i, Y = y_j)$ and n_B^{ik} is the cardinality of elements in B with $(X = x_i, Z = z_k)$.

Whenever n_A^i (resp., n_B^i) is equal to zero, i.e. no observation in A has $(X = x_i)$, (resp., no observation in B has $(X = x_i)$), the value $\mathbf{y}_{j|i}$ (resp., $\mathbf{z}_{k|i}$) is undefined and this specific parameter has no estimation.

If the probabilities $P(S_s)$, $s = 1, 2$, can be elicited, we get a precise assessment $(\mathcal{E}, \mathbf{p})$ with

$$\mathcal{E} = \{(X = x_i), (Y = y_j)|(X = x_i), (Z = z_k)|(X = x_i)\}_{i \in I, j \in J, k \in K},$$
(7)

$$\mathbf{p} = \{\mathbf{x}_i, \mathbf{y}_{j|i}, \mathbf{z}_{k|i}\}_{i \in I, j \in J, k \in K}.$$

Usually, the first step is to check the coherence (see [9]) of $(\mathcal{E}, \mathbf{p})$, that, in the particular context of the statistical matching (see [17]), could be lead back to find at least a solution of a linear system like

$$\begin{cases} \mathbf{y}_{j|i} \sum_{j,k} \alpha_{ijk} = \sum_k \alpha_{ijk} & \text{for any } \mathbf{y}_{j|i} \\ \mathbf{z}_{k|i} \sum_{j,k} \alpha_{ijk} = \sum_j \alpha_{ijk} & \text{for any } \mathbf{z}_{k|i} \\ \mathbf{x}_i = \sum_{j,k} \alpha_{ijk} & \text{for any } \mathbf{x}_i \\ \sum_{i,j,k} \alpha_{ijk} = 1 \\ \alpha_{ijk} \geq 0 \end{cases}$$
(8)

where the unknowns α_{ijk} are associated to events $(X = x_i, Y = y_j, Z = z_k)$ different from the impossible one and represent their probabilities.

In the trivial case of logical independence, coherence is automatically ensured by the following theorem (see [17]):

Theorem 1. *Let X, Y, Z be three finite random variables and $\mathcal{E}_X, \mathcal{E}_Y, \mathcal{E}_Z$ the associated partition generated by X, Y, Z. Consider the following three separately coherent conditional probability assessments $\{\mathbf{x}_i\}_i$, $\{\mathbf{y}_{j|i}\}_j$ and $\{\mathbf{z}_{k|i}\}_k$.*

Then, the assessment

$$\{\mathbf{x}_i, \mathbf{y}_{j|i}\}_{i,j}$$

is coherent (analogously for $\{\mathbf{x}_i, \mathbf{z}_{k|i}\}_{i,k}$).

Moreover, if the partitions $\mathcal{E}_Y, \mathcal{E}_Z$ are logically independent with respect to $\mathcal{E}_X$ (i.e. $(X = x_i, Y = y_j, Z = z_k)$ is possible for any value x_i of X, y_j of Y, z_k of Z s.t. the events $(X = x_i, Y = y_j)$ and $(X = x_i, Z = z_k)$ are possible), then the whole assessment

$$\mathbf{p} = \{\mathbf{x}_i, \mathbf{y}_{j|i}, \mathbf{z}_{k|i}\}_{i,j,k} \text{ on } \mathcal{E}$$

is coherent.

Generally, whenever $(\mathcal{E}, \mathbf{p})$ is coherent there is more than one solution to system (8) and the set of all of them forms a so called "credal set" (see [18]).

In the more worthwhile case of structural zeroes among variables Y and Z (for real applications where these are present refer, e.g., to [12]), coherence of the entire assessment $(\mathcal{E}, \mathbf{p})$ in (7) is not directly ensured by the coherence of the distinct assessments (1), (2), (5). Anyhow, whenever present, inconsistencies focus on conditional events with the same conditioning $(X = x_i)$ (proofs and examples again in [17]).

The check of coherence can be implicitly embedded in the merging procedure that we will present in the last section: if the $L1$ distance of the assessment $(\mathcal{E}, \mathbf{p})$ from those coherent is zero, then $(\mathcal{E}, \mathbf{p})$ is coherent.

Anyhow, in [3] it has been considered also the case whenever the two samples are observed through two different sample schemes S_s and with no relevant information about their probabilities $P(S_s), s = 1, 2$. Consequentially $\mathbf{x}_i$, $i \in I$ cannot be univocally estimated, and coherent values for them are those in the interval

$$\mathbf{lub}_i = [\min\{\mathbf{x}_i^{S_1}, \mathbf{x}_i^{S_2}\}, \max\{\mathbf{x}_i^{S_1}, \mathbf{x}_i^{S_2}\}]. \tag{9}$$

This implies the adoption of an imprecise assessment

$$\mathbf{lub} = \{\mathbf{lub}_i, \mathbf{y}_{j|i}, \mathbf{z}_{k|i}\}_{i,j,k}. \tag{10}$$

on $\mathcal{E}$. In [3] it has been proved that, again, in the trivial case of logical independence of the partitions $\mathcal{E}_Y, \mathcal{E}_Z$ with respect to $\mathcal{E}_X$, coherence is automatically ensured, while, whenever there are some structural zeroes, incoherences can appear but focused among conditional events with the same conditioning event $(X = x_i)$. This result will permit to split the problem of the merging of the two estimates into separate subproblems: one for the unconditional values $\mathbf{lub}_i, i \in I$, and one for each conditioning $(X = x_i)$ about the conditional quantities $\{\mathbf{y}_{j|i}, \mathbf{z}_{k|i}\}$, $j \in J$ and $k \in K$. In each of these subproblems the merging procedure that minimize $L1$ distance can be applied. Let us show how it works in the next section and how it can be used in the statistical matching framework in the subsequent one.

3   An Efficient $L1$ Correct and Merging Procedure

The risk of dealing with incoherent probability assessments is significantly present when the numerical evaluation comes from different sources of information and/or structural constraints limit the possible states (see, e.g., [4, 7, 8, 11, 15, 17]). The basic idea is to "correct" an inconsistent evaluation by finding a coherent one that will be as close as possible to it. This means that a choice for a distance between probability evaluations must be done.

In particular we will deal with the simple and easily understood $L1$-distance, known also as "Manhattan" or "taxi-cab" metric:

$$L1(\mathbf{p}, \mathbf{p}') = \sum_{i=1}^{n} |p(E_i) - p'(E_i)| \tag{11}$$

where E_i, $i = 1, \ldots, n$, are the events of the set $\mathcal{E}$, $\mathbf{p}$ and $\mathbf{p}'$ two numerical evaluations on them.

The main reason for using such metric is because we are able to propose an effective procedure (presented into details in [1]), which is based on integer linear programming and hence is much more efficient than the correction procedures needed for other distances, for instance the quadratic programming for *L*2-distance. *L*1-distance minimization has moreover a simple interpretation, since it implies a direct minimal modification of each single value.

The peculiarity of using *L*1 minimization is the non-uniqueness, in general, of the solution and this could represent an alternative way of legitimating the adoption of imprecise probability models, in addition to the historical ones as stemming from buying/selling prices or desirability of gambles [18], or from extensions of coherent precise initial assessments [9, Chap. 15]. Of course, in some extreme case the imprecise solution could be extremely vague by including all the coherent assessments.

Starting with an initial assessment $(\mathcal{E}, \mathbf{p})$, all the corrections form a convex set $\mathcal{C}(\mathbf{p})$ and can be found by a solving a mixed integer programming (MIP) problem. There exist fast procedures for solving MIP problems, even if this problem is NP-hard. The particular program we can use for our correction purposes has been fully described in [1] and was inspired by a similar one introduced in [10]. We can report here just the main steps on which it is based, demanding to the aforementioned papers the technical details.

Let

$$\delta = L1(\mathbf{p}, \mathbf{p}') \tag{12}$$

be the distance between the original probability vector $\mathbf{p}$ and any of its corrections $\mathbf{p}'$. If $\delta = 0$, $\mathbf{p}$ is already coherent and no correction is needed. Otherwise, we can find the extremal points $\mathbf{q}_1, \ldots, \mathbf{q}_s$ of $\mathcal{C}(\mathbf{p})$. Indeed

$$\mathcal{C}(\mathbf{p}) = \mathcal{Q} \cap \mathcal{B}_{\mathbf{p}}(\delta), \tag{13}$$

where $\mathcal{Q}$ is the set of all coherent assessments $\mathbf{q} \in \mathbb{R}^n$ on $\mathcal{E}$ and $\mathcal{B}_{\mathbf{p}}(\delta)$ is the *ball* of all vectors $\mathbf{q}$ such that $L1(\mathbf{p}, \mathbf{q}) \leq \delta$.

Note that, in general, for conditional probability assessments like $(\mathcal{E}, \mathbf{p})$, the set $\mathcal{Q}$ is not convex (see, e.g., [2]) but, as already anticipated in the previous section and described in the next one, we will split the domain $\mathcal{E}$ into segment of unconditional events or conditioned to the same event, hence for each iteration of the procedure $\mathcal{Q}$ will result a convex polytope (simplex). Since the balls $\mathcal{B}_{\mathbf{p}}(\delta)$ are also convex polytopes, fast procedures for face-enumeration and vertex-enumeration can be used for detecting $\mathcal{C}(\mathbf{p})$.

Computed in this way, the convex set $\mathcal{C}(\mathbf{p})$ results to be *strongly coherent*, i.e. each element $\mathbf{p}' \in \mathcal{C}(\mathbf{p})$ is coherent. The correction can be relaxed to a *coherent lower-upper* assessment by $2n$ minimizations/maximizations, two for each component of $\mathbf{p}' \in \mathcal{Q}$, under the constraint $L1(\mathbf{p}, \mathbf{p}') = \delta$. This can be applied also whenever the initial assessment would be a credal set $\mathcal{P}$ (and in particular one described by lower-upper constraints like **lub** in (10)) by simply generalizing the distance to

$$L1(\mathcal{P}, \mathbf{p}') = \min_{\mathbf{p} \in \mathcal{P}} L1(\mathbf{p}, \mathbf{p}'). \tag{14}$$

This actually results an easier procedure since it does not require the face/vertex enumeration procedures.

The correct procedure can be used as a merging operator by simply putting together two different assessments on sub-domains of $\mathcal{E}$, possibly with some value given on common events. In fact we can take as result of the merging the correction, if needed, of the concatenation of the original assessments.

Since the peculiarity of the structure of $\mathcal{E}$ in the statistical matching problem described in previous section, let us see how the merging procedure can be applied on it.

4   Application of the Merging and Correction Procedures to the Statistical Matching Problem

In the previous section we have (briefly) described the correction procedure that could be used in the statistical matching problem once we have the whole assessment $(\mathcal{E}, \mathbf{p})$ or $(\mathcal{E}, \mathbf{lub})$. But it can be actually used also in the preliminary operation of merging the estimates coming from the two different sampling schemes S_1 and S_2. In particular, since incoherences could be focused only on events conditioned to the same event, we can split the domain $\mathcal{E}$ into sub-domains

$$\mathcal{E}_\Omega = \{(X = x_i)\}_{i \in I}; \tag{15}$$

$$\mathcal{E}_i = \{(Y = y_j)|(X = x_i), (Z = z_k)|(X = x_i)\}_{j \in J, k \in K} \text{ for } i \in I. \tag{16}$$

Since, as described in Sect. 2, variables Y and Z are not jointly observed, on the $\sharp(I)$ domains E_i the two sources of information do not overlap and hence the problem will be to, eventually, correct the estimates $\{\mathbf{y}_{j|i}, \mathbf{z}_{k|i}\}$ obtained through (1) and (2). A proper merging operation is needed for the estimates $\{\mathbf{x}_i^{S_1}\}_{i \in I}$ and $\{\mathbf{x}_i^{S_2}\}_{i \in I}$, both on elements of $\mathcal{E}_\Omega$.

As described in [1], two different merging procedure that uses the efficient $L1$ minimization can be used: the "supervised" procedure that relies on a specific choice of a "weight" ω for the relevance or reliability of sources; or the "unsupervised" one that relies on a duplication of the events that have associated estimates in both sources (hence all events $(X = x_i)$ with non null frequencies if maximum likelihood estimates are used) and consequent addition of structural constraints that express such duplication.

Schematically, we can say that the first approach needs to firstly perform a componentwise "weighted average"

$$\mathbf{x}^{S_1} +_\omega \mathbf{x}^{S_2} = \omega\{\mathbf{x}_i^{S_1}\}_{i \in I} + (1 - \omega)\{\mathbf{x}_i^{S_2}\}_{i \in I} \tag{17}$$

that is a convex combination of the two for a chosen weight $\omega \in [0, 1]$, and consequently apply the correct procedure to $(\mathcal{E}_\Omega, \mathbf{x}^{S_1} +_\omega \mathbf{x}^{S_2})$ obtaining

$$\mathbf{lub} = \mathbf{x}^{S_1} \oplus_\omega \mathbf{x}^{S_2} = \text{Correct}(\mathbf{x}^{S_1} +_\omega \mathbf{x}^{S_2}). \tag{18}$$

If there is some missing value for $\{\mathbf{x}_i^{S_1}\}_{i \in I}$ or for $\{\mathbf{x}_i^{S_2}\}_{i \in I}$ it must be put equal to 0 in (17). Remember that the correct procedure could lead to either a single solution or to a convex set of solutions, hence **lub** in (18) could be either an actually precise coherent assessment $\{x_i\}_{i\in I}$ or a proper lower-upper assessment $\{lub_i\}_{i\in I}$.

Note moreover that, if estimates are taken through frequencies in both samples, $\mathbf{x}^{S_1} +_\omega \mathbf{x}^{S_2}$ in (17) turns out to be directly coherent for any choice of $\omega \in [0,1]$ so that $\mathbf{lub} = \{x_i\}_{i\in I} = \mathbf{x}^{S_1} +_\omega \mathbf{x}^{S_2}$. In particular, choosing $\omega = \frac{n_A}{n_A+n_B}$ we obtain exactly the x_i estimates already described in (6). So the common sampling scheme can be re-interpreted in our method as separate sampling schemes with weights proportional to the different sample dimensions.

The second approach is to let the correct procedure work without any exogenous weight of the sources and contemplating simultaneously the two different estimates $\{\mathbf{x}_i^{S_1}\}_{i\in I}$ and $\{\mathbf{x}_i^{S_2}\}_{i\in I}$. The obvious inconsistencies are solved by duplicating the events in $\mathcal{E}_\Omega$ as

$$\mathcal{E}'_\Omega = \{A_i \equiv (X = x_i), B_i \equiv (X = x_i)\}_{i\in I} \tag{19}$$

and by adding structural zeros induced by the duplicates $A_i = B_i$, $i \in I$. So to the concatenation assessment

$$\mathbf{x}^{S_1} \boxplus \mathbf{x}^{S_2} \tag{20}$$

that assigns $\mathbf{x}_i^{S_1}$ to A_i and $\mathbf{x}_i^{S_2}$ to B_i, for any $i \in I$, the correction procedure can be applied by obtaining a, generally imprecise, assessment

$$\mathbf{lub} = \mathbf{x}^{S_1} \oplus_I \mathbf{x}^{S_2} = \mathrm{Correct}(\mathbf{x}^{S_1} \boxplus \mathbf{x}^{S_2}). \tag{21}$$

Note that with this second method, whenever estimates $\{\mathbf{x}_i^{S_1}\}_{i\in I}$ and $\{\mathbf{x}_i^{S_2}\}_{i\in I}$ are performed through frequencies in both samples, the lower-upper assessments (21) coincide with the min/max bounds already obtained in (9), legitimating in this way its adoption.

As already mentioned, to the other conditioned "strata" $(\mathcal{E}_i, \{\mathbf{y}_{j|i}, \mathbf{z}_{k|i}\}_{j\in J,k\in K})$ the correction procedure can be straightly applied obtaining, generally imprecise, estimates $\{lub_{j|i}, lub_{k|i}\}_{j\in J,k\in K}$, $i = 1,\ldots,\sharp(I)$.

At the end, by collecting all the corrections we get a coherent, generally imprecise and not "strongly coherent" (see [16]), assessment

$$(\mathcal{E}, \{lub_i, lub_{j|i}, lub_{k|i}\}_{i\in I,j\in J,k\in K}) \tag{22}$$

as the merging of the separate estimates based on the two sample schemes S_1 and S_2.

4.1 A Prototypical Example

As a preliminary application of our proposal we resume the example firstly described in [12] (see also [17]). The data are a subset of 2313 employees (people at least 15 years old) extracted from the pilot survey of the Italian Population and Household Census in the year 2000. Three categorical variables have been analyzed: Age, Educational Level and Professional Status. In file A, containing 1148 units, the variables Age and Professional Status are observed, while file B, consisting of 1165 observations, the variables Age and Educational Level are considered. The variables are grouped in homogeneous response categories as follows: $A_1 = 15$–17 years old, $A_2 = 18$–22 years old, $A_3 = 23$–64 years old, $A_4 =$ more than 65; $E_1 =$ None or compulsory school, $E_2 =$ Vocational school, $E_3 =$ Secondary school, $E_4 =$ Degree; $S_1 =$ Manager, $S_2 =$ Clerk, $S_3 =$ Worker.

Logical constraints between the variables Age and Educational level (Age and Professional Status) are denoted by the symbol "–" (to be distinguished from the zero frequencies) in Table 1: for example, in Italy a 17 years old person cannot have a University degree. Table 1 show the distribution of Age and Professional Status in file A, and in file B that related to Age and Educational level.

Table 1. Distribution of Age and Professional Status in file A and of Age and Educational level in file B.

Age	Prof. Status				Age	Educ. level				
	S_1	S_2	S_3	Tot.		E_1	E_2	E_3	E_4	Tot.
A_1	–	–	9	9	A_1	6	0	–	–	6
A_2	–	5	17	22	A_2	14	6	13	–	33
A_3	179	443	486	1108	A_3	387	102	464	158	1111
A_4	6	1	2	9	A_4	10	0	3	2	15
Tot.	185	449	514	1148	Tot.	417	108	480	160	1165

Additional logical constraints involving both the variables Professional Status and Educational level are:

$$S_1 \wedge (E_1 \vee E_2) = \emptyset \text{ and } S_2 \wedge E_1 = \emptyset.$$

By considering a common sampling scheme and the maximum likelihood estimations (6), we get the unconditional assessment $\{\mathbf{x}_i\}_{i \in I}$ for the variable Age:

$$P(A_1) = \frac{15}{2313}, \ P(A_2) = \frac{55}{2313}, \ P(A_3) = \frac{2219}{2313}, \ P(A_4) = \frac{24}{2313}; \quad (23)$$

We recall that to the same result we arrive by applying the first supervised merging procedure (18) with the choice of $\omega = \frac{n_A}{n_A + n_B} = \frac{1148}{2313}$.

On the other hand, by the second merging procedure we obtain the imprecise values $\{\mathbf{lub}_i\}_{i \in I}$ (21):

$$\mathbf{lub}_1 = \left[\frac{11}{1165}, \frac{9}{1148} \right], \ \mathbf{lub}_2 = \left[\frac{22}{1148}, \frac{33}{1165} \right],$$

$$(24)$$

$$\mathbf{lub}_3 = \left[\frac{1111}{1165}, \frac{1108}{1148} \right], \ \mathbf{lub}_4 = \left[\frac{9}{1148}, \frac{15}{1165} \right].$$

About the conditional estimates for the Professional Status given the Age, we get the following $\{\mathbf{y}_j|x_i\}_{j\in J}$, segmented for each $(X = x_i)$:

$$P(S_2|A_2) = \tfrac{5}{22}, P(S_3|A_2) = \tfrac{17}{22},$$

$$P(S_1|A_3) = \tfrac{179}{1108}, P(S_2|A_3) = \tfrac{443}{1108}, P(S_3|A_3) = \tfrac{486}{1108}, \tag{25}$$

$$P(S_1|A_4) = \tfrac{2}{3}, P(S_2|A_4) = \tfrac{1}{9}, P(S_3|A_4) = \tfrac{2}{9};$$

that we have to merge with the conditional estimates for the Educational level given the Age $\{\mathbf{z}_k|x_i\}_{k\in K}$, segmented for each $(X = x_i)$:

$$P(E_1|A_1) = 1, P(E_2|A_1) = 0,$$

$$P(E_1|A_2) = \tfrac{14}{33}, P(E_2|A_2) = \tfrac{6}{33}, P(E_3|A_2) = \tfrac{13}{33},$$

$$P(E_1|A_3) = \tfrac{387}{1111}, P(E_2|A_3) = \tfrac{102}{1111}, P(E_3|A_3) = \tfrac{464}{1111}, P(E_4|A_3) = \tfrac{158}{1111}, \tag{26}$$

$$P(E_1|A_4) = \tfrac{2}{3}, P(E_2|A_4) = 0, P(E_3|A_4) = \tfrac{1}{5}, P(E_4|A_4) = \tfrac{2}{15}.$$

By concatenating these estimates in each segment, we can easily discover that the only incoherences appear in the assessments conditioned to $A4$, as shown in [17], since from logical constraints between Educational Level and Professional Status it follows that $E_1 \wedge S_1 = \emptyset$ and $E_1 \subseteq S_3$, while we have $P(E_1|A_4)+P(S_1|A_4) > 1$ and $P(E_1|A_4) > P(S_3|A_4)$.

Then, we can focus on the minimal set of incoherent merged values

$$\left\{ P(S_1|A_4) = \frac{2}{3}, P(S_3|A_4) = \frac{2}{9}, P(E_1|A_4) = \frac{2}{3} \right\} \tag{27}$$

that, by $L1$ minimal correction, lead to the coherent imprecise probabilities:

$$\mathbf{lub}_{S_1|A_4} = \left\{ \frac{2}{3} \right\}, \mathbf{lub}_{S_3|A_4} = \left[\frac{2}{9}, \frac{1}{3} \right], \mathbf{lub}_{E_1|A_4} = \left[\frac{2}{9}, \frac{1}{3} \right] \tag{28}$$

(note the degenerate interval associated to $S_1|A_4$).

Correction (28) induces on the other events of the same segment the coherent, but not "strongly coherent", bounds:

$$\mathbf{lub}_{S_2|A_4} = \left[0, \frac{1}{9} \right], \mathbf{lub}_{E_2|A_4} = \left[0, \frac{1}{9} \right], \mathbf{lub}_{E_3|A_4} = \left[0, \frac{7}{9} \right], \mathbf{lub}_{E_4|A_4} = \left[0, \frac{7}{9} \right]. \tag{29}$$

More significant numerical merging and correction values on this example framework, involving not only frequencies estimates but also expert evaluations, are under evaluation as well as the extension to cases of statistical matching with misclassification (see [14]).

References

1. Baioletti, M., Capotorti, A.: Efficient L1-based probability assessments correction: algorithms and applications to belief merging and revision. In: ISIPTA 2015 Proceeding of the 9th International Symposium on Imprecise Probability: Theories and Applications, Pescara (IT), pp. 37–46. ARACNE (2015)
2. Biazzo, V., Gilio, A.: Some theoretical properties of conditional probability assessments. In: Godo, L. (ed.) ECSQARU 2005. LNCS, vol. 3571, pp. 775–787. Springer, Heidelberg (2005). doi:10.1007/11518655_65
3. Brozzi, A., Capotorti, A., Vantaggi, B.: Incoherence correction strategies in statistical matching. Int. J. Approximate Reasoning **53**(8), 1124–1136 (2012)
4. Capotorti, A.: Benefits of embedding structural constraints in coherent diagnostic processes. Int. J. Approximate Reasoning **39**(2–3), 211–233 (2005)
5. Capotorti, A.: A further empirical study on the over-performance of estimate correction in statistical matching. In: Greco, S., Bouchon-Meunier, B., Coletti, G., Fedrizzi, M., Matarazzo, B., Yager, R.R. (eds.) IPMU 2012. CCIS, vol. 300, pp. 124–133. Springer, Heidelberg (2012). doi:10.1007/978-3-642-31724-8_14
6. Capotorti, A., Vantaggi, B.: Incoherence correction strategies in statistical matching. In: ISIPTA 2011 Proceeding of the 7th International Symposium on Imprecise Probability: Theories and Applications, Innsbruck, pp. 109–118. SIPTA (2011)
7. Coletti, G.: Numerical and qualitative judgments in probabilistic expert systems. In: Scozzafava, R. (ed.) Proceeding of the International Workshop on Probabilistic Methods in Expert Systems, pp. 37–55. SIS, Roma (1993)
8. Coletti, G.: Coherent numerical and ordinal probabilistic assessments. IEEE Trans. Syst. Man Cybern. **24**, 1747–1754 (1994)
9. Coletti, G., Scozzafava, R.: Probabilistic Logic in a Coherent Setting. Trends in Logic. Kluwer, Dordrecht (2002)
10. Cozman, F.G., Ianni, L.F.: Probabilistic satisfiability and coherence checking through integer programming. In: Gaag, L.C. (ed.) ECSQARU 2013. LNCS, vol. 7958, pp. 145–156. Springer, Heidelberg (2013). doi:10.1007/978-3-642-39091-3_13
11. De Bona, G., Finger, M.: Measuring inconsistency in probabilistic logic: rationality postulates and Dutch book interpretation. Artif. Intell. **227**, 140–164 (2015)
12. D'Orazio, M., Di Zio, M., Scanu, M.: Statistical Matching: Theory and Practice. Wiley, New York (2006)
13. D'Orazio, M., Di Zio, M., Scanu, M.: Statistical matching for categorical data: displaying uncertainty and using logical constraints. J. Off. Stat. **22**, 137–157 (2006)
14. Di Zio, M., Vantaggi, B.: Partial identification in statistical matching with misclassification. Int. J. Approximate Reasoning **82**, 227–241 (2017)
15. Gilio, A.: Probabilistic consistency of knowledge bases in inference systems. In: Clarke, M., Kruse, R., Moral, S. (eds.) ECSQARU 1993. LNCS, vol. 747, pp. 160–167. Springer, Heidelberg (1993). doi:10.1007/BFb0028196
16. Gilio, A., Pfeifer, N., Sanfilippo, G.: Transitivity in coherence-based probability logic. J. Appl. Logic **14**, 46–64 (2016)
17. Vantaggi, B.: Statistical matching of multiple sources: a look through coherence. Int. J. Approximate Reasoning **49**(3), 701–711 (2008)
18. Walley, P.: Statistical Reasoning with Imprecise Probabilities. Chapman and Hall, London (1991)

Interval-Based Possibilistic Logic
in a Coherent Setting

Giulianella Coletti[1], Davide Petturiti[2(✉)], and Barbara Vantaggi[3]

[1] Dip. Matematica e Informatica, Università degli Studi di Perugia, Perugia, Italy
giulianella.coletti@unipg.it
[2] Dip. Economia, Università degli Studi di Perugia, Perugia, Italy
davide.petturiti@unipg.it
[3] Dip. S.B.A.I., "La Sapienza" Università di Roma, Rome, Italy
barbara.vantaggi@sbai.uniroma1.it

Abstract. In probability theory the notion of coherence has been introduced by de Finetti in terms of bets and it reveals to be equivalent to the
notion of consistence of a partial assessment with a finitely additive probability. An important feature of coherent assessments is their coherent
extendibility: in general we obtain a class of coherent extensions, determining a lower and an upper envelope. A similar notion of coherence
has been recently introduced for (T-conditional) possibility measures,
where T is a t-norm. The extendibility of coherent possibility assessments
reveals to be particularly suitable for studying interval-based possibilistic
logic. Our aim is to compare the results implied by the coherent setting
with those obtained in different approaches, in particular, that relying
on classical T-based conditioning.

Keywords: Coherence · Conditional possibility envelopes · Interval-
based possibilistic logic

1 Introduction

The notion of conditioning is a problem of long-standing interest and it involves
different uncertainty measures. In this paper we focus on (finitely maxitive)
possibility measures that can be seen as specific upper probabilities, arising
from a convex set of probabilities or as a result of a generalized probabilistic
inferential process (see, e.g., [12,20]).

Several proposals of conditioning have been introduced for possibility measures [3,4,6,16,18,22,27], most of them by analogy with the Kolmogorovian
probabilistic framework: starting from an unconditional possibility measure, a
conditional possibility is defined as the solution of an equation involving joint
and marginal possibilities. Some criterion, such as the minimum specificity principle (see, e.g., [4,16,19]), is added when the output of the rule is undefined or
not unique.

D. Petturiti—Partially supported by the INdAM-GNAMPA Project 2016 U2016/
000391 and the Italian Ministry of Health grant J52I14001640001.

In [6] a different approach has been considered: a general notion of T-conditional possibility (with T a t-norm) has been directly introduced as a primitive concept. The conditional possibility is a real function on a set of conditional events, satisfying a suitable set of axioms. Referring to the aforementioned axiomatic definition, a comparison with the conditioning notion obtained through the minimum specificity principle (introduced in [19]) has been given in [10] for $T = \min$ and is extended here for T strict. In the following we call such conditioning T-DP-conditioning, showing that it produces particular T-conditional possibilities.

In this paper we refer to the notion of coherence for T-conditional possibilities which allows to consider envelopes of coherent T-conditional possibilities and to face their coherent extension: the envelopes can always be intended as interval assessments. In particular, we highlight that, under T-conditional possibility ($T = \min$ or strict) the set of coherent extensions to a new conditional event is always a closed interval, while for min-DP-conditional possibility connectedness may fail [10]. This leads to a difference with the classical setting relying on minimum specificity in which it is difficult to work with interval assessments when $T = \min$ [5]. By referring to coherent min-conditional possibilities we are enlarging the set of compatible assessments filling the eventual "holes" obtained if only coherent min-DP-conditional possibilities are taken.

2 T-conditional Possibility Envelopes

An *event* E is singled out by a Boolean proposition, that is a statement that can be either true or false. Since in general it is not known whether E is true or not, we are uncertain on the realization of E, which, in this case, is said to be *possible*. We denote with Ω and $\emptyset$ the *certain event* and the *impossible event*, respectively. Such events coincide with the top and the bottom of every Boolean algebra $\mathcal{A}$ of events, i.e., a set of events closed with respect to the Boolean operations of *contrary* ^{c}, *conjunction* $\wedge$ and *disjunction* $\vee$ and equipped with the partial order $\subseteq$ of *implication*. A *conditional event* $E|H$ is an ordered pair (E, H) of events, with $H \neq \emptyset$. In particular any event E can be seen as the conditional event $E|\Omega$.

In what follows, $\mathcal{A} \times \mathcal{H}$ denotes a set of conditional events with $\mathcal{A}$ a Boolean algebra and $\mathcal{H}$ an *additive set* (i.e., closed with respect to finite disjunctions) such that $\mathcal{H} \subseteq \mathcal{A}^0 = \mathcal{A} \setminus \{\emptyset\}$. Recall that any arbitrary set of conditional events $\mathcal{G} = \{E_i | H_i\}_{i \in I}$ can be embedded into a set $\mathcal{A} \times \mathcal{H}$ by taking $\mathcal{A} = \langle \{E_i, H_i\}_{i \in I} \rangle$ and $\mathcal{H} = \langle \{H_i\}_{i \in I} \rangle^{\mathbf{A}}$, which are the Boolean algebra generated by $\{E_i, H_i\}_{i \in I}$ and the additive set generated by $\{H_i\}_{i \in I}$, respectively.

For a t-norm T, in the following we refer to the notion of T-*conditional possibility* (see [6,15]) axiomatically defined as a function $\Pi : \mathcal{A} \times \mathcal{H} \to [0, 1]$ satisfying the following properties:

(CP1) $\Pi(E|H) = \Pi(E \wedge H|H)$, for every $E \in \mathcal{A}$ and $H \in \mathcal{H}$;
(CP2) $\Pi(\cdot|H)$ is a finitely maxitive possibility on $\mathcal{A}$, for any $H \in \mathcal{H}$;
(CP3) $\Pi(E \wedge F|H) = T(\Pi(E|H), \Pi(F|E \wedge H))$, for any $H, E \wedge H \in \mathcal{H}$ and $E, F \in \mathcal{A}$.

A T-conditional possibility is said *full on* $\mathcal{A}$ if its domain is $\mathcal{A} \times \mathcal{A}^0$.

Specific T-conditional possibilities have been studied, focusing on $T = \min$ [14] or a strict t-norm $\odot$ [21] (i.e., a strictly monotone and continuous t-norm), see also [7]. As shown in [15], the continuity of the t-norm T assures the extendibility of every T-conditional possibility on $\mathcal{A} \times \mathcal{H}$ to any superset of conditional events (in particular to $\mathcal{A} \times \mathcal{A}^0$). For that here we only deal with continuous t-norms.

When $T = \min$ in [10] we have shown that the Dubois and Prade definition of conditional possibility based on the *minimum specificity principle* gives rise to a particular min-conditional possibility. The Dubois and Prade approach to conditioning can be generalized also to strict t-norms.

For $T = \min$ or a strict t-norm with associated residuum $\to^T$ (see [23]), a T-*DP-conditional possibility* can be axiomatically defined as a function $\Pi :$ $\mathcal{A} \times \mathcal{H} \to [0,1]$ satisfying the properties *(CP1)-(CP2)* together with

(CP3') for every $E|H \in \mathcal{A} \times \mathcal{H}$ it holds

$$\Pi(E|H) = \begin{cases} 0 & \text{if } E \wedge H = \emptyset, \\ \Pi(H|H_0^0) \to^T \Pi(E \wedge H|H_0^0) & \text{otherwise,} \end{cases}$$

provided $H_0^0 = \bigvee_{H \in \mathcal{H}} H$ belongs to $\mathcal{H}$.

Proposition 1. *For $T = \min$ or a strict t-norm, if Π on $\mathcal{A} \times \mathcal{H}$ is a T-DP-conditional possibility, then Π is a T-conditional possibility.*

Proof. For $T = \min$ the claim has been proved in [10]. If T is a strict t-norm $\odot$ with associated pseudo-division $\oslash$, then for every $x, y \in [0,1]$, we have $x \to^\odot y = y \oslash x$ if $y < x$ and 1 otherwise [23].

We need only to prove that if Π is a $\odot$-DP-conditional possibility on $\mathcal{A} \times \mathcal{H}$, then it satisfies axiom *(CP3)*. Let $H, E \wedge H \in \mathcal{H}$ and $E, F \in \mathcal{A}$. If $E \wedge F \wedge H = \emptyset$ then the claim trivially follows, thus suppose $E \wedge F \wedge H \neq \emptyset$ in which case we have $\Pi(E \wedge F|H) = \Pi(H|H_0^0) \to^\odot \Pi(E \wedge F \wedge H|H_0^0)$, $\Pi(E|H) = \Pi(H|H_0^0) \to^\odot \Pi(E \wedge H|H_0^0)$ and $\Pi(F|E \wedge H) = \Pi(E \wedge H|H_0^0) \to^\odot \Pi(E \wedge F \wedge H|H_0^0)$.

By monotonicity $\Pi(E \wedge F \wedge H|H_0^0) \leq \Pi(E \wedge H|H_0^0) \leq \Pi(H|H_0^0)$ and the claim immediately follows if we have at least an equality. Finally, if all inequalities are strict then *(CP3)* follows since all $\Pi(E \wedge F|H)$, $\Pi(E|H)$ and $\Pi(F|E \wedge H)$ are defined in terms of the pseudo-division $\oslash$.

In the finite case, every T-DP-conditional possibility on $\mathcal{A} \times \mathcal{H}$ can be extended as a full T-DP-conditional possibility on $\mathcal{A}'$, with $\mathcal{A}' \supset \mathcal{A}$ a finite superalgebra (see [10]). Moreover, being a particular T-conditional possibility it can be extended also as a full T-conditional possibility on $\mathcal{A}'$. In both cases the extension is generally not unique but we have two classes of extensions $\mathcal{P}^{\mathbf{DP}}$ and $\mathcal{P}$ such hat $\mathcal{P}^{\mathbf{DP}} \subseteq \mathcal{P}$. As proven in [10], when $T = \min$, $\mathbf{proj}_{E|H}(\mathcal{P}^{\mathbf{DP}})$ is a compact set that can fail connectedness for some $E|H$, while $\mathbf{proj}_{E|H}(\mathcal{P})$ is always a non-empty closed interval, where $\mathbf{proj}_{E|H}$ denotes the projection mapping on $E|H$ in the product topology. Vice versa, for $T = \odot$ both $\mathbf{proj}_{E|H}(\mathcal{P}^{\mathbf{DP}})$ and

$\mathbf{proj}_{E|H}(\mathcal{P})$ are always closed intervals, with $\mathbf{proj}_{E|H}(\mathcal{P}^{\mathbf{DP}})$ possibly reducing to the singleton $\{1\}$. Thus, the envelopes of $\mathcal{P}^{\mathbf{DP}}$ provide a useful information for $T = \odot$ but not for $T = \min$, while the envelopes of $\mathcal{P}$ are always meaningful.

The notion of coherence, originally introduced by de Finetti for (conditional) probability assessments [17] has been introduced also in other frameworks and in particular in possibility theory (see [14,15,21]), by referring to an assessment on an arbitrary set of conditional events $\mathcal{G} = \{E_i|H_i\}_{i\in I}$.

Definition 1. *A function $\Pi : \mathcal{G} \to [0,1]$ is a **coherent T-conditional possibility (assessment)** if there exists a T-conditional possibility $\Pi' : \mathcal{A} \times \mathcal{H} \to [0,1]$ such that $\Pi'_{|\mathcal{G}} = \Pi$, with $\mathcal{A} = \langle\{E_i, H_i\}_{i\in I}\rangle$ and $\mathcal{H} = \langle\{H_i\}_{i\in I}\rangle^{\mathbf{A}}$.*

Notice that in the previous definition it is equivalent to require the existence of a full T-conditional possibility on $\mathcal{A}$ extending Π.

For an arbitrary family of conditional events $\mathcal{G} = \{E_i|H_i\}_{i\in I}$ and $\mathcal{A} = \langle\{E_i, H_i\}_{i\in I}\rangle$, we denote by $T\text{-}\mathbf{CCohe}(\mathcal{G})$ the set of coherent T-conditional possibilities on $\mathcal{G}$, that is:

$$T\text{-}\mathbf{CCohe}(\mathcal{G}) = \{\Pi'_{|\mathcal{G}} : \Pi' \text{ is a full } T\text{-conditional possibility on } \mathcal{A}\}. \quad (1)$$

When $\mathcal{G}$ is finite the class $T\text{-}\mathbf{CCohe}(\mathcal{G})$ can be determined through the solutions of a suitable sequence of non-linear systems [15]. In particular, every $\Pi \in T\text{-}\mathbf{CCohe}(\mathcal{G})$ can be always coherently extended, generally not in a unique way, to a superset of conditional events $\mathcal{G}' \supset \mathcal{G}$. The set of coherent extensions of Π on $\mathcal{G}'$ form a class $\mathcal{P} \subseteq T\text{-}\mathbf{CCohe}(\mathcal{G}')$ which is a compact subset of $[0,1]^{\mathcal{G}'}$ endowed with the product topology [8] and singles out the envelopes $\underline{\Pi} = \min\mathcal{P}$ and $\overline{\Pi} = \max\mathcal{P}$. In particular, when $T = \min$ or a strict t-norm, then for every $E|H \in \mathcal{G}'$, $\mathbf{proj}_{E|H}(\mathcal{P})$ is a non-empty closed interval (see [15]).

3   Envelopes of Coherent T-conditional Possibilities

Imprecision can be introduced in assessing conditional possibilities by referring to coherent T-conditional possibility envelopes defined on an arbitrary set of conditional events $\mathcal{G} = \{E_i|H_i\}_{i\in I}$, according to the following definition.

Definition 2. *A pair of functions $(\underline{\Pi}, \overline{\Pi})$ on $\mathcal{G}$ are **coherent T-conditional possibility envelopes** if there exists a class $\mathcal{P} \subseteq T\text{-}\mathbf{CCohe}(\mathcal{G})$ of coherent T-conditional possibilities on $\mathcal{G}$ such that $\underline{\Pi} = \inf\mathcal{P}$ and $\overline{\Pi} = \sup\mathcal{P}$.*

Notice that no assumption is made about the class $\mathcal{P} \subseteq T\text{-}\mathbf{CCohe}(\mathcal{G})$, which may be a non-closed subset of $T\text{-}\mathbf{CCohe}(\mathcal{G})$: this implies that, in general, the pointwise infimum and supremum of $\mathcal{P}$ could not be reached by elements of $\mathcal{P}$.

Nevertheless, since $T\text{-}\mathbf{CCohe}(\mathcal{G})$ is compact, the closure $\mathrm{cl}(\mathcal{P})$ is a subset of $T\text{-}\mathbf{CCohe}(\mathcal{G})$ and it holds $\inf\mathcal{P} = \min\mathrm{cl}(\mathcal{P})$ and $\sup\mathcal{P} = \max\mathrm{cl}(\mathcal{P})$, thus we can always consider a closed set of coherent T-conditional possibilities on $\mathcal{G}$.

Coherence of $(\underline{\Pi}, \overline{\Pi})$ defined on $\mathcal{G}$ is a necessary and sufficient condition for the coherent extendibility of the envelopes on every superset of conditional events

$\mathcal{G}' \supset \mathcal{G}$. In the extension we search for the pair of envelopes $(\underline{\Pi}', \overline{\Pi}')$ reaching pointwise on $\mathcal{G}'$ the minimum and the maximum coherent values, respectively. We call the pair $(\underline{\Pi}', \overline{\Pi}')$ *natural extension* in analogy to lower and upper conditional probabilities [25, 26]. In detail, by the compactness of T-$\mathbf{CCohe}(\mathcal{G}')$, it holds

$$\underline{\Pi}'(E|H) = \min\left\{\Pi'(E|H) \,:\, \Pi' \in T\text{-}\mathbf{CCohe}(\mathcal{G}'), \underline{\Pi} \le \Pi'_{|\mathcal{G}} \le \overline{\Pi}\right\}, \qquad (2)$$

$$\overline{\Pi}'(E|H) = \max\left\{\Pi'(E|H) \,:\, \Pi' \in T\text{-}\mathbf{CCohe}(\mathcal{G}'), \underline{\Pi} \le \Pi'_{|\mathcal{G}} \le \overline{\Pi}\right\}. \qquad (3)$$

In case of extension on more than one conditional event, then the extension process must be thought as carried on in parallel on each single new conditional event through Eqs. (2) and (3).

Both coherence of $(\underline{\Pi}, \overline{\Pi})$ defined on $\mathcal{G}$ and the computation of its natural extension $(\underline{\Pi}', \overline{\Pi}')$ on $\mathcal{G}' \supset \mathcal{G}$ can be faced in terms of finite subfamilies of $\mathcal{G}$ [11]. In particular, in case of a finite set $\mathcal{G} = \{E_1|H_1, \ldots, E_n|H_n\}$, the coherence of an assessment $(\underline{\Pi}, \overline{\Pi})$ on $\mathcal{G}$ can be characterized in terms of the existence of a finite class $\mathcal{P}^{2n} \subseteq T\text{-}\mathbf{CCohe}(\mathcal{G})$, which is therefore a closed subset of $T\text{-}\mathbf{CCohe}(\mathcal{G})$. The class $\mathcal{P}^{2n}$ is composed at most by $2n$ distinct coherent T-conditional possibilities on $\mathcal{G}$, that can be determined solving, for each event $E_i|H_i$, two suitable sequences of non-linear systems (see [9, 11]). Furthermore, the natural extension on a new conditional event $E|H$ can be computed through two optimization problems over a suitable sequence of non-linear systems [9, 11].

4   Natural Extension of Coherent Possibility Envelopes

Let $\mathcal{E} = \{E_1, \ldots, E_n\}$ be a finite set of events, possibly linked by logical relations, and $\mathcal{A} = \langle \mathcal{E} \rangle$ the generated Boolean algebra, whose set of atoms is $\mathcal{C}_{\mathcal{A}} = \{C_1, \ldots, C_p\}$. In this section we address the problem of computing the natural extension of coherent T-conditional possibility envelopes $(\underline{\Pi}, \overline{\Pi})$ defined on $\mathcal{E} \times \{\Omega\}$ to the whole $\mathcal{A} \times \mathcal{A}^0$, focusing on the case T is the minimum or a strict t-norm.

Such problem has been considered in [5] referring to the Dubois and Prade conditioning and to interval possibility assessments, when $\mathcal{A}$ is the Lindembaum algebra [24] generated by a finite propositional language and $\mathcal{E}$ coincides with the corresponding set of atoms $\mathcal{C}_{\mathcal{A}}$ (so, $p = n = 2^m$, where m is the number of considered propositional variables).

Let $(\underline{\Pi}, \overline{\Pi})$ be defined on $\mathcal{E} \times \{\Omega\}$ as

$$\{(\underline{\Pi}(E_i) = a_i, \overline{\Pi}(E_i) = b_i) \,:\, 0 \le a_i \le b_i \le 1, i = 1, \ldots, n\}.$$

Our first question concerns the coherence of the above assessment that can be verified by the help of the following Boolean operator defined, for $\gamma \in [0, 1]$, as

$$\overline{\mathcal{L}}(\gamma) = \bigwedge\{E_j^c \,:\, \overline{\Pi}(E_j) < \gamma\},$$

where the above conjunction reduces to Ω if the corresponding set is empty. The following theorem generalizes Theorem 1 in [1].

Theorem 1. $(\underline{\Pi}, \overline{\Pi})$ *is a pair of coherent T-conditional possibility envelopes (where T is any continuous t-norm) on $\mathcal{E} \times \{\Omega\}$ if and only if, for every $i = 1, \ldots, n$, we have $\underline{\Pi}(E_i) = \overline{\Pi}(E_i) = 0$ if $E_i = \emptyset$, $\underline{\Pi}(E_i) = \overline{\Pi}(E_i) = 1$ if $E_i = \Omega$, $E_i \wedge \overline{\mathcal{L}}(\overline{\Pi}(E_i)) \neq \emptyset$ and there is no $j \neq i$ such that $E_i \subseteq E_j$ and $\underline{\Pi}(E_j) < \underline{\Pi}(E_i)$ if $\emptyset \neq E_i \neq \Omega$, and if $\bigvee_{i=1}^{n} E_i = \Omega$ then $\max_{i=1,\ldots,n} \overline{\Pi}(E_i) = 1$ and $\underline{\Pi}(E_i) = \overline{\Pi}(E_i) = 1$ whenever there is a unique $i \in \{0, \ldots, n\}$ such that $\overline{\Pi}(E_i) = 1$ and $E_i \supseteq \bigvee\{E_j : \overline{\Pi}(E_j) = 1\}$.*

Proof. The necessity of the condition is trivial thus we prove its sufficiency. The condition allows to build a finite class of possibility measures $\mathcal{Q}^{2n} = \{\Pi^{1,0}, \Pi^{1,1}, \ldots, \Pi^{n,0}, \Pi^{n,1}\}$ on $\mathcal{A}$ such that for $j = 1, \ldots, n$, $\Pi^{j,0}(E_j) = \underline{\Pi}(E_j)$ and $\underline{\Pi}(E_k) \leq \Pi^{j,0}(E_k) \leq \overline{\Pi}(E_k)$, for $k \neq j$, and $\Pi^{j,1}(E_j) = \overline{\Pi}(E_j)$ and $\underline{\Pi}(E_k) \leq \Pi^{j,1}(E_k) \leq \overline{\Pi}(E_k)$, for $k \neq j$. Denoting with $\mathcal{P}^{2n}$ the class of restrictions of elements of $\mathcal{Q}^{2n}$ on $\mathcal{E}$ it follows that $\underline{\Pi} = \min \mathcal{P}^{2n}$ and $\overline{\Pi} = \max \mathcal{P}^{2n}$ by construction.

A straightforward modification of results in [1,2], shows that checking the coherence of an assessment $(\underline{\Pi}, \overline{\Pi})$ can be reduced to a linear number of queries to a SAT solver. The NP-hardness of the problem follows by results in [2].

If $(\underline{\Pi}, \overline{\Pi})$ are coherent, then the largest class of coherent possibilities on $\mathcal{E}$ having $(\underline{\Pi}, \overline{\Pi})$ as envelopes is $\mathcal{P} = \{\Pi' \in T\text{-}\mathbf{CCohe}(\mathcal{E} \times \{\Omega\}) : \underline{\Pi} \leq \Pi' \leq \overline{\Pi}\}$, which is such that $\mathbf{proj}_{E_i \mid \Omega}(\mathcal{P}) = [a_i, b_i]$, for every $i = 1, \ldots, n$.

For every continuous t-norm T, to compute the natural extension of $(\underline{\Pi}, \overline{\Pi})$ on $A \mid B \in \mathcal{A} \times \mathcal{A}^0$ we need to solve two optimization problems over a sequence of non-linear systems $(\mathcal{S}_\alpha)_{\alpha=0,\ldots,k}$ (see [11]). The first system has unknowns $x_r^0 \geq 0$, for $C_r \in \mathcal{C}_\mathcal{A}$, and has form

$$\text{minimize/maximize } \theta$$

$$\mathcal{S}_0 : \begin{cases} \max_{C_r \subseteq A \wedge B} x_r^0 = T\left(\theta, \max_{C_r \subseteq B} x_r^0\right), & \\ \max_{C_r \subseteq E_i} x_r^0 \leq \overline{\Pi}(E_i) & i = 1, \ldots, n, \\ \max_{C_r \subseteq E_i} x_r^0 \geq \underline{\Pi}(E_i) & i = 1, \ldots, n, \\ \max_{r=1,\ldots,p} x_r^0 = 1. \end{cases} \tag{4}$$

For $T = \min$ or T a strict t-norm, the optimal values are determined by the solutions of $\mathcal{S}_0$ and, so, by the values of the natural extension $(\underline{\Pi}', \overline{\Pi}')$ on $\mathcal{A} \times \{\Omega\}$. For this, we first characterize the natural extension of $(\underline{\Pi}, \overline{\Pi})$ on $\mathcal{A} \times \{\Omega\}$.

Theorem 2. *If $(\underline{\Pi}, \overline{\Pi})$ is a pair of coherent T-conditional possibility envelopes (where T is any continuous t-norm) on $\mathcal{E} \times \{\Omega\}$ then its natural extension $(\underline{\Pi}', \overline{\Pi}')$ on $\mathcal{A} \times \{\Omega\}$ is such that, for every $A \in \mathcal{A}$, $\underline{\Pi}(A) = 0$ if $\bigvee\{E_i : E_i \subseteq A\} = \emptyset$ and $\overline{\Pi}(A) = 1$ if $A \wedge \bigwedge_{i=1}^{n} E_i^c \neq \emptyset$, otherwise,*

$$\underline{\Pi}'(A) = \begin{cases} 1 & \text{if } A \supseteq \bigvee\{E_i : \overline{\Pi}(E_i) = 1\} \text{ and } \bigvee_{i=1}^{n} E_i = \Omega, \\ \max_{E_i \subseteq A} \underline{\Pi}(E_i) & \text{otherwise}, \end{cases}$$

$$\overline{\Pi}'(A) = \min\left\{\max_{j \in J} \overline{\Pi}(E_j) : A \subseteq \bigvee_{j \in J} E_j, J \subseteq \{1, \ldots, n\}\right\}.$$

Proof. For every $A \in \mathcal{A}$, we solve the optimization problems on $(\mathcal{S}_\alpha)_{\alpha=0,\ldots,k}$ related to $A|\Omega$. For $\mathcal{S}_0$ defined as in (4), if $\bigvee\{E_i : E_i \subseteq A\} = \emptyset$ a solution $\overline{\xi}^0$ minimizing θ is such that $\max_{C_r \subseteq A} \xi_r^0 = 0$, otherwise if $\bigvee\{E_i : \overline{\Pi}(E_i) = 1\} \wedge A^c \neq \emptyset$ or $\bigvee_{i=1}^n E_i \neq \Omega$, a solution $\overline{\xi}^0$ minimizing θ is such that $\max_{C_r \subseteq A} \xi_r^0 = \max_{E_i \subseteq A} \underline{\Pi}(E_i)$ otherwise, it must be $\xi_r^0 = 1$ for some $C_r \subseteq \bigvee\{E_i : \overline{\Pi}(E_i) = 1\}$. A solution $\overline{\xi}^0$ maximizing θ is such that $\max_{C_r \subseteq A} \xi_r^0 = 1$ if $A \wedge \bigwedge_{i=1}^n E_i^c \neq \emptyset$, otherwise $\max_{C_r \subseteq A} \xi_r^0 = \min\left\{\max_{j \in J} \overline{\Pi}(E_j) : A \subseteq \bigvee_{j \in J} E_j, J \subseteq \{1,\ldots,n\}\right\}$. The next systems in the sequence do not contain the constraint involving θ and their resolution is trivial, so, the claim follows.

The following two theorems characterize the natural extension on the whole set $\mathcal{A} \times \mathcal{A}^0$ just relying on the values of the natural extension on $\mathcal{A} \times \{\Omega\}$ characterized in the previous theorem.

We first cope with the case $T = \min$.

Theorem 3. *If $(\underline{\Pi}, \overline{\Pi})$ is a pair of coherent min-conditional possibility envelopes on $\mathcal{E} \times \{\Omega\}$, then its natural extension $(\underline{\Pi}', \overline{\Pi}')$ on $\mathcal{A} \times \mathcal{A}^0$ is such that, for every $A|B \in \mathcal{A} \times \mathcal{A}^0$, $\underline{\Pi}'(A|B) = \overline{\Pi}'(A|B) = 0$ if $A \wedge B = \emptyset$, $\underline{\Pi}'(A|B) = \overline{\Pi}'(A|B) = 1$ if $A \wedge B = B$, and if $\emptyset \neq A \wedge B \neq B$,*

$$\underline{\Pi}'(A|B) = \begin{cases} 1 & \text{if } \underline{\Pi}'(A \wedge B) > \overline{\Pi}'(A^c \wedge B), \\ \underline{\Pi}'(A \wedge B) & \text{otherwise}, \end{cases}$$

$$\overline{\Pi}'(A|B) = \begin{cases} \overline{\Pi}'(A \wedge B) & \text{if } \overline{\Pi}'(A \wedge B) < \underline{\Pi}'(A^c \wedge B), \\ 1 & \text{otherwise}. \end{cases}$$

Proof. We can restrict to the case $\emptyset \neq A \wedge B \neq B$ since other cases are trivial. For $\underline{\Pi}'(A|B)$, if $\underline{\Pi}'(A \wedge B) > \overline{\Pi}'(A^c \wedge B)$, then every solution $\overline{\xi}^0$ of $\mathcal{S}_0$ in (4) is such that $\max_{C_r \subseteq A \wedge B} \xi_r^0 = \max_{C_r \subseteq B} \xi_r^0 > 0$ and this implies $\underline{\Pi}'(A|B) = 1$. On the converse, there is a solution $\overline{\xi}^0$ of $\mathcal{S}_0$ in (4) such that $\max_{C_r \subseteq A \wedge B} \xi_r^0 = \underline{\Pi}'(A \wedge B) < \max_{C_r \subseteq B} \xi_r^0$ and this implies $\underline{\Pi}'(A|B) = \underline{\Pi}'(A \wedge B)$. Analogous considerations hold for $\overline{\Pi}'(A|B)$.

Now, let T be a strict t-norm $\odot$ with associated pseudo-division $\oslash$.

Theorem 4. *If $(\underline{\Pi}, \overline{\Pi})$ is a pair of coherent $\odot$-conditional possibility envelopes on $\mathcal{E} \times \{\Omega\}$, then its natural extension $(\underline{\Pi}', \overline{\Pi}')$ on $\mathcal{A} \times \mathcal{A}^0$ is such that, for every $A|B \in \mathcal{A} \times \mathcal{A}^0$, $\underline{\Pi}'(A|B) = \overline{\Pi}'(A|B) = 0$ if $A \wedge B = \emptyset$, $\underline{\Pi}'(A|B) = \overline{\Pi}'(A|B) = 1$ if $A \wedge B = B$, and if $\emptyset \neq A \wedge B \neq B$,*

$$\underline{\Pi}'(A|B) = \begin{cases} 0 & \text{if } \underline{\Pi}'(B) = 0, \\ \underline{\Pi}'(A \wedge B) & \text{if } \underline{\Pi}'(B) = 1, \\ \underline{\Pi}'(A \wedge B) \oslash \max\{\underline{\Pi}'(A \wedge B), \overline{\Pi}'(A^c \wedge B)\} & \text{otherwise}, \end{cases}$$

$$\overline{\Pi}'(A|B) = \begin{cases} 1 & \text{if } \underline{\Pi}'(B) = 0, \\ \overline{\Pi}'(A \wedge B) & \text{if } \underline{\Pi}'(B) = 1, \\ \overline{\Pi}'(A \wedge B) \oslash \max\{\overline{\Pi}'(A \wedge B), \underline{\Pi}'(A^c \wedge B)\} & \text{otherwise}. \end{cases}$$

Proof. We can restrict to the case $\emptyset \neq A \wedge B \neq B$ since other cases are trivial. If $\underline{\Pi}'(B) = 0$, then there exists a solution $\overline{\xi}^0$ of $\mathcal{S}_0$ in (4) such that $\max_{C_r \subseteq B} \xi_r^0 = 0$ which implies $\underline{\Pi}'(A|B) = 0$ and $\overline{\Pi}'(A|B) = 1$. If $\underline{\Pi}'(B) = 1$, then every solution $\overline{\xi}^0$ of $\mathcal{S}_0$ in (4) is such that $\max_{C_r \subseteq B} \xi_r^0 = 1$ and then $\underline{\Pi}'(A|B) = \underline{\Pi}'(A \wedge B)$ and $\overline{\Pi}'(A|B) = \overline{\Pi}'(A \wedge B)$. On the remaining cases, every solution $\overline{\xi}^0$ of $\mathcal{S}_0$ in (4) is such that $0 < \max_{C_r \subseteq B} \xi_r^0 \leq 1$, thus the minimum value is obtained choosing a solution $\overline{\xi}^0$, that always exists, such that $\max_{C_r \subseteq A \wedge B} \xi_r^0 = \underline{\Pi}'(A \wedge B)$ and $\max_{C_r \subseteq A^c \wedge B} \xi_r^0 = \overline{\Pi}'(A^c \wedge B)$, which implies $\underline{\Pi}'(A|B) = \overline{\Pi}'(A \wedge B) \oslash \max\{\overline{\Pi}'(A \wedge B), \underline{\Pi}'(A^c \wedge B)\}$. Analogous considerations hold for $\overline{\Pi}'(A|B)$.

Both for T equal to the minimum and a strict t-norm, consider the largest class of full T-conditional possibilities on $\mathcal{A}$ having $(\underline{\Pi}', \overline{\Pi}')$ as envelopes, which is defined as $\mathcal{P}' = \{\Pi' \in T\text{-}\mathbf{CCohe}(\mathcal{A} \times \mathcal{A}^0) : \underline{\Pi}' \leq \Pi' \leq \overline{\Pi}'\}$. By results in [11,15] it follows that, for every $A|B \in \mathcal{A} \times \mathcal{A}^0$, the projection set $\mathbf{proj}_{A|B}(\mathcal{P}')$ is a non-empty closed interval. This leads to a differentiation with classical framework [5] where, for $T = \min$, the connectedness of the set of possibility values for $A|B$ was not guaranteed. This problem, as already pointed out in [10], is essentially due to the imposition of the minimum specificity principle [19] in conditioning.

Example 1. Take the set of events $\mathcal{E} = \{A, B, C, D\}$ where $C = A \wedge B$ and $D = B^c$, together with the coherent T-conditional possibility envelopes (where T is any continuous t-norm): $(\underline{\Pi}(A) = 0.2, \overline{\Pi}(A) = 1), (\underline{\Pi}(B) = 0.3, \overline{\Pi}(B) = 1), (\underline{\Pi}(C) = 0.1, \overline{\Pi}(C) = 1)$ and $(\underline{\Pi}(D) = 0.5, \overline{\Pi}(D) = 0.6)$. The set of atoms generated by $\mathcal{E}$ is $\mathcal{C}_\mathcal{A} = \{C_1, C_2, C_3, C_4\}$ with $C_1 = A \wedge B^c \wedge C^c \wedge D^c$, $C_2 = A \wedge B \wedge C \wedge D^c$, $C_3 = A^c \wedge B \wedge C^c \wedge D^c$ and $C_4 = A^c \wedge B^c \wedge C^c \wedge D$.

Both for $T = \min$ or a strict t-norm, the natural extension on $\mathcal{C}_\mathcal{A} \times \{\Omega\}$ gives rise to the "unconditional" distribution envelopes on the left, while taking $B = C_2 \vee C_3$ we obtain the "updated" distribution envelopes on $\mathcal{C}_\mathcal{A} \times \{B\}$ reported on the right:

$\mathcal{C}_\mathcal{A} \times \{\Omega\}$	C_1	C_2	C_3	C_4
$\underline{\Pi}'$	0	0.1	0	0.5
$\overline{\Pi}'$	1	1	1	0.6

$\mathcal{C}_\mathcal{A} \times \{B\}$	$C_1|B$	$C_2|B$	$C_3|B$	$C_4|B$
$\underline{\Pi}'$	0	0.1	0	0
$\overline{\Pi}'$	0	1	1	0

5 Coherent Interval-Based Possibilistic Logic

Let $\Sigma = \{\sigma_1, \ldots, \sigma_m\}$ be a finite set of propositional variables and $\mathbb{L}^*$ be the propositional language generated by Σ, through $\wedge$, $\vee$ and ^{c}. Let $\Gamma = \{\gamma_1, \ldots, \gamma_t\} \subset \mathbb{L}^*$ be a propositional theory which, as usual, contains formulas intended as "assertions": assume Γ is satisfiable (i.e., $\bigwedge_{i=1}^t \gamma_i$ is satisfiable). The theory Γ is used to define a congruence relation $\equiv_\Gamma$ on $\mathbb{L}^*$, setting, for every $\psi_1, \psi_2 \in \mathbb{L}^*$,

$$\psi_1 \equiv_\Gamma \psi_2 \quad \text{if and only if} \quad \bigwedge_{i=1}^t \gamma_i \models (\psi_1^c \vee \psi_2) \wedge (\psi_2^c \vee \psi_1).$$

The Γ-Lindembaum algebra $\mathcal{A} = \mathbb{L}^*_{/\equiv_\Gamma}$ (see, e.g., [24]) is a finite Boolean algebra whose elements are equivalence classes $[\psi]_{\equiv_\Gamma}$'s that can be identified with events E's. Notice that formulas in Γ correspond to a set of logical constraints and if Γ is empty, then $\mathcal{A}$ reduces to the usual Lindembaum algebra on m propositional variables which is isomorphic to a free Boolean algebra with m generators.

Given Σ, $\mathbb{L}^*$ and Γ, an *imprecise possibilistic knowledge base* is a finite family of triples

$$\{(\psi_i, a_i, b_i) \; : \; \psi_i \in \mathbb{L}^*, 0 \leq a_i \leq b_i \leq 1, i = 1, \ldots, n\},$$

that determines, via the congruence $\equiv_\Gamma$, the envelopes assessment

$$\{(\underline{\Pi}(E_i) = a_i, \overline{\Pi}(E_i) = b_i) \; : \; E_i = [\psi_i]_{\equiv_\Gamma}, 0 \leq a_i \leq b_i \leq 1, i = 1, \ldots, n\}.$$

If the functions $(\underline{\Pi}, \overline{\Pi})$ are coherent T-conditional possibility envelopes (with $T = \min$ or strict), then we can compute their natural extension to the whole $\mathcal{A} \times \mathcal{A}^0$, as seen in Sect. 4. Recall that the set of atoms $\mathcal{C}_\mathcal{A} = \{C_1, \ldots, C_p\}$ of the Boolean algebra $\mathcal{A}$ is in bijection with the set of truth assignments on Σ satisfying the theory Γ. In particular, the natural extension procedure allows to compute the possibility distribution envelopes generated by $(\underline{\Pi}, \overline{\Pi})$

$$\{(\underline{\Pi}'(C_r), \overline{\Pi}'(C_r)) \; : \; r = 1, \ldots, p\},$$

and, fixed $H \in \mathcal{A}^0$, the "updated" possibility distribution envelopes

$$\{(\underline{\Pi}'(C_r|H), \overline{\Pi}'(C_r|H)) \; : \; r = 1, \ldots, p\}.$$

The discussion carried on in Sect. 4 allows to interpret the coherent T-conditional possibility envelopes above as interval-based constraints.

Notice that the introduction of logical constraints through the theory Γ allows to distinguish between "structural zeroes" from "believed zeroes", where the latter are due only to lack of information and can be, therefore, "updated" if new information is acquired. This is explained in detail in [13] where a study of entailment and the axiomatization of System P are faced in the precise case.

References

1. Baioletti, M., Coletti, G., Petturiti, D., Vantaggi, B.: Inferential models and relevant algorithms in a possibilistic framework. Int. J. App. Reas. **52**(5), 580–598 (2011)
2. Baioletti, M., Petturiti, D.: Algorithms for possibility assessments: coherence and extension. Fuzzy Sets Sys. **169**(1), 1–25 (2011)
3. Ben Amor, N., Mellouli, K., Benferhat, S., Dubois, D., Prade, H.: A throretical framework for possibilistic independence in a weakly ordered setting. Int. J. Unc. Fuzz. K.-B. Sys. **10**(2), 117–155 (2002)
4. Benferhat, S., Dubois, D., Prade, H.: Expressing independence in a possibilistic framework and its application to default reasoning. In: Proceeding of ECAI 1994, pp. 150–154 (1994)

5. Benferhat, S., Levray, A., Tabia, K., Kreinovich, V.: Compatible-based conditioning in interval-based possibilistic logic. In: Proceeding of IJCAI 2015, pp. 2777–2783 (2015)
6. Bouchon-Meunier, B., Coletti, G., Marsala, C.: Independence and possibilistic conditioning. Ann. Math. Art. Intell. **35**(1), 107–123 (2002)
7. Coletti, G., Petturiti, D.: Finitely maxitive conditional possibilities, Bayesian-like inference, disintegrability and conglomerability. Fuzzy Sets Sys. **284**, 31–55 (2016)
8. Coletti, G., Petturiti, D.: Finitely maxitive T-conditional possibility theory: coherence and extension. Int. J. App. Reas. **71**, 64–88 (2016)
9. Coletti, G., Petturiti, D., Vantaggi, B.: Coherent T-conditional possibility envelopes and nonmonotonic reasoning. In: Laurent, A., Strauss, O., Bouchon-Meunier, B., Yager, R.R. (eds.) IPMU 2014. CCIS, vol. 444, pp. 446–455. Springer, Cham (2014). doi:10.1007/978-3-319-08852-5_46
10. Coletti, G., Petturiti, D., Vantaggi, B.: Possibilistic and probabilistic likelihood functions and their extensions: common features and specific characteristics. Fuzzy Sets Sys. **250**, 25–51 (2014)
11. Coletti, G., Petturiti, D., Vantaggi, B.: Fuzzy memberships as likelihood functions in a possibilistic framework. Int. J. App. Reas. (in publication). doi:10.1016/j.ijar.2016.11.017
12. Coletti, G., Scozzafava, R., Vantaggi, B.: Inferential processes leading to possibility and necessity. Inf. Sci. **245**, 132–145 (2013)
13. Coletti, G., Scozzafava, R., Vantaggi, B.: Possibilistic and probabilistic logic under coherence: default reasoning and System P. Math. Slovaca **65**(4), 863–890 (2015)
14. Coletti, G., Vantaggi, B.: Possibility theory: conditional independence. Fuzzy Sets Sys. **157**(11), 1491–1513 (2006)
15. Coletti, G., Vantaggi, B.: T-conditional possibilities: coherence and inference. Fuzzy Sets Sys. **160**(3), 306–324 (2009)
16. de Cooman, G.: Possibility theory: conditional possibility. Int. J. Gen. Sys. **25**(4), 325–351 (1997)
17. de Finetti, B.: Sul significato soggettivo della probabilità. Fund. Math. **17**, 298–329 (1931)
18. Dubois, D., del Cerro, L.F., Herzig, A., Prade, H.: An ordinal view of independence with application to plausible reasoning. In: Proceeding UAI 1994, pp. 195–203 (1994)
19. Dubois, D., Prade, H.: Possibility Theory: An Approach to Computerized Processing of Uncertainty. Plenum Press, New York (1988)
20. Dubois, D., Prade, H.: When upper probabilities are possibility measures. Fuzzy Sets Sys. **49**(1), 65–74 (1992)
21. Ferracuti, L., Vantaggi, B.: Independence and conditional possibility for strictly monotone triangular norms. Int. J. Intell. Sys. **21**(3), 299–323 (2006)
22. Hisdal, E.: Conditional possibilities independence and noninteraction. Fuzzy Sets Sys. **1**(4), 283–297 (1978)
23. Klement, E., Mesiar, R., Pap, E.: Triangualr Norms, vol. 8. Kluwer Academic Publishers, Dordrecht (2000)
24. Stoll, R.: Set Theory and Logic. Dover Publications Inc., New York (1979)
25. Walley, P.: Statistical Reasoning with Imprecise Probabilities. Chapman and Hall, London (1991)
26. Williams, P.: Note on conditional previsions. Int. J. App. Reas. **44**, 366–383 (2007)
27. Zadeh, L.: Probability measures of fuzzy events. J. Math. Anal. App. **23**(2), 421–427 (1968)

Conjunction and Disjunction
Among Conditional Events

Angelo Gilio[1] and Giuseppe Sanfilippo[2(⊠)]

[1] Department SBAI, University of Rome "La Sapienza", Rome, Italy
angelo.gilio@sbai.uniroma1.it
[2] Department of Mathematics and Computer Science,
University of Palermo, Palermo, Italy
giuseppe.sanfilippo@unipa.it

Abstract. We generalize, in the setting of coherence, the notions of conjunction and disjunction of two conditional events to the case of n conditional events. Given a prevision assessment on the conjunction of two conditional events, we study the set of coherent extensions for the probabilities of the two conditional events. Then, we introduce by a progressive procedure the notions of conjunction and disjunction for n conditional events. Moreover, by defining the negation of conjunction and of disjunction, we show that De Morgan's Laws still hold. We also show that the associative and commutative properties are satisfied. Finally, we examine in detail the conjunction for a family $\mathcal{F}$ of three conditional events. To study coherence of prevision for the conjunction of the three conditional events, we need to consider the coherence for the prevision assessment on each conditional event and on the conjunction of each pair of conditional events in $\mathcal{F}$.

Keywords: Conditional events · Conditional random quantities · Conjunction · Disjunction · Negation · Quasi conjunction · Coherent prevision assessments · Coherent extensions · De Morgan's Laws

1 Introduction

In probability theory and in probability logic a relevant problem, largely discussed by many authors (see, e.g., [2,6,16]), is that of suitably defining logical operations among conditional events. In [17] it has been proposed a theory for the compounds of conditionals which has been suitably framed in the setting of coherence in [11,12,15]. In these papers, conjunction and disjunction of two conditional events in general are not conditional events but *conditional random quantities*. Moreover, the coherent extensions of a probability assessment (x, y)

Both authors contributed equally to this work.
A. Gilio—Retired
G. Sanfilippo—Partially supported by the INdAM–GNAMPA Project 2016, U 2016/000391.

S. Benferhat et al. (Eds.): IEA/AIE 2017, Part II, LNAI 10351, pp. 85–96, 2017.
DOI: 10.1007/978-3-319-60045-1_11

on two conditional events $\{A|H, B|K\}$ to their conjunction $(A|H) \wedge (B|K)$ and their disjunction $(A|H) \vee (B|K)$ has been studied. In this paper we generalize the notions of conjunction and disjunction of two conditional events to the case of n conditional events. After some preliminary notions and results, in Sect. 3 we study the set of coherent extensions for the probabilities of two conditional events, given the prevision of their conjunction. In Sect. 4 we introduce, in a progressive way, the notions of conjunction and disjunction for n conditional events; we also define the negation of conjunction disjunction; then we show that De Morgan's Laws are satisfied. We define the notion of conjunction (resp., disjunction) for the conjunctions (resp., disjunctions) associated with two families of conditional events, by showing then the validity of commutative and associative properties. In Sect. 5 we examine in detail the conjunction for a family of three conditional events $E_1|H_1, E_2|H_2, E_3|H_3$. We also consider the relation between the notion of conjunction and the notion of quasi-conjunction studied in [1]; see also [13,14]. In Sect. 6 we determine the set of coherent prevision assessments on the whole family $\{E_1|H_1, E_2|H_2, E_3|H_3, (E_1|H_1) \wedge (E_2|H_2), (E_1|H_1) \wedge (E_3|H_3), (E_2|H_2) \wedge (E_3|H_3), (E_1|H_1) \wedge (E_2|H_2) \wedge (E_3|H_3)\}$. In Sect. 7 we give a summary of results. We remark that, due to the lack of space, some aspects on De Morgan's Laws and on disjunction are not illustrated in detail.

2   Some Preliminaries

In this section we recall some basic notions and results on coherence for conditional prevision assessments. In our approach an event A represents an uncertain fact described by a (non ambiguous) logical proposition; hence we look at A as a two-valued logical entity which can be true (T), or false (F). The indicator of A, denoted by the same symbol, is a two-valued numerical quantity which is 1, or 0, according to whether A is true, or false. The sure event is denoted by Ω and the impossible event is denoted by $\emptyset$. Moreover, we denote by $A \wedge B$, or simply AB, (resp., $A \vee B$) the logical conjunction (resp., logical disjunction). The negation of A is denoted $\overline{A}$. Given any events A and B, we simply write $A \subseteq B$ to denote that A logically implies B, that is $A\overline{B}$ is the impossible event $\emptyset$. We recall that n events are logically independent when the number m of constituents, or possible worlds, generated by them is 2^n (in general $m \leq 2^n$). Given two events A and H, with $H \neq \emptyset$, the *conditional event* $A|H$ is defined as a three-valued logical entity which is *true* if AH is true, *false* if $\overline{A}H$ is true, and *void* if H is false.

Coherent Conditional Prevision Assessments. We recall below the notion of coherence (see, e.g., [3–5,7,9,15,21]). Given a prevision function $\mathbb{P}$ defined on an arbitrary family $\mathcal{K}$ of finite c.r.q.'s, consider a finite subfamily $\mathcal{F}_n = \{X_i|H_i, i \in J_n\} \subseteq \mathcal{K}$, where $J_n = \{1, \ldots, n\}$, and the vector $\mathcal{M}_n = (\mu_i, i \in J_n)$, where $\mu_i = \mathbb{P}(X_i|H_i)$ is the assessed prevision for the c.r.q. $X_i|H_i$. With the pair $(\mathcal{F}_n, \mathcal{M}_n)$ we associate the random gain $G = \sum_{i \in J_n} s_i H_i(X_i - \mu_i)$; moreover, we set $\mathcal{H}_n = H_1 \vee \cdots \vee H_n$ and we denote by $\mathcal{G}_{\mathcal{H}_n}$ the set of values of G restricted to $\mathcal{H}_n$. Then, using the *betting scheme* of de Finetti, we have

Definition 1. The function $\mathbb{P}$ defined on $\mathcal{K}$ is coherent if and only if, $\forall n \geq 1$, $\forall \mathcal{F}_n \subseteq \mathcal{K}$, $\forall s_1, \ldots, s_n \in \mathbb{R}$, it holds that: $min\ \mathcal{G}_{\mathcal{H}_n} \leq 0 \leq max\ \mathcal{G}_{\mathcal{H}_n}$.

Given a family $\mathcal{F}_n = \{X_1|H_1, \ldots, X_n|H_n\}$, for each $i \in J_n$ we denote by $\{x_{i1}, \ldots, x_{ir_i}\}$ the set of possible values for the restriction of X_i to H_i; then, for each $i \in J_n$ and $j = 1, \ldots, r_i$, we set $A_{ij} = (X_i = x_{ij})$. Of course, for each $i \in J_n$, the family $\{\overline{H}_i, A_{ij}H_i,\ j = 1, \ldots, r_i\}$ is a partition of the sure event Ω, with $A_{ij}H_i = A_{ij}$, $\bigvee_{j=1}^{r_i} A_{ij} = H_i$. Then, the constituents generated by the family $\mathcal{F}_n$ are (the elements of the partition of Ω) obtained by expanding the expression $\bigwedge_{i \in J_n}(A_{i1} \vee \cdots \vee A_{ir_i} \vee \overline{H}_i)$. We set $C_0 = \overline{H}_1 \cdots \overline{H}_n$ (it may be $C_0 = \emptyset$); moreover, we denote by $C_1, \ldots, C_m$ the constituents contained in $\mathcal{H}_n = H_1 \vee \cdots \vee H_n$. Hence $\bigwedge_{i \in J_n}(A_{i1} \vee \cdots \vee A_{ir_i} \vee \overline{H}_i) = \bigvee_{h=0}^{m} C_h$. With each C_h, $h \in J_m$, we associate a vector $Q_h = (q_{h1}, \ldots, q_{hn})$, where $q_{hi} = x_{ij}$ if $C_h \subseteq A_{ij}, j = 1, \ldots, r_i$, while $q_{hi} = \mu_i$ if $C_h \subseteq \overline{H}_i$; with C_0 it is associated $Q_0 = \mathcal{M}_n = (\mu_1, \ldots, \mu_n)$. Denoting by $\mathcal{I}_n$ the convex hull of $Q_1, \ldots, Q_m$, the condition $\mathcal{M}_n \in \mathcal{I}_n$ amounts to the existence of a vector $(\lambda_1, \ldots, \lambda_m)$ such that: $\sum_{h \in J_m} \lambda_h Q_h = \mathcal{M}_n$, $\sum_{h \in J_m} \lambda_h = 1$, $\lambda_h \geq 0$, $\forall h$; in other words, $\mathcal{M}_n \in \mathcal{I}_n$ is equivalent to the solvability of the system (Σ), associated with $(\mathcal{F}_n, \mathcal{M}_n)$,

$$(\Sigma)\quad \sum_{h \in J_m} \lambda_h q_{hi} = \mu_i,\ i \in J_n;\ \sum_{h \in J_m} \lambda_h = 1; \lambda_h \geq 0,\ h \in J_m. \quad (1)$$

Given the assessment $\mathcal{M}_n = (\mu_1, \ldots, \mu_n)$ on $\mathcal{F}_n = \{X_1|H_1, \ldots, X_n|H_n\}$, let S be the set of solutions $\Lambda = (\lambda_1, \ldots, \lambda_m)$ of system (Σ) defined in (1). Then, assuming the system (Σ) solvable, that is $S \neq \emptyset$, we define:

$$I_0 = \{i : \max_{\Lambda \in S} \sum_{h:C_h \subseteq H_i} \lambda_h = 0\},\ \mathcal{F}_0 = \{X_i|H_i, i \in I_0\},\ \mathcal{M}_0 = (\mu_i, i \in I_0). \quad (2)$$

Then, the following theorem can be proved ([3, Theorem 3])

Theorem 1 [*Operative characterization of coherence*]. A conditional prevision assessment $\mathcal{M}_n = (\mu_1, \ldots, \mu_n)$ on the family $\mathcal{F}_n = \{X_1|H_1, \ldots, X_n|H_n\}$ is coherent if and only if the following conditions are satisfied:

(i) the system (Σ) defined in (1) is solvable;
(ii) if $I_0 \neq \emptyset$, then $\mathcal{M}_0$ is coherent.

By following the approach given in [8,11,12,15] a conditional random quantity $X|H$ can be seen as the random quantity $XH + \mu\overline{H}$, where $\mu = \mathbb{P}(X|H)$. In particular $A|H$ can be interpreted as $AH + xH^c$, where $x = P(A|H)$. Moreover, the negation of $A|H$ is defined as $\overline{A|H} = 1 - A|H = \overline{A}|H$. Coherence can be characterized in terms of proper scoring rules ([4,10]), which can be related to the notion of entropy in information theory ([18,19]).

Quasi conjunction, conjunction and disjunction of two conditional events. The notion of quasi conjunction plays an important role in nonmonotonic reasoning. In particular for two conditional events $A|H, B|K$ the quasi conjunction $QC(A|H, B|K)$ is the following conditional event

$$QC(A|H, B|K) = \min\{\overline{H} \vee A, \overline{K} \vee B\}\,|\,(H \vee K) = [(\overline{H} \vee A) \cdot (\overline{K} \vee B)]\,|\,(H \vee K). \quad (3)$$

Note that: $QC(A|H, B|K)$ is true, when a conditional event is true and the other one is not void; $QC(A|H, B|K)$ is false, when a conditional event is false; $QC(A|H, B|K)$ is void, when $H \vee K$ is false. In other words, the quasi conjunction is the conjunction of the two material conditionals $\overline{H} \vee A, \overline{K} \vee B$ given the disjunction of the conditioning events H, K.

If we replace in formula (3) the material conditionals $\overline{H} \vee A, \overline{K} \vee B$ by the conditional events $A|H, B|K$ we obtain the following [12].

Definition 2. Given any pair of conditional events $A|H$ and $B|K$, with $P(A|H) = x$, $P(B|K) = y$, we define their conjunction as the conditional random quantity $(A|H) \wedge (B|K) = Z \,|\, (H \vee K)$, where $Z = \min\{A|H, B|K\}$, and their disjunction as $(A|H) \vee (B|K) = W \,|\, (H \vee K)$, where $W = \max\{A|H, B|K\}$.

Based on the betting scheme, $(A|H) \wedge (B|K)$ can be seen as the random quantity $1 \cdot AHBK + x \cdot \overline{H}BK + y \cdot AH\overline{K} + z \cdot \overline{H}\,\overline{K}$, where $z = \mathbb{P}[(A|H) \wedge (B|K)]$. Moreover, $(A|H) \vee (B|K)$ can be seen as the random quantity $1 \cdot AH \vee BK + x \cdot \overline{H}\,\overline{B}K + y \cdot \overline{A}H\overline{K} + w \cdot \overline{H}\,\overline{K}$, where $w = \mathbb{P}[(A|H) \vee (B|K)]$. We also recall the following result ([15, Theorem 7]):

Theorem 2. Given any coherent assessment (x, y) on $\{A|H, B|K\}$, with A, H, B, K logically independent, $H \neq \emptyset, K \neq \emptyset$, the extension $z = \mathbb{P}[(A|H) \wedge (B|K)]$ is coherent if and only if the following Fréchet-Hoeffding bounds are satisfied: $\max\{x + y - 1, 0\} = z' \leq z \leq z'' = \min\{x, y\}$.

3   Inference from $(A|H) \wedge (B|K)$ to $\{A|H, B|K\}$

In this section, given a coherent assessment $z = \mathbb{P}((A|H) \wedge (B|K))$, we find the set of coherent extensions (x, y) on $\{A|H, B|K\}$ of the assessment z.

Theorem 3. Given any prevision assessment z on $(A|H) \wedge (B|K)$, with $z \in [0, 1]$, with A, H, B, K logically independent, the extension $x = P(A|H)$, $y = P(B|K)$ is coherent iff $(x, y) \in T_z = \{(x, y) : x \in [z, 1], y \in [z, 1 + z - x]\}$.

Proof. We recall that, by logical independence of A, H, B, K, the assessment (x, y) is coherent for every $(x, y) \in [0, 1]^2$. From Theorem 2, the set Π of all coherent assessment (x, y, z) on $\{A|H, B|K, (A|H) \wedge (B|K)\}$ is $\Pi = \{(x, y, z) : (x, y) \in [0, 1]^2, \max\{x + y - 1, 0\} \leq z \leq \min\{x, y\}\}$. We note that

$$\Pi = \{(x, y, z) : z \in [0, 1], x \in [z, 1], y \in [z, 1 + z - x]\} =$$
$$= \{(x, y, z) : z \in [0, 1], (x, y) \in T_z\}.$$

Then, (x, y) is a coherent extension of z if and only if $(x, y) \in T_z$.

Remark 1. We observe that, given any $z \in [0, 1]$ and defining $\Pi_z = \{(x, y, z) : (x, y) \in T_z\}$, it holds that $\Pi = \bigcup_{z \in [0,1]} \Pi_z$. The set Π is the tetrahedron with vertices the points $(0, 0, 0), (1, 0, 0), (0, 1, 0), (1, 1, 1)$. Hence, contrarily to the general case, for the family $\{A|H, B|K, (A|H) \wedge (B|K)\}$ the set of coherent prevision assessments Π is convex. Indeed, Π is also the (convex) set of coherent probability assessment (x, y, z) on the family of unconditional events $\{A, B, AB\}$. We recall that, assuming $H \wedge K = \emptyset$, the set of coherent prevision assessments (x, y, z) on $\{A|H, B|K, (A|H) \wedge (B|K)\}$ is the surface $\{(x, y, z) : (x, y) \in [0, 1]^2, z = xy\}$, which is a strict non-convex subset of Π (see [12, Sect. 5]).

4 Conjunction and Disjunction of n Conditional Events

We now define the conjunction and the disjunction of n conditional events in a progressive way by specifying the possible values of the corresponding conditional random quantities. Given a family of n conditional events $\mathcal{F} = \{E_1|H_1, \ldots, E_n|H_n\}$, we denote by $C_0, C_1, \ldots, C_m$, with $m + 1 \leq 3^n$, the constituents associated with $\mathcal{F}$, where $C_0 = \overline{H}_1 \overline{H}_2 \cdots \overline{H}_n$. With each C_h, $h = 1, 2, \ldots, m$, we associate a tripartition (S'_h, S''_h, S'''_h) of the set $\{1, \ldots, n\}$, such that, for each $i \in \{1, \ldots, n\}$ it holds that: $i \in J'_h$, or $i \in S''_h$, or $i \in S'''_h$, according to whether $C_h \subseteq E_i H_i$, or $C_h \subseteq \overline{E}_i H_i$, or $C_h \subseteq \overline{H}_i$. In other words, for each $h = 1, 2, \ldots, m$, we have

$$S'_h = \{i : C_h \subseteq E_i H_i\}, \ S''_h = \{i : C_h \subseteq \overline{E}_i H_i\}, \ S'''_h = \{i : C_h \subseteq \overline{H}_i\}.$$

Definition 3 (Conjunction of n conditionals). Let be given a family of n conditional events $\mathcal{F} = \{E_1|H_1, \ldots, E_n|H_n\}$. For each non-empty subset S of $\{1, \ldots, n\}$, let x_S be a prevision assessment on $\bigwedge_{i \in S}(E_i|H_i)$. Then, the conjunction $\mathcal{C}(\mathcal{F}) = (E_1|H_1) \wedge \cdots \wedge (E_n|H_n)$ is defined as

$$Z|(H_1 \vee \cdots \vee H_n) = \sum_{h=0}^{m} z_h C_h, \text{ where } z_h = \begin{cases} 1, & \text{if } S'_h = \{1, \ldots, n\}, \\ 0, & \text{if } S''_h \neq \emptyset, \\ x_{S'''_h}, & \text{if } S''_h = \emptyset \text{ and } S'''_h \neq \emptyset. \end{cases} \tag{4}$$

As shown by (4), the conjunction $(E_1|H_1) \wedge \cdots \wedge (E_n|H_n)$ assumes one of the following possible values: 1, when every conditional event is true; 0, when at least one conditional event is false; x_S, when the conditional event $E_i|H_i$ is void, for every $i \in S$, and is true for every [20] $i \notin S$.

Remark 2. We observe that to introduce the random quantity defined by formula (4) we need to specify the prevision assessments x_S for every $S \subseteq \{1, 2, \ldots, n\}$. In particular, when the conditioning events $H_1, \ldots, H_n$ are all false, i.e. C_0 is true, the associated tripartition is $(S'_0, S''_0, S'''_0) = (\emptyset, \emptyset, \{1, 2, \ldots, n\})$ and the value of the conjunction $\mathcal{C}(\mathcal{F})$ is its prevision $x_{S'''_0} = \mathbb{P}[\mathcal{C}(\mathcal{F})]$. Moreover, we observe that the set of the constituents $\{C_0, \ldots, C_m\}$ associated with $\mathcal{F}$ is invariant with respect to any permutation of the conditional events in $\mathcal{F}$. Then, the operation of conjunction introduced by Definition 3 is invariant with respect to any permutation of the conditional events in $\mathcal{F}$.

Definition 4. Given two finite families of conditional events $\mathcal{F}'$ and $\mathcal{F}''$, based on Definition 3, we set $\mathcal{C}(\mathcal{F}') \wedge \mathcal{C}(\mathcal{F}'') = \mathcal{C}(\mathcal{F}' \cup \mathcal{F}'')$.

Remark 3. By Definitions 3 and 4, the operation of conjunction is associative and commutative. Moreover, we observe that $(A|H) \wedge (A|H) = A|H$.

Given a family of n conditional events $\mathcal{F} = \{E_1|H_1, \ldots, E_n|H_n\}$, we denote by $\overline{\mathcal{F}}$ the family $\{\overline{E_1}|H_1, \ldots, \overline{E_n}|H_n\}$. We also define the negation of the conjunction as $\overline{\mathcal{C}(\mathcal{F})} = 1 - \mathcal{C}(\mathcal{F})$.

Definition 5 (Disjunction of n conditionals). Let be given a family of n conditional events $\mathcal{F} = \{E_1|H_1, \ldots, E_n|H_n\}$. Morever, for each non-empty subset S of $\{1, \ldots, n\}$, let y_S be a prevision assessment on $\bigvee_{i \in S}(E_i|H_i)$.

   Then, the disjunction $\mathcal{D}(\mathcal{F}) = (E_1|H_1) \vee \cdots \vee (E_n|H_n)$ is defined as the following conditional random quantity

$$W|(H_1 \vee \cdots \vee H_n) = \sum_{h=0}^{m} w_h C_h, \text{ where } w_h = \begin{cases} 1, & \text{if } S_h' \neq \emptyset, \\ 0, & \text{if } S_h'' = \{1, 2, \ldots, n\}, \\ y_{S_h'''}, & \text{if } S_h' = \emptyset \text{ and } S_h''' \neq \emptyset. \end{cases} \quad (5)$$

Of course, $y_{S_0'''} = \mathbb{P}[\bigvee_{i=1}^{n}(E_i|H_i)]$. As shown by (5), the disjunction $\mathcal{D}(\mathcal{F})$ assumes one of the following possible values: 1, when at least one conditional event is true; 0, when every conditional event is false; y_S, when the conditional event $E_i|H_i$ is void, for every $i \in S$, and is false for every $i \notin S$.

Remark 4. As it can be easily verified, the random quantities $\mathcal{D}(\mathcal{F})$ and $\overline{\mathcal{C}(\overline{\mathcal{F}})}$ coincide for a family $\mathcal{F}$ of $n = 2$ conditional events. For $n = 3$, by Definitions 3 and (5), $\mathcal{D}(\mathcal{F})$ and $\overline{\mathcal{C}(\overline{\mathcal{F}})}$ coincide when $\mathcal{H}_0 = H_1 \vee H_2 \vee H_3$ is true. Then, the difference $\mathcal{D}(\mathcal{F}) - \overline{\mathcal{C}(\overline{\mathcal{F}})}$ is zero, when $\mathcal{H}_0$ is true, so that $\mathbb{P}(\mathcal{D}(\mathcal{F}) - \overline{\mathcal{C}(\overline{\mathcal{F}})}) = 0$ (see also [15, Theorem 4]) and hence $\mathbb{P}(\mathcal{D}(\mathcal{F})) = \mathbb{P}(\overline{\mathcal{C}(\overline{\mathcal{F}})})$. Therefore $\mathcal{D}(\mathcal{F})$ also coincides with $\overline{\mathcal{C}(\overline{\mathcal{F}})}$ when $\mathcal{H}_0$ is false, so that $\mathcal{D}(\mathcal{F}) = \overline{\mathcal{C}(\overline{\mathcal{F}})}$ for $n = 3$. Thus, by applying a similar reasoning, it can be proved by induction that $\mathcal{D}(\mathcal{F}) = \overline{\mathcal{C}(\overline{\mathcal{F}})}$ for $n > 3$. Moreover, by defining $\overline{\mathcal{D}(\mathcal{F})} = 1 - \mathcal{D}(\mathcal{F})$, it also holds that $\mathcal{C}(\mathcal{F}) = \overline{\mathcal{D}(\overline{\mathcal{F}})}$. Therefore, De Morgan's Laws still hold.

Definition 1. *Given two finite families of conditional events $\mathcal{F}'$ and $\mathcal{F}''$, based on Definition 5, we set $\mathcal{D}(\mathcal{F}') \vee \mathcal{D}(\mathcal{F}'') = \mathcal{D}(\mathcal{F}' \cup \mathcal{F}'')$.*

Remark 5. By Definition 1, one has $(1 - \mathcal{C}(\overline{\mathcal{F}'})) \vee (1 - \mathcal{C}(\overline{\mathcal{F}''})) = \mathcal{D}(\mathcal{F}') \vee \mathcal{D}(\mathcal{F}'') = \mathcal{D}(\mathcal{F}' \cup \mathcal{F}'') = 1 - \mathcal{C}(\overline{\mathcal{F}' \cup \mathcal{F}''})$. By Definitions 5 and 1, disjunction is associative and commutative. Moreover, we observe that $(A|H) \vee (A|H) = A|H$.

5   Conjunction of Three Conditional Events

In this section we develop our analysis for the conjunction of three conditional events. Given a family of three conditional events $\mathcal{F} = \{E_1|H_1, E_2|H_2, E_3|H_3\}$, we set $P(E_i|H_i) = x_i$, $i = 1, 2, 3$, $\mathbb{P}[(E_i|H_i) \wedge (E_j|H_j)] = x_{ij} = x_{ji}$, $i \neq j$, and $x_{123} = \mathbb{P}[Z|(H_1 \vee H_2 \vee H_3)]$. Then, by Definition 3, the conjunction $\mathcal{C}(\mathcal{F}) = (E_1|H_1) \wedge (E_2|H_2) \wedge (E_3|H_3)$ is the conditional random quantity

$$\mathcal{C}(\mathcal{F}) = Z|(H_1 \vee H_2 \vee H_3) = \begin{cases} 1, & \text{if } E_1 H_1 E_2 H_2 E_3 H_3 \text{ is true} \\ 0, & \text{if } \overline{E}_1 H_1 \vee \overline{E}_2 H_2 \vee \overline{E}_3 H_3 \text{ is true,} \\ x_1, & \text{if } \overline{H}_1 E_2 H_2 E_3 H_3 \text{ is true,} \\ x_2, & \text{if } \overline{H}_2 E_1 H_1 E_3 H_3 \text{ is true,} \\ x_3, & \text{if } \overline{H}_3 E_1 H_1 E_2 H_2 \text{ is true,} \\ x_{12}, & \text{if } \overline{H}_1 \overline{H}_2 E_3 H_3 \text{ is true,} \\ x_{13}, & \text{if } \overline{H}_1 \overline{H}_3 E_2 H_2 \text{ is true,} \\ x_{23}, & \text{if } \overline{H}_2 \overline{H}_3 E_1 H_1 \text{ is true,} \\ x_{123}, & \text{if } \overline{H}_1 \overline{H}_2 \overline{H}_3 \text{ is true.} \end{cases} \quad (6)$$

Remark 6. Notice that in the betting scheme x_{123} is the quantity to be paid in order to receive $Z|(H_1 \vee H_2 \vee H_3)$. Assuming that the assessment $(x_1, x_2, x_3, x_{12}, x_{13}, x_{23})$ on $\{E_1|H_1, E_2|H_2, E_3|H_3, (E_1|H_1) \wedge (E_2|H_2), (E_1|H_1) \wedge (E_3|H_3), (E_2|H_2) \wedge (E_3|H_3)\}$ is coherent, we are interested in finding the values x_{123} which are coherent extension of $(x_1, x_2, x_3, x_{12}, x_{13}, x_{23})$. Of course, as $x_i \in [0, 1]$, $i = 1, 2, 3$, and $x_{ij} \in [0, 1]$, $i \neq j$, a necessary condition for coherence is $x_{123} \in [0, 1]$.

From Remarks 2 and 3 the conjunction $\mathcal{C}(\mathcal{F}) = (E_1|H_1) \wedge (E_2|H_2) \wedge (E_3|H_3))$ is invariant with respect to any given permutation (i_1, i_2, i_3) of $(1, 2, 3)$. Moreover, it holds that $[(E_{i_1}|H_{i_1}) \wedge (E_{i_2}|H_{i_2})] \wedge (E_{i_3}|H_{i_3}) = Z|(H_1 \vee H_2 \vee H_3)$, for any permutation (i_1, i_2, i_3) of $(1, 2, 3)$.

Remark 7. We recall that if $x_i = x_j = 1$, then $E_i|H_i \wedge E_j|H_j = QC(E_i|H_i, E_j|H_j)$, and coherence requires that $x_{ij} = 1$ [12]. If $x_i = 1$, $i = 1, 2, 3$, from Theorem 2 it follows that $x_{ij} = 1$ for each $i \neq j$ and (as we will show later) $x_{123} = 1$. We recall that the quasi conjunction of n conditional events $E_1|H_1, \ldots, E_n|H_n$ is the conditional event $QC(E_1|H_1, \ldots, E_n|H_n) = (\bigwedge_{i=1}^{n}(\overline{H}_i \vee E_i H_i))|(\bigvee_{i=1}^{n} H_i)$, with $P(QC(E_1|H_1, \ldots, E_n|H_n)) = 1$ when $x_i = 1$, $i = 1, \ldots, n$. Then, from (6), if $x_i = 1$, $i = 1, \ldots, n$, it holds that

$$(E_1|H_1) \wedge (E_2|H_2) \wedge (E_3|H_3) = \bigwedge_{i=1}^{3}(\overline{H}_i \vee E_i H_i)\Big| \bigvee_{i=1}^{3} H_i = QC(E_1|H_1, E_2|H_2, E_3|H_3).$$

More in general: $(E_1|H_1) \wedge (E_2|H_2) \wedge (E_3|H_3) \leq QC(E_1|H_1, E_2|H_2, E_3|H_3)$, so that: $\mathbb{P}((E_1|H_1) \wedge (E_2|H_2) \wedge (E_3|H_3)) \leq P(QC(E_1|H_1, E_2|H_2, E_3|H_3))$.

6 Set of Coherent Assessments

Based on Sect. 2, we determine the set Π of all coherent assessments $\mathcal{M} = (x_1, x_2, x_3, x_{12}, x_{13}, x_{23}, x_{123})$ on $\mathcal{F} = \{E_1|H_1, E_2|H_2, E_3|H_3, (E_1|H_1) \wedge (E_2|H_2), (E_1|H_1) \wedge (E_3|H_3), (E_2|H_2) \wedge (E_3|H_3), (E_1|H_1) \wedge (E_2|H_2) \wedge (E_3|H_3)\}$. We assume that $E_1, E_2, E_3, H_1, H_2, H_3$ are logically independent. The constituents C_h's and the points Q_h's associated with $(\mathcal{F}, \mathcal{M})$ are illustrated in

Table 1. Constituents C_h's and corresponding points Q_h's associated with $(\mathcal{F}, \mathcal{M})$, where $\mathcal{M} = (x_1, x_2, x_3, x_{12}, x_{13}, x_{23}, x_{123})$ is a prevision assessment on $\mathcal{F} = \{E_1|H_1, E_2|H_2, E_3|H_3, (E_1|H_1) \wedge (E_2|H_2), (E_1|H_1) \wedge (E_3|H_3), (E_2|H_2) \wedge (E_3|H_3), (E_1|H_1) \wedge (E_2|H_2) \wedge (E_3|H_3)\}$.

	C_h	Q_h							
C_1	$E_1H_1E_2H_2E_3H_3$	1	1	1	1	1	1	1	Q_1
C_2	$E_1H_1E_2H_2\overline{E}_3H_3$	1	1	0	1	0	0	0	Q_2
C_3	$E_1H_1E_2H_2\overline{H}_3$	1	1	x_3	1	x_3	x_3	x_3	Q_3
C_4	$E_1H_1\overline{E}_2H_2E_3H_3$	1	0	1	0	1	0	0	Q_4
C_5	$E_1H_1\overline{E}_2H_2\overline{E}_3H_3$	1	0	0	0	0	0	0	Q_5
C_6	$E_1H_1\overline{E}_2H_2\overline{H}_3$	1	0	x_3	0	x_3	0	0	Q_6
C_7	$E_1H_1\overline{H}_2E_3H_3$	1	x_2	1	x_2	1	x_2	x_2	Q_7
C_8	$E_1H_1\overline{H}_2\overline{E}_3H_3$	1	x_2	0	x_2	0	0	0	Q_8
C_9	$E_1H_1\overline{H}_2\overline{H}_3$	1	x_2	x_3	x_2	x_3	x_{23}	x_{23}	Q_9
C_{10}	$\overline{E}_1H_1E_2H_2E_3H_3$	0	1	1	0	0	1	0	Q_{10}
C_{11}	$\overline{E}_1H_1E_2H_2\overline{E}_3H_3$	0	1	0	0	0	0	0	Q_{11}
C_{12}	$\overline{E}_1H_1E_2H_2\overline{H}_3$	0	1	x_3	0	0	x_3	0	Q_{12}
C_{13}	$\overline{E}_1H_1\overline{E}_2H_2E_3H_3$	0	0	1	0	0	0	0	Q_{13}
C_{14}	$\overline{E}_1H_1\overline{E}_2H_2\overline{E}_3H_3$	0	0	0	0	0	0	0	Q_{14}
C_{15}	$\overline{E}_1H_1\overline{E}_2H_2\overline{H}_3$	0	0	x_3	0	0	0	0	Q_{15}
C_{16}	$\overline{E}_1H_1\overline{H}_2E_3H_3$	0	x_2	1	0	0	x_2	0	Q_{16}
C_{17}	$\overline{E}_1H_1\overline{H}_2\overline{E}_3H_3$	0	x_2	0	0	0	0	0	Q_{17}
C_{18}	$\overline{E}_1H_1\overline{H}_2\overline{H}_3$	0	x_2	x_3	0	0	x_{23}	0	Q_{18}
C_{19}	$\overline{H}_1E_2H_2E_3H_3$	x_1	1	1	x_1	x_1	1	x_1	Q_{19}
C_{20}	$\overline{H}_1E_2H_2\overline{E}_3H_3$	x_1	1	0	x_1	0	0	0	Q_{20}
C_{21}	$\overline{H}_1E_2H_2\overline{H}_3$	x_1	1	x_3	x_1	x_{13}	x_3	x_{13}	Q_{21}
C_{22}	$\overline{H}_1\overline{E}_2H_2E_3H_3$	x_1	0	1	0	x_1	0	0	Q_{22}
C_{23}	$\overline{H}_1\overline{E}_2H_2\overline{E}_3H_3$	x_1	0	0	0	0	0	0	Q_{23}
C_{24}	$\overline{H}_1\overline{E}_2H_2\overline{H}_3$	x_1	0	x_3	0	x_{13}	0	0	Q_{24}
C_{25}	$\overline{H}_1\overline{H}_2E_3H_3$	x_1	x_2	1	x_{12}	x_1	x_2	x_{12}	Q_{25}
C_{26}	$\overline{H}_1\overline{H}_2\overline{E}_3H_3$	x_1	x_2	0	x_{12}	0	0	0	Q_{26}
C_0	$\overline{H}_1\overline{H}_2\overline{H}_3$	x_1	x_2	x_3	x_{12}	x_{13}	x_{23}	x_{123}	Q_0

Table 1. Denoting by $\mathcal{I}$ the convex hull generated by $Q_1, Q_2, \ldots, Q_{26}$, the coherence of the prevision assessment $\mathcal{M}$ on $\mathcal{F}$ requires that the condition $\mathcal{P} \in \mathcal{I}$ be satisfied; this amounts to the solvability of the following system

$$(\Sigma) \qquad \mathcal{M} = \sum_{h=1}^{26} \lambda_h Q_h, \quad \sum_{h=1}^{26} \lambda_h = 1, \quad \lambda_h \geq 0, \quad h = 1, \ldots, 26.$$

We observe that

$$Q_3 = x_3 Q_1 + (1 - x_3) Q_2, \quad Q_6 = x_3 Q_4 + (1 - x_3) Q_5,$$
$$Q_7 = x_2 Q_1 + (1 - x_2) Q_4, \quad Q_8 = x_2 Q_2 + (1 - x_2) Q_5,$$
$$Q_9 = x_{23} Q_1 + (x_2 - x_{23}) Q_2 + (x_3 - x_{23}) Q_4 + (x_{23} - x_2 - x_3 + 1) Q_5,$$
$$Q_{12} = x_3 Q_{10} + (1 - x_3) Q_{11}, \quad Q_{15} = x_3 Q_{13} + (1 - x_3) Q_{14},$$
$$Q_{16} = x_2 Q_{10} + (1 - x_2) Q_{13}, \quad Q_{17} = x_2 Q_{11} + (1 - x_2) Q_{14},$$
$$Q_{18} = x_{23} Q_{10} + (x_2 - x_{23}) Q_{11} + (x_3 - x_{23}) Q_{13} + (x_{23} - x_2 - x_3 + 1) Q_{14},$$
$$Q_{19} = x_1 Q_1 + (1 - x_1) Q_{10}, \quad Q_{20} = x_1 Q_2 + (1 - x_1) Q_{11},$$
$$Q_{21} = x_{13} Q_1 + (x_1 - x_{13}) Q_2 + (x_3 - x_{13}) Q_{10} + (x_{13} - x_1 - x_3 + 1) Q_{11},$$
$$Q_{22} = x_1 Q_4 + (1 - x_1) Q_{13}, \quad Q_{23} = x_1 Q_5 + (1 - x_1) Q_{14},$$
$$Q_{24} = x_{13} Q_4 + (x_1 - x_{13}) Q_5 + (x_3 - x_{13}) Q_{13} + (x_{13} - x_1 - x_3 + 1) Q_{14},$$
$$Q_{25} = x_{12} Q_1 + (x_1 - x_{12}) Q_4 + (x_2 - x_{12}) Q_{10} + (x_{12} - x_1 - x_2 + 1) Q_{13},$$
$$Q_{26} = x_{12} Q_2 + (x_1 - x_{12}) Q_5 + (x_2 - x_{12}) Q_{11} + (x_{12} - x_1 - x_2 + 1) Q_{14}.$$

Thus, $\mathcal{I}$ coincides with the convex hull of the points $Q_1, Q_2, Q_4, Q_5,$ $Q_{10}, Q_{11}, Q_{13}, Q_{14}$. For the sake of simplicity, we set: $Q_1' = Q_1, Q_2' = Q_2, Q_3' = Q_4, Q_4' = Q_5, Q_5' = Q_{10}, Q_6' = Q_{11}, Q_7' = Q_{13}, Q_8' = Q_{14}$. Then, the condition $\mathcal{M} \in \mathcal{I}$ amounts to the solvability of the following system

$$(\Sigma') \qquad \mathcal{M} = \sum_{h=1}^{8} \lambda_h' Q_h', \quad \sum_{h=1}^{8} \lambda_h' = 1, \quad \lambda_h' \geq 0, h = 1, \ldots, 8$$

that is

$$(\Sigma') \begin{cases} \lambda_1' + \lambda_2' + \lambda_3' + \lambda_4' = x_1, \quad \lambda_1' + \lambda_2' + \lambda_5' + \lambda_6' = x_2, \quad \lambda_1' + \lambda_3' + \lambda_5' + \lambda_7' = x_3, \\ \lambda_1' + \lambda_2' = x_{12}, \quad \lambda_1' + \lambda_3' = x_{13}, \quad \lambda_1' + \lambda_5' = x_{23}, \quad \lambda_1' = x_{123}, \\ \sum_{h=1}^{8} \lambda_h' = 1, \quad \lambda_h' \geq 0, \quad h = 1, 2, \ldots, 8. \end{cases}$$

System (Σ') can be written as

$$(\Sigma') \begin{cases} \lambda_1' = x_{123}, \quad \lambda_2' = x_{12} - x_{123}, \quad \lambda_3' = x_{13} - x_{123}, \quad \lambda_4' = x_1 - x_{12} - x_{13} + x_{123}, \\ \lambda_5' = x_{23} - x_{123}, \quad \lambda_6' = x_2 - x_{12} - x_{23} + x_{123}, \quad \lambda_7' = x_3 - x_{13} - x_{23} + x_{123}, \\ \lambda_8' = 1 - x_1 - x_2 - x_3 + x_{12} + x_{13} + x_{23} - x_{123}, \quad \lambda_h' \geq 0, \quad h = 1, 2, \ldots, 8. \end{cases}$$

As it can be verified, by non-negativity of $\lambda_1', \ldots, \lambda_8'$ it follows that (Σ') is solvable (with a unique solution) if and only if

$$\begin{cases} x_{123} \geq x_{123}' = \max\{0, x_{12} + x_{13} - x_1, x_{12} + x_{23} - x_2, x_{13} + x_{23} - x_3\}, \\ x_{123} \leq x_{123}'' = \min\{x_{12}, x_{13}, x_{23}, 1 - x_1 - x_2 - x_3 + x_{12} + x_{13} + x_{23}\}, \end{cases} \tag{7}$$

or, in a more explicit way, if and only if

$$
\begin{cases}
(x_1, x_2, x_3) \in [0,1]^3, \\
\max\{x_1 + x_2 - 1, x_{13} + x_{23} - x_3, 0\} \le x_{12} \le \min\{x_1, x_2\}, \\
\max\{x_1 + x_3 - 1, x_{12} + x_{23} - x_2, 0\} \le x_{13} \le \min\{x_1, x_3\}, \\
\max\{x_2 + x_3 - 1, x_{12} + x_{13} - x_1, 0\} \le x_{23} \le \min\{x_2, x_3\}, \\
1 - x_1 - x_2 - x_3 + x_{12} + x_{13} + x_{23} \ge 0, \\
x_{123} \ge \max\{0, x_{12} + x_{13} - x_1, x_{12} + x_{23} - x_2, x_{13} + x_{23} - x_3\}, \\
x_{123} \le \min\{x_{12}, x_{13}, x_{23}, 1 - x_1 - x_2 - x_3 + x_{12} + x_{13} + x_{23}\},
\end{cases}
\tag{8}
$$

Moreover, assuming (Σ') solvable, with the solution $(\lambda_1', \ldots, \lambda_8')$, we associate the vector $(\lambda_1, \lambda_2, \ldots, \lambda_{26})$, with $\lambda_1 = \lambda_1'$, $\lambda_2 = \lambda_2'$, $\lambda_4 = \lambda_3'$, $\lambda_5 = \lambda_4'$, $\lambda_{10} = \lambda_5'$, $\lambda_{11} = \lambda_6'$, $\lambda_{13} = \lambda_7'$, $\lambda_{14} = \lambda_8'$, $\lambda_h = 0, h \notin \{1, 2, 4, 5, 10, 11, 13, 14\}$, which is a solution of (Σ). Moreover, defining $\mathcal{J} = \{1, 2, 4, 5, 10, 11, 13, 14\}$, it holds that $\bigvee_{h \in \mathcal{J}} C_h = H_1 \wedge H_2 \wedge H_3$. Therefore, $\sum_{h \in \mathcal{J}} \lambda_h = \sum_{h: C_h \subseteq H_1 H_2 H_3} \lambda_h = 1$ and hence $\sum_{h: C_h \subseteq H_i} = 1$, $i = 1, 2, 3$, $\sum_{h: C_h \subseteq H_i \vee H_j} = 1$, $i \ne j$, $\sum_{h: C_h \subseteq H_1 \vee H_2 \vee H_3} = 1$; thus, by (2), $I_0 = \emptyset$. Then, by Theorem 1, the solvability of (Σ) is also sufficient for the coherence of $\mathcal{M}$. Finally, Π is the set of conditional prevision assessments $(x_1, x_2, x_3, x_{12}, x_{13}, x_{23}, x_{123})$ which satisfy the conditions in (8). In particular for any coherent assessment $(x_1, x_2, x_3, x_{12}, x_{13}, x_{23})$ the extension x_{123} on $(E_1|H_1) \wedge (E_2|H_2) \wedge (E_3|H_3)$ is coherent iff $x_{123} \in [x_{123}', x_{123}'']$, where x_{123}', x_{123}'' are defined in (7).

7   Conclusions

We generalized the notions of conjunction and disjunction of two conditional events to the case of n conditional events. We also introduced the notion of negation and we showed that De Morgan's Laws still hold. We also showed that the associative and commutative properties are satisfied. We considered the relation between conjunction and quasi-conjunction. Moreover, we studied the set of coherent extensions for the probabilities of two conditional events, given the prevision assessment on their conjunction. Finally, we examined the details of the operation of conjunction for three conditional events. The study of the coherence for the prevision of the conjunction required to consider the coherence for the whole set of prevision assessments on each conditional event and on the conjunction of each pair of conditional events. The results given in Sects. 5 and 6 will be extended to disjunction in a future work.

Acknowledgments. We thank *DFG, FMSH*, and *Villa Vigoni* for supporting joint meetings at Villa Vigoni where parts of this work originated (Project: "Human Rationality: Probabilistic Points of View").

References

1. Adams, E.W.: The Logic of Conditionals. Reidel, Dordrecht (1975)
2. Benferhat, S., Dubois, D., Prade, H.: Nonmonotonic reasoning, conditional objects and possibility theory. Artif. Intell. **92**, 259–276 (1997)

3. Biazzo, V., Gilio, A., Sanfilippo, G.: Generalized coherence and connection property of imprecise conditional previsions. In: Proceeding IPMU 2008, Malaga, Spain, 22–27 June, pp. 907–914 (2008)
4. Biazzo, V., Gilio, A., Sanfilippo, G.: Coherent conditional previsions and proper scoring rules. In: Greco, S., Bouchon-Meunier, B., Coletti, G., Fedrizzi, M., Matarazzo, B., Yager, R.R. (eds.) IPMU 2012. CCIS, vol. 300, pp. 146–156. Springer, Heidelberg (2012). doi:10.1007/978-3-642-31724-8_16
5. Capotorti, A., Lad, F., Sanfilippo, G.: Reassessing accuracy rates of median decisions. Am. Stat. **61**(2), 132–138 (2007)
6. Capotorti, A., Vantaggi, B.: A general interpretation of conditioning and its implication on coherence. Soft. Comput. **3**(3), 148–153 (1999)
7. Coletti, G., Scozzafava, R.: Probabilistic Logic in a Coherent Setting. Kluwer, Dordrecht (2002)
8. Gilio, A., Over, D.E., Pfeifer, N., Sanfilippo, G.: Centering and compound conditionals under coherence. In: Ferraro, M.B., Giordani, P., Vantaggi, B., Gagolewski, M., Gil, M.Á., Grzegorzewski, P., Hryniewicz, O. (eds.) Soft Methods for Data Science. AISC, vol. 456, pp. 253–260. Springer, Cham (2017). doi:10.1007/978-3-319-42972-4_32
9. Gilio, A., Pfeifer, N., Sanfilippo, G.: Transitivity in coherence-based probability logic. J. Appl. Logic **14**, 46–64 (2016)
10. Gilio, A., Sanfilippo, G.: Coherent conditional probabilities and proper scoring rules. In: ISIPTA 2011 - Proceedings of the 7th International Symposium on Imprecise Probability: Theories and Applications, pp. 189–198, Innsbruck (2011)
11. Gilio, A., Sanfilippo, G.: Conditional random quantities and iterated conditioning in the setting of coherence. In: Gaag, L.C. (ed.) ECSQARU 2013. LNCS (LNAI), vol. 7958, pp. 218–229. Springer, Heidelberg (2013). doi:10.1007/978-3-642-39091-3_19
12. Gilio, A., Sanfilippo, G.: Conjunction, disjunction and iterated conditioning of conditional events. In: Kruse, R., Berthold, M., Moewes, C., Gil, M., Grzegorzewski, P., Hryniewicz, O. (eds.) Synergies of Soft Computing and Statistics for Intelligent Data Analysis. AISC, vol. 190, pp. 399–407. Springer, Heidelberg (2013). doi:10.1007/978-3-642-33042-1_43
13. Gilio, A., Sanfilippo, G.: Probabilistic entailment in the setting of coherence: the role of quasi conjunction and inclusion relation. Int. J. Approx. Reason. **54**(4), 513–525 (2013)
14. Gilio, A., Sanfilippo, G.: Quasi conjunction, quasi disjunction, t-norms and t-conorms: probabilistic aspects. Inf. Sci. **245**, 146–167 (2013)
15. Gilio, A., Sanfilippo, G.: Conditional random quantities and compounds of conditionals. Stud. Logica. **102**(4), 709–729 (2014)
16. Goodman, I.R., Nguyen, H.T., Walker, E.A.: Conditional inference and logic for intelligent systems. A theory of measure-free conditioning, North-Holland, Amsterdam (1991)
17. Kaufmann, S.: Conditionals right and left: probabilities for the whole family. J. Philos. Logic **38**, 1–53 (2009)
18. Lad, F., Sanfilippo, G., Agró, G.: Completing the logarithmic scoring rule for assessing probability distributions. AIP Conf. Proc. **1490**(1), 13–30 (2012)

19. Lad, F., Sanfilippo, G., Agró, G.: Extropy: complementary dual of entropy. Stat. Sci. **30**(1), 40–58 (2015)
20. McGee, V.: Conditional probabilities and compounds of conditionals. Philos. Rev. **98**(4), 485–541 (1989)
21. Petturiti, D., Vantaggi, B.: Envelopes of conditional probabilities extending a strategy and a prior probability. Int. J. Approx. Reason. **81**, 160–182 (2017)

A Gold Standards-Based Crowd Label Aggregation Within the Belief Function Theory

Lina Abassi[(⊠)] and Imen Boukhris

LARODEC, Institut Supérieur de Gestion de Tunis,
Université de Tunis, Tunis, Tunisia
lina.abassi@gmail.com, imen.boukhris@hotmail.com

Abstract. Crowdsourcing, in particular microtasking is now a powerful concept used by employers in order to obtain answers on tasks hardly handled by automated computation. These answers are provided by human employees and then combined to get a final answer. Nevertheless, the quality of participants in microtasking platforms is often heterogeneous which makes results imperfect and thus not fully reliable. To tackle this problem, we propose a new approach of label aggregation based on gold standards under the belief function theory. This latter provides several tools able to represent and even combine imperfect information. Experiments conducted on both simulated and real world datasets show that our approach improves results quality even with a high ratio of bad workers.

Keywords: Crowdsourcing · Gold standards · Belief function theory · Error rate · Label aggregation

1 Introduction

Crowdsourcing has attracted a big interest in recent years due to its capacity to distribute work to a large number of people in order to get advantage of the crowd efforts. Crowdsourcing first coined in 2006 in [1] has different forms depending on the type of work. The most known form is called microtasking and has been used in the market to perform through a platform a high variety of small tasks that are hard to be computerized. The problem is microtasking systems is the low results quality caused essentially by the quality of workers. In fact, a worker reliability depends on many factors such as skills, knowledge and motivations. As a basic solution, assigning a task to many workers also called redundancy was proposed by many microtasking platforms. Since this leads to having multiple answers, several methods [7,10,13] addressed the problem of label aggregation. However, answers might be unreliable.

In this paper, we propose a novel approach of label aggregation based on the belief function theory. This theory allows the combination of many pieces of information besides of taking into account the reliability of the various sources providing them. In [14], the belief function theory was also used successfully in a

© Springer International Publishing AG 2017
S. Benferhat et al. (Eds.): IEA/AIE 2017, Part II, LNAI 10351, pp. 97–106, 2017.
DOI: 10.1007/978-3-319-60045-1_12

crowdsourcing environment. Indeed, authors apply the theory of belief function in order to determine a reliable method of identifying experts. Based on the belief model of the workers' labels, they calculate a global degree (including an exactitude and a precision degree) to characterize the expertise level of each labeler.

In this paper, our approach offers a plenary framework that aggregates label besides of calculating and integrating workers expertise based on gold standards (i.e. questions which answers are known by the requester).

The rest of this is organised as follows: Sect. 2, provide an overview of the related works of label aggregation methods. In Sect. 3, we present the fundamental concepts of the belief function. Section 4 introduces our proposed method. Experimentation evaluations are discussed in Sect. 5. Finally, we conclude in Sect. 6.

2   Label Aggregation: Related Works

Many aggregation approaches were proposed in order to improve results quality. One simple solution is to aggregate answers using the majority voting heuristic method (MV) but the problem is that it considers all workers equally reliable. To overcome this problem, the Honeypot (HP) method [7] suggests that unreliable workers are removed in a preprocessing step. Unreliable workers are those who fail to answer some number of gold standards. Providing a framework called Expert Label Injected Crowd Estimation (ELICE), authors in [10] use gold standards to estimate two parameters, the reliability degree of each worker by calculating the ratio of his answers which are similar to true labels of gold standards and the difficulty level of each question is estimated by the number of workers who correctly answer a given number of the gold questions. These two parameters are then integrated into the aggregation process.

The Expectation Maximization (EM) method used in [9] generates both label probabilities and workers levels of expertise iteratively in a sequence of computational rounds. The Generative Model of Labels Ability and Difficulties (GLAD) [17] has the same concept as the EM method but it considers both labelers reliability and the question difficulty of every question. As for the Iterative Learning method [13], it is a sum-product message passing based method that estimates the workers reliability degree and question difficulty.

These existing approaches do not cope effectively with uncertainty. This inspired our previous work, the Belief Label Aggregation (BLA) [8], that adopted the belief function theory to represent and aggregate labels. However, worker expertise was computed considering majority voting. This makes this method highly vulnerable against bad labelers.

3   Belief Function Theory

The theory of belief function was first introduced by Dempster in [2] then described by Shafer in [3] as a model to represent beliefs. Several models have been proposed from this theory. One of the most used is the Transferable Belief Model (TBM) developed by [11] to represent quantified beliefs. It is considered as a powerful tool dealing with uncertainty and has the ability of representing several kinds of imperfections.

3.1 Basic Concepts

The frame of discernment Ω is a finite set of exclusive and exhaustive elements and its power set 2^Ω containing hypotheses about some problem domain is defined by:

$$2^\Omega = \{A : A \subseteq \Omega\}. \tag{1}$$

A basic belief assignment or a mass function $m^\Omega : 2^\Omega \to [0,1]$ represents the degree of belief given to an element A. It affects a real value from $[0, 1]$. It is defined as follows:

$$\sum_{A \subseteq \Omega} m^\Omega(A) = 1 \tag{2}$$

A focal element A is a set of hypothesis with positive mass value (i.e. $m^\Omega(A) > 0$).

In order to express particular situations of imperfection, some special *bbas* have been proposed [3]:

- certain *bba*: in this case a singleton is the only focal element. $m(\{\omega_i\}) = 1$ for one particular element ω_i of Ω.
- vacuous *bba*: Ω is the unique focal element: $m(\Omega) = 1$. This models the case of total ignorance.
- categorical *bba*: The *bba* has a unique focal element A.
- simple support function: The *bba* focal elements are $\{A, \Omega\}$.

When combining *bbas* induced from not fully reliable information sources may lead to a non informative *bba*. It is important then to weaken the masses by the discounting operator also called *discount rate* $\alpha \in [0, 1]$. Accordingly $(1 - \alpha)$ is the degree of reliability of the source. Then the discounted *bba* m becomes:

$$\begin{cases} m^\alpha(A) = (1 - \alpha) \cdot m(A), & \forall A \subset \Omega, \\ m^\alpha(\Omega) = (1 - \alpha) \cdot m(\Omega) + \alpha. \end{cases} \tag{3}$$

3.2 Combination Rules

Let m_1 and m_2 two *bbas* representing two sources of information and having the same frame of discernment Ω. There are several combination rules proposed, each rule has its specificities and its characteristics.

One classical rule is the conjunctive rule of combination. Introduced by Smets [6], it combines data when sources are considered as distinct and reliable. It is noted $\ominus$ and defined as follows:

$$m_1 \ominus m_2(A) = \sum_{B \cap C = A} m_1(B) m_2(C) \tag{4}$$

The Dempster's rule of combination was proposed by [2]. It is equivalent to the conjunctive rule of combination but it does not support the existence of a mass on the empty set. It is denoted by $\oplus$ and defined as follows:

$$m_1 \oplus m_2(C) = \begin{cases} \dfrac{m_1 \bigcirc m_2(C)}{1 - m_1 \bigcirc m_2(\emptyset)} & \text{if } A \neq \emptyset, \forall C \subseteq \Omega \\ 0 & \text{otherwise.} \end{cases} \tag{5}$$

The Combination With Adapted Conflict (CWAC) rule was introduced in [5] proposing an adaptive weighting between the conjunctive and Dempster's rules denoted by $\ominus$.

This latter acts as the conjunctive combination when the belief functions are antonym (opposite), and as the Dempster rule when belief functions are similar and this adaptation is made possible with a measure of dissimilarity between all sources.

The notion of dissimilarity is obtained through a distance measure. The Jousselme distance [4] is one of the most used in the framework of belief functions. It is defined as follows:

$$d(m_1, m_2) = \sqrt{\frac{1}{2}(m_1 - m_2)^t \mathrm{D}(m_1 - m_2)}, \tag{6}$$

where D is the Jaccard index defined by:

$$\mathrm{D}(A, B) = \begin{cases} 0 & \text{if } A = B = \emptyset, \\ \dfrac{|A \cap B|}{|A \cup B|} & \forall A, B \in 2^\Omega. \end{cases} \tag{7}$$

The objective of this rule is to identify if at least one of the sources is in disagreement with the others. This synthesis can be obtained by taking, for example, the maximal value of all the distances. Accordingly, the value of D can be defined as:

$$D = max[d(m_i, m_j)], \tag{8}$$

with $i \in [1, N]$ and $j \in [1, N]$ and N is the total number of mass functions. The combination rule becomes then:

$$m_\ominus(A) = (\ominus m_i)(A) = Dm_\bigcirc(A) + (1 - D)m_\oplus(A) \tag{9}$$

3.3 Decision Process

The Transferable Belief Model (TBM) proposed by [11] is composed by the credal level where evidence is represented by *bbas* and combined and the pignistic level where *bbas* are transformed into pignistic probabilities denoted by *BetP* and defined as follows:

$$BetP(\{\omega_i\}) = \sum_{A \subseteq \Omega} \frac{|A \cap \omega_i|}{|A|} \cdot \frac{m(A)}{(1 - m(\emptyset))} \quad \forall \, \omega_i \in \Omega \tag{10}$$

4   GS-BLA: Belief Label Aggregation Based on Gold Standards

As an attempt to improve the workers expertise estimation due to the unreliability of the majority voting based method [8] in case of the existence of many bad labelers, we came up with the idea of integrating some a priori knowledge in order to make the expertise estimation more accurate. In this context, we introduce our belief label aggregation approach denoted by GS-BLA. We need to mention that to keep it simple and to be able to compare properly with other related work methods, we focused our work on binary labeling but our method can as well handle multi-class labeling.

4.1   Preliminraries

Consider a dataset of N questions that are labeled as either positive $(+1)$ or negative (-1). True label L_i of each question is unknown. There are M workers and the label of the jth worker for the ith question is l_{ij}, $l_{ij} \in \{-1,1\}$.

4.2   Gold Standards-Based Belief Label Aggregation

Our method is composed of five steps as follows:

The first step of our proposed approach is the workers' error rates estimation. Concretely, the error rate is calculated using a subset of n gold standards (i.e., tasks which we know already their answers) from the initial N tasks. These gold standards (GS) can be obtained by expert labeling. So, we compare gold standards labels with labelers' answers on these gold standards and the worker's error rate α_j is estimated as follows:

$$\alpha_j = \frac{Number\_of\_incorrect\_labels}{Number\_of\_gold\_standards} \tag{11}$$

Example 1. Let us consider the case of three distinct workers giving answers to four questions. We calculate their error rates α_j using (Eq. 11).

We suppose that question one and four are the gold standards and their relative ground truth (GT) are respectively (-1) and (1). We see that worker three gave wrong answers on the gold standards. Accordingly, $\alpha_3 = 2/2 = 1$. Results are reported in Table 1.

Table 1. Example of α_j estimation for three workers by GS

Worker (j)	Answer (l_{1j})	Answer (l_{2j})	Answer (l_{3j})	Answer (l_{4j})	α_j
1	−1	1	1	1	0
2	−1	−1	1	−1	0.5
3	1	1	−1	−1	1
GT	−1	X	X	1	X

In the second step, labels are represented under the belief function theory known for its capacity to model several kinds of imperfection. Thus, each label will be transformed into a bba m_{ij}^{Ω} with $\Omega = \{\omega_1, \ldots, \omega_n\}$.

In the case of binary labeling, the frame of discernment is $\Omega = \{-1, 1\}$.

Example 2. Let us consider Example 1 and transform the workers' labels to question 2 into $bbas$. Results are shown in Table 2.

Table 2. Example of label transformation

Worker (j)	Answer (l_{2j})	bba (m_{2j})
1	1	$m_{21}(\{1\}) = 1$
2	-1	$m_{22}(\{-1\}) = 1$
3	1	$m_{23}(\{1\}) = 1$

After modelling labels, workers' error rates are integrated. This third step consists in weakening each bba by the reliability degree $(1 - \alpha_j)$ of its corresponding worker using the discounting operation (Eq. 3) and thus $bbas$ are changed into simple support functions.

Example 3. We consider the bba m_{22} given by the second worker which discount rate is equal to 0.5. The discounting operation, will change the initial certain bba to a simple support function as follows:

$$m_{22}^{\alpha}(\{-1\}) = (1 - 0.5) \cdot 1 = 0.5,$$
$$m_{22}^{\alpha}(\{-1,1\}) = 0.5 + (1 - 0.5) \cdot 0 = 0.5$$

As for the fourth step, we apply the combination with adapted conflict (CWAC) rule to aggregate discounted labels of all workers (i.e. $\ominus m_i = m_{i1}^{\alpha}$ $\ominus m_{i2}^{\alpha} \ominus \ldots m_{ij}^{\alpha}$) as it deals well with conflictual data. In fact, in [12] CWAC turns up to be more accurate than the conjunctive and Dempster's rules in classifier fusion field.

The pignistic probability ($BetP$) (Eq. 10) is then applied in the fifth and final step, and the answer with the greater value is considered as the final decision.

Example 4. Supposing that once aggregating with the CWAC rule we obtain the following bba for the second question:

$$m_2(\emptyset) = 0.1, m_2(\{-1\}) = 0.9$$

Accordingly, we get the following pignistic probability:

$$\text{BetP}(\{-1\}) = 1 \cdot (0.9 \, / \, (1 - 0.1)) = 1,$$
$$\text{BetP}(\{1\}) = 0$$

Thus, the label (-1) is chosen as the final decision.

5 Experimentation and Results

In order to evaluate our Belief Label Aggregation method (GS-BLA) and demonstrate its efficiency at aggregating labelers' answers, we conducted experiments on both synthetic and real world datasets.

5.1 Experimental Protocol

Description of Datasets. In order to evaluate this approach and to be able to compare it with other methods, we require balanced datasets with complete data (i.e. where workers labeled all the questions). Therefore, we based our experiments on two datasets from the UCI repository and a real world dataset. These latter are described in what follows.

UCI Datasets. We selected from the UCI repository [16] the two following datasets:

- **IRIS:** restricted to 2 classes and composed of 100 instances (50 positive and 50 negative)
- **Mushroom:** has a total of 8124 instances (3916 positive and 4208 negative)

Bluebird dataset. This real world dataset is collected by [15] from the Amazon mechanical turk platform. In this dataset, 39 workers were given a task with 108 images containing two species of blue birds and were asked if each image presented at least one Indigo Bunting.

Evaluation Criteria. We evaluate our method according to the two following criteria:

- **Accuracy:** The main measure for evaluating aggregation methods is accuracy defined as the ratio of correctly labeled questions to total questions.
- **Robustness to bad labelers:** This evaluation is achieved by recording the accuracy while changing the ratio of bad labelers.

5.2 Experimental Results

Results on UCI Datasets. In this experiment, 20 labelers were simulated for every instance. We assume that bad labelers make more than 80%. We note that we randomly selected n instances to be our gold standards. In [10], ELICE set the number of gold standards for the IRIS dataset to 4 instances and for the mushroom dataset to 20 instances. We follow the same setup for the GS-BLA method in order to properly compare to ELICE.

This experiment aims to evaluate the method resistance to bad labelers so we increased their ratio from 0% to 100% to be able to see its influence on accuracy.

Figure 1 displaying results on the IRIS dataset, shows that GS-BLA keeps a constant variation of accuracy (an average of 98%) up to 80% bad labelers unlike the other methods. ELICE drops from 60% and records a better average accuracy than MV and BLA but GS-BLA still outperform them all. Figure 2 corresponding to the Mushroom dataset also shows the same observations and GS-BLA remains the best method. Table 3 presents for the two UCI datasets the average accuracies when we have more than 40% of bad labelers.

Table 3. Average accuracies of MV, ELICE, BLA and GS-BLA with more than 40% bad labelers

Dataset	MV	ELICE	BLA	GS-BLA
IRIS	0.14	0.6	0.2	0.74
Mushroom	0.2	0.65	0.3	0.8

Results on Bluebird Dataset. To test our method on a real world dataset, we considered the bluebird dataset [15]. In this experiment, we measured accuracy of each technique while increasing the number of workers per question.

We note that for ELICE and GS-BLA we limited the number of gold standards n to 8. In Fig. 3, accuracies (ratio of true estimated labels to total questions) as function of labelers number are illustrated. Labelers are sampled randomly 100 times to reduce the noise. Clearly, when the number of workers increases, our method GS-BLA achieves higher accuracies than the other approaches. Table 4 presents the average accuracies of the compared methods. It demonstrates that our method outperformed them all in estimation quality hitting the highest values with an average of 60%.

Table 4. Average accuracies of MV, ELICE, BLA and GS-BLA

Dataset	MV	ELICE	BLA	GS-BLA
Bluebird	0.54	0.53	0.56	0.6

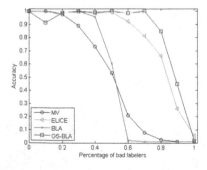

Fig. 1. Effects of bad labelers on accuracy (IRIS dataset)

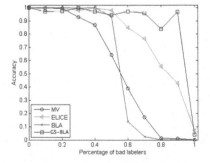

Fig. 2. Effects of bad labelers on accuracy (Mushroom dataset)

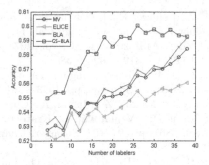

Fig. 3. Accuracies as function of the labelers' number for Bluebird

6 Conclusion and Future Works

Overall, we show that our method (GS-BLA) achieves highest accuracy and works strongly against bad labelers. As future works, we intend to improve the expertise level of workers. We can also consider other correction mechanisms besides the discounting operation such as the reinforcement operation to better manage the integration of workers' reliability.

References

1. Howe, J.: The rise of crowdsourcing. Wired Magaz. **14**(6), 1–4 (2006)
2. Dempster, A.P.: Upper and lower probabilities induced by a multivalued mapping. Annals Math. Stat. **38**, 325–339 (1967)
3. Shafer, G.: A Mathematical Theory of Evidence, vol. 1. Princeton University Press, Princeton (1976)
4. Jousselme, A.-L., Grenier, D., Bossé, É.: A new distance between two bodies of evidence. Inf. Fusion **2**, 91–101 (2001)
5. Lefèvre, E., Elouedi, Z.: How to preserve the confict as an alarm in the combination of belief functions? Decis. Support Syst. **56**, 326–333 (2013)
6. Smets, P.: The combination of evidence in the transferable belief model. IEEE Trans. Pattern Anal. Mach. Intell. **12**(5), 447–458 (1990)
7. Lee, K., Caverlee, J., Webb, S.: The social honeypot project: protecting online communities from spammers. In: International World Wide Web Conference, pp. 1139–1140 (2010)
8. Abassi, L., Boukhris, I.: Crowd label aggregation under a belief function framework. In: Lehner, F., Fteimi, N. (eds.) KSEM 2016. LNCS, vol. 9983, pp. 185–196. Springer, Cham (2016). doi:10.1007/978-3-319-47650-6_15
9. Dawid, A.P., Skene, A.M.: Maximum likelihood estimation of observer error-rates using the EM algorithm. Appl. Stat. **28**, 20–28 (2010)
10. Khattak, F.K., Salleb, A.: Quality control of crowd labeling through expert evaluation. In: The Neural Information Processing Systems 2nd Workshop on Computational Social Science and the Wisdom of Crowds, pp. 27–29 (2011)
11. Smets, P., Mamdani, A., Dubois, D., Prade, H.: Non Standard Logics for Automated Reasoning, pp. 253–286. Academic Press, London (1988)

12. Trabelsi, A., Elouedi, Z., Lefèvre, E.: Belief function combination: comparative study within the classifier fusion framework. In: Gaber, T., Hassanien, A.E., El-Bendary, N., Dey, N. (eds.) AISI 2015. AISC, vol. 407, pp. 425–435. Springer, Cham (2016). doi:10.1007/978-3-319-26690-9_38
13. Karger, D., Oh, S., Shah, D.: Iterative learning for reliable crowdsourcing systems. In: Neural Information Processing Systems, pp. 1953–1961 (2011)
14. Ben Rjab, A., Kharoune, M., Miklos, Z., Martin, A.: Characterization of experts in crowdsourcing platforms. In: Vejnarová, J., Kratochvíl, V. (eds.) BELIEF 2016. LNCS (LNAI), vol. 9861, pp. 97–104. Springer, Cham (2016). doi:10.1007/978-3-319-45559-4_10
15. Welinder, P., Branson, S., Perona, P., Belongie, S.: The multidimensional wisdom of crowds. In: Neural Information Processing Systems, pp. 2424–2432 (2010)
16. Frank, A.: UCI machine learning repository (1987). http://archive.ics.uci.edu/ml
17. Whitehill, J., Wu, T., Bergsma, J., Movellan, R.J., Ruvolo, P.L.: Whose vote should count more: optimal integration of labels from labelers of unknown expertise. In: Neural Information Processing Systems, pp. 2035–2043 (2009)

Experimental Evaluation of the Understanding of Qualitative Probability and Probabilistic Reasoning in Young Children

Jean Baratgin[1], Giulianella Coletti[2], Frank Jamet[3], and Davide Petturiti[4(⊠)]

[1] CHArt (Univesité Paris 8 & EPHE) & IJN (École Normale Supérieure),
Paris, France
jean.baratgin@univ-paris8.fr

[2] Dip. Matematica e Informatica, Università degli Studi di Perugia, Perugia, Italy
giulianella.coletti@unipg.it

[3] CHArt (Univesité Paris 8 & EPHE) & Université de Cergy-Pontoise, Paris, France
frank.jamet@u-cergy.fr

[4] Dip. Economia, Università degli Studi di Perugia, Perugia, Italy
davide.petturiti@unipg.it

Abstract. De Finetti's approach of an event of two levels of knowledge was recently proposed as the model of reference for psychology studies. We show that de Finetti's qualitative probability framework seems to be "natural" to children aged from 3 to 4 as well as to account for children's heuristic approach to probabilistic reasoning.

Keywords: Experimental evaluation · Young children · Comparative degree of belief · Qualitative probability · Probabilistic reasoning

1 Introduction

In the last years, the study of psychology of reasoning has been overthrown by replacing the model of reference of formal logic with the Bayesian model (seen as a probabilistic logic) for coping with deductive inferences under uncertainty (supposed to be applicable to real life). Inside the literature concerning this "new paradigm" for the psychology of reasoning, a convergence toward a common accepted standard Bayesian approach is still lacking (see, e.g., [1]).

In this paper we maintain that the subjective interpretation theorized by de Finetti [8] is the most appropriate model to be considered as a reference in psychological reasoning. First of all, this theory naturally encodes the same objective of the "new paradigm" of reasoning, that is to represent and manage the subjective probability evaluations of individuals [2,3]. Furthermore, it has a

D. Petturiti—Partially supported by the INdAM-GNAMPA Project 2016 U2016/000391, the Italian Ministry of Health grant J52I14001640001, and the trilateral DFG-FMSH-Villa Vigoni Project "Human Rationality: Probabilistic Points of View".

S. Benferhat et al. (Eds.): IEA/AIE 2017, Part II, LNAI 10351, pp. 107–112, 2017.
DOI: 10.1007/978-3-319-60045-1_13

"radically subjective" spirit in the sense that all probability evaluations express a degree of belief (referring to the particular state of knowledge of each individual).

In de Finetti's approach, the probability of an event E can be directly "measured" through the well-known *betting scheme*, i.e., by asking the subject to quantify his degree of belief in a hypothetical coherent bet. Then the notion of *coherence* extended to any combination of bets avoids inconsistencies.

De Finetti's theory has the advantage of offering a complete and robust conceptual-methodological framework, particularly suitable for experimental studies. But what is usually not highlighted is that introducing probability through coherence frees the subject from assessing probability also on events which are irrelevant for him. Nevertheless, sometimes a subject can be unable to attach of numbers to a family of events but he can be only able to provide comparisons expressing the idea of "no more believable than", i.e., a *comparative degree of belief*. De Finetti in [7] proposed the minimal system of (purely qualitative) conditions for a comparative degree of belief to be a *comparative probability* relation. Such conditions are necessary for the existence of an agreeing numerical probability and are sufficient when the elementary events are at most 4 [10]. For larger sets of events the necessary and sufficient condition [4,11] involves indicators of events and so is not purely qualitative.

Our aim is to find a correspondence between de Finetti's theory and the "new paradigm" of reasoning (see [3,12]) by verifying if the intermediate epistemic level of knowledge consisting of comparative probability judgements is actually the primary way in which reasoning is faced by human beings. To see this we focus on pre-school children not disposing of complex quantitative skills (such as, awareness of computation and worth). The experiment is designed to test purely qualitative probabilistic conditions involving 4 elementary events. In the literature only few studies have been addressed in this direction (see [9]).

2   Qualitative Probability and Coherence

Let $\precsim$ be a binary relation on an arbitrary set of events $\mathcal{F} = \{E_i\}_{i \in I}$ expressing the intuitive idea of being "no more believable than". The symbols $\sim$ and $\prec$ represent, respectively, the symmetric and asymmetric parts of $\precsim$. The relation $\precsim$ expresses a qualitative judgement and, as such, we have to set up a system of rules assuring the consistency of the relation with some numerical model.

We recall that a real function φ defined on $\mathcal{F}$ *represents* (or *agrees* with) the relation $\precsim$ if and only if, for every $E, F \in \mathcal{F}$, we have

$$E \precsim F \Longrightarrow \varphi(E) \leq \varphi(F) \quad \text{and} \quad E \prec F \Longrightarrow \varphi(E) < \varphi(F).$$

If we focus on the relations representable (or induced) by a *capacity* (i.e., a function φ monotone with respect to implication $\subseteq$), it is necessary that there exists a weak order extending $\precsim$ on the algebra $\mathcal{B}$ spanned by $\mathcal{F}$ such that:

(c1) $\emptyset \precsim E$ for every $E \in \mathcal{B}$, and $\emptyset \prec \Omega$;
(c2) for every $E, F \in \mathcal{B}$, $E \subseteq F \Longrightarrow E \precsim F$.

In the following we call *comparative degree of belief* a binary relation on an arbitrary set of events $\mathcal{F}$, which admits an extension on $\mathcal{B}$ satisfying (c1)–(c2).

When we specialize the numerical function φ (probability, belief function, lower probability, and so on) agreeing with a relation $\precsim$, then we need to require that there exists an extension of $\precsim$ satisfying a further characteristic condition, proper of the numerical framework of reference.

The most known among these conditions is the *qualitative additivity* axiom (introduced by de Finetti [7] and Koopman [11]), for defining a *qualitative (or comparative) probability*, that reveals to be necessary for the representability of $\precsim$ by a probability:

(p) For every $E, F, H \in \mathcal{B}$, with $(E \vee F) \wedge H = \emptyset$, it must be

$$E \precsim F \Longrightarrow E \vee H \precsim F \vee H \quad \text{and} \quad E \prec F \Longrightarrow E \vee H \prec F \vee H.$$

Notice that, since $\precsim$ is complete on $\mathcal{B}$, then condition (p) can be expressed as $E \prec F \Longleftrightarrow E \vee H \prec F \vee H$. Actually axiom (p) characterizes those comparative degrees of belief representable by a weakly $\oplus$-decomposable measure, with $\oplus$ a suitable strictly increasing binary operation (see [5]).

We recall that, given a function $\varphi : \mathcal{B} \to [0, 1]$ and a commutative binary operation $\oplus$ on $\varphi(\mathcal{B})$ having $\varphi(\emptyset)$ as neutral element, φ is a *weakly $\oplus$-decomposable measure* if the restriction of $\oplus$ to the set $\Gamma = \{(\varphi(A), \varphi(B)) : A, B \in \mathcal{B}, A \wedge B = \emptyset\}$ is associative and increasing, and moreover one has $\varphi(A \vee B) = \varphi(A) \oplus \varphi(B)$.

We recall also that a commutative, associative and increasing operation $\oplus$ on Γ satisfying the equation above is not necessarily extendible to an operation with the same properties on the whole $[0, 1]^2$.

Working with an arbitrary finite set of events $\mathcal{F}$, we can represent a comparative degree of belief $\precsim$ on $\mathcal{F}$ with a coherent probability on $\mathcal{F}$ if and only if $\precsim$ satisfies the following condition (cp) [4], which is the comparative version of de Finetti's numerical coherence condition and is equivalent to those given in [10, 13] if $\mathcal{F}$ is an algebra. Nevertheless, (cp) is not a "pure" qualitative condition, since it does not directly refer to events E_i's but to their truth values $|E_i|$'s and to gambles involving money payoffs:

(cp) For every $n \in \mathbb{N}$ and $A_i, B_i \in \mathcal{F}$ with $A_i \precsim B_i$ (at least a strict comparison) and $\lambda_i > 0$, it must be $\sup \sum_{i=1}^{n} \lambda_i(|B_i| - |A_i|) > 0$.

Condition (cp) is immediately interpretable in terms of bets: if You think $A_i \precsim B_i$, $i = 1, \ldots, n$, with at least a strict degree of belief, then in a combination of bets where You gain λ_i when B_i occurs and You pay λ_i when A_i occurs, You must have a positive global gain in at least a case (i.e., in at least an elementary event generated by the A_i's and B_i's).

3   The Experiment

In the following we provide a short summary of the experimental setting.

Population: We considered 54 children (28 girls and 26 boys) ranging from 3.11 to 4.09 years old. The sample has been reduced of 4 children due to language troubles. All the children were French speaking, schoolarized since 2 years old and coming from middle class families. The experiment was carried on in two pre-schools in the est of the Ile-de-France region.

Material for the experiment: The experiment is carried on individually on a table where the child finds: *(1)* two identical sets of 4 toy cars (6.5 cm × 2.5 cm × 1.8 cm) of different models and colors (red, blue, orange and green); *(2)* two sheets of white paper (A4 format) reporting each a 4-place grid, one of them marked A, B, C, D. The latter is the arrival grid, while the other is the departure grid.

The children are individually examined in an isolated room sitting at a table in front of the experimenter. The experimentation consists of two preliminary activities, followed by the test of qualitative probability axioms. In the first preliminary activity the experimenter submits to the children two glass tubes containing two immiscible liquids, one is transparent ("water") and the other is scarlet red ("orange juice") with ratios 20%:80% and 40%:60%, respectively. The children is asked to indicate which tube assures a "higher chance" to have juice and which assures a "higher chance" to have water. In the second preliminary task, an analogous trial is carried on by means of two glass jars containing toy cars and candies with ratios 5:2 and 2:5, respectively. Both preliminary tasks and both questions in each of them are counter-balanced in between different children and serve for testing the understanding of the "more probable than" concept.

The experiment on qualitative probability axioms is carried on in 3 steps:

Step 1: The experimenter submits to the children the two sheets of paper together with the two identical sets of toy cars. The experimenter shows one of the two sets of toy cars and says that they are engaging in a race, so, the children is asked to position them on the departure grid.

Step 2: Referring to the second set of cars, the children is said that is not going to assist to the race. The experimenter asks which car "has more chance" to win the race and the children has to place the chosen car in position A on the arrival grid. The procedure is repeated iteratively on the remaining set of cars in a way to fill the other positions B, C, D.

Step 3: The arrival positions A, B, C, D of the previous step are used as elementary events. The experimenter proceeds in testing the chosen qualitative probability axioms on events built using A, B, C, D. In each tested axiom the child is asked to indicate a car with his finger providing, therefore, non-verbal answers that are recorded.

In the experiment we test a set of axioms descending from **(cp1)–(cp2)** and **(p)**. We mainly focus on the strict relation $\prec$ and, in particular, on its dual relation $\succ$ expressing the judgement "more probable than". Such relation appears easier to understand to young children and does not present possible linguistic drawbacks. The experiment is designed in order to avoid comparisons involving $\sim$. Table 1 reports the list of tested axioms, where E, F, H, K are distinct events. Let us stress

Table 1. Tested qualitative probability axioms

(P1): Strict comparability	$E \succ F$ or $F \succ E$
(P2): Extreme events	$E \succ \emptyset$
(P2'): Extreme events'	$\Omega \succ E$
(P2"): Extreme events"	$\Omega \succ \emptyset$
(P3): Transitivity	$[E \succ F$ and $F \succ H] \Longrightarrow E \succ H$
(P4): Additivity	$[(E \vee F) \wedge H = \emptyset$ and $E \succ F] \Longleftrightarrow E \vee H \succ F \vee H$
(P4'): Additivity'	$[E \wedge F = \emptyset$ and $H \wedge K = \emptyset$ and $E \succ F$ and $H \succ K]$ $\Longrightarrow E \vee H \succ F \vee K$
(P5): Qualitative Bayes	$[E \subseteq H$ and $F \subseteq H$ and $E \succ F] \Longrightarrow E|H \succ F|H$
(P6): Strict monotonicity	$E \subset F \Longrightarrow F \succ E$
(P7): Negation	$E \succ F \Longrightarrow F^c \succ E^c$

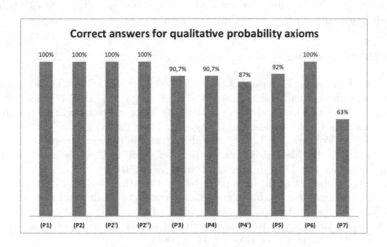

Fig. 1. Experimental results

that axioms **(P1)**–**(P7)** are more restrictive than **(cp1)**–**(cp2)** and **(p)**: if $\succ$ on an algebra $\mathcal{B}$ with at most 4 atoms satisfies them, then we can always find a numerical probability everywhere positive on $\mathcal{B} \setminus \{\emptyset\}$, representing $\succ$. We limit to the case of 4 elementary events for both cognitive manageability and mathematical correspondence between the qualitative and numerical probability models.

Figure 1 shows the inter-individual percentages of correct answers for the tested qualitative probability axioms. It is easily seen that axioms **(P1)** concerning strict comparability, axioms **(P2)**–**(P2")** concerning extreme events, and axiom **(P6)** concerning strict monotonicity, are respected by all children in the sample. Also axiom **(P3)** concerning transitivity, axioms **(P4)**–**(P4')** concerning additivity, and axioms **(P5)** concerning qualitative Bayes, are respected by almost 90% of children. Only axiom **(P7)** concerning negation shows quite distant results that we impute to linguistic issues related to negations. The intra-individual analysis shows that axioms **(P1)**–**(P7)** are completely respected by

24/54 of children, 7/54 violate only 1 axiom ((**P3**) or (**P4**) or (**P7**)), 17/54 violate only 2 axioms, and the remaining 6/54 violate more than 3 axioms.

4   Conclusions and Perspective

As discussed in Sect. 3, condition (**p**) is necessary but not sufficient for the representability of a comparative degree of belief by a probability when the considered events are more than 2^4. On the other hand, limiting the experiments to 4 elementary events appears very restrictive. Actually axiom (**p**) is sufficient (but not necessary) for the representability by both a belief function and a plausibility function (usually not dual). This suggests that the Dempster-Shafer framework could be more suitable: weaker qualitative additivity axioms have been introduced in literature [6,14], characterizing relations representable by a belief or a plausibility function. We plan to extend the experimental study to these axioms since they are purely qualitative and assure a numerical representation in the corresponding framework, for any finite number of elementary events.

References

1. Baratgin J., Douven I., Evans, J.St.B.T., Oaksford, M., Over, D., Polytzer, G.: The new paradigm and mental models. Trends Cogn. Sci. **19**, 547–548 (2015)
2. Baratgin, J., Over, D.E., Politzer, G.: New psychological paradigm for conditionals and general de Finetti tables. Ind. Lang. **29**, 73–84 (2014)
3. Baratgin, J., Politzer, G.: Logic, probability and inference: a methodology for a new paradigm. In: Macchi, L., et al. (eds.) Cognitive Unconscious and Human Rationality, pp. 119–142. MIT Press, Cambridge (2016)
4. Coletti, G.: Coherent qualitative probability. J. Math. Psych. **34**, 297–310 (1990)
5. Coletti, G., Scozzafava, R.: From conditional events to conditional measures: a new axiomatic approach. Ann. Math. Artif. Intell. **32**, 373–392 (2001)
6. Coletti, G., Vantaggi, B.: Representability of ordinal relations on a set of conditional events. Theory Decis. **60**, 137–174 (2006)
7. de Finetti, B.: Sul significato soggettivo della probabilità. Fund. Mat. **17**, 293–329 (1931)
8. de Finetti, B.: Foresight: its logical laws, its subjective sources (1937). Translated in Kyburg, H.E., Smokler, H.E. (eds.) Studies in Subjective Probability, pp. 55–118. Wiley (1964)
9. Huber, B.L., Huber, O.: Development of the concept of comparative subjective probability. J. Exp. Child Psych. **44**, 304–316 (1987)
10. Kraft, C.H., Pratt, J.W., Seidenberg, A.: Intuitive probability on finite sets. Ann. Math. Stat. **30**, 408–419 (1959)
11. Koopman, B.O.: The axioms and algebra of intuitive probability. Ann. Math. **41**, 269–292 (1940)
12. Over, D.E., Baratgin, J.: The 'defective' truth table: its past, present, and future. In: Lucas, E., et al. (eds.) The Thinking Mind: The use of Thinking in Everyday Life. Psychology Press, Alberton (2016)
13. Scott, D.: Measurement structures and linear inequalities. J. Math. Psych. **1**, 233–247 (1964)
14. Wong, S.K.M., Yao, Y.Y., Bollmann, P., Burger, H.C.: Axiomatization of qualitative belief structure. IEEE Trans. Sys. Man Cyb. **21**, 726–734 (1991)

A Set-Valued Approach to Multiple Source Evidence

Didier Dubois[1(✉)] and Henri Prade[1,2]

[1] IRIT, CNRS and University of Toulouse, Toulouse, France
{dubois,prade}@irit.fr
[2] QCIS, University of Technology Sydney, Sydney, Australia

Abstract. This short note studies a multiple source extension of categorical mass functions in the sense of Shafer's evidence theory. Each subset of possible worlds is associated with a subset of information sources and represents a tentative description of what is known. Analogs of belief, plausibility, commonality functions, valued in terms of subsets of agents or sources, are defined, replacing summation by set union. Set-valued plausibility is nothing but set-valued possibility because it is union-decomposable with respect to the union of events. In a special case where each source refers to a single information item, set-valued belief functions decompose with respect to intersection and are thus multiple source necessity-like function. Connections with Belnap epistemic truth-values for handling multiple source inconsistent information are shown. A formal counterpart of Dempster rule of combination is defined and discussed as to its merits for information fusion.

1 Introduction

Qualitative settings (e.g., [4,6]) often refer to approaches where maximum and minimum operations replace sum-product structures. But other kinds of qualitative frameworks exist, in particular where set functions become set-valued rather than being numerical or taking their values on an ordinal scale. An example of such a set-valued counterpart is given in possibility theory by the semantical counterpart of multiple agent logic [2].

In this short paper, we study a set-valued framework that seems to mimic Shafer's evidence theory [7]. We first introduce a multiple source extension of a categorical basic assignment and its intended meaning, from which set-valued belief, plausibility, commonality functions are defined. Actually, these set-valued functions are quite close to the ones of set-valued possibility theory. Then the interest of this setting in information fusion is advocated, and a counterpart of Dempster rule of combination can be defined. Lastly, directions for further research are briefly mentioned.

2 An Evidential Set-Valued Framework

In Shafer's evidence theory, information is represented by a mass function m, originally called 'basic probability assignment', from the power set of a frame of

© Springer International Publishing AG 2017
S. Benferhat et al. (Eds.): IEA/AIE 2017, Part II, LNAI 10351, pp. 113–118, 2017.
DOI: 10.1007/978-3-319-60045-1_14

discernment Ω to the unit interval. Then the mass function is supposed to be such that $\forall A \subseteq \Omega, m(A) \geq 0$ and $\sum_{A \subseteq \Omega} m(A) = 1$ [7].

Set-Valued Mass Function. In the set-valued counterpart we propose here, we start with a set of sources of information (that could be agents) named ALL. In the most elementary setting, each source a proposes a certain view of the real world in the form of a non-empty set $\Gamma(a) = E$ of Ω. Then, the analog of a basic assignment function associates to each set $E \in 2^{\Omega}$ the subset of sources $\mathcal{M}(E) \subseteq$ ALL such that $\Gamma(a) = E$. As usual, the *focal sets* E are non-empty subsets of Ω, such that $\mathcal{M}(E) \neq \emptyset$, forming a collection $\mathcal{F}$. Total ignorance is represented by $\mathcal{M}(\Omega) =$ ALL *and* $\forall E \neq \Omega, \mathcal{M}(E) = \emptyset$, i.e., no source provide information. We assume no inconsistent source, i.e. $\mathcal{M}(\emptyset) = \emptyset$. Since each source in ALL is supposed provide some information, we should have

$$\bigcup_{E \in \mathcal{F}} \mathcal{M}(E) = \text{ALL}$$

This understanding supposes that the piece of information provided by each source is precisely known. Namely,

$$\forall E_1, E_2 \in \mathcal{F}, \text{ if } E_1 \neq E_2 \text{ then } \mathcal{M}(E_1) \cap \mathcal{M}(E_2) = \emptyset \qquad (*)$$

This assumption is not compulsory for the definitions given in the following. In fact, we may extend the setting by assigning to each source a a collection $\tilde{\Gamma}(a)$ of subsets of Ω. Intuitively, it means that the receiver is unsure about what message the source conveys. In this case $\mathcal{M}(E)$ is the set of sources that *possibly* forward information item E (i.e., $\mathcal{M}(E) = \{a : E \in \tilde{\Gamma}(a)\}$). In that case, it is a higher-order model of information source, more similar to a usual mass function. Conversely, $\tilde{\Gamma}(a) = \{E : a \in \mathcal{M}(E)\}$.

Moreover, it is worth mentioning that, provided that condition $(*)$ holds, a regular probability assignment m can be associated in a natural way with a set-valued basic assignment by replacing the subset of sources by their cardinality, namely $m_{\mathcal{M}}(A) = \frac{|\mathcal{M}(A)|}{|\text{ALL}|}$ since then $\sum_A m_{\mathcal{M}}(A) = 1$.

The Four Set-Valued Set Functions. The multiple source counterpart of a numerical belief function $Bel(A) = \sum_{\emptyset \neq B \subseteq A} m(B)$ is $\mathcal{BEL}(A)$, the set of all sources that support A according to the information they convey:

$$\mathcal{BEL}(A) = \bigcup_{E \text{ s.t. } \emptyset \neq E \subseteq A} \mathcal{M}(E)$$

The idea of attaching to propositions sets of sources that support them was already discussed in [1]. Note that $\mathcal{BEL}$ will not change if one adds in $\tilde{\Gamma}(a)$ a set E' containing some set $E \in \tilde{\Gamma}(a)$. So we can modify $\mathcal{M}(E)$ by restricting, for each agent $a \in All$ to minimal subsets for inclusion in $\tilde{\Gamma}(a)$, which leaves $\mathcal{BEL}(A)$ unchanged.

The counterpart $\mathcal{PL}(A)$ of plausibility is the set of sources providing information not inconsistent with A. Namely, we have (without assuming $\mathcal{M}(\emptyset) = \emptyset$):

$$\mathcal{PL}(A) = \bigcup_{E \cap A \neq \emptyset} \mathcal{M}(E).$$

The subset of sources that find A plausible includes the subset of sources that are certain about A, i.e., $\mathcal{PL}(A) \supseteq \mathcal{BEL}(A)$. $\mathcal{PL}(A)$ does not exhibit the usual duality with respect to $\mathcal{BEL}$, that is, $\mathcal{PL}(A) \neq \text{ALL}\backslash(\mathcal{BEL}(\overline{A}) \cup \mathcal{M}(\emptyset))$ where $\overline{A} = \Omega \backslash A$, except if condition $(*)$ holds. Indeed, if $E_1 \neq E_2 \in \tilde{\Gamma}(a)$, then there is an event A such that $a \in \mathcal{PL}(A) \cap \mathcal{BEL}(\overline{A})$ (e.g. $E_2 \cap A \neq \emptyset$, while $E_1 \subseteq \overline{A}$). These set-valued set-functions are monotonic in the sense that if $A \subseteq B$, then $\mathcal{BEL}(A) \subseteq \mathcal{BEL}(B)$ and $\mathcal{PL}(A) \subseteq \mathcal{PL}(B)$.

The counterpart of commonality $Q(A) = \sum_{E \supseteq A} m(E)$ is the set of sources whose information is possibly not more specific than A:

$$\mathcal{Q}(A) = \bigcup_{E \supseteq A} \mathcal{M}(E).$$

If $\mathcal{M}(\Omega) = \emptyset$, letting $\overline{\mathcal{M}}(E) = \mathcal{M}(\overline{E})$, we can see that $\mathcal{Q}_{\mathcal{M}}(A) = \mathcal{BEL}_{\overline{\mathcal{M}}}(\overline{A})$. The dual is $\tilde{\mathcal{O}}(A) = \bigcup_{E \cup A \neq \Omega} \mathcal{M}(E)$, generally not equal to $\text{ALL}\backslash\mathcal{Q}(\overline{A})$, except if condition $(*)$ holds. $\mathcal{Q}$ and $\tilde{\mathcal{O}}$ are anti-monotonic with respect to set inclusion.

Non Unicity of the Function $\mathcal{M}$ in the General Case. Let $\Omega = \{\omega_1, \omega_2, \omega_3\}$, $\text{ALL} = \{a, b\}$. The table below shows four functions $\mathcal{M}_0$, $\mathcal{M}_1$, $\mathcal{M}_2$ and $\mathcal{M}_3$, the associated belief functions of the first three $\mathcal{BEL}_0$, $\mathcal{BEL}_1$ and $\mathcal{BEL}_2$ being equal.

	$\{\omega_1\}$	$\{\omega_2\}$	$\{\omega_3\}$	$\{\omega_1,\omega_2\}$	$\{\omega_1,\omega_3\}$	$\{\omega_2,\omega_3\}$	$\{\omega_1,\omega_2,\omega_3\}$
$\mathcal{M}_0$	$\{a\}$	$\emptyset$	$\{b\}$	$\emptyset$	$\emptyset$	$\emptyset$	$\emptyset$
$\mathcal{M}_1$	$\{a\}$	$\emptyset$	$\{b\}$	$\emptyset$	$\emptyset$	$\emptyset$	$\{a,b\}$
$\mathcal{M}_2$	$\{a\}$	$\emptyset$	$\{b\}$	$\{a\}$	$\{b\}$	$\{b\}$	$\emptyset$
$\mathcal{M}_3$	$\emptyset$	$\emptyset$	$\emptyset$	$\emptyset$	$\emptyset$	$\emptyset$	$\{a,b\}$
$\mathcal{BEL}_0 = \mathcal{BEL}_1 = \mathcal{BEL}_2$	$\{a\}$	$\emptyset$	$\{b\}$	$\{a\}$	$\{a,b\}$	$\{b\}$	$\{a,b\}$
$\mathcal{BEL}_3$	$\emptyset$	$\emptyset$	$\emptyset$	$\emptyset$	$\emptyset$	$\emptyset$	$\{a,b\}$
$\mathcal{PL}_0$	$\{a\}$	$\emptyset$	$\{b\}$	$\{a\}$	$\{a,b\}$	$\{b\}$	$\{a,b\}$
$\mathcal{PL}_1 = \mathcal{PL}_3$	$\{a,b\}$	$\{a,b\}$	$\{a,b\}$	$\{a,b\}$	$\{a,b\}$	$\{a,b\}$	$\{a,b\}$
$\mathcal{PL}_2$	$\{a,b\}$	$\{a,b\}$	$\{b\}$	$\{a,b\}$	$\{a,b\}$	$\{a,b\}$	$\{a,b\}$

$\mathcal{M}_0$ describes the case when each source a and b supply precise information. But $\mathcal{M}_1$ and $\mathcal{M}_2$ violate condition $(*)$ on mass functions. According to $\mathcal{M}_1$, information provided by sources is either precise or vacuous, while for $\mathcal{M}_2$, the receiver has a much more blurred view of source information. It is not always possible to recover $\mathcal{M}$ from $\mathcal{BEL}$ if some focal sets are nested as for $\mathcal{M}_1$ and $\mathcal{M}_2$ that yield the same $\mathcal{BEL}$. But note that plausibility functions differ. Actually given a basic assignment $\mathcal{M}$ and the belief function $\mathcal{BEL}$, then the same belief function is obtained by restricting each set $\Gamma(a)$ to its minimal elements for inclusion. When, $\forall a \in All$, no two focal sets in $\tilde{\Gamma}(a)$ are nested (in particular if condition $(*)$ holds), it can be shown that $\mathcal{M}(E) = \mathcal{BEL}(E)$ if $\mathcal{BEL}(E) \neq \emptyset$ and $\mathcal{BEL}(E\backslash\{\omega\}) = \emptyset, \forall \omega \in E$. This is like focal sets of qualitative capacities [4].

Link with Belnap Epistemic Truth-Values. Belnap logic [3] deals with a set of conflicting sources and assigns to any atomic proposition B an epistemic truth-value in $\{\mathbf{T}, \mathbf{F}, \mathbf{U}, \mathbf{C}\}$, where $\mathbf{T}$ means that B is supported by one source and negated by none, $\mathbf{F}$ means that B is negated by one source and supported by none, $\mathbf{U}$ means that B receives no support, and $\mathbf{C}$ means that B and its negation receive support from some source. It is clear that these assignments can be generalised to any proposition B in terms of set-valued belief functions: $\mathbf{T}$ if $\mathcal{BEL}(B) \neq \emptyset$ and $\mathcal{BEL}(\overline{B}) = \emptyset$, $\mathbf{F}$ if $\mathcal{BEL}(B) = \emptyset$ and $\mathcal{BEL}(\overline{B}) \neq \emptyset$, $\mathbf{U}$ if $\mathcal{BEL}(B) = \mathcal{BEL}(\overline{B}) = \emptyset$, $\mathbf{C}$ if $\mathcal{BEL}(B) \neq \emptyset$ and $\mathcal{BEL}(\overline{B}) \neq \emptyset$.

Behavior with Respect to Combinations of Events. It is worth noticing that if condition (∗) holds,

$$\mathcal{BEL}(A \cap B) = \mathcal{BEL}(A) \cap \mathcal{BEL}(B) \tag{1}$$

Indeed, $\forall a \in All$, $a \in \mathcal{BEL}(A \cap B)$ if and only if $\Gamma(a) \subseteq A \cap B$ if and only if $a \in \mathcal{BEL}(A) \cap \mathcal{BEL}(B)$. However, in general (if some agent is associated to several focal subsets), this equality does not hold, and we only have inclusion due to monotonicity. This is very similar to the graded qualitative capacity setting [4,6] where the union in $\mathcal{BEL}$ is replaced by the max, and only $Bel_q(A \cap B) \leq \min(Bel_q(A), Bel_q(B))$ holds in general, since the maximum over focal sets in $A \cap B$ may be smaller than the minimum of the maxima over A and over B.

A situation when (1) holds without satisfying condition (∗) is when the focal sets are *singletons*. It means that information provided by sources is precise, but each source can propose several information items. Then, $\forall A, \mathcal{BEL}(A) = \mathcal{PL}(A) = \bigcup_{\omega \in A} \mathcal{M}(\{\omega\})$. If, on top, condition (∗) holds, we are in a probabilistic-like situation (one Dirac function per agent), and the numerical mass function $m_{\mathcal{M}}$ induced by counting the proportion of sources supporting a focal set is a probability distribution.

In contrast with (1), we always have

$$\mathcal{PL}(A \cup B) = \mathcal{PL}(A) \cup \mathcal{PL}(B).$$

In particular, $\forall a \in All$, $a \in \mathcal{PL}(A \cup B)$ if and only if $\exists E \in \tilde{\Gamma}(a), E \cap (A \cup B) \neq \emptyset$ if and only if $E \cap A \neq \emptyset$ or $E \cap B \neq \emptyset$, if and only if $a \in \mathcal{PL}(A)$ or $a \in \mathcal{PL}(B)$. Then, $\mathcal{PL}$ can be directly expressed from a set-valued distribution $\pi_{\mathcal{F}}$, from Ω to 2^{ALL}, namely the contour function $\pi_{\mathcal{F}}(\omega) = \mathcal{PL}(\{\omega\}) = \bigcup_{E \ni \omega} \mathcal{M}(E)$ as

$$\mathcal{PL}(A) = \bigcup_{E \cap A \neq \emptyset} \mathcal{M}(E) = \bigcup_{\omega \in A} \pi_{\mathcal{F}}(\omega)$$

where $\pi_{\mathcal{F}}(\omega) = \{a : \exists E, \omega \in E \in \tilde{\Gamma}(a)\}$. Thus, $\mathcal{PL}$ being $\cup$-decomposable is nothing but a set-valued possibility measure $\mathbf{\Pi}$. Its dual is $\mathbf{N}(A) = \overline{\mathcal{PL}(\overline{A})}$ is a multiple-agent necessity measure that satisfies $\cap$-decomposability (1), hence generally different from $\mathcal{BEL}$. Function $\mathbf{N}$ is thus induced by a mass function $\mathcal{M}_{\mathcal{PL}}$ obeying condition (∗), and associated to a set-valued mapping $\Gamma_{\mathcal{PL}}$ such that $\Gamma_{\mathcal{PL}}(a) = \bigcup\{E \in \tilde{\Gamma}(a)\}$ (see mass function $\mathcal{M}_3$ in the previous table). It can be checked that $\omega \in \Gamma_{\mathcal{PL}}(a)$ if and only if $a \in \pi_{\mathcal{F}}(\omega)$. In other words, each agent a has epistemic state $\Gamma_{\mathcal{PL}}(a)$. This is the setting of multiple agent logic [2] briefly recalled below.

In this logic, constraints of the form $\mathbf{N}(A) \supseteq \mathcal{S}$ where $\mathcal{S} \subseteq \text{ALL}$ express that according to at least all sources in $\mathcal{S}$ the true state of the world is in A. Clearly, $\mathbf{N}(A) \supseteq \mathcal{S}$ is the semantical counterpart of a possibilistic logic-like formula $(A, \mathcal{S})$. This formula is associated with the multiple agent ma-distribution:

$$\forall \omega \in \Omega, \pi_{\{(A,\mathcal{S})\}}(\omega) = \begin{cases} \text{ALL} & \text{if } \omega \in A \\ \overline{\mathcal{S}} & \text{if } \omega \in \overline{A}. \end{cases}$$

Indeed the complement of $\mathcal{S}$ is the maximal subset of sources that may find possible that the real world be outside A (since for all sources in $\mathcal{S}$ the true state of the world is in A). More generally, the ma-distribution π_Γ semantically associated to a set of ma-formulas $\mathcal{K} = \{(A_i, \mathcal{S}_i), i = 1, m\}$ is given by

$$\pi_{\mathcal{K}}(\omega) = \begin{cases} \text{ALL} & \text{if } \forall(A_i, \mathcal{S}_i) \in \Gamma, \omega \in A_i \\ \bigcap\{\overline{\mathcal{S}_i} : (A_i, \mathcal{S}_i) \in \Gamma, \omega \in \overline{A_i}\} & \text{otherwise.} \end{cases}$$

Finally, taking advantage of the connection between $\mathcal{BEL}$ and $\mathcal{Q}$, it is easy to see that the property $\mathcal{Q}(A \cup B) = \mathcal{Q}(A) \cap \mathcal{Q}(B)$ holds under condition $(*)$, while $\tilde{\mathcal{O}}(A \cap B) = \tilde{\mathcal{O}}(A) \cup \tilde{\mathcal{O}}(B)$ always holds.

3   Fusion Rules

Dempster rule of combination is central in the theory of evidence. Then, the combination of two mass functions can be viewed as a (normalized) intersection of the two random sets represented by these two basic probability assignments. A kind of counterpart of this rule in the set-valued setting is as follows: $\forall E \neq \emptyset$:

$$(\mathcal{M}_1 \otimes \mathcal{M}_2)(E) = \mathcal{M}_{12}(E) = \bigcup_{A,B \text{ s.t. } E = F \cap G} \mathcal{M}_1(F) \cup \mathcal{M}_2(G)$$

It is especially meaningful to combine two disjoint sets of sources and refine their information. It makes no sense to use $\mathcal{M}_1(F) \cap \mathcal{M}_2(G)$ in the above expression if $\text{ALL} \cap \text{ALL}' = \emptyset$, $\mathcal{M}_1(F) \subseteq \text{ALL}$, $\mathcal{M}_2(G) \subseteq \text{ALL}'$ since then $\mathcal{M}_1(F) \cap \mathcal{M}_2(G) = \emptyset$. In the case where $\text{ALL} = \text{ALL}'$, it means that we have two versions of the information provided by each source, and information items are combined conjunctively. For instance, consider two sources a and b with epistemic states $\Gamma_1(a) = E_a$ and $\Gamma_2(b) = E_b$. The fusion rule gives $\Gamma_{12}(a) = \Gamma_{12}(b) = E_a \cap E_b$, i.e., $\mathcal{M}_{12}(E_a \cap E_b) = \{a, b\}$, and $\mathcal{M}_{12}(E) = \emptyset$ otherwise. Just as Dempster rule of combination amounts to performing the product of commonality functions [7], the above rule corresponds to the union of the set-valued commonality functions, as shown below.

$$\mathcal{Q}_{12}(D) = \bigcup_{C \supseteq D} \mathcal{M}_{12}(C) = \bigcup_{C \supseteq D} \bigcup_{A,B \text{ s.t. } C = A \cap B} \mathcal{M}_1(A) \cup \mathcal{M}_2(B)$$

$$= \bigcup_{A,B \text{ s.t. } A \cap B \supseteq D} \mathcal{M}_1(A) \cup \mathcal{M}_2(B) = \bigcup_{A,B \text{ s.t. } A \supseteq D, B \supseteq D} \mathcal{M}_1(A) \cup \mathcal{M}_2(B)$$

$$= (\bigcup_{A \supseteq D} \mathcal{M}_1(A)) \cup (\bigcup_{B \supseteq D} \mathcal{M}_2(B)) = \mathcal{Q}_1(D) \cup \mathcal{Q}_2(D)$$

Hence, the combination rule is commutative, associative and idempotent. Other combination rules make sense such as the generalized disjunction, replacing $A \cap B$ by $A \cup B$ in the fusion rule. This rule boils down to the union of the set-valued belief functions $\mathcal{BEL}_1(A) \cup \mathcal{BEL}_2(A), \forall A \subseteq \Omega$.

4   Concluding Remarks

There are several lines for further research. First, this set-valued setting has been presented in terms of knowledge, but it might apply as well to preference modeling. Besides, the approach could be generalized by allowing the use of weighted subsets of sources leading to fuzzy set-valued set functions. Moreover, one may follow ideas expressed in [5,8] advocating the interest of a bipolar view of information that can be represented in evidence or in possibility theory, for introducing a similar bipolar setting in set-valued evidence theory. Lastly, the set of sources that are the values of the set functions may be understood in terms of arguments, following an idea already suggested in [1] in a different setting.

References

1. Assaghir, Z., Napoli, A., Kaytoue, M., Dubois, D., Prade, H.: Numerical information fusion: lattice of answers with supporting arguments. In: Proceedings of the 23rd IEEE International Conference on Tools with Artificial Intelligence (ICTAI 2011), Boca Raton, 7–9 November, pp. 621–628 (2011)
2. Belhadi, A., Dubois, D., Khellaf-Haned, F., Prade, H.: Multiple agent possibilistic logic. J. Appl. Non Class. Log. **23**(4), 299–320 (2013)
3. Belnap, N.D.: How a computer should think. In: Ryle, G. (ed.) Contemporary Aspects of Philosophy, pp. 30–56. Oriel Press, Stocksfield (1977)
4. Dubois, D., Prade, H., Rico, A.: Representing qualitative capacities as families of possibility measures. Int. J. Approx. Reason. **58**, 3–24 (2015)
5. Dubois, D., Prade, H., Smets, P.: "Not impossible" vs. "guaranteed possible" in fusion and revision. In: Benferhat, S., Besnard, P. (eds.) ECSQARU 2001. LNCS, vol. 2143, pp. 522–531. Springer, Heidelberg (2001). doi:10.1007/3-540-44652-4_46
6. Prade, H., Rico, A.: Possibilistic evidence. In: Liu, W. (ed.) ECSQARU 2011. LNCS (LNAI), vol. 6717, pp. 713–724. Springer, Heidelberg (2011). doi:10.1007/978-3-642-22152-1_60
7. Shafer, G.: A Mathematical Theory of Evidence. Princeton University Press, Princeton (1976)
8. Smets, P.: The canonical decomposition of a weighted belief. In: Proceedings of the14th International Joint Conference on Artificial Intelligence, Montreal, 20–25 August, Morgan Kaufman, San Mateo, pp. 1896–1901 (1995)

Graphical Models: From Theory to Applications

On the Use of WalkSAT Based Algorithms for MLN Inference in Some Realistic Applications

Romain Rincé[1,2(✉)], Romain Kervarc[1], and Philippe Leray[2]

[1] ONERA – The French Aerospace Lab, Palaiseau, France
{romain.rince,romain.kervarc}@onera.fr
[2] LS2N – Laboratoire des Sciences du Numérique de Nantes,
UMR CNRS 6004 Université de Nantes, Nantes, France
philippe.leray@univ-nantes.fr

Abstract. WalkSAT is a local search algorithm conceived for solving SAT problems, which is also used for sampling possible worlds from a logical formula. This algorithm is used by Markov Logic Networks to perform slice sampling and give probabilities from a knowledge base defined with soft and hard constraints. In this paper, we will show that local search strategies, such as WalkSAT, may perform as poorly as a pure random walk on a category of problems that are quite common in industrial fields. We will also give some insights into the reasons that make random search algorithms intractable for these problems.

Keywords: Complex event processing · Local search · SAT solver · Markov Logic Network · WalkSAT · Chronicles · First-order logic · Temporal logic

1 Introduction

In many industrial fields, it is necessary to manage large temporal streams of raw data that usually represent the first observable layer of a very complex system with a broad variety of interactions between agents. Being able to extract more valuable informations from this data is a major concern, especially in case of critical activities like air traffic safety, market surveillance, or cyber-attack detection. These needs have led to much research about efficient methods for analysing this kind of temporal data and recognising high level information.

In this paper, we focus on a specific formalism from the complex event processing domain known as *Chronicles* [8], more precisely on this latest version [9]. Chronicles are a powerful way to represent and recognise activities on temporal data flows. However, since chronicles are defined with logical formulae, using them on unreliable data may prove hard. Indeed, these streams are usually made of events detected by sensors, which can fatally miss some event or even produce them erroneously making the chronicles inefficient. Our first intent

© Springer International Publishing AG 2017
S. Benferhat et al. (Eds.): IEA/AIE 2017, Part II, LNAI 10351, pp. 121–131, 2017.
DOI: 10.1007/978-3-319-60045-1_15

was to make chronicles able to deal with uncertainty by combining them with Markov Logic.

Markov Logic Networks (MLN), introduced by [10], are graphical models that try to combine the expressiveness of first-order logical formulae and the ability of graphical models to deal with uncertainty. During the last ten years, MLN have been quite popular and have led to many practical and efficient experiments [2, 11,18], ranging over a wide spectrum of fields, including automatic image analysis [2,7] or event recognition [16,17]. The efficiency of MLN inference mainly relies on algorithm MC-SAT [10] which approximates probabilities of different worlds using a sampling technique. This sampling is performed by MaxWalkSAT for sampling plausible worlds. In this paper, we will mostly focus on this algorithm and issues that appear when it is applied to a specific category of problems.

MaxWalkSAT is a SAT solver, extended from WalkSAT, which handles weighted soft and hard constraints. SAT solvers are mainly divided into two families: complete and local search. Complete methods are extensions of the Davis-Putnam-Logemann-Loveland algorithm (DPLL) from [3] that assigns truth values to predicates of a first-order logic (FOL) formula until reaching a satisfactory assignment, known as world. This problem is NP-hard, but different techniques of pruning speed up the resolution.

Local search methods, as WalkSAT, on the other hand, try to find a satisfactory world by solving each inconsistent clause one by one. An advantage of local search strategies is that they are an approximately uniform sampler.

This paper is organised as follows. In Sect. 2, we will present briefly chronicles and their design with a FOL formula in Conjunctive Normal Form (CNF). In Sect. 3, we will introduce the Markov Logic and the WalkSAT algorithm. In Sect. 4, we will narrow chronicles design to a simple but common problem on FOL, for which we will show that trying and finding a satisfiable solution for this structure with WalkSAT strategies is exponential on time, resulting in MLN providing untrustworthy probabilities. In Sect. 5, we will give some insights into the reasons that lead WalkSAT strategies to be intractable in this case.

2   Chronicles

The purpose of chronicles is the detection of meaningful information within temporal data flows. Data is composed of events, called Low Level Events (LLE), together with their detection time. Using these LLE and Allen's operators[1] [1], it is possible to define formulae describing the recognition of specific High Level Events (HLE). These HLE can be reused to compose more complex HLE. Figure 1 presents the recognitions of a chronicle where an event A precedes two events B, without any event C between the two B, which is denoted $A((BB) - [C])$. Here, $(BB) - [C]$ is a sub-chronicle used to define the final chronicle.

As said before, this logical construction needs the analysed data to be lossless or errorless. To make chronicles robust to uncertainty, we modelled them into

---

[1] In fact, chronicles use more than 15 interval operators, including Allen's and some duration-related constraints. For further details, the reader may refer to [9].

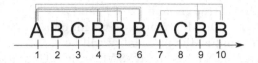

Fig. 1. All recognitions of chronicle $A((BB) - [C])$

Markov Logic. In order to achieve this, we transformed each needed operator into a FOL formula. This step is almost straightforward.

For instance, the *sequence* operator OpSeq may be defined as follows:

$$\mathsf{Ch}(c_1, t_1, t_2) \wedge \mathsf{Ch}(c_2, t_3, t_4) \wedge (t_2 \leq t_3) \implies \mathsf{OpSeq}(c_1, c_2, t_1, t_2, t_3, t_4) \quad (1)$$

$$\neg\mathsf{Ch}(c_1, t_1, t_2) \implies \neg\mathsf{OpSeq}(c_1, c_2, t_1, t_2, t_3, t_4) \quad (2)$$

$$\neg\mathsf{Ch}(c_2, t_3, t_4) \implies \neg\mathsf{OpSeq}(c_1, c_2, t_1, t_2, t_3, t_4) \quad (3)$$

$$\neg(t_2 \leq t_3) \implies \neg\mathsf{OpSeq}(c_1, c_2, t_1, t_2, t_3, t_4) \quad (4)$$

where variables c_i represent the type of a chronicle and t_j instant of time. Ch and OpSeq are predicates that respectively define when a chronicle of a certain type has been recognised and when a sequence between two chronicles is satisfied. For instance, if the predicate $\mathsf{Ch}(c_1, t_1, t_2)$ is valued to true, a recognition of a chronicle of type c_1 has started at time t_1 and terminated at time t_2. OpSeq is valued to true if two chronicles of types c_1, c_2 have been recognized at the given times and if chronicle c_2 happens after the recognition of c_1. Notice that these rules are equivalent to formula (1) with $\iff$ but usually FOL problems are presented in CNF, so we adopt this presentation here.

Once the sequence has been defined, new types of chronicle may be constructed, such as the following (where A and B are chronicles types and AB the new type that defines the sequence of two chronicles A and B):

$$\mathsf{OpSeq}(A, B, t_1, t_2, t_3, t_4) \implies \mathsf{Ch}(AB, t_1, t_4) \quad (5)$$

$$\exists t_2, t_3 \quad \neg\mathsf{OpSeq}(A, B, t_1, t_2, t_3, t_4) \implies \neg\mathsf{Ch}(AB, t_1, t_4) \quad (6)$$

3   MLN and MaxWalkSAT

3.1   Markov Logic

A first-order knowledge base (KB) is a set of clauses, which may be seen as constraints on possible worlds of predicate values. If a rule is violated by a world x, this world does not satisfy the KB. With MLNs, the latter rule is weakened, letting clauses being wrong by associating them to a weight that reflects how strong the constraint is. The higher is the weight, the more probable is the clause to be satisfied. MLNs are Markov random fields where ground predicates are vertices and clauses are cliques on the graph. MLNs are designed using Markov Logic (ML). In ML, each formula F_i is associated to a weight w_i and the probability distribution over possible worlds x is given by

$$P(X = x) = \frac{1}{Z} \exp \left(\sum_i w_i n_i(x) \right) \quad (7)$$

where n_i is the number of true groundings of F_i and $Z = \sum_{X=x} \exp\left(\sum_i w_i n_i(x)\right)$ is the partition function. On ML, an infinite weight on a formula is equivalent to defining a hard constraint as the probability will be zero if the formula is false.

The inference with MLN relies on MC-SAT: a MCMC (Markov Chain Monte-Carlo) technique used to approximate the probability distribution. MC-SAT uses a slice sampling approach to represent the probability distribution over worlds. In this algorithm, it is necessary to be able to sample worlds from the KB. For this purpose, MC-SAT uses SampleSAT [20], to perform approximately uniform samples. SampleSAT consists on taking the solution given by any WalkSAT method, i.e. a SAT solver using random search to find a solution for a FOL formula, smoothed by temperature annealing.

MLN uses MaxWalkSAT which is a weighted version of WalkSAT that allows both soft and hard constraints but the principle remains identical.

3.2 WalkSAT Strategies on Details

In their paper, [20] describe a way to sample approximately uniform solutions from a hard 3-SAT problem using a WalkSAT algorithm.

WalkSAT [14] (Algorithm 1) is an improved version of GSAT [15]: a simple procedure that tries and reaches a solution of a KB with a gradient technique that minimises the number of false clauses. WalkSAT adds a random step probability parameter that sets the chances to take a random step, i.e. flipping a random atom of the selected false clause[2], thus allowing escaping local optima.

Algorithm 1. WalkSAT(KB, m_t, m_f, p)

---

    inputs : KB, a knowledge base in CNF
               m_t, maximum number of tries
               m_f, maximum number of flips
               p, probability of random step
    outputs: *bestSol*, the best solution found
1 **for** $i \leftarrow 1$ **to** m_t
2   *tmpSol* $\leftarrow$ a random assignment for the KB
3   *bestSol* $\leftarrow$ *tmpSol*
4   **for** $i \leftarrow 1$ **to** m_f
5   Choose a random unsatisfied clause c
6   **if** $\boldsymbol{Uniform}(0,1) < p$
7   flip a random atom in c
8   **else**
9   flip best atom in c
10   **if** *tmpSol better than bestSol*
11   *bestSol* $\leftarrow$ *tmpSol*
12 **return** *bestSol*

---

[2] For MaxWalkSAT, the cost function is no longer the number of false clauses, but the sum of their weights.

4   A Simple Intractable Problem for WalkSAT

In this section, we show that using MLNs for solving a chronicle problem is intractable, and more generally, that this happens when the definition of a system with logical formulae contains too many biconditional statements.

4.1   Problem Statement

For the sake of clarity, we show a simplified chronicle problem $\mathcal{F}$. As chronicles may be seen as a succession of deductions at different levels, like a truncated pyramid of deductions, we will choose the following representation:

Given a set of boolean variables $V = \{x_{1,1}, \ldots, x_{i-j+1,j}, \ldots, x_{1,k}\}$ for $j \in \{1, \ldots, k\}$ and $i \in \{1, \ldots, k-j+1\}$ and given the set of clauses $\mathcal{R} = \{c_1, \ldots, c_n\}$, the problem is designed as follows: $\mathcal{F} = \bigwedge_{c_i \in \mathcal{R}} c_i$ and

$$
\begin{cases}
(x_{i,j} \wedge x_{i+1,j} \implies x_{i,j+1}) \in \mathcal{R} \\
(x_{i,j+1} \implies x_{i,j}) \in \mathcal{R} \\
(x_{i,j+1} \implies x_{i+1,j}) \in \mathcal{R}
\end{cases}
\quad \text{with} \quad
\begin{cases}
0 < j \le k; \\
0 < i \le k-j+1
\end{cases}
\tag{8}
$$

where j is the height of a predicates layer, i the position of a predicate on j^{th} layer and k the total number of layers. An example of this problem with a height of three and twelve nodes is shown on Fig. 2. It is worth noting the similarity with the sequence operator definition provided previously on Eq. 1.

To complete this problem, we add all predicates from the first layer as evidences. This simulates the recognition or non-detection of LLE on the data flow; note it will make the number of solutions drop from 2^k to 1.

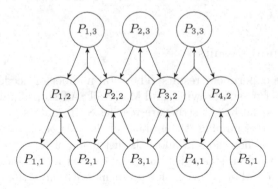

Fig. 2. A simplified chronicles representation with a height of 3 and a base length of 5

4.2   Experimental Setup

For our experiments, we used MaxWalkSAT as a SAT solver implemented in Alchemy 2 [19] Our KB is designed with infinite weights on every clause, so it is supposed to produce equivalent results than WalkSAT [4]. This version uses a TABU implementation which will not let a predicate be flipped twice without n other predicates having been flipped in between[3].

We designed two experiments. In the first one, we want to set the number of nodes but keep control on the length of the first layer. So we ask MaxWalkSAT to solve, at the same time, parallel instances of $\mathcal{F}$ (Eq. 8) with the first layer length equal to the structure height. We set the nodes number to the closest value around 2000 considering previous constraints. This experiment could be seen as a chronicle problem where many distinct chronicles are being recognised on the same data flow.

In the second experiment, we wanted to study the impact of the length of first layer on the resolution time with a fixed height. We launch MaxWalkSAT on a single instance of a problem with height 4.

On both problems, MaxWalkSAT stops if it finds a solution or reaches one million flips[4].

Table 1. Number of flip before depending on the height and length of the structure with 2000 nodes.

Height	2	3	4	5	6	7	8	9	10
Nodes per struct	3	6	10	15	21	28	36	45	55
Structures	666	333	200	133	95	71	55	44	36
Total flips	1505	3530	8265	25324	71567	406655	**980000**	**984068**	**984189**
Percentage solved	100%	100%	100%	100%	100%	100%	50%	10%	0%

4.3   Experimental Results

Table 1 shows the experiment results. The total number of needed flips quickly rises with the structure size growing, and MaxWalkSAT stops finding the optimal solution as soon as the height structure reaches 8. It could seem normal, given that, at constant nodes number, the number of clauses goes up, but keep in mind that this structure is not random and it is just made of repetitions of the same pattern. Usually, random strategies find all solutions for problems of this size. For instance [20], found all solutions for problems with more than 20 000 clauses and almost 5 000 variables.

---

[3] In our case, n was set at 10.

[4] In fact, the solver will stop before reaching the million flips because sometimes, when the algorithm has to flip the best atom, the flip does not occur if it leads to a worse solution than the current one, but this still counts as a flip. Our results just consider *efficient* flips, *i.e.* times when the value of a variable actually changes.

We have indicated the percentage of substructures solved even if the whole problem is not, because random strategies can restart from the beginning (number of tries[5] in Algorithm 1). But we can see that, when reaching a height of ten, restart is not even useful since no structure is solved.

Unfortunately, the algorithm stops with a really low amount of nodes but, looking only at the steps where all the problem is fully solved, it is interesting to note that, per structure, the number of flips is worse in average than a pure random walk strategy on 3SAT known to be exponential regarding the number of nodes, namely $O(1.334^n)$ [12].

One could think height is the main problem, since the algorithm has then to propagate truth along longer deduction layers. So on our second experiment on Table 2, we designed the same case than previously but with dependencies between the structures. Even if we showed that problems with numerous instances of height 4 were easily solved, we have evidenced that, at constant height, the problem becomes quickly intractable; especially if deductions shared a lot of common atoms, letting a predicate having an even small influence on all others.

In the light of the considerations above, it seems that the general structure has as much impact as the number of double implications in the formula.

Table 2. Number of flips needed to solve with the height fixed to 4.

Base length	10	20	25	30	40	50
Total nodes	34	74	94	114	154	194
Total clauses	92	192	232	292	392	592
Flips	6450	62394	386969	**864892**	**886892**	**898827**

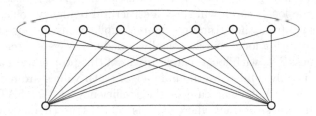

Fig. 3. An instance with strong difference on the node degree

5   Discussion

5.1   General Discussion

In this section, we discuss the reasons that make random walk strategies inefficient when dealing with this kind of logical structure. Structural problems have

---

[5] With MLNs, the number of tries is usually set to 1 due to the cost on the algorithm.

already been isolated like in [13] where GSAT has shown poor experimental results on specific situations. For instance, in a graph colouring problem using only three colours, if the graph presents nodes of a comparatively higher degree, GSAT tends to be stuck. An instance is shown on Fig. 3 where GSAT will often be stuck with the two bottom nodes assigned to the same colour. WalkSAT has been introduced in this same article to solve this problem.

But we have shown that, even in balanced cases, a computational problem may arise, especially when a FOL formula is designed with clauses and their inverse. This substructure allows the solver to flip the same atom a huge number of times without being able to determine when it leads to an improvement.

In a local search, decision is completely correlated to the context around the atom to flip. For instance, in our problem, a node has 18 neighbours, which define the context. It is interesting to know that, on the 2^{18+1} contexts, the WalkSAT algorithm has a 46.2% chance of flipping the atom of interest from the good configuration to the wrong one, and a 36.6% chance the other way around.

If we choose a FOL formula mostly designed with rules of the following kind: $x_1 \wedge \cdots \wedge x_n \iff y$, it CNF will have one clause of size $n+1$ and n clauses of size 2. It is easy to see that in this configuration there are $2^{n+1} - 1$ solutions where y is false and only one when y is true. And if y is used for higher deductions of this kind, putting y to false has a cost only if atoms on the above layer have been already set to true. This make usually WalkSAT more likely to put y to false. More simply, this sub-problem is almost equivalent to the highlighted structure by Selman and Kautz, which is easily solved by WalkSAT. But in our problem, an additional difficulty may account for the poor performance of WalkSAT. Indeed, the structure is repeated many times, with its high-degree nodes serving as low-degree nodes in several higher instances of the structure: this intrication is likely to cause a drop in performance. Assume for instance that such a node of degree n occurs also with a low degree in k structures. There will be $n + k$ clauses where it will occur negatively and $k + 1$ clauses where it will occur positively: consequently, the local search will show a structural tendency to set it to false.

Independently from the structure, double implications are intuitively problematic to solve with a local search. Usually, a deductive system tends to propagate truth values. But, with local search, tracks of this propagation are lost, and the algorithm is only guided by the number of truth values around the node[6]. Figure 4 is a simple but clear case of the inefficiency of WalkSAT on double implications. In this situation, where x_{i-1} is valued true (light gray) and x_{i+1} false (dark gray), determining the value of x_i will be random and meaningless.

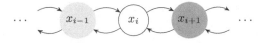

Fig. 4. Conflicting propagation of truth based on local search

---

[6] Especially the number of nodes with a certain truth value.

5.2   Extension of the Problem to MLN

We expressed at the beginning of this article that local search methods lead MLN to give poor probabilities for deductions problems. The reason is straightforward: as the WalkSAT method cannot reach solutions that require a high level of deduction, using it as sampler would result in worlds with only few layers of the deduction consistent with the evidence. Therefore, the sample sets produced for MCSAT will not be reliable enough to produce trustworthy results.

6   Conclusion

Our first intent was to improve chronicles to let them handle uncertainties. But we have shown in this paper that MLNs can not perform well when applied on such problems. This is not due to the MCMC technique they use, but on a deeper problem correlated to the SAT domain. We have highlighted that specific logical problems designed with a lot of biconditional statements may lead local search techniques to be stuck, even on problems with small dimensions compared to other works where these methods have been used.

In the Max-SAT 2016 competition, many benchmarks — whether crafted or industrial — are designed that way. Considering the performances variations between complete and local methods, the highlighted problem might be a reason explaining these differences. We know that many parameters impact the efficiency of SAT-solvers, like the number of solutions or the diameter of the associated neighbourhood graph [6], so, obviously, inner structures might not be the only reason, but seem to be an interesting lead.

Even if complete methods have better results, they still have difficulties to solve large problems and local algorithms are still needed for many tasks. But, for future works, this inner structural problem should be taken in consideration when we design and use local search methods. To help with this design, it would also probably be useful to quantify somehow difficulties linked to structure repetitions evoked in Sect. 5.1. Some other candidates for local search would also have to be assessed in the context of MLN: some algorithms on the Max-SAT competition have sometimes really good results on benchmarks that seem designed as chronicles. It might be interesting to investigate them.

Another possibility will be to look at complete methods; latest improvements on the field made algorithms almost as fast as local search. However, in the context of MLN where it is necessary to make MCMC calculations to compute probabilities, local search methods have a big asset, as they provide approximately uniform samples [20]. On the other hand, to our knowledge, the question whether complete methods also provide such samples has not been studied yet, probably as complete methods used to be too computation time-demanding to be even considered in this context, and would have to be assessed beforehand.

Finally, there are other approaches like the probabilistic logic programming that mix probabilities and logical formulae, Problog [5] for instance. WalkSAT algorithms are sometimes used there too, but many probabilistic logic programming approaches make use of complete methods instead. Hence, investigating these approaches would be an interesting lead to solve the problem arisen here, and we plan to tackle them in future work.

References

1. Allen, J.F.: Maintaining knowledge about temporal intervals. Commun. ACM **26**(11), 832–843 (1983)
2. Biswas, R., Thrun, S., Fujimura, K.: Recognizing activities with multiple cues. In: Elgammal, A., Rosenhahn, B., Klette, R. (eds.) HuMo 2007. LNCS, vol. 4814, pp. 255–270. Springer, Heidelberg (2007). doi:10.1007/978-3-540-75703-0_18
3. Davis, M., Logemann, G., Loveland, D.: A machine program for theorem-proving. Commun. ACM **5**(7), 394–397 (1962)
4. Domingos, P., Lowd, D.: Markov logic: an interface layer for artificial intelligence. Synth. Lect. Artif. Intell. Mach. Learn. **3**(1), 1–155 (2009)
5. Fierens, D., Broeck, G.V.D., Thon, I., Gutmann, B., De Raedt, L.: Inference in probabilistic logic programs using weighted CNF's. Theor. Pract. Log. Program. **15**(03), 258–401 (2012)
6. Hoos, H.H., Stützle, T.: Stochastic Local Search: Foundations and Applications. Morgan Kaufmann Publishers, San Francisco (2005)
7. Kembhavi, A., Yeh, T., Davis, L.S.: Why did the person cross the road (there)? Scene understanding using probabilistic logic models and common sense reasoning. In: Daniilidis, K., Maragos, P., Paragios, N. (eds.) ECCV 2010. LNCS, vol. 6312, pp. 693–706. Springer, Heidelberg (2010). doi:10.1007/978-3-642-15552-9_50
8. Ornato, M., Carle, P.: Reconnaissance d'intentions sans reconnaissance de plan. 2es Journées Francophones d'Intelligence Artificielle Distribuée et Systèmes MultiAgents, p. 29 (1994)
9. Piel, A.: Reconnaissance de comportements complexes par traitement en ligne de flux d'evenements. Ph.D. thesis, U. Paris 13 (2014)
10. Richardson, M., Domingos, P.: Markov logic networks. Mach. Learn. **62**(1–2), 107–136 (2006)
11. Sadilek, A.: Modeling human behavior at a large scale. Ph.D. thesis, Rochester University (2012)
12. Schoning, T.: A probabilistic algorithm for k-SAT and constraint satisfaction problems. In: Proceedings of the 40th Annual Symposium on Foundations of Computer Science, pp. 410–414. IEEE (1999)
13. Selman, B., Kautz, H.: Domain-independent extensions to GSAT: solving large structured satisfiability problems. In: Proceedings of the 13th International Joint Conference on Artifical Intelligence, pp. 290–295. Morgan Kaufmann Publishers Inc. (1993)
14. Selman, B., Kautz, H., Cohen, B., et al.: local search strategies for satisfiability testing. In: DIMACS Series in Discrete Mathematics, vol. 26, pp. 521–532 (1993)
15. Selman, B., Levesque, H.J., Mitchell, D.G., et al.: A new method for solving hard satisfiability problems. In: Proceedings of the 10th National Conference on Artificial Intelligence, vol. 92, pp. 440–446 (1992)
16. Skarlatidis, A., Artikis, A., Filippou, J., Paliouras, G.: A probabilistic logic programming event calculus. Theor. Pract. Log. Program. **15**(02), 213–245 (2015)
17. Skarlatidis, A., Paliouras, G., Vouros, G.A., Artikis, A.: Probabilistic event calculus based on Markov logic networks. In: Olken, F., Palmirani, M., Sottara, D. (eds.) RuleML 2011. LNCS, vol. 7018, pp. 155–170. Springer, Heidelberg (2011). doi:10.1007/978-3-642-24908-2_19

18. Snidaro, L., Visentini, I., Bryan, K.: Fusing uncertain knowledge and evidence for maritime situational awareness via Markov logic networks. Inf. Fusion **21**, 159–172 (2015)
19. Sumner, M., Domingos, P.: The alchemy tutorial (2010)
20. Wei, W., Erenrich, J., Selman, B.: Towards efficient sampling: exploiting random walk strategies. In: Proceedings of the 19th National Conference on Artificial Intelligence, pp. 670–676 (2004)

Applying Object-Oriented Bayesian Networks for Smart Diagnosis and Health Monitoring at both Component and Factory Level

Anders L. Madsen[1,2(✉)], Nicolaj Søndberg-Jeppesen[1], Mohamed S. Sayed[3], Michael Peschl[4], and Niels Lohse[3]

[1] HUGIN EXPERT A/S, Aalborg, Denmark
anders@hugin.com
[2] Aalborg University, Aalborg, Denmark
[3] Loughborough University, Loughborough, UK
[4] Harms & Wende GmbH & Co. KG, Hamburg, Germany

Abstract. To support health monitoring and life-long capability management for self-sustaining manufacturing systems, next generation machine components are expected to embed sensory capabilities combined with advanced ICT. The combination of sensory capabilities and the use of Object-Oriented Bayesian Networks (OOBNs) supports self-diagnosis at the component level enabling them to become self-aware and support self-healing production systems. This paper describes the use of a modular component-based modelling approach enabled by the use of OOBNs for health monitoring and root-cause analysis of manufacturing systems using a welding controller produced by Harms & Wende (HWH) as an example. The model is integrated into the control software of the welding controller and deployed as a SelComp using the SelSus Architecture for diagnosis and predictive maintenance. The SelComp provides diagnosis and condition monitoring capabilities at the component level while the SelSus Architecture provides these capabilities at a wider system level. The results show significant potential of the solution developed.

Keywords: OOBNs · Real-World Application · Software architecture

1 Introduction

A Bayesian network (BN) [1–4,11] is a powerful and popular model for probabilistic inference. Its graphical nature makes it well-suited for representing complex problems where the interactions between entities represented as variables are described using conditional probability distributions (CPDs). A Bayesian network is an efficient knowledge integration tool enabling information from different sources such as mathematical formulas, historical data and domain expert knowledge to be combined into a single model. As such they have been used in a wide range of domains for managing uncertainty.

© Springer International Publishing AG 2017
S. Benferhat et al. (Eds.): IEA/AIE 2017, Part II, LNAI 10351, pp. 132–141, 2017.
DOI: 10.1007/978-3-319-60045-1_16

We describe the application of OOBNs for health monitoring and root-cause analysis of manufacturing systems using a welding controller produced by Harms & Wende (HWH) as an example. HWH serves tens of thousands of welding equipments worldwide. Today, three service technicians are permanently available on phone hotline for solving customer problems. Obviously, one can reduce the load on this personnel by implementing a root-cause analysis solution at the customer service center combined with health monitoring at component level. Several benefits are expected from the successful implementation of such a tool. The average service technician training time is now six months. By implementing and using a service analysis solution this training time can be reduced to two weeks. HWH has about 20 requests per week or about 1000 requests in a year. HWH expects that by using an analytical software solution the average service request processing time will be reduced from 1 h to less than 40 min. This in turn should result in a reduction of load on each employee, improvement of service quality by eliminating human errors, and 333 h of savings annually.

The HWH OOBN model for component-based diagnostic has been encapsulated as a SelComp in the SelSus software architecture to enable system-level diagnostic capabilities [14]. We describe the integration and present the results of a performance evaluation of different levels of integration (direct, local network and wider network). There is a fair amount of related work on the use of OOBNs for diagnosis of industrial equipment including [6,9,12,15].

2 Preliminaries and Notation

A BN [1–4,11] consists of two main components. The first component is a graphical structure specifying dependence and independence relations between the random variables of the model and the second component is a set of CPDs specifying the strengths of the dependence relations. More precisely, a BN is a pair $\langle \mathcal{G}, \mathcal{P} \rangle$, where $\mathcal{G} = (\mathbf{V}, \mathbf{E})$ is an acyclic, directed graph (DAG) over a set of random variables $\mathcal{X} \sim \mathbf{V}$ with directed edges $\mathbf{E}$ that represent probabilistic relationships between variables $\mathcal{X}$ and $\mathcal{P}$ is the set of CPDs. This means that a BN is a decomposition of a joint probability distributions as follows $P(\mathcal{X}) = P(X_1, \ldots, X_n) = \prod_{X_i \in \mathcal{X}} P(X_i | pa(X_i))$. A BN supports the calculation of the posterior probability $P(X_i | \epsilon)$ where ϵ is the observed evidence and X_i is any non-observed variable.

An OOBN can been seen as a Bayesian network augmented with network classes, class instances and an associated notion of interface and private variables [3,5,10]. A class instance is the instantiation of a network class representing a sub-network within another network class. An OOBN can be used to represent a problem domain with repetitive structures more compactly and supports efficient model reuse as well as distributed knowledge elicitation. The variables $\mathcal{X}(C)$ of network class C are divided into disjoint subsets of input $\mathcal{I}$, output $\mathcal{O}$ and hidden/private $\mathcal{H}$ variables such that $\mathcal{X}(C) = \mathcal{I} \cup \mathcal{O} \cup \mathcal{H}$ where the interface variables $\mathcal{I} \cup \mathcal{O}$ are used to link nested class instances.

The OOBN for the HWH welding controller has been developed following a six steps methodology [9] that has proven to be efficient and effective in practice.

The six steps of the model development cycle are *begin, design, implement, test, analysis* and *deploy* as shown in Fig. 1 (taken from [3]). The *begin* and *deploy* steps are usually performed once whereas the remaining four steps are iterated until the model performance requirements are satisfied or until further improvements are not possible or too costly.

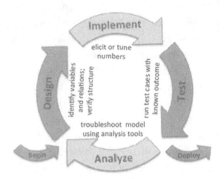

Fig. 1. Model development cycle [3].

3   HWH Welding Controller

The objective of this work has been to realize functionality that allows fast and efficient root-cause analysis of failures and health monitoring of a welding system in the field. Because of the huge amount of components of such a system, e.g., welding gun, transformers, cables, cooling systems and welding control including its sub-components, and their complex interrelationships, root-cause analysis nowadays is a manual task which consumes a lot of time. Often, the root causes can only be identified after several iterations including phone conversations with the customer, logging data analysis or even time-consuming in situ analysis.

Here, we consider the HWH welding controller Genius MFI in combination with the control software XPegasus. The Genius MFI has two separated parts of electronics: the power electronic and the cards electronic. The power electronic provides high power output for performing the welding. The cards electronic is used to control the power electronic and to connect the control with peripheral hardware and software components. The welding controller can be parametrized by the XPegasus PC software. XPegasus also supports documentation and analysis of welding data. The welding controller and XPegasus are connected via TCP/IP over Ethernet. Figure 2(a) shows the XPegasus interface.

XPegasus has a component-oriented software architecture including a huge amount of components, e.g., components for data analysis, quality inspection and client-server connectivity already exist. The objective is to provide the analytical software solution both to HWH service personnel as well as to the customers of HWH. The integration of diagnosis capabilities into the equipment provides the

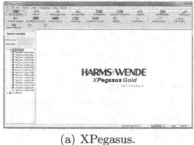

(a) XPegasus.   (b) Diagnosis Capabilities

Fig. 2. The XPegasus start screen and diagnosis capabilities.

following benefits: (1) reaction time in case of failures reduced from up to 12 h to maximum 1 h (due to different time zones), (2) many problems can be solved locally without contacting HWH customer service center. This will result in an additional reduction of the load on service personnel, and (3) the embedded analytical software will support early identification of potential problems/failures and provide warnings to avoid them. This results in a substantial qualitative improvement of the equipment itself. Considering all the factors listed above, the use of OOBNs is expected to substantially improve Overall Equipment Efficiency (OEE) and reduce investments.

4   OOBN for HWH Welding Controller

This section describes the development of the component-level diagnosis model for the welding controller produced by HWH using the method of [9]. The results of the six steps of the method are described next. The model was developed during two physical modelling workshops, numerous web meetings and email exchanges. The process was launched with a physical workshop.

4.1   Begin: Model Choice

The HWH diagnosis model has been developed as an OOBN since it is to be used for root-cause analysis at the component level as well as to be integrated into a larger system-wide model for root-cause analysis at a higher level of abstraction, i.e., shop-floor or even factory level. The model is developed using HUGIN software [7][1]. An OOBN has the advantage of supporting model reuse and can be extended into a dynamic model to support predictive maintenance.

4.2   Design: Structure

As part of the design step, domain experts from HWH and knowledge engineers identified possible root causes, mediating variables and a set of possible

---
[1] http://www.hugin.com.

observables (e.g., an observation by the operator or a sensor reading). Figure 3
shows the top level network class that was the output of the Design-step. The
OOBN reflects root causes, possible observations and whether a problem has
been reported or not. The model contains four instance nodes that represent
instances of embedded components (white boxes with rounded corners). Figure 4
shows the network class representing the Power Electronics of the welding controller. This network class has one instance of the network class representing the
parameter settings. The Power Electronics class is instantiated in the Electronics class (not shown) instantiated in the top level class. The OOBN has a total
of eight network classes and four layers in the class component tree (number of
nested classes). The unfolded model has 24 Boolean root causes, 8 observations,
i.e., sensor readings and operator input and a total of 48 variables with a total
CPD size of 623. Notice that some root causes have parents in the structure and
that the number of observations is relatively low.

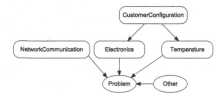

Fig. 3. The top level class of the welding controller model.

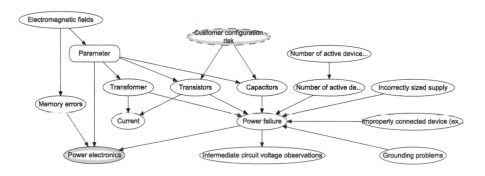

Fig. 4. The power electronics network class.

4.3   Implement: Quantification

In order to assess the root cause probabilities, domain experts were asked to estimate the prior probability of a problem and provide a ranking of the root causes
taking conditional variables into consideration. Each root cause was assigned
a prior probability proportional to its ranking. Since each root cause is represented as a Boolean variable the conditional probability distributions for the

problem defining variables are mainly specified as a logical disjunction of the parent nodes. In some cases, a small leak probability is added to represent that some unlikely or unknown failures are not represented in the model or that a problem is not observed yet even though a root cause is present. Distributions for sensor readings and operator observations have been assessed by experts.

4.4 Test and Analysis

The model was first evaluated qualitatively by domain experts using a web interface and the XPegasus software. Secondly, it was evaluated quantitatively by means of a synthetic data set that was produced by random sampling from the model. For each possible root cause, a set of observations was sampled from the model (given the root cause being set to a failure state and all other causes set to non-failure). Next, the sampled observations and a problem being observed were entered as evidence. The probability of each root cause was retrieved. Ideally, the original root cause would have the highest probability in every case. This evaluation showed that in six cases the true root cause had the highest probability while in 16 out of 21 cases the true root cause was between the five root causes with highest probability.

Due to a low number of sensor readings and operator observations, the model is not able to distinguish between certain root causes. For instance, the model contains no evidence variables to distinguish root cause variables *Grounding problems* and *Incorrectly sized supply* as they share one common sensor reading.

4.5 Deploy

The model has been integrated directly into the control software of the welding controller in order to support diagnosis at the component level as well as deployed inside the SelSus architecture. This is described in more detail in the next section. In addition, a special-purpose web interface [8] for the welding controller model was developed to support the Test-step of the development process[2]. This has served as an important tool in the Test and Analysis-step as the domain experts have been able to interact with the model at their own convenience.

5   The SelSus Architecture

The SelSus architecture is primarily based on the concept of independent smart automation components that can be integrated in a bottom-up fashion into a wider automation system [14]. The underlying intention is to enable the providers of automation components, such as HWH, to offer more encapsulated diagnostic and monitoring functionality as part of their device offering while enabling faster integration and reconfiguration of devices into automation systems.

---

[2] http://selsus.hugin.com.

5.1   The SelComp Concept

The automation components in SelSus are encapsulated using the concept of a SelComp. The aim is to encapsulate the automation component with its own control and sensory capabilities including some embedded data processing, diagnostic and prognostic capabilities. A SelSus system is an integration of a number of SelComps with the added system-level functionalities on the SelSus cloud. This enables diagnostic and prognostic reasoning to be conducted on two levels: locally on the SelComp level where the only issues within the scope of the SelComp itself are possible to be detected and analysed; and System-level reasoning where various SelComps make some or all of their observations available for system-level reasoning. This enables system-level visibility in capturing and analysing the state of the system as a whole covering the various influences between individual SelComps. Figure 5 shows an overview of the generic internal architecture of the SelComp and how it relates to the system-level functionalities within SelSus, while Fig. 2(b) shows how the diagnosis capabilities offered by the model at the SelComp level has been made available to the user of XPegasus. The OOBN approach enables component-based encapsulated modelling at the SelComp level, while enabling the individual SelComp models to be integrated into a wider system-level model that can be used at system level.

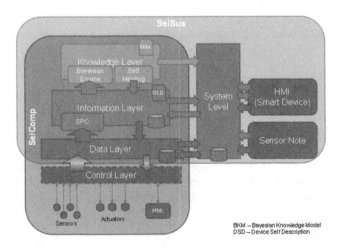

Fig. 5. The SelComp internal architecture concept.

5.2   Wider System Level Diagnosis

Following the notions of component-based modelling the aim here is to enable modular, component-based OOBN models to be constructed on the SelComp level while accommodating for the possibility of integrating these local models into a wider system-level model that covers the overall system. The component models should ideally be self-sufficient and only require information from the available information to the SelComp.

The objective is to enable independent SelComps to operate normally even when they are not connected to an overall SelSus system. This can only be true if the diagnostic and prognostic models along with the reasoning process are entirely self-contained within each individual SelComp and do not depend in their operation on external resources, either in the form of observations or reasoning and computation. The system-level models will be a collection of the constituent component-models. In the context of manufacturing systems, individual component models will typically be connected together through the means of process quality characteristics in order to form system-level diagnostic models.

In the use-case we consider, the SelComp model presented could be linked to other SelComp models representing other components in an integrated system in which the HWH welding controller is deployed. This is ongoing work.

5.3   The HWH Diagnosis Model as a SelSus Cloud Service

In the SelSus architecture, SelComps have the ability to transmit data to and receive data from the SelSus Cloud. The SelSus Cloud is a collection of Software Services from which a SelComp can request (stored) sensor data or it can communicate with, for instance, another Service that is exposing the HUGIN functionality. This latter web service can be equipped with the welding controller model, when requested - thus allowing a SelComp to perform diagnosis and health monitoring on the HWH welding controller. Specifically, this web service communicates using a REST based API where requests can be bundled in JSON objects to minimize the communication overhead.

5.4   Experimental Analysis

This section reports on an experimental analysis of the performance of different levels of integration of the HWH model into the SelSus architecture. The tightest level of integration has been achieved by integrating the model directly into the XPegasus software. In addition, the model has been deployed using a web service inside the SelSus Cloud having the control software and web service running on the same machine as well as having the control software and web service running on machines located far apart (more than 1000 km). In the experiment, one state for each possible observation was propagated and this process was repeated 1000 times producing 8000 propagations. Table 1 shows the time performance results for different configurations. It is clear from the table that direct integration into the control software using save-to-memory[3] is by far the most time efficient solution. Using this approach it is possible to perform thousands of propagations in the model each second using the test computer, which is a standard PC.

---

[3] Save-to-memory is an optimisation option in HUGIN software trading time for space.

Table 1. Average time cost of one belief update across three different setups.

Configuration	Total time (ms)	Average time (ms)
Direct integration	1,508	0.189
Direct integration (w/save-to-memory)	778	0.097
Localhost deployment	10,263	1.283
Network deployment	382,785	47.848

6   Discussion and Conclusion

The use of Bayesian networks for diagnosis at the component level has several benefits to HWH. For HWH, in general, this will result in a substantial qualitative improvement of welding equipment and reduction of costs related to service. A qualitative improvement implies that equipment will become more intelligent, reliable, stable and predictive and human-friendly. In addition, these new capabilities provide competitive advantages.

For the HWH customer service center, the new software will reduce the load related to service problem analysis. It will also improve quality of service, reduce training times for new personnel and reduce requirements to their expertise.

For HWH customers, the usage of embedded analytical software provides several advantages. The welding equipment will become more intelligent with self-awareness and self-diagnosis capabilities. Self-awareness helps in easy integration and configuration into the system while self-diagnosis will help in predicting and preventing failures or finding solutions in case of problems/failures. For the customer this means a substantial simplification of equipment service, improvement of production line efficiency and stability by reducing down-times and failures. All this results in a significant reduction of costs.

The results of the experimental analysis clearly demonstrate that inference is highly efficient using the tightest level of integration and that communication overhead adds significantly to the time cost of the inference process. Even with the deployment of the web service and control software on different machines located far apart, the cost of inference should not be problematic in relation to providing support on root-cause analysis over the phone.

Future work includes development of a system-wide model for diagnosis at line or even factory level combining the HWH welding controller model with models for other components on the line or factory level as well as collecting operational data for parameter estimation in batch and considering algorithms for on-line adjustment of parameters using operational data. Although the modelling methodology is primarily driven by domain expert knowledge, current work focuses on enabling the derivation of Bayesian network models for diagnosis from existing engineering design information such as FMEA data [13].

Acknowledgments. This work is part of the project "Health Monitoring and Life-Long Capability Management for SELf-SUStaining Manufacturing Systems (SelSus)" which is funded by the Commission of the European Communities under the 7th Framework Programme, Grant agreement no: 609382.

References

1. Cowell, R.G., Dawid, A.P., Lauritzen, S.L., Spiegelhalter, D.J.: Probabilistic Networks and Expert Systems. Springer, New York (1999)
2. Jensen, F.V., Nielsen, T.D.: Bayesian Networks and Decision Graphs, 2nd edn. Springer, New York (2007)
3. Kjærulff, U.B., Madsen, A.L.: Bayesian Networks and Influence Diagrams: A Guide to Construction and Analysis, 2nd edn. Springer, New York (2013)
4. Koller, D., Friedman, N.: Probabilistic Graphical Models - Principles and Techniques. MIT Press, Cambridge (2009)
5. Koller, D., Pfeffer, A.: Object-oriented Bayesian networks. In Proceedings of UAI, pp. 302–313 (1997)
6. Lorenzoni, A., Kempf, M.: Degradation processes modelled with dynamic Bayesian networks. In: Proceedings of the 2015 IEEE International Conference on Industrial Informatics (INDIN), p. 6 (2015)
7. Madsen, A.L., Jensen, F., Kjærulff, U.B., Lang, M.: HUGIN - the tool for Bayesian networks and influence diagrams. Int. J. Artif. Intell. Tools **14**(3), 507–543 (2005)
8. Madsen, A.L., Karlsen, M., Barker, G.B., Garcia, A.B., Hoorfar, J., Jensen, F., Vigre, H.: A software package for web deployment of probabilistic graphical models. In: Proceedings of SCAI, pp. 175–184 (2013)
9. Madsen, A.L., Søndberg-Jeppesen, N., Lohse, N., Sayed, M.S.: A methodology for developing local smart diagnostic models using expert knowledge. In: Proceedings of the 2015 IEEE International Conference on Industrial Informatics (INDIN), p. 6 (2015)
10. Neil, M., Fenton, N., Nielsen, L.M.: Building large-scale Bayesian networks. Knowl. Eng. Rev. **15**(3), 257–284 (2000)
11. Pearl, J.: Probabilistic Reasoning in Intelligent Systems: Networks of Plausible Inference. Series in Representation and Reasoning. Morgan Kaufmann Publishers, San Mateo (1988)
12. Sayed, M.S., Lohse, N.: Distributed Bayesian diagnosis for modular assembly systems-a case study. J. Manuf. Syst. **32**(3), 480–488 (2013)
13. Sayed, M.S., Lohse, N.: Ontology-driven generation of Bayesian diagnostic models for assembly systems. Int. J. Adv. Manuf. Technol. **74**(5–8), 1033–1052 (2014)
14. Sayed, M.S., Lohse, N., Søndberg-Jeppesen, N., Madsen, A.L.: SelSus: towards a reference architecture for diagnostics and predictive maintenance using smart manufacturing devices. In: Proceedings of the 2015 IEEE International Conference on Industrial Informatics (INDIN), p. 6 (2015)
15. Weidl, G., Madsen, A.L., Israelson, S.: Applications of object-oriented Bayesian networks for condition monitoring, root cause analysis and decision support on operation of complex continuous processes. Comput. Chem. Eng. **29**, 1996–2009 (2005)

Graphical Representations of Multiple Agent Preferences

Nahla Ben Amor[1], Didier Dubois[2], Héla Gouider[1(✉)], and Henri Prade[2,3]

[1] LARODEC, University of Tunis, Tunis, Tunisie
nahla.benamor@gmx.com, hela.gouider@gmail.com
[2] IRIT, University of Toulouse, Toulouse, France
{dubois,prade}@irit.fr
[3] QCIS, University of Technology, Sydney, Australia

Abstract. A multiple-agent logic, which associates subsets of agents to logical formulas, has been recently proposed. The paper presents a graphical counterpart of this logic, based on a multiple agent version of possibilistic conditioning, and applies it to preference modeling. First, preferences of agents are supposed to be all or nothing. We discuss how one can move from the network to the logic representation and vice-versa. The new representation enables us to focus on networks associated to subsets of agents, and to identify inconsistent agents, or conflicting subsets of agents. The question of optimization and dominance queries is discussed. Finally, the paper outlines an extension where gradual preferences are handled.

Keywords: Possibilistic network · Multiple agent logic · Preferences

1 Introduction

Modeling preferences has been an active research topic in Artificial intelligence for about twenty years. Graphical and logical formalisms have been proposed for describing user's preferences compactly. Graphical representations are appealing for elicitation purposes, and offer a basis for local computation; see, [1] for an overview. Note that only a few graphical models have been proposed for modeling *multiple agent* preferences, based on different extensions of Conditional Preference networks (CP-nets) [5,8], or Generalized Additive Independence networks (GAI-nets) [7]. Besides, a multiple agent logic [2], where formulas are pairs of the form (p, A) made of a proposition p and a subset of agents A, has been advocated for handling beliefs: then (p, A) means '(at least) all agents in A believe that p is true'. But (p, A) may also have a preference reading ('(at least) all agents in A want p to be true').

The strong similarity of multiple agent logic with possibilistic logic and the existence of transformations between possibilistic logic and possibilistic networks [3] suggest to develop a graphical counterpart to multiple agent logic. When modeling preferences, multiple agent networks can be seen as a generalization

© Springer International Publishing AG 2017
S. Benferhat et al. (Eds.): IEA/AIE 2017, Part II, LNAI 10351, pp. 142–153, 2017.
DOI: 10.1007/978-3-319-60045-1_17

of individual π-Pref nets (when possibility degrees are binary valued). In the following we investigate the interest of multiple agent networks (and of their graded extension) for handling preferences.

This paper is organized as follows. Section 2 defines conditioning in case of Boolean possibilities. Section 3 introduces multiple agent logic, and its graphical counterpart in a preference perspective. Section 4 presents the main steps for transforming one model into another. Section 5 discusses queries evaluation for multiple agent network. Section 6 outlines an extension with priority levels of multiple agent logic and network.

2   Conditioning and Possibilistic Networks: Boolean Case

Conditioning is a crucial notion when dealing with possibilistic networks. Here we consider the elementary situation of a single agent and of two-valued possibility distributions. Possibilistic networks [3] are usually defined for non-dogmatic possibility distributions, i.e., taking only positive values in $(0, 1]$. However, in the two-valued case, the only non-dogmatic possibility distribution is the vacuous one with value 1 for all states. So we must use a definition of conditioning that makes sense for dogmatic possibility distributions. Conditioning in this case is defined in the following way: Let Ω be the universe of discourse (set of all interpretations). Then the interpretations known as possible are restricted by a subset $E \neq \emptyset$, $E \subset \Omega$, and the considered possibility measure Π is such that $\Pi(S) = 1$ if $E \cap S \neq \emptyset$ and $\Pi(S) = 0$ otherwise (the possibility distribution being the characteristic function of E). Conditioning obeys the equation:

$$\Pi(S \cap T) = \Pi(S|T) \wedge \Pi(T) \tag{1}$$

where $\wedge$ stands for Boolean conjunction. Then we define $\Pi(\cdot|T)$ as the possibility measure associated with the subset $E_T = T \cap E$ if $T \neq \emptyset$ and $E_T = T$ if $T \cap E = \emptyset$. E_T is the result of revising E by T, the minimally specific solution of the above equation under the success postulate $E_T \subseteq T$. Thus:

$$\Pi(S|T) = 1 \text{ if} \begin{cases} S \cap E_T = S \cap T \cap E \neq \emptyset \ (\Pi(S \cap T) = \Pi(T) = 1) \\ S \cap E_T = S \cap T \neq \emptyset, \ T \cap E = \emptyset \ (\Pi(S \cap T) = \Pi(T) = 0) \end{cases}$$

$$= 0 \qquad\qquad \text{otherwise} \ (\Pi(S \cap T) = 0, \Pi(T) = 1)$$

A Boolean possibility distribution can be decomposed into a combination of conditional possibility distributions. This can be done by applying repeatedly the definition of conditioning. Indeed, taking an arbitrarily order of variables in set $V = \{X_1, \ldots, X_n\}$: $\pi(X_1, \ldots, X_n) = \pi(X_1|X_2, \ldots, X_n) \wedge \cdots \wedge \pi(X_n)$. This decomposition can be simplified when assuming some independence between variables. Graphically, it can be represented by a possibilistic network where each node represents a variable, edges represent the dependencies and conditional distributions define the associated tables.

Example 1. Consider 3 Boolean variables X, Y, Z and π defined by the two interpretations of $x \wedge y$. The possibilistic network associated to the ordering (X, Y, Z)

Table 1. Joint possibility distribution

XYZ	$\pi(Z \mid Y)$	$\pi(Y \mid X)$	$\pi(X)$	$\pi(XYZ)$
$\neg x \neg y \neg z$	1	1	0	0
$\neg x \neg y z$	1	1	0	0
$\neg x y \neg z$	1	1	0	0
$\neg x y z$	1	1	0	0
$x \neg y \neg z$	1	0	1	0
$x \neg y z$	1	0	1	0
$x y \neg z$	1	1	1	1
$x y z$	1	1	1	1

Table 2. Joint possibility distribution

XYZ	$\pi(Z \mid Y)$	$\pi(Y \mid X)$	$\pi(X)$	$\pi(XYZ)$
$\neg x \neg y \neg z$	1	0	0	0
$\neg x \neg y z$	0	0	0	0
$\neg x y \neg z$	1	1	0	0
$\neg x y z$	1	1	0	0
$x \neg y \neg z$	1	0	1	0
$x \neg y z$	0	0	1	0
$x y \neg z$	1	1	1	1
$x y z$	1	1	1	1

corresponding to this possibility distribution is given by columns 2, 3, 4 of Table 1. The original knowledge xy can be recovered from the joint distribution of Table 1 in the last column using the chain rule. In this network, Z is independent from X and Y.

Consider the same ordering of variables with the conditional tables given in Table 2. This illustrates the two first cases above in the definition of $\Pi(S \mid T)$. Note that here Y does not depend on X. The two networks have different tables but correspond to the same possibility distribution. The first network has conditional distributions less specific than the second one. So having fixed the ordering of variables, not only the conditional tables are not unique, but even the network topology is not unique.

3   Multiple Agent Representations

Multiple agent logic has been discussed in details in [2]. Formulas in this logic are pairs of the form (p, A), made of a proposition p and a subset of agents A. In this section, we explain the use of this logic for modeling preferences and present its graphical counterpart. *All* will denote the set of all the agents and capital letters, e.g., A, B, A_i, $\cdots$ denote subsets of *All*. Let $p, q, p_i, \cdots$ denote propositional formulas of a finite language.

3.1   Multiple Agent Logic

A possibilistic logic formula [6] of the form (p, α) is understood as $N(p) \geq \alpha$ (N is a necessity degree), where the higher α, the more imperative p. Multiple agent logic shares formal similarity with possibilistic logic in terms of inference rules, axioms, possibilistic measures and possibility distribution [2]. However, a multiple agent formula (p, A) is understood at the semantic level as a constraint of the form $N(p) \supseteq A$ where N is a *set-valued* mapping that returns the set of agents for whom satisfying p is imperative. Therefore, the formula (p, A) means that at least all the agents in A find p imperative. Set-valued possibility measure and necessity measure are related via duality. Indeed, $\Pi(p) = \overline{N(\neg p)}$, which corresponds to the maximal set of agents for whom the falsity of p is not imperative, which could be expressed as "the truth of p is acceptable". $\Pi(p) \cap \Pi(\neg p)$ represents the set of agents that are indifferent to the truth value of p, and $N(p) \cap N(\neg p)$ represents a set of inconsistent agents, which may be empty or not. It can be checked that the set of agents who think that the truth of p is imperative is a subset of the set of agents who think that its falsity is not imperative, namely, $N(p) \subseteq \Pi(p)$ provided there is no inconsistent agent. The semantics of such a logic is defined by a so-called ma-distribution from a universe of discourse Ω to subsets of agents, formally, $\pi : \Omega \to 2^{All}$. Subsets are partially ordered, which contrasts with a possibilistic logic distribution that maps to a totally ordered scale. A multiple agent formula (p_i, A_i) leads to the following semantic representation by the ma-distribution

$$\pi_{(p_i, A_i)}(\omega) = \begin{cases} All & if \ \omega \models p_i \\ \overline{A_i} \ (= All \setminus A_i) & \text{otherwise.} \end{cases} \quad (2)$$

This expression indicates that agents not in A_i are indifferent to p_i, but agents in A_i find $\neg p_i$ unacceptable. More generally an ma-distribution should be interpreted as follows: $\pi(\omega)$ is the set of all agents that do not find ω unacceptable.

A ma-logic base $\Gamma = \{(p_i, A_i) | i = 1, m\}$ is associated to an ma-distribution, s.t. $\pi_\Gamma(\omega)$ is the intersection of sets of agents $\overline{A_i}$ that find the interpretation ω, for which all formulas p_i are false, acceptable.

$$\pi_\Gamma(\omega) = \begin{cases} All & if \ \forall (p_i, A_i) \in \Gamma, \omega \models p_i \\ \cap \{\overline{A_i} : (p_i, A_i) \in \Gamma, \ \omega \models \neg p_i\} & \text{otherwise.} \end{cases} \quad (3)$$

Two types of normalization exist for π: (i) The *ma-normalization* where $\exists \omega \in \Omega$ s.t. $\pi(\omega) = All$. Thus, all agents are altogether consistent and have at least one common not unacceptable interpretation. This normalization entails the following one. (ii) the *i-normalization* where $\bigcup \{\pi(\omega), \omega \in \Omega\} = All$. This means that each agent is consistent individually by having at least one interpretation that is not rejected. Yet, there may exist some contradictions between subgroups of agents, for instance $\Gamma = \{(p, A), (\neg p, \overline{A})\}$.

Example 2. Let us consider preferences of subsets of agents about drinks and their accompaniments. We consider that the agent population is described by two characteristics namely, being a *Woman* (W) or a *Man* (M) and being *Young* (Y) or *Old* (O). The variables are Drink $= \{\text{Tea}(t), \text{Coffee}(\neg t)\}$, Sugar $= \{\text{Yes}(s), \text{No}(\neg s)\}$. If we consider the ma-base: $\Gamma = \{(\neg t, M), (t, \overline{M \cap Y}), (\neg s, O), (s, Y)\}$, we can check that the ma-normalization is not verified. This is because $N(\neg t) \supseteq M$ and $N(t) \supseteq \overline{M \cap Y}$, hence $N(t) \cap N(\neg t) \supseteq \overline{M \cap Y} \cap M = M \cap O$. The old men demand tea and not tea.

3.2   Graphical Representation of Multiple Agent Preferences

Possibilistic networks are the graphical counterpart of possibilistic logic and one may go from one format to another while preserving semantics [3]. Likewise, given the close similarity between possibilistic and multiple agent logic, we propose a graphical reading of the latter. First, we introduce the multiple agent conditioning rule:

$$\Pi(p \wedge q) = \Pi(p|q) \cap \Pi(q) \quad (4)$$

This means that the set of all agents for whom the truth of $p \wedge q$ is not unacceptable is equal to the intersection between the set of all agents for whom the truth of q is not unacceptable and the set of all agents for whom the truth of p is not unacceptable when q is true. It generalizes the conditioning of Boolean possibilities to multiple agents. As in standard possibilistic networks, the decomposition of a possibility distribution consists in expressing a joint possibility distribution as a combination of conditional possibility distributions, a process that in the two-valued possibility case, does not yield a unique result, even when fixing the ordering of the variables, as shown above. Let E be a subset of $All \times \Omega$ representing an ma-distribution π, and let $E(a)$ the set of interpretations that agent $a \in All$ does not reject. The result of conditioning E by a set of interpretations B will be again defined as the minimally specific revision of $E(a)$ by B that agrees with the definition of conditioning (4), for each agent $a \in All$, namely $E_B(a) = E(a) \cap B$ if this intersection is not empty and B otherwise. Notice that the result differs from $E \cap (All \times B)$ even if this set is not empty. If B contains the set of models $[q]$ of q, then the characteristic function of E_B is denoted by $\boldsymbol{\Pi}(\cdot \mid q)$. The solution of Eq. (4) is then:

$$\boldsymbol{\Pi}(p|q) = \begin{cases} All \text{ if } \boldsymbol{\Pi}(p \wedge q) = \boldsymbol{\Pi}(q) \\ \boldsymbol{\Pi}(p \wedge q) \text{ otherwise.} \end{cases} \tag{5}$$

Let $V = \{X_1, \ldots, X_n\}$ be a set of variables, each variable X_i has a value domain $D(X_i)$. x_i denotes any value of X_i. In coherence with Eq. (4), we can use the chain rule:

$$\pi(X_1, \ldots, X_n) = \pi(X_1|X_2, \ldots, X_n) \cap .. \cap \pi(X_{n-1}|X_n) \tag{6}$$

to decompose a joint ma-distribution into a conjunction of conditional possibility distributions. Now, we introduce a new graphical model for representing multiple agent preferences, called ma-net for short. This model shares similar graphical component and independence relations as possibilistic networks [3]. Formally,

Definition 1 (ma-net). *A multiple agent network $\mathcal{G}$ over a set of variables V consists of two components: (i) Graphical component composed of a directed acyclic graph (DAG). (ii) Numerical component associating to each node X_i a conditional multiple agent distribution for each the context u_i of its parents $Pa(X_i)$.*

Example 3. Let us use the same variables and sets of agents as in Example 2, plus variable Cake $= \{\text{Yes}(c), \text{No}(\neg c)\}$. The network Drink $\rightarrow$ Cake $\leftarrow$ Sugar and the following conditional distributions: $\pi(t) = W$, $\pi(\neg t) = M \cap Y$, $\pi(s) = Y$, $\pi(\neg s) = O$, $\pi(c \mid ts) = M \cap Y$, $\pi(c \mid t\neg s) = O$, $\pi(c \mid \neg ts) = M \cap Y$, $\pi(c \mid \neg t\neg s) = W$, $\pi(\neg c \mid ts) = M \cap O$, $\pi(\neg c \mid t\neg s) = W$, $\pi(\neg c \mid \neg ts) = W$, $\pi(\neg c \mid \neg t\neg s) = M \cap O$ represent conditional preferences of agents. Using the chain rule, we have the following ma-distribution: $\pi(tsc) = \emptyset$, $\pi(ts\neg c) = W \cap Y \cap O = \emptyset$, $\pi(t\neg sc) = W \cap O$, $\pi(t\neg s\neg c) = W \cap O$, $\pi(\neg tsc) = M \cap Y$, $\pi(\neg ts\neg c) = M \cap Y \cap W = \emptyset$, $\pi(\neg t\neg sc) = M \cap Y \cap O \cap W = \emptyset$, $\pi(\neg t\neg s\neg c) = M \cap Y \cap O \cap M \cap O = \emptyset$. In ma-logic, we can encode it by the following base: $\{(t\neg s) \vee (\neg tsc), All), (\neg t \vee s, M \cup Y), (t \vee \neg s \vee \neg c, W \cup O)\}$.

Let us reconstruct the ma-conditional distributions $\pi(\text{Cake}|\text{Drink}, \text{Sugar})$ and the marginals $\pi(\text{Drink}), \pi(\text{Sugar})$ using the conditioning rule:

$\pi(tsc) = \pi(ts\neg c) = \pi(ts) = \emptyset$ so $\pi(c|ts) = \pi(\neg c|ts) = All.$
$\pi(t\neg sc) = \pi(t\neg s\neg c) = \pi(t\neg s) = W \cap O$ so $\pi(c|t\neg s) = \pi(\neg c|t\neg s) = All.$
$\pi(\neg tsc) = \pi(\neg ts) = M \cap Y$ so $\pi(c|\neg ts) = All.$
But $\pi(\neg ts\neg c) = \emptyset, \pi(\neg ts) = M \cap Y$ so $\pi(\neg c|\neg ts) = \emptyset.$
$\pi(\neg t\neg sc) = \pi(\neg t\neg s\neg c) = \pi(\neg t\neg s) = \emptyset$ so $\pi(c|\neg t\neg s) = \pi(\neg c|\neg t\neg s) = All.$
It can be checked that $\pi(s) = M \cap Y$, $\pi(\neg s) = W \cap O$, $\pi(t) = W \cap O$, $\pi(\neg t) = M \cap Y$. We can easily check that even if this network has different conditional tables it again yields the same ma-distribution.

4   Bridging Logical and Graphical Multiple Agent Representations

Transformations between possibilistic graphical and logical representations [3] can be adapted to multiple agent representations.

4.1   Logical Encoding of a Multiple Agent Network

The main idea consists in considering the ma-net $\mathcal{G}$ as a combination of local multiple agent logic bases. Each node $X_i \in V$ is associated to a logic base Γ_{X_i} containing formulas of the form $(x_i \vee \neg u_i, \overline{A})$ and $(\neg x_i \vee \neg u_i', \overline{A'})$ where u_i, u_i' are instantiations of $Pa(X_i)$, and $\pi(x_i|u_i) = A$, $\pi(\neg x_i|u_i') = A'$ appear in the tables of $\mathcal{G}$ and $A, A' \neq All$. Each (conditional) possibility is viewed as a necessity formula expressing the material counterpart of the condition. Indeed, for a single agent $N(\neg p \mid q) = 1 - \Pi(p \mid q) = 1 - \Pi(p \wedge q) = N(\neg q \vee \neg p) = 1$ provided that $\Pi(p|q) = 0$. So, in the multiagent case we can replace $\pi(x_i|u_i)$ by the clause $\neg x_i \vee \neg u_i$ when $A \neq All$. When considered separately, we can see that the conditional possibilities can be recovered from the local possibility distribution such that $\Pi(x_i) = \bigcup_{\omega \models x_i} \pi(\omega)$ since from $\Pi(x_i \wedge u_i) = A$ and $\Pi(u_i) = All$ we get $\Pi(x_i|u_i) = A$ (by solving (4)). A multiple agent network is rarely normalized due to conflicting preferences (which contrasts with standard possibilistic networks), thus each conditional possibility distribution is represented by more than one formula. Combined together, it is clear that the resulting logic base is inconsistent with a degree equal to the intersection of all necessity values associated to formulas. Then, the multiple agent base associated with the ma-net $\mathcal{G}$ is $\Gamma_{\mathcal{G}} = \Gamma_{X_1} \bigcup \cdots \bigcup \Gamma_{X_n}, \forall X_i \in V$. The joint possibility distribution computed from the multiple agent network $\mathcal{G}$ by the chain rule is the intersection of the possibility distributions associated to each node. The possibility distribution associated to $\Gamma_{\mathcal{G}}$ is also an intersection of distributions associated to the formula(s) corresponding to each node. This explains why the two representations are represented by the same ma-distribution. This is the counterpart of the fact that the union of possibilistic logic bases corresponds to the min-based aggregation of their distributions [4]. Thus, the ma-net of Example 3 can be rewritten as the union of the bases $\Gamma_{\text{Cake}} = \{(t \vee \neg s \vee c, All)\}$, $\Gamma_{\text{Drink}} = \{(\neg t, M \vee Y), (t, W \vee O)\}$, $\Gamma_{\text{Sugar}} = \{(\neg s, W \vee O), (s, M \vee Y)\}$.

4.2   Transformation of a Multiple Agent Logic into a Graphical Structure

This converse transformation is more complex. Indeed, the independencies represented by the network are not explicit in logic bases. The transformation consists of two steps: (i) Constructing the network, thus detecting the dependencies, (ii) Computing the conditional possibilities. First, the logic base should be put into a special form, where tautologies are removed (by removing subsumed formulas) each formula should represent a disjunction of a variable value and an instance of all it parents. An algorithm performing this type of transformation is given in [3]. To adapt this algorithm the following definitions are useful:

Definition 2. *Let (p, A) be a formula in Γ. Then (p, A) is said to be subsumed by Γ if $\Gamma_{\supseteq A} \vdash p$, where $\Gamma_{\supseteq A}$ is composed of classical formulas that appear in Γ in association with sets of agents that include A or are equal to A.*

Removing subsumed formulas does not change the possibility distribution. This means that several syntactically different multiple agent logic bases may have the same possibility distribution as their semantic counterpart. For instance, $(x \vee y, A \cap B)$ is subsumed by (x, B), therefore $\Gamma = \{(x \vee y, A \cap B), (x, B)\} = \{(x, B)\}$.

Definition 3. *Let Γ be a multiple agent logic base in a clausal form, where all clauses involve an instance of a variable X. Let $\mathcal{Z}$ be the set of other variables appearing in the clauses of Γ. A clausal completion of Γ with respect to variable X, denoted by $E(\Gamma)$, is the set of clauses of the form $(x \vee \neg\mathbf{z}, A)$ where x is an instance of X, $\mathbf{z}$ is an instance of all variables in $\mathcal{Z}$, and $A = \bigcup\{A_i : (x \vee p_i, A_i) \in \Gamma, \mathbf{z} \models \neg p_i\}$, with $\bigcup(\emptyset) = \emptyset$.*

It can be proved that the two bases Γ and $E(\Gamma)$ are equivalent, i.e. correspond to the same possibility distribution.

The notions of subsumption and clausal completion are instrumental in the procedure (similar to the one in [3]) for finding the dependence graph from the multiple agent logic base. More precisely, for each X_i in V we execute these steps:

- Determination of the local base for X_i: Let $(x_i \vee p, A)$ be a clause of Γ s.t. x_i is an instance of X_i, and p is only built from $X_{i+1}, \ldots X_n$. If $(x_i \vee p, A)$ is subsumed, then remove it from Γ. If $\Gamma \models (p, A)$, then replace $(x_i \vee p, A)$ by (p, A). Let K_i be the set of clauses $(x_i \vee p,)$ in Γ s.t. p is only built from $X_{i+1}, \ldots, X_n$
- The parents of the variable X_i are $Pa(X_i) = \{X_j : \exists c \in K_i \text{ s.t. } c \text{ contains an instance of } X_j\}$
- Compute the clausal completion of K_i: Replace in Γ, K_i by its clausal completion $E(K_i)$
- Remove incoherent data: For each $(x_i \vee p, A)$ of Γ (where p is built from $X_{i+1}, \ldots, X_n$ s.t. $\Gamma \models (p, A)$ replace $(x_i \vee p, A)$ by (p, A).

– Produce Γ_i: Let Γ_i be the set of clauses $(x_i \vee p, A)$ in Γ s.t. p is only built from $X_{i+1}, \ldots, X_n$.

At the end of the procedure, each node X_i of the constructed graph is associated to a local multiple agent base $\Gamma_{X_i} = \{(x_i \vee u_i)|x_i \in D(X_i)$ and u_i an instatiation of $Pa(X_i)\}$ containing only an instantiation of the node and its parents. These local bases are useful to compute the conditional possibilities such that:

$$\pi_A(x_i|u_i) = \begin{cases} \overline{A} & \text{if } (\neg x_i \vee \neg u_i, A) \in \Gamma \\ All & \text{otherwise.} \end{cases} \tag{7}$$

For instance if $\Gamma = \{(x \vee y, A), (x \vee t, B)\}$, this base is equivalent to $\{(x \vee y \vee t, A \cup B), (x \vee \neg y \vee t, B), (x \vee y \vee \neg t, A)\}$, so, $\pi(\neg x|\neg y \neg t) = \overline{A} \cap \overline{B}$, $\pi(\neg x|\neg yt) = \overline{A}$, $\pi(\neg x|y\neg t) = \overline{B}$, $\pi(\neg x|yt) = All$.

5   Specializing Representations and Queries

Before handling queries, we discuss two types of specializations, performed equivalently on ma-nets and ma-logic bases, w.r.t. a subset of agents.

5.1   Sections and Restrictions of Networks and Logic Bases

In some cases, one may need to display preferences that are only related to a subset of agents. Two possible operations are conceivable.

First, one may extract the network with *common* preferences expressed by a subset of agents A, i.e. preferences approved by each element in A. This is called a *section*. The obtained network has the same structure (with possible deletion of nodes or edges) as the original ma-net and its conditional possibilities are computed such that: $\pi_A^\vee(x_i|u_i) = A$ if $A \subseteq \pi(x_i|u_i)$ and $\pi_A^\vee(x_i|u_i) = \emptyset$ otherwise. Its logical counterpart Γ_A is a propositional logic base where only formulas weighted by A_i, such that $A \subseteq A_i$, are retained. This network can be represented by a Boolean one, the same for each agent in A. If the section Γ_A is inconsistent, then, all the interpretations have a possibility degree equal to 0. Second, one may restrain the set of agents to (subsets of) A, that is, forget about preferences of agents out of A. This is called a *restriction*. The corresponding network can be constructed as: $\pi_A^\downarrow(x_i|u_i) = \pi(x_i|u_i) \cap A$. Its logical reading corresponds to a multiple agent logic base containing multiple agent formulas of the form $(\neg x_i \vee \neg u_i, A_i \cap A)$ s.t. $A_i \cap A \neq \emptyset$.

Example 4. In Example 2, the logic base corresponding to the common preferences of the subset $W \cup O$ is $\Gamma_{W \cup O} = \{t\}$. However, the restriction of the multiple-agent base to subset $W \cup O$ corresponds to $\Gamma_{W \cup O}^\downarrow = \{(\neg t, M \cap O), (t, W \cup O), (\neg s, O), (s, W \cap Y)\}$.

5.2   Optimization, Dominance and Other Queries

Optimal configurations for group A of agents in an ma-net exist if the set of preferences of group of agents A is consistent, precisely, if for each node and depending on the parents instantiation, the set of agents represented by the conditional possibility is a superset of A. Finding an optimal configuration is straightforward and linear wrt the number of variables. Starting from the root nodes, we choose each time the value(s) x_i s.t. $A \subseteq \pi(x_i)$. Then, depending on the parents instantiation, each time we again choose a value with a conditional possibility that includes or equals A. In case $\pi(x_i)$ is not a superset of A for some i, then the algorithm stops and the set of agents A have inconsistent preferences. Note that under the ma-normalization, one is always sure to have at least one preferred configuration no matter the set A. In the Boolean setting, dominance queries just amount to testing if each of the two interpretations is accepted or rejected. Another possible query, is to search for the maximal set of agents that prefer a given interpretation. The answer can be obtained by sweeping through the ma-net starting from the roots with the set of agents initialized to *All*, performing, at each node, the intersection of the current evaluation with the ma-possibility corresponding to the value of the node variable for the given interpretation.

6   Extension to Graded Possibilistic Networks. A Brief Outline

Multi-agent possibilistic logic. We can extend multi-agent possibilistic logic to graded preferences of agents using fuzzy set-valued counterparts of the notions of possibility distribution, possibility measure, and necessity measure. Formulas in ma-π logic are of the form $(p, \alpha/A)$ (where α is a necessity measure and A is a subset of agents) expressing that, for at least all agents in A, it is imperative to satisfy p with a minimal priority degree α. Asserting $(p, \alpha/A)$ means that A is the maximal set of agents that tolerate the falsity of p with level at most $1 - \alpha$, while the agents in $\overline{A}$ arc indifferent to the truth or falsity of p, finding both tolerable at level 1. By duality, $\Pi(p)$ is the fuzzy set of agents who do not require the truth of $\neg p$ imperatively. Each possibilistic ma-logic base Γ is associated to an ma-π distribution π_Γ.

$$\pi_\Gamma(\omega) = \begin{cases} 1/All & \text{if } \forall (p_i, \alpha_i/A_i) \in \Gamma, \omega \models p_i \\ \bigcap \{(1 - \alpha_i)/A_i \cup 1/\overline{A_i} \mid (p_i, \alpha_i/A_i) \in \Gamma, \ \omega \models \neg p_i\} & \text{otherwise.} \end{cases} \tag{8}$$

where $\pi_\Gamma(\omega) = \alpha/A$ means that at most all the agents in A find ω acceptable with a maximal satisfaction degree equal to α. The ma-normalization and the i-normalization defined above are still valid. Precisely, ma-normalization is still related to the consistency of the propositional logic base and means that $\exists \omega \in \Omega$, $\pi(\omega) = 1/All$, where $1/All$ is clearly the same as *All*. Moreover, the i-normalization is still defined by $\Pi(\Omega) = \bigcup_{\omega \in \Omega} \pi(\omega) = All$, and means that all the agents are individually consistent.

Example 5. Let us consider a multiple agent possibilistic logic corresponding to the preferences over the variable Drink $\in \{t, \neg t\}$: $\Gamma = \{(\neg t, 0.9/\overline{W}), (t, 0.3/\overline{M \cap Y})\}$. The possibility distribution corresponding to this base is:

$\pi(t) = ((0.1/\overline{W}) \cup (1/W)) \cap (1/All) = (0.1/\overline{W}) \cup (1/W)$,

$\pi(\neg t) = (1/All) \cap ((0.7/\overline{M \cap Y}) \cup (1/M \cap Y)) = 0.7/\overline{M \cap Y} \cup (1/M \cap Y)$.

$\pi(t)$ indicates that women find a cup of tea fully acceptable and men find it tolerable at best to a very low level 0.1. The preference base for women is $\Gamma_W = \{(t, 0.3)\}$.

Multi-agent possibilistic networks. Based on the same conditioning (Eq. (4)) and the same chain rule (Eq. (6)), where intersection is extended to fuzzy sets, we can define multi-agent possibilistic networks (ma-π nets for short) an extension of the above-defined graphical counterpart of ma-logic, that have the same structure as ma-nets.

Example 6. Let us consider the ma-π tables of Table 3, associated to the network **Drink** $\rightarrow$ **Cake** $\leftarrow$ **Sugar**. We can see that the local possibility distribution associated to node 'Drink' corresponds to the logic base of Example 5. It is clear that the network is not ma-normalized and this can be verified on its associated possibility distribution. For instance, $\pi(t\neg sc) = (1/W \cup 0.1/\overline{W}) \cap (1/O \cup 0.2/Y) \cap (1/O \cup 0.1/Y) = (1/W \cap O) \cup (0.1/M \cup Y)$. It is clear that non-sugared tea with cake ($t\neg sc$) is satisfactory at degree 1 only for old women ($W \cap O$).

Table 3. Conditional tables of an ma-π net

$\pi(t)$	$\pi(\neg t)$			$\pi(s)$	$\pi(\neg s)$
$1/W \cup 0.1/\overline{W}$	$1/M \cap Y \cup 0.7/\overline{M \cap Y}$			$1/Y \cup 0.6/O$	$1/O \cup 0.2/Y$

$\pi(.\|.)$	ts	$t\neg s$	$\neg ts$	$\neg t\neg s$
c	$(1/Y) \cup (0.3/O)$	$(1/O) \cup (0.1/Y)$	$(1/M \cap Y) \cup (0.2/\overline{M \cap Y})$	$(1/W) \cup (0.9/M)$
$\neg c$	$(1/O) \cup (0.5/Y)$	$(1/W) \cup (0.6/M)$	$(1/W) \cup (0.1/M)$	$(1/M \cap O) \cup (0.7/\overline{M \cap O})$

From an ma-π net to an instantiated π-Pref net. In contrast with ma-nets, ma-π nets enable us to express levels of preference. Indeed, preferences are no longer all or nothing. Then, the network pertaining to the preferences of a set of agents A, induced as a section of the ma-π net, corresponds to a possibilistic preference network (π-Pref net) with instantiated weights. Its structure is similar to the ma-π net and the local possibility distributions associated to A are defined by: $\pi_A(x_i|u_i) = \alpha$, $\forall A \subseteq B$ s.t. $\pi_\Gamma(x_i|u_i) \subseteq \alpha/B$. Note that the induced net is not always normalized due to the possible lack of normalization of the ma-π net. Clearly, normalization states that the preferences of the set A of agents are consistent and at least one interpretation has a possibility degree equal to 1 for agents in A.

Example 7. Consider the ma-π net defined in Example 6. Its restriction to the set of agents $W \cap O$ are possibilistic tables: $\pi(t) = 1$, $\pi(\neg t) = 0.7$, $\pi(s) = 0.6$, $\pi(\neg s) = 1$,

$\pi(c|ts) = 0.3$, $\pi(c|t\neg s) = 1$, $\pi(c|\neg ts) = 0.2$, $\pi(c|\neg t\neg s) = 1$, $\pi(\neg c|ts) = \pi(\neg c|t\neg s) = \pi(\neg c|\neg ts) = 1$, and $\pi(\neg c|\neg t\neg s) = 0.7$. The resulting network is normalized. The joint possibility distribution too. It can be computed using the standard product-based chain rule, and $t\neg sc$ and $t\neg s\neg c$ are the best interpretations ($\pi(t\neg sc) = \pi(t\neg s\neg c) = 1$).

7   Related Work

Few models exist for representing multiple agent preferences. First, multi-agent CP-nets (mCP-nets) [8] are an extension of CP-nets in a multiple agent setting. They are made of several partial CP-nets representing the preferences of each agent, such that a partial CP-net is a CP-net where some variables may not be ranked when the agent is indifferent about the values of these variables. Graphically, the network is obtained by combining the partial CP-nets. We can reason about an mCP-net by querying each partial CP-net, and then deduce the answer using different voting concepts like Pareto optimality, lexicographic ordering, and quantitative ranking. Second, probabilistic CP-nets (PCP-nets) [5] enable a compact representation of a probability distribution over several CP-nets and stand for a summary of collective preferences. A PCP-net has the same graphical component as a CP-net. Lastly, generalized additive independence (GAI) nets [7] are quantitative graphical models where preferences of agents are expressed by utilities. In a multiple agent framework, each node is characterized by a utility vector where each of its elements represents the utility of the node given by an agent. An aggregation procedure is then applied to these utilities to find the optimal solution.

As shown here, ma-nets represent the collective preferences of agents with a single network, similarly to PCP-nets and GAI nets (and in contrast with mCP-nets), which facilitates the handling of preferences. Besides, it may handle the indifference and non consistency of some agents, and can deal with the agents based on their profiles and not only in terms of proportions contrarily to GAI nets and PCP-nets. The model can be extended to describe preference intensities by adding priorities, unlike mCP-nets and PCP-nets.

8   Concluding Remark

This paper calls for several lines of research. The handling of graded preferences has been only outlined. Algorithms for different types of queries have to be extended to this general case. We may also think of other requests such as identifying non consistent agents directly from multiple agent (possibilistic) networks. Besides, the full strength of the representation power of π-Pref nets comes from a symbolic handling of the priorities yet to be developed.

References

1. Ben Amor, N., Dubois, D., Gouider, H., Prade, H.: Graphical models for preference representation: an overview. In: Scalable Uncertainty Management - 10th International Conference, SUM 2016, Nice, France, 21–23 September 2016, Proceedings, pp. 96–111 (2016)
2. Belhadi, A., Dubois, D., Khellaf-Haned, F., Prade, H.: Multiple agent possibilistic logic. J. Appl. Non-Classic. Logics **23**, 299–320 (2013)
3. Benferhat, S., Dubois, D., Garcia, L., Prade, H.: On the transformation between possibilistic logic bases and possibilistic causal networks. Int. J. Approximate Reasoning **29**(2), 135–173 (2002)
4. Benferhat, S., Dubois, D., Prade, H.: From semantic to syntactic approaches to information combination in possibilistic logic. In: Aggregation and Fusion of Imperfect Information, Physica Verlag, pp. 141–151 (1997)
5. Bigot, D., Zanuttini, B., Fargier, H., Mengin, J.: Probabilistic conditional preference networks. In: Proceeding UAI'21 (2013)
6. Dubois, D., Prade, H.: Possibilistic logic: a retrospective and prospective view. Fuzzy Sets Syst. **144**(1), 3–23 (2004)
7. Dubus, J., Gonzales, C., Perny, P.: Choquet optimization using GAI networks for multiagent/multicriteria decision-making. In: Algorithmic Decision Theory, pp. 377–389 (2009)
8. Rossi, F., Venable, K., Walsh, T.: mCP-nets: representing and reasoning with preferences of multiple agents. In: Proceeding of AAAI, vol. 4, pp. 729–734 (2004)

A Probabilistic Relational Model Approach for Fault Tree Modeling

Thierno Kante[1,2](✉) and Philippe Leray[1](✉)

[1] LS2N (UMR CNRS 6004), DUKe Research Group,
University of Nantes, Nantes, France
{thierno-sadou.kante,philippe.leray}@univ-nantes.fr
[2] EDICIA, Carquefou, France

Abstract. Fault Trees or Bow Tie Diagrams are widely used for system dependability assessment. Some probabilistic extensions have been proposed by using Bayesian network formalism. This article proposes a general modeling approach under the form of a probabilistic relational model (PRM), relational extension of Bayesian networks, that can represent any fault tree, defined as an event tree with possible safety barriers, simply described in a relational database. We first describe an underlying relational schema describing a generic fault tree, and the probabilistic dependencies needed to model the existence of an event given the possible existence of its related causes and eventual safety barriers.

Keywords: Fault trees · Bow Tie diagram · Bayesian network · Probabilistic relational model

1 Introduction

Risk prevention has always been a major concern in many areas such as industrial system, offshore and public security... Nowadays, different approaches for risk analysis in the areas of Dependability (operating reliability) have been proposed in the literature such as preliminary risk analysis (PRA), Petri networks, Bow-Tie method, Fault Tree method.

Fault Trees or Bow Tie Diagrams are widely used for system dependability assessment. Some probabilistic extensions have been proposed by using Bayesian network formalism. This article proposes a general modeling approach under the form of a probabilistic relational model (PRM), relational extension of Bayesian networks, that can represent any fault tree, defined as an event tree with possible safety barriers, simply described in a relational database. We first describe the underlying relational schema describing a generic fault tree, and the probabilistic dependencies needed to model the existence of an event given the possible existence of its related causes and eventual safety barriers.

The rest of the paper is organized as follows: Sect. 2 presents the background about Fault Trees, Probabilistic Graphical Models (PGMs) such as Probabilistic Relational Models, and related works about use of PGMs for reliability. Section 3

© Springer International Publishing AG 2017
S. Benferhat et al. (Eds.): IEA/AIE 2017, Part II, LNAI 10351, pp. 154–162, 2017.
DOI: 10.1007/978-3-319-60045-1_18

presents our contribution, starting from a description of a Fault Tree, and building a generic PRM from its relational schema to the probabilistic dependencies modeling the initial fault tree. We summarize our work and discuss open questions and perspectives offered by our contribution in Sect. 4.

2   Background

2.1   Fault Trees (FTs)

Several formalisms have been proposed in Systems Dependability Assessment. They are classified into two categories: combinatorial models (as fault trees or reliability block diagrams) and state-space models (as Markov chain or Petri nets). Among the combinatorial models, FT is one of the most popular and diffused formalisms for analysis of large, safety critical systems [9]. A FT is synthetically defined by all combinations of events that can lead to failure. This search of combinations of events that can cause a failure continues with a search of minimum cut-sets (sets of basic events, or conditions, necessary and sufficient to produce the failure) and then an evaluation of the likelihood of the occurrence of the failure from the combination of the likelihood that elementary events occur. The FT modeling is based on a descending approach (top-down approach). It is based on the following assumptions: (i) events are binary events (working/not-working); (ii) events are statistically independent; and (iii) relationships between events and causes are represented by means of logical gates [1]. In risk analysis, to assess the impacts of an undesired event, an event tree (ET) is added to the FT, resulting in bow tie model. The goal is to place and assess barriers to prevent or protect from the undesired event. An example of Fault tree associated with safety barriers is described in Fig. 1.

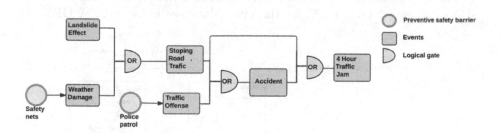

Fig. 1. Example of a Fault Tree with safety barriers.

However, the FTs and Bow tie diagrams are static models. Dynamic fault trees have been proposed to extend standard FTs to dynamic systems [5].

2.2   Probabilistic Relational Models

For representing uncertain knowledge, Probabilistic Graphical Models, in particular, Bayesian networks (BNs) are increasingly used in the field of artificial intelligence [11]. They are a powerful modeling and analysis tool that has been applied in a variety of real-world tasks. Bayesian networks have been extended in order to model more complex problems, such as dynamic ones with Dynamic Bayesian networks, object-oriented ones or relational ones with Probabilistic Relational Models.

As defined in [7], A Probabilistic Relational Model (PRM) Π for a relational schema $\mathcal{R}$ (i.e., set of entities and relations) is defined through a qualitative dependency structure $\mathcal{S}$ and a set of parameters associated with it $\theta_{\mathcal{S}}$. The relational schema $\mathcal{R}$ describes a set of classes $\mathcal{X} = \{X_1, \dots, X_1\}$, each of which has a set of descriptive attributes denoted by $\mathcal{A}(X)$, which take on a range of values $\mathcal{V}(X.A)$ and a set of reference slots denoted by $\mathcal{R}(X) = \{\rho_1 \dots \rho_k\}$. Each $X.\rho$ has X as domain type and Y as a range type, where $Y \in \mathcal{X}$. A sequence of slots $\rho_1 \dots \rho_k$, where $\forall i, Range[\rho_i] = Dom[\rho_{i+1}]$ defines a slot chain K. The notion of aggregation is also adopted from the database theory: an aggregate γ takes a multi-set of values of some ground type, and returns a summary of it, a single-valued attribute is derived from the aggregation function.

Formally, a PRM Π is defined as follows. For each class $X \in \mathcal{X}$ and each descriptive attribute $A \in \mathcal{A}(X)$, we have:

- A set of parents $Pa(X.A) = \{U_1, \dots, U_l\}$, where each U_i has the form $X.B$ if it is a simple attribute in the same relation or $\gamma(X.K.B)$, where K is a slot chain and γ is an aggregation function.
- A legal conditional probability distribution (CPD), $P(X.A|Pa(X.A))$.

An example is described in Fig. 2 (right) for the relational schema depicted in Fig. 2 (left). Probabilistic inference is performed on a *Ground Bayesian Network* (GBN) obtained from a PRM for the given database instance $\mathcal{I}$. A GBN is

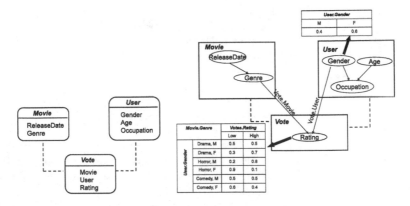

Fig. 2. (left) An example of relational schema. (right) An example of Probabilistic Relational Model.

generated by a process (also called unrolling) of copying the associated PRM for every object in $\mathcal{I}$. Thus a GBN will have a node for every attribute of every object in $\mathcal{I}$ and probabilistic dependencies and CPDs as in the PRM.

2.3 Related Work

The formalism of BNs is well suited to represent complex multi-state systems. Recent works have shown that reliability formalisms such as event trees, fault trees (FTs) or Bow Tie diagram are easy to model by an equivalent BN. For example, [13] has shown that a reliability structure represented as a reliability block diagram can be transformed into a Bayesian network model. This approach makes it possible to compute the reliability of the system using probabilistic inference in the equivalent BN. Similar works have proposed a language allowing to transform fault trees or Bow Tie diagrams into Bayesian networks [1,6,8]. However, these approaches do not allow to model the dynamic aspect of the system. In [2,12,14], a description of a Dynamic fault tree (DFT) with a Dynamic Bayesian network (DBN) has been proposed. These works consider time as a discrete variable and describe temporal probabilistic dependencies with Markov chain. A generalization to continuous time has been proposed by [3,10].

The majority of the previously cited methods deal with Boolean variables (existence of an event). A few of them consider the notion of barrier, and when this barrier is defined, its existence is also Boolean. In addition, BNs are not adapted to model large and complex domains because the structure of the network is fixed in advance. Thus, no part is reusable and therefore explicitly requires rewriting structure or parameter regularity. The data and the model are not decoupled, so taking into account a new component requires updating BN model by an expert or a complete learning of the model. As in the oriented-object framework used in [14], Probabilistic relational models (PRMs) improve the possibilities of generalization in this direction.

3 Contribution

We propose here a general modeling approach under the form of a probabilistic relational model (PRM) that can represent any fault tree, defined as an event tree with possible safety barriers, simply described in a relational database.

3.1 Fault Tree Modeling

We suppose that our FT is defined by a triplet $(\mathcal{E}, \mathcal{G}, \mathcal{B})$.

$\mathcal{E} = \{E_i\}$ is a set of events, with a prior probability $PriorStrength(E_i)$ defined in a set of ordered discrete values $\{absent, low, ...strong\}$.

$\mathcal{G} = \{G_j\}$ is a set of gates, with $Inputs(G_i) \subset \mathcal{E}$, $Output(G_i) \in \mathcal{E}$, $Type(G_i) \in \{OR, AND, ...\}$ and $DependencyStrength(E_i, output(G_j)) \in \{absent, low, ... strong\}$ for each $E_i \in Inputs(G_j)$.

$\mathcal{B} = \{B_k, (E_i, G_j)\}$ is a set of barriers. A barrier B_k is associated to one specific event E_i appearing as an input of a given gate G_j, with a $BarrierStrength(B_k, E_i, G_j) \in \{absent, low, \ldots strong\}$. We can notice here that our definition of barrier is related to one association input-output for a given gate, more general than the usual one where a barrier is only describing an effect on a gate output.

3.2   A PRM for Fault Tree Modeling

Relational Schema. From the previously defined Fault Tree, we propose a relational schema described in Fig. 3 with two entity classes *Event*, class of events, and *Barrier*, class of barriers. and two association classes *CausedBy*, association between events, and *BarrierOf* association between a barrier and one association of events.

Instances of the classes are defined by the following rules: (i) one instance of *Event* for each $E_i \in \mathcal{E}$, (ii) one instance of *Barrier* for each $B_k \in \mathcal{B}$, (iii) one *CausedBy* instance for each $G_j \in \mathcal{G}$ and $E_i \in Inputs(G_j)$ with $Cause = E_i$ and $Effect = Output(G_j)$, and (iv) one *BarrierOf* instance for each $\{B_k, (E_i, G_j)\} \in \mathcal{B}$ with $Barr = B_k$ and $CauseById$ is the instance related to gate G_j and input E_i.

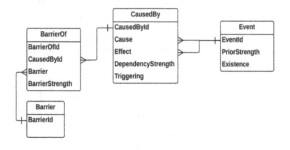

Fig. 3. Relational schema for Fault Tree modeling.

Probabilistic Dependencies. The probabilistic dependencies are defined over the corresponding attributes of the previous classes. $Event.existence \in \{absent, low, \ldots strong\}$ represents the potential existence of an event. This attribute can be observed, or will be estimated depending on its prior strength ($Event.PriorStrength$) and the existence of the events than can raise it in the fault tree.

We propose to model the logical gate between an event and its possible causes by an ICI (independence of causal influence) model [4] by adding $CausedBy.Triggering$ attribute as an inhibitor node between each cause and the effect node. This attribute $Triggering$ has the same domain than $Event.Existence$. This model will correspond to probabilistic dependencies between $CausedBy.Triggering$ and $CausedBy.Cause.Existence$, and deterministic function γ (determined by gate type) between $Event.existence$ and the set of possible triggering associations $Event.Effect^{-1}.Triggering$. For instance the deterministic function corresponding to an OR gate is the max function.

The triggering will be weighted by $CausedBy.DependencyStrength$ or inhibited by the strength of the associated barriers $CausedBy.CauseById^{-1}.BarrierStrength$. As this association can possibly be inhibited by several barriers, we decide here to use the max aggregation function to merge the effects of these possible barriers.

Conditional Probability Distributions. The conditional probability distribution (CPD) $P(Event.Existence \mid PriorStrength, \gamma(Event.Effect^{-1}.Triggering))$ is defined by a simple dependency. When the corresponding event is a root event, $\gamma(Event.Effect^{-1}.Triggering)) = NULL$ and this CPD is an increasing function depending only on $PriorStrength$. In the opposite, when this event is not a root event, this CPD is independent from the $PriorStrength$ and corresponds only to the deterministic function γ.

The conditional probability distribution concerning $CausedBy.Triggering$, $P(CausedBy.Triggering \mid CausedBy.Cause.Existence, \dots CausedBy.DependencyStrength, max(CausedBy.CauseById^{-1}.BarrierStrength))$, is defined by two components. First the dependency between $Caused.Triggering$ and $CausedBy.Cause.existence$ is parametrized like in any ICI model, where the strength of each cause is here weighted by the $CausedBy.DependencyStrength$ or inhibited by the several possible $BarrierStrength$.

The distributions $P(Event.PriorStrength)$, $P(CausedBy.Dependency-Strength)$, $P(Barrier.BarrierStrength)$ correspond to probability distribution of observed root attributes, so their exact definition has no impact in our model. We choose here uniform distributions.

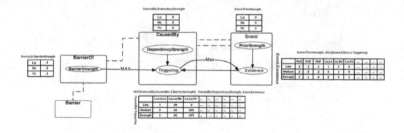

Fig. 4. Probabilistic relational model for Fault Tree modeling.

Ground Bayesian Network. Figure 4 shows the corresponding probabilistic relational model (PRM) defined with its relational schema, its associated probabilistic dependencies and conditional probability distributions. As defined in Sect. 2.2, probabilistic inference is performed on the Ground Bayesian Network

Event

Eventid	PriorStrength	Existence
Landslide effect	low	?
Weather damage	low	?
Stopping road traffic	medium	?
4 hour traffic jam	medium	?
Traffic offense	medium	?
Accident	low	?

BarrierOf

BarrierOfid	Barrierid	CausedById	BarrierStrength
BO1	Safety nets	C2	?
BO2	Police patrol	C5	?

Barrier

Barrierid
Safety nets
Police patrol

CausedBy

CausedById	Cause	Effect	DependencyStrength	Triggering
C1	Landslide effect	Stopping road traffic	strong	?
C2	Weather damage	Stopping road traffic	strong	?
C3	Stopping road traffic	Accident	medium	?
C4	Stopping road traffic	4 hour traffic jam	strong	?
C5	Traffic offense	Accident	medium	?
C6	Accident	4 hour traffic jam	strong	?

Fig. 5. Instantiations of the relational schema describing the FT model of Fig. 1.

obtained from a PRM by unrolling the PRM template model for each instance of each class in the database.

We present here a simple example with the description of a FT (Fig. 1) in the database of Fig. 5 with 6 events, 3 OR gates and 2 barriers. Figure 6 describes the ground BN obtained from our PRM for this FT. Given a set of *Event.Existence* and possible *BarrierOf.BarrierStrength*, the GBN can finally be queried to estimate the probability of other *Event.Existence*.

Figure 6 presents two scenarios in the same context where *Landslide effect* is low, *Weather damage* is medium and *Traffic offense* is strong. In the first scenario, we consider that the two barriers are low, and we observe that the

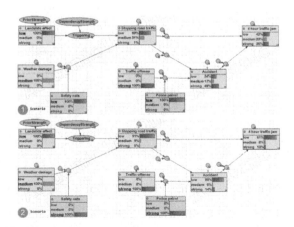

Fig. 6. Ground Bayesian network obtained by unrolling the PRM of Fig. 4 on the instance given in Fig. 5, with two scenarios of probabilistic inference.

probability of having a low *Stopping road traffic* is 69%, the probability of a strong *Accident* is 49%, and the probability of a low *4 h traffic jam* is 42%.

In the second scenario, we consider strong barriers, and we observe that the probability of having a low *Stopping road traffic* is 91% (increasing because of the *Safety net* barrier), the probability of a strong *Accident* is 14% (decreasing because of the *Police patrol* barrier), and the probability of a low *4 h traffic jam* is 81% (because of the cumulative effects of both barriers).

4 Conclusion and Perspectives

This preliminary work proposes a general modeling approach under the form of a probabilistic relational model, that can represent any fault tree, defined as an event tree with possible safety barriers, simply described in a relational database. We first describe the underlying relational schema used to model a generic fault tree, and the probabilistic dependencies needed to model the existence of an event given the possible existence of its related causes and eventual barriers.

The way we model barriers in this work is more general than a simple inhibition of a gate output. Our barriers can (totally or partially) inhibit any input of a logical gate. As already proposed in the literature, we also use ICI models (such as NoisyMax) in order to deal with probabilistic extensions of the logical gates used in Fault Trees. With our proposal, adding new events, gates or barriers simply consists in adding new instances in the database, and generating a new ground Bayesian network where probabilistic inference can then be performed.

References

1. Bobbio, A., Portinale, L., Minichino, M., Ciancamerla, E.: Improving the analysis of dependable systems by mapping fault trees into Bayesian networks. RESS **71**(3), 249–260 (2001)
2. Boudali, H., Dugan, J.B.: A discrete-time Bayesian network reliability modeling and analysis framework. RESS **87**(3), 337–349 (2005)
3. Boudali, H., Dugan, J.B.: A continuous-time Bayesian network reliability modeling, and analysis framework. IEEE Trans. Reliab. **55**(1), 86–97 (2006)
4. Díez, F.J., Druzdzel, M.J.: Canonical probabilistic models for knowledge engineering. Technical report, Research Centre on Intelligent Decision-Support Systems (2000)
5. Dugan, J.B., Bavuso, S.J., Boyd, M.A.: Dynamic fault-tree models for fault-tolerant computer systems. IEEE Trans. Reliab. **41**(3), 363–377 (1992)
6. Duval, C., Fallet-Fidry, G., Iung, B., Weber, P., Levrat, E.: A Bayesian network-based integrated risk analysis approach for industrial systems: application to heat sink system and prospects development. In: Proceeding of the Institution of Mechanical Engineers, Part O: Journal of Risk and Reliability, p. 1748006X12451091 (2012)
7. Friedman, N., Getoor, L., Koller, D., Pfeffer, A.: Learning probabilistic relational models. In: IJCAI, vol. 99, pp. 1300–1309 (1999)

8. Khakzad, N., Khan, F., Amyotte, P.: Dynamic safety analysis of process systems by mapping bow-tie into Bayesian network. Process Saf. Environ. Prot. **91**(1), 46–53 (2013)

9. Leveson, N.G.: System Safety and Computers. Addison-Wesley, Boston (1995)

10. Montani, S., Portinale, L., Bobbio, A., Codetta-Raiteri, D.: RADYBAN: a tool for reliability analysis of dynamic fault trees through conversion into dynamic Bayesian networks. RESS **93**(7), 922–932 (2008)

11. Pearl, J.: Probabilistic Reasoning in Intelligent Systems: Networks of Plausible Reasoning. Morgan Kaufmann Publishers, Los Altos (1988)

12. Portinale, L., Codetta-Raiteri, D., Montani, S.: Supporting reliability engineers in exploiting the power of dynamic Bayesian networks. Int. J. Approximate Reasoning **51**(2), 179–195 (2010)

13. Torres-Toledano, J.G., Sucar, L.E.: Bayesian networks for reliability analysis of complex systems. In: Coelho, H. (ed.) IBERAMIA 1998. LNCS, vol. 1484, pp. 195–206. Springer, Heidelberg (1998). doi:10.1007/3-540-49795-1_17

14. Weber, P., Jouffe, L.: Complex system reliability modelling with dynamic object oriented Bayesian networks (DOOBN). RESS **91**(2), 149–162 (2006)

Incremental Method for Learning Parameters in Evidential Networks

Narjes Ben Hariz[1,2]([⊠]) and Boutheina Ben Yaghlane[2]

[1] Faculté des des Sciences de Gafsa, Université de Gafsa, Gafsa, Tunisia
narjes.benhariz@gmail.com
[2] LARODEC Laboratory, Institut Supérieur de Gestion de Tunis, Tunis, Tunisia
boutheina.yaghlane@ihec.rnu.tn

Abstract. Evidential graphical models are considered as an efficient tool for representing and analyzing complex and real-world systems, and reasoning under uncertainty.

This work raises the issue of estimating the different parameters of these networks. More precisely, we address the problem of updating these parameters when getting new data without repeating the learning process from the beginning. Indeed, we propose a new incremental approach to update the different parameters based on the combination rules proposed in the evidence framework.

Keywords: Parameter estimation · Graphical models · Belief function theory · Incremental learning · Evidential data

1 Introduction

Nowadays, systems in most common application fields become more and more complex, hence graphical models have gained a surge of interest as a flexible and powerful tool for modeling uncertainty. On one hand, these models are able to deal with uncertainty through the use of uncertainty theories. On the other hand, they are able to deal with the complexity through the use of graph theory.

In this paper we are interested in graphical models based on belief function theory, more specifically in Directed EVidential Networks with conditional belief functions (DEVNs). These models are proposed by Ben Yaghlane et al. [4] to generalize other graphical models such as Bayesian Networks (BNs) for handling different types of uncertainty in data.

Generally the different parameters of these models are unknown, they can be defined by experts or estimated from data. Once estimated, an interesting question will be how update these parameters when having new data especially with the fast increase of the amount of collected data in the majority of fields. To take into account the new collected data, two possible solutions can be adopted: repeat the whole learning process from the beginning taking into account both old and new data, or update the different parameters of the existing network. Although the simplicity of the first solution, it has a very high temporal and

© Springer International Publishing AG 2017
S. Benferhat et al. (Eds.): IEA/AIE 2017, Part II, LNAI 10351, pp. 163–170, 2017.
DOI: 10.1007/978-3-319-60045-1_19

spatial complexity. In fact, if we repeat the learning process from the beginning, the total amount of data must be recorded and the computational complexity will increase proportionally with the volume of data.

To resolve this problem, we address in this paper, the problem of updating the different parameters of an evidential network when having new evidential data.

The rest of this document is organized as follows: In Sect. 2, we remind briefly the most important background notions regarding evidence theory, evidential networks and evidential databases. The learning parameters process in DEVNs is summarized in Sect. 3. In Sect. 4, we present the main purpose of the paper which is the incremental algorithm for learning parameters in DEVNs from evidential databases. In the last section we analyze the performance of our incremental approach through a brief experimental study.

2   State of the Art

In the following we introduce briefly the framework of this paper which includes the belief function theory, databases and graphical models based on this theory.

2.1   Evidence Theory

Evidence theory is a general framework for managing different forms of uncertainty in data. This theory, called also belief function theory or Dempster-Shafer theory, is considered as a powerful tool for fusing data through its rules of combination. We review, in this section, some basic concepts of this theory, other details can be found in [12,14].

We call a frame of discernment Ω a finite set of exclusive and exhaustive elements and 2^{Ω} its power set.

The amount of belief supporting a proposition A from 2^{Ω} is called a mass function or a basic belief assignment, it is a function from 2^{Ω} to $[0, 1]$ such that:

$$\sum_{A \subseteq \Omega} m^{\Omega}(A) = 1 \tag{1}$$

A conditional mass function of a proposition A given B, $m^{\Omega}[B](A)$ is defined by Dempster's rule of conditioning as:

$$m^{\Omega}[B](A) = \sum_{C \subseteq \overline{B}} m^{\Omega}(A \cap C), \tag{2}$$

where $\overline{B}$ is the complement of the proposition B. More details about the rules of conditioning in the belief functions theory can be found in [13,15].

One of the most classical rules of combination commonly used in the belief function framework is Dempster's rule of combination. This rule is defined as follows:

$$(m_1 \oplus m_2)(A) = \begin{cases} \frac{\sum_{B \cap C = A} m_1(B).m_2(C)}{1 - \sum_{B \cap C = \emptyset} m_1(B).m_2(C)} & \forall A \subseteq \Omega, A \neq \emptyset \\ 0 & if A = \emptyset \end{cases} \tag{3}$$

More rules of combination can be found in [6,7,17].

2.2 Evidential DataBase

Evidential DataBase (EDB) is a database storing data modeled in the evidence framework [1]. We denote by EDB(L,C) an evidential database with L lines and C columns. Each cell in the lth line and c^{th} column is defined by a mass function m_{lc} from 2^{Ω_c} to $[0, 1]$ such that:

$$m_{lc}(\emptyset) = 0 \; and \sum_{A \subseteq \Omega_c} m_{lc}(A) = 1 \tag{4}$$

2.3 Directed Evidential Networks with Conditional Belief Functions

Directed Evidential Networks with Conditional Belief Functions are graphical models based on the belief function theory to manage uncertainty. As in the majority of graphical models, these networks are defined by two parts:

- **The graphical structure** modeled by a Directed Acyclic Graph (DAG) with a set of nodes $N = \{N_1, ..., N_x\}$ representing the different variables and a set of edges $E = \{E_1, ..., E_y\}$ coding conditional dependencies between variables.
- **The set of parameters** quantified by conditional belief functions.

These models are considered more flexible than Bayesian networks and other evidential networks in the quantification of parameters. In fact, conditional belief functions in DEVNs can be defined in two manners: **per child node** (each child node is defined by a conditional belief function given all its parent nodes) and **per edge** (the conditional relation between a child node and a parent node, represented by an edge, is weighted with a conditional mass function).

3 Learning Parameters in DEVNs

The problem of estimating parameters in directed evidential networks with conditional belief functions from evidential data is studied in [3]. This process is based essentially on the maximum likelihood principle generalized to the belief function theory [8].

As we said previously the quantitative part of a DEVN is characterized by a priori mass function for each node in the graph and a conditional belief function for each child node given its parent nodes, these two metrics are defined respectively by Eqs. 5 and 6:

$$m^{\Omega_{N_i}}(N_i = A_k) = \frac{\sum_{l=1}^{|L|} m_{lc}^{\Omega_{N_i}}(N_i = A_k)}{\sum_{l=1}^{|L|} m_{lc}^{\Omega_{N_i}}(N_i)}, \tag{5}$$

$$m^{\Omega_{N_i}}[PA(N_i) = x](N_i = A_k) = \frac{\sum_{l=1}^{|L|} m_{lc}^{\Omega_{N_i}}(N_i = A_k) * \prod_j m_{lcj}^{\Omega_{pa_j}}(pa_j(N_i) = x_j)}{\sum_{l=1}^{|L|} \prod_j m_{lcj}^{\Omega_{pa_j}}(pa_j(N_i) = x_j)},$$

$$(6)$$

where A_k is a proposition from $2^{\Omega_{N_i}}$, c denotes the column corresponding to the node $N_i \in N$, $m_{lc}^{\Omega_{N_i}}$ is the mass function defining the cell in the lth line and c^{th} column, $PA(N_i) = \{pa_1(N_i), ..., pa_z(N_i)\}$ is the set of parents of the node N_i and x is a configuration of values in which each parent node takes a possible proposition from its frame of discernment.

The detailed description of the learning process in the two cases (per child node and per edge) is presented in [3].

4   Incremental Process for Parameters Estimation in DEVNs

In this section we address the main purpose of this paper which is how to update the different parameters of an evidential network when having new evidential data without repeating the whole learning process from the beginning in order to reduce the complexity of the learning method.

Thus, we propose an incremental method for learning parameters based on combining beliefs using one of the combination rules proposed in the belief function theory. As shown in Algorithm 1, this method includes essentially three steps: the first step consists in learning parameters from the new evidential data according to the structure of the original network and the type of the conditional dependencies in the network (per child node or per edge). The second step involves combining the new estimated parameters with the parameters of the initial network using Dempster's rule of combination[1]. The third step is to update the network by the different calculated parameters obtained in the second step.

In this algorithm, any combination rule other than Dempster's rule of combination can be used in the fusion step. Note that this process can be also applied when having new data from expert opinions. The knowledge of the expert will be considered as new parameters and combined with the parameters of the original network.

It is important to notice, also, that our learning approach can be used to learn the different parameters of a Bayesian network from uncertain data. In fact, after applying our approach to learn each parameter in the network (per child node), we will get for each variable a mass distribution that can be transformed into a probability mass function using the pignistic transformation.

---

[1] The prior mass function of each node will be combined with the prior mass function of the same node and the conditional mass function associated to each configuration of parents with the conditional mass function of the same configuration in the new learned parameters.

Algorithm 1. Incremental method for learning parameters in DEVNs

---

Require: $DEVN1 = (N, E, \theta_p, \theta_c)$, EDB
Ensure: $UPDATED - DEVN = (N, E, \theta_p, \theta_c)$

  Step 1: Learning parameters from new data
  if Parameters are defined per child node **then**
    $DEVN2 \leftarrow Learn - parameters - child - node(DEVN1.DAG, EDB)$
  else if Parameters are defined per edge **then**
    $DEVN2 \leftarrow Learn - parameters - edge(DEVN1.DAG, EDB)$
  end if
  Step 2: Combination of belief
  for each node $N_i \in N$ **do**
    if N_i is a root node **then**
      $m3^{\Omega_{N_i}}(N_i) = m1^{\Omega_{N_i}}(N_i) \oplus m2^{\Omega_{N_i}}(N_i)$
    else
      for each possible configuration $conf_j$ **do**
        $m3^{\Omega_{N_i}}[PA = conf_j](N_i) = m1^{\Omega_{N_i}}[PA = conf_j](N_i) \oplus m2^{\Omega_{N_i}}[PA = conf_j](N_i)$
      end for
    end if
  end for
  Step 3: Updating DEVN
  $UPDATED\_DEVN.N_i.\theta_p \leftarrow m3^{\Omega_{N_i}}(N_i)$
  $UPDATED\_DEVN.N_i.\theta_c \leftarrow m3^{\Omega_{N_i}}[PA](N_i)$

---

5 Discussion and Experimental Study

In this section, we try to demonstrate the performance of our incremental learning approach by comparing the standard learning to the incremental one in terms of computational time and resulted beliefs.

A classical problem that generally encounters people working on evidential networks, is the absence of standard evidential networks used in the real world problems. Thus, we tried to generate some evidential systems that will be used in our experimental study.

Regarding the graphical part of the evidential network, we have adopted two strategies: take the structure of a well known system or generate random DAGs. The set of known systems is formed of four systems: the Asia network [11], the alarm network [2] and two other systems well known in the reliability field (the 2-out-of-3 system and the bridge system [16]). For the generation of DAGs, we have adopted one of the methods proposed in the literature to generate the graphical structure of BNs [9]. For the different parameters of the network, we tried to generate random belief functions [5] for each needed distribution.

This experimental study is based on several steps: (1) Generate from each network an evidential data set. (2) Use these data sets to learn parameters using the standard learning process. (3) Divide each data set into two equal data sets. (4) Use the first part of data to learn new parameters. (5) Update the learned parameters from the second part of data using the incremental learning process.

Table 1. Accuracy of the incremental learning vs standard learning

Networks	Data Set				
	100	500	1000	5000	10000
Asia network	0.456	0.4598	0.654	0.349	0.02
Alarm network	0.564	0.402	0.2798	0.0848	0.0054
2oo3 network	0.7182	0.276	0.05	0.0073	0.0001
Bridge network	0.632	0.067	0.05	0.004	0.0003
Random networks	0.4182	0.31	0.07	0.0098	0.001

(6) Compare the updated parameters with the different parameters resulted from the standard learning (using the whole data set).

To compare the updated parameters and the original ones in the last step, we calculated the dissimilarity between their associated mass functions in each node using Jousselme's distance [10], which is one of the most appropriate measures used for calculating the dissimilarity between mass functions. The different results presented in Table 1 reveal the good accuracy of the incremental process. In fact, the different calculated distances are very low mainly with 10000 instances (last column of the table).

The complexity of the learning process comparing to the standard one is shown in Fig. 1. The speedup of the incremental algorithm (curves in red) is clear with Asia network, 2-out-of-3 (2oo3) system and bridge system. For the alarm network the standard algorithm is faster. These results are justified by the fact that the computational complexity of the conjunctive rule of combination depends essentially on the size of the frame of discernment defining variables. This problem can be resolved by using an approximate rule of combination in the fusion step.

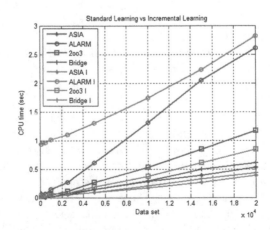

Fig. 1. Standard learning vs incremental learning (Color figure online)

6   Conclusion

We have presented in this paper the idea of updating the different parameters of an evidential network when having new data which is based on learning parameters from the new EDB then combine beliefs to get the updated DEVN. The proposed approach have shown a good accuracy with several networks.

Nevertheless, this work is still subject to improvement and extension. In fact, it will be interesting to use approximate rules of combination in the incremental process in order to decrease the execution time when having complex systems.

References

1. Bach Tobji, M.A., Ben Yaghlane, B., Mellouli, K.: A new algorithm for mining frequent itemsets from evidential databases. In: Proceeding of Information Processing and Management of Uncertainty (IPMU 2008), pp. 1535–1542, Malaga, Spain (2008)
2. Beinlich, I.A., Suermondt, H.J., Chavez, R.M., Cooper, G.F.: The ALARM monitoring system: a case study with two probabilistic inference techniques for belief networks. In: Hunter, J., Cookson, J., Wyatt, J. (eds) AIME 89. Lecture Notes in Medical Informatics, vol 38. Springer, Heidelberg (1989)
3. Ben Hariz, N., Ben Yaghlane, B.: Learning parameters in directed evidential networks with conditional belief functions. In: Cuzzolin, F. (ed.) BELIEF 2014. LNCS, vol. 8764, pp. 294–303. Springer, Cham (2014). doi:10.1007/978-3-319-11191-9_32
4. Ben Yaghlane, B., Mellouli, K.: Inference in directed evidential networks based on the transferable belief model. IJAR 48(2), 399–418 (2008)
5. Burger, T., Destercke, S.: How to randomly generate mass functions. Int. J. Uncertainty Fuzziness Knowl. Based Syst. 21(5), 645–674 (2013)
6. Denœux, T.: The cautious rule of combination for belief functions and some extensions. In: International Conference on Information Fusion (2006)
7. Denœux, T.: Conjunctive and disjunctive combination of belief functions induced by non distinct bodies of evidence. Artif. Intell. 172, 234–264 (2008)
8. Denœux, T.: Maximum likelihood estimation from uncertain data in the belief function framework. Knowl. Data Eng. 25, 119–130 (2013)
9. Ide, J.S., Cozman, F.G.: Random generation of bayesian networks. In: Bittencourt, G., Ramalho, G.L. (eds.) SBIA 2002. LNCS (LNAI), vol. 2507, pp. 366–376. Springer, Heidelberg (2002). doi:10.1007/3-540-36127-8_35
10. Jousselme, A., Grenier, D., Bossée, E.: A new distance between two bodies of evidence. Inf. Fusion 2(2), 91–101 (2001)
11. Lauritzen, S., Spiegelhalter, D.J.: Local computations with probabilities on graphical structures and their application to expert systems. J. R. Stat. Soc. Ser. B 50, 157–224 (1988)
12. Shafer, G.: A Mathematical Theory of Evidence. Princeton University Press, Princeton (1976)
13. Smets, Ph.: Jeffrey's rule of conditioning generalized to belief functions. In: Proceedings of the Ninth International Conference on Uncertainty in Artificial Intelligence (UAI 1993), pp. 500–505, Washington, DC, USA (1993)
14. Smets, P., Kennes, R.: The transferable belief model. Artif. Intell. 66, 191–234 (1994)

15. Tang, Y., Zheng, J.: Dempster conditioning and conditional independence in evidence theory. In: Zhang, S., Jarvis, R. (eds.) AI 2005. LNCS, vol. 3809, pp. 822–825. Springer, Heidelberg (2005). doi:10.1007/11589990_88
16. Villemeur, A.: Reliability, Availability, Maintainability and Safety Assessment: Methods and Techniques. Wiley, New York (1992)
17. Yager, R.: On the Dempster-Shafer framework and new combination rules. Inf. Sci. **41**, 93–137 (1987)

aGrUM: A Graphical Universal Model Framework

Christophe Gonzales, Lionel Torti, and Pierre-Henri Wuillemin[✉]

Sorbonne Universités, UPMC Univ Paris 06, UMR 7606, LIP6, Paris, France
{christophe.gonzales,lionel.torti,pierre-henri.wuillemin}@lip6.fr

Abstract. This paper presents the **aGrUM** framework, a C++ library providing state-of-the-art implementations of graphical models for decision making, including Bayesian Networks, Influence Diagrams, Credal Networks, Probabilistic Relational Models. This is the result of an ongoing effort to build an efficient and well maintained open source cross-platform software, running on Linux, MacOS X and Windows, for dealing with graphical models. The framework also contains a wrapper, pyAgrum, for exploiting **aGrUM** within Python.

1 Introduction

The **aGrUM** project started eight years ago at the artificial intelligence and decision department of University Pierre and Marie Curie (http://www.lip6.fr). Developed by several contributors, in particular the authors of the present paper, the project grew into an extensive open source graphical model framework. This one includes the **aGrUM** C++ library, a Python wrapper and some applications, all running on Linux, MacOS and Windows (supported compilers include g++, clang, mvsc, mingw). The framework is freely available at http://agrum.org[1]. There also exists a dedicated website (http://agrum.org) for the python wrapper: **pyAgrum**.

   The goal of **aGrUM** is the development of an efficient, easy-to-use and well maintained framework for dealing with graphical models for decision making (e.g., Bayesian Networks, Influence Diagrams, *etc.*). The emphasis is set on high standards for performance, code quality and usability. The **aGrUM** framework is now used by academics and industrials around the world, both end-users and algorithm designers. European projects DREAM, MIDAS and SCISSOR as well as French ANR projects SKOOB, INCALIN, LARDONS and DESCRIBE also exploit **aGrUM**. It is a placeholder for its authors' research and more than fifty papers published in international conferences and journals use **aGrUM** for implementation and benchmarking. The framework's name, aGrUM, stands for "A GRaphical Universal Model" but let us be clear that aGrUM does not provide a *universal* model but offers serveral puns in the French language.

---

[1] The website also contains installation instructions, the library's documentation and support.

© Springer International Publishing AG 2017
S. Benferhat et al. (Eds.): IEA/AIE 2017, Part II, LNAI 10351, pp. 171–177, 2017.
DOI: 10.1007/978-3-319-60045-1_20

2   AGrUM Features

The **aGrUM** C++ library is divided into seven modules, the majority of which relate to different graphical models:

- BN: Bayesian Networks.
- Learning: Bayesian Network learning algorithms [2,5].
- CN: Credal Networks [3].
- FMDP: Factorized Markov Decision Processes [4].
- ID: Influence Diagrams.
- PRM: Probabilistic Relational Models [6].
- Core: common data structures and utilities.

The BN module provides flexible and efficient implementations of Bayesian Networks. Those can be read from (and written to) files of different formats (BIF, DSL, net, cnf, BIFXML, UAI). They can also be generated (randomly) from several "generators" or learnt from data using the Learning module. The **aGrUM** library allows users to define BNs using traditional Conditional Probability Tables (CPT), but also using Noisy OR or Noisy AND gates, Logit models, aggregators (and, or, max, min, exists, forall, *etc.*). In addition, for a high level of efficiency, CPTs can be encoded using different representations (arrays, sparse matrices, algebraic decision diagrams, *etc.*). Those are exploited in various inference algorithms like Lazy Propagation, Shafer-Shenoy, Variable Elimination, Gibbs sampling, *etc.*, including relevant reasoning methods.

A specific module is provided for learning the structure and/or parameters of BNs from datasets. Currently, those can be either CSV files or SQL databases. Here again, the library has been designed in order to be as flexible as possible and follows a component-based approach: structure learning algorithms are a combination of a handler for reading the database, a score among (BD, BDeu, K2, AIC, BIC/MDL) with, possibly, some additional *a priori* (smoothing or Dirichlet), a component for scheduling local structure changes and a set of constraints that the user wishes to be satisfied. The latter includes structural constraints like requiring/forbidding arcs, limiting the indegrees and imposing a partial ordering on the nodes. The learning algorithms currently implemented using this framework are greedy hill climbing, local search with tabu list and K2. BN parameters can also be learnt either by maximum likelihood or maximum a posteriori. All the learning algorithms are highly parallelized thanks to the OpenMP library.

Beside BNs, other graphical models have been implemented: Credal Networks (module CN), Factorized Markov Decision Processes (FMDP), Influence Diagrams (ID) and Probabilistic Relational Models (PRM). These modules follow the same philosophy as the BN module: high flexibility, inference efficiency, extended file format support. For instance, all these models are shipped with tailored inference algorithms, e.g., loopy propagation and Monte Carlo for CN, SPUDD for FMDPs, Shafer-Shenoy for IDs.

All the aforementioned modules rely on the core module for their data structures and common algorithms. These include classical data structures like lists,

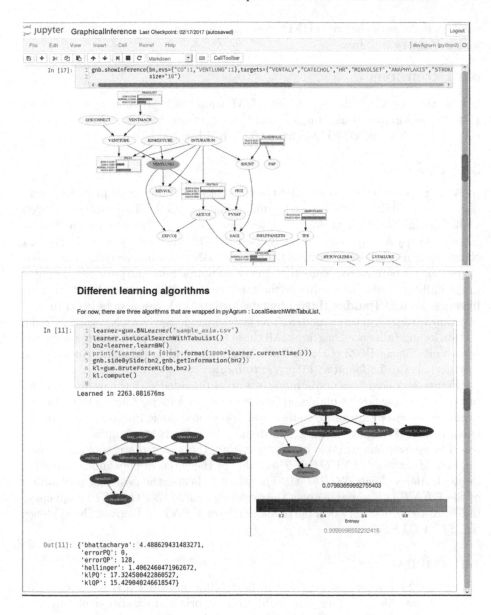

Fig. 1. Some Python notebooks using **pyAgrum**.

hashtables, AVL search trees, sets, heaps, *etc.*, that have been implemented in the library in such a way that they are both safe and particularly efficient. More complex data structures and algorithms are provided, like graph definitions and algorithms (including, e.g., a whole hierarchy of triangulations, notably incremental ones) and the different flavors of multidimensional tables described in the preceding page. The core of the **aGrUM** library also provides some tools used to make sure that **aGrUM**'s code satisfies the highest quality standards and is memory leak free.

3 Extensions

Beside the **aGrUM** library, the **aGrUM** framework provides a wrapper for Python: **pyAgrum**. It also implements the specific probabilistic graphical models (PGM) language **O3PRM** (http://O3PRM.lip6.fr).

3.1 PyAgrum

pyAgrum is a Python wrapper for the C++ **aGrUM** library. It provides a very user friendly high-level interface for manipulating **aGrUM**'s graphical models while keeping the high performance level of the C++ library. Within Python Notebooks, **pyAgrum** can be easily used as a PGM graphical editor. Figure 1 shows such notebooks, illustrating, e.g., how BN structure learning and inferences can be performed. Note that many computations' outputs are provided graphically in order to facilitate their analysis by the users. Other learning libraries, such as **Pandas** (http://pandas.pydata.org), can also be used in conjunction with **pyAgrum**'s models. The latter include Bayesian Networks, Credal Networks and Influence Diagrams. All these features make **pyAgrum** a very versatile and efficient PGM package. Tutorials, demos and downloading/installation instructions can be found at http://agrum.org.

Figure 2 is taken from one of many examples provided with the pyAgrum notebooks (notebooks are available on pyAgrum website http://agrum.org). In this example, we use pyAgrum to iterate over 100 probabilistic inferences to produce these results. Without entering into details, the idea is to visualize the impact of evidence over one variable on another. Here the x axis represents an increasing belief that the $MINVOLSET$ variable of the classical benchmark Bayesian network $Alarm$ equals $NORMAL$. The y axis indicates the posterior probability of the $VENTALV$ variable given the evidence over $MINVOLSET$. Each curve indicates the probability of a particular value of $VENTALV$ given the evidence on $MINVOLSET$.

3.2 O3PRM

The **aGrUM** library contains a specific module named PRM for Probabilistic Relational Models. They are a fully object-oriented extension of Bayesian Networks, as specified in [7]: they implement the notions of classes, interfaces, instances, attributes, reference slots, slot chains, systems, *etc.*. Their object-oriented nature greatly reduces the maintenance and creation costs of complex systems with many repeated subcomponents. Highly efficient inference engines like structured variable elimination (SVE) or SVE with relevant reasoning are provided in the module. A bridge with the BN module exists that enables grounding PRMs into BNs, thereby allowing the exploitation of all the available BN-related algorithms of **aGrUM**. Finally, a domain specific language **O3PRM** has been developed to enable users to easily create PRMs.

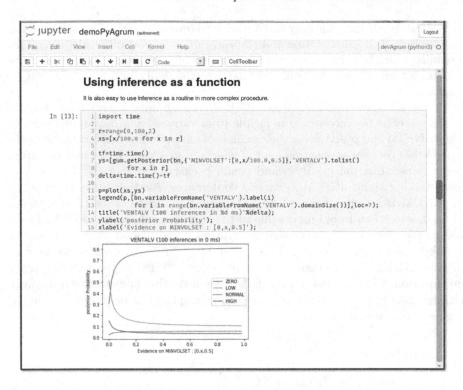

Fig. 2. pyAgrum in action: sensibility analysis

4   Towards aGrUM 1.0

aGrUM is under active development and, even if many of its features are robust and well designed, aGrUM is still missing some fundamental algorithms and useful features that we strive to implement.

Regarding approximate probabilistic inference, we wish to add various Belief Propagation algorithms. For exact inference, we still have to parallelize and further optimize our inference engines. With these additions, aGrUM will offer a wide variety of optimized probabilistic inference algorithms, making it a complete framework for probabilistic inference.

We plan to add the Expectation-Maximization (EM) algorithm and its structural counterpart SEM into aGrUM's learning module. The EM algorithm is widely used in machine learning for finding maximum likelihood or maximum a posteriori estimates of parameters. In conjunction with the learning algorithms already implemented in aGrUM, the framework will offer a broad range of methods for learning Bayesian Networks and other graphical models.

We also plan to add into aGrUM mixed discrete/continuous extensions of Bayesian networks, including, e.g., that proposed in [1], and to provide efficient learning and inference algorithms for these models.

Algorithms are not the only way we wish to improve aGrUM for a first *stable* version. Indeed, documentation and tutorials are as important as algorithms for spreading aGrUM's use. Even if we try to provide the most complete and up-to-date documentation, we still feel that its readability and examples can be improved.

As for all open source projects, aGrUM's community is very important to us and we hope to convince more people from various scientific communities to adopt aGrUM and pyAgrum as their main tool for modeling graphical models. To achieve this goal we are putting a lot of efforts in making aGrUM and pyAgrum easier to use: distributing PyPi and conda packages, porting aGrUM to Windows, talking about aGrUM in various conferences. Another important change for aGrUM is its open source license. Currently, aGrUM is distributed under GPL2.0, which can forbid its use due to the contaminant nature of GPL2.0. We plan to switch to LGPL or another integration friendly open source license.

We hope to release version 1.0 of aGrUM in 2017. Afterwards, we plan to improve aGrUM's performance with integration of GPU support and memory optimization. We also plan to test aGrUM against other open source framework with the goal to provide the most performing graphical model framework in the open source community.

5   Conclusion

This paper has presented **aGrUM**, a powerful framework for manipulating graphical models for decision making. It is designed to be flexible, well maintained and highly efficient. The core of the framework is the C++ **aGrUM** library but wrappers like **pyAgrum** enable users to exploit **aGrUM** within high level and easy-to-use programming languages like Python.

The development of the **aGrUM** framework has not only been stimulated by academic research, it is also the result of different industrial collaborations. For instance, **aGrUM**'s **O3PRM**s are exploited in ongoing projects with EDF (the French national electricity provider) on risk management in nuclear power plants and with IBM on the exploitation of probabilities in rule-based expert systems. The BN learning module is exploited in projects with IRSN, the French Institute for Nuclear Safety, for nuclear incident scenario reconstruction. Other projects with Airbus Research and the Open Turns project use **aGrUM** for structural learning in copules with continuous variables.

References

1. Cortijo, S., Gonzales, C.: Bayesian networks with conditional truncated densities. In: Florida Artificial Intelligence Research Society Conference (FLAIRS 2016), pp. 656–661 (2016)
2. Gonzales, C., Dubuisson, S., Manfredotti, C.E.: A new algorithm for learning non-stationary dynamic Bayesian networks with application to event detection. In: Florida Artificial Intelligence Research Society Conference (FLAIRS 2015), pp. 564–569 (2015)

3. Hourbracq, M., Baudrit, C., Wuillemin, P.H., Destercke, S.: Dynamic credal networks: introduction and use in robustness analysis. In: International Symposium on Imprecise Probability: Theories and Applications (ISIPTA 2013), pp. 159–169 (2013)
4. Magnan, J.: Représentations graphiques de fonctions et processus décisionnels Markoviens factorisés. Ph.D. thesis, University Pierre and Marie Curie, Paris, France (2016)
5. Magnan, J.C., Wuillemin, P.H.: Efficient incremental planning and learning with multi-valued decision diagrams. J. Appl. Logic **22**, 63–90 (2016)
6. Torti, L.: Structured probabilistic inference in object-oriented probabilistic graphical models. Ph.D. thesis, University Pierre and Marie Curie, Paris, France (2012)
7. Torti, L., Wuillemin, P.H., Gonzales, C.: Reinforcing the object-oriented aspect of probabilistic relational models. In: Workshop on Probabilistic Graphical Models (PGM 2010), pp. 273–280 (2010)

Anomaly Detection

Improving Card Fraud Detection Through Suspicious Pattern Discovery

Fabian Braun[1]([✉]), Olivier Caelen[2], Evgueni N. Smirnov[3], Steven Kelk[3], and Bertrand Lebichot[4]

[1] R&D, Worldline GmbH, Aachen, Germany
fabian.braun@worldline.com
[2] R&D, Worldline SA, Brussels, Belgium
[3] Department of Data Science and Knowledge Engineering, Maastricht University, Maastricht, The Netherlands
[4] Université catholique de Louvain, Louvain-la-neuve, Belgium

Abstract. We propose a new approach to detect credit card fraud based on suspicious payment patterns. According to our hypothesis fraudsters use stolen credit card data at specific, recurring sets of shops. We exploit this behavior to identify fraudulent transactions. In a first step we show how suspicious patterns can be identified from known compromised cards. The transactions between cards and shops can be represented as a bipartite graph. We are interested in finding fully connected subgraphs containing mostly compromised cards, because such *bicliques* reveal suspicious payment patterns. Then we define new attributes which capture the suspiciousness of a transaction indicated by known suspicious patterns. Eventually a non-linear classifier is used to assess the predictive power gained through those new features. The new attributes lead to a significant performance improvement compared to state-of-the-art aggregated transaction features. Our results are verified on real transaction data provided by our industrial partner (Worldline http://www.worldline.com).

Keywords: Credit card fraud detection · Supervised learning · Feature engineering · Frequent pattern mining · Bicliques · Graph analysis

1 Introduction

In today's world payments are often effected electronically. Instead of cash, people use credit and debit cards for payments at the point of sale (POS) and can directly issue purchases on shopping websites using their card data (*E-commerce*). However the rise of electronic financial transactions has led to new crime patterns: fraudsters try to misuse the data of legitimate persons to effect payments in their name. Therefore payment processors employ detection techniques to identify fraudulent transactions.

Historically fraud detection is carried out within rule-processing systems where fraudulent transactions are detected if they fulfill certain criteria, e.g. issued

© Springer International Publishing AG 2017
S. Benferhat et al. (Eds.): IEA/AIE 2017, Part II, LNAI 10351, pp. 181–190, 2017.
DOI: 10.1007/978-3-319-60045-1_21

at a specific shop at a specific time of a day. The rules of these systems are crafted manually by human experts or generated by rule learning algorithms [12]. More sophisticated systems use supervised learning to build classification models which learn to identify fraud from known fraudulent transactions in the past [4].

In the best case a fraudulent transaction is immediately detected and rejected by the system. However, even after acceptance of a fraudulent transaction it is useful to detect it because the fraudster is likely to reuse the same card data for further transactions until the card is blocked. Finding compromised cards becomes easier with each further fraudulent transaction from the card in question, under the condition that detection techniques are not solely analyzing individual transactions. Therefore, feature aggregates built from the transaction history of a credit card are heavily used to improve fraud detection in rule-based systems as well as machine learning approaches [17].

The historical rule based approach has the advantage that it allows human investigators to adapt detection systems according to very specific fraud scenarios. The full expertise of the investigator results in very targeted fraud detection with few false alerts. On the other hand non-linear models such as neural networks are not transparent in regard to how they decide on the label of a transaction, but they are able to find hidden meaning in the data, that investigators are not aware of.

In this work we combine the advantages of historical rule learning and non-linear models to outperform existing fraud detection methods. For this purpose we feed the pattern-indicated "suspiciousness" of a transaction into a non-linear classifier. This additional information boosts the classifier performance by 20% in terms of area under precision-recall-curve (AUCPR).

To provide an example assume that we find in historical data that some fraudsters tend to issue their fraudulent transactions always at the shops $\{E, F, G\}$. After further investigation we find out that actually 50% of the cards which have made a transaction at all the shops $\{E, F, G\}$ are compromised. The pattern $\{E, F, G\}$ is therefore highly suspicious—We have identified an anomaly which can be used to find further fraud cases. Therefore we not only provide classical transaction features such as amount and timestamp to our non-linear model but in addition whether the card is used according to a known suspicious pattern. We show that this combined approach leads to a significant performance increase. A similar approach has been applied to identify companies which might go bankrupt deliberately in order to avoid taxation [16]. We extend and adapt the core ideas from this work to the domain of credit card fraud and show that the relationships between cards and card acceptors similarly carry information indicating which cards might be under the control of a fraudster.

Regarding the structure of this paper we first give a detailed description of our contribution (Sect. 2). Subsequently we explain the preprocessing and augmentation of our data based on existing scientific work (Sect. 3). Then we describe the concrete experimental setup (Sect. 4) for testing our contribution. Finally we report our results (Sect. 5) before drawing a conclusion (Sect. 6).

2   Pattern Suspiciousness

Our contribution is based on the hypothesis that compromised credit cards can be identified by inspecting the patterns of card acceptors, e.g. shops, at which they have been used [6]. A pattern is for example "card x has been used in the shops $\{E, F, G\}$" (See Definitions 1 and 2).

Definition 1. *Pattern: Unordered set of acceptors containing at least 2, and at most n, elements, where n is the maximally allowed pattern size. We require that a pattern consists at least of 2 acceptors.*

Definition 2. *Pattern match: A credit card c matches a pattern at moment t if all acceptors of the pattern appear in the transaction history $T_{[t-\Delta t, t]}$ of c. Δt denotes a time difference.*

Definition 3. *Pattern support: The absolute number of cards which match a given pattern.*

With techniques originating from the domain of association rule mining we can identify frequent patterns [1] in the transaction data, i.e. patterns that are common among multiple credit cards. We aim to compute the suspiciousness of such patterns by counting how many of the matching cards are compromised. The underlying assumption is that a pattern which is highly exposed to fraud in the past can be used to detect fraud on future transactions. Thus our approach requires a database of patterns and their suspiciousness. However, we do not want to use the suspicious patterns directly to detect fraudulent cards. Instead we incorporate this information in newly defined transaction features and build a model which also takes into account all other given information to detect fraudulent transactions.

When a new transaction arrives we evaluate whether we recognize a pattern from the database in the transaction history of the card. Then we augment the new transaction with information about the matching patterns' suspiciousness.

2.1   Pattern Enumeration and Scoring

To derive suspiciousness scores for each pattern we need to look at the cards which match the patterns in our historical data. A higher number of compromised cards indicate a higher pattern suspiciousness. For this purpose we introduce the definition of a *biclique* which incorporates a pattern and all its matching cards. We can conclude that for each pattern a corresponding biclique exists and vice versa. The *biclique* definition relies on a graph representation of the data in which the acceptors form a first and the credit cards a second vertex type. A credit card can be linked to an acceptor by a transaction. An example for a *biclique* is depicted in Fig. 1. The representation of a bipartite graph to find suspicious bicliques has already been applied successfully in the domain of bankruptcy fraud, i.e. predicting which companies might go bankrupt deliberately in order to avoid taxation by analyzing the business partners of those companies [16].

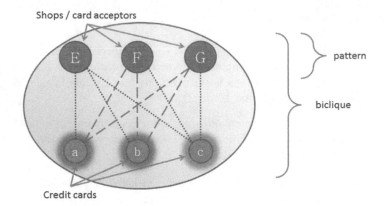

Fig. 1. Example transaction graph to demonstrate the hypothesis of suspicious acceptor patterns. Red long-dashed edges represent fraudulent transactions, blue dotted edges represent genuine transactions. The depicted pattern $\{E, F, G\}$ is suspicious as two out of three (=66%) of its matching cards are compromised (i.e. have fraudulent transactions). (Color figure online)

Definition 4. *Bipartite graph: Let* $G = (N, E)$ *denote a graph consisting of the vertices* N *and edges* E. G *is* bipartite *if* N *can be divided into two sets* U *and* V *such that every edge has one endpoint in* U *and one endpoint in* V.

Definition 5. *Biclique: Let* $G = (V \cup U, E)$ *denote a bipartite graph. A subgraph* $(V' \cup U', E')$ *of* G *is called a* biclique *if* $V' \subseteq V, U' \subseteq U, E' \subseteq E$ *and for every* $u \in U'$ *and* $v \in V'$, $\{u, v\} \in E'$.

The patterns' suspiciousness is directly expressed through the ratio of compromised cards among all cards in its corresponding biclique. The biclique depicted in Fig. 1 contains three cards out of which two are compromised because they have fraudulent transactions. Therefore the suspiciousness score of this biclique is 0.66. In addition to the biclique fraud ratio we store the pattern size and the number of matching cards in the pattern database for later use.

Algorithmically the bicliques are identified in two consecutive steps. First, we identify candidates for suspicious patterns only taking into account compromised cards. In a second step we generate full bicliques from those candidates, now taking into account all cards. The first step can be performed by any appropriate frequent pattern mining algorithm such as the apriori-algorithm [2]. In the second step the bicliques are created by identifying the common cards of each acceptor pattern, which is equivalent to a set intersection operation for each pattern [11, Chap. 10.3.3].

The time complexity of enumerating all maximal bicliques based on frequent itemset mining can be reduced to $O(mnN)$, where m is the number of edges in the graph (credit card transactions), n the number of vertices (cards and acceptors) and N the number of maximal bicliques [9]. The apriori algorithm does not achieve this complexity but has proven to be adequately efficient for our experiments.

2.2   Feature Aggregation

At this point we have identified suspicious patterns on historical transaction data and quantified this suspiciousness in terms of pattern features. In the next step these pattern features will be used to find compromised cards in a target dataset with unknown labels. Therefore the cards in this distinct dataset must be augmented with the pattern information.

We verify for each card which patterns it matches and derive new features from the matched patterns: the number, the mean and the maximum suspiciousness among them. In the domain of credit card fraud we suspect that patterns having the maximum suspiciousness are most important for detecting future fraud. Therefore we add more information about these most suspicious patterns to the new card features: the number of acceptors (pattern size) and the number of matching cards (pattern *support*). The five new features are summarized in Table 1.

Table 1. Newly proposed pattern features. Each transaction is augmented with these five attributes to achieve a better predictive performance.

Attribute	Explanation
Pattern count	Number of patterns matched by the card
Mean suspiciousness	Of all matching patterns
Max suspiciousness	Score of most suspicious matching pattern
Max suspicious pattern's size	Size of m. s. matching pattern
Max suspicious pattern's support	Supporting cards of m. s. matching pattern

3   Real Data and Preprocessing

To assess our approach we use a real-world transaction dataset from our industrial partner. The dataset contains (POS) and E-commerce-transactions. Each day of data comprises on average $517,569.7$ transactions with a standard deviation of 59902.9. Out of these transactions on average 0.152% are fraudulent with a standard deviation of 0.040%.

The dataset provides 21 intrinsic transaction features. Those comprise nominal identifiers of transactions, cards and acceptor and more information related to these entities: for example the transaction amount, the timestamp of the transaction and the merchant category. These attributes are common in the domain of fraud detection [12,13].

A classifier which is only trained on intrinsic attributes is likely to achieve a poor predictive performance. Therefore we augment the given attributes with aggregated new features, which have proven to enhance the prediction performance in other scientific work [3]. The authors derive information on how often the card was used in a similar manner before the current transaction. For example they add the number of transactions issued at the same shop in the past and the average transaction amount of recent payments.

Another approach [5, Chap. 5.1.3] computes the risk of discrete attribute values of being associated to fraud transactions, e.g. the risk that a specific acceptor is used for a fraud transaction. In this work transactions are merged with the risk scores associated with their attribute values.

In total a set of 45 transaction features is used to obtain a baseline performance score for a state-of-the-art fraud detection model. These consist of basic features being intrinsic to each transaction (amount etc.), aggregated card features [3] and risk scores [5, Chap. 5.1.3] for all categorical attributes in our data. As the data used for the referenced work is not publicly available we have fully reimplemented their work to augment our data with the same attributes.

4   Experimental Setup

To estimate the predictive performance gain we compare the performance of a model trained on a state-of-the-art dataset with the performance reached when adding our newly proposed features (Table 1). We choose a random forest model because it is a standard and well-performing model in the domain of fraud detection [3,6]. It allows the construction of sophisticated performance metrics because it is capable of returning class likelihoods instead of hard labels. We use random undersampling for training the random forest model such that each training set contains 1500 fraudulent transactions and 13500 genuine transactions to address the imbalance in the data. We choose a sampling ratio of 10% to compare to [3]. This technique performs well in conjunction with random forest models [15]. A random forest model requires two parameters: we fix the number of trees at 501 and leave the number of split candidate variables at $\sqrt{p}$, where p is the number of transaction attributes in the training set—a common default setting [10]. No further tuning of the parameters is required as we want to compare the performance of multiple random forests trained on different attribute subsets rather than producing one highly tuned classifier. For the performance measures requiring hard labels we set a static cutoff threshold of 0.75, i.e. if a transaction is voted to be fraudulent by less than 75% of the trees, it is classified as genuine.

For computing the newly proposed pattern features we restrict the size of the acceptor patterns to two to six. Patterns of size one (i.e. individual acceptors) are already incorporated in the acceptor risk score [5]. Patterns of larger sizes than six are ignored because they would require that a fraudster issues more than six transactions at different acceptors before they can be detected. Additionally we require that each pattern is matched by at least 4 compromised cards to ensure a minimum evidence for a suspiciousness score (*minimum absolute support*). In summary we only assess bicliques consisting of two to six acceptors and at least four cards.

Another parameter is the size of the time-window Δt from which we derive frequent patterns. We choose a window of five days, relying on the fact that fraudsters try to issue their payments within a short time-frame before the card of the customer is blocked. A larger window could be an interesting subject for future research, because the acceptors used by the legitimate cardholder might also carry important information because in many cases one of those acceptors is the source of the data breach.

4.1 Data Splits

When evaluating our approach we have to be careful about setting up training and test data. The risk score [5] and the newly introduced pattern features require the labels of historical transactions as input which might lead to a biased model when the same transactions are used for training. To ensure that this does not occur we split data into three sets: feature learning set, training set and test set. Additionally we want to assess how good the model behaves in a temporal context, i.e. learning on past transactions for predicting future transactions. Therefore we split based on the timestamp of transaction acceptance. We use five days of transaction data for learning suspicious patterns and risk scores. The subsequent five days of data are used for training the random forest model. Finally we test this model on the subsequent day of data (See Fig. 2). To obtain statistically sound results we generate 40 different learning, training and test sets from our data.

In fraud detection it is trivial to predict the label of transactions once we know that a card is compromised. To avoid an overoptimistic estimate of the performance we remove transactions from known compromised cards from subsequent splits. For example when a card already has a fraudulent transaction in the training set, its transactions are removed from the test set.

4.2 Performance Measures

The choice of adequate performance indicators is highly influenced by the class imbalance of the fraud detection problem. Standard measures as prediction accu-

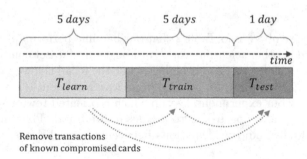

Fig. 2. The transaction dataset is split into three parts: a feature learning dataset, a training set and a test set. The first is used to learn which acceptors patterns are suspicious. The second is used to train a model and the third to test its predictive performance. To avoid reporting already known compromised cards, those are removed from subsequent splits.

racy and area under ROC-curve (AUC) [14] are not suitable because negative and positive instances contribute equally to them while in unbalanced problems the positive class should be emphasized [17].

We base our conclusions on precision and recall which focus on the fraudulent class. In the fraud domain the precision shows how many transactions might be reported erroneously by the model. The recall captures how many fraudulent transactions are completely missed by the system and are eventually detected by the cardholder in their account statement.

Additionally we use the area under precision-recall-curve (AUCPR) as a cutoff-independent measure, which is better suited to imbalanced problems than the classical AUC [7]. The precision among the top-k-ranked alerts is another meaningful performance indicator in fraud detection [3,5]. We fix the parameter k at the number of positive instances in the test set such that a score of 1 indicates perfect prediction.

Table 2. Performance of classifiers: row 1, 3 our baseline; row 2, 4 baseline + contributed features. We report the average performance and std. deviation obtained from 40 different learning-training-test cycles.

Model, attributes	Precision	Prec. at k	Recall	AUCPR	Accuracy	AUC
Random forest baseline	0.333 ± 0.11	0.381 ± 0.09	0.418 ± 0.10	0.323 ± 0.10	0.999	0.971
Random forest + **contribution**	0.371 ± 0.11	0.419 ± 0.09	0.444 ± 0.11	0.387 ± 0.10	0.999	0.971
Logistic regression baseline	0.072 ± 0.04	0.129 ± 0.10	0.338 ± 0.10	0.072 ± 0.056	0.995	0.942
Logistic regression + **contribution**	0.095 ± 0.05	0.183 ± 0.11	0.406 ± 0.11	0.103 ± 0.071	0.996	0.944

5   Results

As a first result we observe in Table 2 that our baseline performance differs from what is reported in other scientific work[1], although our dataset contains the same and more features. Our precision is higher, while the recall is lower, i.e. the alerts of our model are more accurate, but it detects less fraudulent transactions. This may be caused by our experimental setup which is oriented towards a real-world scenario in which we use past data to predict future fraud. The differences may also originate from unknown deviations between the used datasets and model parameters.

Looking at our random forest classifier we observe that the new pattern features lead to an average performance improvement of 0.064 in AUCPR. On

---

[1] [3, Tables 6c, 7c] reports for another dataset a precision of 0.233, a precision at k of 0.494, a recall of 0.747, an accuracy of 0.987 and an AUC of 0.934.

average the area grows by 20%. In the cycle of largest absolute performance improvement the AUCPR grows from 0.157 to 0.357, while in other cycles there is no significant improvement in performance. This indicates that the importance of the new features changes between the different time windows of data. Generally the mean deviation of the performance measurements is high compared to the performance difference between the models. Therefore we apply the Friedman-Nemenyi test [8] on the performance results. For a significance level of $\alpha = 0.05$ the test confirms that the newly proposed pattern features significantly improve the performance regarding *all* different performance measures reported in Table 2. A logistic regression classifier confirms the positive effect of the new features, although performing generally worse than the random forest model.

The performance fluctuation demonstrates the concept drift in the data, i.e. the constant change in the payment behavior of fraudsters. For some days the task of identifying fraudulent transactions can be simple while it becomes more challenging on other days. Likewise for some days fraudsters might act according to previously identified patterns while on others they change their habits and the patterns lose their explanatory power. During the experiments we observe that the generation of suspicious patterns leads to more than 300 patterns for some time windows of data and sometimes only to around 50. We presume that by storing all previously found patterns in a database and only re-estimating their suspiciousness for new time windows could further improve the performance.

6   Conclusion

We have investigated a pattern-based approach to identify fraud among financial transactions. It is common knowledge that the individual transactions of ongoing fraud can seem entirely unsuspicious. The fraudulent activity only becomes evident once the full sequence of transactions is analyzed. In this work we incorporate pattern information in the form of new attributes into a classical machine learning model and show that the predictive performance improves significantly. The area under precision-recall-curve grows on average by 20% when compared to a state-of-the-art baseline. This result shows that fraudsters tend to use compromised cards at the same set of card acceptors over and over again. This knowledge can be exploited to detect fraud more reliably through generating a database of suspicious acceptor patterns.

Our approach can of course be used to reveal suspicious acceptor patterns, but it can also be used in a wider sense too. It can for example be extended to suspicious patterns of point of sale locations or any other categorical transaction attributes. First experiments into this direction based on the merchant category code show promising results.

While looking at several transactions to detect fraud increases the detection performance it has one drawback: compromised cards are only detected once they have been used for transactions at all acceptors in a suspicious pattern. In practice that means that a fraudster is able to issue multiple transactions before the fraud is detected. However, this drawback comes rather from the nature of fraud—Human experts have found that it is in most of the fraud scenarios impossible to detect them on the first fraudulent transaction.

References

1. Aggarwal, C.C., Han, J.: Frequent Pattern Mining. Springer, Heidelberg (2014)
2. Agrawal, R., Imieliński, T., Swami, A.: Mining association rules between sets of items in large databases. In: International Conference on Management of Data (SIGMOD 1993), pp. 207–216. ACM, New York (1993)
3. Bhattacharyya, S., Jha, S., Tharakunnel, K., Westland, J.C.: Data mining for credit card fraud: a comparative study. Decis. Support Syst. **50**(3), 602–613 (2011)
4. Bolton, R.J., Hand, D.J.: Statistical fraud detection: a review. Stat. Sci. **17**(3), 235–249 (2002)
5. Dal Pozzolo, A.: Adaptive machine learning for credit card fraud detection. Ph.D. thesis, Université libre de Bruxelles (2015)
6. Pozzolo, A.D., Caelen, O., Borgne, Y.L., Waterschoot, S., Bontempi, G.: Learned lessons in credit card fraud detection from a practitioner perspective. Expert Syst. Appl. **41**(10), 4915–4928 (2014)
7. Davis, J., Goadrich, M.: The relationship between precision-recall and ROC curves. In: 23rd International Conference on Machine Learning (ICML 2006), pp. 233–240. ACM, New York (2006)
8. Demšar, J.: Statistical comparisons of classifiers over multiple data sets. J. Mach. Learn. Res. **7**, 1–30 (2006)
9. Li, J., Liu, G., Li, H., Wong, L.: Maximal biclique subgraphs and closed pattern pairs of the adjacency matrix: a one-to-one correspondence and mining algorithms. IEEE Trans. Knowl. Data Eng. **19**(12), 1625–1637 (2007)
10. Liaw, A., Wiener, M.: Classification and regression by randomforest. R News **2**(3), 18–22 (2002)
11. Rajaraman, A., Ullman, J.D.: Mining of Massive Datasets. Cambridge University Press, New York (2011)
12. Sánchez, D., Vila, M., Cerda, L., Serrano, J.: Association rules applied to credit card fraud detection. Expert Syst. Appl. **36**(2), 3630–3640 (2009)
13. Shen, A., Tong, R., Deng, Y.: Application of classification models on credit card fraud detection. In: International Conference on Service Systems and Service Management (ICSSSM 2007), pp. 1–4. IEEE (2007)
14. Spackman, K.A.: Signal detection theory: valuable tools for evaluating inductive learning. In: 6th International Workshop on Machine Learning, pp. 160–163. Morgan Kaufmann, San Francisco (1989)
15. Van Hulse, J., Khoshgoftaar, T.M., Napolitano, A.: Experimental perspectives on learning from imbalanced data. In: 24th International Conference on Machine Learning (ICML 2007), pp. 935–942. ACM, New York (2007)
16. Van Vlasselaer, V., Akoglu, L., Eliassi-Rad, T., Snoeck, M., Baesens, B.: Guilt-by-constellation: fraud detection by suspicious clique memberships. In: 48th Hawaii International Conference on System Sciences (HICSS 2015), pp. 918–927. IEEE (2015)
17. Whitrow, C., Hand, D.J., Juszczak, P., Weston, D., Adams, N.M.: Transaction aggregation as a strategy for credit card fraud detection. Data Min. Knowl. Discov. **18**(1), 30–55 (2009)

Contextual Air Leakage Detection in Train Braking Pipes

Wan-Jui Lee[1,2]([envelope])

[1] Maintenance Development, Dutch Railways, 3500 GD Utrecht, The Netherlands
wan-jui.lee@ns.nl
[2] Pattern Recognition and Bioinformatics Group, Delft University of Technology,
2628 CD Delft, The Netherlands
W.J.Lee@tudelft.nl

Abstract. Air leakage in braking pipes is a commonly encountered mechanical defect on trains. A severe air leakage will lead to braking issues and therefore decrease the reliability and cause train delays or stranding. However, air leakage is difficult to be detected via visual inspection and therefore most air leakage defects are run to fail. In this study we present a contextual anomaly detection method that detects air leakage based on the on/off logs of a compressor. Air leakage causes failure in the context when the compressor idle time is short than the compressor run time, that is, the speed of air consumption is faster than air generation. In our method the logistic regression classifier is adopted to model two different classes of compressor behavior for each train separately. The logistic regression classifier defines the boundary separating the two classes under normal situations and models the distribution of the compressor idle time and run time separately using logistic functions. The air leakage anomaly is further detected in the context that when a compressor idle time is erroneously classified as a compressor run time. To distinguish anomalies from outliers and detect anomalies based on the severity degree, a density-based clustering method with a dynamic density threshold is developed for anomaly detection. The results have demonstrated that most air leakages can be detected one to four weeks before the braking failure and therefore can be prevented in time. Most importantly, the contextual anomaly detection method can pre-filter anomaly candidates and therefore avoid generating false alarms.

Keywords: Contextual anomaly detection · Density-based clustering ·
Air leakage · Train braking pipe

1 Introduction

Dutch Railways, the principal railway operator in the Netherlands, operates 178 VIRM (lengthened interregional rolling stock) trains which are a series of electric multiple unit (EMU) double-deck trains. These trains were built between

© Springer International Publishing AG 2017
S. Benferhat et al. (Eds.): IEA/AIE 2017, Part II, LNAI 10351, pp. 191–200, 2017.
DOI: 10.1007/978-3-319-60045-1_22

1994 and 2009 with on-board train management systems continuously logging particular events on the local disk or on a remote disk using wireless data communications. In this work, the switch on and off logs of compressor are used to detect air leakages in braking pipes.

The air pressure of a main reservoir on VIRM trains should be kept in the level between 8.5 and 10 bar at all times. When it drops to below 8.5 bar, the compressor will be switched on to pump air into the main reservoir until the air pressure reaches 10 bar again. After 10 bar is researched, the compressor will be switched off. Air in the main reservoir will be consumed by the braking pipe during service. The time it takes for a compressor to pump air into the main reservoir is defined as the "Compressor Run Time" in this work. The time it takes for the braking pipe to consume air in the main reservoir while the compressor is switched off is defined as the "Compressor Idle Time". It is not difficult to imagine that when the speed of air generation is slower than air consumption there will be insufficient air supply to the braking pipes and therefore braking issues will occur. One of the most possible cause of this phenomenon is air leakage in the braking pipe which is a commonly found mechanical defect on trains. To the best of our knowledge, this is the first work discovering the capability of switch on/off logs of a compressor in detecting air leakage in braking pipes. Such a discovery is extremely valuable since air leakage is one of the most difficult defect to be detected by visual or audio inspection carried out in the workshops. By converting the switch on/off logs of a compressor into duration of compressor run time and idle time, air leakage is finally possible to be continuously monitored and detected from data.

Anomaly detection [4,5,9] is widely applied in many applications where continuous monitoring is available. The goal is to find variants that are different from normal behaviors. In applications where false positives are very expensive, post-processing or human interaction are often required to eliminate false positives. Contextual anomaly detection [3,7] is a newly emerging field of study that aim to detect anomalies that occurs within the context of other meta-information such as spatial or temporal information. For instance, a sensor value 0 during work hours might be normal while it is abnormal during off-work hours. In this study the logistic regression classifier [1,2] is adopted for building context of "Compressor Run Time" and "Compressor Idle Time" separately for each train. The context is used for defining a threshold to filter out non-targeted regions because air leakage are most likely occur in regions where "Compressor Idle Time" is overlapped with "Compressor Run Time". This threshold differs per train due to difference in configuration, age and usage, and therefore the role of the logistic regression classifier is to model the distribution of these two classes in order to identify the decision boundary between them separately for each train and use it as the threshold.

Due to the high variation and noisy nature of the compressor behavior data, clustering techniques [5,6,9] are considered most applicable to our application for anomaly detection. However, during normal services, the air consumption in the braking pipes can be triggered by activities such as braking, door opening and closing and bioreactor usage and so forth. Also the number of carriers of the train has an impact on the duration of air consumption. Therefore there might be sudden and singular occurrences of speedy air consumption due to sudden increase of air consumption demands. This kind of sudden increase of usage demand is defined as an outlier. The most intuitive way to distinguish anomaly from outlier is based on density since a leakage is a mechanical failure which will occur constantly in a certain period of time. On the other hand, a sudden increasing demand is often a single and random event. In this work, we have developed a density-based clustering approach which is inspired by DBSCAN [8] to detect regions of high density. These regions indicate the existence of air leakage. To consider the severity degree of air leakage in anomaly detection, we have defined a dynamic density threshold based on the logistic model describing the context. The result of contextual anomaly detection based on the density-based clustering approach suggest that air leakages in braking pipes can be detected at least one to four weeks before the braking failure.

2   Contextual Air Leakage Detection in Braking Pipes

Due to the difference in configuration and operational use of each train, the range and distribution of "Compressor Idle Time" and "Compressor Run Time" differ per train. However, the physical observation that when the speed of air consumption is faster than the speed of air generation, there might exist an air leakage applies in general to all trains. To find out the region of interest for air leakage detection for each train, the logistic regression classifier is adopted for building context of "Compressor Run Time" and "Compressor Idle Time" separately for each train as a two class problem where "Compressor Run Time" is the positive class and "Compressor Idle Time" is the negative class. By building the context with logistic models, a threshold can be defined at the intersecting point where the probability of the positive class and negative class are both 0.5 to pre-filter non-targeted regions. Since air leakages occur most likely in regions where "Compressor Idle Time" is overlapped with "Compressor Run Time" and therefore only "Compressor Idle Time" with a similarity higher than 0.5 by applying the logistic model of the positive class will be considered for the clustering procedure.

2.1   Learning Context with Logistic Regression Classifier

Logistic regression classifier is a linear model for learning $P(Y|X)$ in the case where Y is the class label and $X = <x_1, x_2, ..., x_m>$ is an input data vector. In our application we only consider the case where Y is a boolean variable (2 class problem) and $m = 1$ which means the data vector is one-dimensional. The parametric model assumed by logistic regression in the 2 class setting is:

$$P(Y = 0|X) = \frac{1}{1 + \exp(w_0 + \sum_{i=1}^{m} w_i x_i)} \tag{1}$$

and

$$P(Y = 1|X) = \frac{\exp(w_0 + \sum_{i=1}^{m} w_i x_i)}{1 + \exp(w_0 + \sum_{i=1}^{m} w_i x_i)}. \tag{2}$$

The goal is to learn the parameters $w_j, \forall j$ from training data. Since the sum of the two probabilities in Eqs. (1) and (2) must equal 1, Eq. (2) can be directly derived from Eq. (1).

In our application, we use the point $\hat{X}$ where $P(Y = 0|\hat{X}) = P(Y = 1|\hat{X})$ as the threshold. That is the point $\hat{X}$ where

$$\frac{1}{1 + \exp(w_0 + w_1\hat{x_1})} = \frac{1}{2}, \tag{3}$$

and $\hat{X} = <\hat{x_1}>$ since the data vector is one-dimensional in our application. By taking the natural log, this becomes

$$w_0 + w_1\hat{x_1} = 0. \tag{4}$$

By transforming Eq. (4), one can derive

$$\hat{x_1} = -\frac{w_0}{w_1}. \tag{5}$$

Therefore, after learning parameters $w_j, \forall j$, the point $\hat{X}$ can also be derived. That is, for all data points in the negative class ("Compressor Idle Time"), only those $\leq \hat{X}$ will be included in the clustering procedure for anomaly detection.

In Fig. 1, an example is given to illustrate the functionality of the logistic regression classifier in our application. From the distribution of 2 classes in Fig. 1(a), the overlapped area can be observed. The logistic regression classifier models these 2 classes with logistic functions as shown in Fig. 1(b) to find the most significant point to distinguish these 2 classes. In this example, the intersecting point of these 2 classes is at 497.4 and it is used as the threshold for filtering out any "Compressor Idle Time" with a duration value larger than 497.4 since these values are very unlikely to be generated from air leakages.

Training Logistic Regression Classifier. One common approach to train a logistic regression model is to choose parameter values that maximize the probability of the observed Y values in the training data, conditioned on their corresponding X values. That is, to choose parameters W satisfying

$$W \leftarrow \operatorname{argmax} \sum_{k=1}^{n} \ln P(Y^k|X^k, W), \tag{6}$$

where $W = <w_0, w_1, ..., w_m>$ is the vector of parameters to be estimated, Y^k denotes the observed value of Y in the kth training example, and X^k demotes the observed value of X in the kth training example. The expression to the right of the argmax is the log of the conditional likelihood.

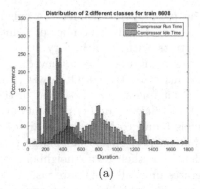
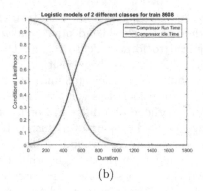

(a)   (b)

Fig. 1. The (a) distribution in histograms, and (b) trained logistic models of "Compressor Run Time" and "Compressor Idle Time" data of train 8608.

By substituting with Eqs. (1) and (2), the log of the conditional likelihood $l(W)$ can be then expressed as:

$$l(W) = \sum_{k=1}^{n} Y^k \ln P(Y^k = 1|X^k, W) + (1 - Y^k)\ln P(Y^k = 0|X^k, W)$$
$$= \sum_{k=1}^{n} Y^k (w_0 + \sum_{i=1}^{m} w_i x_i) - \ln(1 + \exp(w_0 + \sum_{i=1}^{m} w_i x_i)) \qquad (7)$$

where x_i^k denotes the value of x_i for the kth training example.

However, these is no closed form solution to maximizing $l(W)$ with respect to W, and one common approach is to use gradient ascent. The ith component of the vector gradient has the form

$$\frac{\partial l(W)}{\partial w_i} = \sum_{k=1}^{n} x_i^k (Y^k - \hat{P}(Y^k = 1|X^k, W))) \qquad (8)$$

where $\hat{P}(Y^k = 1|X^k, W)$ is the prediction result of the logistic regression classifier. Since the conditional log likelihood is a concave function, this gradient ascent procedure will converge to a global maximum. By beginning with initial weights of zero, the weights are iteratively updated with

$$w_i \leftarrow w_i + \eta \sum_{k=1}^{n} x_i^k (Y^k - \hat{P}(Y^k = 1|X^k, W))) \qquad (9)$$

where η is the step size which is often a small constant.

2.2 A Density-Based Clustering Approach for Anomaly Detection with a Dynamic Density Threshold

For clustering in a noisy dataset, density-based approaches are most commonly adopted. Among them, DBSCAN is one of the most well-known approach which requires two parameters: ϵ and $minPts$. The parameter ϵ defines the neighborhood of a considered point, and $minPts$ is the minimum number of points required to form a dense region. DBSCAN starts with an arbitrary starting point that has not been visited. This point's ϵ-neighborhood is retrieved, and if it contains a sufficient number of points, a cluster is started. Otherwise, the point is considered as a noise. However this point might later be found in the ϵ-neighborhood of a different point containing a sufficient number of points and hence be made a part of a cluster. If a point is found to be a dense part of a cluster, its ϵ-neighborhood is also part of that cluster. Hence, all points that are found within the ϵ-neighborhood are added, as is their own ϵ-neighborhood when they are also dense. This procedure iterates until all points are visited.

In the case of air leakage detection, the detection capability in a severe region needs to be higher than that in a less severe region. Therefore we have defined a dynamic density threshold based on the condition of severity. The procedure of our density-based clustering approach for anomaly detection with a dynamic density threshold is described in the following:

- Step 1: Use the threshold defined in Sect. 2.1 to limit the search range of anomalies.
- Step 2: In the interested region, calculate the neighborhood density of each data point. The neighborhood density of a data point is the number of data points located in its ϵ-neighborhood region. A ϵ-neighborhood region of a data point x_i is defined by:

$$|x_i - x_j| \leq \epsilon, \forall j \tag{10}$$

where ϵ is an user-defined constant.
- Step 3: Classify a data point and all other points located in its ϵ-neighborhood as anomalies if its neighborhood density is higher than the density threshold. The density threshold should be dynamic and vary with the degree of severity. That is, a more severe air leakage (shorter idle duration) should be more easily detected by giving a lower density threshold and vice versa. By giving a user-defined density limit $minPts$, the dynamic density threshold β becomes

$$\beta = 2 * minPts * \frac{1}{1 + \exp(w_0 + \sum_{i=1}^{m} w_i x_i)}, \tag{11}$$

where $\frac{1}{1+\exp(w_0+\sum_{i=1}^{m} w_i x_i)}$ is adopted from Eq. (1).
- Step 4: For a data point, if its neighborhood density $\geq$ its dynamic density threshold β, this data point and all the other data points within the neighborhood of this data points will be labeled as anomalies.

3　Experimental Results

From 178 VIRM trains 632,683 data points were collected in the period from May 2015 to October 2016, in which 6,957 are labeled as "Air Leakage" and 625,726 are labeled as "Normal". The labels are derived from maintenance records of air leakages in the same period. In these 178 trains, 55 trains are mounted with real-time monitoring systems and the data were sent via 4G network directly into the data center. In the rest of 123 trains, the data were read out physically with laptops in the maintenance depot. Due to the manual operations, there were sometimes long gaps in weeks or months between data records.

In the experiments, the logistic regression classifier was built for each train to derive the filtering threshold on "Compressor Idle Time". For anomaly detection, our density-based clustering approach finds clusters in a two-dimensional dataset consisting two features, i.e., "Compressor Idle Time" and date converted into the number of days from January 0, 0000. The ϵ-neighborhood of a data point for the clustering procedure is therefore two-dimensional with ϵ_1 of "Compressor Idle Time" being $0.2 \times \hat{X}$ and ϵ_2 of the number of days being 2 days. The density limit $minPts$ is set to 20 for computing the dynamic density threshold β.

The original "Compressor Run Time" and "Compressor Idle Time" data, thresholds derived from logistic regression classifiers, and the results of contextual anomaly detection for four trains with numbers 8608, 9580, 8652 and 8640, are presented in Figs. 2, 3, 4 and 5, respectively.

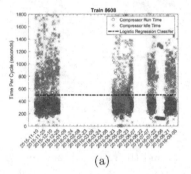
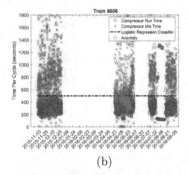

(a)   (b)

Fig. 2. The (a) original compressor duration data and (b) result of the proposed air leakage detection of train 8608.

From the figures, it can be observed that the logistic regression classifier identifies a proper boundary separating the "Compressor Run Time" and "Compressor Idle Time". Please notice that the percentage of air leakage data points is relatively small and therefore it generally does not give a large impact on the logistic regression classifier.

In order to verify the effectiveness of pre-filtering using the logistic regression classifier, a baseline anomaly detection procedure is compared with the proposed procedure. The baseline anomaly detection procedure first adopted the DBSCAN clustering approach to find the dense regions on all "Compressor Idle Time" data points as shown in Fig. 6(a). Then the logistic regression classifier is used for post-filtering to remove detected points above the threshold as given in Fig. 6(b). It can be observed in Fig. 6(b) that several points were wrongly detected as anomaly after post-filtering due to the high density in normal regions.

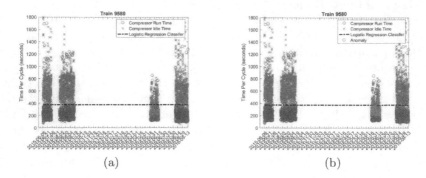

Fig. 3. The (a) original compressor duration data and (b) result of the proposed air leakage detection of train 9580.

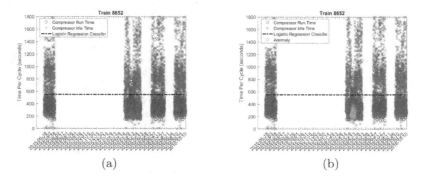

Fig. 4. The (a) original compressor duration data and (b) result of the proposed air leakage detection of train 8652.

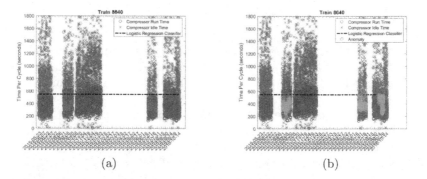

Fig. 5. The (a) original compressor duration data and (b) result of the proposed air leakage detection of train 8640.

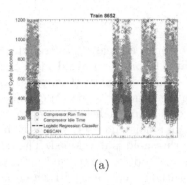
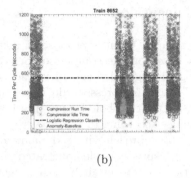

(a)   (b)

Fig. 6. The results of (a) density-based clustering and (b) baseline anomaly detection for train 8652.

Table 1. Confusion matrix of the experimental results of the proposed air leakage detection procedure

	Predicted: Air Leakage	Predicted: Normal
Actual: Air Leakage	5844 (0.840)	1113 (0.160)
Actual: Normal	665 (0.001)	625061 (0.999)

The confusion matrix of the results of our proposed contextual anomaly detection is given in Table 1. The values in brackets are those computed in the form of percentage.

From the confusion matrix, our method for contextual air leakage detection in train braking pipes not only has a high detection capacity of 84% but also a very low false alarm ratio. Without the context modeled with the logistic regression classifier, there will be a large amount of false alarms if a density-based clustering approach is applied. Even applied with a post-filtering threshold as described in the baseline anomaly detection procedure, the amount of false alarms is also significant as shown in Table 2. Moreover, the proposed anomaly detection procedure is computationally much more efficient than the baseline anomaly detection procedure since the proposed anomaly detection procedure pre-filters the "Compressor Idle Time" which resulting in a small subset of data points considered for the density-based clustering while in the baseline anomaly detection procedure, all "Compressor Idle Time" data points were used in density-based clustering.

Table 2. Confusion matrix of the experimental results of the baseline anomaly detection procedure

	Predicted: Air Leakage	Predicted: Normal
Actual: Air Leakage	5892 (0.847)	1065 (0.153)
Actual: Normal	6831 (0.011)	618895 (0.989)

4 Discussion

In this paper, we have proposed a method to detect air leakage in train braking pipes based on the compressor behavior data. In order to avoid false alarms, the logistic regression classifier is adopted to model context of "Compressor Run Time" and "Compressor Idle Time" and use the boundary separating these two classes as the threshold for pre-filtering candidate of anomalies. In order to detect anomalies according to their severity degree in a noisy dataset, a density-based clustering approach with a dynamic density threshold is developed. The experimental results have demonstrated that our method for contextual air leakage detection can detect air leakages effectively without generating false alarms.

References

1. Mitchell, T.: Machine Learning. McGraw Hill, New York (1997)
2. Ng, A.Y., Jordan, M.I.: On discriminative vs. generative classifiers: a comparison of logistic regression and Naive Bayes. In: Advances in Neural Information Processing Systems, vol. 14, pp. 841–848 (2001)
3. Hayes, M.A., Capretz, M.A.: Contextual anomaly detection framework for big sensor data. J. Big Data **2**, 2 (2015)
4. Chandola, V., Banerjee, A., Kumar, V.: Anomaly detection: a survey. ACM Comput. Surv. **41**(3), 1–58 (2009)
5. Khan, L., Awad, M., Thuraisingham, B.: A new intrusion detection system using support vector machines and hierarchical clustering. VLDB J. **16**(4), 507–521 (2007)
6. Upadhyaya, S., Singh, K.: Nearest neighbour based outlier detection techniques. Int. J. Comput. Trends Technol. **3**(2), 299–303 (2012)
7. Mahapatra, A., Srivastava, N., Srivastava, J.: Contextual anomaly detection in text data. Algorithms **4**, 469–489 (2012)
8. Ester, M., Kriegel, H.P., Sander, J., Xu, X.W.: A density-based algorithm for discovering clusters in large spatial databases with noise. In: Proceedings of the Second International Conference on Knowledge Discovery and Data Mining, pp. 226–231 (1996)
9. Behera, S., Rani, R.: Comparative analysis of density based outlier detection techniques on breast cancer data using hadoop and map reduce. In: Proceedings of the International Conference on Inventive Computation Technologies (2016)

K-means Application for Anomaly Detection and Log Classification in HPC

Mohamed Cherif Dani[1], Henri Doreau[2(✉)], and Samantha Alt[1]

[1] Intel, 2 Rue de Paris, Meudon, France
[2] CEA, DAM, DIF, 91297 Arpajon, France
`henri.doreau@cea.fr`

Abstract. Detecting anomalies in the flow of system logs of a high performance computing (HPC) facility is a challenging task. Although previous research has been conducted to identify nominal and abnormal phases; practical ways to provide system administrators with a reduced set of the most useful messages to identify abnormal behaviour remains a challenge. In this paper we describe an extensive study of logs classification and anomaly detection using K-means on real HPC unlabelled data extracted from the Curie supercomputer. This method involves (1) classifying logs by format, which is a valuable information for admin, then (2) build normal and abnormal classes for anomaly detection. Our methodology shows good performances for clustering and detecting abnormal logs.

Keywords: Anomaly detection · HPC · Log processing · K-means

1 Introduction

With the rise of artificial intelligence and intensive simulation in science and engineering, more and more researchers rely on the massive computing power of High Performance Computing (HPC) clusters. Large HPC facilities consist of heterogeneous distributed subsystems, which interact in non-trivial ways. Accidental conditions, hardware or software failures, and sustained heavy load can cause a component in the system to malfunction. Due to the very large number of components within a supercomputer results in significant number of fault occurrences. The fact that HPC systems are designed to maximise performances rather than reliability further increases the risk.

The top-level architectural units, such as storage or compute, are often implemented as interleaved layers of software and hardware that interact together and with numerous services running aside. A single computing cluster operated by CEA at TGCC [1], comprises several thousand compute nodes, which run complex scientific applications and libraries. A job scheduler is in charge of allocating resources and running the tasks as quickly as possible. The nodes communicate together over a high bandwidth/low latency InfiniBand network. External storage servers, connected to the fabric, expose distributed file systems to all clusters of the computing center. The component hierarchy is very deep and the interconnections and dependencies very complex. These subsystems record their activity

© Springer International Publishing AG 2017
S. Benferhat et al. (Eds.): IEA/AIE 2017, Part II, LNAI 10351, pp. 201–210, 2017.
DOI: 10.1007/978-3-319-60045-1_23

using unstructured text lines that constitute a prime source of information for system administrators.

Classical monitoring solutions periodically check whether services are responding[1] [2]. This is indeed essential order to ensure a certain quality of service. The current technology implemented in the HPC system allows for sampling[2] of performance counters at high frequency [3, 4], which supplies the user with highly granular insight into the performance of each node in the system. Both approaches lack the ability to provide system administrators with enough information to understand the nature of the issue they are investigating, only that there is an issue occurring. This information is made available through more detail in the console logs.

Robust tools exist to aggregate and centralise the many log streams of a massively distributed computing infrastructure [5]. Nevertheless, the resulting composite signal is difficult to exploit efficiently because of its high throughput, its unstructured format, and its level of noise and information redundancy. In addition, single messages are incomplete in that they do not contain enough information to fully trace a failure back to the root cause. A task as common as identifying faulty components that generate abnormal behaviour can be extremely time-consuming and has to be done by domain experts. Automatic anomaly detection can be directly coupled with resource management systems to mark faulty components and prevent them from being used in production until the problem is solved.

Nowadays, the need for anomaly detection covers almost every domain in engineering. All these domains converge towards a common definition that the anomaly is a deviation from a normal behaviour, which most of the data form. This definition is extensively explored by Agroual [8] and many other authors [9, 10]. In this context, we refer to abnormal log lines that contain a description and the source of a failure.

As of today, the common approach of analysing logs first consists in writing and maintaining regular expressions to match known patterns [6]. This does not scale well and requires a significant amount of human work and experience. The main drawback of this approach is that it will systematically lead to a situation where the common messages are properly parsed and the unexpected ones cannot be matched against a regular expression despite being highly valuable.

As noted by Ning et al. [7] console logs have a reduced vocabulary, highly skewed word count distribution, and weak syntax. This makes most natural language processing approaches unsuitable for solving the problem. The choice was therefore made to look for anomalies based on the geometrical structure of the messages rather than try to summarise them.

Adding anomaly detection to the system monitoring process leads to healthier and better functioning systems. By applying text mining techniques and unsupervised learning to actual system logs from *petascale* HPC clusters, we have developed an approach to filter the messages and provide the system

---

[1] http://shinken-monitoring.org.
[2] https://graphiteapp.org.

administrators with a selection of the most useful entries to identify and understand anomalies and failures.

2   Problem Statement Within HPC

An HPC environment has domain-specific constraints and characteristics with high component count and complexity. These subsystems change very quickly in order to stay cutting-edge, which leads to frequent firmware and OS upgrades. Therefore, administration and monitoring techniques must be scalable with regard to the number of nodes as well as not be a large impact on performance. Current research is oriented toward the reach of *exascale*. It is expected that future Exascale machines will contain many more base components rather than larger and faster components. This will lead to more failures to investigate within a larger log stream, thus the critical need for efficient automation.

The techniques used to reliably propagate console messages from the nodes that generate them to a log processing cluster is out of the scope of this article. This work explores means to process the logs and present them in a useful way to the system administrators. In particular, identify outliers among the aggregated stream of messages.

We focused on unstructured text messages, so any attempt to apply machine learning techniques on the problem had to come with a matrix representation of the log corpus. The chosen technique had to be efficient, in terms of CPU and memory footprint, so as to be applicable for the very large volume of logs that a HPC cluster can generate.

As scalability of mining algorithms are a large factor in this systems automation, the genomic sequence mining algorithms described in [11] are not applicable due to the scalability limitations. Linking resource usage to console log [12,13] returned interesting results, but failed at identifying problems that are not described by both datasets.

Definitions

A *log message*, or *record*, consists of one or multiple lines of text attached to a timestamp. A record describes an event that occurred on a component of the system at that time. Messages of a component are emitted and recorded sequentially. The sequence of log messages is referred to as system log or log data.

A record can be divided into fields, which in turn fall into two categories. The well-known ones (such as date, time, hostname, process name, etc.) usually prefix the messages and format-free information follows. The latter contains the most relevant information but is by far the hardest to process. Only a small minority of applications publish their log format and specifications.

We call *anomalies* the log records that describe abnormal situations. They are distant from the records that are emitted during nominal operations. The definition of abnormality depends on some terms/tags in the log line *(Fatal, Error, Err, etc.)*, and many other patterns validated by experts.

Log format varies significantly, an example of these logs is described in the following figure:

```
2015-11-xx 15:21:09,568 ERROR tuned.utils.commands:
Executing hdparm error: [Errno 2] No such file or directory

Dec 6 03:56:37 [158XXX] node1789.c-curie.hpc.cea.fr
pengine: error: unpack_resources:          Resource start-up
disabled since no STONITH resources have been defined

141912041 2016 Dec 7 03:35:01 x kern warning kernel
Lustre: DEBUG MARKER: Sun Dec 7 03:35:01
```

Fig. 1. Heterogeneous log format sample

3   Unsupervised Log Clustering and Anomaly Detection

A lot of methods and tools exist in machine learning to analyse and to detect anomalies in data centers, some of them mentioned previously. The simplest rely on regular expressions, while others empower more advanced methods like Natural language processing (NLP) or machine learning [8].

Fig. 2. Different phases before achieving detection

Within an unsupervised environment, where no prior information is available, the detection process of anomalies is complex and challenging. As in every domain, many elements within the data center can lead to an anomaly. Furthermore, the amount of data generated daily is huge. The detection process is defined in Fig. 2.

Our first dataset contains more than 300 log lines of heterogeneous logs, extracted from different templates. Three of these logs are presented in Fig. 1. The entire dataset contains about 15 different log formats. One of these formats constitutes our second dataset, that will be used to demonstrate the concept of the anomaly detection and log clustering. This dataset contains more than 32 million entries used to test the clustering efficiency and scalability, and 1 million log lines used for anomaly detection.

The transformation of the data is an important phase that has a large impact on the quality of clustering. Our goal is to cluster the logs by format and message type using respectively the first and the second datasets. If we consider the log-files analysis process as a classic text mining problem, where we can for example cluster the data by the subject of interest, or extract useful information such as correlated words. Hence, since we assume no prior knowledge of the type of logs to keep consistent with the heterogeneity and rapid changes of the system. The log data are transformed into a frequency matrix that can be easily consumed by machine learning methods. To do so, we keep only the type of logs (error, info, debugging, notices, etc.), and the log description *(cleaned up)*. The cleanup of the message consisted in forcing lowercase, removing punctuation signs, and stemming process. For log messages that contained a file path, we concatenated the path into one word to optimise our representation and to avoid sparse representation by producing too many terms.

The documents term (log-term) matrix, which contains the frequency of terms regarding all the logs, is our first input from the pre-processing phase. The term frequency and inverse document frequency (tfidf) [14] is a widely used matrix in text mining that evaluates how important a term is to a document within a collection of documents. This is defined as:

$tdidf(d,t) = tf(d,t) * log(\frac{|D|}{df(t)})$, where $tf(t)$ is the number of occurrences of term t in a document divided by the total number of terms in the documents.

An example of this transformation is illustrated in Fig. 3:

```
Original log:
    148228XXX 2016 Dec 21 03:35:01 node3435 cron info CROND (root) CMD
    (/usr/bin/test -e /dev/lnet && /usr/sbin/lctl mark >/dev/null 2>&1) 2
Transformed  log:
    info crond root cmd usr-bin-test dev-lnet usr-sbin-lctl mark dev-null
```

Fig. 3. Log transformation

The K-means family methods are used extensively in text mining [9] and outlier and anomaly detection [8]. A performance discussion of K-means clustering in comparison to other approaches such as hierarchical (hclust) and density (dbscan) clustering is done in the next section.

3.1   Log-Files Clustering Using K-means

Our process is illustrated by Fig. 4 where the main input can contain logs with millions of formats. Then for each format group, we apply another clustering to build normal and abnormal classes.

The K-means [15] is an unsupervised algorithm which aims to group the data into K clusters, where K needs to be user defined. The K-means setup can be resumed into major setup: assignment setup and update setup. The knowledge of K is not an obstacle in this study, unlike in many unsupervised problems since we are dealing with known template that generates the logs. So, the number of K can be estimated easily.

Otherwise, an estimation of K is conceivable in the case where new templates are setup or new logs appear. For such estimation, several statistic criteria exist like Akaike Information Criterion [16] or Bayesian Information criterion [17].

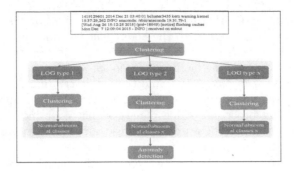

Fig. 4. Log clustering stages and anomaly detection

The classic K-means similarity measure is, in general, the Euclidean distance which is defined as:

$$D_e = (\sum_{t=1}^{n} |w_{t,a} - w_{t,b}|^2)^{1/2}$$

Where $T = t_1, ...t_m$ is the term set and $w_{t,a}$ is the term weights computed using (*tdidf*).

Generally, the document term matrices are known to be highly dimensional. A situation where standard k-means is less powerful than other techniques.

Consequently, we tried during the prepossessing phase to simplify our document term matrix, to get less terms by deleting the least significant ones and merge paths in one word, etc. Also the standard distance definition of k-means based on centroids was replaced by the cosine similarity measure which is more efficient for document term clustering than Euclidian distance [19].

It can be considered as the correlation between two term vectors, with certain independence of document length. So, with two documents t_1, t_2 forming the term-set $T = t_1, ..., t_n$, the cosine is denoted by:

$$D_c = \frac{\overrightarrow{t_1} . \overrightarrow{t_2}}{|t_1||t_2|}$$

In simple manner, when two documents are identical the distance is equal to 1, and if they are very different the distance equals 0. After computing the similarity measures, each data point is assigned to the cluster with the highest cosine similarity measure (the classic k-means steps).

The usage of kmeans for anomaly detection was inspired by many studies [8,9,18] that use the same method for anomaly detection. Before discussing the clustering results, we will explain in the next section the anomaly detection process using K-means.

4 Anomaly Detection and Log Classification Using K-Means

In many anomaly detection problems, the unsupervised part is used for labelling data, then semi-supervised or supervised method like OSVM [9] are used for detection and classification. However, we propose in this part of the work to use K-means centroids and Euclidean distance to classify the new logs as abnormal or not.

In [18] the authors propose to build normal and abnormal classes using K-means. A data point with a distance closer to the normal centroid and under a threshold is labelled as normal. Otherwise the data point is abnormal. This process of detection is adapted to our problematic and used on 1 million of log lines to detect anomalies.

4.1 Results Discussion

First in this section, we will compare the clustering results of different data set. The number of k is known for the three datasets (k = 15 for the 300 logs dataset, and k = 5 or 6 for the other datasets).

Heterogeneous Classification

Clustering the heterogeneous logs is the first relevant information that we can provide to the admin. Technically, because every log is provided from a specific template or system, grouping these logs allows us to link specific anomaly detection to a specific log source, i.e. hardware fault or software application. In addition to K-means, we have also tested dbscan, which is used for clustering logs [7] as well as noise and outlier detection, and hclust with an implementation package of hierarchical clustering in R.

To evaluate the detection and quality of the clustering results, we have chosen to use the common F-measure evaluation criterion. It expresses the performance of an anomaly detection method using the precision P and sensitivity R measures where: $P = \frac{TP}{TP+FP}$ and $R = \frac{TP}{TP+FN}$ and TP, FP, TN, FN are respectively: True Positive, False Positive, True Negative and False Negative.

To measure the performance of our approach, The F-measure is denoted by $F = 2 \times \frac{P \times R}{P+R}$ where $F \simeq 1$ indicates a good performance and $F \simeq 0$ means that the method does not detect any anomaly in the data.

Table 1. Anomaly detection performance (F-measures) in different data sets with different number of clusters.

	Dbscan	Hclust	Kmeans
300 Log	0.39	0.63	0.87
32M Log	0.20	0.64	0.80
01M Log	0.5	0.7	0.94

The original log files are composed of 15 clusters *(k = 15)*. Using dbscan only 9 clusters were formed, with 39% performance. These results are not only due to misclassification of logs, but can also be explained by the particularity of dbscan to not cluster logs that do not respect the density parameters. With an f-score of 63% Hclust misclassified data and returned similar logs with only minor differences. We observe the same thing for K-means, but with a much higher performance (87%) (Fig. 5).

```
Cluster:
info broker master archive old log file
info broker master  move old log file var-log-shinken shinken log to var-log-shinken-archives shinken log
info shinken  poller master  init connection scheduler master https tipasa  tipasa ocre cea
info shinken  poller master  connection ok schedul  schedul  master
info receive master  receive master  stop workers
Cluster:
info crond  root  cmd  usr-bin-test dev-lnet usr-sbin-lctl mark dev-null
cron info crond  root  cmd  usr-bin-test  dev-lnet usr-sbin-lctl mark dev-null
cron info crond  root  cmd  usr-lib64-sa-sa
kern warning kernel
kern warning kernel lustre  debug marker
Cluster:
api ni lnetstartuplndnis     add lni
api ni lnetstartuplndnis     add lni
lprocosc oscwractive     activate   ignore repeat request
lprocosc oscwractive     activate   ignore repeat request
ostosc ffffeaf  communicate operation ostconnect failed
```

Fig. 5. Sample of clustering

Using a classic server to process the original dataset (32 million log lines) which contains only six format families *(k = 6)*. Clustering accuracy for K-means is 80%, 20% for dbscan with heavy processing, and an intermediate score of 64% for hclust. However, these results are accompanied with a great challenge of scalability where execution time took a few minutes for K-means and many hours for dbscan.

Anomaly Detection

To build normal and abnormal classes we followed the definition of anomalies given above. The clustering performances on the training subset of 1 million logs are presented in Table 1. Two global clusters were built manually, the normal cluster contains 5 sub-clusters, and the abnormal one which contains mostly error tags.

To detect anomalies, we extracted (test set) from normal and abnormal clusters about 200 log lines (100 abnormal, 100 normal log lines). And then tried to use the Euclidean distance from centroid to classify the test set. We did not make any assumption or threshold about the normal or abnormal clusters, and the detection process showed very satisfying results. A sample of the results is presented in Fig. 6.

The dataset we used contains only few types of abnormal logs, which explains the good clustering and detection performances. To evaluate the method more efficiently, we would need more types of abnormal logs.

```
Abnormal cluster :
err corosync   totem   marking ringid   interface jobalt faulty
err corosync   totem   marking ringid   interface jobalt faulty
err corosync   totem   marking ringid   interface jobalt faulty
err corosync   totem   marking ringid   interface jobalt faulty
err corosync   totem   marking ringid   interface jobalt faulty
err corosync   totem   marking ringid   interface jobalt faulty


Normal Cluster:
info stonith ng   info stonith command processed stexecute  lrmd
info stonith ng   info stonith command processed stexecute lrmd
info stonith ng   info log operation restofence curiel getting status ipmijo
info stonith ng   info log operation restofence curiel getting status ipmijo
notice corosync   totem automatically recovered ring
notice corosync   totem automatically recovered ring
notice corosync   totem retransmit list
notice corosync   totem retransmit list
notice corosync   totem retransmit list
```

Fig. 6. Sample of abnormal and normal cluster

5 Conclusion and Future Works

This work illustrates the ability to provide system administrators with a useful vision of system logs. It significantly speeds up troubleshooting and failure analysis by clustering heterogeneous logs. The efficiency of the technique, its scalability, and the fact that it works on unlabelled data makes it particularly appropriate for very large and constantly changing data centers such as HPC facilities. The results are limited by the wealth of data, since we have hardly any prior information about the data. Pre-processing is indeed an important phase in such methods and we need to improve the new data representation in order to use more sophisticated algorithms and techniques such as co-clustering or density methods. Abnormal logs detected can serve as a strong input to troubleshoot and identify the root-cause of an anomaly.

References

1. Morey, J.-M.: Numerical simulation at CEA. In: Proceedings of SNA + MC (2013)
2. David, J.: Building a Monitoring Infrastructure with Nagios. Prentice Hall PTR, Upper Saddle River (2007)
3. Bautista, E., Whitney, C., Davis, T.: Big data behind big data. In: Arora, R. (ed.) Conquering Big Data with High Performance Computing, pp. 163–189. Springer, Cham (2016)
4. Sigoure, B.: OpenTSDB scalable time series database (TSDB) (2012)
5. Kreps, J., Narkhede, N., Rao, J., et al.: Kafka: a distributed messaging system for log processing. In: Proceedings of The NetDB, pp. 1–7 (2011)
6. Reelsen, A.: Using elasticsearch, logstash and kibana to create realtime dashboards (2014)
7. Ning, X., Jiang, G., Chen, H., Yoshihira, K.: HLAer: a system for heterogeneous log analysis
8. Aggarwal, C.C., Yu, P.: Outlier detection with uncertain data. In: SDM (2008)
9. Chandola, V., Banerjee, A., Kumar, V.: Anomaly detection: a survey. ACM Comput. Surv. **41**, 15 (2009)
10. Gupta, M., Han, J., Aggarwal, C., Gao, J.: Outlier detection for temporal data: a survey. IEEE Trans. Knowl. Data Eng. **26**, 2250–2267 (2014)

11. Stearley, J.: Towards informatic analysis of syslogs. In: Cluster Computing. IEEE (2004)
12. Chuah, E., Jhumka, A., Narasimhamurthy, S., et al.: Linking resource usage anomalies with system failures from cluster log data. IEEE (2013)
13. Gurumdimma, N., Jhumka, A., et al.: CRUDE: combining resource usage data and error logs for accurate error detection in large-scale distributed systems. IEEE (2016)
14. Rajaraman, A., Ullman, J.D.: Data mining. In: Mining of Massive Datasets (PDF) (2011)
15. MacQueen, J.B.: Some Methods for classification and Analysis of Multivariate Observations. University of California Press, Berkeley (1967)
16. Akaike, H.: Information theory and an extension of the maximum likelihood principle. In: Petrov, B.N., Csáki, F. (eds.) 2nd International Symposium on Information Theory, Tsahkadsor, Armenia, USSR, September 2–8 (1971)
17. Schwarz, G.E.: Estimating the dimension of a model. Ann. Stat. **6**(2), 461–464 (1978)
18. Münz, G., Li, S., Carle, G.: Traffic anomaly detection using k-means clustering. In: GI/ITG-Workshop MMBnet, September 2007
19. Larsen, B., Aone, C.: Fast and effective text mining using linear-time document clustering. In: Proceedings of the Fifth ACM SIGKDD International Conference on Knowledge Discovery and Data Mining (1999)

Information Quality in Social Networks: A Collaborative Method for Detecting Spam Tweets in Trending Topics

Mahdi Washha[1]($\boxtimes$), Aziz Qaroush[2], Manel Mezghani[1], and Florence Sedes[1]

[1] IRIT - Paul Sabatier University, Toulouse, France
{Mahdi.washha,Florence.sedes}@irit.fr, Mezghani.manel@gmail.com
[2] Department of Electrical and Computer Engineering,
Birzeit University, Ramallah, Palestine
Aqaroush@birzeit.edu

Abstract. In Twitter based applications such as tweet summarization, the existence of ill-intentioned users so-called spammers imposes challenges to maintain high performance level in those applications. Conventional social spammer/spam detection methods require significant and unavoidable processing time, extending to months for treating large collections of tweets. Moreover, these methods are completely dependent on supervised learning approach to produce classification models, raising the need for ground truth data-set. In this paper, we design an unsupervised language model based method that performs collaboration with other social networks to detect spam tweets in large-scale topics (e.g. hashtags). We experiment our method on filtering more than 6 million tweets posted in 100 trending topics where Facebook social network is accounted in the collaboration. Experiments demonstrate highly competitive efficiency in regards to processing time and classification performance, compared to conventional spam tweet detection methods.

Keywords: Social spam · Social networks · Collaboration · Topics

1 Introduction

With the enormous popularity of online social networks (OSNs) over the Internet, ill-intentioned users so-called spammers have exploited OSNs for spreading spam content (e.g. advertisements, porn materials, and phishing websites) [1]. Indeed, performing spamming tasks by spammers may cause major problems in different directions, such as: (i) polluting search results by spam information; (ii) degrading statistics accuracy obtained by mining tools; (iii) consuming storage resources; (iv) and violating user's privacy. However, with these serious problems, OSNs' anti-spam mechanisms have failed to end-up the spam problem, raising real concerns about the quality of "crawled" data collections. Hence, besides the importance of OSNs data for tremendous range of areas such as search engines and research field, filtering out noisy data to have high quality information is

© Springer International Publishing AG 2017
S. Benferhat et al. (Eds.): IEA/AIE 2017, Part II, LNAI 10351, pp. 211–223, 2017.
DOI: 10.1007/978-3-319-60045-1_24

the obvious and straight forward solution. Information quality process in social networks is generically summarized in three dependent steps [2]: (i) selecting the data collections (e.g. Facebook accounts, Tweets, Facebook posts) that need improvements; (ii) determining the noise type (e.g. spam, rumor) to be filtered out; (ii) at last, applying pre-designed algorithms depending on the chosen noise type to produce noise free data collections.

In the battle of fighting spam on Twitter, a considerable set of methods [1,3–8] has been designed for detecting spam accounts and spam campaigns with little attention dedicated toward spam tweets detection. The account-level and campaign-level detection methods are time consuming, requiring months to process large collections consisting of millions of Twitter users. The main source of high time consumption is the use of constrained REST APIs[1] to retrieve a required information (e.g. followers, followees, and user time-line) to perform such detection methods. On the other side, the existing tweet-level spam detection methods are grounded on exploiting the features extraction concept combined with supervised machine learning algorithms to build a predictive model using an annotated data-set. The main strength point of tweet-level is the fast detection in regards to time consumption since the detection process is performed on the available information in tweet object only. However, given the fact that spammers are too dynamic in the spam contents, tweet-level detection methods have drawbacks and limitations, including the followings aspects: (i) the use of non-discriminative and ineffective features such as number of words in tweet; (ii) the need for an annotated data-set to build a classification model; (iii) and the use of supervised learning algorithms produces biased models toward the training set adopted.

In this paper, we introduce a design of an unsupervised method for filtering out spam tweets existing in large-scale collections of trending topics. Our method performs collaboration with other OSNs through searching and gathering information relevant to trending topics. Then, a content matching is performed between a desired tweet and retrieved information, like Facebook relevant posts, to decide later the class label of the considered tweet. In this work, we hypothesis that the volume and the content of spam on OSNs vary depending upon the privacy rules followed by OSNs. For instance, Facebook[2] social network adopts restricted rules more than Twitter in opening new accounts such as mobile verification, which impose difficulties to create huge spam campaigns.

The remainder of the paper is organized as follows. Section 2 gives an overview about Twitter-based spam detection methods. Section 3 presents the notations, problem formalization, and design of our collaborative method used in detecting spam tweets. Section 4 describes the data-set used in validating our approach. Section 5 presents the experimental results. Section 6 concludes the paper with providing future perspectives.

---

[1] https://dev.twitter.com/rest/public.
[2] https://www.facebook.com/policies.

2   Related Work

Most of the existing works for fighting spam on Twitter have focused on account and campaign (bot) detection levels with little efforts spent for spam tweet-level detection.

Tweet-Level. At this level, individual tweets are checked for the existence of spam content. Benevenuto [1] extracted a set of simple statistical features from the tweet object such as number of words, number of hashtags, and number of characters. Then, a binary classifier is built on a small annotated data-set. Martinez-Romo and Araujo [9] detected spam tweets in trending topics through employing language models to extract more features such as the probability distribution divergence between a given tweet and other tweets of a trending topic. The major problem at this level of detection is derived from the lack of sufficient information that can be extracted from tweet object itself. In addition, building language models using tweets of trending topics definitely fails when having huge spam attacks. Our work overcomes these shortcomings through exploiting topic relevant information from other OSNs.

Account-Level. Methods designed in [1,3,5,10,11] work firstly through building features vector by extracting hand-designed features such as number of followers, and node betweenness. Then, supervised machine learning algorithms are applied to build a classification model on an annotated data-set. Despite of high detection rate when exploiting such features, extracting them requires significant time to collect information from Twitter's servers through using REST APIs. Indeed, these APIs are constrained to a certain and predefined number of calls, making the extraction of most features not possible in regards to time point of view, especially when treating large-scale data-set.

Campaign-Level. Chu et al. [8] proposed a spam campaign detection method through clustering accounts according to available URLs in tweets. Then, they represented each cluster by a vector of features similar to account-level detection methods. In [12], a classification model was designed to capture differences among bot, human, and cyborg. Regrettably, this level of detection has similar account-level methods drawbacks, making such solutions not scalable for large collections of users or tweets.

3   Collaborative Model Design

Our approach focuses on finding a matched information on other OSNs for a given tweet related to a certain topic. As the obvious purpose of using topic modeling in OSNs is to group similar information, the probability of finding same information talking about same topic on different OSNs is relativity high. Conversely, the probability of finding same spam content posted under the same topic is relativity low because of its dependency on spammers' goals and the openness of OSNs themselves. Therefore, instead of extracting uninformative features (e.g. number of words in tweet) to learn model using machine learning algorithms, we rely on using statistical language model concept to detect spam tweets.

3.1 Notations and Definitions

Let $C_H = \{T_1, T_2, ...\}$ be a collection of tweets for a particular trending topic H, where $T_\bullet$ element represents the tweet object modeled as 2-tuple $T_\bullet = <Text, Actions>$. Also, we model the information retrieved about the topic, H, from defined social networks (e.g. Facebook, Instagram), $SN_\bullet$, as a finite set $S_H = \{SN_{Facbook}, SN_{Instagram}, ...\}$. Each $SN_\bullet$ is modeled as a finite set of posts $SN_\bullet = \{O_1, O_2, ...\}$ where the element $O_\bullet$ is defined by 2-tuple $O_\bullet = <Text, Actions>$. Each element inside the post O and tweet T tuple is defined as follows:

Text. As each post may consist of text, we represent the content of post as a finite set of textual words, $Text = \{w_1, w_2, ...\}$.

Actions. Users of social networks may perform actions on posts as a reaction toward the content of posts or tweets. We define actions as a finite set of 2-tuple, $Actions = \{<a_{name_1}, a_{val_1}>, <a_{name_2}, a_{val_2}>, ...\}$, where a_{name} represents the name of action (e.g. like, share, and comment on Facebook) depending upon the considered social network, and $a_{val} \in \mathbb{N}_{\geq 0}$ is the number of times that the corresponding action performed by social network users on the considered post or tweet.

3.2 Problem Formalization

Given a collection of tweets C_H associated with a trending topic, H, and posted by a set of distinct users U_H such that $U_H \leq |C_H|$, our main problem is to filter out spam tweets in the given collection C_H without involving information requiring REST API calls. More formally, we aim at designing a function f such that it predicts the class label of each tweet in the desired collection, defined as $f(T) : T \rightarrow \{spam, non\text{-}spam\}, T \in C_H$.

3.3 Tweet Likelihood, Post Prior, and Tweet Classification

Tweet Likelihood. We leverage statistical language models [13] to estimate the relevance degree of other OSNs' posts with a given tweet to make a decision later about the tweet. Language modeling method computes the probability $P(D|Q)$ of a document D being generated by a query Q to rank a set of documents. We transform the same concept to get out the most relevant post in other social networks for a given tweet. Thus, we treat tweets as queries and posts as documents, with computing the post O probability of being generated by a tweet T as:

$$P^{SN_i}(O|T) \stackrel{rank}{=} P^{SN_i}(O).P^{SN_i}(T|O) = P^{SN_i}(O). \prod_{w \in T.Text} P^{SN_i}(w|O) \quad (1)$$

$P^{SN_i}(O)$ is the post prior probability such that $O \in SN_i$. The post prior can be viewed as tweet-independent features (i.e. features *not* extracted from tweet object) representing the probability of being non-spam content in the social network SN_i. Estimating the other probability component $P^{SN_i}(T|O)$ can be performed using different models (Jelineck Mercer, Dirichlet) [13] to compute $P^{SN_i}(w|O)$ or (Kullback-Leibler divergence) [14] to calculate the degree of dissimilarity between the tweet and post language models. In this paper, we use the uni-gram language model for representing tweets and posts because of its outstanding performance in information retrieval field. Also, we adopt Kullback-Leibler divergence (KL) method because of its fast computation time compared to others. However, the classical version of KL method cannot be exploited directly in computing the $P^{SN_i}(T|O)$ probability since the zero value of KL means that the language models of tweet and post are completely similar. Moreover, the range of KL method is unbounded, meaning that the ∞ value appears when two language models are dissimilar. Hence, we customize the current version of KL method to inverse the semantic of KL values (i.e. $0 \implies$ dissimilar and $1 \implies$ similar) with bounding its values, where the probability component $P^{SN_i}(T|O)$ is defined as:

$$P^{SN_i}(T|O) = \frac{\log|T.Text| - \sum_{w \in T.Text} P(w|M_T) * min(|\log \frac{P(w|M_T)}{P(w|M_O)}|, \log|T.Text|)}{\log|T.Text|} \quad (2)$$

where $P(w|M_T)$ and $P(w|M_O)$ are the probability of word w being generated by tweet and post language models (M_T, M_O), respectively.

Post Prior. As the retrieved posts of social network, SN_i, may consist of spam content, we estimate the probability of being non-spam through leveraging the actions performed by users on the retrieved posts set (i.e. more actions $\implies$ low probability for being spam post). We assume that actions (e.g. like, comment, and share) are independent features, and thus the general formula for calculating post prior is computed as:

$$P^{SN_i}(O) = \prod_{A \in O.Actions} P(A) \quad (3)$$

where $P(A)$ is estimated using the maximum-likelihood of performing the action A on the post O, computed as $P(A) = \frac{Count(A,O)}{Count(A,SN_i)}$. $Count(A,O) = A.val$ means that the number of times that the action A performed on the post O. $Count(A, SN_i)$ represents the summation of action A over available posts in SN_i.

Tweet Classification. When doing inference for a given tweet over a set of posts in SN_i, we obtain a vector of probability values where each represents the degree of matching between a post and a given tweet. We exploit these values to make a decision about the class label of a given tweet. To do so, we define a thresholded decision function that labels tweets as non-spam in case of finding at least one post on any social network having probability above a fixed threshold.

Table 1. Statistics of Twitter and Facebook crawled data-sets.

Twitter		Facebook	
Property	Value	Property	Value
# of accounts	2,088,131 (4.9% spammers)	# of users	3,122
# of tweets	6,470,809 (11.8% spam)	# of posts	6,880
# of replied tweets	76,393	# of comments	2,398,611
# of re-tweeted tweets	3,129,237	# of reactions	64,083,457

Formally, we define the crisp decision function as follows:

$$F(T, S_H) = \begin{cases} non\text{-}spam & max\{\frac{P^{SN_i}(O|T)}{Sum(SN_i,T)}|SN_i \in S_H, O \in SN_i\} \geq \Delta \\ spam & otherwise \end{cases} \quad (4)$$

where the function $Sum(SN_i, T) = \sum_{O \in SN_i} P^{SN_i}(O|T)$ normalizes the probability of each post retrieved from a certain social network SN_i, making their summation equals to one. Δ is a threshold interpreted as the minimum probability (i.e. matching degree) required to classify the considered tweet T as non-spam.

4   Data-Set Description and Ground Truth

As various social networks available over web, in this paper, we experiment our method through performing collaboration with Facebook social network only. Hence, in this section, we describe the Twitter and Facebook data-sets that have been exploited in validating our method.

Twitter Data-Set. The data-sets used at tweet level detection [1,9] are not publicly available for research use. Also, Twitter's polices allow to publish only the IDs of accounts and tweets of Twitter data-sets. Indeed, in context of social spam problem, using ID is not a solution since Twitter might already have deleted the corresponding object (account or tweet) and thus no information is available to retrieve. Hence, we developed a crawler to collect tweets using real-time streaming method provided by Twitter. Then, we launched our crawler for five months, from 1/Jan/2016 to 31/May/2016, with storing the topics that were trending in the specified period. Afterward, we clustered the crawled tweets based on the available topics in the text of tweets, with discarding the tweets that don't have a trending topic. As thousands of topics available in our tweets collection, we selected the tweets of 100 trending topics randomly sampled to validate our approach. To build an annotated data-set consisting of spam and non-spam tweets, we leverage a widely followed annotation process in the social spam detection researches, named as "Twitter Suspended Spammers (TSS)" [9]. The process checks whether the user of each tweet was suspended by Twitter. In case of suspension, the user is considered as a spammer as well as the corresponding tweet is labeled as a spam; otherwise we assign non-spam and legitimate user for tweet and user, respectively. We performed this process in 1/Nov/2016 to gain large set of spam tweets, annotated around 763,555 as spam tweets and about 102,318 as spammers (spam accounts), as reported in Table 1.

Facebook Data-Set. For the selected 100 trending topics, we crawled the corresponding Facebook posts that contain those topics and posted during the period 1/Jan/2016 to 31/May/2016. It is important to mention that Facebook community has stopped recently post searching APIs in the latest version, v2.8, of Graph API[3] released on August 2016. Thus, we overcome this obstacle through developing a Facebook crawler that searches for a particular topic using a normal Facebook account and then parses the HTML tags of the retrieved posts. We automate this process through using open source Selenium web browser automation tool[4]. In total, as reported in Table 1, we crawled more than 6,880 Facebook posts generated by about 3,122 different users in less than one hour.

5   Results and Evaluations

5.1   Experimental Setup

Performance Metrics. As the ground truth class label about each tweet is available, we exploit accuracy, precision, recall, F-measure, average precision, average recall, and average F-measure, computed according to the confusion matrix of Weka tool [15], as commonly used metrics in classification problems. As our problem is two-class (binary) classification, we compute the precision, recall, and F-measure for the "spam" class, while the average metrics combines both classes based on the fraction of each class (e.g. 11.8% * "spam precision" + 88.2% * "non-spam precision").

Baselines. We define two baselines to compare our method with: (i) baseline "A" which represents the results when classifying all tweets as non-spam directly without doing any kind of classification; (ii) baseline "B" which reflects the results obtained when applying supervised machine learning algorithms on state of the art "tweet" features described in Table 2. As many learning algorithms provided by Weka tool, we exploit Naive Bayes, Random Forest, J48, and support vector machine (SVM) as well-known supervised learning methods to evaluate the performance of the mentioned state of the art features.

Parameter Setting. In computing the post prior probability, $P^{SN_i}(O)$, we adopt "Likes", "Shares", "Comments", "Wow", "Love", "Sad", "Haha", and "Angry" as actions. In our method, Δ is the main variable in classifying tweets and thus we study the impact of changing its value through performing experiments at different values of $\Delta \in [0.1, 1.0]$ with 0.1 increment step. For the Naive Bayes method, we set the "useKernelEstimator" and "useSupervisedDiscretization" options to false value as default values set by Weka. For Random Forest, we set the option max depth to 0 (unlimited), with studying the effect of changing

---

[3] https://developers.facebook.com/docs/graph-api/using-graph-api.
[4] http://docs.seleniumhq.org/.

number of trees $\in \{100, 500\}$. For $J48$ method, we set the minimum number of instances per leaf to 2, number of folds to 3, and confidence factor to 0.2. For the SVM method, we use the LibSVM [17] implementation integrated with Weka tool with setting the kernel function to Radial Basis and examining the impact of gamma $\in \{0.5, 1\}$, where the rest parameters are set to the default ones.

Experiment Procedure. For the baseline "B" experiments, we use the concept of cross validation along the 100 trending topics in our data-set, summarized in the following steps: (i) for each topic, we build a feature vector space using the state of the art features described in Table 2; (ii) then, a feature vector space of a selected topic (training set) only is used to build a predictive model using a chosen learning algorithm; (iii) the feature vector spaces of rest topics (i.e. 99 topics for testing) are validated on the built classification model in the previous step; (iv) the validation results in terms of true positive, true negative, false positive, false negative are extracted and stored; (v) the steps from ii to iv are repeated on each topic in the collection; (vi) at last, using the validation results obtained for each single topic, we calculate the performance metrics mentioned above. It is important to mention that the experiment procedure for the baseline "B" simulates exactly the real scenarios in detecting spam tweets.

In experimenting our method, for each topic we perform the following steps: (i) for a certain value of classification threshold Δ, the designed classification model in Sect. 3 is applied on the considered topic tweets using the correspond-

Table 2. Description of the state of the art "tweet" features used in building supervised classification models [1,9,16].

Feature name	Description
Number of hashtags	Counts the number of hashtags available in the tweet text
Number of spam words	Counts the number of words that listed as spam words in the tweet text
Hashtags ratio	Ratio of number of hashtags with respect to the number of words in the tweet
URLs ratio	Ratio of number of URLs posted in the tweet with respect to the number of tweet words
Number of words	Counts the number of words in the tweet
Number of numeric characters	Counts the number of numeric characters in the tweet text
Number of URLs	Counts the number of URLs posted in the tweet
Number of mentions	Counts the number of accounts (users) mentions in the tweet
Replied tweet	Checks whether the tweet is a replied tweet or not
Tweet and URL content similarity	Measures the similarity between the tweet text and the text of URL posted in Tweet

ing topic Facebook posts to predict the class label of tweets; (ii) then, the results in terms of true positive, true negative, false positive, false negative are extracted and stored for final results computations; (iii) the previous two steps are performed on each topic in the data-set; (iv) in the last step, the results of whole topics are summed together to compute the performance results using the mentioned metrics.

5.2   Experimental Results

According to the results of the baselines reported in Table 3, the supervised classification models have strong failure in filtering out the spam tweets existing in the 100 trending topics. This failure can be easily captured from the low spam recall values (4th column) where the highest value is obtained by *NaiveBayes* learning algorithm. The 10.5% of spam recall obtained by *NaiveBayes* means that less than 80,000 of spam tweets can be detected from around 736,500 spam tweets. The low spam precision values also give an indication that a significant number of "non-spam" tweets has been classified into "spam" ones. Subsequently, as spam F-measure is dependent on recall and precision metrics, the values of spam F-measure are definitely low. The accuracy values of baseline "B" are close to the accuracy value of baseline "A". However, given the low values of spam precision and spam recall, the accuracy metric in this case is not an indicative and useful metric to judge on the supervised learning as winner approach. More precisely, the supervised learning approach does not add significant contribution in increasing the quality of the 100 trending topics tweets. The key idea of using different machine learning algorithms with playing in their parameters is

Table 3. Performance results of baseline A and baseline B in terms of different metrics.

Learning algorithm	Accuracy	Precision	Recall	F-measure	Avg. precision	Avg. recall	Avg. F-measure
Baseline (A): All tweets labeled as non-spam							
————————	88.2%	0.0%	0.0%	0.0.%	88.2%	88.2%	88.2%
Baseline (B): Supervised machine learning approach							
Naive Bayes	81.2%	13.7%	10.5%	11.9%	79.0%	81.2%	80.1%
Random Forest (#Trees = 100)	86.4%	13.2%	2.8%	4.6%	79.0%	86.4%	80.1%
Random Forest (#Trees = 500)	86.5%	12.6%	2.6%	4.7%	79.4%	86.5%	82.8%
J48 (Confidence Factor = 0.2)	86.4%	13.8%	2.9%	4.9%	79.6%	86.4%	82.5%
SVM (Gamma = 0.5)	87.2%	15.7%	0.2%	0.4%	78.3%	87.2%	82.5%
SVM (Gamma = 1.0)	87.0%	15.9%	0.1%	0.3%	77.9%	87.0%	82.2%

Table 4. Our collaborative method performance results in terms of different metrics, showing the impact of post prior probability component when performing collaboration with Facebook social network.

Model (Δ)	Accuracy	Precision	Recall	F-measure	Avg. precision	Avg. recall	Avg. F-measure
Uniform post prior probability							
$\Delta = 0.1$	49.8%	10.8%	48.3%	17.7%	79.7%	49.8%	61.3%
$\Delta = 0.2$	32.3%	10.8%	69.4%	18.7%	79.1%	32.3%	45.9%
$\Delta = 0.3$	26.2%	10.8%	77.0%	18.9%	78.6%	26.2%	39.3%
$\Delta = 0.4$	22.8%	10.9%	82.3%	19.2%	78.5%	22.8%	35.3%
$\Delta = 0.5$	21.0%	11.0%	85.3%	19.4%	78.7%	21.0%	33.2%
$\Delta = 0.6$	19.4%	11.0%	87.9%	19.6%	78.8%	19.4%	31.2%
$\Delta = 0.7$	18.7%	11.1%	89.3%	19.7%	79.1%	18.7%	30.3%
$\Delta = 0.8$	17.5%	11.1%	90.9%	19.8%	79.3%	17.5%	28.7%
$\Delta = 0.9$	17.2%	11.1%	91.5%	19.8%	79.2%	17.2%	28.3%
$\Delta = 1.0$	17.2%	11.1%	91.6%	19.8%	79.4%	17.2%	28.3%
Non-Uniform post prior probability							
$\Delta = 0.1$	80.7%	17.0%	18.8%	17.8%	81.4%	80.7%	81.0%
$\Delta = 0.2$	80.6%	17.2%	19.3%	18.2%	81.5%	80.6%	81.0%
$\Delta = 0.3$	79.3%	15.8%	19.6%	17.5%	81.2%	79.3%	80.2%
$\Delta = 0.4$	77.8%	15.0%	21.1%	17.5%	81.1%	77.8%	79.4%
$\Delta = 0.5$	73.4%	13.5%	24.9%	17.4%	80.8%	73.4%	77.1%
$\Delta = 0.6$	64.0%	12.3%	36.4%	18.5%	80.7%	64.0%	71.4%
$\Delta = 0.7$	57.7%	11.9%	43.4%	18.7%	80.6%	57.7%	67.2%
$\Delta = 0.8$	51.9%	11.5%	49.0%	18.6%	80.3%	51.9%	63.0%
$\Delta = 0.9$	42.2%	11.0%	59.0%	18.6%	79.8%	42.2%	55.2%
$\Delta = 1.0$	34.79%	10.7%	66.0%	18.5%	79.1%	34.79%	48.3%

to highlight the badness of the state of the art tweet features. Overall, the results obtained by the learning models draw various conclusions: (i) the state of the art features are not discriminative among non-spam and spam tweets, ensuring the dynamicity of spam content; (ii) spammers tend to publish tweets almost similar to non-spam ones; (iii) adopting a supervised approach to perform training on an annotated data-set of trending topics and applying the classification model on future or not annotated trending topics is *not* the solution at all.

Taking a look at our method performance results in Table 4, the behavior is completely different in recalling (classifying) "spam" tweets, especially when the value of Δ gets higher. The recall results are completely consistent with the Eq. 4 designed for classifying tweets. For high values of Δ, the major difficulty is in finding at one high matched Facebook post to classify the considered tweet as "non-spam". Thus, this explains the dramatic degradation in the accuracy when increasing the value of Δ. Although of high recall values, the spam precision values of our method are almost similar to the supervised learning approach ones.

Uniform vs. Non-uniform Post Prior. The role of post prior probability component is obvious in detecting spam tweets. Working on the assumption that each Facebook post has same probability (uniform) for being non-spam increases the spam recall values when the value of Δ gets higher, leading to detect most spam tweets. On contrary, a significant number of "non-spam" tweets has been predicted as "spam" ones. We interpret this behavior because of the small value of post prior probability when working on the uniform probability assumption. Indeed, this problem is reduced when considering the actions performed on Facebook post to compute the post prior probability component. Thus, the spam recall has increased without high degradation in the accuracy values. Although of low values of spam precision, the high values of average precision mean that little tweets have been classified as "non-spam" where they are truly "spam".

High Quality vs. False Positive. In email spam filtering, the efforts are directed for the false positive problem that occurs when a truly "non-spam" email is classified as "spam". However, in the context of social spam, the false positive problem is less important because of the availability of large-scale data collections, meaning that classifying "non-spam" tweet as "spam" is not a serious problem to worry about. Thus, the attention is turned in social networks context to increase the quality of data where a wide range of Twitter based applications (e.g. tweet summarization) has high priority to work on noise free collections. Also, the computational time aspect is significant when targeting large-scale collections. Hence, our method is completely suitable to process large-scale collections with providing high quality collections. For instance, the time required to process our Twitter data-set is no more than few hours, distributed between crawling data from Facebook and applying our model. At last, as various experiments are given for different Δ values where no optimal value can satisfy all performance metrics, the selection is mainly dependent on the desired requirements of the final collection. For instance, high Δ value is recommended to have too high quality collection with having high probability to lose not noisy information.

6   Conclusion and Future Directions

In this paper, we study the impact of performing collaboration with social networks to filter out spam tweets in large-scale collections of trending topics. We propose an unsupervised method grounding on the language model concept to find out similar information in other social networks considered in the collaboration. Our method outperforms conventional detection spam methods in regards to time consumption, requiring few hours to process around 6 millions tweets posted in 100 trending topics. With this novel idea in battle of fighting spam, we plan as a future work to study the effect of performing collaboration with additional social networks such as Instagram. Also, we intend to improve the classification performance through extracting more features from users' comments such as sentiment features. Moreover, we plan to study the behavior of using different language models with their estimations.

References

1. Benevenuto, F., Magno, G., Rodrigues, T., Almeida, V.: Detecting spammers on Twitter. In: Collaboration, Electronic messaging, Anti-abuse and Spam Conference (CEAS), p. 12 (2010)
2. Agarwal, N., Yiliyasi, Y.: Information quality challenges in social media. In: International Conference on Information Quality (ICIQ) (2010)
3. Wang, A.H.: Don't follow me: spam detection in Twitter. In: Proceedings of the 2010 International Conference on Security and Cryptography (SECRYPT), pp. 1–10, July 2010
4. Yardi, S., Romero, D., Schoenebeck, G., danah boyd: Detecting spam in a Twitter network. First Monday **15**(1) (2009)
5. Stringhini, G., Kruegel, C., Vigna, G.: Detecting spammers on social networks. In: Proceedings of the 26th Annual Computer Security Applications Conference (ACSAC 2010), pp. 1–9. ACM, New York (2010)
6. Yang, C., Harkreader, R.C., Gu, G.: Die free or live hard? Empirical evaluation and new design for fighting evolving Twitter spammers. In: Sommer, R., Balzarotti, D., Maier, G. (eds.) RAID 2011. LNCS, vol. 6961, pp. 318–337. Springer, Heidelberg (2011). doi:10.1007/978-3-642-23644-0_17
7. Amleshwaram, A.A., Reddy, N., Yadav, S., Guofei, G., Yang, C.: Cats: characterizing automation of Twitter spammers. In: 2013 Fifth International Conference on Communication Systems and Networks (COMSNETS), pp. 1–10. IEEE (2013)
8. Chu, Z., Widjaja, I., Wang, H.: Detecting social spam campaigns on Twitter. In: Bao, F., Samarati, P., Zhou, J. (eds.) ACNS 2012. LNCS, vol. 7341, pp. 455–472. Springer, Heidelberg (2012). doi:10.1007/978-3-642-31284-7_27
9. Martinez-Romo, J., Araujo, L.: Detecting malicious tweets in trending topics using a statistical analysis of language. Expert Syst. Appl. **40**(8), 2992–3000 (2013)
10. McCord, M., Chuah, M.: Spam detection on Twitter using traditional classifiers. In: Calero, J.M.A., Yang, L.T., Mármol, F.G., García Villalba, L.J., Li, A.X., Wang, Y. (eds.) ATC 2011. LNCS, vol. 6906, pp. 175–186. Springer, Heidelberg (2011). doi:10.1007/978-3-642-23496-5_13
11. Cao, C., Caverlee, J.: Detecting spam URLs in social media via behavioral analysis. In: Hanbury, A., Kazai, G., Rauber, A., Fuhr, N. (eds.) ECIR 2015. LNCS, vol. 9022, pp. 703–714. Springer, Cham (2015). doi:10.1007/978-3-319-16354-3_77
12. Chu, Z., Gianvecchio, S., Wang, H., Jajodia, S.: Detecting automation of Twitter accounts: are you a human, bot, or cyborg? IEEE Trans. Dependable Secure Comput. **9**(6), 811–824 (2012)
13. Ponte, J.M., Croft, W.B.: A language modeling approach to information retrieval. In: Proceedings of the 21st Annual International ACM SIGIR Conference on Research and Development in Information Retrieval, pp. 275–281. ACM (1998)
14. Kullback, S.: The Kullback-Leibler distance. Am. Stat. **41**(4), 340–341 (1987)
15. Hall, M., Frank, E., Holmes, G., Pfahringer, B., Reutemann, P., Witten, I.H.: The Weka data mining software: an update. SIGKDD Explor. Newsl. **11**(1), 10–18 (2009)

16. McCord, M., Chuah, M.: Spam detection on Twitter using traditional classifiers. In: Calero, J.M.A., Yang, L.T., Mármol, F.G., García Villalba, L.J., Li, A.X., Wang, Y. (eds.) ATC 2011. LNCS, vol. 6906, pp. 175–186. Springer, Heidelberg (2011). doi:10.1007/978-3-642-23496-5_13
17. Chang, C.-C., Lin, C.-J.: LIBSVM: a library for support vector machines. ACM Trans. Intell. Syst. Technol. **2**, 27:1–27:27 (2011). http://www.csie.ntu.edu.tw/cjlin/libsvm

Agronomy and Artificial Intelligence

Bayesian Model Averaging for Streamflow Prediction of Intermittent Rivers

Paul J. Darwen[(✉)]

James Cook University Brisbane, 349 Queen Street, Brisbane, Australia
paul.darwen@jcub.edu.au

Abstract. Predicting future river flow is a difficult problem. Firstly, models are (by definition) crudely simplified versions of reality. Secondly, historical streamflow data is limited and noisy. Bayesian model averaging is theoretically a good way to cope with these difficulties, but it has not been widely used on this and similar problems. This paper uses real-world data to illustrate why. Bayesian model averaging can give a better prediction, but only if the amount of data is small — if the data is consistent with a wide range of different models (instead of unambiguously consistent with only a narrow range of near-identical models), then the weighted votes of those diverse models will give a better prediction than the single best model. In contrast, with plenty of data, only a narrow range of near-identical models will fit that data, and they all vote the same way, so there is no improvement in the prediction. But even when the data supports a diverse range of models, the improvement is far from large, but it is the *direction* of the improvement that can predict more accurately. Working around these caveats lets us better predict floods and similar problems, using limited or noisy data.

1 Introduction

Least-squares regression finds the model with the highest probability of being correct, given the data. In contrast, Bayesian model averaging [4] is an ensemble method: the predictions of all possible models (weighted by each model's probability of being correct, given the data) gives a prediction at least as good as the single best-fit model [9, p. 175]. The weighted vote of a committee of models that includes the best-fit model plus many others, tends to make better predictions than the best-fit model by itself.

So why doesn't everyone use Bayesian model averaging (apart from the extra computational effort)? This paper will answer that question, by characterizing the circumstances where it can give better predictions than the best-fit model.

Bayesian model averaging has typically used only a tiny number of hand-tuned models [7], as few as nine models [2] or eight [10]. In contrast, this study enumerates up to two million models from each distribution, more than previous studies of water models [6,11,12].

As a sample problem to explore Bayesian model averaging, this paper will attempt to predict the flow of the Warrego River (an intermittent river in the

© Springer International Publishing AG 2017
S. Benferhat et al. (Eds.): IEA/AIE 2017, Part II, LNAI 10351, pp. 227–236, 2017.
DOI: 10.1007/978-3-319-60045-1_25

Australian outback) for four weeks into the future, further out than conventional weather forecasting. The motivation is to help cattle farmers: if the next four weeks will bring a good flow of water, then farmers should keep their calves (and perhaps buy more) to eat the green grass that will grow after the flow.

2   Experimental Set-Up

Given some observed data y, how to tune a model's parameters? Bayes' rule gives the probability that a model with parameters θ is correct [3, p. 8]:

$$P(\theta|y) \propto P(y|\theta)P(\theta) \tag{1}$$

$P(\theta)$ is called the "prior probability", an estimate that a particular set of model parameters θ is correct, prior to seeing any data. This paper assumes a *flat* prior probability: before seeing the data y, any choice of model parameters is presumed to have an equal chance of being correct.

The prior is updated by $P(y|\theta)$ the "likelihood function", the probability of getting the observed data y if the model with parameters θ really was correct.

The likelihood function updates the prior probability to the "posterior probability" $P(\theta|y)$ which is a more accurate estimate of the probability that this choice of model parameters θ is correct, given the data.

For a countable number of observed data points y_i, the probability gets updated by each data point, multiplying the likelihood function for each one:

$$P(\theta|y_1, y_2, ...y_n) \propto P(y_1|\theta)P(y_2|\theta)...P(y_n|\theta)P(\theta) \tag{2}$$

For logistic regression with a linear logit function, the posterior landscape of model parameters has only a single smooth peak, so it's easy to hill-climb up that single peak and find the model with the highest probability of being correct.

This paper uses a complicated model with 11 parameters (Sect. 2.2 below), so unlike least-squares or logistic regression, the landscape of posterior probability over the space of model parameters can have multiple peaks, as in Fig. 4 below. Having a multi-modal landscape of posterior probabilities is what allows Bayesian model averaging to perform better than the single best-fit model.

2.1   Two Approximations to Bayesian Model Averaging

The predictions of all possible models, weighted by each model's probability of being correct, gives a prediction that is at least as good as the single best-fit model [9, p. 175]. This approach is called Bayesian model averaging [4].

For data y and the space of possible parameters θ for a model, the weighted prediction $\tilde{y}$ is given by [3, p. 8]:

$$P(\tilde{y}|y) = \int_\theta P(\tilde{y}|\theta)P(\theta|y)d\theta \tag{3}$$

Equation 3 has two practical difficulties: it requires *integrating* over *all* possible models with non-zero probability of being correct. Here is a brief description of how this paper will approximate Eq. 3 to get around those two problems.

Firstly, instead of integrating where the model is a function, here the model is piece of software that's not easily written as a function. So the continuous integration is approximated with a grid over the model parameters. A more fine-grained grid would be more accurate (as we found that the probability landscape resembles a craggy range of mountainous spikes), but at the cost of more computation time, so there is a trade-off. So the integral in Eq. 3 becomes a large sum.

Secondly, the theorem depends on finding *all* possible models with non-zero probability of being correct. In practice, that's an infeasibly big number of models, and most of them are a terrible fit to the data. This paper merely finds a large number of models with the highest posterior probabilities. To keep run times reasonable, this was limited to the best 150,000 models. Actually finding the best 150,000 models usually required evaluating another couple of million lesser models. This is like taking the mountainous part of a mountain range, but ignoring the wide plains that go all the way down to sea level.

2.2 A Likelihood Function to Cover a Buried Pipe

Figure 1 shows that the Warrego River (like many rivers) has a log-log linear relationship between x = the flow for the previous 7 days, and y = the flow for the future 28 days, with $R^2 = 0.5081$. That's all the data from 1967 to 2017.

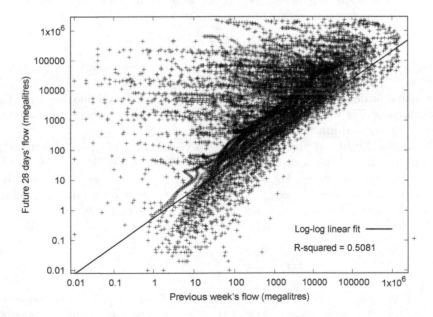

Fig. 1. For the Warrego River's flow near Wyandra (800 km west of Brisbane), this shows a rough linear relationship (in log-log space) between x = last week's flow and y = next month's flow (both in megalitres), with $R^2 = 0.5081$.

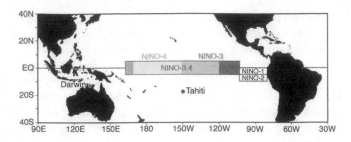

Fig. 2. Nino3 and Nino4 say how hotter or colder than usual are the sea surface temperatures averaged over two vast regions of the tropical Pacific Ocean.

Like many rivers in Australia, the Warrego is intermittent: for months at a time, it has flow so close to zero that it's below the threshold of the measuring equipment. The log of zero would cause an error. This paper kludges it by choosing a number less than 0.001 the minimum detectable flow (namely, the log of 0.0007 GL) and replacing all zero-flow days with that slightly larger value.

Eastern Australia's weather is also influenced by sea surface temperatures in the Pacific Ocean [8]. Nino3 and Nino4 measure how much hotter or colder than usual is the average sea surface temperature over two different regions[1] of the Pacific Ocean, as shown in the Fig. 2 map. This sea temperature data starts in November 1981, when they launched the satellite to measure it.

Putting those together, Eq. 4 predicts μ the log of the streamflow for the next four weeks, taking as inputs $s(t)$ the log of the previous week's streamflow, and the two sea surface temperature anomalies Nino3 $n_3(t)$ and Nino4 $n_4(t)$.

$$\mu(t+4) = a_0 + a_1 s(t) + a_2 n_3(t) + a_3 n_4(t) \tag{4}$$

We need to make the linear Eq. 4 appear at the highest point of a likelihood function $P(y|\theta)$ for Eq. 1, so that it's high along the line and tails off on both sides, like a buried pipe. We want the tails to stretch more on one side than the other, because Fig. 1 is smeared to the left. Figure 3 gives a conceptual view of what the likelihood function should look like.

A suitable likelihood function would be a Gumbel distribution with mode μ given by Eq. 4, and the scale β to adjust the width of the distribution on the sides of the buried pipe in Fig. 3. The Gumbel is one of many extreme value distributions that suit our needs [5, p. 8], and the Gumbel on log data resembles the power-normal distribution, which is also used for streamflow [14].

The Gumbel distribution's probability distribution function $f(x)$ is [5]:

$$f(x) = \frac{1}{\beta} e^{\left(-\frac{x-\mu}{\beta} - e^{\left(-\frac{x-\mu}{\beta}\right)}\right)} \tag{5}$$

---

[1] This paper uses weekly data which is available from November 1981 onwards, from http://ioc-goos-oopc.org/state_of_the_ocean/sur/pac. For a quick introduction to the Nino3 and Nino4 sea surface temperature numbers, please see https://climatedataguide.ucar.edu/climate-data/.

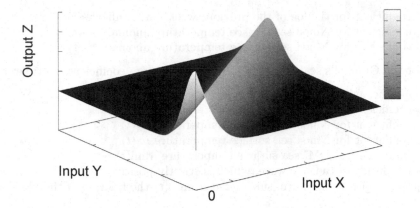

Fig. 3. To capture the log-log line in Fig. 1, this "buried pipe" gives an idea of how likelihoods are calculated. The model predicts streamflow with a truncated Gumbel distribution with mode μ and scale parameter β.

As the flow cannot be zero, we truncate the Gumbel distribution, so that it inflates the remaining non-truncated part. This makes the buried pipe gain a trumpet shape at the bottom end, as in Fig. 3.

For the scale parameter β of the Gumbel distribution in our likelihood function, we follow Eq. 4 and have coefficients for an initial bias, the previous week's flow, and for the Nino3 and Nino4 sea surface temperature anomalies. We also use three more coefficients, one for the Indian Ocean surface temperature, and two more for a seasonal component.

A sea surface temperature index for the Indian Ocean is the Dipole Mode Index (DMI), which measures the east-west temperature gradient across the tropical Indian Ocean[2].

Also, the variance of rainfall in eastern Australia has a strong seasonal component: summer brings either scorching drought or flooding rains, but winters are more boring. For our Gumbel's scale parameter β we add a sine wave component to capture any seasonal changes, with one coefficient for the sine wave's amplitude, and another for the sine wave's offset from the calendar year.

Using those inputs, Eq. 6 is the scale β of a Gumbel distribution:

$$\beta(t+4) = a_4 + a_5 s(t) + a_6 n_3(t) + a_7 n_4(t) + a_8\, \mathrm{dmi}(t) + a_9 \sin(p(t) - a_{10}) \quad (6)$$

So for the buried pipe of our likelihood function, there are eleven coefficients that we must tune to fit the data, a_0 through to a_{10}.

Four of those eleven coefficients are in Eq. 4 for the mode μ of the Gumbel distribution:

– a_0 initial bias or y-intercept

---

[2] See http://ioc-goos-oopc.org/state_of_the_ocean/sur/ind for weekly data on the Indian Ocean sea surface temperature indices, including the DMI.

- a_1 coefficient for the log of the previous week's streamflow $s(t)$
- a_2 coefficient for Nino3 sea surface temperature anomaly $n_3(t)$
- a_3 coefficient for Nino4 sea surface temperature anomaly $n_4(t)$

For the Gumbel's scale β in Eq. 6, there are 7 more coefficients to tune:

- a_4 another initial bias or y-intercept
- a_5 coefficient for the previous week's streamflow $s(t)$
- a_6 coefficient for Nino3 sea surface temperature $n_3(t)$
- a_7 coefficient for Nino4 sea surface temperature $n_4(t)$
- a_8 coefficient for DMI sea surface temperature dmi(t)
- a_9 amplitude of the sine wave, which is strictly positive
- a_{10} offset of the sine wave, subtracted from $p(t)$ the fraction of the year

3   Results

The traditional approach is to find the single best-fit model, i.e., the model coefficients with the maximum probability of being correct, given the data.

In contrast, Bayesian model averaging needs to evaluate all models (to approximate "all", this paper takes merely the best 150,000 models on a discretized grid) and find the weighted average of all their predictions.

Table 1 has the results of predicting the flow of the Warrego River four weeks into the future. At each date (always a Sunday), the data goes from Sunday 15 November 1981 up to the date indicated — this is because 1981 was when those sea surface temperatures were measured by satellite.

So later dates have more data than early dates. We explore dates in the eighties, because there is so little data that a range of models will fit it.

The aim is to predict the probability that the river flow for the following four weeks will exceed 1 GL.

The last column in Table 1 compares the actual flow with the 1 GL prediction: if the Bayesian weighted average gives an exceedance probability that is at least 1% different from the exceedance probability of the best-fit model, and the Bayesian probability's difference is in the correct direction, then the last column has a "yes". The difference of 1% is chosen arbitrarily as the boundary between a trivial and a substantial difference.

For example, the first line in Table 1 has a start date of the sixth of January 1985, or 1985-01-06. The single best-fit model predicts a 47.16% probability of future flow exceeding a gigalitre, and the Bayesian weighted average gives a similar 47.28%, different by only 0.12%. So for 1985-01-06 the last column is empty, because there is only a tiny difference between them.

In contrast, on the third-last line (1989-02-05, the fifth of February 1989), the single best-fit model gives an exceedance probability of 26.35% but the Bayesian weighted average gives an exceedance probability that's more than 4% bigger at 30.89%. The future four weeks gave a flow of 1.925 GL, so yes it really was bigger than 1 GL, in the direction the Bayesian was leaning towards.

So on 1989-02-05, the Bayesian approach predicted an exceedance probability that was both:

Table 1. For the predicted probability of streamflow exceeding 1 GL in the future 4 weeks, this compares the single best-fit model with the weighted average prediction of the best 150,000 models. If the exceedance probability is different by more than 1 % (in bold face) then the Bayesian result is always different in the right direction.

Predicted probability of future flow exceeding 1 GL						
Using data up to this Sunday	Single best fit model	Weighted average	Difference in percent	Actual future flow	Future > 1 GL?	Bayes > 1% in right direction?
1985-01-06	47.16%	47.28%	+0.12%	0.012		
1986-01-05	14.31%	14.78%	+0.47%	17.247		
1987-02-01	100.00%	100.00%	0.00%	69.138		
1988-01-03	29.85%	29.65%	−0.20%	0.000		
1988-02-07	50.49%	49.95%	−0.54%	1.262		
1988-03-06	29.69%	29.69%	0.00%	1.688		
1988-04-03	45.82%	44.73%	**−1.09%**	0.108	Smaller	Yes
1988-11-06	19.46%	18.06%	**−1.40%**	0.000	Smaller	Yes
1989-01-01	42.85%	51.62%	**+8.77%**	9.426	Bigger	Yes
1989-02-05	26.32%	30.89%	**+4.57%**	1.925	Bigger	Yes
1989-07-02	15.63%	13.49%	**−2.14%**	0.810	Smaller	Yes
1989-09-03	9.54%	9.98%	+0.44%	0.000		

- More than 1% *different* from the best-fit probability, and also;
- More *accurate*: if the flow really was more than 1 GL, the probability is more, and if the flow really was less than 1 GL, the probability is less.

As it was both of these criteria, the last column is "yes".

Table 1 shows that it works as advertised: whenever the difference in the predicted exceedance probability is more than 1%, then the Bayesian prediction is different in the direction of the correct outcome.

The problem is that the difference is at best small. It's the *direction* of the difference that gives an accurate prediction. This agrees with similar work on different data [1], which also found that the Bayesian approach gives only a small change, but in the right direction.

3.1 What Causes Bayesian to Do Better? Diverse Models that Fit

The lesson from this article is that the Bayesian approach out-performs the single best-fit model only when the historical data has some ambiguity in what models are a good fit to the data.

As an example, take another look at 1989-02-05 (the fifth of February 1989), the third-last line in Table 1. The Bayesian approach differs from the single best-fit model by more than 1% For the 11-parameter distribution of models, Fig. 4 shows a 2-dimensional cross-section of parameters a_9 and a_{10}. Each vertical line in Fig. 4 is the highest Bayesian posterior probability of all the models with those values of parameters a_9 and a_{10}.

The date 1989-02-05 gives a multi-modal landscape[3] in Fig. 4 and that date's Bayesian weighted average gives a prediction closer to reality than the single best-fit model, in Table 1 above. Checking each date, it turns out that is always true: a unimodal landscape means the two methods give only tiny differences in their prediction, but a multi-modal landscape always gives a more substantial difference (more than 1%) that is closer to the actual future.

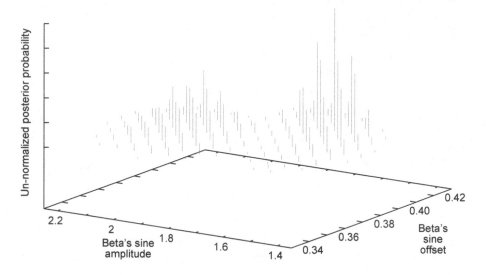

Fig. 4. Here, the vertical axis is the posterior probability (the probability of a model being correct, given the data). From the 11 model parameters, this is a 2-parameter cross-section of a distribution of over 150,000 models. For data up to 1989-02-05, there are two peaks in this posterior landscape: two groups of models both give a reasonably good fit to the data (the single best-fit model is at the highest point). The Bayesian weighted average (i.e., all these models voting, weighted according to the probability of being correct) predicts better than the single best-fit model only if the posterior distribution of models is skewed or multi-modal, like this.

So what makes Bayesian model averaging do better? If there are multiple peaks in the posterior landscape of models (or a single peak that is skewed) then the weighted average of that deformed landscape will be different from the single best-fit model. The best model (the mode) will differ from the weighted average.

On the other hand, if the posterior landscape is unimodal and not skewed, the weighted average will be virtually equal to the best-fit model (the mode), and Bayesian model averaging won't help.

---

[3] The vertical axis in Fig. 4 is the un-normalized posterior probability (assuming a flat prior probability), so while it's a linear scale, we cannot calculate the actual probability without doing the entire distribution of models, and instead we stopped at the best 150,000 models.

4   Discussion and Conclusion

The Warrego River's flow is such that (for the model form in Sect. 2.2) the historical data on some dates is consistent with more than one model, sometimes giving multi-modal landscapes like in Fig. 4, and that's what makes Bayesian model averaging work better.

Watching the posterior landscape at different dates, in which Fig. 4 is one date, reveals an interesting story:

- With a little data, there is only a single peak around a best-fit model, which predicts badly because there is so little data.
- With more data, another peak rises up around another model, so there are two peaks, representing two groups of models that give a reasonably good fit to what little data there is. Weighted voting from these two groups give a prediction that is quite different from that of the single best-fit model.
- With still more data, only a single peak dominates: the posterior probability of any other model declines and the posterior probability of the best-fit model gets higher (assuming it's a stationary distribution that generates the data).

The data used here starts in 1981 and goes to various dates from 1985 to 1989 because that's when there is the right amount of data to show this kind of ambiguity. After 1989, the posterior landscape looks like a single peak, and there is enough data to only match a narrow range of models, with no ambiguity.

4.1   Three Implications

Firstly, this implies that if the data is consistent with only one best-fit model, the Bayesian approach is not worth the extra effort. This may happen with a simple model and plenty of data to tune it.

Even if there are multiple peaks in the probability landscape, some optimization methods will not find them, and you'll see no benefit from Bayesian model averaging. Even if using an optimizer that looks for multiple peaks, many problems won't have them, and again disgruntled practitioners will see no benefit from Bayesian model averaging.

Secondly, the method sometimes lets us infer the presence or absence of ambiguity in our data, to say if there are more peaks that have been overlooked. The theorem [9, p. 175] says that Bayesian model averaging is *at least as good* as the single best-fit model: if instead it does substantially *worse*, then one of the theorem's assumptions have been violated. This is usually the assumption that all models (or a large proportion of them) have been counted.

Thirdly, the improvement from Bayesian model averaging is disappointingly small, at least as performed in this paper. In Table 1, the difference is only a few percent at most. That makes sense, because the difference is a measure of weight of the smaller peak (or peaks) compared to the largest, highest peak. To get a bigger difference needs more models. This paper stopped at the 150,000 models with the highest posterior probability, which is like stopping at the lower reaches of Mount Everest, so the difference is small.

It may be too much work to find millions of models, merely to check the *possibility* of a multi-modal posterior landscape. If you have plenty of data and a simple model form, it's unlikely you'll find a multi-modal posterior landscape. With less data and a complicated model, Bayesian model averaging might help.

One objection is that enumerating a large number of models is only possible in a low-dimensional space, i.e., if the model has a small number of free parameters. This is not a problem for many problems, such as financial risk. [13, p. 114].

In conclusion, Bayesian model averaging can only bring an improvement if the data is in such short supply that it's consistent with multiple models, otherwise it gives virtually identical results to the traditional single best-fit model.

Acknowledgments. The author thanks Matthew Fuller for technical support on the JCUB HPC cluster.

References

1. Darwen, P.J.: Two levels of Bayesian model averaging for optimal control of stochastic systems. Int. J. Syst. Sci. **44**(2), 201–213 (2013)
2. Duan, Q., Ajami, N.K., Gao, X., Sorooshian, S.: Multi-model ensemble hydrologic prediction using Bayesian model averaging. Adv. Water Resour. **30**, 1371–1386 (2007)
3. Gelman, A., Carlin, J.B., Stern, H.S., Rubin, D.B.: Bayesian Data Analysis. Texts in Statistical Science Series, 2nd edn. Chapman-Hall, Boca Raton (2004)
4. Hoeting, J.A., Madigan, D., Raftery, A.E., Volinsky, C.T.: Bayesian model averaging: a tutorial. Stat. Sci. **14**(4), 382–417 (1999)
5. Kotz, S., Nadarajah, S.: Extreme Value Distributions: Theory and Applications. Imperial College Press, London (2001)
6. Madadgar, S., Moradkhani, H.: A Bayesian framework for probabilistic seasonal drought forecasting. J. Hydrometeorol. **14**(6), 1685–1705 (2013)
7. Marshall, L., Nott, D., Sharma, A.: Towards dynamic catchment modelling: a Bayesian hierarchical mixtures of experts framework. Hydrol. Processes **21**(7), 847–861 (2007)
8. Mazzarella, A., Giuliacci, A., Liritzis, I.: On the 60-month cycle of multivariate ENSO index. Theor. Appl. Climatol. **100**, 23–27 (2010)
9. Mitchell, T.M.: Machine Learning. McGraw-Hill, New York (1997)
10. Najafi, M., Moradkhani, H., Jung, I.: Assessing the uncertainties of hydrologic model selection in climate change impact studies. Hydrol. Processes **25**(18), 2814–2826 (2011)
11. Parrish, M.A., Moradkhani, H., DeChant, C.M.: Toward reduction of model uncertainty: integration of Bayesian model averaging and data assimilation. Water Resour. Res. **48**(3), W03519 (2012). doi:10.1029/2011WR011116
12. Qu, B., Zhang, X., Pappenberger, F., Zhang, T., Fang, Y.: Multi-model grand ensemble hydrologic forecasting in the Fu river basin using Bayesian model averaging. Water **9**(2), 74 (2017)
13. Taleb, N.: Dynamic Hedging: Managing Vanilla and Exotic Options. Wiley Finance, New York (1997)
14. Wang, Q.J., Robertson, D.E., Chiew, F.H.S.: A Bayesian joint probability modeling approach for seasonal forecasting of streamflows at multiple sites. Water Resour. Res. **45**, 5407–5425 (2009)

A Mixed Integer Programming Reformulation of the Mixed Fruit-Vegetable Crop Allocation Problem

Sara Maqrot[1], Simon de Givry[1(✉)], Gauthier Quesnel[1],
and Marc Tchamitchian[2]

[1] UR 875 MIAT, Université de Toulouse, INRA, Castanet-Tolosan, France
{sara.maqrot,simon.de-givry,gauthier.quesnel}@inra.fr
[2] UR 767 Ecodéveloppement, INRA, Avignon, France
marc.tchamitchian@inra.fr

Abstract. Mixed fruit-vegetable cropping systems are a promising way
of ensuring environmentally sustainable agricultural production systems
in response to the challenge of being able to fulfill local market requirements. Indeed, they combine productions and they make a better use
of biodiversity. These agroforestry systems are based on a complex set
of interactions modifying the utilization of light, water and nutrients.
Thus, designing such a system must optimize the use of these resources:
by maximizing positive interactions (facilitation) and minimizing negative ones (competition). To attain these objectives, the system's design
has to include the spatial and temporal dimensions, taking into account
the evolution of above- and belowground interactions over a time horizon.
For that, we define the Mixed Fruit-Vegetable Crop Allocation Problem
(MFVCAP) using a discrete representation of the land and the interactions between vegetable crops and fruit trees. First, we give a direct
formulation as a binary quadratic program (BQP). Then we reformulate the problem using a Benders decomposition approach. The master problem has 0/1 binary variables and deals with tree positioning.
The subproblem deals with crop quantities. The BQP objective function
becomes linear in the continuous subproblem by exploiting the fact that
it depends only on the quantity of crops assigned to land units having
shade, root, or nothing. This problem decomposition allows us to reformulate the MFVCAP into a Mixed Integer linear Program (MIP). The
detailed spatial-temporal crop allocation plan is easy to obtain after solving the MIP. Experimental results show the efficiency of our approach
compared to a direct solving of the original BQP formulation.

Keywords: Agroecology · Spatial and temporal crop allocation problem · Binary Quadratic Programming · Mixed integer programming ·
Benders decomposition

1 Introduction

Agroforestry systems are one of the sustainable approaches that have received
considerable research attention over the past with a view to ensure high

© Springer International Publishing AG 2017
S. Benferhat et al. (Eds.): IEA/AIE 2017, Part II, LNAI 10351, pp. 237–250, 2017.
DOI: 10.1007/978-3-319-60045-1_26

productions, ecosystem services and environmental benefits [11]. These systems combine two principal land-use sciences: agriculture and forestry. However, to our knowledge, none of the several studies conducted on agroforestry systems has specifically examined the combination of vegetable crops with fruit trees using a modeling approach. Accordingly, the aim of the present study is to design mixed fruit-vegetable cropping systems, represented as a spatial-temporal crop allocation problem. Nonetheless, unlike existing studies in which allocation concerns only annual crops (see Sect. 2), our approach allocates both annual vegetable crops and perennial fruit trees on the same land while optimizing above- and belowground interactions resulting from this combination [4].

To assess the validity of different modeling choices to design mixed fruit-vegetable cropping systems, we built a first prototype using a Binary Quadratic Programming formulation of the Mixed Fruit-Vegetable Crop Allocation Problem [15]. This model allocates fruit trees and vegetable crops while optimizing interactions between them and minimizing the dispersion of vegetable crops. Such crops must be allocated so that to change their positions between two successive periods (*i.e.,* crop rotation). The aim of this preliminary work was to examine the ability of state-of-the-art exact solver IBM ILOG CPLEX in solving MFVCAP in order to support farmers in their crop allocation strategies. Depending on various modeling simplifications (without crop rotation nor crop dispersion), CPLEX was able to solve in about one hour CPU time a small piece of land divided into 10×10 land units, each one contains either a tree or a crop (among 6 possible ones including bare soil), over a time horizon divided into three periods of four seasons (except the first period with only one season starting in autumn).

We further improved the results by exploiting a Benders decomposition of the problem. The master problem deals with tree positioning and is a 0/1 linear program. The BQP objective function becomes linear in the continuous subproblem by exploiting the fact that it depends on crop quantities assigned to land units having shade, root or nothing. The final spatial-temporal crop allocation is obtained in post-processing. This decomposition allows us to reformulate the MFVCAP into a Mixed Integer linear Program.

Section 2 recaps related work. Section 3 gives an informal definition of MFV-CAP followed by its BQP formulation. Section 4 describes our main contribution by reformulating MFVCAP into MIP. Section 5 presents computational experiments for various scenarii and land sizes. We conclude in Sect. 6.

2   Related Work

Every year, farmers have to allocate their lands to different crops with respect to physical (water use) and chemical (fertilizers, pesticides, etc.) soil properties. To support farmers in these complex decisions, numerous studies [7] have been conducted on cropping plan and crop rotation decisions since they have a major impact on crop productions. Mathematical programming is widely used in this area [9]. For example, Linear Programming (LP) flow models for agricultural planning are proposed in [6,8,10], to find an optimal crop rotation that maximizes profits for a given selection of crops on a given piece of land. Compared to these LP flow models, [2] proposes a MIP flow model that minimizes the surface area needed to cover crop demands (aspect of sustainability) that vary over time rather than maximizing incomes. This problem was proven to be strongly NP-hard in [3] and was reformulated as a 0/1 LP compact formulation based on crop-sequence graphs, then as an extended formulation with a polynomial-time pricing problem and a Branch-and-Price-and-Cut algorithm with adapted branching rules and cutting planes. Many other papers propose a column generation approach [13] to model cropping plan and cropping rotations. In this sense, column generation with Dantzig-Wolfe decomposition was applied in [18] to maximize the land use subject to neighborhood and succession restrictions for crops of the same botanic family. Column generation was also used in [17], but for a more complex MIP: a crop rotation problem with lands divided into plots where the continuous variables represent the surface areas assigned to a given rotation.

Artificial intelligence methods were also employed for solving cropping plan and crop rotation problems. In this direction, [19] used the classical Constraint Satisfaction Problem (CSP) formalism to develop whole-farm crop rotation plans on a specific farm, whereas [1] proposed a Weighted Constraint Satisfaction Problem (WCSP) formalism to solve the spatial-temporal crop allocation planning problem for a medium-size virtual farm. Agent-based simulations are also used in this area. In this sense, [20] presents an application of a multi-agent architecture based on the BDI (Belief-Desire-Intention) paradigm and the belief theory to simulate cropping plan decision-making.

Indeed, to the best of our knowledge, none of the several studies conducted on cropping plan has specifically examined the allocation of annual crops (vegetable) with perennial ones (trees) using a modeling approach. Hence the originality of our model.

3   Mixed Fruit-Vegetable Crop Allocation Problem as BQP

MFVCAP is a spatial-temporal crop allocation problem in which crops are assigned to a piece of land over a time horizon. We discretize the land as a square of $l \times l$ cells; every cell represents a unit land area allocated to a fruit tree, a vegetable crop or a bare soil. In this study, we consider only one type of fruit tree, *apple tree*, which we plant at the beginning of the time horizon. For vegetable crops, we chose a selection that would allow for variable planting dates along the year and would need different cropping durations: *lettuce, tomato, onion, melon* and *carrot*. We added a *green manure* as it is a required practice for the restoration of soil fertility. Indeed, to represent these crops as time passes, we consider a time horizon divided into three periods of four seasons according to tree growth stages: period P1 corresponds to young trees (sprouts), P2 to intermediate growing trees not yet producing fruits (saplings), and P3 to

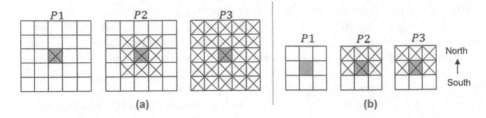

Fig. 1. Surface view of root (a) and shade (b) extensions. Blue cells host trees, and checked cells host roots/shade in periods P1, P2, and P3. (Color figure online)

mature trees. Each tree growing period represents a one-year rotation, except P1 which is represented by only one season for the fact that there are no vegetable crops at this period, only green manure to fertilize the soil. Therefore, we have nine time intervals, and thus nine grids of $l \times l$ land units.

We consider classical interactions observed generally in agroforestry systems, due to root extension dynamics [22,23] as belowground interactions, and microclimate modifications and crop sensitivity to shade (based on solar radiation interception simulation of an apple tree) as above interactions. We model the evolution of the tree root system in three periods as shown in Fig. 1. The shade of a tree takes place only in the spring and summer seasons and we model it as a fixed area orientated to the North of the tree (see Fig. 1).

Moreover, we define operation rules related to the organization of crops in the field: a minimal space between trees allowing them a non-conflict growth and a better light distribution (see Fig. 2), and a minimum (and maximum) number of land units to be allocated to each crop, in order to diversify the food at a given season (see Fig. 3).

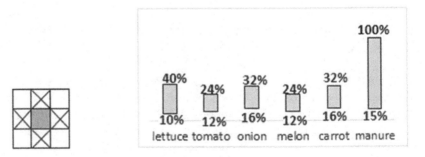

Fig. 2. Minimum space between trees. The blue cell hosts a tree, and checked cells are forbidden for other trees. (Color figure online)

Fig. 3. Minimum and maximum crop quantities as a percentage of the total grid area.

We consider the following binary variables in order to formulate the MFV-CAP as a Binary Quadratic Program (BQP):

- $crop_{x,y}^{t,c} = 1$ iff land unit of coordinates x, y has crop c at time t,
- $tree_{x,y} = 1$ iff land unit of coordinates x, y has a tree,
- $shade_{x,y} = 1$ iff land unit of coordinates x, y has shade,
- $root_{x,y}^p = 1$ iff land unit x, y has roots at period p.

Let $L = \{1, ..., l\}$ be a set of horizontal/vertical land unit positions of a square piece of land discretized as a $l \times l$ grid with top-left (i.e., North-West) corner having coordinates $(x = 1, y = 1)$, ζ a set of crops, T a set of time steps (corresponding to seasons, starting in autumn), and P a set of periods of tree growth stages, with T_p the set of time steps at each period $p \in P$. In our experiments, we vary l and use a fixed ζ, $\zeta = \{onion, melon, lettuce, carrot, tomato, green\ manure, bare\ soil\}$, $T = \{1, ..., 9\}$, $P = \{1, 2, 3\}$, $T_1 = \{1\} \sim \{autumn\}$, $T_2 = \{2, 3, 4, 5\}$, $T_3 = \{6, 7, 8, 9\} \sim \{winter, spring, summer, autumn\}$.

Concerning the objective function, we minimize the following quadratic function (minimization instead of maximization as in [15] and without crop dispersion):

$$\min \sum_{p \in P, t \in T_p, c \in \zeta, x \in L, y \in L} [A^{t,c} \times shade_{x,y} + B^{t,c} \times root_{x,y}^p + C^{t,c}] \times crop_{x,y}^{t,c} \quad (1)$$

with coefficients $A^{t,c}$ related to the degree of crop sensitivity to shade at a particular season (without shade at the first period, i.e., $A^{1,c} = 0$), $B^{t,c}$ related to interactions generated by root systems of trees and vegetable crops at a particular season (competition or sharing for water), and $C^{t,c}$ related to the crop selection whatever presence or absence of shade and tree roots at a given land unit. Specific values of these coefficients have been previously defined by agronomists in [15,21].

To complete the mathematical model, we define the following linear constraints:

A crop or a tree in each land unit

$$tree_{x,y} + \sum_{c \in C} crop_{x,y}^{t,c} = 1 \ (\forall t \in T, \forall x, y \in L^2) \quad (2)$$

Minimal space between trees (see Fig. 2)

$$tree_{x,y} + tree_{x+1,y} \leq 1 \ (\forall x \in L - \{l\}, \forall y \in L) \quad (3)$$

$$tree_{x,y} + tree_{x,y+1} \leq 1 \ (\forall x \in L, \forall y \in L - \{l\}) \quad (4)$$

No trees on East and West borders

$$tree_{x,l} = 0 \ (\forall x \in L) \quad (5)$$

$$tree_{1,y} = 0 \ (\forall y \in L) \quad (6)$$

Definition of shade in the North, East, and West of a tree (Fig. 1)

$$\sum_{\substack{i\in\{\max(1-x,-1),\ldots,\min(l-x,1)\} \\ j\in\{0,\ldots,\min(l-y,1)\}}} tree_{x+i,y+j} - 6shade_{x,y} \leq 0 \ (\forall x,y \in L^2) \quad (7)$$

$$shade_{x,y} - \sum_{\substack{i\in\{\max(1-x,-1),\ldots,\min(l-x,1)\} \\ j\in\{0,\ldots,\min(l-y,1)\}}} tree_{x+i,y+j} \leq 0 \ (\forall x,y \in L^2) \quad (8)$$

Evolution of tree roots (Fig. 1)

$$root^1_{x,y} - tree_{x,y} = 0 \ (\forall x,y \in L^2) \quad (9)$$

$$\sum_{\substack{i\in\{\max(1-x,-1),\ldots,\min(l-x,1)\} \\ j\in\{\max(1-y,-1),\ldots,\min(l-y,1)\}}} root^{p-1}_{x+i,y+j} - 9root^p_{x,y} \leq 0 \ (\forall x,y \in L^2, \forall p \in \{2,3\})(10)$$

$$root^p_{x,y} - \sum_{\substack{i\in\{\max(1-x,-1),\ldots,\min(l-x,1)\} \\ j\in\{\max(1-y,-1),\ldots,\min(l-y,1)\}}} root^{p-1}_{x+i,y+j} \leq 0 \ (\forall x,y \in L^2, \forall p \in \{2,3\}) \quad (11)$$

Vertical symmetry breaking constraint

$$\sum_{x\in\{(l-\lfloor l/2\rfloor+1),\ldots,l\},y\in L} tree_{x,y} - \sum_{x\in\{1,\ldots,\lfloor l/2\rfloor\},y\in L} tree_{x,y} \leq 0 \quad (12)$$

Minimum and maximum crop quantities (Fig. 3)

$$minBalance^{t,c} \leq \sum_{x,y} crop^{t,c}_{x,y} \leq maxBalance^{t,c} \ (\forall t \in T, \forall c \in \zeta) \quad (13)$$

Crops growing during two consecutive seasons

$$crop^{t,c}_{x,y} - crop^{t+1,c}_{x,y} = 0 \ \substack{(\forall p\in P, t=f_c(T_p),\forall x,y\in L^2,\forall c\in \\ \{onion,tomato,carrot,manure\})} \quad (14)$$

where $f_c(T_p)$ returns if available the (unique) time step corresponding to the crop c planting season in T_p at period p for crops growing during two consecutive seasons (manure is planted in autumn, e.g., $f_{manure}(T_1) = 1$, onion and tomato in spring, $f_{onion\vee tomato}(T_2) = 3$, and carrot in summer, $f_{carrot}(T_3) = 8$). Compared to the original formulation in [15], we simplify the problem by removing crop rotation constraints and crop dispersion, and we add a symmetry breaking constraint (Eq. (12)).

4   Reformulation as a MIP by Using a Benders Decomposition with Crop Quantity Variables

We apply a Benders decomposition approach [5,16] in order to separate the MFVCAP into two parts: (i) tree positioning and (ii) crop production optimizing above- and belowground interactions over time. Problem (i) will correspond to the reduced master problem (MP) in the Benders approach and problem (ii) to the subproblem (SP). The master problem keeps the binary variables $tree_{x,y}$, $shade_{x,y}$, and $root^p_{x,y}$, and the associated constraints (3)–(12). The remaining constraints (13) and (14) belong to the subproblem. The master problem communicates with the subproblem by introducing new integer variables (and constraints) corresponding to the number of trees, *i.e.*, $trees = \sum_{x,y\in L^2} tree_{x,y}$, the number of shade land units for crops, $shades = \sum_{x,y\in L^2} shade_{x,y} - trees$, and the number of root land units for crops at each period, $roots_p = \sum_{x,y\in L^2} root^p_{x,y} - trees$. Recall that there are no shade nor roots land units available for crops at the first period (*i.e.*, $roots_1 = 0$).

These extra variables $trees, shades, roots_p$ will be taken as constants in the subproblem. Instead of having $crop^{t,c}_{x,y}$ binary variables here, we replace them by crop quantities for each type of land unit configuration. Because at any land unit, shade at periods 2 and 3 implies roots (see Eqs. (7)–(11) and Fig. 1), we distinguish three possible configurations: land units having shade and roots (sr), land units having roots only ($\bar{s}r$), and land units having no shade and no roots ($\bar{s}\bar{r}$). The corresponding crop quantity non-negative real variables are respectively: $qcrop^{t,c}_{sr}$, $qcrop^{t,c}_{\bar{s}r}$, and $qcrop^{t,c}_{\bar{s}\bar{r}}$, which defines a partition of all the land units excluding trees (the sum of which equals $qcrop^{t,c}$, see Eqs. (16) and (17)). Adding Eqs. (18) and (19) ensures a feasible allocation *w.r.t.* land units having shade or roots and no trees. The subproblem has now a linear objective function,

$$\min \sum_{t\in T, c\in \zeta} (A^{t,c} + B^{t,c})qcrop^{t,c}_{sr} + B^{t,c}qcrop^{t,c}_{\bar{s}r} + C^{t,c}qcrop^{t,c} \tag{15}$$

such that,

$$qcrop^{t,c}_{sr} + qcrop^{t,c}_{\bar{s}r} + qcrop^{t,c}_{\bar{s}\bar{r}} - qcrop^{t,c} = 0 \quad (\forall t \in T, c \in \zeta) \tag{16}$$

$$\sum_{c\in\zeta} qcrop^{t,c} = l^2 - trees \ (\forall t \in T) \tag{17}$$

$$\sum_{c\in\zeta} qcrop^{t,c}_{sr} = shades \quad (\forall t \in T\backslash\{1\}) \tag{18}$$

$$\sum_{c\in\zeta} qcrop^{t,c}_{sr} + qcrop^{t,c}_{\bar{s}r} = roots_p \quad (\forall p \in P, t \in T_p) \tag{19}$$

$$minBalance^{t,c} \leq qcrop^{t,c} \leq maxBalance^{t,c} \quad (\forall t \in T, c \in \zeta) \tag{20}$$

$$qcrop^{t,c} - qcrop^{t+1,c} = 0 \quad \begin{smallmatrix}(\forall p\in P, t=f_c(T_p), \forall c\in\{on-\\ion, tomato, carrot, manure\})\end{smallmatrix} \tag{21}$$

$$qcrop^{t,c}_{sr} - qcrop^{t+1,c}_{sr} = 0 \quad \begin{smallmatrix}(\forall p\in P\backslash\{1\}, t=f_c(T_p), \forall c\in\{on-\\ion, tomato, carrot, manure\})\end{smallmatrix} \tag{22}$$

$$qcrop^{t,c}_{\bar{s}r} - qcrop^{t+1,c}_{\bar{s}r} = 0 \quad \begin{smallmatrix}(\forall p\in P\backslash\{1\}, t=f_c(T_p), \forall c\in\{\\onion, tomato, carrot\})\end{smallmatrix} \tag{23}$$

$$qcrop^{t,manure}_{\bar{s}r} - qcrop^{t+1,manure}_{\bar{s}r} \leq 0 \quad (\forall p\in P, t=f_{manure}(T_p)) \tag{24}$$

Because variables $qcrop^{t,c}_{\bar{s}\bar{r}}$ appear only in Eq. 16, such as slack variables ($qcrop^{t,c}_{\bar{s}\bar{r}} = qcrop^{t,c} - qcrop^{t,c}_{sr} - qcrop^{t,c}_{\bar{s}r}$), we can remove them, replacing Eq. 16 by

$$qcrop^{t,c}_{sr} + qcrop^{t,c}_{\bar{s}r} - qcrop^{t,c} \leq 0 \ (\forall t \in T, c \in \zeta) \tag{25}$$

Notice that the number of land units with shade or roots does not change inside a given period, thus the quantities of crops growing on two consecutive seasons within the same period (except the first) that are allocated to shade or roots must remain the same (Eqs. (22) and (23)). Conversely, two-season duration crops like manure that overlap two periods can be allocated to more land units with roots (and no shade) in their second period than in their first period (Eq. (24)). It makes a supplementary partition between land units having no roots at period 2 and roots at period 3. This will be taken into account when reconstructing a complete allocation plan (see Algorithm 1, line 5 and below).

In conclusion, the subproblem deals with crop production over time but not with crop allocation on every land units, resulting in a linear objective function instead of the original quadratic one. It is easy to verify that Eq. (15) is equivalent to Eq. (1).

Without constraints (21)–(24) dealing with two-season duration crops, the subproblem can easily be cast as a set of independent minimum-cost flow problems for every season with maximum flow equal to $l^2 - trees$, and with demands ($minBalance$) and capacities ($maxBalance$, $l^2 - trees$, $shades$, $roots_p$) given as integer constants. See an example in Fig. 4. It is therefore totally unimodular, with integer optimal solutions. Two-season crops add a chain of equality/inequality binary constraints between crop quantities of consecutive seasons that preserves the integrality property.

To ensure that the subproblem is always feasible, the master problem has to assign trees so as to keep enough land units to be allocated to crops (in the subproblem) satisfying the crop production demands (Eq. 20). This is expressed by the following equations:

$$trees \leq l^2 - \sum_{c \in \zeta} minBalance^{t,c} \quad (\forall t \in T) \tag{26}$$

$$\sum_{c \in \zeta} minBalance^{t,c} \leq l^2 \leq \sum_{c \in \zeta} maxBalance^{t,c} \quad (\forall t \in T) \tag{27}$$

To summarize, we have decomposed the original problem in a master and subproblem by adding extra *channeling* variables ($trees$, $shades$, $roots_p$) also resulting in a linear objective function. Because these variables occur as linear terms in MP and SP (Eqs. (17)–(19)), we can reformulate the initial problem by the conjunction of the master (MP) and subproblem (SP), *i.e.*, Eqs. (3)–(12); (17)–(26) with linear objective Eq. (15), resulting in a Mixed Integer linear Program. This MIP can be solved directly or using a Benders decomposition approach with integer binary variables in the master problem and continuous variables in the subproblem as shown above and implemented in the last version of IBM ILOG cplex solver (v12.7).

Building a Complete Allocation Plan

It remains to build from the MIP solution a complete crop allocation plan with spatial-temporal crop variables $crop_{x,y}^{t,c}$ correctly assigned. The MIP solution gives the positions of trees, shades, and roots at every period. It also gives the crop quantities depending on land unit configurations. In principle, we could

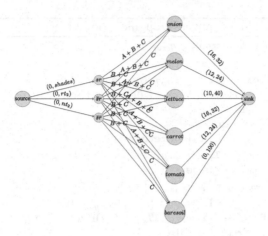

Fig. 4. Crop production in summer at period 2, regardless of two-season crop constraints, for a 10×10 grid as a minimum-cost flow problem with non-zero edge costs and in parentheses, demands and capacities. We define $rt_2 = roots_2 - shades$ and $nt_2 = 100 - trees - roots_2$.

allocate randomly $q_{crop_{sr}}^{t,c}$ (respectively $q_{crop_{\bar{s}r}}^{t,c}$, $q_{crop_{\bar{s}\bar{r}}}^{t,c}$) land units of crop c among free land units having shade and roots (resp. roots only, no shade nor roots) at each time step t and for every crop c. This is not as simple for two-season duration crops. For these crops c, every assignment of a particular land unit x, y at planting time t must be assigned to the same crop at time $t + 1$, i.e., $crop_{x,y}^{t,c} = crop_{x,y}^{t+1,c}$. Moreover, for manure, which spans over two consecutive periods at t and $t + 1$, a specific assignment procedure must be done. In case we have $q_{crop_{\bar{s}r}}^{t,manure} < q_{crop_{\bar{s}r}}^{t+1,manure}$, then we need to find $q_{crop_{\bar{s}r}}^{t+1,manure} - q_{crop_{\bar{s}r}}^{t,manure}$ land units without roots at time t and with roots at time $t + 1$ when allocating $q_{crop_{\bar{s}\bar{r}}}^{t,manure}$ land units to manure at time t in

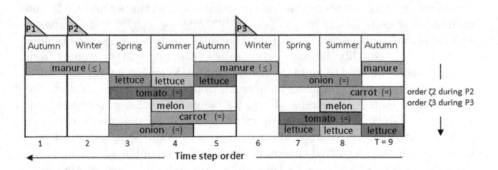

Fig. 5. Rules to build a complete allocation plan. Reverse order of time steps starting from autumn of period 3 to satisfy the equality/inequality constraints of two-season crops. Reverse order of crops between period 2 and period 3 to favor crop rotation.

Algorithm 1. Build a complete crop allocation plan.

Input: $tree_{x,y}, shade_{x,y}, root^p_{x,y}, qcrop^{t,c}_{sr}, qcrop^{t,c}_{\overline{s}r}, qcrop^{t,c}_{\overline{s}\overline{r}}$
Output: $crop^{t,c}_{x,y}$

   Procedure Allocate$(qcrop^{t,c}_{type}, t, c, p, type, p', type')$
     | **if** $(t < \max(T) \wedge twoseason(c) \wedge f_c(T_p) = t)$ **then return** ;
1 | **for** $y \leftarrow 1$ **to** l **do**
2 | | **for** $x \leftarrow 1$ **to** l **do**
         | | **if** $(qcrop^{t,c}_{type} = 0)$ **then return** ;
         | | **if** $(free^t_{x,y} \wedge \texttt{Type}(p,x,y) = type \wedge \texttt{Type}(p',x,y) = type')$ **then**
              | $free^t_{x,y} \leftarrow$ **false**;
              | $qcrop^{t,c}_{type} \leftarrow qcrop^{t,c}_{type} - 1$;
              | $crop^{t,c}_{x,y} \leftarrow 1, \forall c' \in \zeta \setminus \{c\}, crop^{t,c'}_{x,y} \leftarrow 0$;
              | **if** $(twoseason(c) \wedge f_c(T_p) < t)$ **then**
                  | $free^{t-1}_{x,y} \leftarrow$ **false**;
              | $crop^{t-1,c}_{x,y} \leftarrow 1, \forall c' \in \zeta \setminus \{c\}, crop^{t-1,c'}_{x,y} \leftarrow 0$;

Special Boolean array $free^t_{x,y}$ *to identify which land units remain available for crops*;
$\forall x \in L, y \in L, t \in T$, **if** $(tree_{x,y} = 1)$ **then** $free^t_{x,y} \leftarrow$ **false else**
$free^t_{x,y} \leftarrow$ **true**;
3 **for** $t \leftarrow \max(T)$ **to** 2 **do**
  | *Reverse order of crops between periods P2 and P3*;
4 | **if** $(t \geq \min(T_3))$ **then** $\zeta \leftarrow \zeta 3$; $p \leftarrow 3$ **else** $\zeta \leftarrow \zeta 2$; $p \leftarrow 2$;
  | **foreach** $(c \in \zeta)$ **do**
     | Allocate$(qcrop^{t,c}_{sr}, t, c, p, sr, p, sr)$;
5 | **if** $(c = manure \wedge t < \max(T))$ **then**
        | Allocate$(qcrop^{t-1,c}_{\overline{s}r}, t, c, p, \overline{s}r, p-1, \overline{s}r)$;
        | Allocate$(qcrop^{t,c}_{\overline{s}r} - qcrop^{t-1,c}_{\overline{s}r}, t, c, p, \overline{s}r, p-1, \overline{s}\overline{r})$;
     | **else** Allocate$(qcrop^{t,c}_{\overline{s}r}, t, c, p, \overline{s}r, p, \overline{s}r)$;
     | Allocate$(qcrop^{t,c}_{\overline{s}\overline{r}}, t, c, p, \overline{s}\overline{r}, p, \overline{s}\overline{r})$;

---

order to preserve a constant overall quantity of manure at times t and $t+1$. The remaining land units $qcrop^{t,manure}_{\overline{s}\overline{r}} - (qcrop^{t+1,manure}_{\overline{s}r} - qcrop^{t,manure}_{\overline{s}r})$ are chosen arbitrary among land units without roots. Because the two-season crops impose a chain of binary equality/inequality constraints (Eqs. (21)–(24)) spanning from spring to winter, we need to build the allocation plan following a temporal order. We use a decreasing order starting in autumn of period 3 in order to satisfy the more complex manure constraint (Eq. (24)) before the other two-season crop equality constraints (see Fig. 5 and Algorithm 1 line 3). By doing so, our greedy algorithm, Algorithm 1, building the complete allocation plan, is correct and does not require sophisticated constraint propagation techniques.

Instead of allocating crops to land units randomly, we look for the nearest[1] free land unit to the top-left corner of the piece of land when doing the assignment of a given crop quantity to land units. It has the effect to reduce

---

[1] Minimizing the y-axis distance first, then the x-axis. See Algorithm 1 lines 1 and 2.

horizontal crop dispersion. Furthermore, we allocate crops following a reverse order between periods 3 and 2 (see Fig. 5 and Algorithm 1 line 4). It tends to favor crop rotation between two successive periods.

5   Experimental Results

To assess the impact of above and belowground interactions, we performed simulations on three scenarii: scenario Above gives a significant importance to above interactions by multiplying the effect values related to shade by 10, similarly scenario Below attaches a great importance to roots by multiplying their effect values by 10 and the last scenario Equilibrate ascribes equal importance to the impact of both above and belowground interactions.

We solved these scenarii using IBM ILOG cplex v12.7 with its new fully-automatic Benders decomposition strategy for the MIP formulation and with default options for the BQP formulation, except saving the branch-and-bound tree to disk and using 4 cores of an Intel Xeon CPU E5-2680 at 2.5 GHz with 256 GB running Linux Debian 8.7. By comparing the real time taken by BQP formulation and MIP formulation to find an optimal solution and prove its optimality (see Fig. 6), we observed that the MIP is several orders of magnitude faster than the BQP in all scenarii.

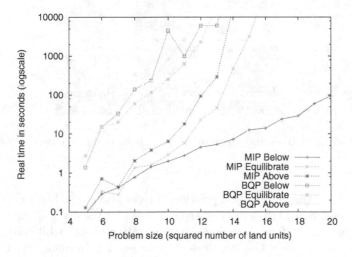

Fig. 6. Solving time in seconds taken by BQP and MIP formulations to solve the MFVCAP.

To analyze the obtained results, Fig. 7 shows as an example the crop allocation plan of a piece of land of 15 × 15 land units for scenarii Equilibrate, Below, and Above. We note that these solutions satisfy the constraints on minimal space between trees and consecutive crops. The main differences between

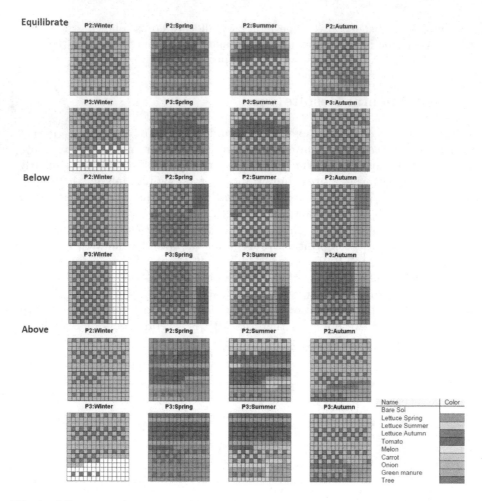

Fig. 7. Allocation of trees and crops on 15 × 15 land units over two periods for all scenarii.

these scenarii are the number and position of trees and crops. For scenario Equilibrate, we observe a high density of trees, caused by the overall negative effect of interactions. Therefore, to reduce these negative effects while ensuring the minimum allowed production of crops, the solver assigns many land units to trees (not penalized in the objective function) at the expense of vegetable crops. For scenario Below, trees are grouped together as in a forest to have less land units related to belowground interactions and thus minimum production of vegetable crops with negative effects. Consequently, this leads to a clear separation between the vegetable garden and the orchard, with insertion of some vegetable crops between trees. This clear separation results in shorter solving times for the MIP formulation, with a piece of land of 20 × 20 land units solved in less than 100 s. Concerning scenario Above, we notice a spaced disposition of apple trees in sparse groves. One reason is to ensure a sufficient number of land units of shade for the benefit of vegetable crops (e.g., tomato is at maximum allowed production in summer).

6   Conclusion and Perspectives

We have proposed a MIP reformulation of the Mixed Fruit-Vegetable Crop Allocation Problem, finding optimal 1-fruit-tree/6-vegetable crop allocation plans for 15 × 15 land units and 9 time steps in less than 1 h for scenario Equilibrate.

Further research remains to be done in order to extend our model, e.g., by taking into account crop rotations in order to avoid soil depletion and to increase pest and disease natural regulation [7]. To be more realistic w.r.t. real land sizes, we have to solve larger instances (going from 20-by-20 to roughly 100-by-100 land units). A possible direction is to try to generalize solutions found at small size to larger sizes by identifying patterns of tree configurations to be repeated. Although it seems easy to generalize for scenario Below, it looks more complex for scenarii Equilibrate and Above. Such a generalization may be further improved by a matheuristic procedure combining local search and linear programming as it is done on block layout design problems [12,14].

References

1. Akplogan, M., De Givry, S., Metivier, J.P., Quesnel, G., Joannon, A., Garcia, F.: Solving the crop allocation problem using hard and soft constraints. RAIRO Oper. Res. **47**(2), 151–172 (2013)
2. Alfandari, L., Lemalade, J., Nagih, A., Plateau, G.: A MIP flow model for crop-rotation planning in a context of forest sustainable development. Ann. Oper. Res. **190**(1), 149–164 (2011)
3. Alfandari, L., Plateau, A., Schepler, X.: A branch-and-price-and-cut approach for sustainable crop rotation planning. Eur. J. Oper. Res. **241**(3), 872–879 (2015)
4. Batish, D., Kohli, R., Jose, S., Singh, H.: Ecological Basis of Agroforestry. CRC Press, New York (2007)
5. Benders, J.F.: Partitioning procedures for solving mixed-variables programming problems. Numerische mathematik **4**(1), 238–252 (1962)
6. Detlefsen, N.K., Jensen, A.L.: Modelling optimal crop sequences using network flows. Agric. Syst. **94**(2), 566–572 (2007)
7. Dury, J., Schaller, N., Garcia, F., Reynaud, A., Bergez, J.E.: Models to support cropping plan and crop rotation decisions. A review. Agron. Sustain. Dev. **32**(2), 567–580 (2012)
8. El-Nazer, T., McCarl, B.A.: The choice of crop rotation: a modeling approach and case study. Am. J. Agric. Econ. **68**(1), 127–136 (1986)
9. Glen, J.: Mathematical models in farm planning: a survey. Oper. Res. **35**(5), 641–666 (1987)
10. Haneveld, W.K., Stegeman, A.W.: Crop succession requirements in agricultural production planning. Eur. J. Oper. Res. **166**(2), 406–429 (2005)
11. Jose, S., Gillespie, A.R., Pallardy, S.G.: Interspecific interactions in temperate agroforestry. In: Nair, P.K.R., Rao, M.R., Buck, L.E. (eds.) New Vistas in Agroforestry, pp. 237–255. Springer, Dordrecht (2004)

12. Kulturel-Konak, S., Konak, A.: Linear programming based genetic algorithm for the unequal area facility layout problem. Int. J. Prod. Res. **51**(14), 4302–4324 (2013)
13. Lbbecke, M.E., Desrosiers, J.: Selected topics in column generation. Oper. Res. **53**(6), 1007–1023 (2005)
14. Maniezzo, V., Sttzle, T. (eds.): Matheuristics. IRIDIA, Brussels (2016)
15. Maqrot, S., de Givry, S., Quesnel, G., Tchamitchian, M.: Designing mixed fruit-vegetable cropping systems by integer quadratic programming. In: Proceedings of iEMSs, Toulouse (2016)
16. Rahmaniani, R., Crainic, T.G., Gendreau, M., Rei, W.: The benders decomposition algorithm: a literature review. EJOR **259**(3), 801–817 (2017)
17. dos Santos, L.M.R., Costa, A.M., Arenales, M.N., Santos, R.H.S.: Sustainable vegetable crop supply problem. Eur. J. Oper. Res. **204**(3), 639–647 (2010)
18. dos Santos, L.M.R., Michelon, P., Arenales, M.N., Santos, R.H.S.: Crop rotation scheduling with adjacency constraints. Ann. Oper. Res. **190**(1), 165–180 (2011)
19. Stone, N., Buick, R., Roach, J., Scheckler, R., Rupani, R.: The planning problem in agriculture: farm-level crop rotation planning as an example. In: AI Applications in Natural Resource Management, USA (1992)
20. Taillandier, P., Therond, O., Gaudou, B.: A new BDI agent architecture based on the belief theory. Application to the modelling of cropping plan decision-making. In: International environmental modelling and software society (iEMSs), Leipzig (2012)
21. Tchamitchian, M., Godin, E.: Designing mixed horticultural systems. Build. Org. Bridges **1**, 179–182 (2014)
22. Vercambre, G., Pag, L., Doussan, C., Habib, R.: Architectural analysis and synthesis of the plum tree root system in an orchard using a quantitative modelling approach. Plant Soil **251**(1), 1–11 (2003)
23. Weaver, J.E., Bruner, W.E.: Root Development of Vegetable Crops, 1st edn. Mcgraw-Hill Book Co., London (1927)

Data Collection and Analysis of Usages from Connected Objects: Some Lessons

Sara Meftah[1], Antoine Cornuéjols[1(✉)], Juliette Dibie[1], and Mariette Sicard[2]

[1] UMR MIA-Paris, AgroParisTech, INRA, Université Paris-Saclay,
75005 Paris, France
{sara.meftah,antoine.cornuejols,juliette.dibie}@agroparistech.fr
[2] Research Cooking and Food, Groupe SEB, 21261 Selongey, France
msicard@groupeseb.com
http://www.springer.com/lncs

Abstract. The emergence of widely available connected devices is perceived as the promise of new added-value services. Companies can now gather, often in real time, huge amounts of data about their customers' habits. Seemingly, all they have to do is to mine these raw data in order to discover the profiles of their users and their needs.

Stemming from an industrial experience, this paper, however, shows that things are not that simple. It appears that, even in an exploratory data mining phase, the usual data cleaning and preprocessing steps are a long shot from being adequate. The rapid deployment of connected devices indeed introduces its own series of problems. The paper shares the pitfalls encountered in a project aiming at enhancing the cooking habits and presents some hard learnt lessons of general import.

Keywords: Data mining · Internet of Things · Data preprocessing

1 Introduction

1.1 The Promise of Gathering Data from Connected Objects

Recent years have witnessed the arrival of a new concept, that of smart connected products and devices, which, all together, will make the *Internet of Things*.

One major driving force is to get a direct access to product usage data. By analyzing massive amounts of data about usages, companies aim at forming new kinds of relationships with customers. The accumulation and analysis of product usage data should enable them to gain fresh insights into how to create new values for the customers, therefore ensuring closer ties and increased loyalty.

This is in this perspective that the industrial project that serves as a case study in this paper has been launched. The project is about cooking devices and habits. It is part of a large undertaking to improve public health by measuring alimentation behaviors. Its goal is to gently try to nudge consumers towards healthier behaviors if needed, and at least to offer and suggest them a more varied diet (see [3] for a related purpose).

© Springer International Publishing AG 2017
S. Benferhat et al. (Eds.): IEA/AIE 2017, Part II, LNAI 10351, pp. 251–258, 2017.
DOI: 10.1007/978-3-319-60045-1_27

This new public health approach, user-centered and in real-time, is enabled by the possibility to equip kitchens with connected devices that both send data about the cooking procedures followed and offer new interfaces to the users. These interfaces provide them with descriptions of recipes and suggestions and gather information from the customers.

In the following, we first present in Sect. 2 the exchanges of data that are possible with the new devices, while Sect. 2.1 reports the kind of questions that are expected to be solved by analyzing the data. Section 3 then turns to the data mining processes that were attempted and shows the difficulties encountered. Section 4 shows that these difficulties are largely intrinsic to the deployment of smart connected devices, independently of the field of cooking study. It is thus beneficial to draw general lessons from this experience.

2   Case Study: Analyzing Data About Cooking Behaviors

2.1   The Questions

When equipping users with smart connected devices, e.g. e-health watches, smartphones, or cooking devices, and then gathering data about the users' habits, companies share general questions such as:

1. Does a *categorization of the users* emerge from the collected data, either
   - directly from their profile available during the buying procedure or before the first interaction with the device
   - or, indirectly, from their measured interactions with the device(s)
2. Is there, and what is, a *typology of the usages*? For instance,
   - from the recipes that are consulted on the application's website
   - from the recipes that are effectively followed
3. Is it possible to identify interesting *relationships between classes of users and classes of behaviors* or classes of recipes?

2.2   The Available Data

When a connected device is rented or sold to a customer, the information gathered by the provider is of two qualitatively different types.

1. The first is akin to a *factual description of the client*. That could be the company or client's name, the revenue, number of employees, number of dependents, age, and so on. Sometimes this description is readily available because the contract cannot be signed without it, sometimes, it comes from the voluntary filling of information from the user.
2. The second type includes all the information that can be collected during the *interactions of the user with the device*, or during the device's operations. Such data can take the form of logs listing temporal actions or procedures, or they can also trace the user's connections to a website purported to provide operating or maintenance information. In that case, the logs of interactions can be completed with the content of the web pages that have been consulted.

As an illustration, in the context of the industrial project on the analysis of cooking habits, data was collected on approximately 100,000 users, covering a period of more than 24 months, from January 2014 to March 2016. Data were obtained when the user voluntarily filled a form. The file describing the *users' profiles* thus provides information about 'age category', 'city', 'gender', 'number of children', 'number of adults' in the family, and 'type of device'.

The behaviors of the users, and their habits, were measured thanks to an application available for smartphones. On one hand, this application allows the users to access a list of recipes approved by nutritionists, to select some of them, to look for information, and to rate them. On the other hand, the application can also be used to remotely control the cooking device in order to automatically perform complex cooking operations. In this way, sophisticated recipes can be realized, but also, data about the user's usage can be gathered. Therefore, each cooking session by a user produces a mixture of operation logs and sequences of textual contents describing the web pages and recipes that had been looked onto during the session and the appreciations possibly provided by the user.

In addition, there is a file recording *relations between users and recipes*, in the form of bookmarks (plus date and time) that each user can put on recipes he/she would like to remember for future use. For instance, this file recorded approximately 9,000 bookmarks put by 2,000 users ($\approx$2% of all users) on 400 recipes ($\approx$11% of the recipes). Conversely, there is also a file about the bookmarks that were removed after a single session.

The users can also evaluate the recipes by grading them. And there are files collecting data about the usages of the cooking devices. One such file contains information about automatic launches of cooking operations. Another file keeps details about the web page navigation by the users on the supplier's website. More than 4,850,000 events were thus recorded from more than 4,500 users at the time of this study. Each event in the file is associated with specific information about the webpage accessed, the time and date, the duration of the consultation, and so on.

2.3   The Methods: Exploratory Data Analysis

In order to better understand how the cooking devices and the associated services are used and how the users' habits are related to the users' profiles, a wealth of machine learning techniques were used, including:

- *Univariate analysis*, e.g. using histograms of distributions for each variable.
- *Visualizations* in 2D or 3D to help discover correlations between variables.
- *Clustering* in order to detect categories in users and in recipes.
- Discovery of *Frequent Item Sets* and *association rules* both within the users' profiles or the habits descriptions.
- Modeling of the dynamics of the user's habits using *Markov chains*.
- *Supervised classification* in order to understand what determined that some recipes would be tagged as "favorites" or "not favorites".

All methods required the use of preprocessing steps before they could be carried out. Some operations were standard, others involved specific knowledge in the form of domain ontologies. Briefly, the following methods were used:

- *Data cleaning.* E.g., lots of variations were encountered in the address fields.
- Processing of *missing information.* As is so unfortunately too often the case, there existed default values for some data fields, like number of children, or number of adults in the household. We devised rules that estimate the probability that these default values were in fact missing values given the answers to other data fields.
- *Data enrichment.* The descriptions of the recipes were too fined grain for useful subsequent data analysis. For instance, there were 483 different ingredients mentioned, such as 'salt', 'oil', 'ham', 'parmesan'. In order to perform clustering or association rules discovery, we decided to derive more abstract description of the recipes, using an ontology[1]. 'Tomato' could thus be replaced by 'vegetable'. (see also [4,5]). In addition, ontologies allowed us also to *add* information, such as the type of diet implied by the use of some ingredient, or the type of course during the meal: entry, main course or dessert.
- *Value imputation.* One important input is whether the user likes or dislikes a process, here a recipe. In our setting, users could provide a grade to the consulted recipe through the interface of the application, however, they were a minority to use this fixture. We thus decided to infer the like/dislike values from the behavior of the customers. One source was the observation of the bookmarks put by the users on recipes. We decided for instance that a user that puts a bookmark on a recipe and consults it at least another time is likely to 'like' this recipe. Conversely, a user that removes a bookmark after a single consultation is viewed as 'disliking' this recipe. Likewise, we decided that a user who launches an automatic cooking session using a recipe probably 'likes' this recipe. Finally, a user sharing a recipe on social networks was also deemed to 'like' this recipe. In this way, we were able to substantially increase the proportion of recipes qualified by like/dislike appreciations.

3   Analyzing the Data

The analysis was organized along three main objectives: *first*, categorizing the users' profiles, *second*, detecting patterns of cooking habits and cooking preferences, and, *third*, see whether there exist some relationships between users's profiles and cooking habits and preferences.

3.1   Analysis of the Data Describing the Users

A preliminary study involved the examination of the distribution of the values for each field: 'age category', 'gender', 'type of device', 'number of adults' and 'number of children' in the household.

[1] We used the TAAABLE ontology [6], which is the most encompassing one for analyzing nutrition and food in general.

In the process of computing statistics for each attribute, it was found that a significant proportion of them were not filled out by the users, or, worse, were filled with a default value. In fact, even the type of the cooking device was not provided by about 10% of the users. This is remarquable since it could be expected that this information should be collected automatically. As was mentioned in Sect. 2.3, we had to resort to heuristic rules to detect and, if possible correct, the values resulting from filling by the default value.

Altogether, these defects in the information collected about the users were detrimental for more refined analyses, such as clustering.

3.2   Analysis of the Data Describing the Cooking Behaviors

In this case study, the idea was to identify typical behaviors measured through the logs of interaction of the users with the devices. The goal was to examine whether there were characteristic temporal patterns in the use of the recipes, for instance during the week or during the year, and, generally, to measure in which way the application's services were used, whether there were steps that were bypassed, others that should be more informative, and so on.

To answer these questions, it is crucial to be able to determine exactly what were the webpages that were consulted, in which order and what was the duration of the consultation for each page. It has been underlined in the literature (for instance, [7]), that there can be impediments from the way Web servers are organized and operate. For instance, because of proxy and local caching, it can be difficult to detect that a user is going back to a page already viewed. With connected devices, however, the operations can be thought anew, and such hindrances should be limited or eliminated.

In our application, it can be determined that a web page has been accessed thanks to the 'page load event'. The duration of consultation of a page can be determined through the records of the 'page load' and 'page unload' events since each is associated with a timestamp.

The application environment draws a distinction between 'content pages', which essentially describe recipe steps, and 'navigational' or 'mobile application pages' which allow the user to navigate between the application services. There are 76 such different types of navigational pages. When trying to analyze the behaviors of the users, it quickly became apparent that problems were looming.

First of all, looking at the content pages, it was readily obvious that the distribution of the durations of consultation exhibited abnormal results. Altogether, 262,488 consultations of pages describing recipe steps were recorded, with a mean duration of consultation of 98 s and a standard deviation of 3,326 s, clearly out of normal range. Actually, it was discovered that the maximal duration time was 119 h! An histogram of the duration times showed that there was a significant proportion of outliers, and that this proportion was higher for the last steps of the recipes that for the first ones. What then was the reason behind this odd and unhelpful set of observations?

After some analysis and discussion with the development team, it was found that the consultation of a page did not have to be formally closed by the user, before he/she was moving to another page, or discontinuing altogether the current cooking session. The current page could be put in the background or the application could be left in its current opened state for days, before another session was started. The confort of use of the application was the foremost concern for the development team, while the demands of any future data analysis was not really considered.

Another source of frustration emerged from the study of the consultations of the 'navigation' pages. There were 1,841,044 pages consulted in the course of 27 months, from January 2014 to March 2016. We quickly discovered that some pages were redundant, having closely related meanings for the users, or providing exactly the same information. We found also that there had been changes in the application navigation system over time, with various modifications in the architecture of the system. For instance, 56 out of the 76 types of navigation pages were added starting from November 2015, without notification to the data analysis team. Again, the changes in the application were driven by concerns about the usage of the device, with no regard for the data analysis needs.

Finally, it was difficult to analyze the search behavior of the users, since if a search conducted among the 'navigation' pages was concluded by a click on a recipe, the search was erased from the user's history, and he/she had to repeat it entirely if needed, causing havoc in the statistics about the viewed pages. When trying to figure out if there were typical search paths, this resulted in obtaining Markov chains that were difficult to interpret.

3.3   Relationships Between Types of Users and Cooking Behaviors

One way to search for relations between the users' characteristics and types of recipes is to perform *clustering*: on the users' description, on the one hand, and on the recipes on the other hand. Another way is to look for *association rules* between user's profiles and types of recipes.

In both analyses, we got interesting and interpretable results. Clustering allowed us to identify marked relationships between clusters of users (2 clusters) and clusters of recipes (3 clusters). Likewise, we uncovered association rules that made sense, like, for instance: women with more than one child look for easy recipes, or men at least 53 years old prefer recipes with less cholesterol.

However, it must be said that these findings are tentative since they rest on fragile and fault prone measurements.

4   Lessons for the Design of IoT for Collecting Data on Usages

Several general lessons can be drawn from the difficulties encountered in analyzing the data about cooking habits and preferences. They are interesting because we believe they potentially apply to many industrial projects that aim at delivering connected devices to their customers in order both to bring them new services and to gather valuable data about their usages. We list them in the following.

1. All too often, *data collected about the users* and their characteristics *are incomplete*, when they are not *erroneous*. The fundamental reason lies in the fact that users will not spend time to fill information if they do not perceive in which way this is critical to the service they get. For instance, users of connected e-health devices, like connected watches, know that they better provide the service with their precise age and weight, because otherwise the assessment of their performance is senseless. In the case of the connected cooking devices, such a link between the information asked to the user and the service provided was far less apparent.

   The remedy is therefore to make obvious to the user that it is in his/her own interest to provide "useful" information in order to get a true benefice from the service. This is what has been done since this study.

2. The *information available from the logs of the device operations and/or the user's interactions was altogether almost useless*. Indeed, the team of designers and developers of the devices and of the user's interface was naturally obsessed with their ease of use and with the technical aspects of the device and interface. If the team was aware of the data collecting role of the devices and interfaces, this role was not a foremost concern.

   One remedy is to mix together in a single team the designers, the technical staff and the data scientists, or, at the very least to ensure a strong communication channel between them. Another remedy is to teach the basics and demands of data science to every one implied in the project.

3. When the data collected over several months of operation was analyzed, it quickly became apparent that there had been *changes in the types of data collected, or, even worse, in the semantics of some measurements*. This was due to the rapid deployment of the devices to the end-users while the design and realization of the device, and above all of the user's interface was not stabilized. Again, the primary concern of the designers and technicians tend to be the proper working of the device and interface. And because the field of connected devices is in such a frenzied state, designers and technicians are in a agile state of mind with rapid prototyping of new softwares and their deployment to the users. The data collecting goal is second.

   One remedy is again to provide education about data science to every one involved. Then, when changes affecting the data available are in order, programs for translating data from one period to another should be produced, or, at least, meta data should accompany any data that is collected.

5   Conclusion

In the last two or three years, the Internet of Things has been widely heralded as a revolution in the making, that could shadow even the already "old" Internet revolution. Nonetheless, among high expectations about what the new area could bring to our lives, some warnings were voiced. For instance, Vinton Cerf, chief inventor of the Internet, observed that a lack of standards could hinder the development and operations of the Internet of Things [1]. Ease of interoperability between different systems, and ease of communication in networks composed of millions of objects, plus resilience in front of possible attacks and privacy preservation were also recognized as essential assets that must be secured if IoT is to become a reality.

But, while all these technical hurdles started to be appraised, other concerns, of as much fundamental importance, have been largely overlooked. Indeed, when connected objects are delivered to a client and installed, the provider and/or the client expect that one prominent service will be the collection, sometimes in real-time, of day to day data. One goal can be to better predict breakdowns, therefore ensuring a smoother service. Quite often, though, it is deemed even more important to gather information about the usage of the connected devices in order to bring improved experience to the users, and possibly new services.

It has been said that the largest challenge for businesses will be determining how to use the tremendous volume of new data that Internet of the Things will generate (see for instance [2]). Ironically, as this paper shows, the data collecting role itself is often overlooked by the people who design and deploy the connected devices. One reason is that they are already overtaxed with trying to solve all the technical problems mentioned above. Another reason is the frantic pace with which the technology evolves, a pace which conducts the technical teams to adopt an agile strategy, with many adaptations along the way. Unfortunately, as our experience demonstrates, these changes and the lack of a clear perception of the demands of data analysis, can ruin the very purpose of the whole operation.

This paper, we hope, will thus help promote a new awareness of the challenges set when the production of exploitable data from connected objects is aimed at.

References

1. Fisher, L.M.: Cerf cites challenges facing the Internet of Things. Commun. ACM (ACM News) (2015)
2. Violino, B.: The 'Internet of things' will mean really, really big data. InfoWorld, 29 July 2013
3. Teng, C., Lin, Y., Adamic, L.: Recipe recommendation using ingredient networks. In: Proceedings of the 4th Annual ACM Web Science Conference, pp. 298–307. ACM (2012)
4. Jonsson, E.: Semantic word classification and temporal dependency detection on cooking recipes (2015)
5. Amano, S., Aizawa, K., Ogawa, M.: Food category representatives: extracting categories from meal names in food recordings and recipe data. In: 2015 IEEE International Conference on Multimedia Big Data (BigMM), pp. 48–55. IEEE (2015)
6. Cordier, A., Dufour-Lussier, V., Lieber, J., Nauer, E., Badra, F., Cojan, J., Gaillard, E., Infante-Blanco, L., Molli, P., Napoli, A., et al.: Taaable : a case-based system for personalized cooking. In: Montani, S., Jain, L.C. (eds.) Successful Case-based Reasoning Applications-2, pp. 121–162. Springer, Heidelberg (2014)
7. Mobasher, B., Cooley, R., Srivastava, J.: Automatic personalization based on web usage mining. Commun. ACM **43**(8), 142–151 (2000)

Assessing Nitrogen Nutrition in Corn Crops with Airborne Multispectral Sensors

Jaen Alberto Arroyo[1], Cecilia Gomez-Castaneda[1], Elias Ruiz[1(✉)], Enrique Munoz de Cote[1,3], Francisco Gavi[2], and Luis Enrique Sucar[1]

[1] Computer Science Department, Instituto Nacional de Astrofísica, Óptica y Electrónica, Luis Enrique Erro No. 1, Sta. María Tonantzintla, 72840 Puebla, Mexico
{j.arroyo,cecilia,elias_ruiz,esucar}@inaoep.mx
[2] Programa de Hidrociencias, Colegio de Posgraduados, Montecillo, Mexico
gavi@colpos.mx
[3] Prowler.io Ltd., Cambridge, UK
enrique@prowler.io

Abstract. This paper presents a method to assess nitrogen levels, a nitrogen nutrition index (NNI), in corn crops (*Zea mays*) using multispectral remote sensing imagery. The multispectral sensors used were four spectral bands only. The experiments were compared with nitrogen levels sensed in the field. The corn crops were divided into three nitrogen fertilization levels (70, 140 and 210 kgN · ha^{-1}) into three replicates. In this sense, we propose a method to infer nitrogen levels in corn crops by using airborne multispectral sensors and machine learning techniques. The presented results offered a simple model to estimate nitrogen with low-cost technologies (UAVs and multispectral cameras only) in small to medium size areas of corn crops.

1 Introduction

Nitrogen (N) is one of the most important nutrients in agriculture to improve the crop yield. In corn crops is especially important. Furthermore, the appropriate dosage is also important since it can be a waste the excess of applying N in crops, but the lack of N implies a compromise in the yield. In this sense, it is important the usage of low-cost strategies to infer the N requirements in order to do a positive impact in the correct supply of N. In addition, it is well known that the excessive use of fertilizers (including N) should be avoided to minimize environmental impacts [3].

For this purpose, N critical concentration term ($\%N_c$) was proposed and used in several articles to estimate the minimum amount of nitrogen required for each crop to produce the maximum aerial biomass at a given time [7,10,11].

Several authors have shown that $\%N_c$ declines as a function of aerial biomass accumulation (W) [1]. Several models have been proposed to estimate N critical concentration. In this paper, the $N_c - W$ model by [11] was used in order to estimate the N critical as a decreasing function of biomass (W). The rule is:

© Springer International Publishing AG 2017
S. Benferhat et al. (Eds.): IEA/AIE 2017, Part II, LNAI 10351, pp. 259–267, 2017.
DOI: 10.1007/978-3-319-60045-1_28

$$\text{If } W < 1 \, t/ha, \, N_c = 3.40 \tag{1}$$

$$\text{If } 1 \, t/ha \leq W \leq 22 \, t/ha, \, N_c = 3.40W^{-0.37} \tag{2}$$

The Nitrogen Nutrition Index (NNI) is the ratio between the actual nitrogen concentration (%Na) and the ideal N concentration (%Nc) of a crop having the same biomass and whose growth is not limited by N availability [8].

$$NNI = \frac{N_a}{N_c} \tag{3}$$

From Eqs. 1–3, we can say that: $NNI = f(N_a, W)$ only if $W \leq 22 \, t/ha$ since $W > 22 \, t/ha$ is not defined.

The Nitrogen concentration is estimated by hyperspectral indices [3] in plants. In this paper, a method with low-cost multispectral cameras is shown for a specific crop (corn). In this sense, several vegetation indices (VIs) have been used to estimate biophysical variables.

Different variables have been used to characterize the nitrogen status of a crop in order to support a decision in fertilization management. Among them, the most popular are the chlorophyll content measurements of the leaves [5].

The main objective of this paper is to assess the nitrogen nutrition in maize crops using multispectral sensors only and machine learning, avoiding the traditional method by estimating nitrogen with higher cost solutions like destructive methods, chlorophyll measurements, studies of soil, among others.

For this purpose, we present in this paper two similar methods to estimate NNI values:

1. Estimate the NNI by its theoretical formula with multispectral sensors and biomass data (W).
2. Estimate the NNI directly by multispectral sensors with machine learning techniques.

At the end, we want to compare these two methods in order to measure the best scenario in terms of accuracy. Ground truth information is provided by measurements of biomass and nitrogen levels produced in a field laboratory. The cheapest scenario is the second since it implies a straightforward inference: we only need multispectral indices and some nitrogen ground truth values. Each pixel of the multispectral images is represented as a function of the form $Y \approx f(X, \beta)$, where X represents the information provided by the multispectral sensors and β are the parameters of the model. It is noteworthy to say that, this model is created for corn crops and the model should be adjusted to others crops since the levels of $\%N_c$ for other crops are different. In addition, the method works in similar regions (similar sea level, latitude, and longitude). The soil type in the region also implies a difference in the study.

2   Materials and Methods

Nine corn plots $25 \, m \times 5 \, m$ were considered. Each block has one kind of nitrogen treatment. Three blocks with $70 \, N \cdot ha^{-1}$, other three blocks with $140 \, N \cdot ha^{-1}$

(which is considered as a normal treatment) and 210 N · ha^{-1} (which is considered as excessive). The crops were considered as temporal. In this sense, additional irrigation was not provided.

The field was sown on June 1, 2016, and the N was applied on July 31, 2016. Two flights with the cameras were done on August 9 and September 2, 2016. A field management plan can be viewed on Fig. 2.

The imagery was captured with easy-acquiring cameras in RGB channels (by a GoPro camera), and NIR band was obtained by a low-cost MaPIR-NIR camera. The composition was performed in Pix4D software. The reason about the usage of a GoPro camera is the weight for the quad-copter. Other cheaper cameras can also be used.

We used two airborne quad-copters equipped with the cameras in two different flights (one by each camera) since the cameras have different exposition times. One of the quad-copters is illustrated in the Fig. 1.

Fig. 1. One of the quad-copters considered (named as "Q1"). Each model requires one li-po battery which perform until 15 min of flight. However, to preserve life of the battery, each flight with the cameras was performed in less than 6 min.

The process to compose the map was conducted with the Datamapper software in order to obtain the ortho-mosaic.

Several multispectral vegetation indices were used. These indices are summarized in the Table 1.

Reflectance for each band (red, green, blue and near-infrared) was obtained with the calibration procedure described in [9]. Reflectance values are given by:

$$R_T(\theta_t) = \frac{DN_T(t)}{DN_R(t_0)} R_R(\theta_{t_0}) \tag{4}$$

where t is time during a flight, t_0 is the time before to the flight and DN_T means digital numbers viewing the crops, DN_R are digital numbers viewing the reference panel, θ_t is the solar zenith angle at the time t, and R_R is the reflectance factor of the reference panel. This procedure is important to normalize the multispectral data in order to reduce the bias originated by the sun position.

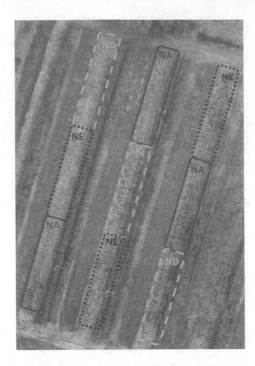

Fig. 2. Nine plots of corn were considered. Three different treatments were applied. In the image, ND is a region with a deficient treatment of N (70 N·ha^{-1}). NA is adequate (140 N · ha^{-1}), and NE is excessive (210 N · ha^{-1}).

2.1 Estimating NNI with Formula

This estimation considers the traditional formula of NNI, where NNI is a ratio between the $\%N_a$ and the $\%N_c$ concentration. In this sense, nine $\%N_a$ ground truth values were taken from leaves with destructive methods. $\%N_c$ were obtained by a regression model and the biomass ground truth values. In the first step, W is estimated by a random forest regression and the N_c is inferred from the Eqs. 1 and 2.

A block diagram of this proposed method is illustrated in the Fig. 3.

For testing, four bands were required as inputs: Red, Blue, Green and NIR. the vegetation indices of the Table 1 are calculated automatically from the four bands.

2.2 Estimating NNI with Machine Learning Techniques

This method is more straightforward (Fig. 4). The estimation is based on a random forest regression method [2] with the NNI ground truth values as labels. The inputs are the same: RGB-Nir values and the vegetation indices from the Table 1. Others methods like SVM (espilon-SVR regression with RBF as base kernel), Multilayer Perceptron (the number of hidden layers was equal to the number of

Table 1. Multispectral vegetation indices that were used in the experiments.

Index name	Formula	Reference
NDVI	$\frac{NIR-R}{NIR+R}$	[14]
GNDVI	$\frac{NIR-G}{NIR+R}$	[4]
OSAVI	$\frac{NIR-R}{NIR+R+0.16}$	[13]
NGRDI	$\frac{G-R}{G+R}$	[16]
MTVI2	$\frac{1.8(NIR-G)-3.75(R-G)}{\sqrt{(2NIR+1)^2-6\left(NIR-5\sqrt{R}\right)-0.5}}$	[6]

Formula-Based Model

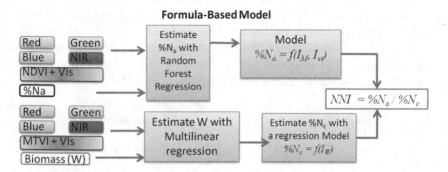

Fig. 3. Block diagram of the Formula-Based model. N_a and N_c are estimated with ML techniques. N_c requires an extra step: the estimation is obtained from biomass and biomass is estimated from four bands and vegetation indices like MTVI.

Machine Learning Based Model

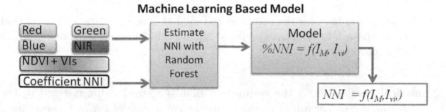

Fig. 4. Block diagram of the machine learning model. This method is a short way to estimate NNI. It only uses NNI ground truth values to perform the estimation. It uses random forest regression with NNI ground truth values as labels.

attributes), and multilinear regression were also tested. Results showed a better performance with random forest method as equal to multilayer perceptrons. We used 100 trees as main parameter of the random forest regression method. To avoid over-fitting problems, we tested initially with 30% of the data for training and the rest for testing. Results were not far with respect to the reported in the paper. The reported ones were with ten fold cross scheme to validate the results. Regression values diminished about 5%. We chose random forest empirically, the model selection problem is not part of our method, in this case, we are more interested in a straightforward and low-cost method to estimate NNI. The goal

is an easy way to learn the method. The model is transferable to other kind
of crops, repeating the training phase with the proper multi spectral and NNI
values.

3   Results

In the Fig. 5 we present a comparison between the two proposed models. The
axis correspond to the NNI values for each NNI estimation values in each flight.
R^2 value is greater than 96% in both flights. The Root Mean Squared Error
(RMSE) is 0.0216 for the first flight and 0.0137 for the second flight. The sum of
squared error of prediction (SSE) is of 0.0033 in the first flight and the SSE in
the second flight is of 0.0013. In this sense we prefer the machine learning based
model since it is easier in terms of training regarding method one. In addition,
we only need some NNI values of ground truth for the training stage, whereas
the Formula-based model requires two values ($\%N_a$ and W).

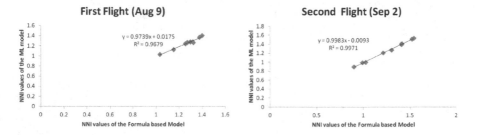

Fig. 5. A comparison between the two proposed models. The correlation suggests that
short model based on ML techniques is almost equal to the formula-based model which
requires extra information.

Numerical results about the estimation of nitrogen are summarized in the
Table 2. A comparison graph of the machine learning model against the ground
truth values is illustrated in the Fig. 6. A comparison between the results of NNI
real values and the estimated values with the two models is illustrated in the
Figs. 7 and 8. It is noteworthy to say that the R^2 value was improved in the
second flight in both methods. The RMSE values for the first flight with the
formula-Based model and the ML model were 0.0367 and 0.0294 respectively.
Analogously, The SSE values were 0.0094 and 0.0061. In the second flight this
values were improved. RMSE values were 0.0351 and 0.0444 for the formula and
the ML model respectively. SSE values were 0.0086 and 0.0138 The reason of the
improvement of R^2 can be due to the N absorption. On the first flight, the dosage
of nitrogen was applied only nine days before. Results about nitrogen are slightly
noisier in the first flight. In the second flight, results were more consistent and
the prediction was improved. The formula based model were better than the
ML model in the second flight, however, the SSE is still low (0.013) and the
correlation values is still high ($R^2 = 96\%$).

Table 2. Results of NNI estimation in the first and second flight. Ground truth and estimated values are shown. Values for the nine plots are shown. D is deficient, A is adequate and E is an excessive amount of dosed nitrogen

Plot	g-truth Aug9	Est. Aug9	g-truth Sep2	Est. Sep2
1-D	0.8026	1.0344	1.5575	1.5116
1-A	1.5694	1.4081	1.4327	1.413
1-E	1.4706	1.3684	0.719	0.9943
2-D	1.2135	1.2442	1.0919	1.2095
2-A	0.8422	1.1307	0.8354	1.0015
2-E	1.3701	1.2675	1.4725	1.3909
3-D	1.3085	1.2698	0.6091	0.8949
3-A	1.3525	1.2786	1.7375	1.5362
3-E	1.3265	1.277	1.3775	1.2706

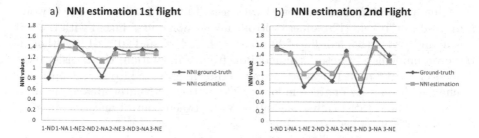

Fig. 6. Comparison between NNI values for each crop region.

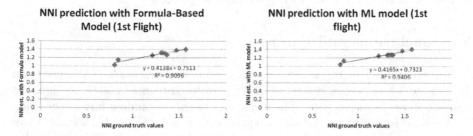

Fig. 7. Results of the NNI estimation via RFR algorithm for the first flight. The ML model improves the results with respect to the formula based model even when the nitrogen dosage was early applied.

4   Discussion

It is interesting the improvement of the model when the dosage of N has more time. The second flight was done in the earring stage of the corn, whereas the first flight was done in the V10 stage. The earring stage is particularly more

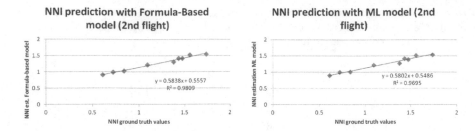

Fig. 8. Results of the NNI estimation via RFR algorithm for the second flight. In the second flight, the formula based model is better as expected, since it uses more information. However, the ML model is also accurate.

stable in prediction. We only have two measurements of N but this information is still enough to predict the NNI values in the crops. One week is not a good time to evaluate the absorption of nitrogen. The reason is due to urea is hydrolyzed (yielding ammonium and ammonia) with a half-life of 1.9 days at 3.5 °C when is applied in the field [12]; under controlled conditions, urea mixed with the soil was hydrolyzed with a half-life of 22, 15 and 6 h at 4, 10 and 20 °C [12]. Although the crop immediately absorbs ammonium from soil solution, the translocation process of N from roots to leaves may take a time in order to be observed optically as change in intensity of green in leaves. The uptake of N after urea application in corn was not statistically different at V6 between control and side-dressing applied in V5 phenology stage [15].

If we observe the two flights, there is an acceptable correlation (better in the second) if we want to predict the absorbed nitrogen in the plants. Although the prediction is local, the cost of flying and training is low.

5   Conclusions and Future Work

A method to infer nitrogen levels in corn crops was proposed. UAVs used can draw up to 5 ha of crops. Since the UAVs performed flights in 50–70 m high, the resolution was 3 cm per pixel. The method is based on random forest regression method and including several linear regressions in order to establish some correlation between biomass and Nitrogen critical values. The method utilizes multi-spectral imagery only with low-cost and easy-acquiring cameras. Results showed that the models predict with an $R^2 = 96\%$ when the nitrogen was absorbed by the crops. There are several future avenues for this model. One of them is the inclusion of other variables in order to expand the inference to chlorophyll and comparing the NNI results with chlorophyll levels (Chlorophyll is usually a common method to infer nitrogen levels in crops). Another avenue is the study of corn in several stages in order to perform a preventive method for applying nitrogen in early stages. It includes the possibility of creating an ML model with several stages included as a whole. Finally, it is important to increase the coverage area of crops. This can be addressed by using fixed wing UAVs.

References

1. Bagheri, N., Ahmadi, H., Alavipanah, S.K., Omid, M.: Multispectral remote sensing for site-specific nitrogen fertilizer management. Pesquisa Agropecuária Brasileira **48**(10), 1394–1401 (2013)
2. Breiman, L.: Random forests. Mach. Learn. **45**(1), 5–32 (2001)
3. Cilia, C., Panigada, C., Rossini, M., Meroni, M., Busetto, L., Amaducci, S., Boschetti, M., Picchi, V., Colombo, R.: Nitrogen status assessment for variable rate fertilization in maize through hyperspectral imagery. Remote Sens. **6**(7), 6549–6565 (2014)
4. Gitelson, A., Merzlyak, M.: Remote sensing of chlorophyll concentration in higher plant leaves. Adv. Space Res. **22**, 689–692 (1998)
5. Guerif, M., Houlés, V., Balet, F.: Remote sensing and detection of nitrogen status in crops. application to precise nitrogen fertilization. In: 4th International Symposium on Intelligent Information Technology in Agriculture, Beijing, October 2007
6. Haboudane, D., Miller, J.R., Pattey, E., Zarco-Tejada, P.J., Strachan, I.B.: Hyperspectral vegetation indices and novel algorithms for predicting green lai of crop canopies: modeling and validation in the context of precision agriculture. Remote Sens. Environ. **90**, 337–352 (2004)
7. Herrmann, A., Taube, F.: The range of the critical nitrogen dilution curve for maize (zea mays l.) can be extended until silage maturity. Agron. J. **96**, 1131–1138 (2004)
8. Lemaire, G., Gastal, F.: N uptake and distribution in plant canopies. In: Lemaire, G. (ed.) Diagnosis of the Nitrogen Status in Crops, pp. 3–43. Springer, Heidelberg (1997)
9. Miura, T., Huete, A.R.: Performance of three reflectance calibration methods for airborne hyperspectral spectrometer data. Sensors **9**(2), 794–813 (2009)
10. Peng, Y., Peng, Y., Li, X., Li, C.: Determination of the critical soil mineral nitrogen concentration for maximizing maize grain yield. Plant Soil **372**(1), 41–51 (2013)
11. Plénet, D., Lemaire, G.: Relationships between dynamics of nitrogen uptake and dry matter accumulation in maize crops. Determination of critical N concentration. Plant Soil **216**(1), 65–82 (1999)
12. Recous, S., Fresneau, C., Faurie, G., Mary, B.: The fate of labelled 15N urea and ammonium nitrate applied to a winter wheat crop. Plant Soil **112**(2), 205–214 (1988)
13. Rondeaux, G., Steven, M., Baret, F.: Optimization of soil-adjusted vegetation indices. Remote Sens. Environ. **55**, 95–107 (1996)
14. Rouse, J.W., Haas, R.H., Schell, J.A., Deering, D.W.: Monitoring vegetation systems in the great plains with ERTS. In: NASA Goddard Space Flight Center 3d ERTS-1 Symposium, pp. 309–317 (1974)
15. Sangoi, L., Ernani, P.R., da Silva, P.R.F.: Maize response to nitrogen fertilization timing in two tillage systems in a soil with high organic matter content. Revista Brasileira de Ci do Solo **31**, 507–517 (2007)
16. Tucker, C.J.: Red and photographic infrared linear combinations for monitoring vegetation. Remote Sens. Environ. **8**, 127–150 (1979)

Multidimensional Analysis Through Argumentation?

Contributions from a Short Food Supply Chain Experience

Rallou Thomopoulos[1(✉)] and Dominique Paturel[2]

[1] INRA IATE Joint Research Unit/INRIA GraphIK, Montpellier, France
rallou.thomopoulos@inra.fr
[2] INRA Innovation Joint Research Unit, Montpellier, France
dominique.paturel@inra.fr

Abstract. The paper introduces a method to evaluate a short food supply chain based on argumentation. It defines an analytical argumentation system using contexts, and introduces indicators to perform analysis. It proposes an evaluation of the experimental device created to observe the short food supply chain mechanisms, based on this analysis methodology. It concludes on the feedback learnt from this analysis, from methodological and application viewpoints.

Keywords: Multicriteria modeling · Risk benefit analysis · Viewpoints

1 Introduction

In recent food-related concerns, short supply chains [3, 6] are considered as a new means of supply that is determined by the close proximity of production to consumption, both geographically and relationally. In 2011–2012, an experimentation was carried out in the department of Hérault in France, to test the feasibility of using short supply chains for the provision of food aid. The aim was to provide a 'proof of concept, the study model being the fruit and vegetable supply of the Hérault branch of the association '*Les restaurants du coeur - relais du coeur*' (denoted AD34).

A need for explanation, analysis and rationalization of the collected results motivated the formal approach proposed in this paper, based on abstract argumentation [1, 5, 7]. In [11], the relevance of the argumentative approach was highlighted regarding cognitive considerations. Recently, several works proved its relevance in social-related concerns, food systems, chains, policies and controversies [2, 4, 8–11]. In the present paper, we revisit argumentation systems to question the meaning of basic notions in a concrete case: What does an extension mean practically? Are rejected arguments not to take into account, as usually considered in the literature? What does the credulous and skeptical semantics express? How can they be exploited from an application point of view? Can argumentation systems enhance the understanding and analysis of the situation?

© Springer International Publishing AG 2017
S. Benferhat et al. (Eds.): IEA/AIE 2017, Part II, LNAI 10351, pp. 268–274, 2017.
DOI: 10.1007/978-3-319-60045-1_29

2 The Experimental Device

The partners involved in the implementation of the device were AD34, Somimon/Mercadis – the managers of the Greater Montpellier National Wholesale Market (MIN) – and the "Innovation" joint research team. In 2011–2012, the dynamic of food supply for the AD34 distribution campaign was monitored chronologically, including all actors: wholesalers, the producers, AD34's volunteers and those who received aid from AD34. The first phase of the evaluation defined the dimensions to be analyzed in the study, namely, the technical, (logistic), economic (added value for producers and wholesalers), social (relations and the sharing of information between stakeholders) and participative (involvement of the actors) dimensions.

In the second phase, information was collected: semi-structured interviews were conducted with producers participating in the device (10 interviews with 8 producers), groupings of producers, coordinators of the agri-food networks in MIN (4 interviews), the two wholesalers (4 interviews), the volunteers responsible for receiving the fruit and vegetables from AD34's warehouse (4 interviews), and other AD34 volunteers (10 interviews with 10 volunteers responsible for the distribution centers). Interviews were conducted throughout the 16 weeks of the distribution campaign.

Moreover, AD34 conducted surveys shortly before the end of the campaign. These were intended for volunteers at the distribution centers and recipients of the food aid, essentially concerned with the technical dimension. For volunteers, all the centers were covered, with a response rate of 77% covering 56 volunteers. For recipients of aid, the survey was conducted on a sample of 10 centers that represented various capacities for aid distribution and for the population group served. 122 people responded. The results of these interviews and surveys provide input for this paper analysis.

3 Formalizing Arguments and Attacks

Arguments discussing the success or failure of the device are presented in Table 1.

Table 1. Arguments about the interest of the device

Arg.	Description	Pro/con	Dimension
A	The device is well accepted when it induces no price loss for producers compared to the classical system	pro	economical
B	Products that are hard to sell in the classical system require little effort for producers in the device	pro	economical
C	Non-standard products are difficult to sell in the classical system	pro	economical
D	Overproduction due to climatic reasons is difficult to sell in the classical system since it leads to an imbalance between supply and demand	pro	economical
E	The device failed when it turned out to be too adverse compared to the classical system	con	economical

(continued)

Table 1. (*continued*)

Arg.	Description	Pro/con	Dimension
F	The device failed when it was too adverse in terms of price	con	economical
G	The device failed when it was too adverse in terms of storage capacity	con	technical
H	The device was a success even with low prices when it took place in a context of low demand, combined with an advantage for producers	pro	economical
I	Reduced transportation cost is a possible advantage	pro	economical
J	The sale of non-standard (e.g. large-size) products is a possible advantage	pro	economical
K	Motivation to participate in a solidarity project is a possible advantage	pro	participative
L	Keeping good business contacts with the wholesalers is a possible advantage	pro	social
M	The device failed when it did not take into account the quantities available on the local market	con	technical
N	For some products, the device was a success despite the inadequacy of the planned dates to the reality of the local market, thanks to the wholesalers' good knowledge of the local market, leading to a new planning proposition	pro	social
O	Large-size products brought logistical difficulties to the volunteers of the distribution centers	con	technical
P	Local fresh products facilitated the volunteers' work from a logistical viewpoint, by avoiding them to sort damaged products	pro	technical
Q	The disposal of products was achieved in reduced time	pro	technical

We can notice that arguments C and D are particular cases of argument B, and that the three of them (B, C, D) disagree with argument A since they express that price is not the only element that may lead to the success of the device. Thus we can note that the attack relation R contains the following attacks: (B, A), (C, A), (D, A).

Arguments I, J, K, L are different variations of argument H. In this set {H, I, J, K, L} all arguments contradict with the prior argument F. Thus we can add the following attacks to the attack relation R: (H, F), (I, F), (J, F), (K, F), (L, F).

Argument N is a counter-example of argument M based on a social benefit of the device. Thus we can add to the attack relation R: (N, M).

Argument O mentions a technical difficulty associated with large-size products. This contrasts with argument J which considers the handling of non-standard products as a positive feature of the device. It also contrasts with argument A which tends to reduce the difficulties encountered by the device to the possible price loss. Thus the following attacks can be added to R: (O, A), (O, J).

Moreover, arguments O and P both focus on logistical aspects of the device. O is a negative one, since it addresses the necessity of cutting large-size products, which is not only time-consuming but also implies space and equipment to do it. On the opposite, P is a positive aspect, since the sorting of damaged products can be avoided in the device. Thus a mutual attack between O and P is declared in R: (O, P), (P, O).

Finally, argument P highlights waste reduction, which counterbalances the economic argument F. Thus we can add to the attack relation R: (P, F).

4   Proposed Model and Indicators

The framework we propose includes several ways of organizing the set of arguments in contexts. Each way provides a partition of A.

Definition 1 (Analytical Argumentation System). An Analytical Argumentation System is a tuple ASS = (A; R; C1 ... Cn) where:

- A is a set of arguments,
- $R \subseteq A \times A$ is an attack relation,
- each Ci is a partition of A. It is thus a breakdown of the set of arguments A into subsets called contexts. By definition of a partition, the set of contexts c belonging to Ci satisfies: $(\cup_{c \in Ci} c = A)$ and $(\cap_{c \in Ci} c = \varnothing)$.
  Several indicators are then associated with the AAS in order to make an analysis.

Definition 2 (Indicators). Given an AAS, the following indicators are computed.

Indicators concerning the polemical status of the system
Let Rej denote the set of rejected arguments, according to [5].

- Ratio of rejected arguments ($|Rej|/|A| \in [0;1]$).
- Number and proportion of rejected arguments per context
- Number of internal and external attacks towards rejected arguments

Indicators concerning the origin of divergent viewpoints
Let Skept the set of skeptically accepted arguments and Cred the set of credulously accepted arguments, according to [5].

- Ratio of skeptically versus credulously accepted arguments ($|Skept|/|Cred| \in [0;1]$).
- Number and proportion of strict credulously accepted arguments per context
- Number of internal and external attacks towards strict credulously accepted arguments

5   Analysis and Discussion

An AAS = (A; R; C1) is instantiated with the following elements:

- A contains the arguments from A to Q described in Sect. 3;
- R contains the attacks indicated in Sect. 3;
- a partition C1 is defined according to the dimensions studied in the device, thus C1 = {economical context, technical context, participative context, social context}.

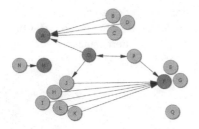

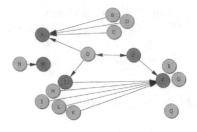

Fig. 1. First preferred extension (Color figure online)

Fig. 2. Second preferred extension (Color figure online)

Figures 1 and 2 show the two preferred extensions (see [5]) of the Dung-style argumentation system AF = (A, R). The arguments displayed in green belong to the extension, those in red do not. We have Rej = {A, F, M} and Cred\Skept = {J, O, P}.

Indicators concerning the polemical status of the system

– Ratio of rejected arguments ($|Rej|/|A| \in [0;1]$).

3 arguments out of 17 are rejected. The ratio of rejected arguments is thus 0.18, which means that a minority of arguments (18%) are attacked without being defended. The first two arguments (A and F) express that the device has to be economically viable to be of interest, the third one (M) claims it has to be aware of the market quantities. Although these arguments express a practical view of the market reality, they were rejected because they needed refining. In summary, the system shows a moderate polemic linked to the refinement of initial common-sense arguments about consideration of the market reality.

– Number and proportion of rejected arguments per context

Figures 3 and 4 show the two preferred extensions partitioned according to C1. The contexts of C1 contain, respectively, {9, 5, 1, 2} arguments, showing the prevalence of economic and technical motivations. The numbers of rejected arguments per context are respectively {2, 1, 0, 0} and their proportions {22%, 20%, 0%, 0%}. We can conclude that the polemic mainly regards economical concerns, and secondarily technical concerns. Indeed, among the rejected arguments, A and F deal with prices, whereas M deals with market quantities.

– Number of internal and external attacks towards rejected arguments

In C1, the numbers of internal attacks (i.e. from the same context) are respectively {6, 0, 0, 0}, and the numbers of external attacks (i.e. from other contexts) are {4, 1, 0, 0}. Surprisingly, economic arguments are mainly internally attacked by other economic arguments, which tends to demonstrate that initial reluctances to consider a possible economic viability of the device had to be revised in the light of the practical implementation of the device and specific conditions (e.g. reduced transportation cost, context of low demand, etc.). External attacks to the economic arguments are quite balanced between the different other contexts (2 from the technical context, 1 from the participative context, 1 from the social context). Their meaning is that economic

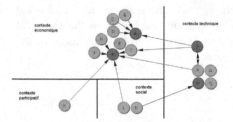 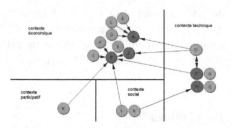

Fig. 3. First preferred extension partitioned according to C1 (the contexts are the dimensions of the study)

Fig. 4. Second preferred extension partioned according to C1 (the contexts are the dimensions of the study)

drawbacks can be counterbalanced by benefits in other concerns (e.g. keeping good business contacts with wholesalers, as expressed by the social argument L). The social context, although containing only 2 arguments, is highly involved in the polemic against rejected arguments, since both social arguments attack a rejected argument. For instance, the technical rejected argument is only attacked by a social one.

Indicators concerning the origin of divergent viewpoints

– Ratio of skeptically *vs* credulously accepted arguments ($|Skept|/|Cred| \in [0;1]$).

14 arguments are credulously accepted, among which 11 are skeptically accepted. The ratio of skeptically versus credulously accepted arguments is 0.79, which expresses a rather consensual debate (79% consensual), although a 21% divergence remains, due to the three arguments that are strict credulously accepted (J, O and P).

The divergence regards two points: (i) whether or not the sale of non-standard size products is a possible advantage, with a divergence between J and O, and (ii) whether the device brings logistic advantage, with a divergence between O and P.

– Number and proportion of strict credulously accepted arguments per context

In C1, the numbers of strict credulously accepted arguments per context are respectively $\{1, 2, 0, 0\}$ and their proportions $\{11\%, 40\%, 0, 0\}$. We can conclude that the technical context plays an important part in divergences. Indeed, among the strict credulously accepted arguments, O and P are technical and deal with logistical issues, whereas J considers the device as an economic opportunity for non-standard products.

– Internal and external attacks towards strict credulously accepted arguments

In C1, the numbers of internal attacks (i.e. from the same context) are respectively $\{0, 2, 0, 0\}$, and the numbers of external attacks (i.e. from other contexts) are $\{1, 0, 0, 0\}$. These figures provide important information: divergences in viewpoints are all related to technical considerations. Indeed, there are no internal discordances except for the technical context, which has an internal dilemma about the logistical benefit of the device (arguments O and P). Moreover, there is only one external attack directed against the economic argument, and this attack is again coming from the technical context (argument O). Thus the technical argument O appears to be a backbone of the divergences expressed in the system.

References

1. Besnard, P., Hunter, A.: Elements of Argumentation, vol. 47. MIT press Cambridge, Cambridge (2008)
2. Bourguet, J.-R., Thomopoulos, R., Mugnier, M.-L., Abécassis, J.: An artificial intelligence based approach to deal with argumentation applied to food quality in a public health policy. Expert Syst. Appl. **40**(11), 4539–4546 (2013). Elsevier
3. Chiffoleau, Y., Degenne, A.: Le développement des circuits courts à l'épreuve de l'analyse des réseaux sociaux. RES **68**(4), 71–78 (2010)
4. Croitoru, M., Thomopoulos, R., Tamani, N.: A practical application of argumentation in French agrifood chains. In: Laurent, A., Strauss, O., Bouchon-Meunier, B., Yager, R.R. (eds.) IPMU 2014. CCIS, vol. 442, pp. 56–66. Springer, Cham (2014). doi:10.1007/978-3-319-08795-5_7
5. Dung, P.M.: On the acceptability of arguments and its fundamental role in nonmonotonic reasoning, logic programming and n-person games. Artif. Intell. J. **77**, 321–357 (1995)
6. Paturel, D., Demarque, F.: Approvisionnement local pour les restaurants du cœur de l'Hérault. Etude de faisabilité réalisée dans le cadre du proa-lr (2011). http://prodinra.inra.fr/ft?id=A3744E7C-9C0C-4973-8560-B25BEC66B152
7. Rahwan I., Simari G. (2009). Argumentation in Artificial Intelligence. Springer
8. Tamani, N., Mosse, P., Croitoru, M., Buche, P., Guillard, V., Guillaume, C., Gontard, N.: An argumentation system for eco-efficient packaging material selection. Comput. Electron. Agric. **113**, 174–192 (2015)
9. Thomopoulos, R., Charnomordic, B., Cuq, B., Abécassis, J.: Artificial intelligence-based decision support system to manage quality of durum wheat products. Qual. Assur. Saf. Crops Foods **1**(3), 179–190 (2009)
10. Thomopoulos, R., Chadli, A., Croitoru, M., Abécassis, J., Brochoire, G., Chiron, H.: Information for decision-making is ubiquitous: revisiting the reverse engineering mode in breadmaking technology. RCIS 2015, pp. 250–261 (2015)
11. Thomopoulos, R., Croitoru, M., Tamani, N.: Decision support for agri-food chains: a reverse engineering argumentation-based approach. Ecol. Inform. **26**(2), 182–191 (2015)

Combined Argumentation and Simulation to Support Decision

Example to Assess the Attractiveness of a Change in Agriculture

Rallou Thomopoulos[1][(✉)], Bernard Moulin[2], and Laurent Bedoussac[3]

[1] INRA UMR IATE/INRIA GraphIK, Montpellier, France
rallou.thomopoulos@inra.fr
[2] Laval University, Quebec, Canada
bernard.moulin@ift.ulaval.ca
[3] ENSFEA/INRA, UMR AGIR, Toulouse, France
laurent.bedoussac@inra.fr

Abstract. Although modeling argument structures is helpful to make involved parties understand the pros and cons of an issue and the context of each other's positions, stakeholders have no means to anticipate the impacts of adopting the debated solutions, let alone to compare them. This is where using simulation approaches would greatly enrich the deliberation process. This paper introduces an approach combining argumentation and simulation. We consider a case study in which both are used to assess and compare cultural options available to farmers.

1 Introduction

Making a decision involving several stakeholders with different objectives requires to take into account qualitative as well as quantitative information: the consequences of each possible decision, the stakeholders' viewpoints and preferences on the decisions, the parameters they considered as indicators. Among public policy decision problems, agri-food chain arbitrations involve various actors, from production to consumption through processing, distribution and recycling. Consequently, besides policy makers' scale, the interests of all the stakeholders of the chain interfere. Given the diversity of their viewpoints, they pursue possibly divergent objectives.

Although international research communities are active both in the argumentation and in the decision fields, most often these domains have been studied separately. [2] can be cited among the earliest formal attempts to combine both. Applications in agronomy have emerged a few years ago and are growing. Recent works have dealt with the interest of argumentation in decisions about agri-food chain steering [6,13,14].

Within this context of argument-supported decision, this paper deals with the combination of qualitative and quantitative approaches. The qualitative model we consider is argumentation. The quantitative one is systems dynamics, which

S. Benferhat et al. (Eds.): IEA/AIE 2017, Part II, LNAI 10351, pp. 275–281, 2017.
DOI: 10.1007/978-3-319-60045-1_30

allows scenario simulation. The difficult point concerns the connections between both formalisms, for which no results are available in the scientific literature. The advance of the proposed approach is to allow for testing the validity of an argument by simulating the scenario resulting from the decision this argument promotes. Therefore it provides a sound way of dealing with a weak point of argumentation in the literature, widely discussed but lacking of practical tools: argument strength evaluation [1,5,6].

2   Formalizing the Decision Problem

Systems dynamics [7] is a mathematical modeling technique which allows analyzing the evolution over time of systems defined by a large number of interdependent variables. One of the variables considered by the system is thus time. We propose the following definition of the studied system.

Definition 1. *The studied **system** is a set $X = \{t, x_1, \ldots, x_n\}$ of variables, where t is time. A **state** of the system is described by an instantiation $V = \{v_t, v_1, \ldots, v_n\}$ of X, where v_t is the value of variable t and for $i \in [1; n]$, v_i is the value of variable x_i.*

We can distinguish three main categories of variables (apart from time):

- constants: their value does not vary over time. They are depicted by black-arrowed circles in the graphical model (see Fig. 1);
- stock variables: they represent the accumulation of a quantity over time and thus correspond to an integral-type function. They are represented as squares in the graphical model;
- the other variables (general case) are depicted by circles in the graphical model.

Definition 2. *X is **partitioned** in two subsets, X_{in} and X_{out}. X_{in} contains the variables whose initial value (in case of constants) or function definition (in case of other variables) can be chosen (or could be in hypothetical scenarios), since they have the meaning of controlled parameters of the system. X_{out} contains the variables of the system on which there is no human control, thus their value is observed but not chosen. Therefore each variable $x_i \in X$ is a function of X_{in}, denoted by F_i.*

To grasp real-world decision schemes, with regard to previous works in multi-criteria decision [4] and argumentation-based decision [2], we integrate within the system description a set of considered options (also called decisions or actions) and a set of considered goals. This yields the following framework:

Definition 3. *A **decision framework** is a couple (x_o, X_G) where:*

- *$x_o \in X_{in}$ is the option variable. Its domain of values is denoted by D_o;*
- *$X_G \subseteq X_{out}$ is a set of goal variables, whose values are to be maximized.*

Decisional approaches of argumentation introduce a distinction between two types of arguments, those justifying beliefs, denoted epistemic arguments, and those justifying actions, denoted practical arguments [8]. In this study we are interested in the latter, on which less literature is available. A formalization is proposed in [2]. To be in accordance with previous works and take into account decision schemes [12], we will consider an argument as a triplet $<Option, Goal, Justification>$. Thus an argument provides a justification for promoting an option in order to achieve a goal. This can be expressed in our framework by the following definition.

An argument is then defined as follows in our framework.

Definition 4. *An **argument** a is a triplet $<o, x_g, J>$, where:*

- *$o \in D_o$, the option promoted by the argument a, is the value chosen for the option variable x_o;*
- *$x_g \in X_G$ is the goal pursued by the argument a;*
- *J, the justification of the argument, is an instantiation of the set of variables $X_{in} \setminus x_o$. It totally defines the state of the system by fixing the values v_i of the variables $x_i \in X_{in} \setminus x_o$.*

Once an argument defined, the next question is how to determine if it sound or not? The principle we propose is to verify if the value of the goal obtained with the settings defined by the argument is the best that would be obtained for any option with the same settings.

Definition 5. *An argument $a = <o, x_g, J>$ is **sound** if $F_g(J \cup \{o\}) = max_{d \in D_o} F_g(J \cup \{d\})$.*

3 Running the Model on the Case Study

In the context of decision support, our work aims at proposing a systematic approach to assess various options available to farmers for cereal-legume intercrops with respect to the corresponding sole crop alternatives. This comparison is possible when considering farmers' gross margin. We specifically address the case of intercropping of durum wheat and legumes.

Intercropping, the simultaneous growth of two or more species in the same field for a significant period, is an application of ecological principles. This practice is particularly suited in low nitrogen input systems where it optimizes the use of nitrogen resources through nitrogen fixation of legumes leading to improved and stabilized yields and increased cereal protein content [3]. Nevertheless, despite their numerous agronomic interests widely demonstrated, intercrops are only slightly adopted by farmers, except for animal feeding and/or in organic farming. Among the main reasons, their potential economic advantage remains questionable because it depends on many factors such as the difference between crop prices, the cost to efficiently separate the grains, but also the input prices and the amount of subsidies. A last issue concerns the way to evaluate the intercrop efficiency by comparing it to sole crops [3]. Indeed, the sole crop reference could be the best sole crop managed with inputs, or with the same amount of inputs as in intercrop, or the average efficiency of the two sole crops. Finally, considering or not the rotation usually leads to strongly different conclusions. A large number of arguments for and against cereal-legume intercropping have been expressed by the main actors of the supply chain [3, 9–11].

Based both on literature review (in particular [3, 10, 11]) and on interviews with domain specialists, various arguments in favor and against cereal-legume intercrops were identified.

"Pro" arguments mainly mentioned:

- the improved soil fertility;
- the reduction of organic nitrogen fertilizers, expensive and unefficient;
- the higher protein content of harvested grain, a quality criterion for durum wheat;
- the better control of weeds;
- the better resistance against plant agressors;
- more stable yields despite climate variability.

"Con" arguments essentially concerned:

- the non-synchronized dates of sow and harvest for the two species;
- the variable composition of harvest;
- the specific sorting operation required;
- the lack of distribution and valorization networks;
- restricted marketing possibilities, due to the absence of a regulatory statute for cereal-legume intercrops;
- discouraging CAP aid policies.

The main indicator that interests us here to reflect the attractiveness of the cultural system for the farmer is the direct gross margin. We consider three value options for the $culturalChoice$ variable: {$soleCereal$, $soleLegume$, $intercrop$}, which respectively correspond to cereal monoculture, legume monoculture and ceral-legume intercrop. Let us examine two economic arguments.

1. The argument in favor of cereal-legume intercrops on the basis of reduced organic nitrogen fertilizers can be formalize as follows: $a_1 = <o_1, x_g1, J_1>$ with $o_1 = intercrop$, $x_g1 = directGrossMargin$, J_1 defined by: unchanged current values for the $publicAids$ variable, adapted values for the $nitrogenInput$ variable (20 nitrogen units economy per year for the intercrop, 40 for sole legume, 0 for sole cereal) and unchanged current values for the $sortingCost$ variable.

2. The argument in favor of sole cereal culture on the basis of avoided sorting operations can be formalize as follows: $a_2 = <o_2, x_g2, J_2>$ with $o_2 = soleCereal$, $x_g2 = directGrossMargin$, J_2 defined by: unchanged current values for the $publicAids$ variable, unchanged current values for the $nitrogenCost$ variable and decreased values (half-reduced) for the $sortingCost$ variable.

Table 1. Results for argument a_1

	Sole cereal option	Sole Legume option	Cereal-legume intercrop option
Goal value (direct gross margin in euro/ha)	977	788	**501**

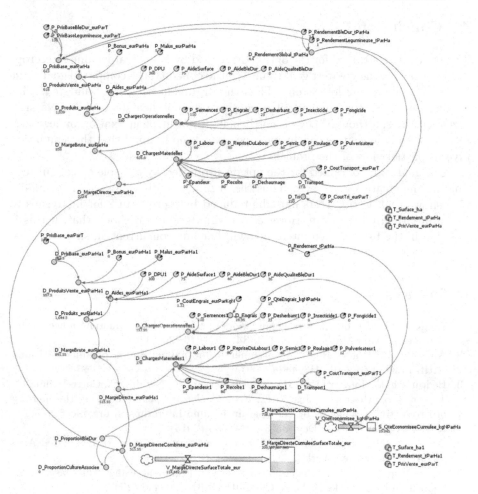

Fig. 1. The generic model run (Anylogic software)

The variable settings of argument a_1 and a_2 are run for the three options. The generic model used is shown in Fig. 1.

Argument a_1 and a_2 obtained the following results (Tables 1 and 2) for a 2-year simulation.

Table 2. Results for argument a_2

	Sole cereal option	Sole Legume option	Cereal-legume intercrop option
Goal value (direct gross margin in euro/ha)	**977**	788	721

4   Conclusion

The goal value obtained for the option promoted by a_1 (cereal-legume intercrop) does not obtain the greatest goal value. On the contrary, the computed goal value for this option is the lowest one. Thus the argument a_1 is not validated. This simulation shows that higher nitrogen costs do not heavily penalize classical cereal cultures, although they do not benefit from nitrogen fixation by legumes. Of course to balance this conclusion, one must keep in mind that the simulation gives a partial view of the problem.

The goal value obtained for the option promoted by a_2 (sole cereal culture) obtains the greatest goal value. Thus the argument a_2 is validated. The simulation shows that sorting costs must be reduced by more than 2 for intercrops to be economivcally attractive. However the simulation also shows that, if this is possible in the future, then intercrops will become concurrential, since the goal value gap is highly reduced.

References

1. Amgoud, L., Cayrol, C.: A reasoning model based on the production of acceptable arguments. Ann. Math. Artif. Intell. **34**, 197–216 (2002)
2. Amgoud, L., Prade, H.: Using arguments for making and explaining decisions. Artif. Intell. **173**(3–4), 413–436 (2009)
3. Bedoussac, L., Journet, E.P., Hauggaard-Nielsen, H., Naudin, C., Corre-Hellou, G., Jensen, E.S., Prieur, L., Justes, E.: Ecological principles underlying the increase of productivity achieved by cereal-grain legume intercrops in organic farming. a review. Agron. Sustain. Dev. **35**(3), 911–935 (2015)
4. Belton, V., Stewart, T.: Multiple Criteria Decision Analysis: An Integrated Approach. Springer, New York (2002)
5. Bench-Capon, T.J.M.: Persuasion in practical argument using value-based argumentation frameworks. J. Logic Comput. **13**(3), 429–448 (2003)
6. Bourguet, J.R., Thomopoulos, R., Mugnier, M.L., Abécassis, J.: An artificial intelligence-based approach to deal with argumentation applied to food quality in a public health policy. Expert Syst. Appl. **40**(11), 4539–4546 (2013)
7. Forrester, J.: Counterintuitive behavior of social systems. Tech. Rev. **73**(3), 52–68 (1971)
8. Harman, G.: Practical aspects of theorical reasoning. In: Mele, A.R., Rawling, P. (eds.) The Oxford Handbook of Rationality, pp. 45–56. Oxford University Press, New York (2004)

9. Magrini, M.B., Triboulet, P., Bedoussac, L.: Pratiques agricoles innovantes et logistique des coopératives agricoles. une étude ex-ante sur l'acceptabilité de cultures associées blé dur-légumineuses. Economie Rurale **338**, 25–45 (2013)
10. Pelzer, E., Bedoussac, L., Corre-Hellou, G., Jeuffroy, M., Métivier, T., Naudin, C.: Association de cultures annuelles combinant une légumineuse et une céréale: retours d'expériences d'agriculteurs et analyse. Innovations Agronomiques **40**, 73–91 (2014)
11. PerfCom Project: Les cultures associées céréale / légumineuse en agriculture "bas intrants" dans le sud de la france (2012). http://www6.montpellier.inra.fr/systerra-perfcom
12. Savage, L.J.: The Foundations of Statistics, 2nd edn. Dover Pub., New York (1972)
13. Tamani, N., Mosse, P., Croitoru, M., Buche, P., Guillard, V., Guillaume, C., Gontard, N.: An argumentation system for eco-efficient packaging material selection. Comput. Electron. Agric. **113**, 174–192 (2015)
14. Thomopoulos, R., Croitoru, M., Tamani, N.: Decision support for agri-food chains: a reverse engineering argumentation-based approach. Ecol. Inform. **26**(2), 182–191 (2015)

Applications of Argumentation

Analysis of Medical Arguments from Patient Experiences Expressed on the Social Web

Kawsar Noor[1]([✉]), Anthony Hunter[1], and Astrid Mayer[2]

[1] Department of Computer Science, University College London, London, UK
kawsar.noor.15@ucl.ac.uk
[2] Department of Oncology, Royal Free London NHS Foundation Trust, London, UK

Abstract. In this paper we present an implemented method for analysing arguments from drug reviews given by patients in medical forums on the web. For this we provide a number of classification rules which allow for the extraction of specific arguments from the drug reviews. For each review we use the extracted arguments to instantiate a Dung argument graph. We undertake an evaluation of the resulting argument graphs by applying Dung's grounded semantics. We demonstrate a correlation between the arguments in the grounded extension of the graph and the rating provided by the user for that particular drug.

1 Introduction

Evidence based medicine stipulates that patients are offered medication and treatment based on scientific evidence published in the medical literature. Whilst patients may find it difficult to relate to medical statistics they are keen to understand benefits, potential side effects and implications on their life and life style. Drug reviews, much like other product reviews on the internet, provide useful insights into the performance and acceptance of the drug amongst patients who have experience of it [2]. Drug review websites contrast with traditional medical resources by providing access to an interesting set of arguments based on personal experiences of the patients. Whilst this reflects the subjective experience of individuals we propose to view the review process as users providing arguments and counter arguments about the drug in question.

If such arguments can be retrieved from drug review websites, it is possible to arrange them using existing argument-theoretic frameworks such as Dung's argument graph [4]. The generation of a Dung graph to represent the arguments in a single drug review, enables one to elicit the overall assessment of the drug based on the evaluation of the argument graph; such evaluations can be achieved using Dung's extensions. In order to validate this assessment it is possible to exploit the rating function provided by drug review websites, which enables users to numerically score the drug. We propose that by correlating the rating, produced by our argument extraction and analysis system, against the numerical rating data given by the drug review author we can ascertain a general measure as to how accurate our analysis was.

© Springer International Publishing AG 2017
S. Benferhat et al. (Eds.): IEA/AIE 2017, Part II, LNAI 10351, pp. 285–294, 2017.
DOI: 10.1007/978-3-319-60045-1_31

We believe this work is a novel contribution because it shows how Dung's approach to analysing arguments is reflected in the way drug review authors evaluate conflicting arguments within a single drug review. This suggests that we could extend the application of our method to those drug review sites that do not have user provided ratings in order to generate analogous ratings. Furthermore our argument-based analysis could provide structured information to patients who are trying to garner an understanding of how the drug was received by previous users. We expect that this tool will provide patients with supplementary reasons for and against the treatment.

Note our method of extracting arguments is not meant as a contribution to argument mining, rather it is a simple method to automate the process of instantiating argument graphs and could potentially be improved by harnessing more advanced argument mining techniques such as those reviewed in [9].

2   Argument Extraction

In the following, we show how simple rule-based information extraction techniques can be harnessed to extract arguments. The implemented system has been written in Python, and makes use of the natural language processing toolkit NLTK[1]. The code and datasets are available on Github[2].

We take reviews from two medical websites (Drugs.com and Webmd.com). Drug reviews on these websites, much like other products tend to focus on a core set of features of the product. We identify a set of common features found across the various reviews. The recurrent themes tend to be centred around the side effects experienced, the overall success of the drug and the general experience with the drug.

> "I get achy$_{side\ effect}$ in the hands and feet, have gained weight$_{side\ effect}$ (20)lbs. and hate$_{negative\ experience}$ the hunger it seems to give me cravings for calorie laden foods."

As can be seen in review above the user's focus is on the side effects of the drug, whilst some words such as 'hate' would indicate that the user had a negative experience with the drug. Similar observations were made when reading a range of different drug reviews. With these observations in mind we identified the following core themes which we use to extract arguments for/against a number of drugs: (1) Presence of side effects; (2) Severity of the side effects; (3) Polarity of experience with the drug; (4) Whether or not supplementary drugs can be taken for side effects from the primary drug.

Each theme is identified through the appearance of key words. Using the example of the theme *presence of side effects*, statements pertaining to this theme are identifiable when a side effect is mentioned; vocabulary for which can be sourced from medical literature. Furthermore each theme can be assessed

---

[1] http://www.nltk.org/.
[2] https://github.com/robienoor/NLTKForumScraper.

for polarity, so continuing the example of the *presence of side effects* theme we say that the resulting argument types are *the absence of a side effect* and *the presence of a side effect*. These argument types thus either favour or oppose the use of that particular drug. Using this approach we formalised 10 classification rules based on the themes mentioned above.

In this paper we assume that each argument is presented in a single sentence. A sentence may convey multiple arguments but no argument requires multiple sentences to convey it. This is a simplifying assumption that we do not further investigate in this paper. The role of the classification rules is to identify the types of argument present in each sentence.

In order to define the classification rules we compiled a number of lists namely `Symptoms`, `Drugs`, `Diseases`, `PosWords`, `NegWords`, `Inverters` and `SideEffects`. The list `SideEffects` contains the term *side effect* in various forms e.g.: *symptoms*, *side-effects* etc. The list `Inverters` contains a list of negating words e.g.: *no*, *not*, *none* etc. These lists serve the purpose of providing quick access to medical and sentiment terminology.

The classification rules below are formalised using first-order logic. Below is a list of predicates that are common across the classification rules.

- `Occur(sentence, wordlist, position)` which holds when there is a word in `wordlist` that occurs at the point `position` in `sentence`
- `ImmediatelyBefore(string1, string2)` which holds when `string1` is the sentence immediately before `string2`.
- `Contains(sentence, wordlist)` which holds when at least one of the words in `wordlist` is in `sentence`.
- `ArgumentType(sentence, type)` which holds when the `sentence` is of type `type`.
- `Score(sentence, wordlist)` is a function that returns the number of words in `wordlist` that occur in `sentence`

With the common predicates defined above we proceed to define all of the individual classification rules. Essentially each rule classifies a sentence to be of a particular type if the conditions of the rule are met for the sentence. A sentence may be classified to be of more than one type (though in practice this is infrequent).

1. **NoSideEffectsI:** This rule looks for an inverter word immediately followed by a side effect string.

    e.g.: *I have* $\underline{no_{inverter}}$ *side* $effects_{sideEffect}$

    $\forall$`sentence, string1, string2`
    `Contains(string1, Inverters)` $\land$ `Contains(string2, SideEffects)`
    $\land$ `ImmediatelyBefore(string1, string2)`
    $\rightarrow$ `ArgumentType(sentence, noSideEffectsType1)`

2. **NoSideEffectsII:** This looks for an inverter word before a side effect string irrespective of its position in the sentence.

e.g.: *During the time I took the medication I did not$_{inverter}$ experience any side effects$_{sideEffect}$ at all*

$\forall$sentence, position1, position2
Occur(sentence, Inverters, position1)
$\land$ Occur(sentence, SideEffects, position2)
$\land$ position1 $<$ position2
$\rightarrow$ ArgumentType(sentence, noSideEffectsType2)

3. **SideEffectsI.** This looks for a side effect string with no inverter words in the preceding words.

e.g.: *The side effects$_{sideEffect}$ outweighed the good*

$\forall$sentence, position1
Occur(sentence, SideEffects, position1)
$\land \neg\exists$position2(
    Occur(sentence, Inverters, position2)
    $\land$ position1 $>$ position2)
$\rightarrow$ ArgumentType(sentence, sideEffectsPresentType1)

4. **SideEffectsII.** This searches for a symptom within a sentence.

e.g.: *The side effects were gradual at first but now they are full blown... fatigue$_{symptom}$ and joint pain$_{symptom}$*

$\forall$sentence
Contains(sentence, Symptoms)
$\land \neg$Contains(sentence, PosWords) $\land \neg$Contains(sentence, NegWords)
$\rightarrow$ ArgumentType(sentence, sideEffectsPresentType2)

5. **BearableSideEffects.** If a side effect and positive word are mentioned we interpret this as meaning that the side effect is present but bearable.

e.g.: *So far my joint pain$_{symptom}$ is better$_{positiveWord}$ and my energy and motivation had noticeably improved$_{positiveWord}$*

$\forall$sentence
Contains(sentence, Symptoms)
$\land$ Score(sentence, Poswords) $>$ Score(sentence, Negwords)
$\rightarrow$ ArgumentType(sentence, bearableSideEffects)

6. **UnbearableSideEffects.** If a side effect and a negative word are mentioned we interpret this as meaning that the side effect is present and unbearable.

e.g.: *I had several fevers$_{symptom}$ and bone pain$_{symptom}$ making it very difficult$_{negativeWord}$ to get up*

$\forall$sentence
Contains(sentence, Symptoms)
$\land$ Score(sentence, Negwords) $>$ Score(sentence, Poswords)
$\rightarrow$ ArgumentType(sentence, unbearableSideEffectsType1)

7. **UnbearableSideEffectsII.** If a side effect is mentioned in a sentence whose sentiment score is neutral we interpret this as meaning that the side effect is present and unbearable.

e.g.: *The constant nightly hot flashes$_{symptomWord}$ and joint pain$_{symptom}$ are irritating$_{negativeWord}$ but yet I'm still hopeful$_{positiveWord}$*

$\forall$sentence
Contains(sentence, Symptoms)
$\land$ Score(sentence, Negwords) = Score(sentence, Poswords)
$\rightarrow$ ArgumentType(sentence, unbearableSideEffectsType2)

8. **PositiveExperience.** The presence of only positive words is interpreted as meaning a positive experience.

e.g.: *I felt much better$_{positiveWord}$ on it*

$\forall$sentence
$\neg$Contains(sentence, Symptoms)
$\land$ Score(sentence, Poswords) > Score(sentence, Negwords)
$\rightarrow$ ArgumentType(sentence, positiveExperience)

9. **NegativeExperience.** The presence of only negative words is interpreted as meaning a negative experience.

e.g.: *Terrible$_{negativeWord}$ terrible$_{negativeWord}$ drug*

$\forall$sentence
$\neg$Contains(sentence, Symptoms)
$\land$ Score(sentence, Negwords) > Score(sentence, Poswords)
$\rightarrow$ ArgumentType(sentence, negativeExperience)

10. **SuppDrugAvailable.** A sentence containing a symptom and another drug, which is not the drug being reviewed, is taken to mean that the patient is taking a supplementary drug. The predicate mainDrug(drug) holds when drug, which the drug being reviewed, is not mentioned in the sentence.

e.g.: *I have anxiety$_{symptom}$ added Ativan$_{suppplementaryDrug}$ to my drugs...*

$\forall$sentence, drug
$\neg$Contains(sentence, Symptoms) $\land$ Contains(sentence, Drugs)
$\land$ $\neg$mainDrug(drug)
$\rightarrow$ ArgumentType(sentence, supplementaryDrugs)

In this section we have formalised 10 classification rules that are used to extract arguments from medical drug reviews. We show in the next section that our classification rules, albeit simple, yield a reasonable performance. The rules could further be improved by harnessing argument mining techniques and natural language processing.

3   Evaluation of Extracted Arguments

The rules mentioned in the previous section were tested against a set of 570 reviews concerning 4 drugs. In order to validate the performance of each of these rules, the extracted arguments were manually checked by a single human annotator (first author) to see if they had been classed correctly. Each extracted argument was marked as being either T (true - the argument was classified correctly), F (false - the argument was classified in the opposite class and could in fact be used as a counter argument) and NA (irrelevant - argument extracted has no relation with its intended class).

Table 1. Accuracy of all arguments pulled out per classification rule

Rule	No. arguments extracted	No. T	% T	%F	%NA
PositiveExperience	368	182	49.46	17.12	33.42
NegativeExperience	446	294	65.92	3.81	30.27
NoSideEffectsI	18	18	100	0	0
NoSideEffectsII	31	17	54.84	22.58	22.58
SideEffectsI	142	114	80.28	7.74	11.97
SideEffectsII	61	52	85.25	4.92	9.84
BearableSideEffects	22	11	50	31.82	18.18
UnbearableSideEffectsI	93	81	87.10	4.30	8.60
UnbearableSideEffectsII	320	261	81.56	7.50	10.94
SuppDrugAvailable	180	21	11.67	2.7	85.56

The results in Table 1 demonstrate that using our classification rules, it is possible to extract relevant arguments regarding treatments. The rules exhibited different precisions (where precision = No. T/No. of Arguments Extracted). For example the rules *NoSideEffectsI* and *PositiveExperience* achieved precisions of 100% and 49.46% respectively. This variability is expected as some of the rules, such as the *PositiveExperience* rule, search for context independent words whereas others search for the occurrence of medical terminology. We also recorded lower precisions when comparing positive sentiment rules to negative ones, e.g.: *BearableSideEffects* vs. *UnbearableSideEffectsI*. We attributed this to our observation that patients rarely mention a side effect without the intent of complaint.

Alongside these difficulties, we encountered a number of natural language challenges, the majority of which were attributed to the casual nature with which authors wrote their reviews. The difficulties encompassed spelling mistakes, adoption of new terms, abbreviations and general violations of English grammar. Another challenge was the use of non-standard terminology to describe side effects. The quote below highlights this kind of issue.

"...my vision seems to be getting weak."

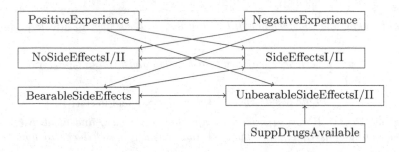

Fig. 1. Argument graph capturing attack relation between the various classification rules.

Discerning a loss of vision from the use of the word *weak* is non-trivial, and is not easily captured using lookup data. Going forward we would seek to improve our classification rules by adopting better natural language processing techniques, and in the case of non standard terminology we could employ techniques such as co-locational data.

4   Evaluation of Argument Graphs

In this section we investigate instantiating an argument graph for each drug review with the arguments extracted from it, we then use Dung's grounded semantics to derive a rating for the drug. We validate these argument-based ratings by correlating them with the numerical ratings given by the authors at the end of their drug reviews.

In order to instantiate the argument graph for a drug review we require a defined set of attack relations for all argument types. In Fig. 1 we specify these attack relations based on observations, of a large number of reviews, of how each argument type influences the numerical ratings provided by the user; more specifically we model the competing levels of influence that the argument types have over the rating with respect to one another. As an example *Positive/Negative Experiences* attack all other arguments of opposing polarity to themselves (e.g.: *NegativeExperience* attacks *NoSideEffectsI/II* and *BearableSideEffects*. This is based on our observation that patients frequently rated in accordance to their overall experience of the drug albeit in the presence/absence of severe/bearable side effects. Other such relationships were observed across the drug reviews and have been represented in our choice of attacks relations.

A consequence of our choice of attack relation is that the grounded extensions of Fig. 1 and any of its subgraphs constitute either entirely positive arguments, negative arguments or an empty set. These three possible sets indicate three polarities (positive, negative and neutral) and serve as our argument-based ratings. In order to validate these ratings we correlate the polarity of a drug review to the numerical value provided by the user. In facilitating this correlation the numerical scale was split into three ranges. We assume that a drug review with a

*I am thankful and consider myself lucky to now be a survivor.*PositiveExperience

↓

*I have experienced major hot flashes day and night.*SideEffectII

↑
↓

*No other side effects at this time.*NoSideEffectsII

Original Post: *"I have experienced major hot flashes day and night..No other side effects at this time..I am thankful and consider myself lucky to now be a survivor"*

Drug: Tamoxifen
User Rating: 8
Grounded Extension: {*PositiveExperience, NoSideEffectsII*}
Argument Evaluation: Positive

Fig. 2. A review for the drug Tamoxifen. Three arguments were extracted. The grounded extension contains only positive arguments and so the argument-based rating is positive.

rating less than 4 to be a negative rating, a drug review with a rating between 5 and 7 to be neutral and any drug review with a rating greater than 7 to be positive. An example of our system in practice, from argument extraction through to analysis, can be seen in Fig. 2.

We ran our experiment using two sets of arguments. In the first set, we used all of the arguments extracted using our classification rules. This was to evaluate the performance of our entire automated process, from argument extraction through to analysis of arguments. In the second set of arguments, we utilised only those extracted arguments which have been annotated as being of type 'T'. By comparing the correlation matrices for both argument sets we are able to measure the effect of inaccuracies in our classification rules on the argument-based ratings.

Table 2. Dung assessment vs. user rating using all posts

Rating	Negative	Neutral	Positive
1–4	0.531	0.443	0.262
5–7	0.198	0.216	0.172
8–10	0.270	0.340	0.566

The results of our experiment in Tables 2 and 3 indicate a positive correlation in the positive and negative classes. It can be seen that there is a notable improvement in correlation in Table 3, given that here we use only validated arguments. The neutral class appears comparatively less correlated with classifications distributed across the ratings scale. What we observed was that reviews

Table 3. Dung assessment vs. user rating using only validated sentences

Rating	Negative	Neutral	Positive
1–4	0.624	0.417	0.129
5–7	0.206	0.202	0.178
8–10	0.170	0.380	0.693

whose constituent arguments predominantly shared the same polarity tended to have a numerical score consistent with this polarity. Drug reviews that have neutral numerical ratings often contained predominantly negative or positive arguments causing us to derive a non-neutral argument-based rating. In other cases it was seen that the author would provide positive and negative statements within a single drug review, and whilst the majority of content was homogeneous in its polarity, one statement may have caused the user to rate otherwise.

5   Discussion and Literature Review

In this paper we have presented an argument-based framework for analysing medical drug reviews to be used by patients who are choosing between multiple treatment options. We have shown how simple domain-specific techniques can be used to extract arguments, but this is only so that we have the necessary input for argument-based analysis. Whilst our work is not intended to be a contribution to argument mining, whose motivation is the automated the extraction of argument components, primarily premises and conclusions, from text [3,6,11], we acknowledge that techniques from argument mining could be employed to improve our system.

Our work resembles [10] which proposes the use of lookup data in conjunction with argument schemes to mine user generated arguments from online camera reviews. Whilst that paper successfully mines arguments for a specific product, it does not provide an evaluation of arguments mined using any argument solver, whereas evaluating arguments is the primary aim of our paper.

Our approach was to identify a small set of argument types common across all drug reviews and then construct classification rules to extract those argument types. This is in contrast to a manual annotation approach as in [5] which extracted arguments from a set of reviews and put them together in a single argument graph. Our approach enabled us to fully automate our entire system, from extraction through to analysis. It also ensured we had to only construct a single set of attack relations which we imposed on all of our drug reviews.

Going forward we will seek to extend the evaluation of the arguments by making use of the quantity of arguments populated for a given argument class. We will also consider using preference-based frameworks [1], probabilistic frameworks [7] and social abstract argumentation [8] to allow us to model argument types that are more frequent and yield greater influence over the overall patient ratings. We will also investigate the possibility of learning the attack relations by analysing the numerical rating of a drug review and attempting to construct an argument graph such that we maximise correlations between our argument-analysis rating and the numerical rating.

Acknowledgements. The first author is grateful to the The Royal Free Charity and the EPSRC for funding his PhD studentship. The authors are grateful to the reviewers for their helpful feedback.

References

1. Amgoud, L., Vesic, S.: Repairing preference-based argumentation systems. In: Proceedings of International Joint Conference on Artificial Intelligence, pp. 665–670 (2009)
2. Cole, J., Watkins, C., Kleine, D.: Health advice from internet discussion forums: how bad is dangerous? J. Med. Internet Res. **18**(1), e4 (2016)
3. Sardianos, G.P.C., Katakis, I., Karkaletsis, V.: Argument extraction from news. In: Proceedings of the 2nd Workshop on Argumentation Mining, Association for Computational Linguistics, pp. 56–66 (2015)
4. Dung, P.M.: On the acceptability of arguments and its fundamental role in non-monotonic reasoning, logic programming, and n-person games. Artif. Intell. **77**, 321–357 (1995)
5. Gabbriellini, S., Santini, F.: A micro study on the evolution of arguments in amazon.com's reviews. In: Chen, Q., Torroni, P., Villata, S., Hsu, J., Omicini, A. (eds.) PRIMA 2015. LNCS, vol. 9387, pp. 284–300. Springer, Cham (2015). doi:10.1007/978-3-319-25524-8_18
6. Huangbo, H., Mercer, R.: An automated method to build a corpus of rhetorically-classified sentences in biomedical texts. In Proceedings of the First Workshop on Argumentation Mining, Association for Computational Linguistics, pp. 19–23 (2014)
7. Hunter, A., Thimm, M.: On partial information and contradictions in probabilistic abstract argumentation. In: Proceedings of the 15th International Conference on Principles of Knowledge Representation and Reasoning, pp. 53–62 (2016)
8. Leite, J., Martins, J.: Social abstract argumentation. In: Proceedings of the Twenty-Second International Joint Conference on Artificial Intelligence, vol. 3, pp. 2287–2292 (2011)
9. Lippi, M., Torroni, P.: Argumentation mining: state of the art and emerging trends. ACM Trans. Internet Technol. **16**, 1–25 (2016)
10. Schneider, J.: Semi-automated argumentative analysis of online product reviews. In: Proceedings of COMMA 2012: Computational Models of Arguments, pp. 43–50 (2012)
11. Teufel, S.: Argumentative zoning: Information extraction from scientific text. PhD Thesis, School of Cognitive Science, University of Edinburgh, Edinburgh, UK (1999)

A Dynamic Logic Framework
for Abstract Argumentation:
Adding and Removing Arguments

Sylvie Doutre[1(✉)], Faustine Maffre[1], and Peter McBurney[2]

[1] IRIT, Université Toulouse 1 Capitole, Toulouse, France
doutre@irit.fr
[2] King's College London, London, UK

Abstract. A dynamic framework, based on the Dynamic Logic of Propositional
Assignments (DL-PA), has recently been proposed for Dung's abstract argument
system. This framework allows the addition and the removal of attacks, and the
modification of the acceptance status of arguments. We here extend this framework in order to capture the addition and the removal of arguments. We then
apply the framework on an access control case, where an agent engages in an
argued dialogue to access some information controlled by another agent.

1 Introduction

In Dung's approach to argumentation [7], an argument system is represented as a set
of (abstract) arguments and a binary attack relation between these arguments. Several
semantics—ways to evaluate which arguments should be accepted—have been developed from this model (see [2]), some of them referred as "extension-based". These are
semantics which define acceptable sets of arguments, called extensions.

Logical representations of Dung's approach of argumentation have been presented,
based for instance on propositional logic [3], or more recently on dynamic logic [6]. In
these contributions, the argument system is described by a boolean formula and each
type of semantics is also represented by a boolean formula; for a given semantics, any
interpretation of the propositional variables for which both formulas are true characterizes an extension. In [6], the use of a dynamic logic (DL-PA—Dynamic Logic of
Propositional Assignments [1]) furthermore allows us to model updates of the argument system, such as addition or removal of an attack, or modification of extensions.
[6] is not the only approach which has tackled the question of the dynamics of argument systems (see [5,15] for instance), but this one provides a single framework which
encompasses at the same time the argument system, the logical definition of the change
to enforce, and the change operations to perform. Moreover, the logic it is based on
is non-specific to argumentation since it has already been applied in various contexts
[8,12].

Following an idea that was triggered in [6], we extend [6]'s framework to capture
addition and removal of arguments. An extension of Dung's system is proposed to take
into account, within the set of arguments, those which are currently considered, or,

say, enabled. The formulas that describe the argument system and the semantics are modified to take into account this new notion of enabled arguments. We illustrate our contribution with an example from [14], in which the authors present a protocol for agents engaging in an argued dialogue to access some information.

The paper is organized as follows. In the next section we introduce the example of access control dialogue that we will use throughout the paper. In Sect. 3 we show how to extend the framework of [6] to capture addition and removal of arguments. In Sect. 4 we show how this extension can be used to formalize updates of the argument system during the dialogue. Section 5 concludes.

2   Our Running Example

In this example taken from [14], an agent, called the *client* (here, Brussels agent), wants to access some information. He engages a dialogue with the agent controlling it—the *server* (London agent)—in order to convince him to grant authorization to access this information. The second agent explains the reasons why he cannot give this access by presenting all the arguments attacking the client's arguments that he knows.

"Robert is a British businessman visiting Brussels for a meeting. During his visit he becomes ill and is taken unconscious into hospital. The staff of the hospital suspect Robert has had a heart attack and seek to prescribe appropriate drugs for his condition. Unfortunately the safe choice of drugs depends upon various factors, including prior medical conditions that Robert might have and other drugs he may be taking. The hospital's agent is given the goal of finding out the required information about Robert, from the agent representing his London doctor.

In order to gain access to information about Robert, the agent of Brussels Hospital (B. agent) establishes the following dialogue with the London agent (L. agent):

0. **B. agent:** I would like to dialog with the agent of Robert's British doctor; I request Robert's health record.
1. **L. agent:** I cannot provide you Robert's health record because Robert has only given his British doctor limited consent to pass on his personal information (argument a_1).
2. **B. agent:** This record could possibly include information that could affect the treatment of Robert's heart failure. I request it, Robert's life may be at stake (argument a_2)!
3. **L. agent:** I cannot divulge this information, because British law prohibits passing on information without the consent of the provider of the information (argument a_3).
4. **B. agent:** EC law takes precedence over British law when it would be in the interests of the owner to divulge the information (argument a_4). You should allow me to access the record.
5. **L. agent:** Only Robert could decide what would be in his interests (argument a_5).
6. **B. agent:** Robert's doctor owes a duty of care to Robert and, should he die, the doctor might be sued by his family, or the Brussels hospital, or both (argument a_6).
7. **L. agent:** OK. I provide you the requested record: Robert's history of diabetes is..."

Some arguments are directly in favor of giving the permission to access the information (a_2 and a_6), some are directly against this permission (a_1 and a_3), while others are not directly linked to the permission (a_4 and a_5) but contradict other arguments. The dialogue ends after London agent has implicitly considered acceptable Brussels' final argument (a_6), which supports the permission to give the requested information to Brussels. No such argument was acceptable for London agent earlier in the dialogue.

In this paper, we focus on capturing the evolution of the acceptability of arguments for London agent, after each addition of argument. This can be seen as an a posteriori analysis of the dialogue, that allows us to understand the reasons why the permission to access the information was first refused, and then given.

3   Representing Argument Systems

We extend here the definition of an argument system, and of its logical formalization [6]. We present DL-PA logic and how to compute extensions with DL-PA programs.

3.1   Logical Representation of an Argument System

Argument System. In order to capture addition and removal of arguments, we add a component to Dung's argument system [7]: the set of currently considered ("enabled") arguments, among all the arguments of the system. These arguments are those which are known, at some step, in the context of a dialogue.

Definition 1. *An* argument system for enablement *is a tuple* $\mathcal{F} = (\mathcal{A}, \mathcal{A}^{En}, R)$ *where* $\mathcal{A}$ *is a finite set of abstract arguments;* $\mathcal{A}^{En} \subseteq \mathcal{A}$ *is the set of* enabled *arguments, and* $R \subseteq \mathcal{A} \times \mathcal{A}$ *is the attack relation:* $(a, b) \in R$ *means that a attacks b.*

$\mathcal{A}$ contains all possible arguments that may arise during the dialogue, while $\mathcal{A}^{En}$ constitutes the set of arguments that have been uttered until now.

An argument system for enablement is represented by a directed graph whose nodes are enabled arguments and edges are attacks between enabled arguments: there is an edge between a and b if $(a, b) \in R$, $a \in \mathcal{A}^{En}$ and $b \in \mathcal{A}^{En}$. Hence the representation contains less information than the original model. Note that as soon as an argument is enabled, all its attacks from (resp. to) other arguments are considered. When $\mathcal{A}^{En} = \mathcal{A}$, the argument system for enablement comes down to Dung's argument system.

Example 1. In our running example, six arguments were presented during the dialogue: $\mathcal{A} = \{a_1, a_2, a_3, a_4, a_5, a_6\}$. Let us write $\mathcal{F}_i = (\mathcal{A}, \mathcal{A}_i^{En}, R)$ the argument system at step i (steps are numbered as in Sect. 2, from 0 to 6). The attack relation, from the point of view of London agent, and according to [14], is $R = \{(a_1, a_2), (a_3, a_2), (a_4, a_3), (a_5, a_4), (a_6, a_1), (a_6, a_3)\}$.

At step 0, no argument is considered: $\mathcal{A}_0^{En} = \emptyset$. Then, a_1 is uttered: $\mathcal{A}_1^{En} = \{a_1\}$. This argument is not attacked nor attacks any enabled argument; the graph that represents the argument system thus is:

$$a_1$$

Then a_2 is presented ($\mathcal{A}_2^{En} = \{a_1, a_2\}$) and the graph becomes:

$$a_1 \longrightarrow a_2$$

The dialogue goes on until all arguments are presented:

$$a_1 \longrightarrow a_2 \longleftarrow a_3 \longleftarrow a_4 \longleftarrow a_5$$
$$a_6$$

The set of enabled arguments $\mathcal{A}_6^{En}$ is then equal to $\mathcal{A}$.

In order to logically represent an argument system for enablement $\mathcal{F}$, we extend the language of [6]. As in [6], a set of attack variables is used to represent attacks:

$$\text{ATT}_{\mathcal{A}} = \{\text{Att}_{a,b} : (a, b) \in \mathcal{A} \times \mathcal{A}\}.$$

$\text{Att}_{a,b}$ means that a attacks b. We consider in addition a set of *enablement variables*:

$$\text{EN}_{\mathcal{A}} = \{\text{En}_a : a \in \mathcal{A}\},$$

where En_a means that a is enabled (or "considered").

Let $\mathcal{L}_{\text{Att,En}}$ be the set of all formulas that are built variables from $\text{ATT}_{\mathcal{A}} \cup \text{EN}_{\mathcal{A}}$. The *theory* describing the framework $\mathcal{F} = (\mathcal{A}, \mathcal{A}^{En}, R)$ is the following boolean formula:

$$\text{Th}_{\mathcal{F}} = \left(\bigwedge_{(a,b)\in R} \text{Att}_{a,b} \right) \wedge \left(\bigwedge_{(a,b)\notin R} \neg\text{Att}_{a,b} \right) \wedge \left(\bigwedge_{a\in\mathcal{A}^{En}} \text{En}_a \right) \wedge \left(\bigwedge_{a\notin\mathcal{A}^{En}} \neg\text{En}_a \right)$$

Note that in the theory, $\text{Att}_{a,b}$ is true even if a or b are not enabled. This is required to not loose any information, and will be important for updates (see Sect. 4).

Example 2. We have 6 arguments in our running example. This means that $\text{ATT}_{\mathcal{A}}$ contains 36 variables and $\text{EN}_{\mathcal{A}}$ contains 6 variables. Therefore, whatever the step i of the dialogue, $\text{Th}_{\mathcal{F}_i}$ is a conjunction of 42 literals. For simplification, we do not write explicitly every attack literal $\text{Att}_{a,b}$ and $\neg\text{Att}_{a,b}$ (Att_{a_1,a_2}, Att_{a_3,a_2}, and $\neg\text{Att}_{a_1,a_3} \ldots$) but we keep the expression $(\bigwedge_{(a,b)\in R} \text{Att}_{a,b}) \wedge (\bigwedge_{(a,b)\notin R} \neg\text{Att}_{a,b})$. Note that, since in our case the attack relation R is constant, this expression remains constant.

As examples, the theory at step 0 is:

$$\text{Th}_{\mathcal{F}_0} = \left(\bigwedge_{(a,b)\in R} \text{Att}_{a,b} \right) \wedge \left(\bigwedge_{(a,b)\notin R} \neg\text{Att}_{a,b} \right) \wedge \neg\text{En}_{a_1} \wedge \neg\text{En}_{a_2} \wedge \neg\text{En}_{a_3} \wedge \neg\text{En}_{a_4} \wedge \neg\text{En}_{a_5} \wedge \neg\text{En}_{a_6}$$

and the theory at step 3 is:

$$\text{Th}_{\mathcal{F}_3} = \left(\bigwedge_{(a,b)\in R} \text{Att}_{a,b} \right) \wedge \left(\bigwedge_{(a,b)\notin R} \neg\text{Att}_{a,b} \right) \wedge \text{En}_{a_1} \wedge \text{En}_{a_2} \wedge \text{En}_{a_3} \wedge \neg\text{En}_{a_4} \wedge \neg\text{En}_{a_5} \wedge \neg\text{En}_{a_6}$$

Argumentation Semantics. Given an argument system, an acceptability semantics identifies a set of extensions, i.e., acceptable sets of arguments. There may be none, one or several extensions. As in [6], we characterize extensions thanks to a set of *acceptability* variables:

$$IN_{\mathcal{A}} = \{In_a : a \in \mathcal{A}\}$$

where In_a stands for "argument a is in the extension".

Without the notion of enabled arguments (that is, when all arguments are always considered), it has already been shown how to encode the stable, admissible and complete semantics with propositional formulas [6]. These definitions can be adapted to consider enabled arguments only. In this case, extensions are subsets of $\mathcal{A}^{En}$ and only attacks between arguments from $\mathcal{A}^{En}$ are considered. In the corresponding formulas, we only include an argument if it is enabled. Also, attacks must be considered only if they link enabled arguments. To this end, we define the following formula: $Att_{a,b}^{En} = Att_{a,b} \wedge En_a \wedge En_b$. Now we can easily transform formulas from [6]: we check if the argument is enabled, otherwise it will not be included in the extension, and we replace attacks variables $Att_{a,b}$ by formulas $Att_{a,b}^{En}$ to ensure they are indeed present. We illustrate this transformation to capture the *stable* semantics. Let $\mathcal{L}_{Att,En,In}$ be the language of formulas built from $\mathbb{P} = ATT_{\mathcal{A}} \cup EN_{\mathcal{A}} \cup IN_{\mathcal{A}}$.

Definition 2. *Let* $\mathcal{F} = (\mathcal{A}, \mathcal{A}^{En}, R)$ *be an argument system for enablement. Let* $S \subseteq \mathcal{A}^{En}$ *be a set of enabled arguments.* S *is* conflict-free *if* $\forall a, b \in S$, $(a, b) \notin R$. S *is a* stable extension *if* S *is conflict-free and* $\forall b \in \mathcal{A}^{En} \backslash S$, $\exists a \in S$ *such that* $(a, b) \in R$ *(any considered argument outside the extension is attacked by at least one in the extension).*

Note that we do not need to restrict R to the set of considered arguments as a and b both belong to S which is a subset of $\mathcal{A}^{En}$.

The following formula captures the stable semantics[1]:

$$Stable_{\mathcal{A}} = \bigwedge_{a \in \mathcal{A}} \left(\left(En_a \rightarrow \left(In_a \leftrightarrow \neg \bigvee_{b \in \mathcal{A}} (In_b \wedge Att_{b,a}^{En}) \right) \right) \wedge \left(\neg En_a \rightarrow \neg In_a \right) \right)$$

Extensions and Valuations. A *valuation* is a subset of the set of variables $\mathbb{P} = ATT_{\mathcal{A}} \cup EN_{\mathcal{A}} \cup IN_{\mathcal{A}}$: the variables that are currently true. The set of all valuations is $2^{\mathbb{P}}$. Valuations are denoted by v, v', v_1, v_2, etc. A given valuation determines the truth value of the boolean formulas of the language $\mathcal{L}_{Att,En,In}$ in the usual way. For a formula φ, a valuation where φ is true is called a *model of* φ and the set of models of φ is denoted by $\|\varphi\|$. A formula is propositionally valid if it is true in all valuations, i.e., if $\|\varphi\| = 2^{\mathbb{P}}$. The following results are adapted from [6].

Proposition 1. *Let* $\mathcal{F} = (\mathcal{A}, \mathcal{A}^{En}, R)$ *be an argument system for enablement. Let* $E \subseteq \mathcal{A}^{En}$. *Consider* $v_E = \{Att_{a,b} : (a, b) \in R\} \cup \{En_a : a \in \mathcal{A}^{En}\} \cup \{In_a : a \in E\}$. E *is a* stable *extension of* $\mathcal{F}$ *if and only if* v_E *is a model of* $Th_{\mathcal{F}} \wedge Stable_{\mathcal{A}}$.

---

[1] An equivalent way to express these formulas would be to use the set of enabled arguments. For example, to describe the stable extensions, we would write: $Stable_{\mathcal{A}, \mathcal{A}^{En}} = \bigwedge_{a \in \mathcal{A}^{En}} (In_a \leftrightarrow \neg \bigvee_{b \in \mathcal{A}^{En}} (In_b \wedge Att_{b,a})) \wedge \bigwedge_{a \notin \mathcal{A}^{En}} \neg In_a$. This highlights the fact that when all arguments are enabled, i.e., when $\mathcal{A}^{En} = \mathcal{A}$, we indeed retrieve formulas presented in [6].

Example 3. Let us consider $\mathcal{F}_3 = (\mathcal{A}, \mathcal{A}_3^{En}, R)$ with $\mathcal{A}$ and R as in Example 1 and $\mathcal{A}_3^{En} = \{a_1, a_2, a_3\}$.

$$a_1 \longrightarrow a_2 \longleftarrow a_3$$

Let $v_{Th} = \{Att_{a,b} : (a, b) \in R\} \cup \{En_{a_1}, En_{a_2}, En_{a_3}\}$. Note that the theory $Th_{\mathcal{F}_3}$ (see Example 2) is true in v_{Th}. $\mathcal{F}_3$ has only one stable extension: $\{a_1, a_3\}$. Hence $v_{\{a_1, a_3\}} = v_{Th} \cup \{In_{a_1}, In_{a_3}\}$ is a model of $Th_{\mathcal{F}_3} \wedge Stable_{\mathcal{A}}$.

3.2   DL-PA: Dynamic Logic of Propositional Assignments

Dynamic Logic of Propositional Assignments DL-PA [1, 10] is a variant of Propositional Dynamic Logic PDL [9], with operators for sequential and nondeterministic composition of programs, test and iteration (the Kleene star), but where atomic programs are assignments of truth values to propositional variables. Modal operators associated to programs can express that some property holds after the modification of the current valuation by the program. In our case, they will allow us to update the theory associated to the argument system as the dialogue progresses.

We will see that the results from [6] are still applicable in our framework. Hence we also consider the star-free version of DL-PA [10] with the converse operator.

Language. The language DL-PA is defined by the following grammar:

$$\pi ::= p \leftarrow \top \mid p \leftarrow \bot \mid \varphi? \mid \pi; \pi \mid \pi \cup \pi \mid \pi^-$$
$$\varphi ::= p \mid \neg\varphi \mid \varphi \vee \varphi \mid \langle\pi\rangle\varphi$$

where p ranges over $\mathbb{P}$.

The formula $\langle\pi\rangle\varphi$ reads "after some execution of the program π formula φ holds". The formula $[\pi]\varphi$, abbreviating $\neg\langle\pi\rangle\neg\varphi$, reads "after every execution of the program π formula φ holds". The *atomic programs* $p \leftarrow \top$ and $p \leftarrow \bot$ respectively make p true and make p false. The operators of sequential composition (";"), nondeterministic composition ("$\cup$") and test ("(.)?") are from PDL. The operator "(.)$^-$" is the converse operator: the formula $\langle\pi^-\rangle\varphi$ reads "before some execution of the program π formula φ was true". Other boolean operators are abbreviated as usual. Like in PDL, skip abbreviates $\top$? ("nothing happens").

Semantics and Validity. Models of DL-PA formulas are subsets of the set of propositional variables $\mathbb{P}$, i.e., valuations. DL-PA programs are interpreted by means of a relation between valuations. Atomic programs $p \leftarrow \top$ and $p \leftarrow \bot$ are interpreted as update operations on valuations, and complex programs are interpreted just as in PDL by mutual recursion. Table 1 gives the interpretation of the DL-PA connectives.

Two formulas φ_1 and φ_2 are *formula equivalent* if $\|\varphi_1\| = \|\varphi_2\|$. Two programs π_1 and π_2 are *program equivalent* if $\|\pi_1\| = \|\pi_2\|$. In that case we write $\pi_1 \equiv \pi_2$. An expression is a formula or a program; equivalence is preserved under replacement of a sub-expression by an equivalent expression [1]. A formula φ is DL-PA *valid* if it is true in all valuations, i.e., if $\|\varphi\| = 2^{\mathbb{P}}$.

Table 1. Interpretation of the DL-PA connectives

$$\|p \leftarrow \top\| = \{(v_1, v_2) : v_2 = v_1 \cup \{p\}\} \qquad \|p\| = \{v : p \in v\}$$
$$\|p \leftarrow \bot\| = \{(v_1, v_2) : v_2 = v_1 \setminus \{p\}\} \qquad \|\neg\varphi\| = 2^{\mathbb{P}} \setminus \|\varphi\|$$
$$\|\varphi?\| = \{(v, v) : v \in \|\varphi\|\} \qquad \|\varphi \vee \psi\| = \|\varphi\| \cup \|\psi\|$$
$$\|\pi; \pi'\| = \|\pi\| \circ \|\pi'\| \qquad \|\langle\pi\rangle\varphi\| = \{v : \text{ there is } v' \text{ s.t.}$$
$$\|\pi \cup \pi'\| = \|\pi\| \cup \|\pi'\| \qquad (v, v') \in \|\pi\| \text{ and } v' \in \|\varphi\|\}$$
$$\|\pi^-\| = \|\pi\|^{-1}$$

3.3 Constructing Extensions with DL-PA

As in [6], we can build extensions of an argument system by means of DL-PA programs. We recall the program vary(P), from [6], with $P = \{p_1, \ldots, p_n\}$ a set of variables:

$$\text{vary}(P) = (p_1 \leftarrow \top \cup p_1 \leftarrow \bot); \ldots; (p_n \leftarrow \top \cup p_n \leftarrow \bot)$$

vary(P) is a sequence of subprograms, each step i of the sequence nondeterminiscally setting the value of p_i to true or to false. (Note that the ordering of the p_i does not matter.) Executing vary(P) from a valuation v will lead to any valuation where variables from $\mathbb{P} \setminus P$ have the same value than in v, while variables from P can have any value.

Given an argument system $\mathcal{F}$, the idea of [6] is to start from a valuation where the theory $\text{Th}_{\mathcal{F}}$ is verified, and vary accessibility variables In_a; this leads to several valuations, some corresponding to an extension. To "filter" these valuations to keep stable extensions only, we test the formula capturing the semantics (see Sect. 3.1). More formally, we use the following program to build stable extensions:

$$\text{makeExt}_{\mathcal{A}}^{\text{Stable}} = \text{vary}(\text{IN}_{\mathcal{A}}); \text{Stable}_{\mathcal{A}}?$$

Example 4. In Example 3, we have seen that $v_{\{a_1,a_3\}} = v_{\text{Th}} \cup \{\text{In}_{a_1}, \text{In}_{a_3}\}$ is the only stable extension. $\text{Th}_{\mathcal{F}_3}$ is true in this valuation thanks to v_{Th}, and the values of the accessibility variables describe the extension. Executing $\text{makeExt}_{\mathcal{A}}^{\text{Stable}}$ from, e.g., v_{Th}, will lead exactly to $v_{\{a_1,a_3\}}$; $\text{Stable}_{\mathcal{A}}$ is not true for any other valuation linked by vary($\text{IN}_{\mathcal{A}}$).

The following results are adapted from [6].

Lemma 1. *Let $\mathcal{F}$ be an argument system for enablement. Let v_1 be a model of $\text{Th}_{\mathcal{F}}$. Then $(v_1, v_2) \in \|\text{makeExt}_{\mathcal{A}}^{\text{Stable}}\|$ if and only if v_2 is a model of $\text{Th}_{\mathcal{F}} \wedge \text{Stable}_{\mathcal{A}}$.*

The main result about the construction of extensions with DL-PA is as follows.

Proposition 2. *Let $\mathcal{F} = (\mathcal{A}, \mathcal{A}^{En}, R)$ be an argument system for enablement. The following equivalence is DL-PA valid:*

$$\text{Th}_{\mathcal{F}} \wedge \text{Stable}_{\mathcal{A}} \leftrightarrow \langle(\text{makeExt}_{\mathcal{A}}^{\text{Stable}})^-\rangle\text{Th}_{\mathcal{F}}$$

Remember that $\langle\pi^-\rangle\varphi$ means "before some execution of the program π formula φ was true". This indeed corresponds to the update of $\text{Th}_{\mathcal{F}}$ by $\text{makeExt}_{\mathcal{A}}^{\text{Stable}}$.

4   Updating the Argument System Throughout the Dialogue

With the extended framework, we are now able to model changes that may happen in a dialogue, that is, addition, and possibly, removal of arguments. We update the theory corresponding to an argument system to this end:

$$\text{Th}_{\mathcal{F}} \diamond \text{En}_a = \langle (\text{En}_a \leftarrow \top)^- \rangle \text{Th}_{\mathcal{F}}$$

$$\text{Th}_{\mathcal{F}} \diamond \neg \text{En}_a = \langle (\text{En}_a \leftarrow \bot)^- \rangle \text{Th}_{\mathcal{F}}$$

where $\text{Th}_{\mathcal{F}} \diamond \text{En}_a$ refers to updating the system to add (enable) argument a and $\text{Th}_{\mathcal{F}} \diamond \neg \text{En}_a$ to updating the system to remove (disable) argument a. Since attacks are already in the theory even if arguments are not considered, we do not need to include them in our update: all the attacks from (resp. to) a to (resp. from) other enabled arguments, are considered. The framework, being an extension of [6], however allows us to remove some of these attacks, or add extra ones, if necessary.

Example 5. In our running example, at step 0, $\mathcal{A}_0^{En} = \emptyset$, and $\text{Th}_{\mathcal{F}_0}$ is as described in Example 2. At step 1, argument a_1 is enabled. The theory is thus updated as follows:

$$\text{Th}_{\mathcal{F}_0} \diamond \text{En}_{a_1} = \langle (\text{En}_{a_1} \leftarrow \top)^- \rangle \text{Th}_{\mathcal{F}_0}$$

Using properties of DL-PA, we explain in details this update. First, it is shown in [6] that $(p \leftarrow \top)^-$ is equivalent to $p? \cup (p?; p \leftarrow \bot)$ (p is now true and was either already true or was false). Hence:

$$\text{Th}_{\mathcal{F}_0} \diamond \text{En}_{a_1} \equiv \langle \text{En}_{a_1}? \cup (\text{En}_{a_1}?; \text{En}_{a_1} \leftarrow \bot) \rangle \text{Th}_{\mathcal{F}_0}$$

DL-PA shares most properties about program operators with PDL [1], such as:

$$\langle \pi \cup \pi' \rangle \varphi \leftrightarrow \langle \pi \rangle \varphi \vee \langle \pi' \rangle \varphi \qquad \langle \pi; \pi' \rangle \varphi \leftrightarrow \langle \pi \rangle \langle \pi' \rangle \varphi \qquad \langle \chi? \rangle \varphi \leftrightarrow \chi \wedge \varphi$$

Using these, we can transform our updated theory:

$$\text{Th}_{\mathcal{F}_0} \diamond \text{En}_{a_1} \equiv (\text{En}_{a_1} \wedge \text{Th}_{\mathcal{F}_0}) \vee (\text{En}_{a_1} \wedge \langle \text{En}_{a_1} \leftarrow \bot \rangle \text{Th}_{\mathcal{F}_0})$$

The first part of the disjunction is equivalent to $\bot$ since $\text{Th}_{\mathcal{F}_0}$ is a conjunction of literals and one is $\neg \text{En}_{a_1}$. For the second part, we consider two properties of DL-PA [1]:

$$\langle p \leftarrow \top \rangle (\varphi \wedge \varphi') \leftrightarrow \langle p \leftarrow \top \rangle \varphi \wedge \langle p \leftarrow \top \rangle \varphi' \qquad \langle p \leftarrow \top \rangle \neg \varphi \leftrightarrow \neg \langle p \leftarrow \top \rangle \varphi$$

With these equivalences, we know that in $\langle \text{En}_{a_1} \leftarrow \bot \rangle \text{Th}_{\mathcal{F}_0}$, the operator $\langle \text{En}_{a_1} \leftarrow \bot \rangle$ can distribute over the conjunction and be placed before every literal of $\text{Th}_{\mathcal{F}_0}$, and that for negative literals, $\langle \text{En}_{a_1} \leftarrow \bot \rangle$ can be "pushed" against the variable. We obtain:

$$\text{Th}_{\mathcal{F}_0} \diamond \text{En}_{a_1} \equiv \text{En}_{a_1} \wedge \left(\bigwedge_{(a,b) \in R} \langle \text{En}_{a_1} \leftarrow \bot \rangle \text{Att}_{a,b} \right) \wedge \left(\bigwedge_{(a,b) \notin R} \neg \langle \text{En}_{a_1} \leftarrow \bot \rangle \text{Att}_{a,b} \right)$$

$$\wedge \neg \langle \text{En}_{a_1} \leftarrow \bot \rangle \text{En}_{a_1} \wedge \neg \langle \text{En}_{a_1} \leftarrow \bot \rangle \text{En}_{a_2} \wedge \neg \langle \text{En}_{a_1} \leftarrow \bot \rangle \text{En}_{a_3}$$

$$\wedge \neg \langle \text{En}_{a_1} \leftarrow \bot \rangle \text{En}_{a_4} \wedge \neg \langle \text{En}_{a_1} \leftarrow \bot \rangle \text{En}_{a_5} \wedge \neg \langle \text{En}_{a_1} \leftarrow \bot \rangle \text{En}_{a_6}$$

We finally use a last DL-PA property [1]:

$$\langle p \leftarrow \bot \rangle q \leftrightarrow \begin{cases} \bot & \text{if } p = q \\ q & \text{otherwise} \end{cases}$$

Most of the conjuncts fall in the second category and thus are not affected by the program, except $\neg \langle En_{a_1} \leftarrow \bot \rangle En_{a_1}$ which is equivalent to $\neg \bot$, that is, to $\top$, and thus will disappear from the conjunction. We end with:

$$Th_{\mathcal{F}_0} \diamond En_{a_1} \equiv En_{a_1} \wedge \left(\bigwedge_{(a,b) \in R} Att_{a,b} \right) \wedge \left(\bigwedge_{(a,b) \notin R} \neg Att_{a,b} \right)$$

$$\wedge \neg En_{a_2} \wedge \neg En_{a_3} \wedge \neg En_{a_4} \wedge \neg En_{a_5} \wedge \neg En_{a_6}$$

which is the theory $Th_{\mathcal{F}_1}$, i.e., for $\mathcal{A}_1^{En} = \{a_1\}$.

Example 6. We can finally fully run through our main example. $\mathcal{A}$ and R remain constant and are as described in Example 1. We are going to run the example from step 0 to step 6, hence showing the addition/enablement of arguments step after step. Notice that it may be run the other way round, from step 6 to step 0; the removal/disablement of arguments would then be illustrated.

At step 0, $\mathcal{A}_0^{En} = \emptyset$, and $Th_{\mathcal{F}_0}$ is as in Example 2. The execution of

$$\langle (makeExt_{\mathcal{A}}^{Stable})^- \rangle Th_{\mathcal{F}_0}$$

allows one to get the only stable extension of $\mathcal{F}_0$: $\emptyset$.

When a_1 is uttered, the set of enabled arguments becomes $\mathcal{A}_1^{En} = \{a_1\}$. As we have seen in Example 5:

$$Th_{\mathcal{F}_1} = \langle (En_{a_1} \leftarrow \top)^- \rangle Th_{\mathcal{F}_0}$$

Executing $makeExt_{\mathcal{A}}^{Stable}$ from any valuation satisfying $Th_{\mathcal{F}_1}$ will lead to one valuation, where In_{a_1} is true and every In_{a_i} for $i \in \{2, \ldots, 6\}$ is false; this means we obtain one stable extension: $\{a_1\}$.

We summarize the results at each step of the dialogue in Table 2. Numbers in the first column are steps. In the second column, we write, first, the DL-PA formula describing the updated theory, and second, the DL-PA formula true in valuations corresponding to (stable) extensions. Then in the third column we give the current graph representing the argument system, and the set of extensions.

After the server (London agent) has presented all his arguments, we end up with one extension: $\{a_2, a_5, a_6\}$. In this setting, he accepts to provide the information as argument a_6, which directly supports the permission, belongs to at least one extension (following the principle of trustfulness of [14]).

5   Conclusion

This paper presents an extension of the formal framework of [6], which allows us to update the argument system by adding or removing an argument. We achieve this by

Table 2. Evolution of the argument system and of the set of extensions during the dialogue

Step	DL-PA formulas	Graph and extensions
0	$\mathrm{Th}_{\mathcal{F}_0}$	
	$\langle(\mathrm{makeExt}_{\mathcal{A}}^{\mathrm{Stable}})^-\rangle\mathrm{Th}_{\mathcal{F}_0}$	$\{\emptyset\}$
1	$\langle(\mathrm{En}_{a_1}\leftarrow\top)^-\rangle\mathrm{Th}_{\mathcal{F}_0} = \mathrm{Th}_{\mathcal{F}_1}$	a_1
	$\langle(\mathrm{makeExt}_{\mathcal{A}}^{\mathrm{Stable}})^-\rangle\mathrm{Th}_{\mathcal{F}_1}$	$\{\{a_1\}\}$
2	$\langle(\mathrm{En}_{a_2}\leftarrow\top)^-\rangle\mathrm{Th}_{\mathcal{F}_1} = \mathrm{Th}_{\mathcal{F}_2}$	$a_1 \longrightarrow a_2$
	$\langle(\mathrm{makeExt}_{\mathcal{A}}^{\mathrm{Stable}})^-\rangle\mathrm{Th}_{\mathcal{F}_2}$	$\{\{a_1\}\}$
3	$\langle(\mathrm{En}_{a_3}\leftarrow\top)^-\rangle\mathrm{Th}_{\mathcal{F}_2} = \mathrm{Th}_{\mathcal{F}_3}$	$a_1 \longrightarrow a_2 \longleftarrow a_3$
	$\langle(\mathrm{makeExt}_{\mathcal{A}}^{\mathrm{Stable}})^-\rangle\mathrm{Th}_{\mathcal{F}_3}$	$\{\{a_1, a_3\}\}$
4	$\langle(\mathrm{En}_{a_4}\leftarrow\top)^-\rangle\mathrm{Th}_{\mathcal{F}_3} = \mathrm{Th}_{\mathcal{F}_4}$	$a_1 \longrightarrow a_2 \longleftarrow a_3 \longleftarrow a_4$
	$\langle(\mathrm{makeExt}_{\mathcal{A}}^{\mathrm{Stable}})^-\rangle\mathrm{Th}_{\mathcal{F}_4}$	$\{\{a_1, a_4\}\}$
5	$\langle(\mathrm{En}_{a_5}\leftarrow\top)^-\rangle\mathrm{Th}_{\mathcal{F}_4} = \mathrm{Th}_{\mathcal{F}_5}$	$a_1 \longrightarrow a_2 \longleftarrow a_3 \longleftarrow a_4 \longleftarrow a_5$
	$\langle(\mathrm{makeExt}_{\mathcal{A}}^{\mathrm{Stable}})^-\rangle\mathrm{Th}_{\mathcal{F}_5}$	$\{\{a_1, a_3, a_5\}\}$
6	$\langle(\mathrm{En}_{a_6}\leftarrow\top)^-\rangle\mathrm{Th}_{\mathcal{F}_5} = \mathrm{Th}_{\mathcal{F}_6}$	$a_1 \longrightarrow a_2 \longleftarrow a_3 \longleftarrow a_4 \longleftarrow a_5$ a_6
	$\langle(\mathrm{makeExt}_{\mathcal{A}}^{\mathrm{Stable}})^-\rangle\mathrm{Th}_{\mathcal{F}_6}$	$\{\{a_2, a_5, a_6\}\}$

including a set of currently enabled arguments to the argument system and a new set of propositional variables reflecting this set in the logical representation. With new appropriate formulas for the argument system and semantics, the formalization of [6] is general enough to transpose well to this extension. Our new framework allows us to easily model the evolution of the argument graph during dialogue, as shown with the example of [14]. It is interesting to note that while we focused on the stable semantics, any semantics that can be described by a logical formula can be encoded in our framework.

Implemented theorem proving methods for **DL-PA** have not yet been developed, **DL-PA** being quite recent, but a paper such as the present on applications motivates implementation work.

The evolution of the argument system and the set of extensions during the dialogue, as illustrated in Table 2, is similar to the key idea of Discourse Representation Theory (DRT) [11] in linguistics. This idea is that the semantics of a dialogue may be constructed by the participants, jointly and incrementally as the dialogue proceeds. Other work in multi-agent systems has also drawn on these ideas, for example, [4, 13].

The dialogue analysis has been made from the point of view of one agent in this paper, and a posteriori. A perspective is to extend it to several agents, and to capture some ongoing strategy each one of them may have to fulfill own goals. In this case, agents may or may not agree on the set of arguments and on the set of attacks. For every of his arguments, an agent could compute the set of extensions for the current graph plus this argument, and thereby identify the argument that brings him closer to his personal goal. This is similar to the update of extensions in [6] but with a different approach (modifying arguments rather than attacks). We leave this to future work.

Acknowledgements. This work benefited from the support of the AMANDE project (ANR-13-BS02-0004) of the French National Research Agency (ANR).

References

1. Balbiani, P., Herzig, A., Troquard, N.: Dynamic logic of propositional assignments: a well-behaved variant of PDL. In: Logic in Computer Science (LICS). IEEE (2013)
2. Baroni, P., Giacomin, M.: Semantics of abstract argument systems. In: Simari, G., Rahwan, I. (eds.) Argumentation in Artificial Intelligence, pp. 25–44. Springer, US (2009)
3. Besnard, P., Doutre, S.: Checking the acceptability of a set of arguments. In: 10th International Workshop on Non-Monotonic Reasoning (NMR 2004), pp. 59–64 (2004)
4. Bratu, M., Andreoli, J.-M., Boissier, O., Castellani, S.: A software infrastructure for negotiation within inter-organisational alliances. In: Padget, J., Shehory, O., Parkes, D., Sadeh, N., Walsh, W.E. (eds.) AMEC 2002. LNCS, vol. 2531, pp. 161–179. Springer, Heidelberg (2002). doi:10.1007/3-540-36378-5_10
5. Coste-Marquis, S., Konieczny, S., Mailly, J.G., Marquis, P.: On the revision of argumentation systems: minimal change of arguments statuses. KR **14**, 52–61 (2014)
6. Doutre, S., Herzig, A., Perrussel, L.: A dynamic logic framework for abstract argumentation. In: KR 2014, pp. 62–71. AAAI Press (2014)
7. Dung, P.M.: On the acceptability of arguments and its fundamental role in nonmonotonic reasoning, logic programming and n-person games. Artif. Intell. **77**(2), 321–357 (1995)
8. Gaudou, B., Herzig, A., Lorini, E., Sibertin-Blanc, C.: How to do social simulation in logic: modelling the segregation game in a dynamic logic of assignments. In: Villatoro, D., Sabater-Mir, J., Sichman, J.S. (eds.) MABS 2011. LNCS, vol. 7124, pp. 59–73. Springer, Heidelberg (2012). doi:10.1007/978-3-642-28400-7_5
9. Harel, D.: Dynamic logic. In: Gabbay, D.M., Günthner, F. (eds.) Handbook of Philosophical Logic, vol. II, pp. 497–604. D. Reidel, Dordrecht (1984)
10. Herzig, A., Lorini, E., Moisan, F., Troquard, N.: A dynamic logic of normative systems. In: IJCAI 2011, pp. 228–233 (2011). www.irit.fr/ Andreas.Herzig/P/Ijcai11.html
11. Kamp, H., Reyle, U.: From Discourse to Logic: Introduction to Modeltheoretic Semantics of Natural Language, Formal Logic and Discourse Representation Theory, Studies in Linguistics and Philosophy, vol. 42. Kluwer Academic, Dordrecht, The Netherlands (1993)
12. Maffre, F.: Ignorance is bliss: observability-based dynamic epistemic logics and their applications. Ph.D. thesis, University of Toulouse (2016)
13. McBurney, P., Parsons, S.: Posit spaces: a performative theory of e-commerce. In: AAMAS 2003, pp. 624–631. ACM Press (2003)
14. Perrussel, L., Doutre, S., Thévenin, J.-M., McBurney, P.: A persuasion dialog for gaining access to information. In: Rahwan, I., Parsons, S., Reed, C. (eds.) ArgMAS 2007. LNCS, vol. 4946, pp. 63–79. Springer, Heidelberg (2008). doi:10.1007/978-3-540-78915-4_5
15. de Saint-Cyr, F.D., Bisquert, P., Cayrol, C., Lagasquie-Schiex, M.C.: Argumentation update in YALLA (yet another logic language for argumentation). Int. J. Approximate Reasoning **75**, 57–92 (2016)

Combining Answer Set Programming with Description Logics for Analogical Reasoning Under an Agent's Preferences

Teeradaj Racharak[1,2(✉)], Satoshi Tojo[2], Nguyen Duy Hung[1],
and Prachya Boonkwan[3]

[1] School of Information, Computer, and Communication Technology,
Sirindhorn International Institute of Technology,
Thammasat University, Pathum Thani, Thailand
r.teeradaj@gmail.com, hung@siit.tu.ac.th
[2] School of Information Science,
Japan Advanced Institute of Science and Technology, Ishikawa, Japan
{racharak,tojo}@jaist.ac.jp
[3] National Electronics and Computer Technology Center,
Pathum Thani, Thailand
prachya.boonkwan@nectec.or.th

Abstract. Analogical reasoning makes use of a kind of resemblance of one thing to another for assigning properties from one context to another. This kind of reasoning is used quite often by human beings, especially in unseen situations. The key idea of analogy is to identify a good similarity; however, similarity may be varied on subjective factors (*i.e.* an agent's preferences). This paper studies an implementation of this phenomena using an answer set programming with Description Logics. The main idea underlying the proposed approach lies in the so-called *Argument from Analogy* developed by Walton [1]. Finally, the paper relates the approach to others and discusses future directions.

Keywords: Analogical argumentation · Argumentation schemes · Argument from analogy · Answer set programming · Description logics

1 Introduction and Motivation

Analogical reasoning makes use a kind of resemblance of one thing to another for assigning properties from one context to another. This kind of reasoning is used quite often by human beings in real-life situations, especially when humans encounter an unseen situation. To have an intuitive understanding of the mechanism, let us take a look on the following case where attorney Gerry Spence reasons in the case of Silkwood v. Kerr-McGee Corporation (1984) [2].

Example 1 (The Silkwood case). Karen Silkwood was a technician who had the job of grinding and polishing plutonium pins used to make fuel rods for nuclear

© Springer International Publishing AG 2017
S. Benferhat et al. (Eds.): IEA/AIE 2017, Part II, LNAI 10351, pp. 306–316, 2017.
DOI: 10.1007/978-3-319-60045-1_33

reactors. Tests in 1974 showed that she had been exposed to dangerously high levels of plutonium radiation. After she died in an automobile accident, her father brought an action against Kerr-McGee in which the corporation was held to be at fault for her death on the basis of strict liability. In strict liability, a person can be held accountable for the harmful consequences of some dangerous activity he was engaged in, without having to prove that he intended the outcome.   □

Spence's closing argument uses the analogy of the escaping lion, which had great rhetorical effect on the jury. According to his speech (p. 129 of [2]), he emphasized the statement *If the lion got away, Kerr-McGee has to pay.*

> Some guy brought an old lion in a cage – lions are dangerous – and through no negligence of his own, the lion got away. Nobody knew how – like in the Silkwood case, *nobody knew how.* And, the lion ate up some people. And they said, you know: *Pay. It was your lion and it got away.* And, the man says: *But I did everything that I could and it isn't my fault that it got away.* They said: *You have to pay.* You have to pay because it was your lion – unless the person who was hurt let the lion out himself.

Roughly, reasoning by analogy is a form of non-deductive reasoning in which we infer a conclusion based on similarity of two situations. There is substantial work on methodology ranging from a kind of introspective folk psychology [1,3] to partial identity of Horn clause logic interpretations [4]. There are some contributions which include elements of both, *e.g.* [5,6]; and also, work which provides a form of analogical reasoning in terms of a system of hypothetical reasoning based on mathematical logic [7]. While there is a diversity of methodology, there is some consensus, *i.e.* using similarity information to support an inference which cannot be deductively inferred.

In this work, we base our study on the result of argumentation studies called *argumentation schemes* for Argument from Analogy (*cf.* Subsect. 2.1). Our usage of argumentation schemes is also based on the assumption that the proponent and the opponent have the same ground-truth preferences. Our primary motivation is a formalization of argumentation schemes for Argument from Analogy as a logic program. Answer set semantics for logic programs [8] is one of the most widely adopted semantics for logic programs. It provides the theoretical foundation for answer set programming (ASP) [9,10] which has proved to be useful in several applications such as diagnosis, bioinformatics, planning, and is proven in [11] to coincide with the stable semantics of argumentation framework.

As aforementioned, the key idea of using analogy is to identify similarity of two situations. This work exploits benefits of two different formalisms, *i.e.* Description Logics (DLs) and rules. In particular, DLs are used for reasoning about conceptual schemata whereas rules are applied to data-centric problems. Both formalisms exhibit certain shortcomings that can be compensated for by advantages of the other. Using DLs, situations are defined in form of concept definitions, and similarity under preferences is identified by the use of a concept similarity measure under the preference profile (*i.e.* $\stackrel{\pi}{\sim}_T$) [12,13]. In this paper, we are attempting to incorporate the notion $\overset{\pi}{\sim}_{\mathcal{T}}$ with ASP for deriving *plausible conclusions by analogy* (*cf.* Sect. 3). Section 2 is its preliminaries; Sect. 4 discusses its relationship to argumentation framework; Sect. 5 relates to existing models of analogical reasoning; and Sect. 6 is the conclusion. This work is an extended study of the papers [12,13] for analogical reasoning.

2   Preliminaries

In this section, we review the basics of argumentation schemes and concept similarity measure under preference profile in Description Logics (DLs).

2.1   Argumentation Schemes: Argument from Analogy

Argumentation schemes [1] are stereotypical non-deductive patterns of reasoning, consisting of a set of premises and a conclusion that is *presumed* to follow from the premises. Use of argumentation schemes is evaluated by a specific set of critical questions corresponding to each scheme. Let us illustrate this with the argumentation scheme called *Argument from Analogy* as follows:

1. A situation is described in C_1.
2. A is plausibly drawn as an acceptable conclusion in C_1.
3. Generally, C_1 is similar to C_2.

Therefore, A is plausibly drawn as an acceptable conclusion in C_2.

The following set of critical questions matches the scheme:

1. Are there respects in which C_1 and C_2 are different that would tend to undermine the similarity cited?
2. Is A the right conclusion to be drawn in C_1?
3. Is there some other situation C_3 that is also similar to C_1, but in which A is not drawn as an acceptable conclusion?

The first critical question relates to differences between the two situations that could detract from the strength of the argument from analogy. The second critical question nicely ensures the right conclusion. Lastly, the third critical question is associated with a familiar type of counter-analogy. The function of this critical question is to suggest doubt that could possibly lead to a plausible counter-argument that could be used to rebut the original conclusion.

2.2   Concept Similarity Measure Under an Agent's Preferences in Description Logics

In DLs, we assume countably infinite sets CN of concept names and RN of role names that are fixed and disjoint. The set of concept descriptions, or simply concepts, for a specific DL $\mathcal{L}$ is denoted by $\mathsf{Con}(\mathcal{L})$. The set $\mathsf{Con}(\mathcal{L})$ is inductively defined on CN and RN with the use of concept constructors in the standard way. An ontology $\mathcal{O}$ is usually defined as $\langle \mathcal{T}, \mathcal{A} \rangle$ where $\mathcal{T}$ is a terminological component or TBox and $\mathcal{A}$ is an assertional component or ABox. However, some practical ontologies may exclude $\mathcal{A}$ from $\mathcal{O}$. In the following, we give formal definitions of a concept similarity measure under a preference profile in DLs.

Definition 1 (Preference Profile [12]**).** *Let* $\mathsf{CN}^{\mathsf{pri}}(\mathcal{T})$, $\mathsf{RN}^{\mathsf{pri}}(\mathcal{T})$, *and* $\mathsf{RN}(\mathcal{T})$ *be a set of primitive concept names occurring in* $\mathcal{T}$, *a set of primitive role names occurring in* $\mathcal{T}$, *and a set of role names occurring in* $\mathcal{T}$, *respectively. A* preference profile, *denoted by* π, *is a quintuple* $\langle \mathfrak{i}^{\mathfrak{c}}, \mathfrak{i}^{\mathfrak{r}}, \mathfrak{s}^{\mathfrak{c}}, \mathfrak{s}^{\mathfrak{r}}, \mathfrak{d} \rangle^1$ *where*

- $\mathfrak{i}^{\mathfrak{c}} : \mathsf{CN} \rightarrow [0,2]$ *where* $\mathsf{CN} \subseteq \mathsf{CN}^{\mathsf{pri}}(\mathcal{T})$ *is primitive concept importance;*
- $\mathfrak{i}^{\mathfrak{r}} : \mathsf{RN} \rightarrow [0,2]$ *where* $\mathsf{RN} \subseteq \mathsf{RN}(\mathcal{T})$ *is role importance;*
- $\mathfrak{s}^{\mathfrak{c}} : \mathsf{CN} \times \mathsf{CN} \rightarrow [0,1]$ *where* $\mathsf{CN} \subseteq \mathsf{CN}^{\mathsf{pri}}(\mathcal{T})$ *is primitive concepts similarity;*
- $\mathfrak{s}^{\mathfrak{r}} : \mathsf{RN} \times \mathsf{RN} \rightarrow [0,1]$ *where* $\mathsf{RN} \subseteq \mathsf{RN}^{\mathsf{pri}}(\mathcal{T})$ *is primitive roles similarity; and*
- $\mathfrak{d} : \mathsf{RN} \rightarrow [0,1]$ *where* $\mathsf{RN} \subseteq \mathsf{RN}(\mathcal{T})$ *is role discount factor.*

We discuss the interpretation of each above function in order. Firstly, for any $A \in \mathsf{CN}^{\mathsf{pri}}(\mathcal{T})$, $\mathfrak{i}^{\mathfrak{c}}(A) = 1$ captures an expression of normal importance on A, $\mathfrak{i}^{\mathfrak{c}}(A) > 1$ ($\mathfrak{i}^{\mathfrak{c}}(A) < 1$) indicates that A has higher (and lower, respectively) importance, and $\mathfrak{i}^{\mathfrak{c}}(A) = 0$ indicates that A is of no importance for the consideration. Secondly, we define the interpretation of $\mathfrak{i}^{\mathfrak{r}}$ in the similar fashion as $\mathfrak{i}^{\mathfrak{c}}$ for any $r \in \mathsf{RN}(\mathcal{T})$. Thirdly, for any $A, B \in \mathsf{CN}^{\mathsf{pri}}(\mathcal{T})$, $\mathfrak{s}^{\mathfrak{c}}(A, B) = 1$ captures an expression of total similarity between A and B and $\mathfrak{s}^{\mathfrak{c}}(A, B) = 0$ captures an expression of total dissimilarity between A and B. Fourthly, the interpretation of $\mathfrak{s}^{\mathfrak{r}}$ is defined in the similar fashion as $\mathfrak{s}^{\mathfrak{c}}$ for any $r, s \in \mathsf{RN}^{\mathsf{pri}}(\mathcal{T})$. Lastly, for any $r \in \mathsf{RN}(\mathcal{T})$, $\mathfrak{d}(r) = 1$ captures an expression of total importance on a role (over a corresponding nested concept) and $\mathfrak{d}(r) = 0$ captures an expression of total importance on a nested concept (over a corresponding role).

Definition 2 ([13]**).** *Given a preference profile* π, *two concepts* $C, D \in \mathsf{Con}(\mathcal{L})$, *and a TBox* $\mathcal{T}$, *a concept similarity measure under preference profile w.r.t. a TBox* $\mathcal{T}$ *is a function* $\sim^{\pi}_{\mathcal{T}} : \mathsf{Con}(\mathcal{L}) \times \mathsf{Con}(\mathcal{L}) \rightarrow [0,1]$. *A function* $\sim^{\pi}_{\mathcal{T}}$ *is called* preference invariance *w.r.t equivalence if* $C \equiv D \Leftrightarrow (C \sim^{\pi}_{\mathcal{T}} D = 1$ *for any* $\pi)$.

There is substantial research on concept similarity measure in the context of DLs; however, a notable measure is sim^{π} which addresses concept similarity under an agent's preferences. We refer the readers to [13] for detail.

3   The Formal System: Analogical Reasoning

In this section, we introduce a knowledge base $\mathcal{K}$ which makes it possible to find analogical consequences. We note that, whenever we refer to a knowledge base $\mathcal{K}$, we mean our setting defined in this section. Informally, $\mathcal{K}$ has three components, *viz.* a logic program $\mathcal{LP}$, a DL-based ontology $\mathcal{O}$, an instance of concept similarity measure under preference profile $\sim^{\pi}_{\mathcal{T}}$. Subsection 3.1 introduces a *declarative language* for the specification of $\mathcal{LP}$ and gives a formal definition of $\mathcal{K}$. Subsection 3.2 addresses the problem of computing conclusions from analogy.

---

[1] In the original definition of preference profile [12,13], both $\mathfrak{i}^{\mathfrak{c}}$ and $\mathfrak{i}^{\mathfrak{r}}$ are mapped to $\mathbb{R}_{\geq 0}$ which is a minor error.

3.1   The Knowledge Base Setting

The object language of $\mathcal{LP}$ conforms to the familiar logic-programming-like style. That is, let $\Sigma = \langle \mathcal{C}, \mathcal{V}, \mathcal{P} \rangle$ be a signature with a finite set of constants $\mathcal{C}$, an infinite set of variables $\mathcal{V}$, and a finite set of predicate symbols $\mathcal{P}$. Let L_Σ be the first-order language constructed over Σ. There are two types of literals. A *strong* literal is an atomic first-order formula A (of L_Σ) or such a formula preceded by classical negation, *i.e.* $\neg A$. A *weak* literal is a literal of the form *not* A, where A is a strong literal and *not* denotes *negation-as-failure* (or default negation). Informally, *not* A reads as *there is no evidence that A is the case* whereas $\neg A$ reads as *A is definitely not the case*. In what follows, we use the standard typographic conventions of Logic Programming.

Definition 3 (Program Clause). *A definite program clause is a clause of the form $A_0 \leftarrow L_1, \ldots, L_n$ where A_0 is a strong literal and L_i ($1 \le i \le n$) is a literal. If $n = 0$, it is referred to as a* fact. *Otherwise, it is referred to as a* rule.

Definition 4 (Logic Program). *A definite logic program $\mathcal{LP}$ is a finite set of definite program clauses.*

Example 2 (Continuation of Example 1). We translate the Silkwood case into our logic program $\mathcal{LP}$. For the sake of clarity, we distinguish in $\mathcal{LP}$ the legal rules $\mathcal{LP}_L$, the hypothetical case $\mathcal{LP}_H$, and the current case $\mathcal{LP}_C$, *i.e.* $\mathcal{LP} = \mathcal{LP}_L \cup \mathcal{LP}_H \cup \mathcal{LP}_C$. The literal *exception(X)* means *X is an exception to inactivate the goal*. To avoid confusion, we separate each program clause by a semicolon.

$\mathcal{LP}_L = \{defendant(X) \leftarrow owner(X, Y), danger(Y), killer(Y, Z); \; liable(X) \leftarrow defendant(X), not \; exception(X);\}$
$\mathcal{LP}_H = \{danger(X) \leftarrow lion(X); \; lion(l_1); \; owner(guy, l_1); \; person(man); \; killer(l_1, man);\}$
$\mathcal{LP}_C = \{plutonium\_plant(p_1); \; owner(kerr\_mcgee, p_1); \; person(silkwood); \; killer(p_1, silkwood).\}$ □

We note that there could be many ways to transform a problem domain into $\mathcal{LP}$. Addressing this issue is also important but it is outside the scope of this paper. Our intention is to determine the similarity of two predicate symbols from a DL-based ontology by using the notion $\overset{\pi}{\sim}_\mathcal{T}$. The following gives a formal definition of our knowledge base setting.

Definition 5 (Knowledge Base). *A knowledge base $\mathcal{K}$ is a triple $\langle \mathcal{LP}, \mathcal{O}, \overset{\pi}{\sim}_\mathcal{T} \rangle$, where $\mathcal{LP}$ is a logic program, $\mathcal{O}$ is a DL-based ontology, $\overset{\pi}{\sim}_\mathcal{T}$ represents an instance of concept similarity measure under preference profile in DLs.*

One may observe that not every knowledge base is meaningful to give conclusions from analogy, *e.g.* when the set Pred($\mathcal{LP}$) of predicate symbols appearing in $\mathcal{LP}$ and the set CN($\mathcal{O}$) of concept names appearing in $\mathcal{O}$ do not intersect.

Example 3 (Continuation of Example 2). We assume that our working ontology $\mathcal{O}$ has been modeled as follows:

$$\text{lion} \sqsubseteq \text{carnivore} \sqcap \text{wild}$$
$$\text{plutonium\_plant} \sqsubseteq \text{power\_plant} \sqcap \text{radiation}$$
$$\text{carnivore} \sqsubseteq \text{harm}$$
$$\text{radiation} \sqsubseteq \text{harm}$$

A knowledge base $\mathcal{K}$ may be represented as a triple $\langle \mathcal{LP}, \mathcal{O}, \text{sim}^\pi \rangle$. We note that sim^π is shown to be an instance of $\approx_{\mathcal{T}}^\pi$ in [13]. □

3.2 Computing Analogical Conclusions

One may observe from Example 3 that $\mathcal{K}$ successfully models the decision of the hypothetical case by having logical conclusions *defendant(guy)* and *liable(guy)*. However, $\mathcal{K}$ does not model the decision of the current case stated in Spence's closing argument. $\mathcal{K}$ can be twisted a bit with additional rules (*e.g.* rules representing extra evidences) so that *liable(kerr_mcgee)* is logically concluded. Nevertheless, this approach does not correctly reconstruct Spence's analogical argument, which is not based on purely logical models.

In this subsection, we assume that there is no extra evidence about the case. To reconstruct Spence's argument, we extend $\mathcal{K}$ with analogical knowledge extracted from the ontological component. This extension is technically defined as the operator $\cdot^+$. Intuitively, $\cdot^+$ provides transforming steps to extend $\mathcal{LP}$ with $\mathcal{O}$ via $\approx_{\mathcal{T}}$. The result of executing $\cdot^+$ on $\mathcal{K}$, *i.e.* $\mathcal{K}^+$, conforms to the input language of grounder **gringo** [14] and can be used with an answer set engine.

Transforming Logic Program $\mathcal{LP}$. We achieve this by transforming each clause of $\mathcal{LP}$ as a set of answer set program clauses in $\mathcal{K}^+$. Our transformation uses the predicate symbol *atom* as a basic predicate symbol. For each $\varphi_0 \leftarrow \varphi_1, \ldots, \varphi_n$ $(0 \le i \le n) \in \mathcal{LP}$ and let φ_0' :- $\varphi_1', \ldots, \varphi_n'$ $(0 \le i \le n)$ be a corresponding clause in $\mathcal{K}^+$, then the transformation is performed as follows:

- If $\varphi_i = A_i(X_0, \ldots, X_m)$, then $\varphi_i' = atom(X_0, \ldots, X_m, A_i)$;
- If $\varphi_i = \neg A_i(X_0, \ldots, X_m)$, then $\varphi_i' = \text{-}atom(X_0, \ldots, X_m, A_i)$;
- If $\varphi_i = not\ A_i(X_0, \ldots, X_m)$, then $\varphi_i' = not\ atom(X_0, \ldots, X_m, A_i)$.

Extending with Similarity from Ontology $\mathcal{O}$. Let Sim be a set of pairs of predicates whose similarity is maximal among each matching predicate, *i.e.* $\text{Sim} = \{(\varphi, \psi) \mid \forall \varphi \in \Lambda : (\varphi \approx_{\mathcal{T}}^\pi \psi = \max_{\psi \in \Lambda}\{\varphi \approx_{\mathcal{T}}^\pi \psi\})\}$ where $\Lambda = \text{Pred}(\mathcal{LP}) \cap \text{CN}(\mathcal{O})$ and $\varphi \not\equiv \psi$. Let $arity(\varphi, \psi)$ gives the number of arguments that both φ and ψ take. We note that *dsim* is additionally reserved. For each $(\varphi, \psi) \in \text{Sim}$:

- $\mathcal{K}^+ := \mathcal{K}^+ \cup \{dsim(\varphi, \psi); atom(A_1, \ldots, A_m, \varphi)$:- $atom(A_1, \ldots, A_m, \psi), dsim(\varphi, \psi).\}$ where $m = arity(\varphi, \psi)$.

It is worth to observe that φ is fixed for each $\varphi \in \Lambda$ to determine the maximal pair. Thus, either a symmetric measure or an asymmetric measure can be employed by the same rule of extending with similarity. We refer the readers to [12,13] for useful discussion about inherited properties of concept similarity measures in DLs, *e.g.* sim^π [13] is symmetric.

Example 4 (Continuation of Example 3). Let $\mathcal{K}^+$ be the result of transforming the logic program (*i.e.* the first step of $\cdot^+$). Then, we enrich $\mathcal{K}^+$ by the following additional set of clauses. That is, $\mathcal{K}^+ = \mathcal{K}^+ \cup \{$

> $dsim(lion, plutonium\_plant);$
> $atom(X, lion) :\!- atom(X, plutonium\_plant), dsim(lion, plutonium\_plant);$
> $dsim(plutonium\_plant, lion);$
> $atom(X, plutonium\_plant) :\!- atom(X, lion), dsim(plutonium\_plant, lion).\}$ □

Using Critical Questions as Constraints. It is not difficult to see that the first critical question and the second one are automatically configured by $\sim_\mathcal{T}^\pi$ and the logic program, respectively. Also, counter-analogies can be discovered through answer set semantics. These make $\mathcal{K}^+$ to incorporate critical questions.

Finding Logical Entailment. We successfully explain each execution step of $\cdot^+$. As we can use an answer set engine (*e.g.* **clasp** [14]) to determine answer sets as analogical conclusions from $\mathcal{K}^+$, we include the original definition of entailment w.r.t answer set semantics here for self-containment. For a logic program Π and a ground atom a, Π entails a w.r.t. answer set semantics (in symbols, $\Pi \models a$) if $a \in S$ for every answer set S of Π. Similarly, for a logic program Π and a ground atom a, Π entails $\neg a$ w.r.t. answer set semantics (in symbols, $\Pi \models \neg a$) if $\neg a \in S$ for every answer set S of Π. If neither $\Pi \models a$ nor $\Pi \models \neg a$, then we say that a is *unknown* w.r.t. Π. Hence, we say an atom $A(X_0, \ldots, X_m)$ is an *analogical conclusion* from $\mathcal{K}$ if $\mathcal{K}^+ \models atom(X_0, \ldots, X_m, A)$.

4   Relationship to Argumentation Framework

Now, our intention is to analyze the underlying mechanisms of $\mathcal{K}$ and $\mathcal{K}^+$ under the lens of argumentation framework. It is not difficult to see that logical conclusions obtained from $\mathcal{K}$ and $\mathcal{K}^+$ can be seen as proof trees constructed from $\mathcal{K}$ and $\mathcal{K}^+$, respectively. Each proof tree represents an argument supporting the conclusion at its root. For instance, possible proof trees for $defendant(guy)$ and $liable(guy)$ are depicted on the left-hand side and the right-hand side of Fig. 1, where T_1 denotes a proof tree for $defendant(guy)$. This explains that the guy is a defendant for the lion case and the guy is liable for the case.

As discussed in Subsect. 3.2, $\mathcal{K}$ cannot successfully model the legal rules with the current case. To achieve this, $\mathcal{K}$ is extended to $\mathcal{K}^+$ so that $\mathcal{K}^+ \models atom(ker\_mcgee, defendant)$. Figure 2 depicts a proof tree for $atom(ker\_mcgee,$

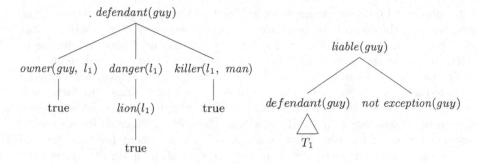

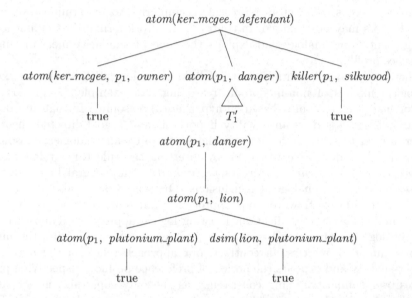

Fig. 1. Possible proof trees for *defendant(guy)* and *liable(guy)*

Fig. 2. Proof trees for *atom(ker_mcgee, defendant)* and *atom(p₁, danger)*

defendant) from $\mathcal{K}^+$, where T_1' denotes a proof tree for *atom*(p_1, *danger*). Such trees represent *arguments from analogy* supporting the conclusion at their roots.

It is not difficult to see that our proposed operator formalizes the form of Walton's scheme. That is, when desired conclusions cannot be logically inferred from a knowledge base, that knowledge base is extended with similarity information. Conclusions obtained from the extended one are called *analogical conclusions*.

5   Related Work

After surveying the literature on Argument from Analogy in many fields, such as logic, law, philosophy of science, and computer science, it appears to us that there are two different forms of Argument from Analogy. The first form (*cf.* Subsect. 2.1), on which our work is based, is the most widely accepted version whereas the second one compares factors of two cases (*e.g.* [15,16]), which may be regarded as an instance of the first form. As the second one makes no reference to the notion of similarity, it becomes simpler to use, such as in standard case-based reasoning. The method of evaluating an argument from analogy in case-based reasoning (CBR) uses respects (*i.e.* dimensions and factors) in which two cases are similar or different. In CBR, the decision in the best precedent case is then taken as the decision into the current case. A dimension is a relevant aspect of the case whereas a factor is an argument favoring one side or the other in relation to the issue being disputed. The HYPO system [15] uses dimensions. CATO [16] is a simpler CBR system that uses factors. Systems which employ factors use pro factors to represent similarities for supporting an argument whereas con factors represent dissimilarity to undermine the argument. Factors may be weighted. In contrast, this work formalizes the first form of Argument from Analogy and exploits the concept similarity measure under preference profile in DLs.

There are also substantial efforts of linking analogical reasoning to existing logical models of non-monotonic reasoning. For example, [7] proposes a form of analogical reasoning based on hypothetical reasoning. In that approach, similarity is expressed as an equality hypothesis and a goal-directed theorem prover is used to search relevant hypotheses. In [5,6], an analogical reasoning is considered as deductive reasoning by inserting the rule (in our language): $has\_property(t, p) \leftarrow has\_property(s, p), similar(s, t)$ as general knowledge to be used in deriving analogical conclusions. Our operator $\cdot^+$ also has a rule similar to the above. However, our approach is different to those on the constraint and similarity identification. Existing logical approaches require consistency on logic programs and employs a preference, *i.e.* maximizing the number of common properties. In contrast, our approach relies on the notion of counter-analogy and exploits the notion of preference profile for specifying preferences over similarity. Using consistency as the only constraint is not sufficient. For instance, let us exemplify a counter-example (in our language): $\mathcal{LP} = \{danger(X) \leftarrow lion(X); \neg danger(X) \leftarrow solar\_plant(X); plutonium\_plant(p_1).\}$ and $\mathcal{O} = \{$lion $\sqsubseteq$ harm $\sqcap$ wild; plutonium_plant $\sqsubseteq$ power_plant $\sqcap$ harm; solar_plant $\sqsubseteq$ power_plant $\sqcap$ green_environment$\}$. Most of existing approaches conclude either $danger(p_1)$ or $\neg danger(p_1)$ from the logic program. However, our approach concludes nothing as a counter-analogy is discovered. Using the number of common properties to identify preferred similarity also has less flexibility than using preference profile, *e.g.* it is not able to express importance over different names.

Also, inspired by Walton's [1], like ours, [17] introduces a framework based on a declarative language for analogical reasoning. However, this work intends to bring together the benefits of existing similarity measures in DLs with answer set programming. Thus, their practical applications can be different.

6 Conclusion

We make contributions to the logical study of analogical reasoning using the combination of answer set programming with DLs. The key idea behind our approach lies in the scheme proposed by Walton [1]. The strong point of this study is to exploit benefits of extensive tools from answer set programming; and also, is to embody the existing notion $\sim_{\mathcal{T}}^{\pi}$ in DLs for establishing analogy.

As analyzed in Sect. 4, we discuss the relationship of our extended logic programs with argumentation framework. One may notice that the approach does not preserve similarity degrees on the computation of analogical conclusions. Our future task is to extend this study to value-based argumentation [18].

Acknowledgments. This research is part of the JAIST-NECTEC-SIIT dual doctoral degree program.

References

1. Walton, D., Reed, C., Macagno, F.: Argumentation Schemes. Cambridge University Press, Cambridge (2008)
2. Lief, M.S., Caldwell, H.M., Bycel, B.: Ladies and Gentlemen of the Jury: Greatest Closing Arguments in Modern Law. Scribner, New York (2000)
3. Hofstadter, D., Mitchell, M.: Concepts, analogies, and creativity. In: Proceedings of CSCSI-88, pp. 94–101, June 1988
4. Haraguchi, M., Arikawa, S.: Reasoning by analogy as a partial identity between models. In: Jantke, K.P. (ed.) AII 1986. LNCS, vol. 265, pp. 61–87. Springer, Heidelberg (1987). doi:10.1007/3-540-18081-8_86
5. Greiner, R.: Learning by understanding analogies. In: Greiner, R. (ed.) Machine Learning: A Guide to Current Research, vol. 12, pp. 81–84. Springer, Heidelberg (1986)
6. Winston, P.H.: Learning and reasoning by analogy. Commun. ACM **23**(12), 689–703 (1980)
7. Goebel, R.: A sketch of analogy as reasoning with equality hypotheses. In: Jantke, K.P. (ed.) AII 1989. LNCS, vol. 397, pp. 243–253. Springer, Heidelberg (1989). doi:10.1007/3-540-51734-0_65
8. Gelfond, M., Lifschitz, V.: The stable model semantics for logic programming. In: LPICS, pp. 1070–1080 (1988)
9. Marek, V.W., Truszczyński, M.: Stable models and an alternative logic programming paradigm. In: Apt, K.R., Marek, V.W., Truszczynski, M., Warren, D.S. (eds.) The Logic Programming Paradigm: A 25-Year Perspective. Artificial Intelligence, pp. 375–398. Springer, Heidelberg (1999)
10. Niemelä, I.: Logic programs with stable model semantics as a constraint programming paradigm. Ann. Math. Artif. Intell. **25**(3–4), 241–273 (1999)
11. Dung, P.M.: On the acceptability of arguments and its fundamental role in non-monotonic reasoning, logic programming and n-person games. Artif. Intell. **77**(2), 321–358 (1995)
12. Racharak, T., Suntisrivaraporn, B., Tojo, S.: Identifying an agent's preferences toward similarity measures in description logics. In: Qi, G., Kozaki, K., Pan, J.Z., Yu, S. (eds.) JIST 2015. LNCS, vol. 9544, pp. 201–208. Springer, Cham (2016). doi:10.1007/978-3-319-31676-5_14

13. Racharak, T., Suntisrivaraporn, B., Tojo, S.: sim$^\pi$: a concept similarity measure under an agent's preferences in description logic $\mathcal{ELH}$. In: Proceedings of the 8th International Conference on Agents and Artificial Intelligence, pp. 480–487 (2016)
14. Potsdam answer set solving collection. http://potassco.sourceforge.net/. Accessed 13 Dec 2016
15. Ashley, K.: Case-based reasoning. In: Lodder, A.R., Oskamp, A. (eds.) Information Technology and Lawyers: Advanced Technology in the Legal Domain, from Challenges to Daily Routine, pp. 23–60. Springer, Dordrecht (2006)
16. Aleven, V.: Teaching case-based argumentation through a model and examples. Ph.D. diss., University of Pittsburgh, Pittsburgh, Pennsylvania (1997)
17. Racharak, T., Tojo, S., Hung, N.D., Boonkwan, P.: Argument-based logic programming for analogical reasoning. In: New Frontiers in Artificial Intelligence (JSAI-isAI Workshops, JURISIN2016), LNAI. Springer (2017, to appear)
18. Bench-Capon, T.J.M.: Value based argumentation frameworks. CoRR cs.AI/0207059 (2002)

Modeling Data Access Legislation with Gorgias

Nikolaos I. Spanoudakis[1]([✉]), Elena Constantinou[2], Adamos Koumi[2],
and Antonis C. Kakas[2]

[1] Applied Mathematics and Computers Laboratory,
Technical University of Crete, Chania, Greece
nispanoudakis@isc.tuc.gr
[2] Department of Computer Science, University of Cyprus, Nicosia, Cyprus

Abstract. This paper uses argumentation as the basis for modeling and implementing the relevant legislation of an EU country relating to medical data access. Users can consult a web application for determining their allowed level of access to a patient's medical record and are offered an explanation based on the relevant legislation. The system can also advise a user on what additional information is required for a higher access level. The system is currently in the process of an extensive evaluation through a pilot trial with a special focus group of medical professionals. The development methodology that we have used is generally applicable to any other similar cases of decision making based on legislative regulations. The main advantage of using argumentation is the ability to explain the solutions drawn and the high modularity of software facilitating the extension and adaptation of the system when new relevant legislation becomes available.

Keywords: Argumentation · Legal systems · Modular software

1 Introduction

Modern systems aim to automate compliance to laws, policies (or business rules) and regulations. In many cases the problem would involve several of such policies to be applied together creating the need for internal coherence amongst the different policies of the integrated system. The main challenge in building such systems is to develop software that is close to the high-level specification of the policies involved so that (1) the information can be easily acquired and faithfully represented, and, (2) changes in the policies could be easily propagated to the software. The resulting software should also be able to provide information explaining why a particular case is compliant or not, how its compliance is affected by the various policies involved and how new information about the case at hand can change the degree of compliance.

A particular case of the problem of policy compliance is that of *data sharing*. In such problems data may belong and be private to a particular owner or institution but, yet, it is often necessary to share (at least part of) this data. Data sharing agreements are enforced when the data is used to identify if a

© Springer International Publishing AG 2017
S. Benferhat et al. (Eds.): IEA/AIE 2017, Part II, LNAI 10351, pp. 317–327, 2017.
DOI: 10.1007/978-3-319-60045-1_34

user/application is granted access to the data and at what level of access. The problem of such data access and usage control is well studied [11,16,18], but existing solutions are restricted in allowing conflicting rules, together with a solution to the conflicts. Recent projects like *CoCo Cloud*[1] aim to automate data sharing activities by analyzing the various policies involved in order to identify possible conflicts and then propose algorithms for conflict resolution.

An important case of data sharing is that of *accessing a patient's medical data* where, although the data belongs to the patient, it is necessary for doctors or other medical staff to access parts of this data when the patient needs treatment. The decision of what data can be shared should follow legal regulations that pertain on the one hand to the general data protection and privacy rights of individuals and on the other hand to rights and obligations that are specific to medical data.

In this paper we study the problem of medical data access as specified by the relevant European Union and national regulations in one of its member states (Cyprus). These regulations are modeled in terms of argumentation drawing from the theory and practice of argumentation in Artificial Intelligence (see e.g. [5,8,17]). Compliance of access with respect to the regulations is thus mapped into a decision problem of what level of access has, according to the argumentation theory that models the legislation, an acceptable argument that supports the option to grant this level of access. Arguments that support different levels of access dialectically compete with each other and only the stronger argument(s) are used to grant access. Our approach follows a long tradition of linking argumentation in AI with Law (see [6,14,15] for reviews) but where the emphasis is on the development of a practical system for a relatively simple, yet real-life, piece of legislation.

In contrast with conventional approaches to data sharing the approach through argumentation is not based on a procedural analysis for finding and resolving conflicts but on a high-level declarative representation of the policies themselves. Through a systematic evaluation that we are currently carrying out using an appropriate focus group for this real-life application of medical data access we aim to examine and understand the possible added value of argumentation for this type of applications.

The next section presents the legislation that regulates medical data access and analyses this in a suitable way for our model. In Sect. 3 we briefly review the argumentation framework and the methodology we will use in modeling the problem. Section 4 shows how the legislation is mapped into argumentation and how the application system is build. The final section concludes with our plans for future work of more extensive evaluation and the development of other similar applications.

2   Legal Framework for Medical Data Access

In this section we will present the legal framework that we aim to model. For this we had to consider two law documents, one for personal data protection [2]

---

[1] http://rissgroup.org/coco-cloud-confidential-and-compliant-clouds/.

and one on the rights of the patients [1]. We will start by defining some domain knowledge that will aid in the development of the argumentation theory. Then we will present the different users and types of access. Finally we will outline the policies defined in the legal framework.

2.1 Definitions

We will start by defining what is/constitutes a *medical record*. The medical record contains data related to the mental and physical health of the owner in the past, the present, and, sometimes, the future. Specifically, it contains:

- *Demographic data*, used to identify the owner, e.g. name, surname, date of birth, telephone number, address, identity and social security numbers.
- *Socioeconomic data*, personal data, such as marital status, profession, employer, religion, nationality, personal habits (e.g. smoking).
- *Clinical data*, such as illnesses endured, lab tests, x-rays, drug prescriptions, surgeries, temperature and blood pressure readings.

The type of access to the medical record depends on the following concepts:

- *Patient*: An individual that requests/receives medical service.
- *Medical service provider*: Medical doctor, pharmacist, dentist, nurse, obstetrician, paramedical or administrative staff working for a medical institution.
- *Personal data*: Any information related to an individual whose identity is known or can be established.
- *Data Processing and archiving*: Any series of activities applied to medical or personal data, including: *collection, modification, storage, transformation, retrieval, search, use, transfer, copy, encryption, deletion or destruction.*
- *Medical data*: Information about the health of an individual, also information in close connection with the medical domain.
- *Medical files*: Files produced by a medical service provider in printed or digital form related to the health of an individual, containing information that can be used to establish the identity of the individual.
- *Third party*: A legal or physical entity, public authority, service or any other body other than the person to whom the data refers.
- *Legal representative*: An individual hired to perform an action in place of someone else or to represent someone in a transaction with a third party.
- *Consent*: The owner of the personal data gives clearly and in full knowledge consent for their processing.
- *Controller*: Decides on the purpose and means of processing a data file.

The users of the medical data are those with the right to process them. They are expected to be medical doctors, nurses, paramedical and administrative personnel of state-owned or private medical institutions and hospitals. The administrative personnel can also use the system aiming to provide access to a patient, the patient's family or a legal representative.

Before the user can access a medical record of a patient, he is expected to establish his/her identity and explain the circumstances under which he/she is requesting access. There are several types of access granted to a specific user:

- *Full access*: The user can add, remove data of a medical record. The user can access all the medical files in the record and the personal data.
- *Limited plus access*: Limited plus access aims to allow access to data for determining the general status of the owner's health without much detail but allowing a good diagnosis and drug prescription. The user can have limited access to the medical files, i.e. those related to the current treatment of the owner and to personal data. The user can access information related to the allergies of the owner, chronic diseases and medication received. The user can add a medical file related to the current treatment of the owner.
- *Limited plus, read-only access*: Same as previous, with the exception that the user cannot add a medical record.
- *Limited access*: The user can have limited access to the medical files related to the medical history of the owner with respect to a specific therapy followed in the past. Specifically, the user can access information relating to the treating medical personnel, the diagnosis, medication received, results of clinical examinations and the resulting conclusions.
- *Suspended access*: This type of access is only valid for the owner of the medical record. Access to specific data is refused for a specific time-span determined by a medical doctor (who has determined that the patient must not know yet a specific issue regarding his/her health because this might be a hazard for his/her health).
- *No access*: No information is disclosed to the user.

2.2   Policies for Determining Access Type

The access type depends on three main contexts. Firstly it depends on *who is asking to get access* to the medical record. According to that we have the following types of users and **default** access types:

- {owner} → full access
- {family doctor} → full access
- {doctor} → limited plus access
- {family member} → limited plus access
- {legal representative person} → full access
- {patient involved to owner's treatment} → limited plus read only access
- {person holding order from the high court} → limited plus read only access
- {other person} → no access

Then, access type depends on *the purpose of asking for access* (that the user must disclose along with his/her identity) posing limitations:

- {research purpose} → limited access
- {processing purpose} → limited plus access
- {for publishing purposes in medical journals} → limited access
- {treatment purpose} → limited plus read only access
- {teaching purpose} → limited read only access
- {order from the Medical Association} → limited plus read only access

Thirdly, access type depends on other *specific circumstances*:

- {written consent from owner} → full access
- {owner is dead} → no access
- {owner, doctor restriction} → suspended access

These factors are considered together, generally from the first (person asking) to the third (circumstances).

3 Argumentation Theory for Policy Applications

In this section we review the basic theory of argumentation which we will use to model regulation and other policies. The theory will be presented from a general point of view of applying argumentation to real-life compliance problems viewed as decision problems under an argumentation policy. We will also overview the *Gorgias* system as an environment for developing applications of argumentation and on which our case study of medical data access will be based.

Policies will be represented within the preference-based argumentation framework proposed in [9]. In this, application problems are captured via argumentation theories composed of different levels. **Object level arguments support** the possible decisions, or **options**, in a specific application domain, while **first-level priority arguments** express preferences on the object level arguments in order to resolve possible conflicts. **Higher-order priority arguments** are also used to resolve potential conflicts between priority arguments of the first (or subsequent) levels.

Formally, an **argumentation theory** is a pair $(\mathcal{T}, \mathcal{P})$ whose sentences are formulae in the background monotonic logic, $(\mathcal{L}, \vdash)$, of the form $L \leftarrow L_1, \ldots, L_n$, where $L, L_1, \ldots, L_n$ are positive or negative ground literals. The derivability relation, $\vdash$, is given simply by the inference rule of modus ponens. The head literal L can also be empty. Rules in $\mathcal{T}$ capture argument schemes for building **object level arguments**, or denials when the head is empty. On the other hand, rules in $\mathcal{P}$ represent argument schemes for building **priority arguments**. The head L of these rules has the general form, $L = h\_p(rule1, rule2)$, where $rule1$ and $rule2$ are atoms naming two rules and h_p refers to an (irreflexive) *higher priority* relation amongst the rules of the theory.

The semantics of an argumentation theory is defined via an abstract argumentation framework $<Args, Att>$ associated to any given theory $(\mathcal{T}, \mathcal{P})$. The **arguments** in $Args$ are given by the composite subsets, (T, P), of the given theory, where $T \subseteq \mathcal{T}$ and $P \subseteq \mathcal{P}$. An argument (T, P) **supports** its conclusions, of either a literal, L, or a priority (ground) atom, $h\_p(r, r')$, where r and r' are the names of two rules in the theory, when $T \vdash L$ or $T \cup P \vdash h\_p(r, r')$.

The **attack relation**, Att, allows an argument, (T, P), to attack another argument, (T', P'), when (i) these arguments derive contrary conclusions (i.e. derive L and $\neg L$, or $h\_p(r, r')$ and $h\_p(r', r)$) and (ii) (T, P) makes the rules of its counter proof at least "as strong" as the rules of the proof of the argument (T', P') that is attacked. The detailed formal definition of the attacking relation can be found in [9]. The **admissibility** of (sets of) arguments, Δ, is defined in the usual way [8], i.e. that Δ does not attack itself and that it attacks back any argument that attacks it.

It is important to note that typically for an argument (T, P) to be *admissible* its object level part, T, has to have along with it priority arguments, P (from $\mathcal{P}$), in order to make itself at least "as strong" as its opposing counter-arguments. This need for priority rules can repeat itself when the initially chosen ones can themselves be attacked by opposing priority rules. In that case, higher-order priority rules need to be used to make these priority rules at least "as strong" as their opposing priority ones.

The multi-layered nature of an argumentation theory $(\mathcal{T}, \mathcal{P})$ and the process of deciding on the admissibility arguments mirror the structure of the legislation and the process of legal reasoning to decide on a valid legal position. Basic articles of the law give the information for object-level rules, in the argumentation theory, for general default decisions while articles describing contextual-based exceptional decisions are captured via the priority rules of the theory.

The above theoretical framework of argumentation has been implemented in the open source *Gorgias* system (http://www.cs.ucy.ac.cy/~nkd/gorgias/). *Gorgias* has been, since 2004, successfully applied by different users for developing real life applications (see e.g. portfolio management [13], provision of services in ambient intelligence [12], management of firewall policies [3], conflicts resolution in pervasive services [4]) (see http://gorgiasb.tuc.gr/Apps.html for a list of applications).

Based on this experience a new software methodology [19] and tool to support this, called *Gorgias-B* (http://gorgiasb.tuc.gr), has been recently developed so that such applications of argumentation can be developed in a systematic and principled way. The proposed *"Software Development for Argumentation" (SoDA)* methodology aims to provide a general software development framework that can be used by application domain experts, with little or no knowledge of argumentation theory, to develop application software based on argumentation. The methodology guides the developer through his/her application problem by an incremental refinement of application scenarios, where he/she considers the several (usually conflicting) alternatives (e.g., different diagnostic results, judicial decisions, recommendation options, risk management decisions, etc.) and evaluates them according to some criteria/features of the problem and context dependent (meta)-knowledge. The *Gorgias-B* tool helps the developer to consider his/her application according to the *SoDA* methodology and offers a high-level environment through which the software code of the underlying argumentation theory is automatically generated. The *Gorgias-B* system also supports *abductive reasoning* integrated with argumentation [7,10] thus enabling the possibility for solving, using the same application software, *reverse decision problems* of identifying extra information needed to make a certain desired decision possible, i.e. supported by an admissible argument.

4   Medical Data Access System

In this section we will describe how we have modeled the legislation for medical data access using *Gorgias* according to the *SoDA* methodology and give the high-level architecture of the developed application system.

4.1   Decision Policy Development

The first task is to model the options of the problem, i.e. the different types of access (see Sect. 2.2). We use the option predicate *access(User, Data, Level)* where the first parameter denotes the user, the second the data (or file) asking for permission and the third the permission type for this data. The next task is to define the contextual hierarchy from the most general to the most specific, of the various application scenarios. In our case (see Sect. 2) this is given by:

1. Person requesting access
2. Purpose of access
3. Special circumstances

We then proceed to define the Gorgias rules that defined the argumentation theory starting from general scenarios and considering refinements of these. For example these object rules will be generated for two different types of access:

$$r_1(P, F, T) : access(P, F, no\_access) \leftarrow true$$
$$r_2(P, F, T) : access(P, F, limited\_plus\_access) \leftarrow true$$

According to the *SoDA* methodology, we consider conflicting options in pairs. For the pair *no_access* and *limited_plus_access* we have at the second level two possibilities. One defaulting to the *no_access* captured by the rule $c_{1,2}^2$ and one selecting *limited_plus_access* when the person requesting it is a medical doctor, captured by $c_{2,1}^2$:

$$c_{1,2}^2(P, F, T) : h\_p(r_1(P, F, T), r_2(P, F, T)) \leftarrow true$$
$$c_{2,1}^2(P, F, T) : h\_p(r_2(P, F, T), r_1(P, F, T)) \leftarrow doctor(P)$$

At a higher-level of priority we capture that $c_{1,2}^2$ is generally stronger, and we move to consider the purpose of requesting access. If a doctor wants access for medical purpose then the *limited_plus_access* is granted:

$$c_{1,2}^3(P, F, T) : h\_p(c_{1,2}^2(P, F, T), c_{2,1}^2(P, F, T)) \leftarrow true$$
$$c_{2,1}^3(P, F, T) : h\_p(c_{2,1}^2(P, F, T), c_{1,2}^2(P, F, T)) \leftarrow medical$$

At yet a higher-level of priority we capture that $c_{2,1}^3$ is stronger and that it forms the default at this higher level. However, in the special circumstance that the owner is dead, this priority is again reversed:

$$c_{2,1}^4(P,F,T) : h\_p(c_{2,1}^3(P,F,T), c_{1,2}^3(P,F,T)) \leftarrow true$$
$$c_{1,2}^4(P,F,T) : h\_p(c_{1,2}^3(P,F,T), c_{2,1}^3(P,F,T)) \leftarrow owner(X,F), dead(X)$$

Finally, at a fifth level of priority we capture that $c_{2,1}^4$ is generally stronger:

$$c_{1,2}^5(P,F,T) : h\_p(c_{1,2}^4(P,F,T), c_{2,1}^4(P,F,T)) \leftarrow true$$

When all such pairs have been considered for all possible ranked contexts the argumentation theory is ready and the *Gorgias-B* tool automatically generates the *Gorgias* Prolog source code.

4.2　System Design/Architecture

The Prolog source code is invoked by a Java module for getting the facts for any situation for which we want to find the access rights. This Java module is used by a web application built using standard HTML/CSS and PHP technologies[2]. The architecture of our system is depicted in Fig. 1 where the numbers on the arrows show the sequence of execution for each user query.

A user typically logs in and uses a form to request for the access rights to a patient's record. The Java module then writes the result of the Prolog query to a database that is used by the web application along with the explanation in predicate form. In the database the predicates are mapped to legislation articles and paragraphs (e.g. the request by a doctor for medical reasons will respond with *limited_plus_access* rights based on article 15, paragraph 2b of [1]) so that a user-understandable text is shown to the user by the web-application.

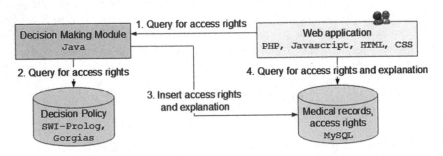

Fig. 1. The *Medical Data Access Control* application's architecture

A user can also use the system to ask what circumstances should hold so that he/she can have a different access level. To support this query, facts are defined as abducibles, i.e. unless the system is informed otherwise, they can be assumed as true, and the system can reply with the possible context for such use. For example if a doctor wants to access a file he gets *no_access*. However,

---

[2] The MEDICA web application has been deployed at: http://medica.cs.ucy.ac.cy.

if he asks whether he could get *limited_plus_access* rights he will get the answer that he needs to have a *medical* reason.

4.3 First Evaluation of System

The developed system is the result of Elena Constantinou's diploma thesis for her Computer Science B.Sc. degree. A first evaluation with (23) classmates was carried out, aiming to determine how easy it was to learn and use it. Through a questionnaire, 78% of the students agreed that the system is easy to learn, 70% agreed that the system menus and functionality is well designed. Moreover, through this survey a number of ideas to enhance the system were suggested.

We are currently in the process of evaluating the system with a focus group of specialists to assess the applicability of the system for usage in hospitals and health centers. We are working closely with a team of medical informatics which advises the government of Cyprus on IT systems for the national health service. This team will first evaluate our system from their own IT perspective and then proceed for an evaluation through pilot trial at appropriate medical centers.

5 Conclusions

We have shown how the technology of argumentation can be used to model and implement the real-life legal regulations pertaining to access to patient data. Using the high-level declarative approach of argumentation we can develop in a principled way application software that is modular and flexible in accommodating changes in the problem requirements. In contrast to a carefully crafted set of rules for capturing the legislation, argumentation provides a direct mapping of the legislation where the representation of one part of legislation does not need to explicitly safeguard against the other parts of legislation that might be in conflict with this. We claim that this results in application software where the effort required to update the software to changes in the legislation is comparable to that of changing the old legislation document to the new one.

The direct representation of the legislation is particularly facilitated by the simplicity of the representation language of the *Gorgias* framework (not found in other structured argumentation frameworks). This simplicity allows the developer to follow the *SoDA* methodology where s/he does not need to consider the application at the lower-level of the structured argumentation representation language but rather only at the higher level of application scenarios and the possible relative preferred decisions available in the different scenarios.

Apart from a more extensive evaluation of the system, including the strengthening of confidence in its legal correctness, we are working to provide a natural dialogue interface with the user for explaining and guiding as to the available levels of access. We are also considering, in collaboration with the *RISS* group at Imperial College, other real-life applications of data sharing where a more heterogeneous set of policies is involved such as business policies, shared party agreements, as well as national and international legal regulations.

Acknowledgements. We thank the *RISS* group at Imperial College for useful discussions.

References

1. Cyprus law on patient rights, 1(I) (2005)
2. Cyprus law on personal data protection, 138(I) (2001)
3. Bandara, A.K., Kakas, A.C., Lupu, E.C., Russo, A.: Using argumentation logic for firewall configuration management. In: Integrated Network Management (IM 2009), 11th IFIP/IEEE International Symposium on Integrated Network Management, June 1–5, 2009, pp. 180–187. Hofstra University, Long Island (2009)
4. Benazzouz, Y., Boyle, D.: Argumentation-based conflict resolution in pervasive services. In: Negotiation and Argumentation in Multi-Agent Systems: Fundamentals, Theories, Systems and Applications, pp. 399–419. Bentham Science (2014)
5. Bench-Capon, T.J.M., Dunne, P.E.: Argumentation in artificial intelligence. Artif. Intell. **171**(10–15), 619–641 (2007)
6. Bench-Capon, T., Prakken, H., Sartor, G.: Argumentation in legal reasoning. In: Simari, G., Rahwan, I. (eds.) Argumentation in Artificial Intelligence, pp. 363–382. Springer, Heidelberg (2009)
7. Demetriou, N., Kakas, A.C.: Argumentation with abduction. In: 4th Panhellenic Logic Symposium (PLS 2003), 7–10 July, Thessaloniki, Greece, pp. 38–43 (2003)
8. Dung, P.M.: On the acceptability of arguments and its fundamental role in non-monotonic reasoning, logic programming and n-person games. Artif. Intell. **77**, 321–357 (1995)
9. Kakas, A.C., Moraitis, P.: Argumentation based decision making for autonomous agents. In: The Second International Joint Conference on Autonomous Agents & Multiagent Systems (AAMAS), Proceedings, 14–18, 2003, Melbourne, Victoria, Australia, pp. 883–890 (2003)
10. Kakas, A.C., Moraitis, P.: Adaptive agent negotiation via argumentation. In: 5th International Joint Conference on Autonomous Agents and Multiagent Systems (AAMAS 2006), Hakodate, Japan, 8–12 May, 2006, pp. 384–391 (2006)
11. Matteucci, I., Petrocchi, M., Sbodio, M.L.: CNL4DSA: a controlled natural language for data sharing agreements. In: Proceedings of the ACM Symposium on Applied Computing (SAC), Sierre, Switzerland, 22–26 March, pp. 616–620 (2010)
12. Moraitis, P., Spanoudakis, N.I.: Argumentation-based agent interaction in an ambient-intelligence context. IEEE Intell. Syst. **22**(6), 84–93 (2007)
13. Pendaraki, K., Spanoudakis, N.I.: Portfolio performance and risk-based assessment of the PORTRAIT tool. Oper. Res. **15**(3), 359–378 (2015)
14. Prakken, H., Sartor, G.: Law and logic: a review from an argumentation perspective. Artif. Intell. **227**, 214–245 (2015)
15. Prakken, H.: AI & law, logic and argument schemes. Argumentation **19**(3), 303–320 (2005)
16. Pretschner, A., Hilty, M., Basin, D., Schaefer, C., Walter, T.: Mechanisms for usage control. In: Proceedings of the 2008 ACM Symposium on Information, Computer and Communications Security (ASIACCS 2008), pp. 240–244. ACM (2008)
17. Rahwan, I., Simari, G.R.: Argumentation in Artificial Intelligence, 1st edn. Springer, Heidelberg (2009)

18. Ruiz, J.F., Petrocchi, M., Matteucci, I., Costantino, G., Gambardella, C., Manea, M., Ozdeniz, A.: A lifecycle for data sharing agreements: how it works out. In: Schiffner, S., Serna, J., Ikonomou, D., Rannenberg, K. (eds.) APF 2016. LNCS, vol. 9857, pp. 3–20. Springer, Cham (2016). doi:10.1007/978-3-319-44760-5_1
19. Spanoudakis, N.I., Kakas, A.C., Moraitis, P.: Applications of argumentation: the SoDA methodology. In: 22nd European Conference on Artificial Intelligence (ECAI 2016), 29 August–2 September, The Hague, The Netherlands, pp. 1722–1723 (2016)

dARe – Using Argumentation to Explain Conclusions from a Controlled Natural Language Knowledge Base

Adam Wyner[1]([⊠]) and Hannes Strass[2]

[1] Department of Computing Science, University of Aberdeen, Aberdeen, UK
azwyner@abdn.ac.uk
[2] Computer Science Institute, Leipzig University, Leipzig, Germany
strass@informatik.uni-leipzig.de

Abstract. We present an approach to reasoning with knowledge bases comprised of strict and defeasible rules over literals. A controlled natural language is proposed as a human/machine interface to facilitate the specification of knowledge and verbalisation of results. Techniques from formal argumentation theory are employed to justify conclusions of the approach; this aims at facilitating human acceptance of computed answers.

1 Introduction

Approaches to artificial intelligence in general and to automated problem solving in particular should be – in virtue of their intelligence – able to explain and justify their conclusions and actions in a rational discourse. This is not always done: the Go playing computer program *AlphaGo* [22], while very proficient in choosing the right move (i.e. solving a range of problems), cannot explain to a human user *why* it chose that particular move (i.e. justifying its solution). A recent Nature editorial concluded that "[t]he machine becomes an oracle; its pronouncements have to be believed" (Nature 529, p. 437).

To make believable, useful results, they have to be communicated to human users, which implies that the formal knowledge models used in efficient inference mechanisms ought to be translatable into a form that is familiar and relevant for humans. In this paper, we aim at addressing specific problems of usability of knowledge-based intelligent systems in a particular, restricted setting. The restricted setting is that of reasoning with non-monotonic semantics of knowledge bases (KBs) that are given in the form of strict and defeasible rules, since people reason non-monotonically about many matters. For this, we make use of several techniques. Firstly, to address the communication issue (between humans and machines), we employ a *controlled natural language* as specification language for the input of the model as well as the output of inferences. Controlled natural languages (CNLs) are subsets of natural language that have been restricted in lexicon and grammar, thereby eliminating ambiguity and reducing complexity [17]. Some systems automatically translate sentences into formal,

S. Benferhat et al. (Eds.): IEA/AIE 2017, Part II, LNAI 10351, pp. 328–338, 2017.
DOI: 10.1007/978-3-319-60045-1_35

machine-readable semantic representations; they are useful in, for example, conversational intelligence analysis, so support distributed sense-making [25]. We adapt one such system, AceRules [16], for user specification of defeasible theories. Secondly, to address the explanation issue (justifying answers), we employ techniques from formal argumentation theory. Argumentation studies determine which arguments are acceptable, that is, which arguments can be defended in rational discourse, where arguments consist of prerequisites, a claim, and an inference between the two, along with their relationships with other arguments, such as rebuttal. Formal argumentation theory and its implementations formally and automatically construct conclusions from a knowledge base. The CNL interface allows a user to build the knowledge base and to receive justified conclusions in natural language. Importantly, as we argue, a CNL enables an *engineering approach* to argumentation and reasoning in natural language. This is in contrast to most existing approaches to formal argumentation, which do not strongly tie-in to intuitions about natural language. It also contrasts with argument mining [18], which, while promising, requires extensive preprocessing and normalisation to support formal inference.

On the reasoning side, there are approaches to reasoning with knowledge bases consisting of strict and defeasible rules [1,2,6–8,10,21,23,26]. We subscribe to none in particular and opt to make our approach parametric, abstracting from the concrete reasoning back-end that is used. We only assume that the back-end receives as input a set of strict and defeasible rules, provides output in the form of conclusions with respect to some semantics, and yields (upon request) justifications of the conclusions.

The novel contributions of this paper are that we propose a new interface between natural language, defeasible knowledge bases, and defeasible reasoning, which is either non-existent in other approaches or does not correlate with intuitive semantic judgements. Our proposal is the first to facilitate automatic reasoning from inconsistent knowledge bases in natural language [12,13,16]. It takes the idea of "convincing by explaining" one step further, as explanations can be expressed in a natural language text. We can apply and propose to extend an existing controlled natural language (CNL) tool that largely provides the requisite translation to defeasible theories, which can be further processed by background reasoning engines. We dub our system *dARe* for "*d*efeasible *AceRules* with *explanations*". In the rest of the paper, we provide a motivating example, introduce the formal language on which the actual reasoning is done, then outline our natural language interface. The picture below illustrates the overall process which is discussed over the course of the paper. Our aim is to provide a high level outline of the issues relating to defeasible reasoning and CNLs; a detailed or formal presentation is beyond the scope of this work and can be better appreciated from the references. We close with some discussion and notes on future work.

2   A Motivating Example

For human-machine communication, there are CNL tools which translate natural language into first-order logic formulas and interface to (non-monotonic) inference engines [11–13,16]. Yet, there are still issues with defeasible and/or conflicting information. More pointedly, defeasible propositions are modelled using "not provably not", which we show has a different interpretation than the natural expression "usually" or "it is usual that", which are normative quantifier expressions over contexts [15]. The following running example is paraphrased from Pollock [20] and illustrates these matters.

Example 1 (Moustache Murder)

> *Jones is a person. Paul is a person. Jacob is a person. Usually, a person is reliable. If Jones is reliable then the gunman has a moustache. If Paul is reliable then Jones is not reliable. If Jacob is reliable then Jones is reliable.*

Clearly not both Paul and Jacob can be reliable. Crucially, any semantics should provide a choice between the different (and mutually exclusive) consistent viewpoints of this narrative. An interpretation of "usually" should facilitate such choices.

In the approaches of [11,13], the adverb of quantification "usually" is translated as "not provably not" (perhaps along with an abnormality predicate), e.g. a paraphrase for "usually, a person is reliable" is along the lines of "if a person is not provably not reliable then the person is reliable". However, this formalisation can be incorrect, as demonstrated by its straightforward ASP implementation:

```
1: person(jones). person(paul). person(jacob).
2: has(gunman,moustache) :- reliable(jones).
3: -reliable(jones) :- reliable(paul).
4: reliable(jones) :- reliable(jacob).
5: reliable(X) :- person(X), not -reliable(X).
```

This answer set program is inconsistent. The literal $-$`reliable(jacob)` cannot ever be derived from the program, so `reliable(jacob)` must be in every answer set by (5) and (1). Thus `reliable(jones)` must be in every answer set by (4). However, the same holds for `paul`, whence the literal `reliable(paul)` must be in every answer set. Thus $-$`reliable(jones)` must be in every answer set by (3). Consequently, any answer set would have to contain both `reliable(jones)` and $-$`reliable(jones)`, therefore no answer set exists.[1] Yet, a correctly formalized logic program ought to produce the intended interpretations as stable models. Thus, the "not provably not" reading of "usually, ⟨*statement*⟩" phrases is not always correct.[2] In contrast, the correct reading is obtained by interpreting

---

[1] While ASP can deal with this example, the common "not provably not" reading of "usually, ⟨*statement*⟩" phrases is not always correct.

[2] Adding an abnormality atom into the body of line 5 (like in rule (12) of [5]) would address inconsistency, but not get us our intended reading. It would introduce the issue of having to create abnormality predicates from language input, where such predicates are not explicit.

"usually, ⟨*statement*⟩" as a defeasible rule in a defeasible theory. In the following section, we outline our approach to defeasible theories.

3 Defeasible Theories

For a set $\mathcal{P}$ of atomic propositions, the set $\mathcal{L}_\mathcal{P}$ of its literals is $\mathcal{L}_\mathcal{P} = \mathcal{P} \cup \{\neg p \mid p \in \mathcal{P}\}$. A *rule* over $\mathcal{L}_\mathcal{P}$ is a pair (B, h) where the finite set $B \subseteq \mathcal{L}_\mathcal{P}$ is called the *body* (premises) and the literal $h \in \mathcal{L}_\mathcal{P}$ is called the *head* (conclusion). For $B = \{b_1, \ldots, b_k\}$ with $k \in \mathbb{N}$, we can write rules thus: a *strict* rule is of the form "$b_1, \ldots, b_k \to h$"; a *defeasible* rule is of the form "$b_1, \ldots, b_k \Rightarrow h$". In case $k = 0$ we call "$\to h$" a *fact* and "$\Rightarrow h$" an *assumption*. The intuitive meaning of a rule (B, h) is that whenever we are in a state of affairs where all literals in B hold, then also literal h (always/usually, depending on the type of rule) holds. A *defeasible theory* is a tuple $\mathcal{T} = (\mathcal{P}, \mathcal{S}, \mathcal{D})$ where $\mathcal{P}$ is a set of atomic propositions, $\mathcal{S}$ is a set of strict rules over $\mathcal{L}_\mathcal{P}$, and $\mathcal{D}$ is a set of defeasible rules over $\mathcal{L}_\mathcal{P}$. In this paper, we will also consider defeasible theories with first-order predicates, variables, and constants, and treat them as short-hand versions of their ground instantiations. More details can be found in a previous workshop paper [24].

The semantics of defeasible theories are a topic of ongoing work in argumentation theory [1,2,6–8,10,21,23,26]. For the purposes of this paper, we express no preference, abstracting away from any concrete manifestations of existing approaches. For our approach to work, we make a few (mild) assumptions about the approach to assigning semantics to defeasible theories that is used to draw inferences (the "back-end"). More specifically, we assume that the reasoning back-end:

1. ... accepts a defeasible theory $\mathcal{T} = (\mathcal{P}, \mathcal{S}, \mathcal{D})$ as input. We consider this a mild assumption since only in some cases an additional step might be needed to transform $\mathcal{T}$ into the reasoner's native input format. (Some approaches distinguish rules with empty and non-empty bodies [2,10,21], which can be achieved by a simple syntactic preprocessing step; in ABA [6], there are no defeasible rules with non-empty body, this can be checked before passing the theory to the reasoner.)
2. ... can produce "interpretations" (consistent viewpoints, e.g. extensions) and/or (sets of) credulous/sceptical conclusions of the defeasible theory with respect to one or more semantics, e.g. stable, complete, preferred, grounded [9].
3. ... can produce graph-based justifications for its conclusions. For most approaches, this will be easy as they use structured (mostly tree-shaped) arguments, and when queried for the justification for a single conclusion, can just return a derivation of that literal as obtained from an argument extension. We assume only graph-based justifications in our approach to be most general, as more recent approaches [8,24] diverge from the traditional tree-shaped view for computational reasons.

It may be more or less straightforward to lift these restrictions, depending on the concrete approaches. Our assumptions cover considerable common ground of the various approaches in the literature; they are a meaningful and non-trivial starting point for our own work. While there are several roles for argumentation, for our purposes, it serves to provide graph-based justifications for conclusions, which contrasts to other approaches. We illustrate the formal back-end language with our running example.

Example 1 (Continued). The text on the gunman mystery leads to the below defeasible theory with variables, where Π is a set of (first-order) predicates, C is a set of constant symbols, V is a set of variables, S is a set of strict rules, D is a set of defeasible rules, and T a theory constructed from the other components (using atoms over Π, C, and V):

$$\Pi = \{person/1, reliable/1, has/2\}, \quad C = \{jones, paul, jacob, gunman, moustache\}$$
$$T = (atoms(\Pi, V, C), S, D) \text{ with } D = \{person(x_1) \Rightarrow reliable(x_1)\}, \text{ and}$$
$$S = \{\rightarrow person(jones), \quad \rightarrow person(paul), \quad \rightarrow person(jacob),$$
$$reliable(jones) \rightarrow has(gunman, moustache),$$
$$reliable(paul) \rightarrow \neg reliable(jones), \quad reliable(jacob) \rightarrow reliable(jones)\}.$$

Intuitively, this defeasible theory ought to have two different "interpretations":

$$M_1 = M \cup \{reliable(jacob), reliable(jones), has(gunman, moustache)\} \text{ and}$$
$$M_2 = M \cup \{reliable(paul), \neg reliable(jones)\}, \text{ with}$$
$$M = \{person(jones), person(paul), person(jacob)\}.$$

In particular, either of these two sets makes a choice whether Jacob is reliable or Paul is reliable, avoiding inconsistency.

4   Obtaining Defeasible Theories from Controlled Natural Language

In the subsections below, we justify CNLs for argumentation and knowledge bases, outline an existing CNL and required modifications, and then discuss our running example. Our aim is to provide a high level outline of the issues, as a detailed or formal presentation of a CNL and associated inference engine is beyond the scope of this work and can be better appreciated from the cited literature.

4.1   The Role of a CNL in Argumentation

We claim that a CNL is an important, perhaps essential, interface to argumentation, wherein natural language input is automatically analysed (parsed and semantically represented), returning a formal representation suitable for reasoning; the results are then verbalised in natural language. Our proposal is the first to facilitate automatic reasoning from inconsistent knowledge bases in natural language [12,13,16].

Our approach is complementary to argument mining, where texts are extracted from unstructured natural language corpora, then mapped to arguments for reasoning in Dungian AFs [18], given some sense of what counts as an argument [26]. In current argument mining approaches, machine learning techniques are often applied to identify topics, classify statements as claim or justification, or relate contrasting statements. However, natural language is highly complex and diverse in lexicon, syntax, semantics, and pragmatics. Current mining approaches do not systematically address matters of synonymy, contradiction, or deductions. They treat extracts from texts as atomic propositions, so do not provide *fine-grained* analysis into a formal language suitable for knowledge representation and reasoning such as predicate logic, where predicates and individuals are articulated (also see the *recognizing textual entailment* tasks [3]). Therefore, it is difficult to account for a range of patterns of reasoning that are fundamental to argumentation in natural language.

In contrast to argument mining, we adopt a CNL-based approach, where a CNL is an engineered language that reads as a natural language, yet has a constrained lexicon and grammar [17]. We are particularly interested in CNLs which translate the input language to machine-readable, first-order logic expressions and which interface with inference engines for model generation and theorem proving. Such a CNL facilitates an *engineered solution* to argumentation in NL by addressing three critical issues. First, it provides *normalised language* which, in principle, can serve as target expressions for information extracted by argument mining; thus we can process arguments and reason in the requisite way. For example, a CNL can homogenise diverse linguistic forms, e.g. passive and active sentences, and disambiguate expressions using interpretation rules. Second, we can *scope, experimentally control, and systematically augment the language* as needed. Finally, ACE gives us an *essential experimental interface with inference engines*, enabling testing of different forms and combinations of transformations from natural language to a formal language, then the interaction with alternative inference engines. Thus, in our view, a CNL is not only compatible with approaches to argument mining, but arguably a prerequisite processing pipeline element to instantiate substantive and articulated knowledge bases that facilitate inference.

While there are, in our view, clearly advantages to working with a CNL, it is important to acknowledge its limitations as well. As an engineered language, there are lexical items and grammatical constructions that are not available from the source natural language. Relatedly, there are interpretive, contextual, or idiomatic matters that a CNL does not address. Users of a language must learn to work with a CNL in ways that they do not in natural languages. Despite these limitations, we believe the advantages of an engineered language outweigh them.

4.2   AceRules

We work with AceRules [16], which is a sublanguage of Attempto Controlled English (ACE)[3] [12,16] (also see RACE [12], PENG-ASP [13], and ITA Controlled English [19]). For our purposes, the main advantage of AceRules over ACE is that AceRules allows us to access and redirect the inference engine, facilitating comparison between existing proposals and our alternative proposal. While many functionalities of AceRules are currently available and useful, other key components have been identified as to be implemented and are as of yet manually produced.

AceRules has a range of lexical components: proper names, common nouns, logical connectives, existential and universal quantifiers, one and two place predicates, and relative clauses. Construction rules define the admissible sentence structures, e.g. declarative or conditional sentences. The admissible sentences are translated into *Discourse Representation Structures* [4,14], which can be translated into predicate logic and which support the semantic representation of aspects of discourse such as pronominal anaphora. For instance, a sentence such as *"Every man is happy."* is automatically parsed and semantically represented along the lines of $\forall x[man(x) \rightarrow happy(x)]$. Interpretation rules restrict input such that each sentence is provided a single, unambiguous translation into a semantic representation; a user must evaluate whether this representation is the intended interpretation. There are further lexical elements and syntactic constructions to use as needed. Verbalisation generates natural language expressions from the formal representations, which fulfils the basic objective of making the results of inference accessible. A range of auxiliary axioms (from ACE) can be optionally added to treat generic linguistic inferences, e.g. interpretations of "be", relations between the plural and the singular form of nouns, lexical semantic inferences such as *throw* implying *move*, and a range of presuppositions relating to proper names or definite descriptions. Domain knowledge must be added as well into AceRules. To use AceRules, the user has to have some familiarity with the vocabulary, grammar, and interpretation rules. There are a range of support tools to input statements correctly, represent them in different forms, and process them further such as for reasoning or information extraction.[4]

For the semantics, AceRules has linguistic expressions and correlated first-order representations for strong negation, negation-as-failure, the strict conditional, and the adverb "usually", which is a predicate of events. It connects to different inference engines (courteous logic programs, stable models, and stable models with strong negation) and allows others, e.g. our direct semantics from [24].[5] These features are sufficient to reason non-monotonically. However, there are two key problems with AceRules as is (and shared with RACE and PENG-ASP): it cannot reason from inconsistent knowledge bases (e.g. as in the

---

[3] http://attempto.ifi.uzh.ch/site/description/.

[4] See [27,28] for an example of several natural language statements that are worked with ACE and related to an instantiated argumentation framework.

[5] RACE and PENG-ASP have the same expressions [12,13]. RACE is based on *Satchmo* (written in Prolog), while PENG-ASP uses ASP.

Nixon diamond example), and it does not incorporate the defeasible conditional. We have argued that both are essential for human-like reasoning. We have shown (see Example 1) that a conditional with "not provably not" is not semantically equivalent to the natural interpretation of "usually ⟨*statement*⟩" as the defeasible conditional. More relevant to the discussion of a natural language interface to arguments to explain conclusions, AceRules does not parse, semantically represent, or verbalise the discourse connectives such as "because" or "except", which are essential for natural expressions of explanation and justification (neither does ACE).

To address these matters, it is necessary to modify AceRules in several ways. Some of the modifications are as yet to be integrated for automatic processing. AceRules allows modal operators as sentential modifiers, e.g. "It is possible that" as well as the modal auxiliary "may", which may only be applied to atomic sentences. There is no sentential adverb "usually", but there is a manner adverb "usually", which is a predicate of events that does not provide the intended interpretation. To avoid problematic polysemy, we have created a new lexical item "usual" that is a predicate of atomic sentences as in "It is usual that P", where P is an atomic sentence; sentences of such forms are parsed by the revised AceRules. Further revisions are under development. In particular, expressions of the form "It is usual that P" are to be semantically represented with the defeasible conditional: where we have "It is usual that P" appears as a defeasible rule without a body; where we have "If Q then it is usual that P", we have a defeasible rule with Q as the body and P as the head. In addition, the semantic representation of a knowledge base with defeasible rules is to be processed with an inference "back-end" as described in Sect. 3, e.g. [24].[6] Finally, as previously noted, AceRule's verbalisation must be augmented to present structured explanations for extensions, which are arguments for conclusions; that is, we would like expressions such as "P because Q." to indicate what is concluded from the knowledge base, e.g. P, along with its justification, e.g. Q. In this way, we can fulfil the goal of defeasible reasoning in natural language along with justifications for conclusions.

4.3 Worked Example

In this section, we discuss our running example further, showing some of the revised linguistic forms needed to make the original example into expressions that are compatible with AceRules. The original statement from [20] is provided in the first portion below, followed by our paraphrase as given previously, and then an additional paraphrase written so as to be compatible with AceRules.

Example 1 (Continued). Moustache Murder

---

[6] An integration to AceRules is feasible; see, in a related setting, *If Nixon is a quaker then Nixon usually is a pacifist.* in https://argument-pipeline.herokuapp. com/, which is based on [26]. However, that work relied on ad-hoc manipulations of semantic representations.

Source: Jones says that the gunman had a moustache. Paul says that Jones was looking the other way and did not see what happened. Jacob says that Jones was watching carefully and had a clear view of the gunman.

Paraphrase 1: Jones is a person. Paul is a person. Jacob is a person. It is usual that a person is reliable. If Jones is reliable then the gunman has a moustache. If Paul is reliable then Jones is not reliable. If Jacob is reliable then Jones is reliable.

Paraphrase 2: Jones is a person. Paul is a person. Jacob is a person. If X is a person then it is usual that X is reliable. If Jones is reliable then the gunman has a moustache. If Paul is reliable then Jones is not reliable. If Jacob is reliable then Jones is reliable.

Our paraphrase 1 takes into consideration some of our caveats above about the introduction and translation of "usually", translating it instead as "it is usual that P". Note the obvious difference between the source and paraphrase 1. The paraphrase is intended to capture the core reasoning in the example, which has as conclusion whether or not the gunman has a moustache. This conclusion depends on the testimony of Jones; this is represented in terms of Jones' reliability. In turn, Jones' reliability is contingent on the testimony of Paul and Jacob, who may or may not be reliable. The rationale for such a paraphrase in our context is that AceRules, in its current form, cannot reason about the contents of subordinate clauses, i.e. the phrase "Jones was looking the other way and did not see what happened", which follows "Paul says that". Moreover, AceRules cannot process the complexity of predicates such as "looking the other way" and "did not see what happened"; similarly for the witness statement of Jacob. The paraphrase has introduced statements about the reliability with respect to 'person', which then requires individuals "Jones", "Paul", and "Jacob" to be asserted as of this class. Finally, considering paraphrase 2, we note that the expression of defeasibility has been represented as a rule about persons "If X is a person then it is usual that X is reliable." The conditional with "it is usual" in the consequence is translated into defeasible rule. As noted above, we model the syntactic form of our natural language treatment of defeasibility "it is usual that" on the form "it is possible that", though with a different form of semantic representation. This discussion highlights that what appear to be relatively simple statements, e.g. the source above, have several complex elements that need systematic treatment. Other standard examples from the argumentation literature, e.g. the Nixon, Tweety, and Tandem Bicycle examples, also raise issues about representation in AceRules but can nevertheless be treated by our approach.

5   Discussion and Future Work

The paper has outlined an approach to defeasible reasoning in a human-readable way using a CNL, which we justified as a way to *engineer* the range of issues about natural language that must be addressed to facilitate defeasible reasoning. We sketched a motivating example as well as a defeasible inference engine. We articulated the justification for CNLs, outlined AceRules, then highlighted several issues about argumentation in natural language that a CNL must address in future work. Nonetheless, the discussion serves to make the point that simply mining arguments from source text will encounter at least such related problems to instantiate knowledge bases for defeasible reasoning.

While this paper makes foundational progress in argument processing using a CNL, stronger justification for the approach will require working with more substantial and complex knowledge bases. Thus, a major area of future work is to advance the overall pipeline from natural language, formal representation, argument semantics, to verbalised explanations in natural language; such an advance would overcome the limitations of [28]. This will require a systematic, correlated, and iterated development of each component of the processing pipeline. This requires further examples, testing of outputs, identification of translation issues, likely extension of the expressivity of the CNL or argumentation semantics. Relatedly, an important step is to draw upon data derived from argument mining and working to normalising the data into forms suitable to AceRules/dARe. We anticipate that such a step will encounter familiar issues, e.g. pragmatics, ellipsis, and linguistic variation, that arise in formalising natural language.

References

1. Amgoud, L., Besnard, P.: A formal characterization of the outcomes of rule-based argumentation systems. In: Liu, W., Subrahmanian, V.S., Wijsen, J. (eds.) SUM 2013. LNCS (LNAI), vol. 8078, pp. 78–91. Springer, Heidelberg (2013). doi:10.1007/978-3-642-40381-1_7
2. Amgoud, L., Nouioua, F.: Undercutting in argumentation systems. In: Beierle, C., Dekhtyar, A. (eds.) SUM 2015. LNCS (LNAI), vol. 9310, pp. 267–281. Springer, Cham (2015). doi:10.1007/978-3-319-23540-0_18
3. Androutsopoulos, I., Malakasiotis, P.: A survey of paraphrasing and textual entailment methods. J. Artif. Intell. Res. **38**, 135–187 (2010)
4. Asher, N.: Reference to Abstract Objects in Discourse. Kluwer Academic Publishers, Amsterdam (1993)
5. Baral, C., Gelfond, M.: Logic programming and knowledge representation. J. Log. Program. **19**(20), 73–148 (1994)
6. Bondarenko, A., Dung, P.M., Kowalski, R.A., Toni, F.: An abstract, argumentation-theoretic approach to default reasoning. Artif. Intell. **93**, 63–101 (1997)
7. Caminada, M., Amgoud, L.: On the evaluation of argumentation formalisms. Artif. Intell. **171**(5–6), 286–310 (2007)
8. Craven, R., Toni, F.: Argument graphs and assumption-based argumentation. Artif. Intell. **233**, 1–59 (2016)
9. Dung, P.M.: On the acceptability of arguments and its fundamental role in nonmonotonic reasoning, logic programming and n-person games. Artif. Intell. **77**(2), 321–358 (1995)
10. Dung, P.M., Son, T.C.: An argument-based approach to reasoning with specificity. Artif. Intell. **133**(1–2), 35–85 (2001)

11. Fuchs, N.E.: Reasoning in attempto controlled english: non-monotonicity. In: Davis, B., Pace, G.J.J., Wyner, A. (eds.) CNL 2016. LNCS (LNAI), vol. 9767, pp. 13–24. Springer, Cham (2016). doi:10.1007/978-3-319-41498-0_2

12. Fuchs, N.E., Kaljurand, K., Kuhn, T.: Attempto controlled english for knowledge representation. In: Baroglio, C., Bonatti, P.A., Małuszyński, J., Marchiori, M., Polleres, A., Schaffert, S. (eds.) Reasoning Web. LNCS, vol. 5224, pp. 104–124. Springer, Heidelberg (2008). doi:10.1007/978-3-540-85658-0_3

13. Guy, S., Schwitter, R.: The PENG^{ASP} system: architecture, language and authoring tool. Lang. Resour. Eval. 1–26 (2016)

14. Kamp, H., Reyle, U.: From Discourse to Logic: Introduction to Model-Theoretic Semantics of Natural Language: Formal Logic and Discourse Representation Theory. Springer, Dordrecht (1993)

15. Kratzer, A.: Modals and Conditionals. Oxford University Press, Oxford (2012)

16. Kuhn, T.: AceRules: executing rules in controlled natural language. In: Marchiori, M., Pan, J.Z., Marie, C.S. (eds.) RR 2007. LNCS, vol. 4524, pp. 299–308. Springer, Heidelberg (2007). doi:10.1007/978-3-540-72982-2_24

17. Kuhn, T.: A survey and classification of controlled natural languages. Comput. Linguist. 40(1), 121–170 (2014)

18. Lippi, M., Torroni, P.: Argumentation mining: state of the art and emerging trends. ACM Trans. Internet Technol. 16(2), 10:1–10:25 (2016)

19. Mott, D.: The ITA controlled english report (Prolog version). Technical report, Emerging Technology Services, Hursley, IBM UK (2016)

20. Pollock, J.L.: Reasoning and probability. Law Prob. Risk 6, 43–58 (2007)

21. Prakken, H.: An abstract framework for argumentation with structured arguments. Argum. Comput. 1(2), 93–124 (2010)

22. Silver, D., Huang, A., Maddison, C.J., Guez, A., Sifre, L., van den Driessche, G., Schrittwieser, J., Antonoglou, I., Panneershelvam, V., Lanctot, M., Dieleman, S., Grewe, D., Nham, J., Kalchbrenner, N., Sutskever, I., Lillicrap, T., Leach, M., Kavukcuoglu, K., Graepel, T., Hassabis, D.: Mastering the game of Go with deep neural networks and tree search. Nature 529, 484–489 (2016)

23. Strass, H.: Instantiating rule-based defeasible theories in abstract dialectical frameworks and beyond. J. Log. Comput. (2015)

24. Strass, H., Wyner, A.: On automated defeasible reasoning with controlled natural language and argumentation. In: AAAI-17 Workshop on knowledge-based Techniques for Problem Solving and Reasoning (KnowProS 2017), February 2017

25. Toniolo, A., Preece, A.D., Webberley, W., Norman, T.J., Sullivan, P., Dropps, T.: Conversational intelligence analysis. In: Proceedings of the 17th International Conference on Distributed Computing and Networking, Singapore, 4–7 January 2016, pp. 42:1–42:6 (2016)

26. Wyner, A., Bench-Capon, T., Dunne, P., Cerutti, F.: Senses of 'argument' in instantiated argumentation frameworks. Argum. Comput. 6(1), 50–72 (2015)

27. Wyner, A., Engers, T., Bahreini, K.: From policy-making statements to first-order logic. In: Andersen, K.N., Francesconi, E., Grönlund, Å., Engers, T.M. (eds.) EGOVIS 2010. LNCS, vol. 6267, pp. 47–61. Springer, Heidelberg (2010). doi:10.1007/978-3-642-15172-9_5

28. Wyner, A.Z., van Engers, T.M., Hunter, A.: Working on the argument pipeline: through flow issues between natural language argument, instantiated arguments, and argumentation frameworks. Argum. Comput. 7(1), 69–89 (2016)

Intelligent Systems in Healthcare and mHealth for Health Outcomes

Exploring Parameter Tuning for Analysis and Optimization of a Computational Model

Julia S. Mollee[✉], Eric F.M. Araújo, and Michel C.A. Klein

VU University Amsterdam, De Boelelaan 1081, 1081 HV Amsterdam, Netherlands
{j.s.mollee,e.araujo,m.c.a.klein}@vu.nl

Abstract. Computational models of human processes are used for many different purposes and in many different types of applications. A common challenge in using such models is to find suitable parameter values. In many cases, the ideal parameter values are those that yield the most realistic simulation results. However, there are situations in which the goodness of fit is not the main or only criterion to evaluate the appropriateness of a model, but where other aspects of the model behavior are also relevant. This is often the case when computational models are employed in real-life applications, such as mHealth systems. In this paper, we explore how parameter tuning techniques can be used to analyze the behavior of computational models systematically and to investigate the reasons behind the observed behavior. We study a computational model of psychosocial influences on physical activity behavior as an in-depth use case. In this particular case, an important measure of the feasibility of the model is the diversity in the simulation outcomes. This novel application of parameter tuning techniques for analysis and understanding of model behavior is transferable to other cases, and is therefore a valuable new approach in the toolset of computational modelers.

Keywords: mHealth systems · Behavior change · Computational modeling · Dynamic modeling · Model analysis · Model optimization · Parameter tuning

1 Introduction

Computational models of human processes are used for many different purposes and in many different types of applications. A common use case of computational models is the analysis and understanding of the modeled processes. Another application area of such models is human support systems, in which the model provides the understanding of the user. Examples of such systems are behavior change support systems [1] or systems that provide support during demanding tasks.

A challenge when developing these models is to find parameter sets that result in adequate behavior of the model. Usually, background knowledge and (psychological) literature is used to determine the values in these models. In other situations, especially when empirical data about actual human behavior is available, automated parameter estimation techniques are used to find suitable parameter values. To test the appropriateness of the parameterized model, the goodness of fit is determined by comparing the generated values with the observed values.

© Springer International Publishing AG 2017
S. Benferhat et al. (Eds.): IEA/AIE 2017, Part II, LNAI 10351, pp. 341–352, 2017.
DOI: 10.1007/978-3-319-60045-1_36

However, there are situations in which the goodness of fit is not the only criterion to evaluate a model. When the data is noisy, goodness of fit might lead to incorrect outcomes [2], but it is also possible that other aspects of model behavior are important. For example, in this paper we use a model (that is deployed in an mHealth system) as case study in which the variety in the outcomes is an important measure of the feasibility of the model (see Sect. 3.2 for further explanation). When this aspect of the model behavior is suboptimal, the question arises how this can be explained. This is a non-trivial problem to which analytical techniques could contribute.

In this paper, we exploit parameter tuning techniques to investigate the behavior of the model and to investigate the reasons behind the observed behavior. Specifically, we do an in-depth analysis of a computational model that is expected to show diverse outcomes. We investigate the question about the cause of this lack of diversity in outcomes: is it due to the data that is used (for initial values) or due to (an inadequate choice of) parameter values? The application of the parameter tuning techniques leads to a better understanding of the model behavior and provides answers to these questions. It can be used to gain more insight in the structural properties of the model.

2   Background

In this section, we describe related work on optimization problems and parameter tuning, as well as the novelty of the current work.

Parameter Tuning. Parameter tuning is a widely used optimization approach. It is often used in machine learning applications, to find optimal parameters for the learning process [3], but also in evolutionary computing applications [4]. In addition, these algorithms are broadly used in dynamic modeling, in order to fit model predictions to actual data. We can find applications of parameter tuning strategies in several domains. For instance, in hydrology, parameter tuning strategies are used in hydrologic models, which are defined by parameters and states. Here, parameters are physical and generally time-invariant descriptions of surface and subsurface characteristics, while states are fluxes and storages of water and energy that are propagated in time by the model physics [5].

Parameter tuning techniques also have many applications in the simulation of human systems or agent-based models [6]. Simulations of crowd behavior [7, 8], organizations, and emotion contagion [9] are examples of scenarios for parameter tuning. Individual and group behaviors rely on many aspects, which can be captured in models that will need to be fitted to real data obtained from empirical experiments.

Simulated Annealing. The computational model investigated in this paper has many continuous variables. The presence of continuous variables in an optimization problem increases the complexity of the problem solving mechanism due to the infinite number of possibilities in the solution space, which makes it an NP-hard combinatorial problem. Often, parameter tuning tasks with continuous variables are limited by time constraints, making it impossible to identify the globally best result. Therefore, many optimizations algorithms are designed to yield good solutions in a limited time period, but do not guarantee that the solution found is the globally best solution. Examples of such algorithms include simulated annealing (SA), gradient descent, and evolution-based, swarm-based and ecology-based algorithms [10–13].

For our analysis, we use the simulated annealing algorithm. This technique is able to find the global optimum when the variables are discrete. In case of continuous variables, SA is preferable over alternatives (like gradient descent), because of its fast convergence and easy implementation. This is the reason that NP-hard combinatorial optimization problems can be successfully addressed with SA [14].

Novelty. In this work, we also apply parameter tuning in the domain of human behavior models. However, in contrast with the research described above, we do not use parameter tuning techniques with the aim to find a best fitting model (as is done in most other applications of parameter optimization in computational models). Instead, we use parameter tuning as a means to analyze the behavior of the model. The tuning algorithm is used to investigate to what extent a model can produce different simulation outcomes. We compare the outcomes of the simulations with the structural aspects of the model. This provides us with an additional tool that helps to increase our understanding of the behavior of the model in relation to the structural characteristics.

3   Use Case: Model of Influences on Physical Activity Based on Social Cognitive Theory

The use case studied in this paper concerns a computational model of psychosocial influences on physical activity behavior. It describes the relations between several psychological determinants, such as self-efficacy, intentions and social norms, and their influence on physical activity behavior. The model under investigation is an adaptation of the computational model presented in [15]. Therefore, the concepts and the relations of the model described in Sect. 3.1 are explained in more detail in the original publication. Revisions between the two versions of the model were motivated by a decrease in conceptual detail and computational complexity of the model, and by suggestions of experts in the domain of behavior change.

The details of the computational model are described in depth in Sect. 3.1. The objective of the model and its application are described in Sect. 3.2.

3.1   Detailed Specification of the Model

The computational model is largely based on the social cognitive theory by Albert Bandura [16]. This is a well-established theory of behavior change, with high applicability in the domain of health behavior [17]. The theory has proven to account for a large proportion of the variance in physical activity [18], and is therefore very suitable as a basis to describe the dynamics underlying physical activity behavior.

All concepts are modeled numerically, as real values in the interval [0, 1], and the relations are formalized as differential equations. The relations express the influence of the source concept on the target concept by increasing or decreasing the value of the target concept in the direction of the source target, moderated by a parameter named

$\beta_{source,target}$. The increase or decrease of the target concept is also relative to its current value (e.g., for concept SE, a decrease is relative to $SE(t)$ and an increase is relative to $(1-SE(t))$), in order to ensure that the concept values stay in the interval [0, 1]. The constant Δt indicates the step size of the model, and is set at 0.1 to ensure smooth results. An example of the formal relation between the concepts is given below, for the concept Behavior (Beh). Figure 1 shows a graphical representation of the dynamic relations between all concepts in the model.

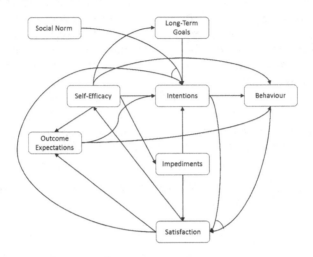

Fig. 1. Graphical representation of the model.

$$Change\_Beh(t) = \left(\beta_{SE,Beh} \cdot (SE(t) - Beh(t)) + \beta_{Int,Beh} \cdot (Int(t) - Beh(t)) + \beta_{OE,Beh} \cdot (OE(t) - Beh(t)) - \beta_{Imp,Beh} \cdot Imp(t)\right)$$
$$if\ (Change\_Beh(t) \geq 0): Beh(t+1) = Beh(t) + (Change\_Beh(t)) \cdot \Delta t \cdot (1 - Beh(t))$$
$$if\ (Change\_Beh(t) < 0): Beh(t+1) = Beh(t) + (Change\_Beh(t)) \cdot \Delta t \cdot Beh(t)$$

The values of all parameters (β) can be adjusted by the modeler. In the current implementation, the parameters were chosen based on correlations between the concepts found in literature [18–20], in order to keep the ratio between the parameters in accordance with empirical findings. This original parameter set is shown in Table 1.

Table 1. Parameter settings.

Parameter	$\beta_{Sat,SE}$	$\beta_{Imp,Int}$	$\beta_{SE,Int}$	$\beta_{SE,Imp}$	$\beta_{Imp,Sat}$	$\beta_{Int,Beh,Sat}$	$\beta_{SE,Beh}$	$\beta_{Int,Beh}$
Value	0.50	0.08	1.00	0.43	0.25	0.50	0.17	0.60
Parameter	$\beta_{Imp,Beh}$	$\beta_{SE,LTG}$	$\beta_{LTG,Int}$	$\beta_{Sat,OE}$	$\beta_{SE,OE}$	$\beta_{OE,Int}$	$\beta_{OE,Beh}$	$\beta_{SN,Sat,Int}$
Value	0.25	0.05	0.20	0.10	0.05	0.02	0.01	0.02

3.2   Practical Application of the Model

The computational model described above was created in the context of a behavior change system for encouraging physical activity among young adults [21]. The system monitors the users' behavior through an activity tracker, and combines this with various other sources of information (e.g., location data, weather forecasts, personality questionnaires, social network information) to provide tailored coaching.

The role of the model is to run simulations to estimate the effect of different coaching strategies on the behavior. Thus, the model is run for each user and each possible strategy, and outcomes for the behavior are compared. The strategy that yields the highest result for the behavior concept (Beh) is considered to be the most promising.

In context of developing the behavior change system, eight coaching strategies were defined. Each of the strategies targets one of the psychological concepts in the model, and consists of coaching messages that are sent to the user through a smartphone app during one week. The presumed effect of the possible coaching strategies is implemented as a subtle boost of 5% in the first three days of the simulation. For example, if the simulated coaching strategy targets the self-efficacy, the value of the self-efficacy concept is increased with 5% of the potential improvement (i.e., its distance to the maximum), as in Eq. 1.

$$if \ (coaching\_strategy \ == \ SE): SE(t) = SE(t) + 0.05 \cdot (1 - SE(t)) \tag{1}$$

Since the outcomes of these simulations are used in a real-life application, their closeness to reality is not the only relevant measure. Specifically, for the behavior change intervention to be both effective and engaging to the user, the outcomes (which determine the activated coaching strategy) should be diverse.

Figure 2 shows an example of two simulations for a certain person from our dataset, with on the left side the concept targeted by the simulated coaching strategy and on the right side the change in the behavior based on that coaching strategy. The simulated effect of the coaching strategy is visible in the first half of the graphs on the left hand side. Since the behavior value increases most in Fig. 2(a), that coaching strategy (self-efficacy) would be preferred over the other (intentions).

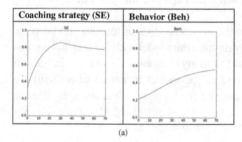
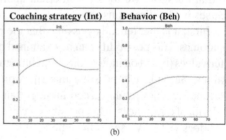

Fig. 2. Example of two model simulations, showing the concept targeted by the coaching strategy and its effect on the behavior. The targeted concepts are self-efficacy (a) and intentions (b). The vertical axis represents the simulation values; the horizontal axis represents the time.

4 Methods

When investigating the model behavior with respect to its application in a behavior change intervention, it is important to base this analysis on realistic combinations of values for concepts in the model. Therefore, we collected data about the state of the concepts from ten potential users with varying levels of physical activity. These initial values were obtained from extensive validated questionnaires for assessing the psychological constructs (e.g., [18, 22]). That way, we collected a set of reliable assessments for the combinations of initial values of the concepts. Four users in the data set were male and six were female. The average age was 30.1 years (range [21, 42]).

When running the model simulations for this user set with the parameter values based on correlations found in literature (see Sect. 3.1), the results yield very little diversity. When sorting the eight coaching strategies based on the predicted outcome of the behavior concept, only three different strategies appear in the first two positions for all ten users. Overall, it appears that some strategies are more often among the best options, while others occur only towards the end of the order (see Fig. 3).

```
User 1:  ['Sat', 'SE', 'Int', 'LTG', 'OE', 'Imp', 'SRS', 'SN']
User 2:  ['Sat', 'SE', 'Int', 'LTG', 'OE', 'Imp', 'SRS', 'SN']
User 3:  ['Int', 'Sat', 'SE', 'LTG', 'Imp', 'SRS', 'OE', 'SN']
User 4:  ['SE', 'Sat', 'LTG', 'Int', 'OE', 'Imp', 'SRS', 'SN']
User 5:  ['Sat', 'SE', 'Int', 'LTG', 'OE', 'Imp', 'SRS', 'SN']
User 6:  ['SE', 'Int', 'Sat', 'LTG', 'OE', 'Imp', 'SRS', 'SN']
User 7:  ['SE', 'Int', 'LTG', 'Sat', 'OE', 'Imp', 'SRS', 'SN']
User 8:  ['Sat', 'SE', 'Int', 'LTG', 'OE', 'Imp', 'SRS', 'SN']
User 9:  ['Sat', 'SE', 'LTG', 'OE', 'Imp', 'SRS', 'SN', 'Int']
User 10: ['SE', 'Sat', 'LTG', 'Int', 'OE', 'Imp', 'SRS', 'SN']
```

Fig. 3. Initial outcomes of model simulations.

The surprising lack of diversity among these findings raises the question: what factors cause the stability of the model's simulation outcomes? In order to find an answer to that question, we took a numerical approach, and explored the possible underlying causes in two directions.

First, it is theoretically possible that the initial values are too uniform to yield diverse outcomes. This possibility can be examined by running the model with the original parameter values (based on indications from literature) on many combinations of random starting values. Second, it is possible that the structure of the model in combination with the parameter values implies a certain importance of the concepts, which is stronger than the individual differences. This possibility can be examined by searching for a parameter set that does yield diverse results among the collection of realistic initial values.

4.1 Quantifying the Lack of Diversity

In order to evaluate the (lack of) diversity of the simulation outcomes, it has to be quantified systematically. In this research, the lack of diversity is computed by comparing all coaching strategy sequences for each pair of users, and applying a 0.01 penalty each time a strategy occurs in the same position. This choice is motivated by the particular application of the computational model in our use case. Other operationalizations of diversity or other measures (e.g., entropy, variance) could be more relevant in other applications. The currently adopted approach implies a maximum cost of $(N(N-1))/2 \cdot 8 \cdot 0.01 = 3.6$. For the results shown in Fig. 3, the cost is 1.8.

4.2 Analyzing the Influence of the Initial Values

To test whether the set of combinations of initial values plays a role in the constancy of the simulation results, we generate a set of 1,000 times 10 different combinations of random starting values for the concepts of the model, to mimic sets of 10 users. Then, we run the computational model on each of these initializations with the original parameter settings (see Table 1). For each of these simulations, we compute the cost as specified in Sect. 4.1.

4.3 Analyzing the Influence of the Parameter Set

To investigate whether the lack of diversity in the simulation results is caused by the model's parameter settings, we explore the ability of the model to produce diverse outcomes for the dataset of real users. This exploration is done by searching the parameter space with a simulated annealing algorithm [10], in which we optimize for a reduction in the cost as specified in Sect. 4.1.

The solution space in this instance of the simulated annealing algorithm is represented by the possible values of the 16 parameters. Each solution is a set of parameter values (see Table 1), which describe the strength of the relations between the concepts. A neighboring solution is generated by adding a (positive or negative) change drawn from a normal distribution to each parameter value, while bounding them to the range [0, 1]. The costs corresponding to each solution are calculated by running the model with the parameter values, and computing the costs of the outcomes according to Sect. 4.1. The probability of accepting a solution with a higher cost depends on the difference between the current cost and the new cost and the "temperature" T, as in Eq. 2. The temperature decreases with a factor 0.9 with each 100 iterations, and stops the algorithm when the initial temperature of 1.0 has decreased to a value below 0.00001. The final parameter set is used to run the model once more and calculate the corresponding costs, and the results are stored. The entire search process was repeated 75 times.

$$acceptance\_probability = e^{(old\_cost - new\_cost)/T} \tag{2}$$

4.4 Hypothesized Outcomes

The experimental setup described above yielded a number of anticipated outcomes, enumerated below.

Hypothesis H1: Because of the diverse combinations of values for the ten users and the extraordinary stability of the initial simulation results (in Fig. 3), we expect that these starting values do not cause the stable outcomes. Therefore, we expect similar or lower levels of diversity when running the model on random sets of input values (see Sect. 4.2).

Hypothesis H2: Since the parameter values determine the influence of the different concepts, we expect that they play a key role in the stability of the initial simulation results. Therefore, we expect more diversity when running the model on parameter sets found through simulated annealing (see Sect. 4.3).

Hypothesis H3: Because of the computational model's complexity, and the corresponding large number of degrees of freedom, we expect that many different parameter sets that are obtained through the simulated annealing search can lead to similar outcomes in terms of cost.

Hypothesis H4: However, we still expect to see some global pattern in the parameter sets on average, i.e. that some parameters generally end up in the lower part of the range and some parameters in the higher part of the range.

Hypothesis H5: If indeed such overall patterns are found, we expect that we will be able to explain them based on the underlying meaning of the concepts and the structure of the model.

As mentioned before, the combination of the dataset of real users with the original parameter values yielded a cost of 1.8 out of a possible 3.6. (See Sect. 4.1.)

5 Results

As mentioned before, the combination of the dataset of real users with the original parameter values yielded a cost of 1.8 out of a possible 3.6. (See Sect. 4.1.)

5.1 Influence of Initial Values

When running the model with the original parameter set on 1,000 different sets of 10 combinations of random initial values, the average cost of the simulation results is 2.21 out of 3.6. Even though in the set of 1,000 different outcomes there are some runs that produce more diversity than in the original situation, 92.5% of the results produce less diversity and correspondingly have a higher cost than the 1.8 of the initial solution. See Table 2 for an overview of the results.

Table 2. Results of original parameter settings and random initial values over 1,000 runs.

Measure	Value
Average cost	2.21459
Range of costs	[1.33, 2.96]
Standard deviation of cost	0.261168
Percentage where cost > 1.8	92.5%

5.2 Influence of Parameter Set

After 75 runs of the simulated annealing algorithm, the average cost of the model on the dataset of real users is 0.85 out of 3.6. The standard deviation is quite low, indicating that most of the outcomes are close to the average. See Table 3 for an overview of the results.

Table 3. Results of real initial values and parameters found through simulated annealing.

Measure	Value
Average cost	0.853867
Range of costs	[0.66, 0.99]
Standard deviation of cost	0.033898

When further exploring the parameter sets that yield these results, we see a large variety in the found parameter values for largely similar cost outcomes. Most parameters cover (almost) the full range of [0, 1] in the 75 runs, with 14 out of 16 parameters approaching or reaching the limits in both directions within 0.1. The average parameter value is 0.5268, and the average standard deviation of each parameter is 0.2564, further supporting the observation that their values vary widely. Hence, there is no clear pattern of the parameter values for each individual solution found.

However, when looking at the parameter values averaged over the 75 runs, it appears that there are some patterns visible. That is, for some of the parameters, the average values deviates from the overall average of 0.5268. Table 4 shows the parameter values averaged over all 75 runs.

Table 4. Parameter settings.

Parameter	$\beta_{Sat,SE}$	$\beta_{Imp,Int}$	$\beta_{SE,Int}$	$\beta_{SE,Imp}$	$\beta_{Imp,Sat}$	$\beta_{Int,Beh,Sat}$	$\beta_{SE,Beh}$	$\beta_{Int,Beh}$
Avg. value	0.5932	0.2760	0.5102	0.5321	0.8258	0.8320	0.3319	0.3086
Parameter	$\beta_{Imp,Beh}$	$\beta_{SE,LTG}$	$\beta_{LTG,Int}$	$\beta_{Sat,OE}$	$\beta_{SE,OE}$	$\beta_{OE,Int}$	$\beta_{OE,Beh}$	$\beta_{SN,Sat,Int}$
Avg. value	0.3677	0.6865	0.7381	0.4348	0.3042	0.5703	0.4610	0.6563

6 Discussion

The results provide grounds to investigate the hypothesized outcomes from Sect. 4.4. As expected, the results presented in Sect. 5.1 show that the lack of diversity in the original simulation is not caused by the initial values in our dataset. Although some of the sets of initial values produce more diversity than in the original simulation, the vast majority (92.5%) yields higher costs. Therefore, hypothesis H1 can be confirmed. On the contrary, the costs found in Sect. 5.2 are considerably lower than in the original simulations. This confirms hypothesis H2, and indicates that the potential for more diversity in the simulation results is related to the parameter values.

The results described in Sect. 5.2 also showed a large variety in the parameter sets found through the optimization algorithm. This is in line with hypothesis H3, and can be explained by the model's complexity. The high number of degrees of freedom in the model implies that many different parameter sets may produce similar results in terms of cost. However, when analyzing the found parameters in more detail, we do discern patterns in their values: some parameter values are generally high (e.g., $\beta_{Imp,Sat}$), while others are low (e.g., $\beta_{SE,Beh}$). This finding confirms hypothesis H4.

By looking at the meaning of the parameters with relatively low or high values, we attempt to explain why they end up with these values. Since we're optimizing for high diversity in the effect on the behavior, it can be expected that concepts with a structurally high influence on the behavior will be dampened, while concepts with a structurally low influence will be increased. Indeed, we see that the parameters in Table 4 tend to weaken the path from the self-efficacy (the central notion of the social cognitive theory) to the behavior. For example, $\beta_{SE,Beh}$ and $\beta_{Int,Beh}$ are relatively low on average, thus decreasing the effect of the self-efficacy on the behavior. Similarly, $\beta_{Imp,Sat}$ has a relatively high value, but since the impediments have a negative effect on the satisfaction, this will ultimately lead to a decrease in the self-efficacy. At first sight, the low average value of $\beta_{Imp,Int}$ is surprising: one would expect that a strong (negative) influence on the intentions will transfer to the behavior. However, when taking a closer look at the data, the impediments seem to have generally low values (average: 0.29, minimum: 0.10, maximum: 0.39), so a high parameter would in fact cause an increase in the intentions and consequently a stronger influence on the behavior. In summary, hypothesis H5 is confirmed as well.

The observation of the surprising value for $\beta_{Imp,Int}$ indicates that the outcomes are still dependent on the values in the dataset of users. Therefore, although we demonstrated that the relatively small set of users does not cause the lack of diverse outcomes, it would be interesting to see whether the findings scale to larger populations of users, or that the global patterns of the parameters change. Another limitation to the generalizability of this work concerns the dependency of the results on the structure of our model and the specific implementation of the relations between the concepts. Also, we have restricted ourselves to the simulated annealing algorithm, and further research should reveal whether the results are dependent on our choice of algorithm. However, our use case has demonstrated that applying parameter tuning techniques to analyze and better understand models has indeed given us insight in the model behavior. This novel use of parameter tuning is also transferable to other applications, with different underlying models and different evaluation (cost) measures.

In the context of the application of the model (see Sect. 3.2), we strive for both a close fit to reality and diverse outcomes. In other words, we look for a balance between keeping the parameters close to the indications found in literature and searching for a parameter set that yields diverse results. Therefore, we ran the algorithm described in Sect. 4.3 again, but with constraints to the generation of neighboring solutions, forcing them to stay within a distance of ± 0.1 from the original parameters. This approach allowed us to increase the diversity of the outcomes (reducing the cost from 1.8 to 1.06), while keeping the literature-based parameters to some extent intact.

7 Conclusion

This research has established that applying parameter tuning techniques to analyze and better understand the behavior of dynamic computational models has indeed the potential to provide more insight in the structural properties of the models. In our use case, where we tried to increase the diversity in the results of the model simulations, we successfully demonstrated the cause of the initial lack of diversity. Subsequently, we were able to show that diverse outcomes can be achieved by finding suitable parameter values through simulated annealing, and that the global patterns of these parameter sets provide information about (or can be explained by) the structure of the model and the meaning of its concepts and relations. This novel application of parameter tuning techniques is transferable to other cases, with different underlying models and different evaluation (cost) measures, and is therefore a valuable new approach in the toolset of computational modelers and designers of mHealth systems.

References

1. Oinas-Kukkonen, H.: Behavior change support systems: a research model and agenda. In: Ploug, T., Hasle, P., Oinas-Kukkonen, H. (eds.) PERSUASIVE 2010. LNCS, vol. 6137, pp. 4–14. Springer, Heidelberg (2010). doi:10.1007/978-3-642-13226-1_3
2. Pitt, M., Myung, I.: When a good fit can be bad. Trends Cognit. Sci. **6**(10), 421–425 (2002)
3. Chapelle, O., Vapnik, V., Bousquet, O., Mukherjee, S.: Choosing multiple parameters for support vector machines. Mach. Learn. **46**(1–3), 131–159 (2002)
4. Eiben, A.E., Smit, S.K.: Parameter tuning for configuring and analyzing evolutionary algorithms. Swarm Evol. Comput. **1**(1), 19–31 (2011)
5. Moradkhani, H., Sorooshian, S., Gupta, H.V., Houser, P.R.: Dual state–parameter estimation of hydrological models using ensemble Kalman filter. Adv. Water Resour. **28**(2), 135–147 (2005)
6. Bonabeau, E.: Agent-based modeling: methods and techniques for simulating human systems. Proc. Natl. Acad. Sci. **99**(3), 7280–7287 (2002)
7. Sun, Q., Wu, S.: A crowd model with multiple individual parameters to represent individual behaviour in crowd simulation. In: Proceedings of the 28th ISARC (2011)
8. Bosse, T., Hoogendoorn, M., Klein, M.C., Treur, J., van der Wal, C.N., van Wissen, A.: Modelling collective decision making in groups and crowds: integrating social contagion and interacting emotions, beliefs and intentions. Auton. Agents Multi Agent Syst. **27**(1), 52–84 (2013)
9. Tsai, J., Bowring, E., Marsella, S., Tambe, M.: Empirical evaluation of computational emotional contagion models. In: Vilhjálmsson, H.H., Kopp, S., Marsella, S., Thórisson, Kristinn R. (eds.) IVA 2011. LNCS, vol. 6895, pp. 384–397. Springer, Heidelberg (2011). doi:10.1007/978-3-642-23974-8_42
10. Kirkpatrick, S., Gelatt Jr., C., Vecchi, M.: Optimization by simulated annealing. Science **220**(4598), 671–680 (1983)
11. Černý, V.: Thermodynamical approach to the traveling salesman problem: an efficient simulation algorithm. J. Optim. Theory Appl. **45**(1), 41–51 (1985)
12. Bertsimas, D., Tsitsiklis, J.: Simulated annealing. Stat. Sci. **8**(1), 10–15 (1993)
13. Binitha, S., Siva Sathya, S.: A survey of bio inspired optimization algorithms. Int. J. Soft Comput. Eng. **2**(2), 13751 (2012)

14. Boulcimen, K., Lecocq, H.: A new efficient simulated annealing algorithm for the resource-constrained project scheduling problem and its multiple mode version. Eur. J. Oper. Res. **149**(2), 268–281 (2003)

15. Bandura, A.: Health promotion from the perspective of social cognitive theory. Psychol. Health **13**, 623–649 (1998)

16. Mollee, J.S., Wal, C.N.: A computational agent model of influences on physical activity based on the social cognitive theory. In: Boella, G., Elkind, E., Savarimuthu, B.T.R., Dignum, F., Purvis, Martin K. (eds.) PRIMA 2013. LNCS, vol. 8291, pp. 478–485. Springer, Heidelberg (2013). doi:10.1007/978-3-642-44927-7_37

17. Bandura, A.: Health promotion by social cognitive means. Health Educ. Behav. Off. Publ. Soc. Publ. Health Educ. **31**(2), 143–164 (2004)

18. Rovniak, L., Anderson, E., Winett, R., Stephens, R.: Social cognitive determinants of physical activity in young adults: a prospective structural equation analysis. Ann. Behav. Med. **24**(2), 149–156 (2002)

19. Plotnikoff, R., Lippke, S., Courneya, K., Birkett, N., Sigal, R.: Physical activity and social cognitive theory: a test in a population sample of adults with type 1 or type 2 diabetes. Appl. Psychol. **57**(4), 628–643 (2008)

20. Plotnikoff, R., Costigan, S., Karunamuni, N., Lubans, D.: Social cognitive theories used to explain physical activity behavior in adolescents: a systematic review and meta-analysis. Preventive Med. **56**(5), 245–253 (2013)

21. Klein, M.C.A., Manzoor, A., Middelweerd, A., Mollee, J.S., te Velde, S.J.: Encouraging physical activity via a personalized mobile system. IEEE Internet Comput. **19**(4), 20–27 (2015)

22. Frank, L.D., Sallis, J.F., Saelens, B.E., Leary, L., Cain, K., Conway, T.L., Hess, P.M.: The development of a walkability index: application to the neighborhood quality of life study. Br. J. Sports Med. **44**(13), 924–933 (2010)

Empirical Validation of a Computational Model of Influences on Physical Activity Behavior

Julia S. Mollee[(✉)] and Michel C.A. Klein

VU University Amsterdam, De Boelelaan 1081,
1081 HV Amsterdam, The Netherlands
{j.s.mollee,m.c.a.klein}@vu.nl

Abstract. The adoption and maintenance of a healthy lifestyle is a fundamental pillar in the quest towards a healthy society. Modern (mobile) technology allows for increasingly intelligent systems that can help to optimize people's health outcomes. One of the possible directions in such mHealth systems is the use of intelligent reasoning engines based on dynamic computational models of behavior change. In this work, we investigate the accuracy of such a model to simulate changes in physical activity levels over a period of two to twelve weeks. The predictions of the model are compared to empirical physical activity data of 108 participants. The results reveal that the model's predictions show a moderate to strong correlation with the actual data, and it performs substantially better than a simple alternative model. Even though the implications of these findings depend strongly on the application at hand, we show that it is possible to use a computational model to predict changes in behavior. This is an important finding for developers of mHealth systems, as it confirms the relevance of model-based reasoning in such health interventions.

Keywords: Computational modeling · Dynamic modeling · Model validation · mHealth systems · Behavior change · Physical activity

1 Introduction

It is well known that engaging in sufficient physical activity has many beneficial effects on physical and mental health [1, 2]. On the contrary, low levels of physical activity have been associated with increased risks of cardiovascular diseases, cancer, diabetes, and mental illness [3]. Despite these prominent advantages, a large proportion of the Western population does not meet the guidelines of being moderately to vigorously active for at least 30 min on at least five days a week [4].

It is believed that mobile technology provides an opportunity to support people with increasing their level of physical activity [5–7], and there is also some initial evidence that this is effective [8]. However, just monitoring physical activity is not sufficient to achieve a durable improvement [9]. There is a need for development of evidence-informed mobile apps that apply advanced technological features in order to yield long-term effects [7].

© Springer International Publishing AG 2017
S. Benferhat et al. (Eds.): IEA/AIE 2017, Part II, LNAI 10351, pp. 353–363, 2017.
DOI: 10.1007/978-3-319-60045-1_37

In [10], we described how we developed an intelligent system to stimulate physical activity for young adults. Part of the intelligence lies in the fact that it uses a computational model of behavior change to predict the effect of different intervention strategies on the activity level of the users. The model consists of temporal-dynamic relations between determinants of behavior change. The model predictions are used for deciding on the support messages for specific users in each phase of the intervention. We believe that this can result in a highly tailored and personalized intervention.

The model is based on a number of different theories on behavior change [11]. Most of these theories have been validated independently, and there also have been validations of integrated frameworks [12]. However, these validations usually look at correlations between the different constructs in the theories. Hence, we do not yet know whether the dynamic computational representation of our integrated model provides a valid description of the process of behavior change. Therefore, we would like to know to what extent the model is a valid way to predict the most effective coaching strategies. This paper describes a first step towards such a validation. We use empirical data collected in the effectiveness study to compare the prediction of the model based on the initial questionnaire with the actual change in physical activity that has been measured in the study. In addition, we compare the actually measured behavior with predictions of an alternative simple model. The results provide an initial answer about the validity of the model.

The remainder of this paper is organized as follows. In Sect. 2, the details of the computational model under consideration are presented. Section 3 describes the methods used to provide a validation of the computational model. The results are presented in Sect. 4, and reflected upon in Sect. 5.

2 Computational Model of Psychosocial Influences on Physical Activity Based on Social Cognitive Theory

The computational model investigated in this paper was designed in context of the development of an intelligent behavior change support system [10]. The reasoning engine of this system uses the model to predict what available coaching strategies are the most promising to improve the user's behavior (For more information, see [10].).

The model captures the dynamics between psychosocial influences on physical activity behavior. It describes the relations between several psychological determinants, such as self-efficacy, intentions and social norms, and their influence on physical activity behavior. The model under investigation in this paper is an adaptation of the computational model presented in [13]. Therefore, the concepts and the relations of the model described below are explained in more detail in the original publication. The revision was motivated by a decrease in conceptual detail and computational complexity of the model, and by suggestions of experts in behavior change.

The computational model is largely based on the social cognitive theory by Albert Bandura [14]. This is a well-established theory of behavior change, with high applicability in the domain of health behavior [15]. The theory has proven to account for a large proportion of the variance in physical activity [16], and is therefore very suitable as a basis to describe the dynamics underlying physical activity behavior.

All concepts are modeled numerically, as real values in the interval [0,1], and the relations are formalized as differential equations. The relations express the influence of the source concept on the target concept by increasing or decreasing the value of the target concept in the direction of the source target, moderated by a parameter named $\beta_{source,target}$ (or occasionally $\beta_{source1+source2,target}$). The increase or decrease of the target concept is also relative to its current value: e.g., $SE(t)$ in case of a decrease and $(1 - SE(t))$ in case of an increase. This consideration of the current value also ensures that the concept values stay in the interval [0,1]. The constant Δt indicates the step size of the model, and is set at 0.1 to ensure smooth results. Figure 1 shows a graphical representation of the dynamic relations between all concepts in the model.

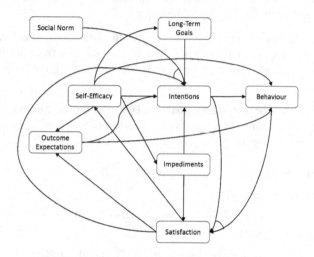

Fig. 1. Graphical representation of the model.

Below, the meaning of the concepts in the model are explained and the formal relations are specified.

Self-Efficacy: The self-efficacy (SE) is a key element of the process described by the social cognitive theory. It represents the confidence in one's own ability to achieve certain goals, which plays a fundamental role in the acquisition and maintenance of some desired behavior. The self-efficacy increases with high satisfaction of the current behavior, and it decreases if one is dissatisfied with his/her behavior.

$$if\ (SE(t) \geq Sat(t)):$$
$$SE(t+1) = SE(t) + \beta_{Sat,SE} \cdot (Sat(t) - SE(t)) \cdot \Delta t \cdot SE(t)$$
$$if\ (SE(t) < Sat(t)):$$
$$SE(t+1) = SE(t) + \beta_{Sat,SE} \cdot (Sat(t) - SE(t)) \cdot \Delta t \cdot (1 - SE(t))$$

Impediments: Impediments (Imp) are the (personal, situational or systemic) factors that form an obstacle to the desired behavior. The self-efficacy plays a role in how insurmountable one views those obstacles. Therefore, the personal impediments (Input_Imp) are adjusted based on the level of the self-efficacy.

$if\ (SE(t) \geq Input\_Imp(t))$:
$$Imp(t) = Input\_Imp(t) - (\beta_{SE,Imp} \cdot (SE(t) - Input\_Imp(t))) \cdot \Delta t \cdot Input\_Imp(t)$$
$if\ (SE(t) < Input\_Imp(t))$:
$$Imp(t) = Input\_Imp(t) - (\beta_{SE,Imp} \cdot (SE(t) - Input\_Imp(t))) \cdot \Delta t \cdot (1 - Input\_Imp(t))$$

In the system, these personal 'input impediments' are assessed through a questionnaire, so they reflect the user's overall experience of barriers on a scale of 0 (no impediments) to 1 (very strong impediments).

Social Norm: The social norm (SN) represents the behavioral standards that one's social connections impose on him or her. It is derived directly from information about the user's social network, and it assumed to be stable for the duration covered by the simulations.

Long-Term Goals: The long-term goals (LTG) can be interpreted as the overall motivation to achieve change in the behavior. The levels of self-efficacy can increase or decrease the long-term goals.

$$Change\_LTG(t) = (\beta_{SE,LTG} \cdot (SE(t) - LTG(t)))$$
$if\ (Change\_LTG(t) \geq 0)$:
$$LTG(t+1) = LTG(t) + Change\_LTG(t) \cdot \Delta t \cdot (1 - LTG(t))$$
$if\ (Change\_LTG(t) < 0)$:
$$LTG(t+1) = LTG(t) + Change\_LTG(t) \cdot \Delta t \cdot LTG(t)$$

Intentions: The intentions (Int) denote the user's aims for the desired behavior. They provide focus and a measure for evaluation. The intentions are influenced by the self-efficacy, the social norm and the outcome expectations, and adjusted by the perceived impediments.

$$Change\_Int(t) = (\beta_{SE,Int} \cdot (SE(t) - Int(t)) + \beta_{LTG,Int} \cdot (LTG(t) - Int(t)) + \beta_{OE,Int} \cdot (OE(t) - Int(t))$$
$$+ \beta_{SN+Sat,Int} \cdot (Sat(t) - SN(t)) - \beta_{Imp,Int} \cdot Imp(t))$$
$if\ (Change\_Int(t) \geq 0)$:
$$Int(t+1) = Int(t) + (Change\_Int(t)) \cdot \Delta t \cdot (1 - Int(t))$$
$if\ (Change\_Int(t) < 0)$:
$$Int(t+1) = Int(t) + (Change\_Int(t)) \cdot \Delta t \cdot Int(t)$$

Behavior: The behavior (Beh) describes the level of physical activity that someone is engaged in: its value is 0 if someone is not physically active at all, and 1 if someone is maximally active. It is mainly influenced by the self-efficacy, outcome expectations, intentions and the impediments.

$$Change\_Beh(t) = (\beta_{SE,Beh} \cdot (SE(t) - Beh(t)) + \beta_{Int,Beh} \cdot (Int(t) - Beh(t)) + \beta_{OE,Beh} \cdot (OE(t) - Beh(t))$$
$$- \beta_{Imp,Beh} \cdot Imp(t))$$

if $(Change\_Beh(t) \geq 0)$:

$Beh(t+1) = \quad Beh(t) + (Change\_Beh(t)) \cdot \Delta t \cdot (1 - Beh(t))$

if $(Change\_Beh(t) < 0)$:

$Beh(t+1) = \quad Beh(t) + (Change\_Beh(t)) \cdot \Delta t \cdot Beh(t)$

Satisfaction: The satisfaction (Sat) denotes one's perception of his/her own behavior, i.e. an evaluation of the behavior. It is based on the difference between one's intentions and current behavior, and adjusted with the perceived impediments.

$$Change\_Sat(t) = \left(\beta_{Int+Beh,Sat} \cdot (Beh(t) - Int(t)) + \beta_{Imp,Sat} \cdot Imp(t)\right)$$
$$if \; (Change\_Sat(t) \geq 0) :$$
$$Sat(t+1) = Sat(t) + (Change\_Sat(t)) \cdot \Delta t \cdot (1 - Sat(t))$$
$$if \; (Change\_Sat(t) < 0) :$$
$$Sat(t+1) = Sat(t) + (Change\_Sat(t)) \cdot \Delta t \cdot Sat(t)$$

Outcome Expectations: The outcome expectations (OE) represent the anticipated results of performing the behavior, on a physical, personal and social level. They are influenced by one's satisfaction with the current behavior and the self-efficacy.

$$Change\_OE(t) = (\beta_{Sat,OE} \cdot (Sat(t) - OE(t)) + \beta_{SE,OE} \cdot (SE(t) - OE(t)))$$
$$if \; (Change\_OE(t) \geq 0) :$$
$$OE(t+1) = OE(t) + (Change\_OE(t)) \cdot \Delta t \cdot (1 - OE(t))$$
$$if \; (Change\_OE(t) < 0) :$$
$$OE(t+1) = OE(t) + (Change\_OE(t)) \cdot \Delta t \cdot OE(t)$$

The values of all parameters (β) can be adjusted by the modeler. In the current implementation of the model, the parameters were chosen based on correlations between the concepts found in literature [16–18], in order to keep the ratio between the parameters in accordance with empirical findings. This parameter set is shown in Table 1. Additionally, one day was chosen to correspond with 10 time steps.

Table 1. Parameter settings.

Parameter	$\beta_{Sat,SE}$	$\beta_{Imp,Int}$	$\beta_{SE,Int}$	$\beta_{SE,Imp}$	$\beta_{Imp,Sat}$	$\beta_{Int+Beh,Sat}$	$\beta_{SE,Beh}$	$\beta_{Int,Beh}$
Value	0.50	0.08	1.00	0.43	0.25	0.50	0.17	0.60
Parameter	$\beta_{Imp,Beh}$	$\beta_{SE,LTG}$	$\beta_{LTG,Int}$	$\beta_{Sat,OE}$	$\beta_{SE,OE}$	$\beta_{OE,Int}$	$\beta_{OE,Beh}$	$\beta_{SN+Sat,Int}$
Value	0.25	0.05	0.20	0.10	0.05	0.02	0.01	0.02

3 Methods

In order to assess the validity of the computational model described above, empirical data is collected, preprocessed and analyzed. These steps are described in this section.

3.1 Data Collection

The data was collected in context of a user study, in which three (versions of) physical activity promotion apps were tested. Each of the participants ($N = 108$) used one of the apps for at least 12 weeks, in the period between March and October 2016.

At the start of the experiment, the participants were asked to fill in an extensive intake questionnaire. This questionnaire included questions about their demographics (e.g., gender, age), about their daily life patterns (e.g., occupation, important locations, travel options), and about psychological concepts underlying behavior (e.g., intentions, self-efficacy). Each of the eight psychological constructs is assessed by a number of items on a four- or five-point Likert scale, or by one item on a scale of 1 to 10. The items were based on extensive, validated questionnaires (e.g., [16, 19, 20]).

All participants received a Fitbit One activity tracker that monitored their physical activity and synchronized their data wirelessly to their assigned app. The tracker registers steps, floors climbed, distance, calories burned and active minutes. As mentioned before, the participants measured their physical activity via the Fitbit One for a minimum of 12 weeks (that is, apart from possible dropouts). The data from the first week was used to assess the initial physical activity, whereas the subsequent eleven weeks were used as ground truth to compare with the model's predictions.

3.2 Data Preprocessing

In order to obtain the initial values for the concepts of the computational model, the responses to the questionnaire items for assessing the psychological constructs were aggregated per concept. As the model assumes numerical values between 0 and 1, all responses were rescaled and averaged per concept in order to fit in that same range.

The initial value of the behavior concept was based on the Fitbit step data, rather than self-reported questionnaire answers. This value was calculated in three steps. First, the number of steps in the first seven days of participation was averaged, while discarding any days with no recorded steps (e.g., because the participant forgot to wear the activity tracker). Then, the average number of steps was capped off at 15,000 steps per day, as that represents amply complying with the guideline of 10,000 steps per day. Finally, the initial value of the behavior concept was obtained by normalizing the average number of steps. This way, a behavior value of 1.0 corresponds with 15,000 (or more) daily steps, which is regarded as "optimal" behavior. The calculation of this initial behavior value is shown in Eq. 1.

$$Beh(t_0) = \frac{\min(15,000, NumSteps)}{15,000} \qquad (1)$$

where *NumSteps* is the average number of steps for the days in the first week, discarding any days with no recorded steps.

3.3 Analyses

In order to investigate the validity of the computational model, the assessments of the psychological constructs and the normalized average number of steps in the first week were used to initialize the computational model (as described in Sect. 3.2). Starting from these values, the model was run to predict the physical activity behavior in the second week, third week, etc., up to the twelfth week of the experiment. As for the calculation of the initial behavior value, the actual behavior values for these subsequent weeks were determined as well. Then, the actual change in behavior and the predicted change in behavior were calculated.

The accuracy of the model's predictions was assessed by comparing the predicted differences to the actual differences in the behavior values. This was done by means of calculating Spearman rank-order correlations.

In order to exclude the possibility that the model's performance relies on certain underlying pattern in the data (e.g., high values will probably decrease, and vice versa), it was evaluated by comparing it to the results of a simple alternative model. In this 'random model', for each user a random value in [0,1] is drawn as predicted behavior value. This random model will also show that high values generally decrease and vice versa, as the probability of drawing a value below (for example) 0.8 is higher than drawing a value above 0.8. Spearman correlations were calculated for the random predictions as well. To avoid flukes, the random model was applied and evaluated 100 times, and the resulting correlation coefficients and p-values were averaged.

Although 108 participants filled out the intake questionnaire and wore the Fitbit One for an intended period of 12 weeks, not all participants had step data for each subsequent week (e.g., dropouts). Those were not considered in the analyses.

4 Results

The 108 people that participated in the user study were between 18 and 30 years old at the time of the data collection. Of those, 22 were male and 86 were female. However, the number of participants with usable data varied each week. Table 2 shows the number of users whose data was included in the analyses.

Table 2. Number of users included and excluded in the analyses for each predicted week.

Week number	2	3	4	5	6	7	8	9	10	11
No. included users	92	88	87	85	82	78	79	79	74	72
No. discarded users	16	20	21	23	26	30	29	29	34	36

The results of the Spearman rank-order correlation tests are summarized in Table 3. It shows the correlation coefficient (r_s) and corresponding p-value for the predictions of both the computational model and the random model. The results of the random model are based on 100 draws of a random prediction for each user.

Table 3. Results of the Spearman rank correlation for week 2 up to week 12.

Week	Computational model		Random model (avg)	
	Spearman's r_s	p-value	Spearman's r_s	p-value
2	.4134	<.001	.2592	.0524
3	.4019	<.001	.2164	.1038
4	.3001	.0047	.1523	.2376
5	.3957	<.001	.1866	.1754
6	.3064	.0051	.1692	.2146
7	.5522	<.001	.2835	.0543
8	.3173	.0044	.1658	.2384
9	.3201	.0040	.1745	.2056
10	.2841	.0142	.1631	.2741
11	.2319	.0499	.1364	.3325
12	.3510	.0039	.1978	.2028

To illustrate, Fig. 2 shows a scatter plot of the changes in the behavior values of 85 included users as predicted by the model (on the vertical axis) and the corresponding changes according to the empirical data (on the horizontal axis). The scatter plot for the random model shows the predictions of one of the 100 repeated runs.

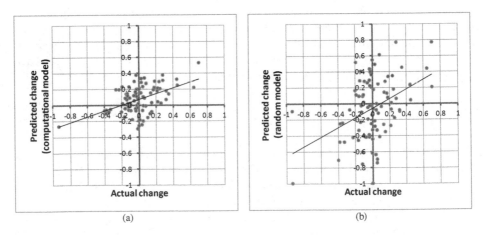

(a)   (b)

Fig. 2. Correlation plots with the predictions of the computational model (a) and the random model (b) on the vertical axis and the empirical data on the horizontal axis for week 5.

5 Discussion

The results presented in Sect. 4 reveal that the computational model performs quite well in predicting the change in physical activity level. The predictions show a weak to moderate positive correlation with the actual data, which is statistically significant ($p < .05$) for all predicted weeks. In contrast, the random model has both weaker and non-significant correlations with the empirical data. However, the random model performs relatively well on some of the weeks (i.e., week 2 and week 7). This indicates that some characteristics of the data can make it easier to predict the change right. Further investigation into this finding should reveal why this happens.

The work presented in this paper clearly is only a first step in the direction of validating computational models that are applied in mHealth systems. For instance, it would be interesting to see whether the computational model is also able to predict the course of the behavior on a more detailed (i.e., daily) level, rather than considering the errors for its predictions per week. On the other hand, the steady good performance for each week suggests that the model captures the dynamics of the behavior over time quite well. Also, the current work is limited to 12 weeks, which might not be transferrable to longer periods. The model's performance on predicting the underlying psychological constructs would be an interesting further exploration as well. Moreover, as Table 2 shows, the dataset contained a substantial number of missing observations, for example because of dropouts or participants forgetting to wear the activity tracker. This could have affected the results, and therefore replicating the analyses on a more complete dataset would be another valuable endeavor.

Several directions for further analysis could reveal whether the computational model is able to perform even better than the results found in this work. For example, the current model uses global parameters (based on indications from literature), but it is plausible that better results could be obtained when the parameters are tuned to the users in the dataset, either globally or individually. In addition, the computational model does not account for the fact that the participants in the study were exposed to an intervention during the data collection: they were using a physical activity promotion app (see Sect. 3.1). By taking a potential effect of the intervention into account, the model's predictions could arguably be improved even further.

Validation of dynamic computational models is an important endeavor, as it allows researchers to better understand the dynamics of the modeled behavior through simulations. Moreover, this work presents a step in the direction of more reliable and effective mHealth systems. After all, if the computational models underlying their reasoning engines are proven trustworthy, this increases the dependability of the support provided by the mHealth systems.

References

1. Conn, V.S., Hafdahl, A.R., Mehr, D.R.: Interventions to increase physical activity among healthy adults: meta-analysis of outcomes. Am. J. Public Health **101**(4), 751–758 (2011)
2. Eime, R.M., Young, J.A., Harvey, J.T., Charity, M.J., Payne, W.R.: A systematic review of the psychological and social benefits of participation in sport for children and adolescents: informing development of a conceptual model of health through sport. Int. J. Behav. Nutr. Phys. Act. **10**(98), 1 (2013)
3. Lee, I.M., Shiroma, E.J., Lobelo, F., Puska, P., Blair, S.N., Katzmarzyk, P.T., Lancet Physical Activity Series Working Group: Effect of physical inactivity on major non-communicable diseases worldwide: an analysis of burden of disease and life expectancy. Lancet **380**(9838), 219–229 (2012)
4. Haskell, W.L., Lee, I.M., Pate, R.R., Powell, K.E., Blair, S.N., Franklin, B.A., Macera, C.A., Heath, G.W., Thompson, P.D., Bauman, A.: Physical activity and public health: updated recommendation for adults from the American College of Sports Medicine and the American Heart Association. Circulation **116**(9), 1081 (2007)
5. Sieverdes, J.C., Treiber, F., Jenkins, C., Hermayer, K.: Improving diabetes management with mobile health technology. Am. J. Med. Sci. **345**(4), 289–295 (2013)
6. Payne, H.E., Lister, C., West, J.H., Bernhardt, J.M.: Behavioral functionality of mobile apps in health interventions: a systematic review of the literature. JMIR mHealth uHealth **3**(1), e20 (2015)
7. Knight, E., Stuckey, M.I., Prapavessis, H., Petrella, R.J.: Public health guidelines for physical activity: is there an app for that? A review of android and apple app stores. JMIR mHealth uHealth **3**(2), e43 (2015)
8. Stephens, J., Allen, J.: Mobile phone interventions to increase physical activity and reduce weight: a systematic review. J. Cardiovasc. Nurs. **28**(4), 320 (2013)
9. Gierisch, J.M., Goode, A.P., Batch, B.C., Huffman, K.N., Hall, K.S., Hastings, S.N., Allen, K.D., Shaw, R.J., Kanach, F.A., McDuffie, J.R., Kosinski, A.S.: The impact of wearable motion sensing technologies on physical activity: a systematic review. Department of Veterans Affairs (US), Washington (DC) (2015)
10. Klein, M.C.A., Manzoor, A., Middelweerd, A., Mollee, J.S., te Velde, S.J.: Encouraging physical activity via a personalized mobile system. IEEE Internet Comput. **19**(4), 20–27 (2015)
11. Michie, S., Johnston, M.: Theories and techniques of behaviour change: developing a cumulative science of behaviour change. Health Psychol. Rev. **6**(1), 1–6 (2012)
12. Cane, J., O'Connor, D., Michie, S.: Validation of the theoretical domains framework for use in behaviour change and implementation research. Implementation Sci. **7**(1), 1 (2012)
13. Mollee, J.S., van der Wal, C.N.: A computational agent model of influences on physical activity based on the social cognitive theory. In: PRIMA 2013: Principles and Practice of Multi-Agent Systems (2013)
14. Bandura, A.: Health promotion from the perspective of social cognitive theory. In: Psychology and Health (1998)
15. Bandura, A.: Health promotion by social cognitive means. Health Educ. Behav. **31**(2), 143–164 (2004). The official publication of the Society for Public Health Education
16. Rovniak, L., Anderson, E., Winett, R., Stephens, R.: Social cognitive determinants of physical activity in young adults: a prospective structural equation analysis. Ann. Behav. Med. **24**(2), 149–156 (2002)

17. Plotnikoff, R., Lippke, S., Courneya, K., Birkett, N., Sigal, R.: Physical activity and social cognitive theory: a test in a population sample of adults with type 1 or type 2 diabetes. Appl. Psychol. **57**(4), 628–643 (2008)
18. Plotnikoff, R., Costigan, S., Karunamuni, N., Lubans, D.: Social cognitive theories used to explain physical activity behavior in adolescents: a systematic review and meta-analysis. Prev. Med. **56**(5), 245–253 (2013)
19. Frank, L.D., Sallis, J.F., Saelens, B.E., Leary, L., Cain, K., Conway, T.L., Hess, P.M.: The development of a walkability index: application to the Neighborhood quality of life study. Br. J. Sports Med. **44**(13), 924–933 (2010)
20. Sallis, J., Pinski, R., Grossman, R., Patterson, T., Nader, P.: The development of self-efficacy scales for healthrelated diet and exercise behaviors. Health Educ. Res. **3**(3), 283–292 (1988)

Detecting Drinking-Related Contents on Social Media by Classifying Heterogeneous Data Types

Omar ElTayeby[1], Todd Eaglin[1], Malak Abdullah[1], David Burlinson[1],
Wenwen Dou[1], and Lixia Yao[2(✉)]

[1] University of North Carolina at Charlotte, Charlotte, USA
{oeltayeb,teaglin,mabdull5,dburlins,wdou1}@uncc.edu
[2] Department of Human Sciences Research, Mayo Clinic, Rochester, USA
Lixia.yao@mayo.edu

Abstract. One common health problem in the US faced by colleges and universities is binge drinking. College students often post drinking related texts and images on social media as a socially desirable identity. Some public health and clinical research scholars have surveyed different social media sites manually to understand their behavior patterns. In this paper, we investigate the feasibility of mining the heterogeneous data scattered on social media to identify drinking-related contents, which is the first step towards unleashing the potential of social media in automatic detection of binge drinking users. We use the state-of-the-art algorithms such as Support Vector Machine and neural networks to classify drinking from non-drinking posts, which contain not only text, but also images and videos. Our results show that combining heterogeneous data types, we are able to identify drinking related posts with an overall accuracy of 82%. Prediction models based on text data is more reliable compared to the other two models built on image and video data for predicting drinking related contents.

Keywords: Binge drinking · Social media · Machine learning · Text classification · Image classification · Video classification

1 Introduction

Abusive alcohol consumption and underage drinking are serious, chronic problems faced by US colleges and universities. According to epidemiological studies, about 25% of American college students report having academic difficulties due to drinking, with problems ranging from missing classes to doing poorly on exams or papers (Engs et al. 1996; Wechsler et al. 2002). Nationwide, around 599 thousand college students each year sustain alcohol-related injuries, and 1,825 of these students die as a result of their injuries. In addition, there are approximately 696 thousand alcohol-related non-sexual assaults each year among college students and 97 thousand cases of alcohol-related sexual assault or rape (Hingson

© Springer International Publishing AG 2017
S. Benferhat et al. (Eds.): IEA/AIE 2017, Part II, LNAI 10351, pp. 364–373, 2017.
DOI: 10.1007/978-3-319-60045-1_38

et al. 2009). College students with a heavy drinking problem are also much more likely to abuse other substances, leading to more complex social and medical consequences (Jones et al. 2001).

In contrast to older age groups with drinking problems, college students often perceive drinking as an integral part of their higher education experience and a ritual to becoming an independent adult. Studies show that college students embrace the "drinker" image on social media websites, such as Facebook, Twitter, Pinterest and Instagram, valuing it as a socially desirable identity (Ridout et al. 2012; Fournier and Clarke 2011). They also tend to overestimate the amount and frequency with which their peers drink (Fournier et al. 2013; Haug et al. 2011), and this perception generates internal pressure to conform to the false norm. Since students conclude that heavy drinking is normal, they do not seek preventive or intervention health care at student health centers or elsewhere (Foote et al. 2004; Moreno et al. 2012). Thus, in addition to community-based prevention efforts (e.g., limiting alcohol availability, increasing supervision from parents and other adults, and enforcing underage drinking laws), innovative approaches are needed to use social media more effectively to identify college students with heavy drinking problems and simultaneously help them to reduce drinking and seek proper treatment. Due to the "social network" property of those websites, those approaches could also educate students who now do not have heavy drinking problems, but at risk due to their peer groups' influence.

Further research show that between 94% and 98% of college students maintain a social media profile, and most report daily use (Lewis et al. 2008) of various social media platforms (Buffardi and Campbell 2008; Ross et al. 2009). The majority of college students do post drinking related images or text on their profiles (Moreno et al. 2009; Moreno et al. 2010; Egan and Moreno 2011), and alcohol manufacturers spend heavily on marketing and advertising on social media (Winpenny et al. 2014; Jernigan and Rushman 2014). To counter a "drinking culture", public health and clinical research scholars are also utilizing social media platforms (Moreno et al. 2014; Bull et al. 2012). For example, Morgan et al. (Morgan et al. 2010) analyzed photos and comments from MySpace and videos from YouTube to locate images and videos showing people drinking alcohol or engaging in recreational drug use. They were able to identify general themes and patterns using an open coding technique. Moreno et al. [Moreno et al. 2012] categorized 244 Facebook profiles into 3 groups, and found that 64% of the profiles have no alcohol references, 20% of the profiles include 1 or more references to alcohol use but not intoxication and 16% of the profiles have 1 or more references to drinking problems. Hanson et al. (Hanson et al. 2013) aimed to leverage twitter data to better understand Adderall (a psychostimulant drug) abuse among college and university students. Lovecchio et al. (Lovecchio et al. 2010) evaluated the short-term impact of an online alcohol course for first year students and found that compared to the control group, the treatment group reported significantly lower levels of alcohol use, fewer negative consequences, and less positive attitudes towards alcohol. However, these studies have been designed to survey a small number of participants to qualitatively understand the use of social media among drinking college students, or to test certain intervention methods in small-scale randomized controlled trials. Both require manual analysis of the participants' profiles on specific social media websites. Effective interventions on social media require accurate detection of targeted audience in an economical, fast, accurate and automatic fashion. There is an urgent need to investigate advanced machine learning, natural language processing, text mining and image mining techniques for detecting drinking-related contents on social media in the format of text, image and video clips.

From the field of computer science, various machine learning and statistical techniques have been developed for text classification for many other applications. Commonly used machine learning algorithms include k-Nearest Neighbor, decision tree, neural network, Bayesian classifiers, expectation-maximization and Support Vector Machine (SVM). Colas et al. (Colas and Brazdil 2006) compared SVM to k-Nearest Neighbor and naive Bayes and found that SVM has better overall performance especially in non-linear classification tasks. Similarly Joachims et al. demonstrated that SVM produced the better accuracy compared to naive Bayes and maximum entropy in text categorization (Joachims 1998). In a nutshell, SVM projects the training data in the feature space onto a high-dimension space in order to separate two classes using a kernel function. Joachims and colleagues (Joachims 1998; Joachims 1999) illustrated in their work on how SVM can be adapted to suit textual data. Images and videos are more complicated to analyze than text, because they are represented by a collection of 2-D pixels. Previously, many systems utilized the SVM (Chapelle et al. 1999) to classify images. Now neural network-based deep learning methods are gaining popularity after a decade of recession (Vincent et al. 2010). The process of training the neural network starts with forward propagation to assign weights to the perceptrons inside the layers, and then an optimization algorithm propagates backwards on these weights to reduce errors. We adopted SVM for textual data and AlexNet (Vincent et al. 2010), a popular neural network algorithm for image classification in this project.

Our goal is to investigate the feasibility of identifying heavy drinking by mining the heterogeneous data on social media, such as textual post, comments, images and video clips. We want to answer three major research questions: (1) How feasible it is to use social media data for detecting posts about drinking? (2) What is the best-performing technique for analyzing each heterogeneous data type on social media? and (3) Can we improve the prediction by combining those data and methods together? In other words, we aim to examine the state-of-the-art machine learning methods to automatically classify social media posts in the format of image, video and text to tell if they contain drinking-related content. This is the first step towards identifying college students with heavy drinking problems and simultaneously help them to reduce drinking and seek proper treatment using social media data. In the next section, we introduce our dataset and describe our methodology. We then show the results in Sect. 3. Lastly, we conclude the paper and highlight our future work.

2   Data and Methods

Data Collection

We crawled and de-identified posts from self-identified college students on Facebook and Twitter pages of an entertainment group called "I'm Shamacked" (http://imshmacked.com/). "I'm Shmacked" is a company that targets on high school and college students, organizes entertainment events and video-records college parties in the United States. The company's Facebook page is liked by over 118,000 users and has thousands of posts. Using Facebook's Graph API (Version 2.1) (https://developers.facebook.com/docs/graph-api) and Facebook Platform Python SDK (https://github.com/mobolic/facebook-sdk), we developed a Python application to retrieve all public visible content posted on the timeline of "I'm Shmacked" Facebook page. The returned posts were in JSON format with the multimedia contents presented in the form of hyperlinks. We ran the application on November 3, 2014 and collected 4,266 posts as the study cohort for this study.

Textual and Media Content Annotation

We have two rounds of annotations by four graduate students at UNC Charlotte, to determine whether or not each entry contained drinking content independently. In each round, each annotator assigns separate labels to the textual and media contents. Then a final label (e.g., "Yes", "No", "Maybe") is assigned to a given entry. 78.5% of the final labels during the 1st and 2nd round of annotations are identical. For the inconsistent 918 cases out of 4,266 entries, the annotators discussed to come up with the final labels. The graduate students also explained how they made their decision by giving keywords, features or hints, such as mentioning of colloquial expressions for drinking (i.e., arrived, blackout, crazy, drunk, hammered, high, hype, wasted, twisted) and appearance of red cup or beer can in the image.

We split our dataset into 4,000 posts for building the prediction models and 266 for testing them based on the posting date. The testing data was held out for independent evaluation of model performance. Each record is tabulated to contain 7 columns, which are timestamp, user ID, message (text), link (to the image or video), post type (text, image, video, links and questions), label and hints. In Table 1, we report the percentages of the post types within each label. Around 61% of the posts are text only without images or videos, while 18% and 11% of the posts are text with images and videos respectively.

Workflow and Methods

We summarize the steps of our workflow as in Fig. 1. The workflow starts with collecting the Facebook posts, where many of them refer to Twitter, YouTube, and Instagram links. Then we have our annotators to label each post into three classes (Yes, No, Maybe). In the data preprocessing step, we randomly split the 4,000 posts into 5 folds and perform 5-fold cross-validation when building various machine models. In each round, we use 80% of the 4,000 posts, which is 3,200 to train a machine learning model, and use the remaining 20% as validation dataset for performance evaluation and parameter tuning.

Table 1. Percentages of post types within each label.

Dataset	Attribute	Yes	No	Maybe
Training	Total	11.3%	79.1%	9.6%
	Text	3.6%	88.6%	7.8%
	Image	28.9%	60.1%	11.1%
	Video	15.2%	75.8%	9.1%
	Links	22.5%	58.5%	19%
	Questions	0%	0%	100%
Testing	Total	22.3%	62.3%	14.3%
	Text	3.2%	87.3%	9.5%
	Image	28.2%	67.6%	4.2%
	Video	33.7%	59%	7.2%
	Links	20.8%	29.2%	50%
	Questions	0%	0%	0%

In order to apply our various machine learning models on top of the heterogeneous data types, we first build one model per post type (i.e., text, images, videos) separately, then sort the priority of the models according to the descending order of their performance on the validation dataset. In the end, we apply the top-performing trained models on the hold-out test dataset for final evaluation.

Fig. 1. The workflow shows the steps of collecting and annotating the data, followed by training and evaluating the classification models.

When building the text classification model using SVM, we filter out the links and hashtags inside the text, because they contain special characters, which are considered as noise (Hu and Liu 2012). After that, we create a feature vector expressing the term frequency-inverse document frequency (TF-IDF) for each post, as the input of the SVM algorithm using a linear kernel.

When building the image classification model, we first resize all input images to the size of 256×256 pixels in order to fit them into the neural network (AlexNet). To enhance the performance of the model, we also parsed more images from the videos. One image was extracted for every 100 frames from each of the 462 videos, and then added to the training dataset. After the forward propagation of the images through the neural network in batches, the back propagation was performed using Nestrov's accelerated gradient descent solver. The training process iterated for 30 epochs over all of the images. The test data was resized similarly and then forward passed into the neural network for classification. On the other hand for the video classification, we used one image per 10 frames as the training set. We applied the same process for images, using AlexNet with Nestrov's accelerated gradient solver for 30 epochs.

3 Results

Using 5-fold cross-validation, the average accuracy of the SVM model is 85.52% on the text data. On the independent test data that is held out when building the model, the accuracy of the trained SVM model equals to 82% without using the content from the crawled links. Using the content from the crawled links decrease the accuracy, probably due to the fact that the contents from the crawled websites are very noisy and sometimes irrelevant to the context of the Facebook posts (i.e., commercial advertisements).

When training in the image classification model we used 5-fold cross-validation. We ended up at the last epoch with around 72% average accuracy, while on the test data that is held-out, the accuracy is less than 50%, which is insignificant. This suggests that the machine learning model based on image data is not useful for the prediction of drinking related contents. After the images from the videos were resized to 256×256, the video classification model achieved a high accuracy of 86%, which might be attributed to the larger number of images generated from video in the training dataset. Since each video might have different classification outcomes according to the different images we extract and use for building the prediction models, we finalize the classification by considering the most frequent class labels. The accuracy on the test data reached 78.8%. The low accuracy of the image classifier might be due to the lack of amount of training examples given as input to the neural network. The image classifier had 4350 images for training and 1449 for validation, while the video classifier had almost 4 times that amount (i.e., 15189 extracted images for training and 5065 extracted image for validation).

Table 2 shows the confusion matrix for the three models separated by a comma in each cell in the order of text, images, and videos on the independent test dataset. Since the image classification model has less than 50% accuracy, we combined the results from text and video only for the final predictions. Since the video classifier had the highest accuracy from the cross-validation experiment, we used the video's predictions with a higher priority over the text's predictions in the combined model. Then came the text classifier as the second and the image classifier as the third. In other words, if a post has both video and text contents, the prediction from the video classifier decides the final label. In contrast, if a post has both image and text content, the text classifier's prediction is the final decision.

The confusion matrix for the combined model is shown in Table 3. The accuracy of the combined model on the test dataset is around 81%, which is slightly less than the text model's accuracy when used solely. However, from the perspective of confusion matrix, both (the text and combined models) perform similarly.

Table 2. Confusion matrix representing the number of predicted labels (column) corresponding to the ground truth (row) in the order of text, image, and video.

True/Prediction	Yes	Maybe	No	Total
Yes	38, 12, 26	7, 0, 0	15, 10, 2	15, 10, 2
Maybe	5, 17, 1	21, 0, 0	13, 7, 0	39, 24, 1
No	2, 25, 4	6, 0, 0	159, 23, 0	167, 48, 4
Total	45, 54, 31	34, 0, 0	187, 40, 2	266, 94, 33

Table 3. Confusion matrix using the combined model, the table shows the number of predicted labels (column) corresponding to the ground truth (row).

True/Prediction	Yes	Maybe	No	Total
Yes	39	6	15	60
Maybe	5	21	13	39
No	7	4	156	167
Total	51	31	184	266

4   Conclusions

In conclusion, we find that automating the detection of binge drinking habits through social media posts is feasible using text, image and video classification techniques. We applied SVM on the text portions of the collected posts, and AlexNet on the images and videos in order to build prediction models to classify between drinking and non-drinking posts. The accuracy of the text model and video model reached 82% and 78.8% on the hold-out dataset respectively. The image model's accuracy is less than 50% on the test dataset, and thus we didn't use it in the combined model. We also find that the text classification model is the most reliable compared to the other two models, due to the number of training posts provided (i.e. 61% of the posts are text only). At the end, the text classification model performed almost the same as the combined model, because the video classification model did not improve on the misclassified posts from the text model. Our original expectations were that the video classifier would have corrected those misclassified posts. But unfortunately, the results did not support it.

There might be two challenges of building high-performance models based on mining heterogeneous data types. First, there is much higher abundance of text posts than image or video posts on Facebook. Secondly we observe that college student users do not keep the drinking-related images or video clips on their profile for long period of time. As soon as they realize that their posts contain inappropriate image or video clips, they remove them. So truly powerful and reliable prediction models should be able to monitor users' activities in a real-time fashion, with the presence of more images and videos.

5   Future Work

This first feasibility study on detecting drinking-related contents on social media by classifying heterogeneous data types demonstrates promising results and encourages us to invest more efforts in this route. We envision that an ultimate social media-based application will provide a number of advantages relative to current practices: (1) It overcomes patients' reluctance to admit and report their drinking problems to authority figures. (2) When students resist participating in public alcohol education programs or treatment plans an intelligent application can deliver targeted information in a private and comfortable setting to students with drinking problems whenever and wherever they need such help. (3) A machine intelligence-based solution is economical and easy to scale up once a useful solution is known. A directed, but non-intrusive, intervention program is desired by many stakeholders who care about the growth and development of college students while considering privacy rights of individuals.

The underlying technologies are also transferrable to address other public health issues, such as illegal drug use, depression, suicide and eating disorders, crime prevention, and to improve students' adjustment to college. However, there are several challenges we need to address before achieving the grand goal. First, although the Substance Abuse and Mental Health Services Administration of U.S. defines heavy drinking as drinking 5 or more drinks on the same occasion on each of 5 or more days in the past 30 days, this term needs to be further quantified when transforming into users' online activities on social media. We need to conduct more studies with behavioral and substance-abuse scholars to determine what online behaviors count as unhealthy, heavy drinking and who can be the target users for social media-based intervention. Another avenue of interest is to implement near-real-time classification, which is sensitive and reliable enough to catch all relevant and risky drinking activities posted on social media, as observed in our study that social media users often delete inappropriate contents, particularly in the format of image and video after impromptu posting. Last but not least, the posting of drinking-related contents on social media is still a rare event by nature. Such imbalance inevitably impedes the performance of machine learning algorithms. We did not address much of this issue in this project. In future, we aim to develop techniques that perform undersampling or oversampling of asymmetric categories to create more balanced training datasets and improve model performance (Nguyen et al. 2011; Liu et al. 2009).

Acknowledgments. We show our gratitude and thank our colleagues at UNC Charlotte: Boshu Ru, Jingyi Shi, Yi Zhen, Charles Warner-Hillard and Kimberly Harris, for their hard work in annotating the dataset.

References

Buffardi, L.E., Campbell, W.K.: Narcissism and social networking web sites. Pers. Soc. Psychol. Bull. **34**(10), 1303–1314 (2008)

Bull, S.S., Levine, D.K., Black, S.R., Schmiege, S.J., Santelli, J.: Social media-delivered sexual health intervention: a cluster randomized controlled trial. Am. J. Prev. Med. **43**(5), 467–474 (2012)

Chapelle, O., Haffner, P., Vapnik, V.N.: Support vector machines for histogram-based image classification. IEEE Trans. Neural Netw. **10**(5), 1055–1064 (1999)

Colas, F., Brazdil, P.: Comparison of SVM and some older classification algorithms in text classification tasks. In: Bramer, M. (ed.) IFIP AI 2006. IIFIP, vol. 217, pp. 169–178. Springer, Boston, MA (2006). doi:10.1007/978-0-387-34747-9_18

Egan, K.G., Moreno, M.A.: Alcohol references on undergraduate males' Facebook profiles. Am. J. Men's Health 5, 413–420 (2011). 1557988310394341

Engs, R.C., Diebold, B.A., Hanson, D.J.: The drinking patterns and problems of a national sample of college students, 1994. J. Alcohol Drug Educ. **41**, 13–33 (1996)

Foote, J., Wilkens, C., Vavagiakis, P.: A national survey of alcohol screening and referral in college health centers. J. Am. Coll. Health **52**(4), 149 (2004)

Fournier, A.K., Clarke, S.W.: Do college students use facebook to communicate about alcohol? an analysis of student profile pages. Cyberpsychology **5**(2), 1–12 (2011)

Fournier, A.K., Hall, E., Ricke, P., Storey, B.: Alcohol and the social network: online social networking sites and college students' perceived drinking norms. Psychol. Popular Media Cult. **2**(2), 86 (2013)

Hanson, C.L., Burton, S.H., Giraud-Carrier, C., West, J.H., Barnes, M.D., Hansen, B.: Tweaking and tweeting: exploring twitter for nonmedical use of a psychostimulant drug (adderall) among college students. J. Med. Internet Res. **15**(4), e62 (2013)

Haug, S., Ulbricht, S., Hanke, M., Meyer, C., John, U.: Overestimation of drinking norms and its association with alcohol consumption in apprentices. Alcohol Alcohol. **46**(2), 204–209 (2011)

Hingson, R.W., Zha, W., Weitzman, E.R.: Magnitude of and trends in alcohol-related mortality and morbidity among us college students ages 18–24, 1998–2005. J. Stud. Alcohol Drugs, Suppl. **16**, 12–20 (2009)

Hu, X., Liu, H.: Text analytics in social media. In: Mining Text Data, pp. 385–414. Springer, USA (2012)

Jernigan, D.H., Rushman, A.E.: Measuring youth exposure to alcohol marketing on social networking sites: challenges and prospects. J. Public Health Policy **35**(1), 91–104 (2014)

Joachims, T.: Text categorization with Support Vector Machines: Learning with many relevant features. In: Nédellec, C., Rouveirol, C. (eds.) ECML 1998. LNCS, vol. 1398, pp. 137–142. Springer, Heidelberg (1998). doi:10.1007/BFb0026683

Joachims, T.: Transductive inference for text classification using support vector machines. In: ICML, vol. 99, pp. 200–209 (1999)

Jones, S.E., Oeltmann, J., Wilson, T.W., Brener, N.D., Hill, C.V.: Binge drinking among undergraduate college students in the united states: Implications for other substance use. J. Am. Coll. Health **50**(1), 33–38 (2001)

Lewis, K., Kaufman, J., Christakis, N.: The taste for privacy: an analysis of college student privacy settings in an online social network. J. Comput. Mediated Commun. **14**(1), 79–100 (2008)

Liu, X.-Y., Wu, J., Zhou, Z.-H.: Exploratory undersampling for class-imbalance learning. IEEE Trans. Syst. Man Cybern. Part B (Cybernetics), **39**(2), 539–550 (2009)

Lovecchio, C.P., Wyatt, T.M., DeJong, W.: Reductions in drinking and alcohol-related harms reported by first-year college students taking an online alcohol education course: A randomized trial. J. Health Commun. **15**(7), 805–819 (2010)

Moreno, M.A., Briner, L.R., Williams, A., Brockman, L., Walker, L., Christakis, D.A.: A content analysis of displayed alcohol references on a social networking web site. J. Adolesc. Health **47**(2), 168–175 (2010)

Moreno, M.A., Christakis, D.A., Egan, K.G., Brockman, L.N., Becker, T.: Associations between displayed alcohol references on facebook and problem drinking among college students. Arch. Pediatr. Adolesc. Med. **166**(2), 157–163 (2012)

Moreno, M.A., DAngelo, J., Kacvinsky, L.E., Kerr, B., Zhang, C., Eickhoff, J.: Emergence and predictors of alcohol reference displays on facebook during the first year of college. Comput. Hum. Behav. **30**, 87–94 (2014)

Moreno, M.A., Parks, M.R., Zimmerman, F.J., Brito, T.E., Christakis, D.A.: Display of health risk behaviors on myspace by adolescents: prevalence and associations. Arch. Pediatr. Adolesc. Med. **163**(1), 27–34 (2009)

Morgan, E.M., Snelson, C., Elison-Bowers, P.: Image and video disclosure of substance use on social media websites. Comput. Hum. Behav. **26**(6), 1405–1411 (2010)

Nguyen, H.M., Cooper, E.W., Kamei, K.: Borderline over-sampling for imbalanced data classification. Int. J. Knowl. Eng. Soft Data Paradigms **3**(1), 4–21 (2011)

Ridout, B., Campbell, A., Ellis, L.: Off your face (book): alcohol in online social identity construction and its relation to problem drinking in university students. Drug Alcohol Rev. **31**(1), 20–26 (2012)

Ross, C., Orr, E.S., Sisic, M., Arseneault, J.M., Simmering, M.G., Orr, R.R.: Personality and motivations associated with facebook use. Comput. Hum. Behav. **25**(2), 578–586 (2009)

Vincent, P., Larochelle, H., Lajoie, I., Bengio, Y., Manzagol, P.-A.: Learning useful representations in a deep network with a local denoising criterion. J. Mach. Learn. Res. **11**, 3371–3408 (2010)

Wechsler, H., Lee, J.E., Kuo, M., Seibring, M., Nelson, T.F., Lee, H.: Trends in college binge drinking during a period of increased prevention efforts: findings from 4 harvard school of public health college alcohol study surveys: 1993–2001. J. Am. Coll. Health **50**(5), 203–217 (2002)

Winpenny, E.M., Marteau, T.M., Nolte, E.: Exposure of children and adolescents to alcohol marketing on social media websites. Alcohol Alcohol. **49**(2), 154–159 (2014)

Estimating Disease Burden Using Google Trends and Wikipedia Data

Riyi Qiu[1], Mirsad Hadzikadic[1], and Lixia Yao[1,2(✉)]

[1] Department of Software and Information Systems,
University of North Carolina at Charlotte, Charlotte, NC 28223, USA
[2] Department of Health Sciences Research,
Mayo Clinic, Rochester, MN 55905, USA
yao.lixia@mayo.edu

Abstract. Data on disease burden is often used for assessing population health, evaluating the effectiveness of interventions, formulating health policies, and planning future resource allocation. We investigated whether Internet usage data, particularly the search volume on Google and page view counts on Wikipedia, are correlated with the disease burden, measured by prevalence and treatment cost, for 1,633 diseases over an 11-year period. We also applied the method of least absolute shrinkage and selection operator (LASSO) to predict the burden of diseases, using those Internet data together with three other variables we quantified previously. We found a relatively strong correlation for 39 of 1,633 diseases, including viral hepatitis, diabetes mellitus, other headache syndromes, multiple sclerosis, sleep apnea, hemorrhoids, and disaccharidase deficiency. However, an accurate analysis must consider each condition's characteristics, including acute/chronic nature, severity, familiarity to the public, and presence of stigma.

Keywords: Disease burden · Prevalence · Treatment cost · Search query volume · Page review · Least absolute shrinkage and selection operator (LASSO)

1 Introduction

The term "disease burden" refers to the financial, medical, or socio-economic impact of a disease or health problem [1]. Researchers in public health frequently measure the burden of various diseases or health problems across different geographic locations or at different time points, for purposes such as assessing population health, evaluating the effectiveness of interventions, formulating health policies, and planning future resource allocation.

There is no consensus on the best measure of disease burden; the choice often depends on individual value or specific need. One common measure is financial cost. It summarizes the direct and indirect costs due to illness, which can be nontrivial for the low-income population. For example, Paez *et al.* examined the out-of-pocket expenses, which are the economic burden for patients and their family, for more than 100 chronic conditions in

© Springer International Publishing AG 2017
S. Benferhat et al. (Eds.): IEA/AIE 2017, Part II, LNAI 10351, pp. 374–385, 2017.
DOI: 10.1007/978-3-319-60045-1_39

both adults and children. What they revealed was that the annual out-of-pocket expenses increased by 39.4% from 1996 to 2005 in the US, after inflation adjustment [2].

Another measure of disease burden is mortality rate. It counts the number of deaths due to a specific medical condition in a particular population, scaled to the size of that population, in unit time. In one study on the correlation between diabetes and ischemic heart disease (IHD), Laing *et al.* found that young adult women with diabetes were more than 8 times more likely to die of IHD than those without diabetes were. Similar trends were observed among young adult men, older men, and older women; and patients with Type I diabetes were found to have a relatively higher IHD mortality rate than patients with Type II diabetes [3].

By contrast, morbidity rate describes the frequency with which a disease occurs in a population and is often calculated by incidence rate and prevalence rate. Incidence rate refers to the proportion of newly diagnosed cases of a disease in a population, while prevalence rate accounts for both newly diagnosed and pre-existing cases of a disease. Corbett *et al.* found that worldwide, among 0.9 million cases of newly diagnosed adult cases of tuberculosis (TB) in 2000, 9% were attributable to HIV. In selected African countries and United States, 31% and 26% of TB cases were attributable to HIV, respectively. However, TB led to about 11% of adult deaths from AIDS [4]. This study indicated the comorbidity of TB and HIV, and highlighted the need for a targeted intervention strategy in countries with a high prevalence of HIV and TB.

A more sophisticated measure of disease burden is Disability Adjusted Life Years (DALYs). It is defined as the Years Lived with Disability (YLDs) plus the Years of Life Lost (YLLs) owing to a disease or health problem. Both YLDs and YLLs are age-weighted to reflect productivity and societal investment (e.g., years lived as a young adult are valued more than years spent as a young child or older adult). DALYs is the primary measure of disease burdens developed for the most comprehensive worldwide observational epidemiological study to date – the Global Burden of Disease Study [5], in which researchers have been estimating DALYs among populations of different ages, sex, and countries for more than 200 diseases and causes of death since 1990. Several developed countries, including the Netherlands [6] and Australia [7], use DALYs to survey and compare their nationwide burden of diseases for public policymaking.

Obviously, each of these established measures of disease burden has its own limitations. The financial cost of a disease, for instance, does not reflect health-related quality of life and untreated cases [8]. Mortality rate does not capture the disease burden prior to death [9], and in practice, it is often difficult to determine the actual cause of death as it is often the consequence of multiple diseases or injuries [10]. Morbidity does not adjust for the severity and impact of diseases. DALYs require a large amount of time and resources to calculate. This situation has led to many pandemic and rare diseases being left unstudied, and made it barely possible to compare the disease burden across a large number of diseases over time [11, 12]. Further, the estimates of disease burden from different studies sometimes conflict with each other. The prevalence of Parkinson's disease in Spain was reported to be 1.5%, 0.6%, and 0.2% in 1994, by three separate groups [13–15].

In recent years, new data from the Internet have revealed novel utility in different fields. For instance, Ginsberg *et al.* used some search query keywords describing

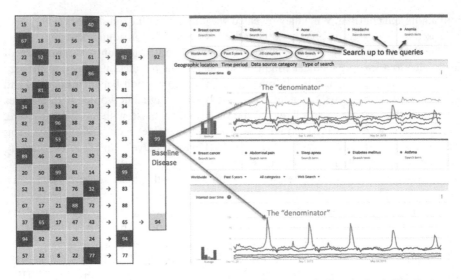

Fig. 1. Strategy to retrieve relative search volume from Google Trends for 1,633 diseases.

influenza-like illness on Google to predict influenza epidemics, as they were highly correlated with the actual influenza prevalence data reported by Centers for Disease Control and Prevention [16]. Similarly, Moat *et al.* identified correlations between the stock prices of 30 Dow Jones Industrial Average component companies and weekly Wikipedia page review data, and were able to increase their portfolio return by 65% using Wikipedia page review data instead of conventional strategies to build prediction models [17]. Therefore, we investigated whether mining these new data sources, primarily Google Trends and Wikipedia page review data, would allow the estimation of disease burden for a large number of diseases in an *automated* and *cost-efficient* way. Specifically, we examined the alignment of disease burden in terms of disease prevalence and financial cost for 1,633 diseases over 11 years with Google Trends and Wikipedia data. We also applied the least absolute shrinkage and selection operator (LASSO), a regression method that accomplishes variable selection and regularization, to predict the burden of diseases, using the Internet data along with other variables that we quantified in a previous study [18] for four specific diseases.

2 Data and Methods

2.1 Data Collection

Google Trends and Wikipedia are two publicly available data sources that record searching and browsing activities related to various diseases and health conditions on the Internet. On Google Trends (https://www.google.com/trends/), users enter one to five key words to retrieve their *relative* search volume. The upper-right panel of Fig. 1 shows the output of querying "breast cancer," "obesity," "acne," "headache," and "anemia" in the interactive user interface. The x-axis gives the timeline and the y-axis gives the normalized search volume in percentages, where the denominator is the highest search volume among all queried terms in the given time frame (e.g., in Fig. 1, the highest search volume is for breast cancer around October 2012). Google Trend also allows users to specify the geographic location, time period, data source category (i.e., Arts & Entertainment, Books & Literature, Health), and the type of search (i.e., web search, image search, news search), or to use their Application Programming Interface (API) for batch queries. In our experiment, these parameters were set to worldwide, from 2004 (earliest available year for Google Trends) to 2014, all categories, and web search, respectively. Further, we developed a two-step strategy to retrieve the relative search volume for 1,633 diseases from 2004 to 2014. As shown in the left panel of Fig. 1, the first step was to find the disease with the highest search volume during the defined time framework among all our diseases of interest and set it as the baseline disease. Thereafter, we categorized all the diseases into 5-disease groups, with the baseline disease inserted into each group, and queried Google Trends again (shown on the right panel, Fig. 1). Hence, the normalization denominator for each group was the same. Wikipedia provides a simpler API that allows us to download the weekly page review counts of each disease term from 2008 to 2014. We computed the annual Wikipedia review counts by adding up all 52 weeks of a year.

2.2 Disease Nomenclature

When diseases or medical conditions are mentioned in different online contexts, they can be abbreviated, exhibit various morphological or orthographical variations, or have multiple synonyms. For example, medical professionals refer to stroke as cerebrovascular accident, cerebrovascular insult, or brain attack. To ensure the completeness and consistency of the query results, we used the metathesaurus of the unified medical language system (UMLS) [19], which unifies more than one million medical concepts and five million names from more than a hundred biomedical controlled vocabularies and terminologies. For each of the 1,633 diseases of interest, we queried Google Trends and Wikipedia using all of its synonyms and defined its search volume as the highest search volume among all its synonyms.

2.3 Benchmark Data on Disease Burdens

We obtained the benchmark data on disease burdens during 2004 and 2010 from our previous study [18], and the data for 2011 to 2014 from a large medical claims database —MarketScan®—offered by Truven Health. Using the UMLS, we set the disease terminology for our analysis to be PheWAS codes as they represent clinically meaningful phenotypes with appropriate granularity [20]. More specifically, for 1,633 diseases defined by PheWAS codes from medical claims databases with non-zero Internet or disease burden data, we calculated the relative prevalence and the relative treatment cost, together with the relative number of publications and the relative number of clinical trials using the method introduced in our previous study [18]. The "relative" treatment cost, for instance, is defined as a given disease's treatment cost divided by the total treatment cost of all the 1,633 diseases. This way, different factors become unitless and comparable.

2.4   Analytic Method

We denote the relative search volume of disease i in year j on Google as $G_{i,j}$, where $\sum_{i=1}^{n} G_{i,j} = 1$. Thus, the vector $G_{,j}$, which can be extended as $(G_{1,j}, G_{2,j}, G_{3,j}, \ldots, G_{n,j})$, represents the relative search volume of all n diseases in year j on Google, and the vector $G_{i,}$, which represents $(G_{i,1}, G_{i,2}, G_{i,3}, \ldots G_{i,m})$, denotes the relative search volume of disease i in all m years of interest on Google. Similarly, we define the relative page review counts of disease i in year j on Wikipedia as $W_{i,j}$, the relative prevalence of disease i in year j as $P_{i,j}$, and the relative treatment cost of disease i in year j as $C_{i,j}$.

To determine whether the information from Google Trends and Wikipedia can approximate the burden of diseases from three dimensions, we first examined the correlations between the Internet data and disease burdens measured by relative prevalence and relative treatment cost for all the diseases of interest as a whole. We did so by computing the Pearson correlation coefficients of $(G_{,k}, P_{,l})$ and $(G_{,k}, C_{,l})$ for years from 2004 to 2014 and the Pearson correlation coefficients of $(W_{,k}, P_{,l})$ and $(W_{,k}, C_{,l})$ for years from 2008 to 2014. We also computed Spearman Rank correlation coefficients and the p values, to test the null hypothesis that the Internet data is not correlated with those disease burden measures.

Second, we determined whether the Internet data could forecast the disease burden during the same year, one year later, and two years later on an individual disease level. Mathematically, for each disease i, we computed the Pearson correlation coefficients between the relative search volume on Google and relative disease prevalence $(G_{i,}, P_{i,})$ $(G_{i,}, \tilde{P}_{i,})$, $(G_{i,}, \tilde{\tilde{P}}_{i,})$, between the relative page reviews on Wikipedia and relative disease prevalence $(W_{i,}, P_{i,})$, $(W_{i,}, \tilde{P}_{i,})$, $(W_{i,}, \tilde{\tilde{P}}_{i,})$, between the relative search volume on Google and relative treatment cost $(G_{i,}, C_{i,})$, $(G_{i,}, \tilde{C}_{i,})$, $(G_{i,}, \tilde{\tilde{C}}_{i,})$, and between the relative page reviews on Wikipedia and relative treatment cost $(W_{i,}, C_{i,})$, $(W_{i,}, \tilde{C}_{i,})$, $(W_{i,}, \tilde{\tilde{C}}_{i,})$, where $\tilde{P}_{i,} = P_{i,2}, P_{i,3}, P_{i,4}, \ldots, P_{i,m+1}$ $\tilde{\tilde{P}}_{i,} = (P_{i,3}, P_{i,4}, P_{i,5}, \ldots P_{i,m+2})$, $\tilde{C}_{i,} = (C_{i,2}, C_{i,3}, C_{i,4}, \ldots, C_{i,m+1})$, and $\tilde{\tilde{C}}_{i,} = (C_{i,3}, C_{i,4}, C_{i,5} \ldots C_{i,m+2})$.

Finally, we used a LASSO-based regression model to predict the *relative* disease burden $(\tilde{P}_{i,}, \tilde{C}_{i,})$ or using $G_{i,}, W_{i,}$, and three other variables introduced in our previous work [18], namely the relative number of scientific articles from PubMed $(L_{i,})$, relative number of clinical trials $(T_{i,})$, and relative funding from the NIH $(F_{i,})$. LASSO is more powerful than traditional linear regression as it uses variable (feature) selection and regularization [21]. The diseases we chose are viral hepatitis, diabetes mellitus, other headache syndrome, and multiple sclerosis, whose relative burdens demonstrated the biggest correlations with relative search volume on Google and relative page review on Wikipedia in the second step. All these computations were performed in the R programming environment, in which LASSO is simulated by the "glmnet" package [22].

3   Results

First, for all the diseases as a whole, we analyzed the correlations between disease burdens, measured by relative disease prevalence $(P_{,t})$ and relative treatment cost $(C_{,t})$, and the relative search volume on Google at different years. Table 1 lists the Pearson correlation coefficients. The coefficients in Table 1(a) are all greater than the corresponding values in Table 1(b), indicating that the prevalence of diseases is more correlated to search volume than treatment cost. This can be explained by the definitions of those two measures. The treatment cost of a disease equals to its prevalence times the average treatment fees for each patient with the disease diagnosis in a given year. When all diseases are evaluated as a whole, the treatment cost estimate will have a larger variation than disease prevalence, therefore reducing its correlation with the *relative* search volume data on Google.

We were also interested in the relationship between the relative search volume on Google in a given year t and the relative prevalence of a disease in year t-1 (the highlighted area under the diagonal lines in Table 1), as we initially assumed that individuals search the Internet once they receive a diagnosis. However, we did not observe such a trend. This might be owing to the fact that not all patients with a certain diagnosis will search the Internet and not all people who search for a particular disease on the Internet are diagnosed patients, or the fact that the computation of prevalence includes both newly diagnosed and pre-existing cases. An observable trend is that the Pearson correlation coefficients in the diagonal and right under the diagonal increase slowly with time, despite a few downward instances during 2009 and 2011. Such a weak increase suggests that it is becoming increasingly common to search the Internet for health-related topics.

We also tested the null hypotheses that $cor\left(G_{,k}, P_{,l}\right) = 0$ and $co\left(G_{,k}, C_{,l}\right) = 0$ and found that all the computed p values were less than 0.05. Therefore, we concluded that the relative search volume on Google and the relative disease prevalence (or the treatment cost) are unlikely to be uncorrelated. The correlations between the relative page reviews on Wikipedia and relative disease burdens showed similar trends during 2008 and 2014. The p values of the hypothesis testing (https://cci-hit.uncc.edu/resources/rqJan2017TableS1.xlsx) and correlation analyses between the relative page reviews on Wikipedia and relative disease burdens (https://cci-hit.uncc.edu/resources/rqJan2017TableS2.docx) can be found on our website.

Overall, the correlation coefficients between relative search volume on Google (or relative page reviews on Wikipedia) and relative disease burden measures are small—all are less than 0.35. We thus assessed the correlations between relative search volume on Google (G_i) and relative disease burdens (P_i, C_i) with 0-year, 1-year, and 2-year intervals for *individual* diseases. Filtering by $p < 0.05$ on all the six correlation coefficients left 60 diseases. Twenty-one diseases that had high correlations owing to missing values in either Google Trends or disease burden data were then excluded, and the remaining 39 diseases and their Pearson correlation coefficients are listed in Table 2. Black and white values refer to positive and negative correlations, respectively.

Table 1. The correlations between relative search volume on Google $(G_{,k})$ and relative disease burdens $(P_{,l}$ and $C_{,l})$ during 2004-2014

(a) Correlations between relative search volume on Google and relative disease prevalence										
	$G_{,04}$	$G_{,05}$	$G_{,06}$	$G_{,07}$	$G_{,08}$	$G_{,09}$	$G_{,10}$	$G_{,11}$	$G_{,12}$	$G_{,13}$	$G_{,14}$
$P_{,04}$	0.277	0.278	0.272	0.272	0.277	0.262	0.274	0.279	0.284	0.283	0.284
$P_{,05}$	0.281	0.283	0.276	0.275	0.282	0.272	0.279	0.283	0.288	0.288	0.289
$P_{,06}$	0.286	0.287	0.281	0.28	0.285	0.272	0.281	0.286	0.29	0.29	0.29
$P_{,07}$	0.284	0.286	0.279	0.279	0.283	0.27	0.28	0.284	0.289	0.288	0.288
$P_{,08}$	0.287	0.29	0.284	0.282	0.286	0.279	0.283	0.287	0.292	0.291	0.291
$P_{,09}$	0.295	0.299	0.293	0.29	0.294	0.298	0.29	0.295	0.3	0.301	0.301
$P_{,10}$	0.274	0.275	0.27	0.269	0.27	0.254	0.267	0.272	0.276	0.276	0.275
$P_{,11}$	0.279	0.281	0.276	0.274	0.275	0.265	0.273	0.278	0.282	0.282	0.281
$P_{,12}$	0.278	0.28	0.275	0.273	0.274	0.263	0.271	0.277	0.281	0.281	0.28
$P_{,13}$	0.285	0.288	0.283	0.281	0.281	0.275	0.278	0.283	0.287	0.288	0.287
$P_{,14}$	0.291	0.293	0.289	0.286	0.286	0.279	0.283	0.288	0.292	0.293	0.292
(b) Correlations between relative search volume on Google and relative treatment cost										
	$G_{,04}$	$G_{,05}$	$G_{,06}$	$G_{,07}$	$G_{,08}$	$G_{,09}$	$G_{,10}$	$G_{,11}$	$G_{,12}$	$G_{,13}$	$G_{,14}$
$C_{,04}$	0.203	0.201	0.197	0.195	0.192	0.176	0.186	0.189	0.191	0.191	0.188
$C_{,05}$	0.206	0.205	0.2	0.199	0.195	0.181	0.19	0.193	0.195	0.195	0.192
$C_{,06}$	0.207	0.206	0.201	0.2	0.196	0.181	0.191	0.194	0.195	0.195	0.192
$C_{,07}$	0.213	0.211	0.207	0.205	0.201	0.185	0.195	0.198	0.199	0.199	0.195
$C_{,08}$	0.213	0.212	0.207	0.205	0.201	0.187	0.195	0.198	0.199	0.199	0.195
$C_{,09}$	0.214	0.214	0.209	0.207	0.203	0.194	0.197	0.2	0.202	0.201	0.198
$C_{,10}$	0.208	0.205	0.201	0.199	0.191	0.173	0.183	0.185	0.185	0.186	0.181
$C_{,11}$	0.217	0.214	0.21	0.207	0.199	0.183	0.19	0.193	0.193	0.194	0.188
$C_{,12}$	0.216	0.214	0.21	0.207	0.199	0.182	0.19	0.193	0.193	0.194	0.188
$C_{,13}$	0.228	0.226	0.222	0.218	0.209	0.195	0.2	0.203	0.202	0.204	0.198
$C_{,14}$	0.24	0.238	0.234	0.23	0.22	0.205	0.21	0.213	0.212	0.214	0.207

In Fig. 2, we also plotted the correlation patterns for four representative diseases. Figure 2(A) shows that viral hepatitis is becoming less and less popular in Google Search, which corresponds to its decreasing prevalence and treatment costs. Figure 2(B) shows that diabetes mellitus is searched less and less frequently on Google, but both its prevalence and treatment cost are increasing with time. This might indicate that as a chronic condition, diabetes mellitus requires long-term treatment but is underestimated by the public. "Other headache syndromes" in Fig. 2(C) exhibits a rising popularity in Google Search, but both its prevalence and treatment cost went down from 2004 to 2014. According to our communication with clinicians, one

Table 2. 39 diseases demonstrate strong correlations between relative search volume on Google and disease burden measured by relative prevalence and relative treatment cost

PheWAS name	Pearson Correlation Coefficient					
	(G_i, P_i)	(G_i, C_i)	$(G_i, \tilde{P}_i)$	$(G_i, \tilde{C}_i)$	$(G_i, \tilde{\tilde{P}}_i)$	$(G_i, \tilde{\tilde{C}}_i)$
Other non-epithelial cancer of skin	0.683	0.795	0.78	0.871	0.8	0.91
Prostate cancer	0.692	0.693	0.812	0.828	0.957	0.961
Neoplasm of uncertain behavior	0.88	0.899	0.854	0.909	0.697	0.719
Sleep apnea	0.625	0.854	0.731	0.865	0.921	0.898
Other peripheral nerve disorders	0.933	0.844	0.951	0.889	0.975	0.98
Congestive heart failure	0.846	0.886	0.951	0.94	0.927	0.958
Heart failure	0.833	0.877	0.953	0.964	0.933	0.898
Asthma	0.975	0.883	0.968	0.929	0.962	0.95
Other diseases of lung	0.71	0.823	0.877	0.942	0.937	0.989
Irritable bowel syndrome	0.919	0.896	0.93	0.909	0.941	0.934
Other disorders of liver	0.911	0.911	0.968	0.974	0.893	0.873
Urinary tract infection	0.695	0.68	0.641	0.643	0.831	0.873
Vaginitis and vulvovaginitis	0.895	0.897	0.926	0.978	0.777	0.763
Arthropathy NOS	0.945	0.929	0.974	0.972	0.97	0.964
Osteoporosis	0.817	0.878	0.821	0.88	0.813	0.833
Symptoms of nervous and musculoskeletal systems	0.844	0.867	0.918	0.959	0.687	0.797
Viral hepatitis	0.974	0.982	0.982	0.98	0.949	0.943
Viral warts & HPV	0.866	0.891	0.769	0.929	0.809	0.849
Asphyxia, respiratory failure, nervousness, and debility	0.935	0.797	0.901	0.758	0.736	0.728
Infectious mononucleosis	0.897	0.702	0.78	0.83	0.738	0.792
Other malignant neoplasm	-0.88	-0.87	-0.951	-0.936	-0.864	-0.84
Diabetes mellitus	-0.906	-0.903	-0.962	-0.957	-0.919	-0.966
Obesity	-0.831	-0.862	-0.887	-0.921	-0.911	-0.957
Epilepsy, recurrent seizures, convulsions	-0.862	-0.864	-0.867	-0.87	-0.767	-0.777
Disaccharidase deficiency	-0.783	-0.757	-0.887	-0.898	-0.87	-0.837
Other headache syndromes	-0.884	-0.93	-0.785	-0.846	-0.681	-0.782
Otalgia	-0.843	-0.77	-0.981	-0.957	-0.899	-0.912
Varicose veins	-0.621	-0.745	-0.679	-0.739	-0.872	-0.778
Hemorrhoids	-0.755	-0.884	-0.815	-0.776	-0.697	-0.74
Acute tonsillitis	-0.889	-0.887	-0.843	-0.973	-0.819	-0.9
Acute bronchitis & bronchiolitis	-0.782	-0.769	-0.874	-0.869	-0.707	-0.794
Dental caries	-0.635	-0.817	-0.738	-0.853	-0.781	-0.681
Constipation	-0.753	-0.719	-0.746	-0.689	-0.804	-0.707
Missed abortion /Hydatidiform mole	-0.83	-0.859	-0.743	-0.784	-0.882	-0.866
Rash & other nonspecific skin eruption	-0.769	-0.701	-0.723	-0.667	-0.78	-0.722
Acne	-0.865	-0.877	-0.809	-0.817	-0.801	-0.833
Viral enteritis	-0.926	-0.656	-0.979	-0.847	-0.919	-0.892
Abdominal pain	0.952	-0.961	0.853	-0.914	0.703	-0.811
Multiple sclerosis	0.825	-0.892	0.868	-0.826	0.886	-0.829

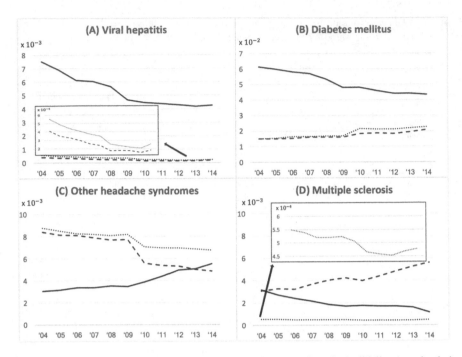

Fig. 2. The correlations between relative search volume on Google (solid lines) and relative disease prevalence (dotted lines) and treatment cost (dashed lines), for (A) viral hepatitis, (B) diabetes mellitus, (C) other headache syndromes, and (D) multiple sclerosis.

reasonable explanation is that headache is underdiagnosed as many people do not seek medical consultation for headache. Instead, patients simply turn to the Internet for information. In Fig. 2(D), the relative search volume for multiple sclerosis on Google aligns well with its prevalence but the treatment cost has been rising dramatically, possibly owing to the increase in the cost of medication, which occurred in the same period [23].

Finally, we explored whether the relative search volume on Google ($G_{i,}$), relative page review on Wikipedia ($W_{i,}$), relative disease prevalence ($P_{i,}$), relative treatment cost ($C_{i,}$), and three other variables we quantified in our previous study [18], namely the relative number of scientific articles from PubMed ($L_{i,}$), relative number of clinical trials ($T_{i,}$), and relative funding from the NIH ($F_{i,}$) for year t could predict the relative disease prevalence ($\tilde{P}_{i,}$) or relative treatment cost ($\tilde{C}_{i,}$) for year $t + 1$, using LASSO for each of the 39 diseases we identified in the previous step. Figure 3 shows the LASSO cross validation curves and variable selection results for the treatment cost prediction of sleep apnea, hemorrhoid, disaccharidase deficiency, and diabetes mellitus. With the shrinkage of lambda (bottom horizontal axis; log scale), mean-squared error (MSE, left vertical axis) decreases until the minimum value (close to 0 in Fig. 3) is reached at the left vertical line. The right vertical line gives the optimal model where the error is within one standard deviation from the minimal MSE. The correlation coefficients and intercept of the fittest model are listed in each panel. It seems that not all five variables

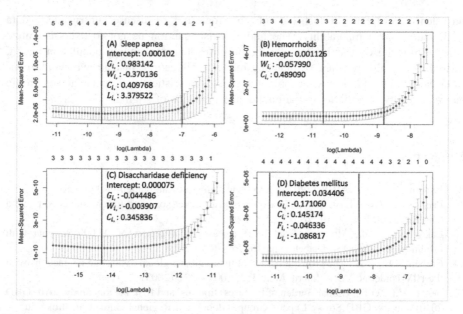

Fig. 3. LASSO cross validation curves and estimated coefficients of four diseases. (A) Sleep apnea, (B) Hemorrhoids, (C) Disaccharidase deficiency, and (D) Diabetes mellitus.

are related to treatment cost prediction in each case, but the relative treatment cost from the previous year is most useful, which is consistent with our previous findings [18]. We repeated the analysis for relative disease prevalence ($\tilde{P}_{i,}$) (https://cci-hit.uncc.edu/resources/rqJan2017FigS1.jpeg). The results confirmed that the predictive powers of the aforementioned factors vary in accordance with each case.

4   Discussion and Conclusions

In the present study, we investigated the correlation between search volume on Google and page view counts on Wikipedia with disease burden, measured by prevalence and treatment cost, for 1,633 diseases over an 11-year-period. Our analysis revealed that disease prevalence is more strongly correlated to search volume on Google and page view counts on Wikipedia than treatment cost. A relatively stronger correlation exists for 39 out of 1,633 diseases, including viral hepatitis, diabetes mellitus, other headache syndromes, multiple sclerosis, sleep apnea, hemorrhoids, and disaccharidase deficiency. However, the relative search volume on Google and page view counts on Wikipedia for different diseases displayed different correlation patterns with their prevalence and treatment costs. Further, the LASSO regression analysis showed that the relative search volume on Google, relative page review on Wikipedia, relative disease prevalence, relative treatment cost, relative number of scientific articles from PubMed, relative number of clinical trials, and relative funding from the NIH have various power for predicting future disease burdens. However, our analysis is limited to prevalence and treatment cost, but not other measures of disease burden due to data availability and comparability. The findings also caution us not to over-generalize when estimating disease burdens for the purpose of understanding population health, formulating health policies, or planning resource allocation. Instead, we should consider each individual disease according to its characteristics, such as the acute/chronic nature, severity, familiarity to the public, and presence of stigma.

References

1. Burden of disease (AIHW) (2016). http://www.aihw.gov.au/burden-of-disease/
2. Paez, K.A., Zhao, L., Hwang, W.: Rising out-of-pocket spending for chronic conditions: a ten-year trend. Health Aff. **28**, 15–25 (2009)
3. Laing, S., et al.: Mortality from heart disease in a cohort of 23,000 patients with insulin-treated diabetes. Diabetologia **46**, 760–765 (2003)
4. Corbett, E.L., et al.: The growing burden of tuberculosis: global trends and interactions with the HIV epidemic. Arch. Intern. Med. **163**, 1009–1021 (2003)
5. Feigin, V.L., et al.: Global Burden of Diseases, Injuries, and Risk Factors Study 2010 (GBD 2010) and the GBD Stroke Experts Group. Global and Regional Burden of Stroke during 1990-2010: Findings from the Global Burden of Disease Study 2010. Lancet **383**, 245–254 (2014)
6. Melse, J.M., et al.: A national burden of disease calculation: dutch disability-adjusted life-years. dutch burden of disease group. Am. J. Public Health **90**, 1241 (2000)
7. Mathers, C., Vos, T., Stevenson, C.: The Burden of Disease and Injury in Australia. Australian Institute of Health and Welfare (1999)
8. Thacker, S.B., et al.: Measuring the public's health. Public Health Rep. **121**, 14–22 (2006)
9. Michaud, C.M., Murray, C.J., Bloom, B.R.: Burden of disease—implications for future research. JAMA **285**, 535–539 (2001)
10. McGinnis, J.M., Foege, W.H.: Actual causes of death in the United States. JAMA **270**, 2207–2212 (1993)
11. Murray, C.J.: Quantifying the burden of disease: the technical basis for disability-adjusted life years. Bull. World Health Org. **72**, 429 (1994)
12. Mason, V., Bridgwood, A.: Methods of Collecting Morbidity Statistics: Revised Report to the Eurostat Task Force on 'Health and Health-related Survey Data' (2003)
13. Clavería, L.E., et al.: Prevalence of parkinson's disease in cantalejo, Spain: a door-to-door survey. Mov. Disord. **17**, 242–249 (2002)
14. Benito-León, J., et al.: Prevalence of PD and other types of parkinsonism in three elderly populations of central Spain. Mov. Disord. **18**, 267–274 (2003)
15. Errea, J.M., et al.: Prevalence of Parkinson's disease in lower aragon. Spain. Mov. Disord. **14**, 596–604 (1999)
16. Ginsberg, J., et al.: Detecting influenza epidemics using search engine query data. Nature **457**, 1012–1014 (2009)
17. Moat, H.S., et al.: Quantifying wikipedia usage patterns before stock market moves. Sci. Rep. **3**, Article number 1801 (2013)
18. Yao, L., et al.: Health ROI as a measure of misalignment of biomedical needs and resources. Nat. Biotechnol. **33**, 807–811 (2015)
19. Schuyler, P.L., et al.: The UMLS metathesaurus: representing different views of biomedical concepts. Bull. Med. Libr. Assoc. **81**, 217 (1993)

20. Denny, J.C., et al.: PheWAS: demonstrating the feasibility of a phenome-wide scan to discover gene-disease associations. Bioinformatics **26**, 1205–1210 (2010)
21. Tibshirani, R.: Regression shrinkage and selection via the lasso. J. R. Stat. Soc. Ser. B Stat. Methodol. **58**, 267–288 (1996)
22. Friedman, J., Hastie, T., Tibshirani, R.: glmnet: Lasso and Elastic-Net Regularized Generalized Linear Models. R Package Version 1 (2009)
23. Hartung, D.M., et al.: The cost of multiple sclerosis drugs in the US and the pharmaceutical industry: too big to fail? Neurology **84**, 2185–2192 (2015)

Knowledge-Based Approach for Named Entity Recognition in Biomedical Literature: A Use Case in Biomedical Software Identification

Muhammad Amith, Yaoyun Zhang, Hua Xu[✉], and Cui Tao[✉]

University of Texas Health Science Center, Houston, TX 77030, USA
cui.tao@uth.tmc.edu

Abstract. Statistical and machine learning approaches to named entity recognition have risen to prominence in the field of natural language processing. Certain named entities, specifically biomedical software, is a challenge to identify as a named entity. One direction is investigating the use of contextual semantic information to assist in this task as alluded to by previous researchers. We introduce an ontology-driven method that experiments with both information extraction and inherited features of ontologies (e.g., embedded semantic relationships and links to entities) to automatically identify familiar and unfamiliar software names. We evaluated this method with a set of biomedical research abstracts containing software entities. Our proposed approach could be used to further augment other named entity recognition methods.

1 Introduction

Ontology researchers often recognize the symbiotic relationship between the fields of ontology and natural language processing. Both are concerned with terminology and the contextual meaning of terms, including how to make these terms interpretable by and interactive with machines. This study describes a system in which both ontology and natural language processing methods attempt to solve a known text mining challenge named entity recognition (NER). We will discuss a unique method that could harness some of the features of an ontology, specifically terms and properties of an entity, and unsupervised open information extraction (OIE) methods to identify and estimate probable software terms in a corpus. While NER has various use cases in biomedical research [23,24], one current and practical use case is utilizing named entity recognition for indexing documents of a corpus, specifically for biomedical software [10–12].

According to Gruber, an ontology is an explicit specification of a conceptualization [15]. The basic information handled by ontologies are knowledge triples, factual statements about the domain in subject-verb-object format. The manifestation of the ontology comprise triples ontology languages such as RDF (Resource Description Format)[1] and OWL (Web Ontology Language)[2]. Relating to knowledge triples and supporting the complementary nature of natural

---

[1] https://www.w3.org/TR/2014/REC-rdf11-concepts-20140225/.
[2] http://www.w3.org/TR/owl2-overview/.

© Springer International Publishing AG 2017
S. Benferhat et al. (Eds.): IEA/AIE 2017, Part II, LNAI 10351, pp. 386–395, 2017.
DOI: 10.1007/978-3-319-60045-1_40

language processing (NLP) and ontology, natural language tools like information extraction can assist in extracting triples from a corpus.

Past studies have used ontologies for NER tasks. In the biomedical domain, ontology-based NER have mined text using the Unified Medical Language System (UMLS) for protein names [27], gene identification with the Gene Ontology tool [6], or general biomedical information (BioAnnotator) [22]. These studies mainly used the ontology as a dictionary of terms (gazetteer) to identify familiar entities, assisted with supplementary statistical or rule-based systems. However, a gazetteer technique weaknesses is how the term is represented between the ontology source and the text. Outside the biomedical domain, Hassell et al. introduced an NER study of researchers' names from an online source using an RDF-coded ontology of researchers [16], and Cimiano and Volker explored NER with a tourism domain ontology [7]. DBpedia Spotlight is another service for automated ontology-based corpus annotation [21].

There is renewed stress that published research be replicable and on the idea of open-curated research data for disclosure[3]. The latter not only applies to datasets but also to other artifacts of research that supplement research workflow. One of these includes software deployed in the research workflow, particularly the software tools used to generate data (and perhaps reproduce the data to replicate the study). Additionally, there is a growing need to benchmark biomedical research to identify elements within a research study to encourage replication of results and offer viable resources to further expand on a study. Also, an expanding corpus of biomedical research literature needs to be indexed and identified to highlight various resources. These resources (or resourceome) could include databases and software important for other biomedical researchers to further their own studies and determine future best practices.

Currently, there are several tools, either directories or ontologies, to index resources [1,4,28]. However, to efficiently identify and handle these resources within the biomedical literature is challenging and requires automated text-mining methods [5]. Specifically, NER has successfully demonstrated recognizing specific entities in biomedical literature, like proteins and genes [17–19,25,26].

University of Manchester researchers have published studies utilizing text mining of bioinformatics software and database entities. Duck et al. developed the bioNerDS system, which used a scoring method based on the word pattern and clues of the entity to determine the software entity [12], and depending on the corpus, *f-measure* varied between 63–91%. Later, Duck and coworkers introduced a supervised machine-learning approach for NER that averaged 58–63% for strict and 65–70% for less strict identification of software and database on a corpus of 60 documents [11]. This approach specifically experimented with CRF++ with orthogonal, lexical, dictionary, and syntactic features. However, the researchers suggested that if contextual information has been accounted for, potential improvements could be made.

Biomedical software is primarily involved in analyzing and producing data and therefore, like datasets and documented workflows, is critical for study repro-

---

[3] https://bd2k.nih.gov/.

ducibility. This led Malone et al. to develop a formal ontology of biomedical software for the purpose of describing "resources used in storing, managing and analyzing data" (Malone et al. 2014:3) [20]. Curating requirements from a series of workshops, through an agile-like software engineering process, an ontology encoded in OWL was developed with 4067 classes, 56 objects and data properties, and 119 individual instances, based on figures from the National Center for Biomedical Ontologies' BioPortal[4]. In our study, we used the published Software Ontology (SWO) to help define the identification of software that could harness the ontology for dictionary-based NER and other experimental approaches.

If one is given a document to identify or to annotate specific entities, it is possible to use a gazetteer approach to match an entity's exact or similar terms. However, if an entity's term is not listed in the gazetteer, either by lack of updates or of familiarity, it would be difficult to annotate it. Using the biomedical software literature example, while some research may contain terms that are associated with commonly known software, e.g., Weka, Ubuntu Linux, or Protégé, others may use terms from an *ad hoc* software tool or a lesser-known software name. Therefore, using an ontology that contains a list of named entities as the gazetteer may be limiting. Despite this, an ontology also describes the entity's properties and relationships to other concepts. The additional information could identify unfamiliar entities without the need of the exact or a similar term. Unlike the aforementioned ontology-based, "dictionary lookup" (gazetteer) approaches, the semantic relationships and properties may serve as embedded decision rules to identify unfamiliar entities. Our proposed approach relies on the knowledge triples upon which the formal ontologies are built, and the unique advantage is that even if the ontology is not updated with new entities, the system can still recognize terms based on semantic information.

Figure 1 illustrates an scenario wherein a NER system used a gazetteer of software terms, and the term "BioPerl" is encountered. The system then recognizes the entity as a software name and identifies it as software. In a different document, the same NER system encounters another software name, but the name is unrecognized because it is not listed in the system dictionary. Yet within the document, there exist semantic relational information pertaining to the entity:

- the entity has interface "application programing interface"
- the entity has version "2.1.0", and
- the entity has license "Apache License v2"

Based on the information, one can reasonably assume that the unknown entity is a software. While an ontology can be a source of exact or similar terms to denote entities, it can also be the source of the entities' properties and relational information to distinguish a term belonging to a concept, like software. Overall, we assume that an unsupervised knowledge-based approach, driven by ontology-based tools, could identify familiar (known) or unfamiliar (unknown) named entities.

---

[4] http://bioportal.bioontology.org/ontologies/SWO.

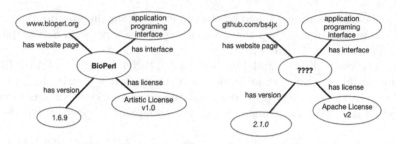

Fig. 1. Hypothetical software entities. Familiar name (left) and unfamiliar name (right) with the same properties and relationships.

To demonstrate, we identified software entities using the ontology-based approach described herein. We experimented with both open information extraction (OIE) and inherited features of ontologies to automatically annotate familiar and unfamiliar software names. This system utilized the published SWO to provide the ontology support for this study. After software names from research abstracts are annotated, we will evaluate the accuracy by manual inspection of the results and calculate its *precision, recall,* and *f-measure.*

2   Materials and Methods

We developed Java-based software that imports a set of biomedical abstracts in plain text format and automatically annotates terms that are estimated to be software based on a sample ontology and extracted knowledge triples. The system utilizes natural language components for the knowledge triple extraction and word similarity algorithms. Ontology components, OWL API (application program interface)[5] and SWO, are also incorporated into the system.

2.1   Ontology Components

For the system to interact with an NER ontology, the OWL API is required to help find the relevant software names, all associated object properties, and any connected non-software terms. Additionally with the OWL API, the system builds gazetteers of types of terms for matching and term similarity. We will use the recent SWO in OWL2 format as the subject ontology.

2.2   Natural Language Processing Components

The fundamental element of an ontology is a triple which expresses a basic statement of knowledge as subject-verb-object. The ClausIE Java-based library [9] is an unsupervised open information extraction module that produces knowledge

---

[5] http://owlapi.sourceforge.net/.

triples (called prepositions) based on decision rules from the grammatical structure of the sentences and the utilization of dependency parsing, and surpassing
the accuracy of other OIE methods.

Both the ws4j library[6] and MIT's Java WordNet Interface (JWI) [13] are
additional utilities. Our system harnesses term similarity metrics to find similarity between the ontology properties and the extracted knowledge triple verb.
Our system uses JWI for lemmatization due to lack of support for this feature
in ws4j.

Each of the eight word similarity algorithms[7] had its own scale, 0 to 1, 0 to
infinity, etc. Furthermore, there is not uniform agreement of similarity among
algorithms if two terms are said to be similar. The challenge was to select one or
a few algorithms to determine similarity or to devise an aggregate score from all
eight algorithms. Based on earlier experimentation, the latter was chosen and
a simple composite of the score was used where each result of the metric was
equally weighted. It was determined that if the similarity score was higher than
a set threshold, then the similarity is found between terms. In this study, we set
the threshold to 0.6.

Other utilities include the Apache Commons[8] library and Google's Guava[9].
Guava is used for string-based manipulation, and Apache Commons provides
string similarity, specifically Jaro-Winkler, which is said to be appropriate for
proper name matching [8,14]. Jaro-Winkler produces a score between 0 and 1,
with a higher score indicating similarity. Arbitrarily for the study, the threshold
for similarity was set at 0.85. The tool was developed using Eclipse's e4 platform[10] for GUI (graphical user interface) interaction and reporting. We collected
194 abstracts of biomedical studies that described the use of software, and we
included the titles in plain text format for input.

2.3   Implementation

The software implementation was developed in Java 8 SDK. The University of
Texas Health Science Center faculty provided the corpus of 185 random biomedical abstracts with titles from PubMed (MeSH term "Software"). The system
tokenized each sentence and imported the merged version of the SWO. Then, the
system generated a gazetteer based on the terms from the "software" class and
subclasses. Also, the system extracted the software class's (and its subclasses)
object and data properties, including the domain objects connected to the class
and subclass. The system is bifurcated by subsystems - gazetteer match and
ontology rule-based match.

---

[6] https://code.google.com/p/ws4j/.

[7] Hirst and St-Onge (1988), Leacock and Chodorow (1988), Banerjee and Pedersen
(2002), Wu and Palmer (1994), Resnik (1995), Jiang and Conrath (1997), Lin (1998),
and ws4J's PATH.

[8] http://commons.apache.org/.

[9] https://github.com/google/guava.

[10] http://eclipse.org.

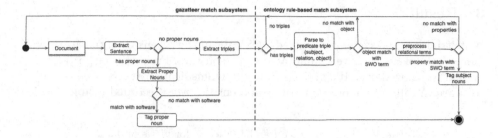

Fig. 2. Core process to discover and collect software names from corpus.

Gazetteer Match: After the system was initialized, it preformed a batch processing of each document and iterated through each sentence. A sentence level summary of the process is presented in Fig. 2. With each sentence, the proper nouns are extracted and each is matched, either using Jaro-Winkler string similarity or an exact match with a software term in the ontology-based gazetteer. If the exact match is made or the similarity score is above 0.85, the match is recorded. This is called a simple gazetteer approach for NER.

Ontology Rule-Based Match: After knowledge triples were obtained and their parts recorded, the system continued with the same sentence to seek out unfamiliar software terms. With the object part of the knowledge triples, the system matched the main nouns from the object part with either the non-software terms or the software terms. If a match was found, the system notes a match with the subject. In the example $bs4jx > is\ encoded\ in > Java$, where "Java" is the object and "bs4jx" (fictitious software) is an unfamiliar software entity, we want to discover if "Java" is matched with the same term described in SWO under the "programming language" class.

In order for "bs4jx" to be noted as a software entity, the system must match the predicate ("is encoded in") with a predicate associated with "Java" from the SWO. After which, "bs4jx" would be annotated as a software entity. Continuing, with the extracted relation (verb) term(s), unnecessary words, like "are" and "a" were removed and the main term was reduced to its lemma form using JWI. Once the relation term preprocessing is prepared, the tool then queries the relationship terms for the "software" class and compares it with relational terms from the sentence using word similarity metrics from the ws4j library. For this step, the tool retrieves a normalized total score from each of the semantic similarity algorithms. If the normalized score is above the threshold (0.6), the relational term from the sentence and the property term are noted to be similar. Then, the subject would be recorded as a software entity. Finally, the identified terms are collected and output to the system user.

3   Results

In its trial run, the system outputted a CSV file of the tokens from the abstracts, along with tokens that were annotated to be software. From the output file, the system recognized over 100 entities from the biomedical abstracts deemed to be software. A tally of annotated entities and entities were recorded (Table 1).

Table 1. *Precision, recall* and *f-measure* for views of data.

	Precision	*Recall*	*f-measure*
Basic results	0.66	0.32	0.43
Removed stop words	0.66	0.36	0.47
Removed stop words + referred software entities	0.66	0.44	0.53

Overall, there were 176 software entities in the corpus, and the system correctly annotated 116. Table 1 presents the *precision, recall,* and *f-measure* for different views of the data. Basic results represents the unembellished data gathered from the trial.

The system did not implement any stop words removal that were domain independent (e.g., *the, we, our*). Removing stop words filters the stop words that were incorrectly identified as software, which slightly improved the recall. Viewing the data further, we noted nouns (*software, tools, programs*) or pronouns (*this, it, their*) that referred to the primary software entity discussed in the document, and we filtered the data, resulting in improved *recall* and overall *f-measure*.

Of interest was the number of software entities annotated as the result of relational-based matching, instead of the direct software name matching from the ontology. Fifty-eight nouns and pronouns were deduced by the system as software, solely through the use of corresponding with the ontology's properties and relational terms.

4   Discussion

The unique aspect of this study is that it utilized a combination of state-of-the-art information extraction methods and ontology-based tools for NER. Another unique contribution, we used semantic relationships in our study, which served as foundational decision rules to identify unfamiliar entities. Previously, one ontology-based study yielded an *f-measure* of 0.66 using domain-specific string matching and the UMLS ontology for protein names [27]. With Cimiano and Volker's study, the *precision, recall,* and *f-measure* was 0.37, 0.29, and 0.33, respectively [7]. Mendes et al. evaluated DBpedia Spotlight with randomly selected paragraphs from the New York Times, and depending on annotation configuration, the *f-measure* was 0.45 and 0.56 [21]. Hassell et al.'s research [16], which involves identifying scientific researchers' names from DBWorld online postings, specifically the researcher's co-authorship with others. For that specific use case, *precision* was 0.97 and *recall* was 0.79 [16].

Limitations. Our study was limited in that each document was an abstract and thus provided limited information from which to deduce entities. We assumed that with a full document that contained more information about the specific software, the system could improve in its pinpointing software entities, particularly unfamiliar ones. An abstract may have one or no sentence that describes the software, which would make it challenging for this system to determine software entities in the documents. Additionally, the processing speed could also be improved with parallel threading or big data technologies, like Apache Spark.

The SWO had a substantial number of class and property terms, but it is possible that the ontology, like most ontologies, was limited and may not cover the domain beyond the software names or the properties and attributes. For this method to be effective, we need a comprehensive ontological description of what constitutes software. But this, compounded by what software engineering researchers like Brooks [2] and Budgen [3] call the "invisibility" feature of software, makes modeling difficult.

Future Direction. Aside from the technical improvements, this study has the potential to promote the use of ontology for natural language research and thereby improve these results. Another possibility is to update ontology terminology with new entities whenever a new entity name is discovered. We found, for example, an abstract with a labeled entity, but the same entity in another abstract was not labeled. This might have been avoided if the ontology had been updated upon successful disambiguation.

There is also an option to experiment with alternative term similarity methods. The current subroutine that handles term similarity between properties using similarity metrics is time consuming. In the future, it would be ideal to utilize alternate, faster methods to compare terms. Also, the system could be enhanced by using common nouns and pronouns that refer to the entities, thereby improving accuracy, and by incorporating support ontologies into the system process.

5   Conclusion

We have introduced a system that harnesses several natural language and ontology components, including lightweight information extraction and ontology-based technology. NER is a fundamental research challenge in NLP and text mining, with implications for biomedical researchers. Annotating datasets for research and analysis is expensive, but automating some of the process or augmenting the manual process of annotating could be less costly. Although we applied the approach in software entity extraction and annotation, it could be modified to distinguish other entity types from other domain ontologies or to augment other NER methods and techniques to improve entity identification.

Acknowledgements. Research was partially supported by the National Library Of Medicine of the National Institutes of Health under Award Number R01LM011829 and R01AI130460, by the National Institutes of Health (NIH) through the NIH Big Data to Knowledge, Grant 1U24AI117966-01, and by the Cancer Prevention Research Institute of Texas (CPRIT) Training Grant #RP160015.

References

1. Brazas, M.D., Yim, D.S., Yamada, J.T., Ouellette, B.F.F.: The 2011 bioinformatics links directory update: more resources, tools and databases and features to empower the bioinformatics community. Nucl. Acids Res. **39**(suppl), W3–W7 (2011). http://nar.oxfordjournals.org/lookup/doi/10.1093/nar/gkr514
2. Brooks, F.P.: The Mythical Man-Month, vol. 1995. Addison-Wesley, Reading (1975)
3. Budgen, D.: Software Design. Pearson Education, Harlow (2003)
4. de la Calle, G., Garca-Remesal, M., Chiesa, S., de la Iglesia, D., Maojo, V.: BIRI: a new approach for automatically discovering and indexing available public bioinformatics resources from the literature. BMC Bioinform. **10**(1), 320 (2009). http://www.biomedcentral.com/1471-2105/10/320
5. Cannata, N., Merelli, E., Altman, R.B.: Time to organize the bioinformatics resourceome. PLoS Comput. Biol. **1**(7), e76 (2005)
6. Chiang, J.H., Yu, H.C.: MeKE: discovering the functions of gene products from biomedical literature via sentence alignment. Bioinformatics **19**(11), 1417–1422 (2003)
7. Cimiano, P., Vlker, J.: Towards large-scale, open-domain and ontology-based named entity classification. In: Proceedings of the International Conference on Recent Advances in Natural Language Processing (RANLP) (2005)
8. Cohen, W., Ravikumar, P., Fienberg, S.: A comparison of string metrics for matching names and records. In: KDD Workshop on Data Cleaning and Object Consolidation, vol. 3, pp. 73–78 (2003). https://www.cs.cmu.edu/afs/cs/Web/People/wcohen/postscript/kdd-2003-match-ws.pdf
9. Del Corro, L., Gemulla, R.: ClausIE: clause-based open information extraction. In: Proceedings of the 22nd International Conference on World Wide Web, pp. 355–366. International World Wide Web Conferences Steering Committee (2013). http://dl.acm.org/citation.cfm?id=2488420
10. Duck, G., Nenadic, G., Brass, A., Robertson, D.L., Stevens, R.: Extracting patterns of database and software usage from the bioinformatics literature. Bioinformatics **30**(17), i601–i608 (2014). http://bioinformatics.oxfordjournals.org/cgi/doi/10.1093/bioinformatics/btu471
11. Duck, G., Kovacevic, A., Robertson, D.L., Stevens, R., Nenadic, G.: Ambiguity and variability of database and software names in bioinformatics. J. Biomed. Semant. **6**(1), 29 (2015). http://www.jbiomedsem.com/content/6/1/29
12. Duck, G., Nenadic, G., Brass, A., Robertson, D.L., Stevens, R.: bioNerDS: exploring bioinformatics database and software use through literature mining. BMC Bioinform. **14**(1), 194 (2013). http://www.biomedcentral.com/1471-2105/14/194
13. Finlayson, M.A.: Java libraries for accessing the princeton wordnet: comparison and evaluation. In: Proceedings of the 7th Global Wordnet Conference, pp. 78–85 (2014)
14. Grannis, S.J., Overhage, J.M., McDonald, C.: Real world performance of approximate string comparators for use in patient matching. Medinfo **11**, 43–47 (2004)

15. Gruber, T.R.: Toward principles for the design of ontologies used for knowledge sharing? Int. J. Hum. Comput. Stud. **43**(56), 907–928 (1995). http://www.sciencedirect.com/science/article/pii/S1071581985710816

16. Hassell, J., Aleman-Meza, B., Arpinar, I.B.: Ontology-driven automatic entity disambiguation in unstructured text. In: Cruz, I., et al. (eds.) ISWC 2006. LNCS, vol. 4273, pp. 44–57. Springer, Heidelberg (2006). doi:10.1007/11926078_4

17. Hirschman, L., Yeh, A., Blaschke, C., Valencia, A.: Overview of BioCreAtIvE: critical assessment of information extraction for biology. BMC Bioinform. **6**(Suppl 1), S1 (2005). http://www.ncbi.nlm.nih.gov/pmc/articles/PMC1869002/

18. Kolluru, B., Hawizy, L., Murray-Rust, P., Tsujii, J., Ananiadou, S.: Using workflows to explore and optimise named entity recognition for chemistry. PLoS ONE **6**(5), e20181 (2011). http://dx.doi.org/10.1371/journal.pone.0020181

19. Lei, J., Tang, B., Lu, X., Gao, K., Jiang, M., Xu, H.: A comprehensive study of named entity recognition in Chinese clinical text. J. Am. Med. Inform. Assoc. **21**(5), 808–814 (2014). http://jamia.oxfordjournals.org/content/21/5/808

20. Malone, J., Brown, A., Lister, A.L., Ison, J., Hull, D., Parkinson, H., Stevens, R.: The Software Ontology (SWO): a resource for reproducibility in biomedical data analysis, curation and digital preservation. J. Biomed. Semant. **5**(1), 25 (2014). http://www.jbiomedsem.com/content/5/1/25/abstract

21. Mendes, P.N., Jakob, M., Garca-Silva, A., Bizer, C.: DBpedia spotlight: shedding light on the web of documents. In: Proceedings of the 7th International Conference on Semantic Systems, pp. 1–8. ACM (2011). http://dl.acm.org/citation.cfm?id=2063519

22. Mukherjea, S., Subramaniam, L.V., Chanda, G., Sankararaman, S., Kothari, R., Batra, V., Bhardwaj, D., Srivastava, B.: Enhancing a biomedical information extraction system with dictionary mining and context disambiguation. IBM J. Res. Dev. **48**(5.6), 693–701 (2004)

23. Nadeau, D., Sekine, S.: A survey of named entity recognition and classification. Lingvisticae Investigationes **30**(1), 3–26 (2007). http://www.ingentaconnect.com/content/jbp/li/2007/00000030/00000001/art00002

24. Sekine, S.: Extended named entity ontology with attribute information. In: LREC, pp. 52–57 (2008). http://nlp.cs.nyu.edu/sekine/papers/lrec08.pdf

25. Settles, B.: ABNER: an open source tool for automatically tagging genes, proteins and other entity names in text. Bioinformatics **21**(14), 3191–3192 (2005). http://bioinformatics.oxfordjournals.org/content/21/14/3191

26. Spasic, I., Ananiadou, S., McNaught, J., Kumar, A.: Text mining and ontologies in biomedicine: making sense of raw text. Brief. Bioinform. **6**(3), 239–251 (2005). http://bib.oxfordjournals.org/content/6/3/239.short

27. Tsuruoka, Y., Tsujii, J.: Improving the performance of dictionary-based approaches in protein name recognition. J. Biomed. Inform. **37**(6), 461–470 (2004). http://linkinghub.elsevier.com/retrieve/pii/S1532046404000814

28. Yamamoto, Y., Takagi, T.: OReFiL: an online resource finder for life sciences. BMC Bioinform. **8**(1), 287 (2007). http://www.biomedcentral.com/1471-2105/8/287

Interweaving Domain Knowledge and Unsupervised Learning for Psychiatric Stressor Extraction from Clinical Notes

Olivia R. Zhang[1], Yaoyun Zhang[2], Jun Xu[2], Kirk Roberts[2],
Xiang Y. Zhang[3], and Hua Xu[2(✉)]

[1] St. John's School, Houston, TX 77019, USA
[2] School of Biomedical Informatics,
The University of Texas Health Science Center at Houston,
Houston, TX 77030, USA
hua.xu@uth.tmc.edu
[3] Department of Psychiatry and Behavioral Sciences,
The University of Texas Health Science Center at Houston,
Houston, TX 77030, USA

Abstract. Mental health is an increasingly important problem in healthcare. Psychiatric stressors are one of the major contributors of mental disorders. Very few studies have investigated stressor data in electronic health records, mostly because they are recorded in narrative texts. This study takes the initiative to develop a natural language processing system to automatically extract psychiatric stressors from clinical notes. Our approach integrates domain knowledge from multiple sources and unsupervised word representation features generated from deep learning based algorithms, to address the context dependence and data sparseness challenges caused by idiosyncratic psychosocial backgrounds. Experimental results on psychiatric notes from the CEGS N-GRID 2016 challenge demonstrate that the proposed approach is promising. The best performing configuration achieved a precision of 90.5%, a recall of 65.5%, and a F-measure of 76.0% for inexact matching.

1 Introduction

Mental health is an increasingly important problem in healthcare [21] As one of the major contributors of mental disorders, psychiatric stressors are defined as psychosocial or environmental factors (e.g. loss of a loved one, job issues, etc.) that can profoundly impact cognition, emotion, and behavior of patients [5,18]. There is a major category of trauma and stressor-related mental disorders, including adjustment disorders, acute stress disorder, posttraumatic stress disorder, dissociative disorders, etc. [5] However, due to the diverse and subjective nature of the patients' psychosocial situations, psychiatric stressors are often recorded in narrative text in electronic health record (EHR) systems and are not directly available for further analyses. To enable large-scale quantitative analysis of psychiatric stressors, mental disorder risks and treatment outcomes

© Springer International Publishing AG 2017
S. Benferhat et al. (Eds.): IEA/AIE 2017, Part II, LNAI 10351, pp. 396–406, 2017.
DOI: 10.1007/978-3-319-60045-1_41

using EHR data, it is critical to develop automated approaches to extract and structure stressor information from clinical text.

Recently emerging research activities have used natural language processing (NLP) techniques to unlock information in psychiatric text in EHRs for various applications. For example, Gorrell et al. (2013) applied active learning based algorithms for negative symptom recognition of schizophrenia [6]. In addition, Pestian et al. (2015) used NLP features and semi-supervised machine learning methods to discriminate between the conversation of suicidal and non-suicidal individuals [20]. Patel et al. (2015) used NLP techniques to identify cannabis use that was documented in free text clinical records [19]. Further, Rumshisky et al. (2016) used features generated from the Latent Dirichlet Allocation (LDA) model to enhance the accuracy of predicting early psychiatric readmission [22]. McCoy et al. (2016) also used NLP features extracted from discharge summaries and regression models to predict the risk of suicides [13].

However, few studies have been devoted to extraction of psychiatric stressors from clinical notes. As illustrated by the examples in Fig. 1, psychiatric stressors have several distinctive attributes, making automatic extraction of the information from text extremely challenging. Firstly, stressors are highly unique to individuals and come from a broad range of psychosocial environments, leading to very sparse distribution of stressors across different patients and clinical notes. In addition, the identification of stressors is highly dependent on and constrained by contextual information, such as the co-occurrence with psychiatric symptoms or a worsened mental disorder. Furthermore, stressors usually consist of complex phrases or clauses, and the exact boundaries of stressors are difficult and sometimes ambiguous to identify. Due to the fact that most expressions of psychiatric stressors are not typical biomedical concepts, current major sources of biomedical terminologies such as the Unified Medical Language System (UMLS) [2] have a very limited coverage of psychiatric stressors. Moreover, existing named entity recognition tools such as MetaMap [1] and DNorm [11] are not specifically designed for the sublanguages in psychiatric notes and stressors, which may differ greatly from other types of clinical notes and biomedical literature [12].

S1: 66 yo man with history of cocaine abuse now in remission, persistent marijuana use, worsening mood and anxiety symptoms over past several years in setting of *father's death* and *legal battle with sister and mother*.

S2: Patient relays having some sadness throughout childhood secondary to *bullying in school for being overweight*, but otherwise describes essential euthymia until about age 23 when *she became involved with her partner and had significant relational difficulties*.

Fig. 1. Examples of sentences with stressors in psychiatric notes. The mentions of stressors are underlined.

To address this problem, this study takes the initiative to extract psychiatric stressor information from clinical notes. Specifically, extraction of psychiatric stressors was treated as a typical named entity recognition (NER) task, and machine learning systems based on the conditional random field (CRF) algorithm were developed. In addition to common NLP features used for NER [24, 26] domain knowledge from multiple sources such as online healthcare knowledge repositories and sentiment analysis lexicons were also collected as context features and candidate stressor indicators. Furthermore, to address the idiosyncrasy and data sparseness issues, unsupervised word representation features were generated from a large unlabeled clinical corpus by using a novel binarized word embedding method [7]. Experimental results show that the proposed approach is promising, demonstrating the feasibility of conducting large-scale psychiatric stressors analysis using NLP for narrative text in EHR. To the best of our knowledge, this is one of the first studies to extract psychiatric stressors from clinical text using novel NLP approaches, by combining specialized knowledge sources, corpora and unsupervised feature representation methods.

2 Materials and Methods

2.1 System Overview

Psychiatric stressor extraction from clinical text could be treated as a typical NER task. Figure 2 shows an overview of our psychiatric stressor extraction system. First, the mentions of stressors are annotated in psychiatric notes. Based on the observation of the annotations, a set of features were designed and extracted to generate the machine-learning based models for stressor recognition. Three major types of features were employed in this study: (1) the most common NLP features widely used for NER [24, 26]; (2) domain knowledge based features obtained from multiple sources; and (3) Distributional word representation features generated from deep-learning based word embedding models [4]. Based on the extracted features, ten-fold cross validation was used to evaluate the performance of machine learning models. The key components of the systems are presented in the following sections in detail.

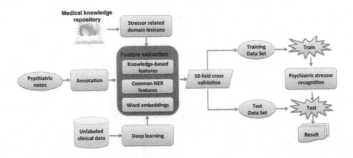

Fig. 2. Study design of our psychiatric stressor extraction system.

2.2 Dataset

A corpus of 246 psychiatric notes was collected from the CEGS N-GRID 2016 shared task[1]. We developed an annotation guideline and recruited two annotators, who manually annotated all the psychiatric stressor mentions in each note by following the guideline. First, 20 psychiatric notes were annotated by the two annotators, and the kappa value between them was 0.75. A domain expert manually reviewed these 20 notes and resolved the dis-agreements between the two annotators. Problems present in this initial annotation were noted in the guideline, based on which the second round of annotation was conducted. In total, 1,225 stressors were annotated.

2.3 Machine Learning-Based NER

In the machine learning-based NER, the problem was converted into a sequence labeling task by representing each word using specific labels [3]. In our study, we used the BIO labels, a typical representation for named entities, to represent stressor entities, where "B", "I" and "O" denote the beginning, inside and outside of an entity respectively. Therefore, the stressor recognition problem was converted into a sequence labeling task, assigning one of the three labels to each word. Figure 3 shows an example of the BIO representation, where the stressor entity "father's death" is represented as "father/B '/I s/I death/I" after tokenization.

Sentence: worsening mood and anxiety symptoms over past several years in setting of *father's death* and $\cdots$

Tokenized sentence: worsening mood and anxiety symptoms over past several years in setting of *father ' s death* and $\cdots$

BIO representation: worsening/O mood/O and/O anxiety/O symptoms/O over/O past/O several/O years/O in/O setting/O of/O *father*/B '/I *s*/I *death*/I and/O $\cdots$

Fig. 3. An example of BIO annotation for psychiatric stressors.

In this study, we employed CRF [10], a state-of-the-art machine learning algorithm for NER, to extract stressors using the implementation in CRFsuite[2]. Our experiments are primarily focused on investigating the effects of the three different types of features:

Baseline Features: The most common NER features including bag-of-words, orthographic information (word patterns, prefixes and suffixes), syntactic information (POS [part of speech] tags) as well as n-grams of words, POS tags and their combinations (unigrams, bigrams, and trigrams) [24].

---

[1] https://www.i2b2.org/NLP/RDoCforPsychiatry.
[2] http://www.chokkan.org/software/crfsuite/.

Features from Domain Knowledge Bases: Features collected from domain knowledge bases related to various aspects of stressors as described below:

- Mental disorders: Mental disorder terms, including both mental diseases and symptoms, are important context information for stressor recognition, because stressors are usually the cause of changes in the severity status of mental disorders. Therefore, mental disorders in the psychiatric notes were labeled by a dictionary lookup program in the automate clinical text processing toolkit CLAMP[3], based on lexicons from UMLS. They were used as contextual features.
- Common disorders: Common disorders (i.e., non-mental disorders) of the patients or the people having social relations with the patients could potentially be psychiatric stressors, which were also identified by CLAMP as features and stressor candidates.
- Negative words: Negative words refer to the words expressing negative emotions (e.g., "sad"), evaluations (e.g., "bad"), and stances (e.g., "against"), which may indicate the presence of stressors. The comprehensive list of negative words generated by Wilson et al. (2005) was adopted in this study [25].
- Keywords of psychosocial environments: Since psychiatric stressors happen in a broad range of psychosocial environments, related keywords were collected from WordNet [15], including: (1) keywords of family members (e.g., "family, father, mother, sibling"); (2) social environments (e.g., "job, school, work, college"); and (3) keywords of social relations (e.g., "employer, boyfriend, supervisor").
- Keywords of stressors: The cause sections of webpages about mental disorders in online healthcare knowledge repositories (e.g., APA, Mayo Clinic online, MedLinePlus, etc.) usually contain lists of stressors, from where stressor keywords were collected (e.g., "bully, trauma, war, abuse").
- Cues of discourse relations: In addition, cues of cause-effect discourse relations such as "in setting of", "in the context of", "secondary to" were used as a strong indication of stressors, especially with the co-occurrence of psychiatric disorders.

In total, eight types of features based on domain knowledge were employed in this study. As can be seen from the example sentences in Fig. 4, keywords of different types of domain knowledge act as important contextual features to indicate the presence of stressors.

Unsupervised Word Representation Features: Word representation features were generated from a corpus of unlabeled clinical documents. Specifically, we used word embeddings producing a distributional word representation for each word in an unlabeled corpus as a real-valued vector using neural networks [4,14,16]. We used the binarized word embedding feature proposed in 2014 by Guo et al. [7]. The intuition of the binarized embedding feature is to discretize the

---

[3] http://clamp.uth.edu/.

S1: 66 yo man with history of cocaine abuse now in remission, persistent marijuana use, worsening mood and anxiety symptoms over past several years in setting of *father's death* and *legal battle with sister and mother.*

S2: Patient relays having some sadness throughout childhood secondary to *bullying in school for being overweight,* but otherwise describes essential euthymia until about age 23 when *she became involved with her partner and had significant relational difficulties.*

Fig. 4. Examples of sentences with stressors in psychiatric notes. The stressor expressions are in italics and underlined. Keywords from different types of domain knowledge are highlighted by different colors. Specifically, the red color stands for mental disorders; the blue color stands for cue strings of discourse relations; the green color stands for keywords of psychosocial environments; the orange color stands for keywords of stressors; and the brown color stands for the psychiatric stressors. (Color figure online)

original real-valued matrix of word embeddings [14] and omit the insignificant dimensions. Thus, the less frequent terms are generalized together with other syntactically/semantically relevant terms of higher frequency. Word embedding features were derived from the entire set of MIMIC II [23] corpus. To generate word embedding features, we implemented the ranking-based deep neural network algorithm according to the paper from Collobert [4] using Java. The 50-dimension binarized word embeddings of each word are used as word representation features.

2.4 Experiments and Evaluation

In this study, we started with a baseline system that implemented common features including bag-of-word, orthographic information, morphological information and POS. Then, we evaluated the effects of the two sets of features: domain knowledge features and unsupervised word representation features, by adding each of them incrementally to the baseline system. Ten fold cross validation was employed for each model, and the performance of the system was evaluated using precision, recall and F-measure with the exact matching criteria. Considering that the boundaries of stressors could be flexible and ambiguous, performance based on in-exact matching, i.e., partial string matching, with gold standard annotations is also reported.

3   Results and Discussion

As shown in Table 1, the overall performance of exact matching is relatively poor. Adding domain knowledge features enhanced both the precision and recall, and yielded a F-measure of 0.426. The word embedding features further enhanced the recall (0.347 vs. 0.320) and increased the F-measure to 0.443. As illustrated more explicitly in Fig. 5, in terms of the results of in-exact matching, the baseline CRF model yielded high precision, while the recall was still very low (precision: 0.869, recall: 0.424). Integrating domain knowledge into CRF significantly enhanced the recall (0.593 vs. 0.424). The word embedding features further improved the recall (0.655 vs. 0.593), with a slight drop in the precision (0.905 vs. 0.919). Overall, the system incorporating both domain knowledge and unsupervised word representation features achieved the optimal F-measure of 0.760.

Table 1. Experimental results of CRF-based psychiatric stressor extraction systems using baseline NLP features, with incremental inclusion of domain knowledge based features and word embedding features. Both the performance of exact matching and in-exact matching are reported. (%)

		Precision	Recall	F-measure
Baseline	Exact	51.9	21.6	30.5
	In-exact	86.9	42.4	57.0
+Knowledge	Exact	63.6	32.0	42.6
	In-exact	91.9	59.3	72.1
+Word embeddings	Exact	62.4	34.7	44.3
	In-exact	90.5	65.5	76.0

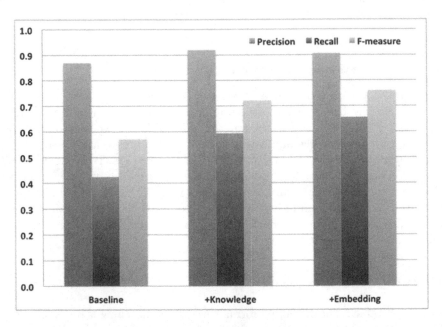

Fig. 5. Experimental results of in-exact matching using baseline NLP features, and incremental addition of domain knowledge and word embedding features into the CRF models.

Table 2. Examples of false positives from psychiatric stressor recognition. The false positive stressors are in italics.

Reasons	Example sentences
Resultant from mental disorders	Substance use difficulties resulted in her loss of job subsequently
Wrong context	With a DSM-IV diagnosis of Alcohol Abuse (1 sx of *abuse*)
Wrong subject	His father was an esthetician and returned to Tuvalu due to *difficulty obtained work permit in the US*

Although our system showed reasonable performance using in-exact matching, challenges remain for stressor information extraction. First, accurate boundary determination of stressor expressions is still difficult, as shown in the results of exact matching. However, manual review of boundary errors showed that some of the boundary errors were not critical, in terms of recognizing essential stressor entities. An example is the recognition of "parents divorced" in the sentence "parents divorced when he was 3 years old". Therefore, we argue that in-exact matching could be reasonable in stressor recognition.

We also conducted manual analysis on false positive and false negative errors by the system. As illustrated by example sentences in Table 2, the major causes of false positive errors include mistaken identification of the outcomes (instead of causes) of mental disorders as the stressors. Some cues of disorder outcomes such as "leading to" and "resulted in" should be added as features. Moreover, the discourse directions of the cause-effective relations between mental disorders and candidate stressors should also be identified. Further, some keywords are very general and often mistakenly recognized as stressors, although they are used in contexts. In addition, some stressors that do not belong to the patient are also recognized by the system, which are false positives according to our current annotation guideline. On the other hand, as illustrated by example sentences in Table 3, the major cause of false negative errors is the sparseness of the corpus, arising due to the following two reasons: (1) the diversity in both the scope of stressors and the personalized expressions of stressors; (2) the unbalanced dataset, in which most of the sentences do not contain any mention of stressors. In addition, some stressors present in conjunctive structures are not recognized completely. A post-processing step to handle such common errors may help increase recall. Other causes of false negative errors include failing to detect the negation scope modifying stressor keywords and sentences describing stressors without explicit context information.

As shown in Table 1, both domain knowledge and unsupervised work representation features improved the system's performance. Domain knowledge features improved both precision and recall. We plan to expand our system to include more knowledge sources. Adding word representation features from

Table 3. Examples of false negatives from psychiatric stressor recognition. The false negative stressors are in italics.

Reasons	Example sentences
Rare patterns of stressors	· · · in the context of a number of stressors/transitions, including *the birth of her two children within a year of each other, marriage to her college boyfriend at the age of 39,* and ensuing conflicts with her mother as a result of the marriage
Wrong scope of negations (adversative discourse relation)	There are no clear stressors in Farris' life though *the inconsistency of his father's involvement* may be a contributing factor
Lack of context	*Parents would often scream and yell when his dad did visit*

MIMIC II reduced precision slightly, but improved recall. Based on our observation, MIMIC II may not be the ideal corpus for stressor information, as it mainly contains clinical notes from ICUs. Other large corpora such as collections of Twitter and psychiatric forum postings would be more appropriate and should be investigated in the future for further recall enhancement.

One limitation of our current work is that our annotated corpus is not comprehensive enough to cover all the patterns of stressor expressions, which led to a much lower recall than the precision (0.655 vs. 0.905). Additional lexical patterns and syntactic patterns would be explored as features next to improve the recall. Furthermore, a post-processing step could be added using frequent patterns to improve the boundary detection of stressors. In addition, based on the above error analysis, more advanced methods probably need to be exploited to address the unbalanced corpus issue for NER [9,17]. It would be also very valuable to further classify stressors into different categories based on source (e.g., family, workplace, military). On one hand, implementing automatic recognition systems for each specific stressor category would potentially further improve the performance. On the other hand, it will facilitate large-scale population based investigation of psychiatric stressors and related risks and outcomes.

4   Conclusion

Psychiatric stressors are critical factors that contribute to personalized medicine in mental disorders [8]. This is the first study to automatically extract psychiatric stressors from clinical notes and our system showed reasonable performance, indicating the feasibility to leverage narrative data for mental health research.

Acknowledgement. We thank the organizers of the CEGS N-GRID 2016 challenge for providing the corpus.

References

1. Aronson, A.R., Lang, F.M.: An overview of MetaMap: historical perspective and recent advances. J. Am. Med. Inf. Assoc. **17**(3), 229–236 (2010)
2. Bodenreider, O.: The unified medical language system (UMLS): integrating biomedical terminology. Nucleic Acids Res. **32**(suppl 1), D267–D270 (2004)
3. Cho, H.C., Okazaki, N., Miwa, M., Tsujii, J.: Named entity recognition with multiple segment representations. Inf. Process. Manag. **49**(4), 954–965 (2013)
4. Collobert, R., Weston, J.: A unified architecture for natural language processing: deep neural networks with multitask learning. In: The 25th International Conference on Machine Learning, pp. 160–167. ACM (2008)
5. Friedman, M.J., Resick, P.A., Bryant, R.A., Strain, J., Horowitz, M., Spiegel, D.: Classification of trauma and stressor-related disorders in DSM-5. Depression and anxiety **28**(9), 737–749 (2011). http://onlinelibrary.wiley.com/doi/10.1002/da.20845/full
6. Gorrell, G., Jackson, R., Roberts, A., Stewart, R.: Finding negative symptoms of schizophrenia in patient records. In: Proceedings of the NLP Med Biol Work (NLPMedBio), Recent Adv Nat Lang Process (RANLP), pp. 9–17 (2013)
7. Guo, J., Che, W., Wang, H., Liu, T.: Revisiting embedding features for simple semi-supervised learning. In: Proceedings of the 2014 Conference on Empirical Methods in Natural Language Processing (EMNLP), pp. 110–120 (2014)
8. Insel, T.R.: The NIMH research domain criteria (RDoC) project: precision medicine for psychiatry. Am. J. Psychiatry (2014). http://ajp.psychiatryonline.org/doi/abs/10.1176/appi.ajp.2014.14020138
9. Kazama, J., Makino, T., Ohta, Y., Tsujii, J.: Tuning support vector machines for biomedical named entity recognition. In: Proceedings of the ACL-02 Workshop on Natural Language Processing in the Biomedical Domain, vol. 3, pp. 1–8. Association for Computational Linguistics (2002)
10. Lafferty, J., McCallum, A., Pereira, F.C.N.: Conditional random fields: probabilistic models for segmenting and labeling sequence data (2001)
11. Leaman, R., Doğan, R.I., Lu, Z.: DNorm: disease name normalization with pairwise learning to rank. Bioinformatics, p. btt474 (2013)
12. Leaman, R., Lu, Z.: TaggerOne: joint named entity recognition and normalization with semi-Markov Models. Bioinformatics **32**(18), 2839–2846 (2016)
13. McCoy, T.H., Castro, V.M., Roberson, A.M., Snapper, L.A., Perlis, R.H.: Improving prediction of suicide and accidental death after discharge from general hospitals with natural language processing. Jama Psychiatry **73**(10), 1064–1071 (2016)
14. Mikolov, T., Chen, K., Corrado, G., Dean, J.: Efficient estimation of word representations in vector space. arXiv preprint arXiv:1301.3781 (2013)
15. Miller, G.A.: WordNet: a lexical database for English. Commun. ACM **38**(11), 39–41 (1995)
16. Mnih, A., Hinton, G.E.: A scalable hierarchical distributed language model. In: Advances in Neural Information Processing Systems, pp. 1081–1088 (2009)
17. Nadeau, D., Turney, P.D., Matwin, S.: Unsupervised named-entity recognition: generating gazetteers and resolving ambiguity. In: Lamontagne, L., Marchand, M. (eds.) AI 2006. LNCS, vol. 4013, pp. 266–277. Springer, Heidelberg (2006). doi:10.1007/11766247_23
18. Organization, W.H., et al.: Prevention of mental disorders: effective interventions and policy options: Summary report (2004). http://apps.who.int/iris/handle/10665/43027

19. Patel, R., Wilson, R., Jackson, R., Ball, M., Shetty, H., Broadbent, M., Stewart, R., McGuire, P., Bhattacharyya, S.: Cannabis use and treatment resistance in first episode psychosis: a natural language processing study. Lancet **385**, S79 (2015)
20. Pestian, J.P., Grupp-Phelan, J., Bretonnel Cohen, K., Meyers, G., Richey, L.A., Matykiewicz, P., Sorter, M.T.: A controlled trial using natural language processing to examine the language of suicidal adolescents in the emergency department. Suicide and Life-threatening Behavior (2015)
21. Proctor, E.K., Landsverk, J., Aarons, G., Chambers, D., Glisson, C., Mittman, B.: Implementation research in mental health services: an emerging science with conceptual, methodological, and training challenges. Adm. Policy Ment. Health Ment. Health Serv. Res. **36**(1), 24–34 (2009)
22. Rumshisky, A., Ghassemi, M., Naumann, T., Szolovits, P., Castro, V.M., McCoy, T.H., Perlis, R.H.: Predicting early psychiatric readmission with natural language processing of narrative discharge summaries. Transl. Psychiatry **6**(10), e921 (2016)
23. Saeed, M., Villarroel, M., Reisner, A.T., Clifford, G., Lehman, L.W., Moody, G., Heldt, T., Kyaw, T.H., Moody, B., Mark, R.G.: Multiparameter Intelligent Monitoring in Intensive Care II (MIMIC-II): a public-access intensive care unit database. Crit. Care Med. **39**(5), 952 (2011)
24. Tang, B., Feng, Y., Wang, X., Wu, Y., Zhang, Y., Jiang, M., Wang, J., Xu, H.: A comparison of conditional random fields and structured support vector machines for chemical entity recognition in biomedical literature. J. Cheminform. **7**(supplement 1), S8 (2015)
25. Wilson, T., Wiebe, J., Hoffmann, P.: Recognizing contextual polarity in phrase-level sentiment analysis. In: Proceedings of the Conference on Human Language Technology and Empirical Methods in Language Processing, pp. 347–354. Association for Computational Linguistics (2005)
26. Zhang, Y., Wang, J., Tang, B., Wu, Y., Jiang, M., Chen, Y., Xu, H.: UTH_CCB: A Report for SemEval 2014 Task 7 Analysis of Clinical Text. SemEval 2014, pp. 802–806 (2014)

Innovative Applications of Textual Analysis Based on AI

Active Learning for Text Mining from Crowds

Hao Shao[(✉)]

Shanghai University of International Business and Economics, Shanghai, China
flyingmouse820@gmail.com

Abstract. The benefits of crowdsourcing have been widely recognized in active learning for text mining. Due to the lack of golden ground-truth, it is crucial to evaluate how trustworthy of "noisy" labelers when labeling informative instances. Despite recent achievements made on active learning with crowdsourcing, most of the research works are involved in tuning a considerable amount of parameters, and also sensitive to noise. In this paper, a novel framework to select both the best-fitting labeler and the most informative instance is proposed, with the help of the minimum description length principle which is acknowledged as noise-tolerant and parameter-free. The algorithm is proved to be effective through extensive experiments on texts.

Keywords: Active learning · Crowdsourcing · Text mining · Minimum encoding

1 Introduction

Traditional active learning framework assumes that there always exists a "perfect" labeler who annotates instances with 100% accuracy. However, it is not always the case in real applications, due to the high cost of obtaining faultless labels from experts. Moreover, in the big data era, the burgeoning new data makes it inapplicable to rely on precise labeling. The success of crowdsourcing shed lights on the path to solve the problem of label insufficiency, such applications include the "Amazon Mechanical Turk", "Label Me" and "Quora" [24].

Recently, a number of research works focus on this emerged learning paradigm known as "Active Learning with Crowdsourcing" (ALC). The omniscient expert in active learning is replaced by several imperfect labelers that may possibly obtain wrong labels for a portion of the unlabeled instances. On the one hand, the cost will be dramatically reduced in such a way, on the contrary, more attention should be paid to evaluate how reliable of each labeler. Meanwhile, effective strategy to alleviate the negative influences of noise should also be carefully designed. Therefore, the two key issues in ALC that should be concerned are: (1) How to select the informative instance and (2) How to select a labeler to label the instance.

Several research works have been done for ALC [5,6,11,12,18,22–24]. Despite substantial achievements, a common difficulty is the overfitting problem in the initial stage of active learning. As pointed out in [1,13], given only a few labeled

© Springer International Publishing AG 2017
S. Benferhat et al. (Eds.): IEA/AIE 2017, Part II, LNAI 10351, pp. 409–418, 2017.
DOI: 10.1007/978-3-319-60045-1_42

instances in the beginning, the initial hypotheses are not reliable since they may deviate from the optimal hypothesis with respect to the input distribution in the end of the classification procedure. Without prior knowledge of the true underlying distribution of the data, it is difficult for labelers to select the most representative and informative instance. Another disadvantage for these research works is the mechanism to tune a considerable amount of parameters. It is widely known that a method with many parameters is subject to overfitting and the user has to tune parameters prior to learning [4]. To the best of our knowledge, none of the existing methods are free from parameters and robust to noise. Moreover, most of the research works deal with labeler selection and instance selection separately.

We are motivated to develop a method that is noise-tolerant and without parameters. The Minimum Description Length Principle (MDLP) possesses the desired properties, which has a solid theoretical framework and a clear interpretation, is able to avoid overfitting and requires no parameter specification, thus is desirable to evaluate different models. The proposed algorithm aims to solve the two key issues in ALC by incorporating MDLP to evaluate labelers in each iteration, as well as to select informative instances through minimum encoding. The informative measurements adaptively combine the labeler selection and the instance selection as an integration process. It is proved to perform better than the state-of-the-art methods through extensive experiments.

2   Related Work

Active learning (AL) [13] tries to obtain a satisfactory classifier by annotating as few instances as possible where the labeling cost is high. It consists of two categories that are the stream-based active learning [7] and the pool-based active learning [2]. The former one scans the data sequentially and makes query decisions individually, while the pool-based active learning makes one decision each time from the entire collection of the unlabeled pool. The proposed algorithm belongs to the pool-based active learning scenario. Extensive research works have been done on active learning. For example, the Query by Committee (QBC) model [14] assumes a correct Bayesian prior on the set of hypotheses, and the committee members are all trained on the current labeled set. However, existing active learning methods commonly assume that there exists a perfect labeler, which is not the case in real applications. Crowdsourcing is an emerged learning paradigm which aims to alleviate the problem of label insufficiency of active learning [24]. In active learning with crowdsourcing, labels of instances are collected by several noisy labelers. Early works include [6,11,12,18]. The authors in [18] proved that crowdsourcing is helpful in active learning and showed that repeated-labeling improved the data quality directly and substantially. The authors in [22,23] extended these works and firstly used graphical model representation for ALC and tried to extract the expertise of annotators through probabilistic models. It is assumed that the expertise can be represented by the input data and their unknown true labels. These algorithms contain a considerable amount of parameters and separately deal with labelers selection and instance selection, which tend to overfit in the initial stage of learning. Algorithm proposed in [5] adopted the same problem settings as [22] to minimize labeling costs and labeling errors, in which weak labelers can learn from strong labelers. We argue that in real applications such as "Amazon Mechanical Turk", labelers will not possibly update their abilities given only a small number of diverse instances in a limited time. Our proposed algorithm is based on MDLP [9]. It states that the best hypothesis is the one that minimizes the sum of the code length of the hypothesis and the code length of the data given the hypothesis. It was successfully applied in the classification problems such as [3,20]. It was also incorporated in transfer learning [15,16] and active learning [17]. In this paper, MDLP is firstly extended in active learning with crowdsourcing.

3   Preliminary

3.1   Problem Setting

There exist a target data set T which consists of a small potion of labeled instances called L, and a large number of unlabeled instances set UL. $T = \{\mathbf{x}_1, ..., \mathbf{x}_N\}$, where $\mathbf{x}_i \in \mathbb{R}^M$. There exist K labelers $\{l_1, ..., l_K\}$. The label given by the labeler for instance $\mathbf{x}$ is denoted by $z^{(k)}$, for the k-th labeler. Y is the set of all possible labels for an instance $\mathbf{x}$, and the j-th class is denoted by y_j, where $y_j \in Y = \{y_1, ..., y_d\}$. The ground-truth label for $\mathbf{x}$ is $y*$. The objective is to produce an estimate for the ground-truth label for new instances.

3.2   Preliminary

Active learning aims to select the most informative unlabeled instance by some information measurements. The key issue is to measure the "usefulness" of an unlabeled instance using only a small amount of available information. In the framework of Query by Committee (QBC) [14], a committee of t members are maintained which are all trained using re-sampled data from the labeled data L. Each member will vote on the candidates and decide the most informative instance to query. The key issue is to design an effective information measurement, which can represent the "disagreement" of every committee member. The most informative instance is shown to be the one with the maximum *vote entropy* [2].

In our works, MDLP is extended to accommodate to the active learning scenario. We provide here the preliminaries for MDLP, which may be viewed as a principle for avoiding overfitting, i.e., it is a means to balance the simplicity of a classifier and its goodness-of-fit to the data [10,21]. It states that the best classifier h_{best} is given as follows.

$$h_{\text{best}} = \arg\min_h \left(-\log P(h) - \log P(D|h) \right) \tag{1}$$

where h is a hypothesis on a data set D, and $P(h)$ and $P(D|h)$ represent the probability that h occurs and the conditional probability that D occurs given h, respectively.

We then consider a problem of encoding a binary string of length a which consists of b binary 1s and $(a - b)$ binary 0s under the framework of the sender and the receiver problem. An obvious method is to send the number b of binary 1s with the code length $\log(a+1)$ then specify the positions of binary 1s [10,21]. We denote the required code length with $\Theta(a, b)$ as follows (We assume the receiver knows $b > 0$).

$$\Theta_0(a, b) \equiv \log a + \log \binom{a}{b}$$

Lastly we consider a problem of sending an integer a under the assumption that $a = b$ is most likely and the occurrence probability $P(i)$ of $a = i$ is given by $P(b)\phi^{|b-i|}$, where ϕ is a constant given by the user.

$$\sum_{i=0}^{\infty} P(i) = 1 \Leftrightarrow P(b) = \frac{1 - \phi}{1 + \phi - \phi^{b+1}}$$

ϕ is set to be $\frac{1}{2}$ and this choice may be interpreted as the length for sending a is longer than that for sending b by $|b - a|$ bits. We denote the length $-\log\left[P(b)\phi^{|b-a|}\right]$ required to send a given b by $\Lambda(a, b)$, which can be easily obtained as

$$\Lambda(a, b) \equiv -\log\left[P(b)\phi^{|b-a|}\right] = \log\left[3 - \left(\frac{1}{2}\right)^b\right] + |b - a|$$

4   Our Proposal

4.1   Labeler Selection Procedure

Without lose of generality, we define a crowd labeler in the form of a linear function as follows: A crowd labeler $y = \mathbf{w}^T x + b$, has a fixed $\mathbf{w}$ and b that does not change in each iterations. In real cases, a crowd labeler does not improve her labeling skills with a limited number of instances in a limited period of time, but rather relies on her personal expertise. The code length consists of two parts, including the code length of the labeler and the code length of the data given the labeler.

Firstly let us consider the code length of a labeler $y = \mathbf{w}^T + b$. To encode the coefficient vector $\mathbf{w}$, in a sender-receiver problem, the sender needs to send the number of non-zero weights in $\mathbf{w}$, by $\Lambda(m, 0)$, where m is the number of non-zero weights in $\mathbf{w}$. Secondly, the sender specifies the exact position of these weights by $\Theta_0(M, m)$, where M is the number of attributes in the data. The values of weights are encoded by $\Lambda(v, 0)$, where v is the value of the specified weight. The sender also need to send the value of b by $\Lambda(b, 0)$. Therefore, The code length of a labeler h is then given by

$$-\log P(h) = \Lambda(m, 0) + \sum_{i=1}^{m} [\Theta_0(M, m) + \Lambda(v, 0)] + \Lambda(b, 0)$$

Secondly let us consider the code length $-\log P(D|h)$ of data D with the help of a labeler h. Similarly to the MDLP for classification, we send a binary string which indicates the misclassified examples in D by h. For example, if D contains five examples and the class labels of them are $(1,1,0,0,1)$, with the classification result of h on D as $(1,1,0,0,0)$, we only need to specify the wrong class label in the fifth position to the receiver, which corresponds to sending a binary string of length 5 which contains one binary 1. Let $\omega(h,D)$ denote the number of misclassified examples,

$$-\log P(D|h) = \Theta_0(|D|, \omega(h,D))$$

4.2   Select Informative Instances

The strategy of selecting the most informative instance to query is also based on minimum encoding. We extend the concept of QBC, in which each labeler is regarded as a committee member. In the conventional framework of QBC, a committee of members are maintained that are all trained using re-sampled data from L in the target task [13], and the query is chosen according to the maximum disagreement among all members. However, without solid prior knowledge of the target task, the initial model induced from the few labeled instances is possibly inappropriate and may deviate from the model in the end of the learning process. In such a circumstance, the distributions of the committee members that sampled from these few labeled instances will have a large discrepancy towards the distribution underlying the data set. We are motivated to borrow the strength of the crowds, and let each labeler as well as the model induced from the target task to be a committee member. Therefore, given the objective to find the most informative instance, we propose a novel weighted disagreement measure to deal with the "inferior" models in the learning stage.

During the learning process, the most informative instance is selected based on the disagreement of all committee members. In the conventional QBC setting [8], all members are treated equally important. However in ALC, some models may fit the data better while some models have totally different distributions. Therefore, instead of assigning equal weights to every member, a more flexible way is to use different weights.

Given the code length of each model, it is necessary for committee members to vote for the most informative instance. We illustrate our weighting strategy below.

$$x_{VE}^* = \arg\max_x -\sum_i \frac{VT(y_i)}{C} \log \frac{VT(y_i)}{C} \tag{2}$$

where $VT(y_i) = \sum_{j=1}^{|C|} w_j V(y_i)$ and $w_j = \left(\frac{CL_j}{\sum_j CL_j} \right)^{-1}$, y_i ranges over all possible labels, CL_j is the code length for the jth committee member, and $V(y_i)$ is the number of "votes" that a label receives from the committee members, and C is the committee size. This can be regarded as a QBC generalization of entropy-based uncertainty sampling.

5   Experiments

We performed experiments on both the synthetic data sets [19] and the real data sets. Our algorithm is compared to the state-of-the-art multi-labeler ALC algorithm [22], denoted as "MLALC", as well as the modified ALC that the label of the informative instance is labeled by the majority vote from all labelers, denoted as "ALCMV". The ALC with random query (ALCRQ) is also included for comparison. Our algorithm is denoted as Active Learning from Crowds with Minimum Encoding (ALCME). The baseline method is chosen as Naive Bayes. A labeler is generated by change the value of the coefficient vector in a random position, and 4 labelers are generated for each experiment. In the initial stage, 3% labeled instances are provided.

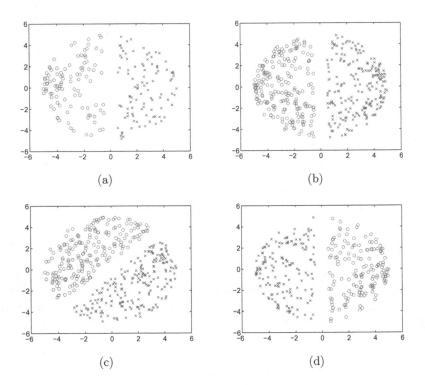

(a)   (b)

(c)   (d)

Fig. 1. Structures of the synthetic data sets

The two-dimensional synthetic data sets from [19] are adopted. The 4 data sets are generated with specific structures that are easy to analyze, as shown in Fig. 1. All the data sets are linearly separable so that the performances of different algorithms can be illustrated clearly. The error rates of all competing algorithms are presented in Fig. 2. As shown in the figure, the performances of all algorithms fluctuate initially, and become stable after about 10 queries.

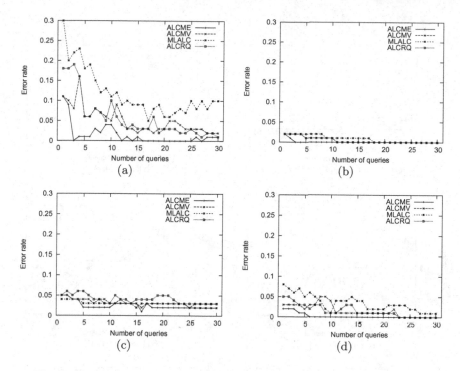

Fig. 2. Error rates on synthetic data sets for different number of queries

The underlying reason is that, given noisy labelers, an informative instance may not be annotated with the correct label in the beginning. Our ALCME is able to perform better than other methods especially after about 20 queries. As a general tendency, the errors rates of all methods are larger in data set (a) than the others. In the first data set, there are only 160 instances generated, and initially, there is only 4 labeled instances are given to the labelers. We also note that, the ALCRQ are better than ALCMV in most circumstances, the possible reason is that, a noisy labeler that is not suitable for the data will decrease the overall accuracy by voting on the informative instance. Another observation is that, with the exitance of noisy labelers, the error rates sometimes will not decrease even more labeled instances are added to the data set.

We evaluate the algorithms on UCI data sets include iris and diabetes. The iris data set has 2 dimensions and the diabetes data set has 8 dimensions. For more complex data sets, we choose text data sets include 20 Newsgroups and the Universities data sets. Two categories are chosen from the 20 Newsgroups data sets which are *rec* vs. *sci* and *sci* vs. *talk*. For example, in the *rec* vs. *sci* data set, all the positive instances are from category *rec*, while the negative ones are from category *sci*. The 8,282 pages of the universities data sets were manually classified into several categories including student, faculty, course, etc. For each class the data set contains pages from the universities such as Cornell and Texas. The results of all algorithms are illustrated in Fig. 3. As the dimension of the

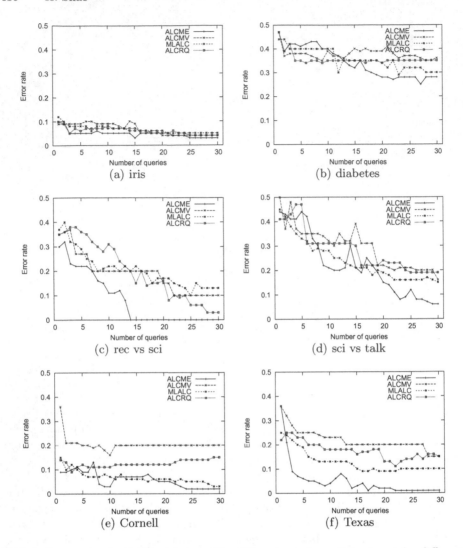

Fig. 3. Error rates for the Real data set for different numbers of queries under different categories

data decreases, the performances get better for all algorithms. It is obvious that the error rates in iris data set are the lowest among all the figures, because there are only 2 dimensions in this data set. Generally speaking, the performances of all algorithms become stable after about 20 queries. Similarly to the synthetic data sets, the accuracies sometimes do not increase even more instances are labeled due to the existence of inaccurate labelers. Our ALCME is superior than other methods especially with text data sets while the dimensions are high. For example in the Texas data set, our algorithms is able to obtain an error rate nearly to zero after about 20 queries, which are 10% better than the state-of-the-art methods. Also we note that the ALCRQ is better than ALCMMV.

6   Conclusions

Crowdsourcing, as an emerged learning paradigm, is proved to be effective in active learning for text mining. In this paper, we propose a novel ALC framework by adopting the MDLP for evolutions of labelers, as well as the selection of informative instances. Our algorithm is able to solve the two key issues in ALC by minimum encoding which is parameter-free and noise-tolerent. Experiments on both the synthetic data sets and the real texts data sets show that the proposed algorithm is better than others in most circumstance. For future research directions, we believe that a detailed mathematical analysis of the lower bound and the upper bound is necessary to develop more robust algorithms for active learning with crowdsourcing.

Acknowledgment. This work was supported by the National Natural Science Foundation of China(61603240), the Humanity and Social Science Youth foundation of Ministry of Education of China (No. 13YJC630126), SRF for ROCS, SEM, WTO chair program and SC-GTEG.

References

1. Balcan, M.F., Beygelzimer, A., Langford, J.: Agnostic active learning. In: ICML, pp. 65–72 (2006)
2. Dagan, I., Engelson, S.P.: Committee-based sampling for training probabilistic classifiers. In: ICML 2006, pp. 150–157 (2006)
3. Dhillon, P.S., Ungar, L.: Transfer learning, feature selection and word sense disambiguation. In: NLP/CL ACL-IJCNLP (2009)
4. Lonardi, S., Keogh, E., Ratanamahatana, C.A.: Towards parameter-free data mining. In: KDD 2004, pp. 206–215 (2004)
5. Fang, M., Zhu, X., Li, B., Ding, W., Wu, X.: Self-taught active learning from crowds. In: Machine Learning and Knowledge Discovery in Databases, pp. 858–863 (2012)
6. Grammer, K., Kearns, M., Wortman, J.: Learning from multiple sources. J. Mach. Learn. Res. **9**, 1757–1774 (2008)
7. Lewis, D.D., Gale, W.A.: A sequential algorithm for training text classifiers. In: SIGIR 1994, pp. 3–12 (1994)
8. McCallum, A., Nigam, K.: Employing EM in pool-based active learning for text classification. In: ICML 1998, pp. 350–358 (1998)
9. Grünwald, P.D.: The Minimum Description Length Principle. MIT Press, Cambridge (2007)
10. Quinlan, J.R., Rivest, R.L.: Inferring decision trees using the minimum description length principle. Inf. Comput. **80**(3), 227–248 (1989)
11. Raykar, V.C., Yu, S., Zhao, L.H., Jerebko, A., Florin, C., Valadez, G.H., Bogoni, L., Moy, L.: Supervised learning from multiple experts: whom to trust when everyone lies a bit. In: ICML, pp. 889–896 (2009)
12. Raykar, V.C., Yu, S., Zhao, L.H., Valadez, G.H., Florin, C., Bogoni, L., Moy, L.: Learning from crowds. J. Mach. Learn. Res. **11**, 1297–1322 (2010)
13. Settles, B.: Active learning literature survey. Technical Report No. 1648 (2010)

14. Seung, H.S., Opper, M., Sompolinsky, H.: Query by committee. In: Computational Learning Theory, pp. 287–294 (1992)
15. Shao, H., Suzuki, E.: Feature-based inductive transfer learning through minimum encoding. In: SDM 2011, pp. 259–270 (2011)
16. Shao, H., Tong, B., Suzuki, E.: Compact coding for hyperplane classifiers in heterogeneous environment. In: ECML PKDD 2011, pp. 207–222 (2011)
17. Shao, H., Tong, B., Suzuki, E.: Query by committee in a heterogeneous environment. In: Zhou, S., Zhang, S., Karypis, G. (eds.) ADMA 2012. LNCS (LNAI), vol. 7713, pp. 186–198. Springer, Heidelberg (2012). doi:10.1007/978-3-642-35527-1_16
18. Sheng, V.S., Provost, F., Ipeirotis, P.G.: Get another label? Improving data quality and data mining using multiple, noisy labelers. In: KDD, pp. 614–622 (2008)
19. Shi, X., Fan, W., Ren, J.: Actively transfer domain knowledge. In: ECML PKDD 2008, pp. 342–357 (2008)
20. Suzuki, E.: Negative encoding length as a subjective interestingness measure for groups of rules. In: Theeramunkong, T., Kijsirikul, B., Cercone, N., Ho, T.-B. (eds.) PAKDD 2009. LNCS (LNAI), vol. 5476, pp. 220–231. Springer, Heidelberg (2009). doi:10.1007/978-3-642-01307-2_22
21. Wallace, C., Patrick, J.: Coding decision trees. J. Mach. Learn. **11**(1), 7–22 (1993)
22. Yan, Y., Rosales, R., Fung, G., Dy, J.G.: Active learning from crowds. In: ICML, pp. 385–392 (2011)
23. Yan, Y., Rosales, R., Fung, G., Schmidt, M., Hermosillo, G., Bogoni, L., Moy, L., Dy, J.G.: Modeling annotator expertise: learning when everybody knows a bit of something. In: AISTATS, pp. 932–939 (2010)
24. Zhao, Z., Cheng, J., Wei, F., Zhou, M., Ng, W., Socialtransfer, Y.: Transferring social knowledge for cold-start crowdsourcing. In: CIKM (2014)

Chinese Lyrics Generation Using Long Short-Term Memory Neural Network

Xing Wu[1,2(✉)], Zhikang Du[1], Mingyu Zhong[1], Shuji Dai[1], and Yazhou Liu[2]

[1] School of Computer Engineering and Science, Shanghai University, Shanghai 200444, China
{xingwu,duzhikang,zhongmingyu,daishuji}@shu.edu.cn
[2] Key Laboratory of Image and Video Understanding for Social Safety,
Nanjing University of Science and Technology, Nanjing 210094, China
yazhouliu@njust.edu.cn

Abstract. Lyrics take a great role to express users' feelings. Every user has its own patterns and styles of songs. This paper proposes a method to capture the patterns and styles of users and generates lyrics automatically, using Long Short-Term Memory network combined with language model. The Long Short-Term memory network can capture long-term context information into the memory, this paper trains the context representation of each line of lyrics as a sentence vector. And with the recurrent neural network-based language model, lyrics can be generated automatically. Compared to the previous systems based on word frequency, melodies and templates which are hard to be built, the model in this paper is much easier and fully unsupervised. With this model, some patterns and styles can be seen in the generated lyrics of every single user.

Keywords: Lyric generation · Long Short-Term memory · Language model · Sentence vector

1 Introduction

Writing songs is a good way for users to express their personal emotions, lives, hopes, and attitudes towards things. Lyrics take a great role to do that job, as well as rhythms. All the writers have their own patterns and styles, and their own ways to show their love, dreams and so on. Writing lyrics is not an easy task for human and it usually comes with rhythms. Automatic lyric generation tasks always start from defining keywords, choosing a template, matching the rhythm and generating words using ontologies with these kinds of constraints, it's hard for system construction and maintenance, and to capture the patterns and styles of a single user.

The work of this paper tries to learn the patterns and styles of every single user automatically, using state-of-art machine learning algorithms, and generate lyrics of specified singers automatically, using recurrent neural network-based language modeling. With Long Short-Term Memory network (LSTM), context information of long texts can be captured into the memory (the parameters of the network). The context information gathered from the previous texts is useful for the model to generate new texts with context support. The model takes all the lyrics of a person as input, to capture

S. Benferhat et al. (Eds.): IEA/AIE 2017, Part II, LNAI 10351, pp. 419–427, 2017.
DOI: 10.1007/978-3-319-60045-1_43

its statistical patterns and generates new lyrics just like its own style. Contrary to the previous work, this model doesn't need to rely on other kinds of techniques and resources like ontologies, rhymes, templates, word frequencies and so on, thus it's easy to implement and train, and gain better result based on the formal evaluation methods.

The remaining paper is separated into four parts. Section 2 shows some related work on poem and lyric generation, which are mainly based on ontologies, templates and word frequencies. Some work uses machine translation approach to generate lyrics line by line. Section 3 shows the details of the model of this paper, training the context representations of words and sentences, and generating lyrics word by word using Long Short-Term Memory neural network-based language model. Section 4 shows some experimental results on lyrics of three Chinese singers, which seems good to capture some styles of them. Section 5 draws the conclusion on this model, to show that it is easy to be built and trained, with the help of word embedding trained on Chinese Wikipedia data, the model can generate many other words, which makes it more flexible.

2 Related Work

The generation of lyrics are much more like the generation of poems, which has been popular for many years. Most of the work is based on word frequency, melodies or templates, which seems to have gained many difficulties. The report of Manurung et al. [1] shows that most of the difficulties comes from the difficulty of natural language generating system, the problems of architectural rigidness, lack of resources supplied to satisfy the multitude of syntactic and semantic constraints, and the objective evaluation of the output text.

To deal with all these kinds of difficulties, many researchers proposed their own methods in different aspects. Diaz-Agudo et al. [2] uses case-based reasoning ontology to design a knowledge intensive system to capture knowledge in cases of texts provided by user, and tries to gather the knowledge to form a regular line of texts using ontologies indexing, this system has a highly dependency on the quality of the ontology knowledge base, which is hard for construction and maintains. Manurung [3] then utilities an evolutionary algorithm approach to generate poems, which uses a linguistic representation based on Lexicalized Tree Adjoining Grammar, the structure of the tree adjoining grammar is complicated and may even be bad when the text becomes oral. Oliveira et al. [4] uses a kind of system to generate lyrics automatically for given melodies, they present two strategies to generate words for this system, random words and generative grammar, tests show that the later one gains better result, it may be a good idea but it takes the melodies into consideration. Tosa et al. [5] proposes a method to combine user queries with rules extracted from a corpus and additional lexical resources to generate new poems, the quality of rules definition of the corpus shows a highly influence on the poem generation. Colton et al. [6] describes a full-face corpus-based poetry generation system which uses templates to construct poems according to given constraints on rhyme, meter, stress, sentiment, word frequency and word similarity. The full-face poetry generator takes advantages of many previous techniques, thus it's complicated and hard to be implemented.

There are also some researches use summarization methods to do the text-generation job inspired by the statistical machine techniques. Genzel et al. [7] implements the ability to produce translations with meter and rhyme for phrase-based MT to gather the poetic constraints. He J et al. [8] uses a phrase-based SMT approach which translates the first line into the second, to generate Chinese poems.

The above methods take a lot about knowledge and rules extracted by human into consideration, which may take a great deal of time for the preparation work to construct their systems. Compared with all these methods, our method is a totally automatic and unsupervised one. With the help of recurrent neural network model like Long Short-Term Memory (LSTM), Gated Recurrent Units (GRU), the system can automatically capture the semantic meanings and grammatic structures of lyrics from users, then generate new lyrics word by word using recurrent neural network-based language model.

3 Lyric Generation

The work of generating lyrics of specified users can be separated of 3 parts. Section 3.1 shows a way to learn the vector representations of words using word2vec model, to capture some semantic meanings of words and word similarities. Section 3.2 tries to learn the vector representations of sentences using long short-term memory neural networks. The sentence vectors learned from the recurrent neural network model signif-icantly captures the semantic meanings of sentences which are useful to introduce the context information into the generative model. Section 3.3 tells the detail about the recurrent neural network-based language model to generate lyrics from the vocabulary list of word2vec model given the lyrics data of users. The model uses a LSTM neural network to train the higher representation of the sequential input and maps the repre-sentation to a single word (phrase level) index in the vocabulary list, using a softmax classifier. Section 3.4 and 3.5 shows the details of how to train the LSTM context model and LSTM generative model, and how to generate new words with the combination of these two models.

3.1 Learning Context of Words

In order to capture some semantic meanings of words and word similarities, we use word embedding to represent words. The concept of word embedding was first introduced in neural probabilistic language model [9] to learn a distributed representation for words. In 2013 a fast training method of word embedding called word2vec was proposed by Mikolov et al. [10] The word embedding of a word is a dense vector, the paper shows that words with similar context seems to be closer in vector space.

Another advantage of using word embedding is that it is a dense vector of a fixed size, always with a dimension of 128, 256 and so on. The traditional one-hot represen-tation of words is a very large vector of vocabulary size, where there is only one 1 in the vector and others are all 0. It loses a lot of semantic meanings of words like word order and word similarities, and the large size of vector may even lead to the curse of dimensions, as it is hard to perform the matrix calculation in the neural networks. Word embedding is a great way to fix all these problems and gain good result among many applications.

For English, words are separated by space, and each word always represent one meaning. But for Chinese, words are connected together, and the meaning of a sentence is always represented by two or more words, one-word level word embedding is meaningless than phrases. In order to train Chinese word embedding, we first segment all the data into two or more words-level phrases, and feed them to the word2vec model, so each word embedding represents a phrase, other than only one character. The result word vectors trained from Chinese Wikipedia data shows that similar words are closer, as shown in Table 1.

Table 1. Five most similar words of four words

Words	Five most similar words				
幸福	快乐	美好	甜蜜	喜乐	欢乐
Happy	Happy	wonderful	sweet	happy	joyful
流行	风行	盛行	普及	风靡	受欢迎
Popular	Popular	popular	popular	popular	popular
美丽	迷人	可爱	漂亮	最美	优美
Beautiful	Fancy	cute	beautiful	most beautiful	beautiful
句子	短语	语句	词语	词组	问句
Sentence	Phrase	sentence	word	phrase	question

3.2 Learning Context of Sentences

Recurrent neural network is a kind of artificial neural network where connections between units form a directed cycle. Unlike feedforward neural networks, recurrent neural networks can use their internal memory to process sequence of inputs, and store all the internal states in the memory as useful information. With the help of the internal memory, researchers even find out that it can capture some context information of words like word orders, word meanings and even some grammatic structure, thus it can be a good solution for our model to capture the style of users.

With the great improvements of computation performance, some deep learning recurrent neural networks like Long Short-Term Memory (LSTM) and Gated Recurrent Unit(GRU) become popular among these years. Long Short-Term memory was first published by Hochreiter and Schmidhuber [11] in 1997. Traditional RNNs that suffer from the vanishing gradient problem, when the sequential data is too long, the context information will be lost, it's not very suitable to deal with long data. LSTM is augmented by recurrent gates called forget gates to prevent backpropagated errors from vanishing or exploding, which makes it suitable to deal with very long texts and time steps, and can still capture the context information into the memory. For now LSTM is a very popular deep learning neural network in the field of natural language processing, like machine translation and language modeling. Gated Recurrent Unit [12] is another kind of recurrent neural network which simplify the process of LSTM network.

This paper tries to train a LSTM-RNN context model to capture the context information of every line of lyrics from a user. Every line of lyrics is segmented into phrases list, and then fed into the model word by word (phrase level), and it will generate a context vector representation of this line. The LSTM context model is shown in Fig. 1. As we can see, this model takes a sequence of word vectors as input and output a sequence of vector representations, we take the last output vector as the context of the input line of lyrics, and then feed it into a fully connected neural network layer (the number of the units in this layer is the number of lines in the lyrics data), to project the context vector to the vector space in the line index level. A softmax classifier is then been introduced to predict which line of index it is given the input sample. The softmax classifier layer can be seen as an activation layer to predict the most probable index. The probability of each unit can be calculated using softmax function as it is shown in (1).

$$\sigma(z)_j = \frac{e^{z_j}}{\sum_{k=1}^{K} e^{z_k}}$$ (1)

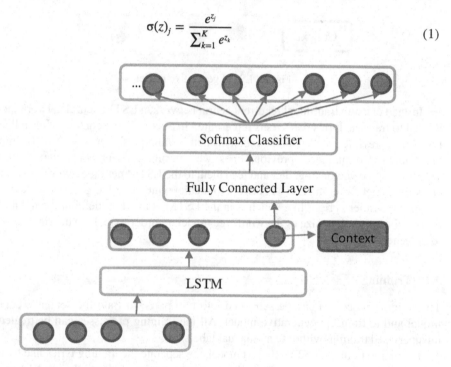

Fig. 1. LSTM context model

3.3 Generating Lyrics Word by Word

In 2010 Mikolov et al. [13] proposed a method to deal with language modeling using vanilla recurrent neural networks. This RNN-based model uses sequence of previous words as input and predict the next word using softmax classifier, which outperforms the standard backoff n-gram models and traditional feedforward neural networks. We take the inspiration of RNN-based language model to generate lyrics word by word, and automatically segmented them line by line using some predefined marks. The generative model is shown in Fig. 2.

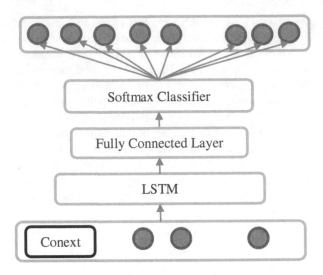

Fig. 2. LSTM generative model

Instead of using traditional recurrent neural network, a LSTM neural network model is used to train the lyrics data. As is represented in Sect. 3.2, the context of each line of lyrics is represented by a context vector, which is called a sentence vector. To import the context information of previous lines, we combine its sentence context with the sequential word vectors together and feed them to the LSTM neural network. A softmax classifier is right after the LSTM network to predict which word to generate at next. The softmax classifier is right like which is in the LSTM context model, but the number of units is the vocabulary size of the word2vec model, in order to pick up the rightful word to be generated.

3.4   Training

The training processes can be separated into two parts, to train the sentence context model and to train the generative model. All the training processes can be treated as unsupervised training without any manual labels.

In order to train the LSTM context model, we separate the training lyrics line by line, each line represents one index. Thus, the input is a sentence fed into the model word by word, and the target output is a class represented as a single line. After the training is done, the context of vector of each line can be saved for the use of LSTM generative model.

As for the training of LSTM generative, not only the word vectors of the current line are fed into the LSTM network, the context vector of the previous line is also imported to capture the context information of previous lyrics. To train the language model, we also need to separate the training lyrics into the input data and the target data. Each line of lyrics is concatenated with a start token and an end token, to specify the start and the end of a line, and then cut into a fixed length of sequential list, the target data is the word right next to the word sequence.

The LSTM context model and the LSTM generative model look quite similar as is shown in Figs. 1 and 2, but there are some main differences. Firstly, the input line of lyrics doesn't need to be cut into fixed length in the LSTM context model, but for the LSTM generative model, the input data should be cut into fixed length to satisfy the need of the language model. Secondly, the LSTM context model is used to train the sentence context vector of every single line of lyrics, which is then fed into the LSTM generative model to capture the context information of the previous line of lyrics. Finally, the target output of the LSTM context model is the index of a line of lyrics, but for the LSTM generative model, it is a word index in the vocabulary, to predict the next word of the current line.

3.5 Generating

The process of generating lyrics is a feedforward neural network which inputs a sequential data and outputs a word index in the vocabulary list. After the training process is done, the model randomly picks some start words (also called as seed words) and looks up to their word vectors to form a sequential input, combined with the previous sentence context. At first time the sentence context is a zero vector since there is no previous word. But later, the sentence vector can be calculated using the LSTM context model, then it can be used to generate the word for now. The LSTM generate model takes the sequential input and outputs a densely-connected vector with the dimension of vocabulary size of the word2vec model, a softmax function is then given to calculate the probability of each word to be generated. The generative model can go again and again to generate as many words as possible. Remember that we introduce the start token, the end token and the unknown token in Sect. 3.4, we can simply separate the generated words line by line using these tokens.

4 Experimental Results

We experiment our models on three famous Chinese singers, Jay Chou, Eason Chan and Faye Wong. The system first segments the lyrics data from each singer line by line, and extracts the vocabularies, then represents each line of lyrics as a sequence of word vectors. As it is shown in Sect. 3.1, the word vectors have been pre-trained on Chinese Wikipedia data using word2vec model, which are quite helpful to capture the word meaning of each sentence. And for the words not shown in the vocabularies of the word2vec model, they are represented as an unknown token. The sequences of word vectors representation of sentences are then fed into the LSTM context model line by line. After training the sentences for many epochs, all the sentence vectors can be projected into a latent vector space, where similar lyric lines are closer to each other.

As the context vector of the previous line has been introduced into the LSTM generative model just as the vector representation of each word, it is fairly easy to train the language model and use softmax classifier to predict the most possible word to be generated. After training for many epochs, the generative model is able to generate some lines of lyrics with a good manner. For example, the generative model learned from 243 songs from Jay Chou, and generated some lyrics in Table 1, which seems to be funny and mysterious, just like the style of himself. As for Eason Chan, 325 songs have been fed into the model to learn his styles, the generated lyrics is shown in Table 2, which seems more mature and sad. And for Faye Wong, 215 songs have been trained to learn her pattern, the lyrics shown in Table 3 express her style of songs, which is nature and free of love, sometimes mysterious (Table 4).

Table 2. Generated lyrics of Jay Chou

童话 猫 跟你 静静 在 教室 想 了解 初恋
Fairy cat in classroom with you quietly, wants to know first love
千里 沉默 送你 离开 **爱**着 大海 可怕
See you off silently for a long way, you love scary see
青花 香残 **满**地 一种 神秘 空气
Green floral residue all over the floor of a mysterious air

Table 3. Generated lyrics of Eason Chan

沉默 **难**舍 像我 不能 入睡
Silence and hard to drop like me, can't sleep
苦痛 挽回 太**难** **换**取 一只 手表
Recovery from suffering is hard, to exchange a watch
残酷喜**剧实**在嘲**讽**路人可惜**岁**月太沉重
The comedy is a crucial sarcasm to stranger, it's a pity that life is heavy

Table 4. Generated lyrics of Faye Wong

思念 梦中人 **爱** 得 **单纯** 天真
Missing the man in the dream, love is pure and naive
生命 无罪 但 偏要 怨 半世 年**华**
Life is innocent, but one insist on complaining for half of life
故事 **结**尾 如**风** 偏离 **轨**迹
The end of the story is like a wind off-track

5   Conclusion

The results of the generated lyrics of the above three singers show that the models can significantly captures some patterns and styles of the input users automatically. Although the patterns and styles of singers are latent as parameters in their own trained models, they can be shown by generating some lyrics with the generative model. With more times of training and validation, our models can perform even better. One remarkable thing is that the models try to train the previous line of context to improve the performance of the generative model. Introducing the previous context into the current generating process might be a significant way.

Long Short-Term Memory neural network plays a great role in the context model. With its help, sequential text data can be processed line by line to get the context representation of sentences. The results in this paper show it useful in generating lyrics given previous context. This may be a very good method for other applications like text classification, sentiment analysis and so on.

Besides, with the help of word vectors trained on Chinese Wikipedia data, the model can generate words not just from a given singer's lyrics, but some words with similar semantic meanings, so it can generate purely new songs, and it is more flexible.

Acknowledgement. This paper is supported by the Science and Technology Commission of Shanghai Municipality (16511102400), by Innovation Program of Shanghai Municipal Education Commission (14YZ024), and by the Jiangsu Key Laboratory of Image and Video Understanding for Social Safety (Nanjing University of Science and Technology), Grant No. 30920140122007.

References

1. Manurung, H., Ritchie, G., Thompson, H.: Towards a computational model of poetry generation. The University of Edinburgh (2000)
2. Díaz-Agudo, B., Gervás, P., González-Calero, Pedro A.: Poetry generation in COLIBRI. In: Craw, S., Preece, A. (eds.) ECCBR 2002. LNCS, vol. 2416, pp. 73–87. Springer, Heidelberg (2002). doi:10.1007/3-540-46119-1_7
3. Manurung, H.: An evolutionary algorithm approach to poetry generation (2004)
4. Oliveira, H.G., Cardoso, F.A., Pereira, F.C.: Exploring different strategies for the automatic generation of song lyrics with tra-la-lyrics. In: Proceedings of 13th Portuguese Conference on Artificial Intelligence, EPIA, pp. 57–68 (2007)
5. Tosa, N., Obara, H., Minoh, M.: Hitch haiku: an interactive supporting system for composing haiku poem. In: Stevens, S.M., Saldamarco, S.J. (eds.) ICEC 2008. LNCS, vol. 5309, pp. 209–216. Springer, Heidelberg (2008). doi:10.1007/978-3-540-89222-9_26
6. Colton, S., Goodwin, J., Veale, T.: Full face poetry generation. In: Proceedings of the Third International Conference on Computational Creativity, pp. 95–102 (2012)
7. Genzel, D., Uszkoreit, J., Och, F.: Poetic statistical machine translation: rhyme and meter. In: Proceedings of the 2010 Conference on Empirical Methods in Natural Language Processing, pp. 158–166. Association for Computational Linguistics (2010)
8. He, J., Zhou, M., Jiang, L.: Generating Chinese classical poems with statistical machine translation models. In: AAAI (2012)
9. Bengio, Y., Ducharme, R., Vincent, P., et al.: A neural probabilistic language model. J. Mach. Learn. Res. **3**(Feb), 1137–1155 (2003)
10. Mikolov, T., Sutskever, I., Chen, K., et al.: Distributed representations of words and phrases and their compositionality. In: Advances in Neural Information Processing Systems, pp. 3111–3119 (2013)
11. Hochreiter, S., Schmidhuber, J.: Long short-term memory. Neural Comput. **9**(8), 1735–1780 (1997)
12. Chung, J., Gulcehre, C., Cho, K.H., et al.: Empirical evaluation of gated recurrent neural networks on sequence modeling. arXiv preprint arXiv:1412.3555 (2014)
13. Mikolov, T., Karafiát, M., Burget, L., et al.: Recurrent neural network based language model. Interspeech **2**, 3 (2010)

CN-DBpedia: A Never-Ending Chinese Knowledge Extraction System

Bo Xu[1], Yong Xu[1], Jiaqing Liang[1,2], Chenhao Xie[1,2], Bin Liang[1],
Wanyun Cui[1], and Yanghua Xiao[1,3(✉)]

[1] Shanghai Key Laboratory of Data Science, School of Computer Science,
Fudan University, Shanghai, China
{xubo,yongxu16,jqliang15,xiech15,liangbin,shawyh}@fudan.edu.cn,
wanyuncui1@gmail.com
[2] Data Eyes Research, Shanghai, China
[3] Shanghai Internet Big Data Engineering and Technology Center, Shanghai, China

Abstract. Great efforts have been dedicated to harvesting knowledge bases from online encyclopedias. These knowledge bases play important roles in enabling machines to understand texts. However, most current knowledge bases are in English and non-English knowledge bases, especially Chinese ones, are still very rare. Many previous systems that extract knowledge from online encyclopedias, although are applicable for building a Chinese knowledge base, still suffer from two challenges. The first is that it requires great human efforts to construct an ontology and build a supervised knowledge extraction model. The second is that the update frequency of knowledge bases is very slow. To solve these challenges, we propose a never-ending Chinese Knowledge extraction system, **CN-DBpedia**, which can automatically generate a knowledge base that is of ever-increasing in size and constantly updated. Specially, we reduce the human costs by reusing the ontology of existing knowledge bases and building an end-to-end facts extraction model. We further propose a smart active update strategy to keep the freshness of our knowledge base with little human costs. The 164 million API calls of the published services justify the success of our system.

1 Introduction

With the boost of Web applications, WWW has been flooded with information on an unprecedented scale. However, most of which are readable only by human but not by machines. To make the machines understand the Web contents, great efforts have been dedicated to harvesting knowledge from online encyclopedias, such as Wikipedia. A variety of knowledge graphs or knowledge bases thus

This paper was supported by National Key Basic Research Program of China under No. 2015CB358800, by the National NSFC (No. 61472085, U1509213), by Shanghai Municipal Science and Technology Commission foundation key project under No. 15JC1400900, by Shanghai Municipal Science and Technology project under No. 16511102102.

S. Benferhat et al. (Eds.): IEA/AIE 2017, Part II, LNAI 10351, pp. 428–438, 2017.
DOI: 10.1007/978-3-319-60045-1_44

have been constructed, such as Yago [7], DBpedia [1] and Freebase [2]. These knowledge bases play important roles in many applications, such as question answering [3] and recommendation systems [10].

Nowadays, English language dominates the existing knowledge bases. Non-English knowledge bases, such as Chinese ones, are still very rare. For example, DBpedia is a community effort to extract structured, multilingual knowledge from 111 different language editions of Wikipedia. Its English version contains more than 3.7 million entities while its Chinese version contains only about one million entities [4]. The popularity of Chinese applications demands more Chinese knowledge bases.

Although there already exists many construction methods for knowledge bases, such as Yago [7], DBpedia [1] and zhishi.me [5] (a Chinese knowledge base), we still face two challenges:

1. First, *how to reduce human cost?* In general, it is not trivial to construct a knowledge base with only little human cost. Many hand-crafted knowledge bases greatly rely on human efforts. For example, DBpedia uses crowd sourcing method to construct an ontology [4], which is used for typing entities. Yago uses human specified patterns to enrich ontology [7]. Furthermore, many supervised methods are used to enrich knowledge bases, and most of them rely on hand-crafted features.
2. Second, *how to keep the freshness of knowledge bases?* The update frequency of existing knowledge bases are very low. For example, the update frequency of DBpedia is 6 months. However, emerging entities appear very fast, leading to the obsoleteness of knowledge bases. One direct solution to ensure the freshness of a knowledge base is synchronizing the knowledge base with the data source with a high frequency. However, a high synchronization frequency usually leads to a costly and wasteful update since most entities keep unchanged. Hence, we need a smart active update strategy, which can automatically identify the emerging entities and the changed facts of an entity already in the knowledge base.

To solve these problems, we propose a never-ending Chinese knowledge extraction system: CN-DBpedia. Our contributions are as follows:

1. First, we reduce the human cost in constructing the Chinese knowledge bases. We first propose to reuse an existing ontology to alleviate the difficulties to build a high-quality ontology. We also propose an end-to-end deep learning model without any human supervision to automatically extract structured facts from encyclopedia articles.
2. Second, we propose a smart active update strategy to keep the freshness of knowledge base with little update cost.

The rest of this paper is organized as follows. In Sect. 2, we present the architecture of CN-DBpedia. In Sect. 3, we introduce how we reduce the human efforts in building CN-DBpedia, including reusing the ontology of DBpedia and building an end-to-end extraction models to enrich the infobox of entities. In

Sect. 4, we elaborate our update strategies. Section 5 presents the statistic of our system, including the distribution of the extracted knowledge and the usage of information. Finally, we conclude our paper in Sect. 6.

2 System Architecture

The system architecture of CN-DBpedia is shown in Fig. 1. The system uses Baidu Baike, Hudong Baike and Chinese Wikipedia (which are the three largest Chinese encyclopedia websites) as the main data sources. We first extract raw knowledge from the articles of those encyclopedia websites. Different with Wikipedia, Baidu Baike and Hudong Baike do not provide any dump files. Hence, we need to use a crawler to fetch those articles. Encyclopedia articles contain many structured information, such as abstract, infobox and category information. We extract facts from those structured information directly and populate them into a Chinese knowledge base.

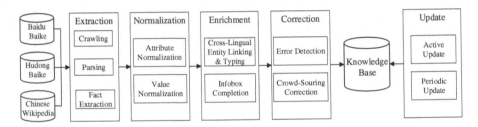

Fig. 1. System architecture of CN-DBpedia.

However, the quality of the knowledge base derived so far is still not good enough yet. There are three additional steps to improve the quality of the knowledge base.

- *STEP 1: Normalization.* Since online encyclopedias are user-generated content websites, the descriptions of contents are usually diverse. Different contributors may use different names and formats to describe the same attributes and values. For example, in order to describe a person's birth, one editor may use attribute `birthday`, another editor may use `date of birth` or something else. Hence, we need to normalize the attributes and values in the knowledge base.
- *STEP 2: Enrichment.* Current knowledge base is incomplete since no entities contain type information and some entities lacking of infobox information. To enrich entities with types, we reuse the ontology (especially the taxonomy of types) in DBpedia and type Chinese entities with DBpedia types. We complete the infobox information of entities by finding more SPO (Subjecte-Predicate-Object) triples from their article texts. The details are elaborated in Sect. 3.

– *STEP 3: Correction.* Current knowledge base might contain wrong facts. We propose two main steps to correct them. The first is error detection and the second is error correction. We use two methods for error detection. The first is rule-based detection. For example, we can use the domain and range of properties to find errors, the range of attribute `birthday` is date, any other types of values are wrong. The second way of error detection is based on user feedbacks. CN-DBpedia provides a user exploration interface to browse the knowledge in our system[1]. The interface allows users to provide feedbacks on the correctness of an SPO fact. The interface is shown in Fig. 2. After error detection, we mainly use crowd-sourcing for error correction. We assign error facts to different contributors and aggregate their corrections. The challenge is how to aggregate the multiple, noisy contributor inputs to create a consistent data [6]. A simple-yet-effective method is majority vote.

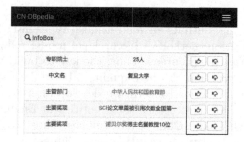

Fig. 2. The interface of `CN-DBpedia` allows users to provide feedbacks

3   Human Effort Reduction

Our first idea of human efforts reduction is reusing the ontology of existing knowledge bases and typing Chinese entities with the types in the existing knowledge base. The second idea is building an end-to-end extractor to complete the infobox. Next, we elaborate these two ideas.

3.1   Cross-Lingual Entity Typing

Building a widely accepted taxonomy requires huge human effort. To avoid this, we reuse the taxonomy of DBpedia because it is well defined and widely acknowledged. The first step of the taxonomy reuse is typing Chinese entities with English DBpedia types. To solve the problem, we propose a system, CUTE [9] (**C**ross-ling**U**al **T**ype inf**E**rence).

Figure 3 is the system architecture of CUTE. The system builds a supervised hierarchical classification model, which accepts an untyped Chinese entity (with

---

[1] http://kw.fudan.edu.cn/cndbpedia/search/.

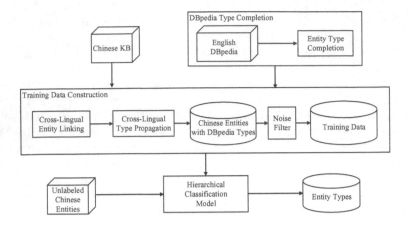

Fig. 3. Framework of CUTE

its features) as input and outputs all valid English types in DBpedia. Compared with the flat classification method, a hierarchical model reduces the classification time and increases the accuracy. Thus, the key to build an effective model is reduced to the construction of a high quality labeled data set. Since reducing the human efforts is our major concern, we develop an automatic labeled data generation procedure. We notice that some entities in English/Chinese knowledge bases may have the same Chinese label names. Thus, we can pair a Chinese entity with the English entity sharing the same Chinese label names. The Chinese entity as well as the types of the paired English entity is naturally a labeled sample. However, the quality of the training data constructed in the way above still has many problems:

- The types of English DBpedia entities in many cases are incomplete, which leads to the labeled samples with incomplete types.
- The types of English DBpedia entities in some cases are wrong, which leads to some samples with wrong types.
- Entity linking by Chinese label name is subject to errors, which leads to wrong samples. For example, The Hunger Games is a novel's label name in DBpedia, while in Chinese knowledge base, it is a label name of a film.
- The features of Chinese entities are usually incomplete. For example, some actors may only contain some basic information, such as birthday and height, which disables an effective inference to their fine-grained types, such as Actor.

To improve the quality of training data, we propose two approaches:

- To solve the incompleteness problem, we first complete the types for English DBpedia entities.
- To solve the last three problems, we execute a noisy filter step on training data to get rid of all wrong samples.

3.2 Infobox Completion

Infobox completion is the key step to enrich CN-DBpedia. The automation of this step is critical for the reduction of human effort. Infoboxes contain structured ⟨*subject, predicate, object*⟩ (i.e. ⟨s,p,o⟩ triple) facts about an entity, such as ⟨Leonardo DiCaprio, BirthPlace, Hollywood⟩. Infobox completion is a task to extract *object* for a given pair of entity and predicate from encyclopedia articles. We model the extraction problem as a seq2seq learning problem [8]. The input is a natural language sentence containing tokens, the output is the label of each token. The label is either 1 or 0, predicting whether a token is a part of the object for the predicate. We train an extractor $\mathcal{E}_p$ for each *predicate*. For example, the sentence in Fig. 4 occurs in the Wikipedia page of Leonardo DiCaprio. The extractor of BirthPlace will label Hollywood and California as True for Leonardo DiCaprio.

There are two key issues to build an effective extractor. The first is how to construct the training data. The second is how to select the desired extraction model. For the first issue, we use distant supervision method. The basic idea is that the Wikipedia infobox contains many structured facts about entities and many of these facts are also mentioned in the free text part in the entity article. Thus, we can use the sentences that express the facts in the infobox as our training data. For example, if ⟨Leonardo DiCaprio, BirthPlace, Hollywood⟩ occurs in the infobox of Leonardo DiCaprio, we can easily find the sentences (shown in Fig. 4) and correctly label the object in the sentence.

... DiCaprio was born in Hollywood, California, the only child of ...
   0   0   0   0   1   0   1   0   0   0   0 0

Fig. 4. Hollywood and California extracted as *objects*.

For the second issue, we employ Long Short-Term Memory Recurrent Neural Network (LSTM-RNN) for information extraction. LSTM-RNN has been proved effective in modeling and processing complex information, and it has achieved the state-of-the-art results in many natural language processing tasks. However, LSTM-RNN has been rarely used for information extraction. We envision that LSTM-RNN could be a powerful tool for information extraction for the following reasons. First, given labeled data, it is possible for the deep learning framework to derive the features and representation, which saves the cost of feature engineering in large scale, multiple predicates information extraction. Second, LSTM-RNN can better handle long distance dependency, and is capable of generalization of syntactic patterns of natural language.

The model structure is shown in Fig. 5. The input text is treated as a token sequence. Our final output is a labeled sequence (with a TRUE or FALSE label), which has an equal length with the input token sequence. We use a hybrid representation for each token in the input token sequences, to cover as many

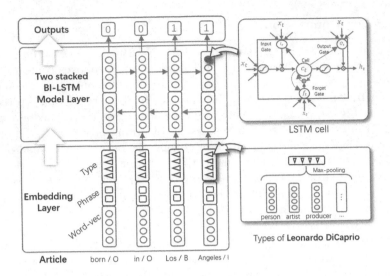

Fig. 5. Model structure [8]

as possible useful information towards knowledge base construction. The vector representation is the concatenation of three vectors: *word embedding vector (V), phrase information(P), type information (T)*. V represents the literal word information. P represents our prior knowledge about how words are combined into a phrase. T is the type representation for entity e. The representation for each token derived in the previous step is now fed into the LSTM recurrent neural network. Clearly, the label of a token in a natural language sentence is related to both its preceding tokens and its successive tokens. This motivates us to use *bi-directional hidden LSTM* layers to make use of the past and future input features.

Finally we use *binary cross entropy loss* function as the objective function to train the model:

$$Loss = \sum_{t=0}^{len} \hat{y}_t \log(y_t) + (1 - \hat{y}_t) \log(1 - y_t) \tag{1}$$

where $\hat{y}_t$ (0 or 1) is the ground-truth for the t-th token. We derive $\hat{y}_t$ in the training data generation phrase.

4   Knowledge Base Update

In this section, we elaborate our update mechanisms. We first present a widely used update strategy, then we present a more smart update strategy.

Periodical Update. The update policy is critical for the freshness of a knowledge base. The most preliminary update policy is periodical update. Existing knowledge bases such as DBpedia and Yago mostly use this update strategy. That is replacing the current knowledge bases completely with a new version after a certain period. In periodical update, the period is a key issue. A long update period means a low update cost, but the knowledge bases are likely to contain more obsolete facts about entities. A short update period can keep the freshness of the knowledge bases, but has a huge update cost. How to set a best update period is a challenging problem.

To solve this problem, CN-DBpedia supports not only periodical update but also a more smart update strategy which actively updates the knowledge bases by monitoring the changes of entities and updates an entity only when its facts change. We refer to this update strategy as *active update*, which will be elaborated in the following texts.

Active Update. The key issue of active update is to identify new entities (such as `iPhone 7s`) or an old entity (already existing in knowledge bases) that is likely to contain new facts (such as `Donald Trump`). We resort to two sources to identify these entities:

- First, entities mentioned in recent hot news.
- Second, entities mentioned in popularly searched keywords of search engines or other popular websites.

Hot news usually is about a timely and important event. The entities mentioned in the hot news are either new entities or entities whose facts tend to change. For example, Donald Trump was elected as the 45th President of the United States. His occupation in the knowledge bases should be updated to `President`. To find entities mentioned in hot news, we build a real-time news monitor, to collect the titles of latest hot news. Then, we identify the entities in the news titles and retrieve the entity from the encyclopedia source.

The popular search key words or sentences in the search engine websites usually contain the target entities. Many Chinese search engines, such as Baidu, Sogou, etc., have a panel for the real-time hot queries or topics. Moreover, some search engines such as Sogou even show the top-10 searched movies, songs, games, etc. They are also high-quality sources from which to find emerging entities or recent updated entities.

The only remaining problem is extracting entity names from news titles or search queries. To ensure our solution misses no new entities, we do not use a new phrase detection algorithm. Instead, we employ a simple greedy entity extraction method. We first do a word segmentation, to convert the sentences/phrases into a word list. Then we select all sub-lists of this list, and concatenate each sub-list into a string. In this way, we get many sub-strings. Some of them are entity names, and some others are sentence fragments. No matter what a sub-string is, we search it in the encyclopedia website. Then we can judge whether it is an entity name (there are hit results) or a meaningless fragments (no results returned). In addition, some sub-strings with low IDF (Inverse Document Frequency) could be filtered because they are usually non-meaningful entities.

5   Statistics for CN-DBpedia

We present the statistics of our system in this section. Since CN-DBpedia is continually updated. The entities and facts in CN-DBpedia are continuously growing. By December 2016, CN-DBpedia contains 10,341,196 entities and 88,454,264 relations. Table 1 shows the distribution of entities over different types (only top-15 most popular types are shown). We can see that our knowledge base in general covers entities from a variety of different domains. Table 2 further shows the distribution of structured facts. It is clearly to see that facts in infobox play a dominant role.

Table 1. Top-15 most popular types in CN-DBpedia.

Types	Count	Rank
dbo:Work	2,529,054	1
dbo:Agent	2,004,923	2
dbo:Person	1,217,988	3
dbo:Place	1,197,263	4
dbo:WrittenWork	1,098,019	5
dbo:Book	1,056,106	6
dbo:Organisation	790,974	7
dbo:PopulatedPlace	616,022	8
dbo:ArchitecturalStructure	492,580	9
dbo:Settlement	462,082	10
dbo:Building	454,448	11
dbo:Company	417,010	12
dbo:Species	211,536	13
dbo:Eukaryote	207,771	14
dbo:Food	178,689	15

Table 2. Relations in CN-DBpedia.

Relation types	Count	Rank
Entity Infobox	41,140,062	1
Entity Tags	19,865,811	2
Entity Types	19,846,300	3
Entity Information	4,003,901	4
Entity SameAs	142,448	5

Table 3. APIs and their descriptions.

API name	Description	Rank	Count
mention2entity	given mention name, return entity name	1	59,277,949
entityAVP	given entity name, return all its attribute-value pairs	2	35,812,420
entityTag	given entity name, return all its tags	3	27,334,278
entityInformation	given entity name, return its description information	4	22,698,972
entityType	given entity name, return all its types	5	17,608,266
entityAttribute	given entity and attribute names, return all values	6	36,936

We also publish a lot of APIs[2] to make our knowledge base accessible from Web. By December 2016, these APIs have already been called 164 million times since it is published on December 2015. Table 3 shows the function of each API and their usage statistics. We can see that `mention2entity` service which returns an entity for a certain mention of the entity in text is the most popular one. We envision that most of these APIs are serving many big data analytic applications as the underlying knowledge services.

6   Conclusion

In this paper, we propose a never-ending Chinese Knowledge extraction system: `CN-DBpedia`. Compared with other knowledge bases, `CN-DBpedia` relies quite few human efforts and provides the freshest knowledge with a smart active update strategy. The 160 million API calls of knowledge services provided by `CN-DBpedia` justify the rationality of our system design. We will further integrate more knowledge sources to increase the coverage of `CN-DBpedia` in the near future.

References

1. Auer, S., Bizer, C., Kobilarov, G., Lehmann, J., Cyganiak, R., Ives, Z.: DBpedia: a nucleus for a web of open data. In: Aberer, K., et al. (eds.) ASWC/ISWC - 2007. LNCS, vol. 4825, pp. 722–735. Springer, Heidelberg (2007). doi:10.1007/978-3-540-76298-0_52
2. Bollacker, K., Evans, C., Paritosh, P., Sturge, T., Taylor, J.: Freebase: a collaboratively created graph database for structuring human knowledge. In: Proceedings of the 2008 ACM SIGMOD International Conference on Management of Data, pp. 1247–1250. ACM (2008)
3. Cui, W., Xiao, Y., Wang, W.: KBQA: an online template based question answering system over freebase. In: Proceedings of the Twenty-Fifth International Joint Conference on Artificial Intelligence, IJCAI 2016, New York, NY, USA, 9–15 July, pp. 4240–4241 (2016)
4. Lehmann, J., Isele, R., Jakob, M., Jentzsch, A., Kontokostas, D., Mendes, P.N., Hellmann, S., Morsey, M., van Kleef, P., Auer, S., et al.: Dbpedia-a large-scale, multilingual knowledge base extracted from wikipedia. Semant. Web J. **5**, 1–29 (2014)
5. Niu, X., Sun, X., Wang, H., Rong, S., Qi, G., Yu, Y.: Zhishi.me - weaving Chinese linking open data. In: Aroyo, L., Welty, C., Alani, H., Taylor, J., Bernstein, A., Kagal, L., Noy, N., Blomqvist, E. (eds.) ISWC 2011. LNCS, vol. 7032, pp. 205–220. Springer, Heidelberg (2011). doi:10.1007/978-3-642-25093-4_14
6. Sabou, M., Bontcheva, K., Scharl, A.: Crowdsourcing research opportunities: lessons from natural language processing. In: Proceedings of the 12th International Conference on Knowledge Management and Knowledge Technologies, p. 17. ACM (2012)

---

[2] http://kw.fudan.edu.cn/cndbpedia/apiwiki/.

7. Suchanek, F.M., Kasneci, G., Weikum, G.: Yago: a core of semantic knowledge. In: Proceedings of the 16th International Conference on World Wide Web, pp. 697–706. ACM (2007)

8. Xie, C., Liang, J., Chen, L., Xiao, Y.: Towards End-to-End Knowledge Graph Construction via a Hybrid LSTM-RNN Framework

9. Xu, B., Zhang, Y., Liang, J., Xiao, Y., Hwang, S., Wang, W.: Cross-lingual type inference. In: Navathe, S.B., Wu, W., Shekhar, S., Du, X., Wang, X.S., Xiong, H. (eds.) DASFAA 2016. LNCS, vol. 9642, pp. 447–462. Springer, Cham (2016). doi:10.1007/978-3-319-32025-0_28

10. Yang, D., He, J., Qin, H., Xiao, Y., Wang, W.: A graph-based recommendation across heterogeneous domains. In: Proceedings of the 24th ACM International on Conference on Information and Knowledge Management, pp. 463–472. ACM (2015)

Aspect-Based Rating Prediction on Reviews Using Sentiment Strength Analysis

Yinglin Wang[1(✉)], Yi Huang[2], and Ming Wang[1]

[1] Department of Computer Science and Technology,
Shanghai University of Finance and Economics, Shanghai, China
wang.yinglin@shufe.edu.cn

[2] Department of Computer Science and Engineering, Shanghai Jiao Tong University,
Shanghai, China
hy890916@gmail.com

Abstract. This paper aims at demonstrating sentiment strength analysis in aspect-based opinion mining. Previous works normally focused on reviewers' sentiment orientation and ignored sentiment strength that users expressed in the reviews. In order to offset this disadvantage, two methods for sentiment strength evaluation were proposed. Experiments on a huge hotel review dataset show how sentiment strength analysis can improve the performance of aspect rating prediction.

Keywords: Opinion mining · Sentiment strength analysis · Aspect-based rating

1 Introduction

With the rapid extension and advancement of internet, increasing number of people are attracted to be involved in e-commerce for its facility and convenience. And most e-commerce websites allow internet users to share their viewpoints and opinions about the products on sale with other users. The reviews, feedbacks or ratings about products play a significant role in the customer choice. Besides, sellers can improve their products or services according to feedbacks from customers.

However, reviews or feedbacks on the web are commonly long and redundant, and users usually care about some certain aspects/features of the products only. It would be tedious and fruitless to scan all of these reviews. As focusing on just the overall ratings will not be sufficient for a user to make decisions, the research of mining different aspects of the reviews is in great demand.

Aspect-based opinion mining aims to extract major aspects of a product and predict the rating of each aspect from the product reviews [1]. Hu and Liu proposed a feature-based opinion mining framework for product reviews [2]. Their research focused on the features of the product, but the features extracted from reviews are complicated and trivial. Aspects are attributes or components of products, and some similar features will be clustered into an aspect (e.g., "breakfast", "snack" in "food" aspect).

In early period, most works about aspect-based opinion mining focus on the feature extraction and aspect identification. The works on aspect-based opinion mining are

© Springer International Publishing AG 2017
S. Benferhat et al. (Eds.): IEA/AIE 2017, Part II, LNAI 10351, pp. 439–447, 2017.
DOI: 10.1007/978-3-319-60045-1_45

feature-based approaches [1–5]. These approaches are mostly based on some rules or constraints to find high-frequency noun phrases and identify product aspects. Apparently, this type of approach would result in a loss of features expressed in low frequency. Moreover, it requires much manual tuning to filter many non-aspect features.

In order to reduce manual cost and improve the adaptability to cross-domain dataset, some works apply automatic learning method to estimating the model parameters from dataset. And most of the current models are based on Latent Dirichlet Allocation(LDA) [6]. LDA methods use the bag-of-words representation of documents and focus on the co-occurrences at the document level. However, some topics generated from the LDA methods are not valid. Additionally, when given some ratable aspects, the topics and the aspects cannot match properly.

Fine-grained aspect extracting system has recently attracted increasing attention. Titov proposed a multi-grain topic models based on LDA [3]. They solved the task in a two-step process. At first they applied LDA method on document level to infer the overall topics which were referred to as global topics. Then they proposed a sliding windows method on sentence level to infer local topics. The local topics are close to the aspects. Wang and Lu proposed a latent variable model to extract sentiments related to each aspect [7]. In this model, they assumed that reviewers first decided which aspects they commented on; and then for each aspect they chose word to express their opinion. The overall rating depends on a weighted sum of all ratings. Their model could estimate the weight and the sentiment strength for each aspect in an unsupervised way.

The main goal of sentiment analysis is to predict the sentiment orientation (*i.e.*, positive or negative) in sentences and documents. To determine which words or phrases are positive or negative, many works are based on sentiment lexicons or manual resources. Turney proposed an unsupervised learning technique based on the mutual information between phrase and the words "excellent" and "poor" [8], whose detail will be mentioned later. To assign the sentiment orientation on document level, many supervised learning techniques were used in early studies. Pang and Lee compared three machine learning methods: Naive Bayes, Maximum Entropy classification and SVM and proved that SVM outperformed the other two learning approaches [9]. Sentence level sentiment analysis is much sophisticated and linguistic knowledge are usually required to get accurate results.

Much work has been completed to build a fine-grained probabilistic model to address the problem of aspect-based opinion mining [1, 3, 4]. In contrast, few researches focus on the sentiment strength that users expressed in the reviews. In most previous work, the sentiment analysis of an aspect in one review is often considered as a binary classification problem: positive or negative, ignoring the sentiment strength. In fact, the word "*wonderful*" apparently expresses more positive sentiment than "*good*".

Based on sentiment analysis, sentiment strength analysis further explores the emotional intensity of reviewers toward the entity they rate on, which is likely be contributive to the aspect-based opinion mining.

Rather than simply predict whether a review is positive or negative, Pang and Lee [10] proposed an algorithm based on a metric labeling formulation to predict the strength of ratings on a scale of 1 to 5. Experiments show that this algorithm improves the prediction over both multi-class and regression of SVM. And SVM regression performs slightly better than multi-class SVM because SVM regression uses ordering of classes in an implicit way.

Wilson and Wiebe accomplished some work on classifying the intensity of opinions and the subjectivity of deeply nested clause [11]. They defined three levels(low, medium and high) for the subjective sentences or clauses, which is similar to sentiment strength analysis. They employed a wide range of features including syntactic features, and achieved more satisfactory performance.

In this paper, we bridge the gap between aspect-based opinion mining and sentiment strength analysis. Comparing with the binary classification method, we propose two methods to measure the sentiment strength. The experiment demonstrate how sentiment strength analysis can improve the prediction of aspect rating. The rest of the paper is structured as follows. Section 1 describes our aspect identification and clustering method. Section 2 presents the two sentiment strength analysis methods. Section 3 shows the experiment results and according evaluation. Finally, Sect. 4 concludes the paper and provides a summary of our work and a discussion of future work.

2   Feature Identification and Aspect Extraction

Among large amount of features we can extract from the reviews, we need to classify these features into ratable aspects. As outlined in introduction, topic models, including LDA model, are commonly employed to cluster the features.

2.1   Latent Dirichlet Allocation

Latent Dirichlet allocation is a generative probabilistic model for collections of discrete data such as text corpora. The basic idea is that documents are represented as random mixtures over latent topics, where each topic is characterized by a distribution over words [6].

LDA assumes the following generative process for each review in the corpus:

(1) Sample ~ $Dir()$
(2) For each of the N words w_n:
    (a) Choose a topic Z_n ~ $Multinomial$
    (b) Choose a word w_n from, $p(w_n \mid z_n)$, a multinomial probability conditioned on the topic z_n.

We apply Latent Dirichlet allocation approach on a hotel review dataset that will be used in the following experiment as well. As for deciding topic number in LDA model training stage, repeated experiments have shown that relatively higher performance can be obtained by 10 topics. Before utilizing LDA model, we removed the opinion words in the corpus to avoid unnecessary workload. An opinion word is an adjective that conveys reviewers' emotion toward an object. For instance, in the sentence "This phone has an amazing and big screen", the "screen" is the opinion target and the "amazing", "big" are opinion words for this particular review.

After feature extraction with certain methods, LDA is employed to conduct features clustering and the results are demonstrated in Table 1.

Table 1. Top 5 groups of words from LDA topics for hotel reviews

I	II	III	IV	V
Service	Hotel	Internet	Noise	Room
Room	Room	Access	Room	Bed
Desk	Booked	Rooms	Night	Manager
Size	Made	Wedding	Floor	Desk
Ice	Reservation	Wireless	Street	Staff
Breakfast	Parking	Beach	Airport	Market
Coffee	Hotel	Pool	Shuttle	Downtown
Room	Car	Ocean	Hotel	Place
Day	Room	View	Minutes	Location
Fruit	Park	Resort	Bus	Walk

The result of LDA model reveals its major drawbacks although there are some reasonable topic clusters generated. Specifically, many clusters are not understandable since the model simply formulates various clusters but not provide labels. For example, it is tricky to determine the topic of a cluster that contains *noise, room, night, floor* and *street*. In addition, the model automatically generates clusters without any human choice of topics, which leads to low flexibility.

2.2 Semi-automatic Aspect Extraction

A semi-automatic classification approach can effectively conquer the main shortcoming of the above full automatic method. Concretely, we adopt a bootstrapping approach similar to the aspect segmentation algorithm in Ref. [7].

The bootstrapping approach is carried out with the following steps: first of all, we manually select some keywords that are specific enough to describe the aspect as seed words (*i.e.*, *room, bed* for the *room* aspect). Then given the seed words for each aspect, we split the reviews into sentences and assign each sentence to the aspect that most terms correspond to. After that, we calculate the dependencies between aspects and words by Chi-square statistic with which we could rank the words under each aspect. We join the top words into their corresponding aspect keyword list. The above-mentioned steps will be repeated until the keyword list remains unchanged or the iteration number exceeds the limits.

We apply the bootstrapping approach to the same hotel reviews dataset. The seed words and top word list for each aspect is presented in Table 2. After filtering out stop words, the outcome seems rather reasonable, significantly outperforming the LDA approach. Additionally, given a feature word, we can easily obtain which aspect it belongs to.

Table 2. Top words from aspect segmentation

Aspect	Seed Words	Top Words
Value	Value, price, quality, worth	Cheap, cost, expectation, money, …
Room	Room, suite, view, bed	Sleep, bathroom, bed, size, …
Location	Location, traffic, minute	Market, train, site, facility, …
Cleanliness	Clean, dirty, smell, tidy	Smoke, valet, linen, maintain, …
Service	Service, food, breakfast	Restaurant, food, cafe, drink, …

3   Sentiment Strength Analysis

After feature clustering and aspect identification for each cluster, we need to distinguish opinion words so as to further analyze the precise opinion of reviewers. It is worth mentioning that attention should be paid to negation forms in a review sentence since they can reverse the final analysis result. Based on the above work, we can discuss the process of sentiment strength analysis.

There are various methods for identifying opinion words. Compared with the word distance based or part-of-speech pattern based method, the method we adopt turns out to perform relatively better by considering syntactic patterns. We first apply Stanford Parser to each sentence and then we can extract different dependencies through grammatical relations in a sentence. One type of dependency relation patterns, including adjectival modifiers (AMOD) and nominal subjects (NSUBJ), is effective to detect opinion words in adjective form. Another type containing conjunction (CONJ) prepositional modifier (PREP) is also contributive for opinion words identification when conjunctions and prepositions appear in the review sentences. In terms of negation dependency (NEG) in the sentence, we normally add a "negation" tag to the according opinion words in order to attain the necessary information expressed by reviewers.

With the opinion words identification accomplished, we can explore the sentiment strength of reviews' viewpoint by making use of two methods based on pointwise mutual information and fuzzy set. Comparison between the two methods' performance is made after the experiments.

3.1   PMI-IR Algorithm

The pointwise mutual information (PMI) between two words, *word1(w1)* and *word2(w2)*, is defined as follows:

$$PMI(w1, w2) = \log_2 \left[\frac{p(w1 \ \& \ w2)}{p(w1)p(w2)} \right] \tag{1}$$

In the equation, $p(w1 \& w2)$ is the probability that *word1* and *word2* co-occur. If *word1* is independent to *word2*, their mutual information value is zero. The ratio between $p(w1 \& w2)$ and $p(w1)p(w2)$ is a measure of the degree of dependence between these two words.

In order to acquire the sentiment strength value of a phrase, the semantic orientation (SO) has defined as a computation form as follows [8]:

$$SO(phrase) \quad PMI(phrase, "excellent") \quad PMI(phrase, "poor") \tag{2}$$

PMI-IR estimates PMI by issuing queries to a search engine(hence the IR in PMI-IR) and returning the number of hits(matching documents). Let hits(*query*) be the number of hits returned, given the *query*, the following estimate of SO can be derived from Eqs. (1) and (2).

$$SO(\text{phrase}) = \log_2 \frac{hits(phraseNEAR"excellent")hits("poor")}{hits(phraseNEAR"poor")hits("excellent")} \tag{3}$$

Based on the features and their according opinion words, we can employ PMI-IR to generate the sentiment strength. The sentiment strength of some words show in Fig. 1.

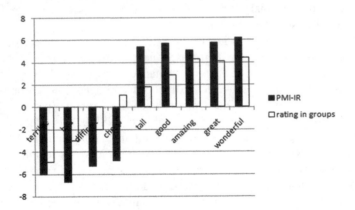

Fig. 1. Sentiment strength score calculated in PMI-IR and Rating in Groups

3.2   Rating in Groups

Another approach of computing sentiment strength of an opinion word is related to the rating of a particular review which it appears in. If an opinion word always appears in reviews with a certain rating, we could intuitively infer its sentiment strength. However, plenty of opinion words appear in reviews with varied ratings. Under this circumstance, their sentiment strength value is closely relevant to the ratio in reviews with different ratings. Based on this assumption, we propose a method to calculate opinion words' sentiment strength.

The initial step is to divide the review dataset into five groups by its overall rating, namely G1, G2, G3, G4, G5, representing a rating of 1 to 5 respectively. We extract the opinion words which are tagged as adjectives (ADJ). Then the frequency distribution among the five groups of each word is calculated. The relative frequency distribution of some frequent opinion words is presented in Table 3. As an example, most '*good*' are located in G4 and G5, which indicates its positive sentiment. By making use of the frequency distribution acquired above, we can utilize the fuzzy sets model to predict sentiment strength of an opinion word and compute the weighted sum of the group rating. Figure 1 shows the sentiment strength of some words calculated by this algorithm.

Table 3. Frequency distribution of some opinion words

Frequency distribution	G1	G2	G3	G4	G5
Good	3.9%	14.4%	12.6%	40.4%	28.8%
Quiet	5.2%	1.7%	0.0%	50.0%	43.1%
Great	2.2%	5.3%	13.0%	38.9%	40.5%
Terrible	25.0%	33.3%	8.3%	16.7%	16.7%

The major issue for now is how to assemble the sentiment strength of all the opinion words belonging to one aspect. The most straightforward approach is adopted, where we simply compute the average sentiment strength of all the opinion words describing the same aspect. Consequently, given a review and an overall rating, we can obtain all the aspect ratings by employing the several methods mentioned above.

4   Experiment Results

4.1   Dataset and Pre-processing

The hotel reviews of TripAdvisor are selected as our dataset. In addition to the free-text reviews and an overall rating, reviewers can also optionally rate predefined 8 aspects of the hotel in each review: service, value, sleep quality, location, cleanliness, room, spa, and breakfast. The ratings can be varied from 5 levels of 1 to 5 stars, which can serve as ground-truth for our aspect rating prediction.

We crawled 198,982 hotel reviews as raw dataset, with some being lack of data integrity. Specifically, among the 8 optional ratable aspects, most people would rate value, room, location, cleanliness and service. Hence, there is a need for data filtering. After that, we attain 111,443 reviews which contain all these 5 aspect ratings. In addition, some other data pre-processings including removing punctuations, stop words and stemming are conducted before we finally carry out the experiments.

4.2   Quantitative Experiments

In previous studies about aspect-based opinion mining, there has been little attention on sentiment strength conveyed by reviewers. The reason is that focusing merely on sentiment orientation can guarantee a relatively high correctness. At the same time, it becomes complicated when evaluating sentiment strength analysis. In order to explore how both sentiment orientation and sentiment strength affect performance, we design the following experiment about aspect rating prediction.

First of all, we set up two baseline methods for comparison. One, namely BASE-LINE, treats the overall rating given as the rating of every aspect. The other, namely Sentiment Orientation, combine the overall rating and sentiment orientation for each aspect to train a supervised model. As for improvement, we similarly take the overall rating and sentiment strength into consideration to train two models, where sentiment strength is measured by PMI-IR and Rating in groups respectively.

During the experiment, support vector regression (SVR) is chosen as learning method and implemented with LIBSVM toolkit [12]. In order to ensure the comparability of the four different methods, we adopt mean square error (MSE) for quantitative evaluation, which is illustrated in Table 4.

Table 4. Results of experiments

Experiment result	MSE
BASELINE	0.74507
Sentiment orientation	0.62771
PMI-IR	0.59514
Rating in groups	0.55206

4.3   Result Analysis

As shown in the table, transparent improvement triggered by sentiment analysis can be discovered. Concretely, the latter baseline method which takes into account sentiment orientation outperforms the former one. Further, the latter two experiments has proved that sentiment strength is more contributive to aspect rating prediction compared to sentiment orientation.

Besides, in the comparison between PMI-IR and Rating in groups, prediction of the latter is comparatively accurate, about which we can find a hint from Fig. 1. The sentiment strength measured by PMI-IR tends to polarize. In contrast, the strength measured by Rating in Groups is rather refined. However, it should be admitted that the dataset has affected the result to some extent.

5   Conclusions

In this paper, we explore the contribution of sentiment strength analysis to aspect rating prediction with two proposed methods. Experiments reveal that sentiment strength plays an important role in enhancing the performance of aspect rating prediction, despite these two methods provide slightly varied outcomes.

There is space for further improvement. It is probably influential to fully take advantage of those long and complicated sentences with pronoun in it. Besides, some semantic parser methods might also be valuable for this work.

Acknowledgements. We would like to thank the National Natural Science Foundation of China (Grant No. 61375053) for part of the financial support of this paper.

References

1. Moghaddam, S., Ester, M.: On the design of LDA models for aspect-based opinion mining. In: 21st ACM International Conference on Information and Knowledge Management, Maui, Hawaii, USA, pp. 803–812. ACM Press, New York (2012)
2. Hu, M.Q., Liu, B.: Mining and summarizing customer reviews. In: 10th ACM SIGKDD International Conference on Knowledge Discovery & Data Mining, Seattle, WA, USA, pp. 168–177. ACM Press, New York (2004)
3. Titov, I., McDonald, R.: Modeling online reviews with multi-grain topic models. In: 17th International Conference on World Wide Web, Beijing, China, pp. 111–120. ACM Press, New York (2008)
4. Moghaddam, S., Ester, M.: The FLDA model for aspect-based opinion mining: addressing the cold start problem. In: 22nd International Conference on World Wide Web, Rio de Janeiro, Brazil, pp. 909–918, ACM Press, New York (2013)
5. Yang, Y., Pedersen, J.O.: A comparative study on feature selection in text categorization. In: 14th International Conference on Machine Learning, Nashville, TN, USA, pp. 412–420, Morgan Kaufmann Publishers Inc., San Francisco (1997)
6. Blei, D.M., Ng, A.Y., Jordan, M.I.: Latent Dirichlet allocation. J. Mach. Learn. Res. **3**, 993–1022 (2003)
7. Wang, H., Lu, Y., Zhai, C.: Latent aspect rating analysis on review text data: a rating regression approach. In: 16th ACM SIGKDD International Conference on Knowledge Discovery and Data Mining, Washington, USA, pp. 783–792, ACM Press, New York (2010)
8. Turney, P.D.: Thumbs up or thumbs down? Semantic orientation applied to unsupervised classification of reviews. In: 40th annual meeting on association for computational linguistics, Philadelphia, PA, USA, pp. 417–424, Association for Computational Linguistics, Stroudsburg (2002)
9. Pang, B., Lee, L., Vaithyanathan, S.: Thumbs up? Sentiment classification using machine learning techniques. In: ACL-02 Conference on Empirical Methods in Natural Language Processing, EMNLP 2002, Philadelphia, PA, USA, pp. 79–86. Association for Computational Linguistics, Stroudsburg (2002)
10. Pang, B., Lee, L.: Seeing stars: exploiting class relationships for sentiment categorization with respect to rating scales. In: 43rd Annual Meeting on Association for Computational Linguistics, Michigan, USA, pp. 115–124. Association for Computational Linguistics, Stroudsburg (2005)
11. Wilson, T., Wiebe, J., Hwa, R.: Recognizing strong and weak opinion clauses. Comput. Intell. **22**(2), 73–99 (2006)
12. Chang, C.-C., Lin, C.-J.: LIBSVM: a library for support vector machines. ACM Trans. Intell. Syst. Technol. (TIST) **2**(3), 389–396 (2011)

Using Topic Labels for Text Summarization

Wanqiu Kou, Fang Li[✉], and Zhe Ye

Department of Computer Science and Engineering,
Shanghai Jiaotong University, Shanghai 200240, People's Republic of China
Autumn2012@qq.com, {fli,yezhejack}@sjtu.edu.cn

Abstract. Multi-document summarization is a difficult natural language processing task. Many extractive summarization methods consist of two steps: extract important concepts of documents and select sentences based on those concepts. In this paper, we introduce a method to use the Latent Dirichlet Allocation (LDA) topic labels as concepts, instead of n-gram or using external resources. Sentences are selected based on these topic labels in order to form a summary. Two selection methods are proposed in the paper. Experiments on DUC2004 dataset has shown that Vector-based methods are better, i.e. map topic labels and sentences to a word vector and a letter trigram vector space to find those sentences which are syntactically and semantically related with the topic labels in order to form a summary. Experiments show that the produced summaries are informative, abstractive and better than the baseline method.

Keywords: Text summarization · Topic labels · Word vectors

1 Introduction

With the rapid development of the Internet, information has witnessed explosive growth. To browse and search information in an effective way has become an important issue in natural language processing. Automatic text summarization can compress document information and help users absorb mass information. Such technologies can decrease information overload effectively.

Extractive and abstractive ways are usually two kinds methods for automatic summarization (Ani Nenkova and Kathleen McKeown 2011). Considering the difficulty of abstractive way, most researchers use many different extractive methods to extract some important sentences as text summarization, such as supervised method (Li et al. 2013), graph based method (Erkan and Dragomir 2004), global optimization method (Dimitrios et al. 2012) and concept based method (Gillick and Favre 2009).

It has been assumed that the value of a summary is the sum of the values of the unique concepts it contains. Concepts could be words, named entities, syntactic subtrees or semantic relations. The goal is to maximize the sum of the weights of those concepts that will be chosen to appear in the summary (Gillick and Favre 2009).

In this paper, we propose a method for concept based multi-document text summarization. LDA topic labels are used as concepts. Our method consists of three steps: use LDA topic model to generate LDA topics, then generate topic labels by vector based method, select sentences that are semantically related with topic labels as final summaries.

© Springer International Publishing AG 2017
S. Benferhat et al. (Eds.): IEA/AIE 2017, Part II, LNAI 10351, pp. 448–457, 2017.
DOI: 10.1007/978-3-319-60045-1_46

Our contributions in this work are: (1) the proposal of LDA topic labels as concepts in a concept based text summarization method; (2) the proposal of vector based methods to select sentences as extractive text summarization.

The rest of the paper is organized as follows. Section 2 summarizes some of the recent works in text summarization and topic labelling. Section 3 proposes our concept based method. Experimental results and conclusions are discussed in Sects. 4 and 5.

2   Related Work

There are two types of summarization methods: extractive and abstractive. Extractive summaries are produced by concatenating several sentences taken exactly as they appear in the documents being summarized. Abstractive summaries are written to convey the main information of the documents and may reuse phrases or clauses from it, but the summaries are different from the sentences in the documents. Carenini (2006) has compared these two types of methods and found that they performed equally well relative to each other, each has different strengths and weaknesses. Extractive methods are suitable for summarization of factual documents, while abstractive methods deal with documents that contain inconsistent information. Past extractive methods focused on assigning value to individual sentence to select informative and not redundant sentences as summary. Gillick and Favre (2009) presented an Integer Linear Program for exact inference under a maximum coverage model. They use bigrams as concepts, weighted by the number of input documents in which they appear. Berg-Kirkpatrick et al. (2011) proposed a combined linear model to jointly extract and compress. There is a common assumption that a good summary is those sentences which contain as many of the important concepts as possible.

Topics are usually interpreted by their top terms (Blei et al. 2003). Topic labelling aims at generating labels to represent topics, such labels can be words, phrases and sentences. Blei (2003) use terms ranked by p(w|z) in LDA topic as label, where z represents LDA topic. Lau et al. (2010) re-rank LDA top terms by features including PMI, WordNet relationship and Wikipedia feature. Some other methods use phrases as topic label. Blei and Lafferty (2009) extend LDA model to generate multi-word distribution of topics. Cano et al. (2014) experimented summarization methods for topic labeling. We think that topic labels can also be used in text summarization.

Our technique is inspired by the concept based extractive method and word vector based method. The basic intuition is that a good summary is semantically related to important concepts and concepts can be represented by LDA topic labels.

3   Methodology

3.1   Preliminary

LDA model has widely used in finding the hidden topics of documents. Those topics are semantic meanings of the documents. A summary should represent the core meaning of the documents. The framework of our method contains two steps: 1.

Generate LDA topic labels by vector based methods; 2. Calculate the similarity between each sentence and LDA topic labels, select top 5 sentences that has the highest similarity as final summary. Four topic labelling methods and two similarity measures are proposed in the paper.

3.2   LDA Topic Label Generation

We use vector based method to generate LDA topic labels, the framework is shown in the Fig. 1. The method contains three steps: generate candidate phrase labels; map LDA topics and candidate labels to vector space; calculate the correlation between LDA topics and their candidate labels by cosine similarity and select topic labels based on the highest similarity (Kou et al. 2015).

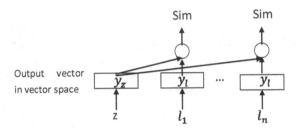

Fig. 1. Vector based topic labelling method

Three kinds of vectors are applied to generate labels: letter trigram vector (Huang et al. 2013); continuous bag-of-word model and skip-gram model (Mikolov et al. 2013). LDA top 1 term is used to show the topics.

3.3   Sentence Selection

LDA topics are hidden semantic meanings of a document set. The label for a topic can represent a concept of this document set. A good summary should be highly related to those important concepts of documents. Two methods are used to evaluate the similarity in order to select sentences as the final summaries.

Topic label Coverage:
According to (Berg-Kirkpatrick et al. 2011), a good summary should contain as many important concepts as possible. Topic labels are regarded as important concepts, the coverage calculation of a sentence is shown as follow:

$$\sum_{i}^{N} weight(l_i) * count(l_i) \tag{1}$$

Where a weight represents the importance of a label, a count represents the number of labels in a sentence. A label weight is calculated by LDA model output as follows:

$$\text{weight}(l_z) = \frac{\sum \theta_d(z)}{N_d} \tag{2}$$

where l_z represents a label of a topic z, $\theta_d(z)$ represents the weight of a topic z in a document d, N_d represents the number of documents.

Word Vector Similarity:
Each word has been represented by a vector in vector space. A naive intuition is that calculation of the similarity between LDA topic labels and sentences by word vector distance can find important sentences.

Based on researches on extending word vector to phrase and sentence vector (Mikolov et al. 2013), Weighted additive method (Mitchell and Lapata 2010) is used to transfer a word vector into a topic label vector and a sentence vector. The formulas are shown as follows

$$y_s = \sum_{w_j \in s} y_{w_j} \tag{3}$$

$$y_l = \sum_{w_j \in l} y_{w_j} \tag{4}$$

Where s represents a sentence and l represent a LDA topic label, y represents a vector. After generation of a LDA topic label vector and a sentence vector, we then calculate the similarity between them by cosine measure as follows.

$$Sim(y_s, y_l) = \text{cosine}(y_s, y_l) = \frac{y_s^T y_l}{\|y_s\| \|y_l\|} \tag{5}$$

The score of each sentence is the sum of its Sim with all LDA topic labels in the document cluster. Top 5 sentences with the highest scores are selected as the final summary.

4 Experiments

4.1 Dataset

We test our methods on DUC (Document understanding conference)2004 dataset. There are five tasks of DUC2004. Task 2 focused on generating short multi-document summaries of TDT events. The data of task2 is used in our experiments. It consists of 50 TDT English document clusters, each cluster contains 10 documents. The dataset also provides human generated summaries for each cluster.

We train LDA topics of each document cluster. The parameter α. LDA model is set as 50/K and β. set as 0.01. Considering the size of documents is limited, we set K as 3 for each cluster.

4.2   Evaluation Metrics

ROUGE (Recall-Oriented Understudy for Gisting Evaluation) measure is used to evaluate the effectiveness of our method. Specifically ROUGE-1, ROUGE-2 and ROUGE-3 are used. These measures correlate well with human judgement in general.

4.3   Experiment Result Evaluation

In generating LDA topic labels, we use nlp chunker[1] to extract chunks for candidate label selection. Word2vec toolbox is used to train CBOW and skip-gram vectors. The window size is set as 5 for both models. The dimensions of CBOW and skip-gram models are 100. The dimension of letter trigram is 18252.

Table 1 shows the result of using topic label coverage to select sentences. Table 2 shows the result of using vector-based method. Comparing with the result of Task 2 in 2004, our method using vector-based topic label and similarity calculation is better than their median value. The median values evaluated by R-1, R-2, R-3 are 0.34251, 0.07135 and 0.02289 respectively. We analysis and summarize the results in the following:

Table 1. ROUGE evaluation result of 'topic label coverage' method

Topic label	R-1 (95% conf.)	R-2 (95% conf.)	R-3 (95% conf.)
Letter trigram	0.28	0.059	0.018
CBOW	0.26	0.056	0.016
Skip-gram	0.26	0.051	0.014
LDA top word	0.32	0.056	0.013

Table 2. ROUGE evaluation result of 'word vector similarity' method

Topic label	R-1 (95% conf.)	R-2 (95% conf.)	R-3 (95% conf.)
Letter trigram	0.35	0.072	0.023
CBOW	0.32	0.060	0.017
Skip-gram	0.29	0.044	0.010

---

[1] http://opennlp.apache.org/.

- Among three different vector-based topic labels, the label using letter trigram are the best of all experiments, skip-gram and LDA top word perform the worst. The topic label using CBOW outperforms those of using skip-gram. The reason is that representation of using letter trigram can reduce the dimension of word space with few collisions, compared with the unlimited word space. More importantly, letter trigram vector map morphologically variations of a same word to points that are close to each other. Representation of using CBOW vector can benefit not only those syntactic features, but also those semantic features hidden in a text. The evaluation of word vectors has shown that CBOW is better than all other word vectors in some similarity tasks (Yulia Tsvetkov et al. 2015). Skip-gram performs better in corpus which has highly semantic concentration degree, i.e. the context is all about the same event or the similar things. DUC corpus is a variety of news corpus whose semantic concentration is not too high, thus skip-gram performs not well.
- Sentence selection using 'word vector similarity' outperforms 'topic label coverage' in all evaluations. The method using topic label coverage only catches whether the concepts are in the sentence or not, omitting their morphologic similarity and semantic similarity. The vector-based selection method can project both the sentences and topic labels to a morphological similarity and semantic word space in order to find their true relationship between them. Our experiment has shown that the word vector space can catch the semantic relationship of two vectors.

4.4   Comparison with a Baseline Method

MDSES (Multi-document Summarization based on Explicit Semantics of Sentences) (Zheng et al. 2015) is used as our baseline method. It is a concept based method, which explicitly considers conceptual relations of sentences. In addition, MDSES builds a sentence-concept graph and proposes a graph weighting algorithm to rank sentences. Based on their results on DUC2004, the comparison is shown on Table 3.

Table 3. Baseline comparison result

Method	R-1 (95% conf.)
Letter trigram + word vector similarity	0.35
MDSES	0.34

Our result of using topic labels as concepts and select sentences based on letter trigram vector is a little bit better than the baseline method, which takes conceptual relations of sentences into consideration and utilizes explicit semantics of sentences. More importantly, the baseline also uses concept-concept semantic relation based on Wikipedia textual content and hyperlink structure to eliminate redundancy. Our method does not use any external sources and only use word vectors to represent both the concepts and sentences.

4.5   Summarization Result

To show the effectiveness of our method, some results of sample document clusters are shown as follows. There are three parts: LDA topics from document clusters; topic labels generated from LDA topics using three different vectors; sentences selected based on the methods in 3.3. Because of space limitation, we list a part of document cluster, LDA topics, topic labels and summaries. Table 4 shows two data sample with our result in the following:

Table 4. Two examples of summarization result

DUC document (partial): The outcome of the Microsoft antitrust case may be a long way off, but one thing is already clear: This is the first major e-mail trial. The government's prosecution and Microsoft Corp.'s defense, to a striking degree, are legal campaigns waged with electronic messages. The human testimony often pales next to the e-mail evidence. **LDA topics:** Topic 1 'aol' 'sun' 'netscape' 'software' 'microsoft' 'browser' 'executives' 'deal' 'technology' Topic 2 'online' 'america' 'netscape' 'companies' 'commerce' 'services' 'software' 'electronic' 'business' 'consulting' Topic 3 'microsoft' 'government' 'mail' 'case' 'antitrust' 'gates' 'trial' 'netscape' 'site' 'line' **Topic labels:** Topic 1 Cbow: netscape , sun and aol Skip-gram: sun sun microsystems Letter trigram: internet browser software Topic 2 Cbow: america online and netscape Skip-gram: america online argues Letter trigram: electronic commerce services and software Topic 3 Cbow: antitrust trial microsoft Skip-gram: antitrust trial microsoft Letter trigram: antitrust trial Microsoft **Summary (partial):** Executives representing Netscape, AOL and Sun Microsystems are government wit-

nesses at the Microsoft trial. The Netscape deal, if consummated, would realign three businesses at the forefront of the modern economy _ on - line services, Internet software and electronic commerce .

DUC document (partial):

In a surprise move, nations adopting the new European currency, the euro, dropped key interest rates Thursday, effectively setting the rate that will be adopted throughout the euro zone on Jan. 1. Ten of the 11 countries adopting the euro dropped their interest rate to 3 percent. Italy dropped to 3.5 percent from 4 percent. The coordinated move was a key step in preparing for economic union.

LDA topics:

Topic 1

'percent' 'euro' 'rate' 'cuts' 'france' 'duisenberg' 'currency' 'germany' 'nations' 'markets'

Topic 2

'european' 'london' 'market' 'europe' 'euro' 'exchange' 'german' 'paris' 'create' 'joining'

Topic 3

'european' 'business' 'french' 'ago' 'europeans' 'common' 'italian' 'work' 'job' 'union'

Topic labels:

Topic 1

Cbow: busy financial markets

Skip-gram: coordinated rate cut

Letter trigram: germany and france pressed

Topic 2

Cbow: london stock exchange

Skip-gram: french , greek , spanish , german

Letter trigram: european stock exchange

Topic 3

Cbow: european university students

Skip-gram: common european currency

Letter trigram: common european currency

Summary (partial):

27 of nine other European exchanges to discuss ``the steps and conditions needed to create a unifying and competitive pan - European equity market." The two announcements show how the introduction of the currency, the euro, is reshaping Europe' s financial landscape , requiring Europeans to think in Continental rather than national terms in finance and business.`` It' s the beginning of a new era ."

5   Conclusion

We propose a new concept-based multi-document summarization method. It uses topic labels as concepts and applies vector-based methods to select sentences as text summarization. The method first extract topic labels as important concepts of documents, then select sentences that are semantically related to topic labels as summaries. We propose two methods to select sentences using our four topic labelling methods.

Experiments show that topic label using the letter trigram vector and sentence selection using word vector has achieved the best result.

Experiments on DUC data show that our method can get better result than the baseline and the summarization result is also understandable and reasonable. It is also better than the median value of the competition results in 2004.

The limitation of our method is that the topic labels will affect the quality of summarization, while the quality of topic labels is also affected by a corpus size and the number of topics. In the future, we plan to test more corpora and use more word vectors for text summarization.

Acknowledgement. We would like to thank the National Natural Science Foundation of China (Grant No. 61375053) for part of the financial support of this paper.

References

Nenkova, A., McKeown, K.: Automatic summarization. Found. Trend Inform. Retrieval **5**(2–3), 103–233 (2011)

Li, C., Qian, X., Liu, Y.: Using supervised bigram-based ILP for extractive summarization. In: Proceedings of ACL, Sofia, Bulgaria (2013)

Erkan, G., Radev, D.R.: Lexrank: Graph-based centrality as salience in text summarization. Jair, 2004, 22 (2004)

Galanis, D., Lampouras, G., Androutsopoulos, I.: Extractive multi-document summarization with integer linear programming and support vector regression. In: Proceedings of the COLING (2012)

Gillick, D., Favre, B.: A scalable global model for summarization. In: Proceedings of ACL Workshop on Integer Linear Programming for Natural Language Processing (2009)

Kou, W., Li, F., Baldwin, T.: Automatic labelling of topic models using word vectors and letter trigram vectors. In: Zuccon, G., Geva, S., Joho, H., Scholer, F., Sun, A., Zhang, P. (eds.) AIRS 2015. LNCS, vol. 9460, pp. 253–264. Springer, Cham (2015). doi:10.1007/978-3-319-28940-3_20

Carenini, G., Cheung, J.C.K., Pauls, A.: Multi-document summarization of evaluative text. Comput. Intell. **29**(4), 545–576 (2006)

Berg-Kirkpatrick, T., Gillick, D., Klein, D.: Jointly learning to extract and compress. In: Proceedings of ACL, Portland, USA (2011)

Blei, D.M., Ng, A.Y., Jordan, M.I.: Latent dirichlet allocation. J. Mach. Learn. Res. **3**, 993–1022 (2003)

Lau, J.H., Newman, D., Karimi, S., et al.: Best topic word selection for topic labelling. In: Proceedings of the 23rd International Conference on Computational Linguistics: Posters. Association for Computational Linguistics, pp. 605–613 (2010)

Blei, D.M., Lafferty, J.D.: Visualizing topics with multi-word expressions (2009). arXiv preprint arXiv:0907.1013

Cano Basave, A.E., He, Y., Xu, R.: Automatic labelling of topic models learned from Twitter by summarisation. Association for Computational Linguistics (ACL) (2014)

Huang, P.S., He, X., Gao, J., et al.: Learning deep structured semantic models for web search using clickthrough data. In: Proceedings of the 22nd ACM International Conference on Information & Knowledge Management, pp. 2333–2338. ACM (2013)

Mikolov, T., Sutskever, I., Chen, K., et al.: Distributed representations of words and phrases and their compositionality. In: Advances in Neural Information Processing Systems, pp. 3111–3119 (2013)

Mitchell, J., Lapata, M.: Composition in distributional models of semantics. Cogn. Sci. **34**(8), 1388–1429 (2010)

Tsvetkov, Y., Faruqu, M., et al.: Evaluation of word vector representations by subspace alignment. In: Proceedings of the 2015 Conference on Empirical Methods in Natural Language Processing, Lisbon, Portugal, 17–21 September 2015, pp. 2049–2054 (2015)

Zheng, H.-T., Gong, S.-Q., Guo, J.-M., Wu, W.-Z.: Exploiting conceptual relations of sentences for multi-document summarization. In: Dong, X.L., Yu, X., Li, J., Sun, Y. (eds.) WAIM 2015. LNCS, vol. 9098, pp. 506–510. Springer, Cham (2015). doi:10.1007/978-3-319-21042-1_51

Pair-Aware Neural Sentence Modeling for Implicit Discourse Relation Classification

Deng Cai[1,2] and Hai Zhao[1,2(✉)]

[1] Department of Computer Science and Engineering,
Shanghai Jiao Tong University, Shanghai, China
thisisjcykcd@gmail.com, zhaohai@cs.sjtu.edu.cn
[2] Key Lab of Shanghai Education Commision for Intelligent Interaction
and Cognitive Engineering, Shanghai Jiao Tong University, Shanghai, China

Abstract. Implicit discourse relation recognition is an extremely challenging task, for it lacks of explicit connectives between two arguments. Currently, most methods to address this problem can be regarded as to solve it in two stages, the first is to extract features from two arguments separately, and the next is to apply those features to some standard classifier. However, during the first stage, those methods neglect the links between two arguments and thus are blind to find pair-specified clues at the very beginning. This paper therefore makes an attempt to model sentence with its targeted pair in mind. Concretely, an LSTM model with attention mechanism is adapted to accomplish this idea. Experiments on the benchmark dataset show that without the help of feature engineering or any external linguistic knowledge, our proposed model outperforms previous state-of-the-art systems.

1 Introduction

Discourse parsing has been shown helpful for many downstream natural language process (NLP) tasks, such as summarization, question answering. While recently the field of discourse parsing has been widely studied, implicit discourse relation classification remains a significant challenge and becomes a performance bottleneck of such systems [9,11]. The main reason that makes implicit discourse relation classification so difficult is that the absence of discourse connectives (e.g., *so*, *but* et al.), which can explicitly indicate the relation between its governed arguments with few ambiguousness [18,21]. In other words, implicit discourse relation classification requires semantic understanding of both two text arguments [6].

This paper was partially supported by Cai Yuanpei Program (CSC No. 201304490199 and No. 201304490171), National Natural Science Foundation of China (No. 61170114, No. 61672343 and No. 61272248), National Basic Research Program of China (No. 2013CB329401), Major Basic Research Program of Shanghai Science and Technology Committee (No. 15JC1400103), Artand Science Interdisciplinary Funds of Shanghai Jiao Tong University (No. 14JCRZ04), and Key Project of National Society Science Foundation of China (No. 15-ZDA041).

S. Benferhat et al. (Eds.): IEA/AIE 2017, Part II, LNAI 10351, pp. 458–466, 2017.
DOI: 10.1007/978-3-319-60045-1_47

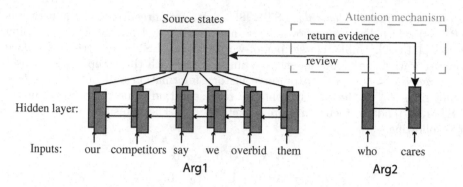

Fig. 1. Illustration of our model. The processes of modeling two **Arg**uments are connected via an attention mechanism.

Until now, related works focus on identifying an ideal set of features to better represent two arguments, such as exploiting handcrafted features obtained from external linguistic knowledge [9,12,14,16,20,27,30], feature combination optimization [19], and using neural network for automatic feature learning [32]. Data selection or augmentation is also applied [3,10,31].

However, in previous works, either of two arguments is simply transformed into vector representation according to feature designing individually [22–24]. The modeling processes of two arguments are parallel running and independent to each other. For one who is asked what the relation is between the current and the previous sentences, one highly possible strategy is to look back into the previous sentence and find some relevant evidence to make the decision, i.e., goal-directed observation makes better judgment. Moreover, as plain text of arguments can be so long that redundant and needless words may also be contained, conventional models can easily overfit on training corpus. Previous work has primarily applied attentive neural models to generating text for their capability of target-guided feature extraction, advancing several fields such as machine translation [1,15] and sentence summarization [26]. In this work, we extends these techniques to modeling text pair for discourse relation classification. Specifically, we adapt an LSTM model with attention mechanism for sentence modeling in implicit discourse relation classification, which intends to filter out useless information and capture critical evidence via pair-guided feature extraction.

2   Model

The overall model architecture is illustrated in Fig. 1. Without any feature engineering, we just use the original word information as input. Those symbolic data will first be transformed into distributed vectors (word embeddings) [2] through an embedding layer.

Bi-LSTM Sentence Modeling. LSTM [8] is a variant of recurrent neural networks (RNNs) which has been shown to be an effective tool for sequence modeling tasks [4,13,29]. Unlike classic bag-of-words model, LSTM constructs sentence representations as an order-sensitive function. At each time step t, LSTM uses a *memory cell* $\mathbf{c}_t \in \mathbb{R}^H$ to preserve history information and output a *hidden state* $\mathbf{h}_t \in \mathbb{R}^H$ as the current sentence representation (Due to the structure of LSTM, it tends to focus on more recent inputs). The transition equations are the following:

$$\mathbf{i}_t = \sigma(\mathbf{W}^i \mathbf{x}_t + \mathbf{U}^i \mathbf{h}_{t-1} + \mathbf{b}^i)$$
$$\mathbf{f}_t = \sigma(\mathbf{W}^f \mathbf{x}_t + \mathbf{U}^f \mathbf{h}_{t-1} + \mathbf{b}^f)$$
$$\mathbf{o}_t = \sigma(\mathbf{W}^o \mathbf{x}_t + \mathbf{U}^o \mathbf{h}_{t-1} + \mathbf{b}^o)$$
$$\hat{\mathbf{c}}_t = \tanh(\mathbf{W}^c \mathbf{x}_t + \mathbf{U}^c \mathbf{h}_{t-1} + \mathbf{b}^c)$$
$$\mathbf{c}_t = \mathbf{f}_t \odot \mathbf{c}_{t-1} + \mathbf{i}_t \odot \hat{\mathbf{c}}_t$$
$$\mathbf{h}_t = \mathbf{o}_t \odot \tanh(\mathbf{c}_t)$$

where x_t is the input at the current time step (e.g., t-th word representation), σ denotes the sigmoid function and $\odot$ denotes element-wise multiplication.

To fully capture the semantics of natural language, a bidirectional LSTM [7] is used to modeling the first argument (Arg1) which consists of two LSTMs: one takes the input word sequence in its original order and the other takes the sequence in the reverse order. Therefore, the outputs of bi-LSTM include a sequence of *forward hidden states* $(\overrightarrow{\mathbf{h}_1}, \ldots, \overrightarrow{\mathbf{h}_{T_1}})$ and a sequence of *backward hidden states* $(\overleftarrow{\mathbf{h}_1}, \ldots, \overleftarrow{\mathbf{h}_{T_1}})$, where T_1 is the length of Arg1. We then concatenate those two sequence into one sequence as $\bar{\mathbf{h}}_j = [\overrightarrow{\mathbf{h}_j}^T; \overleftarrow{\mathbf{h}_j}^T]^T$. In this way, each annotation $\bar{\mathbf{h}}_i$ contains summarized information about the whole input sentence, but with a strong attention to the details surrounding the i-th word. The resulted vectors $(\bar{\mathbf{h}}_1, \ldots, \bar{\mathbf{h}}_{T_1})$ not only stand as a representation of Arg1 but also serve as an information source, so called *source states*, to the followed modeling of the second argument (Arg2).

Attentive LSTM Sentence Modeling. To generate the representation of Arg2, one can also use an LSTM to achieve it (See Sect. 3). However, since we already have the representation of Arg1 and the ultimate goal is to classify the relation between those two arguments, it should be better to make more purposeful feature extraction so that more targeted evidence could be detected and focused. In our model, an attentive LSTM [1] is adapted to fulfill this requirement, which uses the source states as another input. Concretely, at each time step t, the actual input to feed the attentive LSTM is calculated as:

$$\mathbf{x}_t = g(\mathbf{c}_t, \mathbf{w}_t)$$

where $g(\cdot)$ is a nonlinear, potentially multi-layered function that mixes the information of $\mathbf{c}_t$ and $\mathbf{w}_t$, while $\mathbf{c}_t$ is the *collaborate vector* detected from source states and $\mathbf{w}_t$ is the word representation of the t-th word in Arg2.

The collaborate vector is computed as weighted sum of source states $\bar{\mathbf{h}}_i$:

$$\mathbf{c}_t = \sum_{j=1}^{T_1} \alpha_{tj} \bar{\mathbf{h}}_j$$

the weight α_{tj} of source state $\bar{\mathbf{h}}_j$ is computed by:

$$\alpha_{tj} = \frac{\exp(s(\mathbf{h}_{t-1}, \bar{\mathbf{h}}_j))}{\sum_{i=1}^{T_1} \exp(s(\mathbf{h}_{t-1}, \bar{\mathbf{h}}_i))}$$

where $s()$ is a function to score the importance of each source state based on previous hidden state $\mathbf{h}_{t-1}$:

$$s(\mathbf{h}_{t-1}, \bar{\mathbf{h}}_j) = \mathbf{v}_\alpha^T \tanh(\mathbf{W}_\alpha [\mathbf{h}_{t-1}^T; \bar{\mathbf{h}}_j^T]^T + \mathbf{b}_\alpha)$$

where $\mathbf{v}_\alpha, \mathbf{b}_\alpha \in \mathbb{R}^V$ and $\mathbf{W}_\alpha \in \mathbb{R}^{V \times (H_1 + H_2)}$ are trainable parameters, H_1, H_2 are the dimensionality of source states and hidden states, respectively. Intuitively, this score function implements a mechanism of attentive comparison between the both details of arguments.

After obtaining the hidden states of attentive LSTM, i.e., $(\mathbf{h}_1, \ldots, \mathbf{h}_{T_2})$, to deal with variable argument lengths and reduce the dimensionality for final classification, we average the vector representations of both arguments and concatenate them into one vector:

$$\mathbf{h}^* = [(\frac{1}{T_1} \sum_{i=1}^{T_1} \bar{\mathbf{h}}_i)^T; (\frac{1}{T_2} \sum_{j=1}^{T_2} \mathbf{h}_j)^T]^T$$

where $\mathbf{h}^*$ is the final hidden layer representation of both arguments. Upon the hidden layer, we stack a Softmax layer for relation classification. During training, the traditional cross-entropy error combined with an ℓ_2 regularization is used as the loss function:

$$J(\theta) = \frac{1}{m} \sum_{k=1}^{m} -\log \operatorname{Softmax}_{y_{(k)}}(\mathbf{h}_{(k)}^*) + \frac{\lambda}{2} ||\theta||_2^2$$

where m is the size of training set, $y_{(k)}$, $\mathbf{h}_{(k)}^*$ are the golden relation and final representation for the k-th training instance respectively, λ is the regularization coefficient and θ is the parameter set in our model. The diagonal variant of AdaGrad [5] with minibatchs is used for the training procedure.

3   Experiments

To evaluate the proposed model, we conducted a series of experiments on the Penn Discourse Treebank (PDTB) dataset [25]. Following the conventions of most previous works, we used sections 2–20 in the PDTB as training set, sections 0–1 as development set for hyper-parameter tuning and sections 21–22 as test set.

Table 1. Distribution of the second level relation types of implicit relations from training sections.

Level 1 class	Level 2 type	Training instances	%
Comparison	Concession	184	1.43
	Contrast	1610	12.54
	Pragmatic concession	1	0.01
	Pragmatic contrast	4	0.03
Contingency	Cause	3277	25.53
	Condition	1	0.01
	Pragmatic cause	64	0.50
	Pragmatic condition	1	0.01
Expansion	Alternative	151	1.18
	Conjunction	2882	22.46
	Exception	2	0.02
	Instantiation	1102	8.59
	List	338	2.63
	Restatement	2458	19.15
Temporal	Asynchronous	555	4.32
	Synchrony	204	1.59

Setup. The PDTB [25] provides a multi-level hierarchy of discourse relations. The first level roughly categorizes the relations into four major classes. For each class, a second level of types is available to make more distinct and pragmatic description on the relation. However, most of recent works only concern about recognizing of the first level classes, in the "one-versus-all" binary classification setting (in fact, at present only two papers are available presenting results on second level classification). The neglect of deeper processing may be due to the following reasons: (1) the distribution of second level discourse relation is unbalanced; (2) the training instances for each relation type are relatively small. The distribution of 16 second level relation types of implicit relations from training sections is shown in Table 1.

In this paper, we attack the second level relation classification as it is more challenging but more relevant for the ultimate use of discourse parsing, and the more general multi-classes classification setting is adopted.

Implement Details. Pre-training the word embeddings on large unlabeled data has been found to benefit the performance of neural network models on many tasks. We therefore use word2vec[1] [17] toolkit to initialize the word embedding matrix $\mathbf{M}$. According to early experiments on development set, we empirically set $d = 300$, $H_1 = 300$, $H_2 = 300$ and $V = 100$. We also found that dropout

---

[1] http://code.google.com/p/word2vec/.

Table 2. Performance comparisons of baseline models.

Models	Accuracy (%)
Most common class	26.63
Arg1 only	36.38
Arg2 only	40.81
Arg1 + Arg2	42.93
Arg2 + attentive Arg1	45.14
Arg1 + attentive Arg2	45.81

Table 3. Comparisons with previous models.

Models	Accuracy (%)
[12]	–
+ Surface features	40.20
+ Brown cluster	40.66
[9]	36.98
+ Surface features	43.75
+ Entity semantics	37.63
+ Both	44.59
This work	**45.81**

[28] on the embedding layer with dropout rate 0.5 can significantly improve the overall performance.

Model Analysis. To reveal the effect of pair-aware sentence modeling, we re-implemented several simplified versions of our model as baseline models: one without the attention mechanism, one only uses features in Arg1 and the other only uses Arg2. We also tried swapping the positions of two arguments. The results are listed in Table 2. As we can see, the performance is significantly boosted by exploiting pair-aware sentence modeling. Moreover, it is interesting to see that the Arg2-only one yields similar results compared to none attention model, and attentive model has substantial improvements on both of them. It demonstrates that pair-specific evidence can be easily ignored without guiding information.

Results. The comparisons of previous models and our model are shown in Table 3. Note that previous methods exploited massive hand-crafted *surface features* (word pair features, constituent parse features, dependency parse features, and contextual features), or other external linguistic knowledge such as Brown clusters and entity semantics [9], while our proposed model simply uses word information. However, with the ability of extracting pair-specified features, our model achieves even better results against them.

4   Conclusion and Future Work

This paper presents a pair-aware sentence modeling method for implicit discourse relation classification. Unlike previous works, the proposed model generates sentence representations via pair-specified feature extraction. Experiments on benchmark dataset show that with an attention mechanism, our model achieves improved performance over baseline models and outperforms previous state-of-the-art methods in the way without any feature engineering.

Although the proposed method is originally designed for implicit discourse relation, it can be easily generalized to other text relation classification tasks, such as paraphrase detection.

References

1. Bahdanau, D., Cho, K., Bengio, Y.: Neural machine translation by jointly learning to align and translate. arXiv preprint arXiv:1409.0473 (2014)
2. Bengio, Y., Ducharme, R., Vincent, P., Janvin, C.: A neural probabilistic language model. J. Mach. Learn. Res. **3**, 1137–1155 (2003)
3. Braud, C., Denis, P.: Combining natural and artificial examples to improve implicit discourse relation identification. In: Proceedings of the 25th International Conference on Computational Linguistics: Technical papers, Dublin, Ireland, pp. 1694–1705 (2014)
4. Cai, D., Zhao, H.: Neural word segmentation learning for Chinese. In: Proceedings of the 54th Annual Meeting of the Association for Computational Linguistics, Berlin, Germany, vol. 1, Long Papers, pp. 409–420 (2016)
5. Duchi, J., Hazan, E., Singer, Y.: Adaptive subgradient methods for online learning and stochastic optimization. J. Mach. Learn. Res. **12**, 2121–2159 (2011)
6. Forbes-Riley, K., Webber, B., Joshi, A.: Computing discourse semantics: the predicate-argument semantics of discourse connectives in D-LTAG. J. Semant. **23**(1), 55–106 (2006)
7. Graves, A., Jaitly, N., Mohamed, A.R.: Hybrid speech recognition with deep bidirectional LSTM. In: 2013 IEEE Workshop on Automatic Speech Recognition and Understanding (ASRU), pp. 273–278 (2013)
8. Hochreiter, S., Schmidhuber, J.: Long short-term memory. Neural Comput. **9**(8), 1735–1780 (1997)
9. Ji, Y., Eisenstein, J.: One vector is not enough: entity-augmented distributed semantics for discourse relations. Transactions of the Association for Computational Linguistics (2015)
10. Lan, M., Xu, Y., Niu, Z.: Leveraging synthetic discourse data via multi-task learning for implicit discourse relation recognition. In: Proceedings of the 51st Annual Meeting of the Association for Computational Linguistics, Sofia, Bulgaria, vol. 1, Long Papers, pp. 476–485 (2013)
11. Li, Z., Zhao, H., Pang, C., Wang, L., Wang, H.: A constituent syntactic parse tree based discourse parser. In: Proceedings of the CoNLL-16 Shared Task, pp. 60–64 (2016)
12. Lin, Z., Kan, M.Y., Ng, H.T.: Recognizing implicit discourse relations in the Penn discourse treebank. In: Proceedings of the 2009 Conference on Empirical Methods in Natural Language Processing, vol. 1, pp. 343–351 (2009)

13. Liu, P., Qiu, X., Chen, X., Wu, S., Huang, X.: Multi-timescale long short-term memory neural network for modelling sentences and documents. In: Proceedings of the 2015 Conference on Empirical Methods in Natural Language Processing, pp. 2326–2335 (2015)
14. Louis, A., Joshi, A., Prasad, R., Nenkova, A.: Using entity features to classify implicit discourse relations. In: Proceedings of the 11th Annual Meeting of the Special Interest Group on Discourse and Dialogue, pp. 59–62 (2010)
15. Luong, T., Pham, H., Manning, C.D.: Effective approaches to attention-based neural machine translation. In: Proceedings of the 2015 Conference on Empirical Methods in Natural Language Processing, Lisbon, Portugal, pp. 1412–1421 (2015)
16. McKeown, K., Biran, O.: Aggregated word pair features for implicit discourse relation disambiguation. In: Proceedings of the 51st Annual Meeting of the Association for Computational Linguistics, pp. 69–73 (2013)
17. Mikolov, T., Chen, K., Corrado, G., Dean, J.: Efficient estimation of word representations in vector space. arXiv preprint arXiv:1301.3781 (2013)
18. Miltsakaki, E., Dinesh, N., Prasad, R., Joshi, A., Webber, B.: Experiments on sense annotations and sense disambiguation of discourse connectives. In: Proceedings of the Fourth Workshop on Treebanks and Linguistic Theories, Barcelona, Spain, December 2005
19. Park, J., Cardie, C.: Improving implicit discourse relation recognition through feature set optimization. In: Proceedings of the 13th Annual Meeting of the Special Interest Group on Discourse and Dialogue, pp. 108–112 (2012)
20. Pitler, E., Louis, A., Nenkova, A.: Automatic sense prediction for implicit discourse relations in text. In: Proceedings of the Joint Conference of the 47th Annual Meeting of the ACL and the 4th International Joint Conference on Natural Language Processing of the AFNLP, vol. 2, pp. 683–691 (2009)
21. Pitler, E., Raghupathy, M., Mehta, H., Nenkova, A., Lee, A., Joshi, A.: Easily identifiable discourse relations. In: Proceedings of the 22nd International Conference on Computational Linguistics, Manchester, UK, pp. 87–90 (2008)
22. Qin, L., Zhang, Z., Zhao, H.: Implicit discourse relation recognition with contextaware character-enhanced embeddings. In: the 26th International Conference on Computational Linguistics, Osaka, Japan, December 2016
23. Qin, L., Zhang, Z., Zhao, H.: Shallow discourse parsing using convolutional neural network. In: Proceedings of the CoNLL-16 Shared Task, pp. 70–77 (2016)
24. Qin, L., Zhang, Z., Zhao, H.: A stacking gated neural architecture for implicit discourse relation classification. In: Proceedings of the 2016 Conference on Empirical Methods in Natural Language Processing, Austin, USA, November 2016
25. Prasad, R., Nikhil Dinesh, A., Webber, B.: The Penn discourse treebank 2.0. In: Proceedings of the Sixth International Conference on Language Resources and Evaluation. Marrakech, Morocco (2008)
26. Rush, A.M., Chopra, S., Weston, J.: A neural attention model for abstractive sentence summarization. In: Proceedings of the 2015 Conference on Empirical Methods in Natural Language Processing, Lisbon, Portugal, pp. 379–389 (2015)
27. Rutherford, A., Xue, N.: Discovering implicit discourse relations through brown cluster pair representation and coreference patterns. In: Proceedings of the 14th Conference of the European Chapter of the Association for Computational Linguistics, Gothenburg, Sweden, pp. 645–654 (2014)
28. Srivastava, N., Hinton, G., Krizhevsky, A., Sutskever, I., Salakhutdinov, R.: Dropout: a simple way to prevent neural networks from overfitting. J. Mach. Learn. Res. 15(1), 1929–1958 (2014)

29. Sutskever, I., Vinyals, O., Le, Q.V.: Sequence to sequence learning with neural networks. In: Advances in Neural Information Processing Systems, pp. 3104–3112 (2014)
30. Versley, Y.: Subgraph-based classification of explicit and implicit discourse relations. In: Proceedings of the 10th International Conference on Computational Semantics (IWCS 2013)-Long Papers, pp. 264–275 (2013)
31. Wang, X., Li, S., Li, J., Li, W.: Implicit discourse relation recognition by selecting typical training examples. In: Proceedings of the 24th International Conference on Computational Linguistics: Technical papers, pp. 2757–2772 (2012)
32. Zhang, B., Su, J., Xiong, D., Lu, Y., Duan, H., Yao, J.: Shallow convolutional neural network for implicit discourse relation recognition. In: Proceedings of the 2015 Conference on Empirical Methods in Natural Language Processing, Lisbon, Portugal, pp. 2230–2235 (2015)

Author Index

Abassi, Lina II-97
Abdelkhalek, Raoua I-315
Abdullah, Malak II-364
Acharya, U. Rajendra I-259
Adam, Muhammad I-259
Afshar-Nadjafi, Behrouz I-102
Alami, Reda I-182
Alanazi, Eisa I-51
Alexandre, Frederic I-235
Alomari, Khaled Mohammad I-602
Alpar, Orcan I-267, I-289
Alt, Samantha II-201
Amith, Muhammad II-386
Androvitsaneas, Vasilios P. I-295
Appel, Orestes I-628
Araújo, Eric F.M. II-341
Arieli, Ofer I-455
Arroyo, Jaen Alberto II-259
Atas, Muesluem I-21, I-335
Ayachi, Raouia I-325
Ayadi, Manel I-325

Bacchini, Alessandro I-513
Badreddine, Ahmed I-446
Baioletti, Marco II-65
Baratgin, Jean I-559, II-107
Bardelli, Alessandro Pietro I-513
Bargsten, Vinzenz I-543
Barrero, David F. I-149
Bedoussac, Laurent II-275
Beierle, Christoph I-477, I-488
Bekrar, Abdelghani I-124
Ben Abdrabbah, Sabrine I-325
Ben Amor, Nahla I-325, II-142
Ben Hariz, Narjes II-163
Ben Hariz, Nassima I-171
Ben Hassen, Mariam I-407
Ben Mahmoud, Hajer I-383
Ben Messaoud, Montassar I-345
Ben Romdhane, Taieb I-383, I-446
Ben Yaghlane, Boutheina II-163
Bennour, Imed I-124
Berzins, Gundars I-359, I-426
Boonkwan, Prachya II-306

Bordogna, Gloria I-466
Borg, AnneMarie I-455, I-507
Borri, Dino I-553
Bosse, Tibor I-611, I-620
Boukhris, Imen I-315, I-595, II-97
Boulas, Konstantinos I-295
Bradle, Jiri I-569
Bratko, Ivan I-41
Braun, Fabian II-181
Bui-The, Duy II-3
Burlinson, David II-364

Caelen, Olivier II-181
Cai, Deng II-458
Camarda, Domenico I-553
Capotorti, Andrea II-65
Carter, Jenny I-628
Chaib Draa, Ismat I-242
Chakchouk, Fadoua I-136
Chaouch, Imen I-112
Charnbumroong, Suepphong II-47
Chiclana, Francisco I-628
Cho, Hyuk I-277
Chraibi Kaadoud, Ikram I-235
Chua, Kok Poo I-259
Chua, Kuang Chua I-259
Chung, Paul W.H. II-55
Clarke, Dwaine I-227
Çoba, Ludovik I-305
Codocedo, Victor II-12
Coletti, Giulianella II-75, II-107
Collado-Villaverde, Armando I-149
Constantinou, Elena II-317
Cornuéjols, Antoine II-251
Couwenberg, Maik I-611
Cui, Wanyun II-428

Dai, Shuji II-419
Dani, Mohamed Cherif II-201
Danovics, Vadims I-359, I-426
Darwen, Paul J. II-227
de Cote, Enrique Munoz II-259
de Gea Fernández, José I-543
de Givry, Simon II-237

De Lucia, Caterina   I-553
De Meuter, Wolfgang   I-394
De Pessemier, Toon   I-345
Dhouib, Amira   I-371
Dibie, Juliette   II-251
Doreau, Henri   II-201
Dou, Wenwen   II-364
Dounias, Georgios   I-295
Doutre, Sylvie   II-295
Driss, Olfa Belkahla   I-112
Du, Zhikang   II-419
Dubois, Didier   II-113, II-142
Dvorak, Jan   I-141

Eaglin, Todd   II-364
Eichhorn, Christian   I-488
El Mernissi, Karim   I-433
Elouedi, Zied   I-160, I-315, I-595
ElSherif, Hatem M.   I-602
ElTayeby, Omar   II-364
Erdeniz, Seda Polat   I-21, I-335

Feillet, Pierre   I-433
Felfernig, Alexander   I-21, I-335
Formolo, Daniel   I-620
Frey, Daniel   I-507
Fujita, Hamido   I-259, I-628

Galochkin, M.   I-635
Garci, Eya   I-345
García-Martinez, Ramón   I-221
Gargouri, Faïez   I-407
Gavi, Francisco   II-259
Ghedira, Khaled   I-112, I-136
Gilio, Angelo   II-85
Gomez-Castaneda, Cecilia   II-259
Gómez-Martín, Marco Antonio   II-33
Gómez-Martín, Pedro Pablo   II-33
Gonos, Ioannis F.   I-295
Gonzales, Christophe   II-171
González-Calero, Pedro A.   II-33
Gouider, Héla   II-142
Grislin-Le Strugeon, Emmanuelle   I-242
Guo, Yi-Hong   I-31

Hadzikadic, Mirsad   II-374
Hagiwara, Yuki   I-259
Halfawy, Mahmoud   I-51
Hammer, Hugo Lewi   I-92, I-202

Hossain, Md Shafaeat   I-249
Hsieh, Fu-Shiung   I-31
Huang, Yi   II-439
Hung, Nguyen Duy   II-306
Hunter, Anthony   II-285

Jamet, Frank   I-559, II-107
Jemai, Abderrazak   I-124
Jenhani, Ilyes   I-345
Jeran, Michael   I-21
John, Tracey   I-227
Jonassen, Tore Møller   I-92

Kakas, Antonis C.   II-317
Kambona, Kennedy   I-394
Kante, Thierno   II-154
Karampotsis, Evangelos   I-295
Karampotsis, Evangelos   I-295
Kassahun, Yohannes   I-543
Kaytoue, Mehdi   II-12
Kelk, Steven   II-181
Kern-Isberner, Gabriele   I-488
Kervarc, Romain   II-121
Khoufi, Hela   I-171
Klein, Michel C.A.   II-341, II-353
Koh, Jia-Ling   I-579
Koitz, Roxane   I-440
Kolski, Christophe   I-371
Kou, Wanqiu   II-448
Koumi, Adamos   II-317
Krejcar, Ondrej   I-141, I-267, I-289, I-569
Kuca, Kamil   I-569
Kuntz, Pascale   I-182
Kutsch, Steven   I-477

Labernia, Quentin   II-12
Lagrue, Sylvain   II-3
Lebichot, Bertrand   II-181
Lee, Wan-Jui   II-191
Lefevre, Eric   I-160, I-595
Leitner, Gerhard   I-335
Leray, Philippe   II-121, II-154
Le-Thanh, Ha   II-3
Li, Fang   II-448
Li, Pengyu   I-192
Li, Xiaoqing   I-72
Liang, Bin   II-428
Liang, Jiaqing   II-428
Liang, Yuxuan   I-61
Liu, Shiang-Tai   I-283

Liu, Weijia   I-82
Liu, Yazhou   II-419
Liu, Yifan   I-192
Lohse, Niels   II-132
Lüftenegger, Johannes   I-440

Ma, Nang Laik   I-211
Madsen, Anders L.   II-132
Maffre, Faustine   II-295
Majlesi, Mahyar   I-102
Mallek, Sabrine   I-595
Mandiau, René   I-136
Mansfield, Adam   I-277
Maqrot, Sara   II-237
Martin, Ana Paula   I-523
Martyna, Jerzy   I-118
Masson, Olivier   I-559
Mastrodonato, Giulia   I-553
Mastroleo, Marcello   I-513
Ma-Thi, Chau   II-3
Maudet, Nicolas   I-433
Mayer, Astrid   II-285
McBurney, Peter   II-295
Meftah, Sara   II-251
Menapace, Marco   I-502
Meng, Qinggang   II-55
Meng, Zhenyu   I-72
Merlino, Hernán   I-221
Mesicek, Jakub   I-569
Meyer, Frank   I-182
Mezghani, Manel   II-211
Mollee, Julia S.   II-341, II-353
Mouhoub, Malek   I-51
Moulin, Bernard   II-275
Muangmoon, Ob-orm   II-27
Muñoz, Pablo   I-533
Murakami, Harumi   II-40

Nechval, Nicholas   I-359, I-426
Neji, Mahmoud   I-371
Nemeckova, Veronika   I-141
Nguyen-Thanh, Thuy   II-3
Niar, Smail   I-242
Noor, Kawsar   II-285

Oh, Shu Lih   I-259
Oka, Ikuo   II-40
Ouerdane, Wassila   I-433
Oukhay, Fadwa   I-383
Oyola, Angely   I-131

Pan, Jeng-Shyang   I-72
Pandolfo, Laura   I-495
Paturel, Dominique   II-268
Peschl, Michael   II-132
Petturiti, Davide   II-75, II-107
Piechowiak, Sylvain   I-136
Prade, Henri   II-113, II-142
Pulina, Luca   I-495

Qaroush, Aziz   II-211
Qin, Zengchang   I-82, I-192
Qiu, Riyi   II-374
Quesnel, Gauthier   II-237

Racharak, Teeradaj   II-306
Rahman, Khandaker Abir   I-249
Rateau, Aymeric   I-513
Rattanakhum, Mongkhol   II-22
Renaux, Thierry   I-394
Rincé, Romain   II-121
R-Moreno, María D.   I-149, I-533
Robardet, Céline   II-12
Roberts, Kirk   II-396
Rodriguez, Daniel   I-149
Romero, Dennis G.   I-131
Ropero, Fernando   I-533
Rottoli, Giovanni Daián   I-221
Rougier, Nicolas   I-235
Ruiz, Elias   II-259

Safi-Samghabadi, Marjan   I-523
Sagredo-Olivenza, Ismael   II-33
Sanfilippo, Giuseppe   II-85
Santos, Paulo E.   I-523
Sassi, Federico   I-513
Sayed, Mohamed S.   II-132
Sedes, Florence   II-211
Selamat, Ali   I-141, I-569
Šešelja, Dunja   I-507
Shaalan, Khaled   I-602
Shao, Hao   II-409
Siblini, Wissam   I-182
Sicard, Mariette   II-251
Smirnov, Evgueni N.   II-181
Šoberl, Domen   I-41
Søndberg-Jeppesen, Nicolaj   II-132
Sosnin, P.   I-635
Soui, Makram   I-136
Souli, Mounira   I-446
Spanoudakis, Nikolaos I.   II-317

Stathopulos, Ioannis A.   I-295
Sterlacchini, Simone   I-466
Stettinger, Martin   I-21, I-335
Straccia, Umberto   I-3
Strass, Hannes   II-328
Straßer, Christian   I-455, I-507
Sucar, Luis Enrique   II-259
Sudarshan, Vidya K.   I-259
Sun, Yuyan   I-61
Sureephong, Pradorn   II-22, II-27, II-47

Tabia, Karim   II-3, II-27
Tacchella, Armando   I-502
Tan, Jen Hong   I-259
Tao, Cui   II-386
Tchamitchian, Marc   II-237
Thomopoulos, Rallou   II-268, II-275
Tojo, Satoshi   II-306
Tongpaeng, Yootthapong   II-22, II-47
Torti, Lionel   II-171
Trabelsi, Abdelwaheb   I-371
Trabelsi, Asma   I-160
Tran, Thi Ngoc Trang   I-21, I-335
Turki, Mohamed   I-407
Tzanetos, Alexandros   I-295

Ueda, Hiroshi   II-40

van der Borght, Wim   I-513
van der Torre, Leendert   I-9
van der Wal, C. Natalie   I-611, I-620
van Zee, Marc   I-9
Vantaggi, Barbara   II-75
Vaquerizo, Daniel   I-533
Vintimilla, Boris X.   I-131
Vion, Julien   I-136

Wan, Tao   I-82, I-192
Wang, Han   I-579

Wang, Jiahai   I-61
Wang, Ming   II-439
Wang, Yinglin   II-439
Washha, Mahdi   II-211
Whitbrook, Amanda   II-55
Wicha, Satichai   II-22
Wotawa, Franz   I-440
Wu, Xing   II-419
Wuillemin, Pierre-Henri   II-171
Wyner, Adam   II-328

Xiao, Yanghua   II-428
Xie, Chenhao   II-428
Xu, Bo   II-428
Xu, Hua   II-386, II-396
Xu, Huarong   I-72
Xu, Jun   II-396
Xu, Yong   II-428

Yamada, Kuniko   II-40
Yao, Lixia   II-364, II-374
Yazdani, Mehdi   I-102
Yazidi, Anis   I-92, I-202
Ye, Zhe   II-448
Yu, Bingbin   I-543

Zagrouba, Ezzeddine   I-171
Zanker, Markus   I-305
Zarrouk, Rim   I-124
Zhan, Fu-Min   I-31
Zhang, Olivia R.   II-396
Zhang, Xiang Y.   II-396
Zhang, Yaoyun   II-386, II-396
Zhang, Zizhen   I-61
Zhao, Hai   II-458
Zhao, Hanqing   I-82
Zhong, Mingyu   II-419
Zhou, Bing   I-277

Printed in the United States
By Bookmasters